REMAINS

OF

BISHOP COVERDALE.

The Parker Society.

Instituted A.D. M.DCCC.XL.

For the Publication of the Works of the Fathers
and Early Writers of the Reformed
English Church.

REMAINS

OF

MYLES COVERDALE,

BISHOP OF EXETER.

CONTAINING

PROLOGUES TO THE TRANSLATION OF THE BIBLE.
TREATISE ON DEATH.
HOPE OF THE FAITHFUL.
EXHORTATION TO THE CARRYING OF CHRIST'S CROSS.
EXPOSITION UPON THE TWENTY-SECOND PSALM.
CONFUTATION OF THE TREATISE OF JOHN STANDISH.
DEFENCE OF A CERTAIN POOR CHRISTIAN MAN.
LETTERS.
GHOSTLY PSALMS AND SPIRITUAL SONGS.

EDITED FOR

The Parker Society,

BY THE

REV. GEORGE PEARSON, B.D.

RECTOR OF CASTLE CAMPS,

AND LATE CHRISTIAN ADVOCATE IN THE UNIVERSITY OF CAMBRIDGE.

CAMBRIDGE:

PRINTED AT

THE UNIVERSITY PRESS.

M.DCCC.XLVI.

JOHNSON REPRINT CORPORATION
111 Fifth Avenue, New York, N.Y. 10003

JOHNSON REPRINT COMPANY LTD.
Berkeley Square House, London, W.1

First reprinting, 1968, Johnson Reprint Corporation
Printed in the United States of America

CONTENTS.

BIOGRAPHICAL NOTICE

BISHOP COVERDALE.

THE early history of eminent persons is often involved
in much obscurity: and this observation is remarkably
verified in the instance of the illustrious subject of this
memoir. Bishop Myles Coverdale is supposed to have been
born in the year of our Lord 1488, in the district of
Coverdale in the parish of Coverham, near Middleham, in the
North Riding of Yorkshire; and it is the opinion of the
learned historian of Richmondshire[1], that it is an assumed,
and not a family name. Whatever may be the truth in this
respect, it is perhaps impossible in the present day accurately
to determine it.

Of the history of his early life every thing is equally
obscure. When he was of a proper age for an academical
education, he was sent to the monastery of the Augustines at
Cambridge, of which the celebrated Dr Robert Barnes was
at that time Prior; from whom he imbibed those sound prin-
ciples of learning and religion, which fitted him afterwards to
take so conspicuous a lead in the events connected with the
Reformation; and his name is mentioned amongst the principal persons in the University at this period who favoured these
opinions, the most celebrated of whom were Bilney, Stafford,
and Latimer[2]. He appears even at this early period to have
attracted the notice of lord Crumwell; and during the time that
he was an inmate of this house, we find him in correspondence
with him, and enjoying the confidence of this eminent person[3].

He is said by Tanner to have been admitted to Priests'
Orders by John Bishop of Chalcedon at Norwich, A. D.
1514[4], and to have taken the degree of Bachelor of Canon
Law at Cambridge, A. D. 1531. He is stated on the same

---

[1] Whitaker, History of Richmondshire, Vol. I. p. 17.

[2] Strype's Parker, Vol. I. p. 12. Ed. 1822; Memorials, Vol. I. p.
568.

[3] See Letters I. II.

[4] Tanner, Bibliotheca Britanno-Hibernica.

authority to have been admitted to the degree of D.D. at Tubingen.

Upon the occasion of Dr Barnes being arrested in the Convocation-house and carried before Wolsey for preaching heretical doctrines, we find Coverdale accompanying him, to support him under his trials. The next intelligence that we hear of him is amongst the earlier leaders of the Reformation in the northern parts of Essex. Among the parishes in this part of the country, which are mentioned as having been favourable to the cause of the Reformation, are those of Birdbrook, Steeple-Bumpstead[1], and the adjoining parish of Stoke-Clare in the county of Suffolk; and this effect seems to have been produced by the circulation of portions of the New Testament, which had existed in manuscript long before the publication of Tyndale's New Testament, and had prepared the minds of men for the reception of it, when it appeared[2]. In one of these parishes, Steeple-Bumpstead, Richard Foxe, the minister of the parish, was among the most zealous preachers of the doctrines of the Reformation in this district[3]; and we

---

[1] Anciently called Bumpstead ad Turrim, as having one of the round towers, so common in Norfolk and Suffolk. Some account of these towers is contained in the Archæologia, Vol. I. pp. 305—7, and II. pp. 80, 82.

[2] Anderson, Annals of the English Bible, Vol. I. p. 176. In alluding to this valuable work, and with a desire to acknowledge in the fullest manner the great learning and research, which he has brought to bear on the history of our English Bible, the Editor feels it to be due to the memory of Coverdale to protest against the view which he has given of Coverdale's character; a view, which he believes not to be borne out by an impartial estimate of his life, and of the transactions in which he was engaged.

[3] An interesting account is given by Anderson, ibid. p. 177, from the Register of bishop Tunstall, (which contains the confessions of various persons, who were apprehended on different charges of heresy, and for being concerned in the circulation of the scriptures,) of the events connected with the progress of the reformed doctrines in this district, and of the conversion of Foxe, and also of Topley and Gardiner, two Augustine friars of Stoke-Clare, from the perusal of Tyndale's New Testament; of which copies had been procured by two countrymen, who travelled to London from this place on purpose, where they procured them from Dr Barnes. The following is the interesting narrative, which is given by Topley, of his conversion, and of the connexion of Coverdale with it: "It fortuned," he relates, "about half a year ago, that the said Sir Richard Foxe went forth,

find the name of Coverdale mentioned in a prominent manner
in connexion with these transactions, and with the distribution
of the scriptures at this period.

Wickliffe's translation of the scriptures had now for
nearly two centuries been before the public, and two editions
of Tyndale's New Testament had been published at Worms
as early as A. D. 1525 ; and in 1530 he published his translation of The five books of Moses.   There appears to be no
foundation for the story, which was circulated by Foxe, and
has since that time been adopted by many other writers, that
in this work he was assisted by Coverdale.   They do not
appear to have been associated together during this period ;
and it is probable that Coverdale was labouring by himself
in retirement in the same vocation, as we lose sight of him
almost entirely after the year 1528 till 1535, when he published, on the fourth of October, his translation of the whole
Bible ; a work, on which it is probable that he had been
employed for some years, although we have no evidence at
what time he commenced it.   There is great uncertainty also
with regard to the place at which this Bible was printed :

and desired me to serve his cure for him; and as I was in his chamber,
I found a certain book called "Wickliffe's Wicket," whereby I felt in my
conscience a great wavering for the time that I did read upon it, and
afterwards also, when I remembered, it wounded my conscience very
sore.   Nevertheless I consented not to it, till I heard him preach, and
that was upon St Anthony's day.   Yet my mind was much troubled
with the said book, (which did make the sacrament of Christ's body in
the form of bread but a remembrance of Christ's passion,) till I heard
Sir Miles Coverdale preach ; and then my mind was sore withdrawn
from the blessed sacrament, insomuch that I took it then but for the
remembrance of Christ's body.   Furthermore he said and confessed,
that in the Lent last passed, as he was walking in the fields at Bumpstead with Sir Miles Coverdale, late friar of the same order, going in
the habit of a secular priest, who had preached the fourth Sunday in
Lent, (29th March 1528,) at Bumpstead, they did commune together of
Erasmus's works, and also upon Confession.   This Sir Miles said, and
did hold, that it was sufficient for a man to be contrite for his sins
betwixt God and his conscience, without confession made to a priest;
which opinion this respondent thought to be true, and did affirm and
hold the same at that time.   Also he saith, that at the said sermon
by the said Sir Miles Coverdale at Bumpstead, he heard him preach
against worshipping of images in the church, saying, that men should
in no wise honour or worship them; which likewise he thought to be
true, because he had no learning to defend it."

but the best and most approved opinions assign it to Froschover, a learned bookseller at Zurich, one of the earliest
and most eminent publishers of writings connected with the
Reformation.

It has been a subject of dispute, whether the translation
of Coverdale ever had the express sanction of the king.
From a review of the circumstances, as they have been
related by Coverdale himself, and from the fact, that in
the following year, in June 1536, we find the Convocation
petitioning the king for a new translation, it would appear
probable that it never had this sanction[1].

In 1537, two years afterwards, two other editions of
Coverdale's Bible were published by James Nycolson, a
bookseller in Southwark.

In the same year also the Bible appeared, which bears
the name of Thomas Mathewe, but which was really edited
by John Rogers, the friend and fellow-labourer of Tyndale.
This book, to the end of the books of Chronicles, is Tyndale's
translation, and from thence to the end of the Apocrypha,
with the exception of the book of Jonah, which is Tyndale's,
is Coverdale's version; and the whole of the New Testament
is Tyndale's translation. This Bible appears to have been
a private speculation of Grafton, the printer: the publication
of it was a subject of great joy to Cranmer, and through his
interest with the king it obtained the royal sanction, and
is said to have been "set forth with the king's most gracious
licence[2]."

In 1538 we find Coverdale in Paris, engaged there
under Lord Crumwell's direction with Grafton, in carrying
through the press another edition of this Bible; and we have
letters written at this period from Coverdale and Grafton to
Crumwell with respect to annotations, which it was proposed
to annex to this Bible, and other matters connected with
it. But the printing of it was suddenly interrupted by
an order from the Inquisition, before which Regnault, the

[1] See Memorials of Coverdale, chap. v.; Fulke, Defence of the
English Translations of the Bible, p. 98. Parker Soc. Ed.; Strype's
Cranmer, Vol. i. p. 638; Jenkyns, Preface to Cranmer's Remains,
p. xxviii.

[2] Lewis, History of Translations, p. 105; Strype's Cranmer, Book
i. c. 21; Annals ii. i. p. 324; Memorials of Coverdale, chap. vi.

printer, was summoned to appear on the seventeenth of December. However by the activity of Coverdale the greater part of the impression, together with the types, was removed to London, where it was published in April 1539, and was presented by Cranmer to the king. This edition of the Bible must be distinguished both from the former edition of 1537, and from those which were set forth in 1540 and the following years, under the express patronage and authority of Cranmer. It appears to have been undertaken and carried through the press at the sole risk and charge of lord Crumwell: and is a noble instance of his zeal in the cause of the scriptures[3].

About this period, and during his absence at Paris, the first New Testament of Coverdale was published by Nycolson of Southwark, professing to contain Coverdale's translation and the Latin in parallel columns. It appears, that Coverdale wrote a Dedication to Henry VIII. and a Prologue to the reader, to be prefixed to this volume, entrusting the task of carrying the work through the press to Nycolson. But upon its appearance it was found to be so full of errors, that Coverdale published in December a new edition at Paris, which was printed by Regnault under his own immediate direction; to which he prefixed a Dedication to Lord Crumwell and a Prologue to the reader, complaining of the errors of the first edition[4]. Nycolson published in 1538 another edition of this Testament, (although without the sanction of Coverdale,) in which the mistakes of the former edition were corrected, with the name of John Holybushe prefixed to it; who probably was also the real editor of the former edition.

In the early part of the year 1539 we find Coverdale resident at Newbury in Berkshire, and engaged under Lord Crumwell's directions in the detection of popish books and other abuses connected with religion in that neighbourhood[5].

In 1540 Cranmer set forth his Bible, and in the same year Lord Crumwell was executed and Dr Barnes brought to the stake. It is probable from a letter written in 1548

[3] For a full account of the circumstances connected with this Bible, see Anderson's Annals of the English Bible, Vol. II. pp. 22, &c. Compare also Letters III, IV, V, VII.

[4] See pp. 32—36.

[5] See Letters IX., X., pp. 498, 500.

to Calvin, when he was on the point of returning to England, in which he mentions that he had been in exile eight years[1], that Coverdale, having lost in Lord Crumwell his friend and protector, and having been so closely connected with Dr Barnes, in this year left England for Germany; where he resided in the first instance at Tubingen[2], and afterwards at Bergzabern in the duchy of Deux-ponts, supporting himself at this place by keeping a school and by his pastoral charge, to which he had been promoted in consequence of his knowledge of the German language. At this place he lived in very straitened circumstances, till on the accession of Edward VI. he was recalled to England[3]. Shortly after he left England he married a person of Scotch extraction, named Elizabeth Macheson; a connexion, which appears to have been to him a source of great comfort. During his residence at Bergzabern the principal part of the letters in this collection were written; and they give an interesting picture of his condition at this period[4].

An ancient friendship had existed between Cranmer and Coverdale; and his great exertions, first, in translating the

---

[1] Letter XXIII. p. 525.

[2] Godwin De præsulibus Angliæ, p. 413.

[3] See Letter XXIII.

[4] The following account is given of him at this time in a letter from Richard Hilles to Henry Bullinger, in the Third Series of Letters relative to the English Reformation published by the Parker Society, Letter CXIV. p. 247 : "* * * has requested me to obtain for him the testimonials of at least two Englishmen of sufficiently known reputation and piety. One of them is * * *. The other, I think, is somewhat known to you, both by my commendation and also his own letters sent to you some time since. He is called Myles Coverdale, and is truly one who is very dear, and honourably esteemed by all the ministers of the word and other learned men in these parts. He is the master of a grammar-school at Bergzabern, a town not far from Weissemberg, and where, by translating in his leisure hours, for the sake of the extensive advancement of the kingdom of Christ, various religious works into our language, partly yours, and partly those of other learned men, he is of very great service in promoting the scriptural benefit of those persons in the lower ranks of life, who are anxious for the truth, and inflamed with zeal and desire of obeying the will of God. He is one of those, who, after the example of Moses, rather choose to be banished, than with a wounded conscience enjoy the pleasures of sin in their native Egypt."

scriptures, and afterwards in carrying Lord Crumwell's Bible through the press, as well as his various writings, had marked him as one of the leading men of his day : and therefore on his return to England he was appointed one of the king's chaplains, and almoner to the queen Catharine; and in January 1550 he was nominated in conjunction with the archbishop, and the bishops of Ely, London, Lincoln, Sir John Cheke, Latimer, and Dr Parker, afterwards archbishop of Canterbury, on a commission against the anabaptists and such like sectaries. These persons were authorised to punish all anabaptists, and such as did not duly administer the sacraments according to the Book of Common Prayer[5].

In 1550 Coverdale brought out a new edition of his Bible, which was printed by Froschover at Zurich, and published in London by Andrew Hester. The same book was re-issued in London in 1553, with a new title-page and the Dedication and Prologue reprinted, by Richard Jugge.

In 1551 he was sent to accompany Lord Russell into Devonshire, to preach to the rebels, and he subsequently preached a thanksgiving sermon after the victory[6]. He was shortly afterwards appointed coadjutor to Veysey, bishop of Exeter, and was finally on the thirtieth of August consecrated bishop of that see, Scory at the same time being consecrated bishop of Rochester; his first-fruits, on the ground of his poverty, having been forgiven him by the king[7]. He was in the same year appointed on a commission for the reformation of the ecclesiastical laws[8].

In 1553 king Edward died, and together with the other protestant bishops Coverdale was deprived of his bishoprick[9]; and by an order dated August 20th he was summoned to

[5] Strype, Memorials, II. i. p. 385; Parker, I. p. 55.

[6] Strype, Cranmer, Vol. I. p. 382; Memorials, IV. ii. p. 268; Cheke, p. 175.

[7] Strype says (Cranmer, Vol. I. p. 389. August 30th): "John Scory, Ponet being translated to Winchester, was consecrated bishop of Rochester at Croydon, by the archbishop of Canterbury, assisted by Nicholas, bishop of London, and John, suffragan of Bedford. Myles Coverdale was at the same time consecrated bishop of Exeter, all with their surplices and copes, and Coverdale so habited also." See also Rymer, Vol. XV. p. 289.

[8] Strype, Cranmer, Vol. I. p. 388.

[9] Strype, Cranmer, Vol. I. p. 443; Memorials, Vol. III. i. p. 77.

appear before the council at Richmond. On the 31st of the same month he appeared in obedience to the summons, and on the first of September he was directed to wait the council's further pleasure[1].

It has been mentioned, that Coverdale, during his first exile, had married a lady of Scotch descent, named Macheson. A sister of this lady had married Dr John Macbee, or, as he was better known abroad, Machabæus, who was chaplain to the king of Denmark, and high in his favour, having had a very prominent share in the Danish version of the scriptures. Through the intercession of this person with the king of Denmark, his majesty personally interceded with queen Mary for the release of Coverdale. The queen pretended, that he was not detained on the ground of any reasons connected with religion, but for a personal debt due to her majesty; and for some time no notice was taken of the application. However, upon a second application from the king, after some delays, an order was finally made out for his release in February 1555[2]. Upon this Coverdale retired to Denmark; but was subsequently appointed preacher to the exiles at Wesel in Friesland[3], where he remained for a short time, till he was invited by the duke of Deux-ponts to his former charge at Bergzabern.

In 1555 the works of Coverdale were included in a general proscription, which was issued against the writings of several of the Reformers, including those of Cranmer, Latimer, Becon, Frith, and others[4].

In 1558 he was at Geneva; from whence he joined in the letter addressed by the exiles at that place to those at Basle, Strasburgh, Frankfort, and other places, for peace and an amicable agreement on their return home in such measures as should be agreed upon by authority with reference to religion[5]; and afterwards in the same year he returned to England.

[1] Minutes of Privy Council, MSS. Cecil, Vol. I. pp. 177—8.

[2] The circumstances connected with this discharge are related by Strype, Memorials, Vol. III. i. p. 240; by Foxe, Acts and Monuments, Vol. III. pp. 102, &c.; in the Memorials of Coverdale, pp. 157, &c.; and by Anderson, Annals of the English Bible, Vol. II. p. 293.

[3] Strype, Memorials, Vol. III. i. pp. 233, 410.

[4] Strype, Memorials, Vol. III. i. pp. 417—18.

[5] Strype, Annals, Vol. I. i. chap. VII. pp. 150—4.

The fact of his returning to England in this year, appears to be conclusive against the supposition that he was engaged in the Geneva version of the bible, which was not published till 1560.

We find him spoken of on his return in terms of great respect as preaching on different occasions at Paul's Cross[6]; and on the 17th of December he assisted with bishops Barlow, Scory, and Hodgkin, the suffragan of Bedford, at the consecration of archbishop Parker[7].

In 1563 he was recommended to secretary Cecil by bishop Grindal for the bishoprick of Llandaff, in a letter in which the bishop states that he had offered him different pieces of preferment, which had been declined by him[8] : and it is probable that he refused this also. But in 1564 he was presented by the bishop to the living of St Magnus, London bridge, the first-fruits having been remitted to him by the queen on account of his poverty, on the intercession of archbishop Parker and secretary Cecil[9]. This living he resigned in 1566[10].

In 1563 he took the degree of D. D. at Cambridge, having previously taken it at Tubingen ; and in April 1564 he was commissioned by the vice-chancellor of Cambridge to admit bishop Grindal to the same degree[11].

When Coverdale returned from his second exile, he felt the scruples relating to the habits, which had been adopted by many of the reformers. It does not however appear, that he experienced any molestation on this account[12]; and

[6] Strype, Annals, Vol. I. i. pp. 200, 300, 408; Grindal, p. 40.

[7] Strype, Parker, Vol. I. Book II. c. 1. pp. 107, &c. ; where the account of this consecration is given from the original MS. in the library of Corpus Christi College, Cambridge, which has been published in a separate form by the Cambridge Antiquarian Society. See also archbishop Bramhall's Works, p. 449.

[8] See this letter XXXVI. p. 529. note 2.

[9] The letters relating to this transaction are found pp. 529—32. The real date of his presentation is 1564, i. e. 1563 old style.

[10] September 24, 1566, John Young is mentioned as having been appointed to St Magnus, on the resignation of M. Coverdale. Newcourt's Repertorium, Vol. I. p. 398.

[11] Strype, Grindal, pp. 139, 140.

[12] Strype, Parker, Vol. I. p. 409. See also Coverdale's Letter to the Rev. Mr Robinson, chaplain to archbishop Parker, Letter XXXIX. p. 532, which appears to relate to this subject.

he was much followed as a preacher by persons attached to these opinions[1]. Nevertheless, whatever might have been his scruples with respect to vestments and other subjects of controversy at this period, it is evident that he never renounced his episcopal character; as his signature always retains the addition of his former dignity to the time of his death[2]. He died in February, 1569[3], at the age of eighty-one years, and was buried in the church of St Bartholomew behind the Exchange, on the 19th of the same month. This church having been taken down in 1840, to make room for the new Exchange, the remains of bishop Coverdale were removed to St Magnus, where they were finally interred.

We will conclude this memoir with some brief remarks,

I.   First, On the writings of bishop Coverdale;

II.   And secondly, on his Translation of the scriptures.

I.   The writings of bishop Coverdale are partly original, and partly translations. It does not appear certain, that any of them were published before the completion of his bible, in 1535. One of the earliest of his writings appears to have been the *Old Faith*, which is translated from a treatise of Bullinger, and which is expressly alluded to in his *Confutation of Standish*[4]; and it is probable, that during his first residence abroad the principal part of his writings was published. But as most of the earlier editions are without the name either of the author or the printer, and bear neither the date nor place of their publication, the exact period of their first publication is involved in great uncertainty; and the circumstances of Coverdale's writings having been proscribed in the reign of queen Mary will probably account for the great scarcity of some of them, and renders it probable that others may be altogether lost. The works of bishop Coverdale are some of them historical; others are connected with the religious controversies of the time; and others again are of a strictly practical character,

---

[1] Strype, Parker, Vol. I. p. 480.

[2] Myles Coverdale, *quondam Exon.*

[3] "Myles Coverdale, Doctor of Divinity, was buried anno 1568, the 19th of February." Register of burials of St Bartholomew behind the Exchange. The date being of the old style, is correctly 1569.

[4] P. 340.

although bringing to bear upon the subject in question much varied and recondite learning. It is a distinguishing mark of the humility of this great man, that he has not scrupled to adopt the labours of others, where he thought them superior to his own : but even in these he has shewn the hand of a master, and has generally improved upon his original author.

II. With respect to the merits of bishop Coverdale, as a translator of the scriptures, it does not appear that he derived assistance from any person in his labours, whatever countenance and support he may have received in other respects from lord Crumwell, who appears to have been his constant and steady friend : and making every allowance for the greatest possible time that he could have devoted to the task, considered as the unassisted work of an individual, it must be regarded as a very remarkable effort of industry and learning. With regard to the supposition of his having assisted Tyndale in his labours, it appears, as we have seen, to have been satisfactorily established that this is a mistake; that during this period they scarcely met[5]; and that while Tyndale was pursuing his labours abroad amidst trials and persecution, Coverdale was probably labouring at home in privacy and retirement. Indeed, even a cursory examination will convince us, that the two translations are cast in an entirely different mould.

It is not consistent with the object of the present publication, to enter into an elaborate discussion of the merits of Coverdale as a translator ; yet it may be permitted to remark, that although he professes to have consulted both the Latin and German translations, his version throughout bears marks of a close attention to the original : and ample justice has been done to his qualifications, and to the general ability with which he has executed his task[5].

[5] This appears to be clearly established by Anderson, Annals of the English Bible, Vol. i. pp. 240, 554.

[6] Coverdale's translation is expressly mentioned in the directions to king James's translators, as one of those which were to be used by them in preparing the new translation. Lewis, History of the Translations, p. 318. And ample justice is done to his merits, in an examination of different passages, by Dr Whittaker, vicar of Blackburn, in his *Historical and Critical Enquiry into the Interpretation of the Hebrew Scriptures,* pp. 48, &c.

When Rogers, who had been the friend and fellow-labourer
of Tyndale, brought forth the bible which bears the name
of Mathewe, it was natural, even independently of other
considerations, that he should adopt the translation of Tyndale, as far as it went: but it still remains to the honour
of Coverdale, that his version was selected to supply the
portion, and that no inconsiderable and unimportant portion,
which was wanting to the completion of that great work:
and when lord Crumwell determined upon the reprint of
this edition, we find Coverdale engaged with Grafton the
printer in the laborious task of carrying it through the
press. To the energy which he shewed in this work, and
his ability for the task, his letters written to lord Crumwell at this period bear ample testimony; and he would
gladly see his own labours in some degree overlooked in the
accomplishment of so important a work, as the presenting
another edition of the scriptures under so high a sanction to
his countrymen. It does not appear that Cranmer was in
any way concerned in bringing forth Mathewe's bible, which
he describes as having come upon him in the way of delightful surprise; but upon its appearance he took it up with
great energy, and pleaded its cause both with lord Crumwell,
and with the king[1]: nor are we exactly aware, how far he
countenanced the reprint of Mathewe's bible under lord
Crumwell's direction at Paris; but it seems probable that
it had his sanction, as in the year following its publication
the same book came out again under his own immediate
sanction. If he gave this preference deliberately to Tyndale's translation, (which in truth forms the basis of our
present authorised version,) he only anticipated the judgment
of posterity; although the eminent persons, who had the
conduct of our present version, have done ample justice to
the merits of Coverdale. The merits of eminent men, and
especially of persons who have been placed under the trying
circumstances which marked the age in which Coverdale
lived, must be estimated by an impartial survey of their
conduct under the various trials to which they were ex-
posed: and whatever different opinions may prevail with

[1] This point appears to be clearly established by Anderson, Annals,
Vol. I. p. 576. Cranmer's correspondence on this subject is contained
in Strype's Cranmer, Book I. c. 15.

regard to him, yet when we consider his character in all
its different bearings, and, above all, his labours in presenting to the inhabitants of this country, and all the nations
of the world who speak the English language, the scriptures
in their native tongue; the name of Coverdale is one which
will be always mentioned with veneration and respect.

The following account of bishop Coverdale and his works
has been given by bishop Tanner in his *Bibliotheca Bri-
tannico-Hibernica*[2]:

Coverdalus [Milo] patria Eboracensis in Cantabrigiensi
academia studia philosophica et theologica sedulo excoluit.
Dein unus ex primis doctrinæ reformatæ prædicatoribus.
Frater eremita Augustinianus A. MDXCIV. Norwici per Jo.
Calcidonensem episcopum suffrag. ordinatus presbyter. [A.
MDXLVII. in ecclesia S. Pauli London. prædicabat, cum multi
Anabaptistæ palinodiam canebant. Stow, *Hist.* p. 596. Et
A. MDXLIX. dominum Russel comitatus est in expeditione
contra rebelles Devon. Hooker ad Hollinsh. iii. 1023.] S.
theol. doctor Tubingæ in Germania creatus. A. MDLI. 20
Aug. consecrabatur episcopus Exon. Post biennium in car-
cerem detrusus, ægre, Danorum regis opera, flammas evasit,
et solum vertit (Fox, I. edit. 1081). Post obitum reginæ
Mariæ e Germania in patriam rediit, sedem vero suam re-
petere non curavit, quia Calvinistarum dogmatibus in Germania imbutus, ceremoniis et vestibus sacris in ecclesia Anglicana infensissimus erat. A. MDLXIII. per episcopum Grindal
ad episcopatum Landavensem commendabatur (Strype in *Vita
Grindall.* p. 91.) Et hoc anno 3 Martii collatus fuit ad
ecclesiam S. Magni ad pedem pontis Londin. quam resignabat
A. MDLXVI. *Reg.* Grind. Newc. i. 396. A. MDLXIV. 15 April.
Edmundum Grindall. episc. Londinensem ad gradum doc-
toratus virtute mandati procancellarii universitatis admisit,
Strype in *Vita Grindall.* p. 95. Scripsit Anglice, *Confutation of J. Standish his treatise made against the pro-
testation of Dr Barnes, anno* MDXL. Marp. MDXLVII. 8vo.
Foxius hunc inter libros prohibitos recenset, 1 edit. 573.
Calvinum de eucharistia cum constitutionibus quibusdam

---

[2] In the preceding volume of bishop Coverdale's works a list of his
writings is given in a more compendious form, for which the Editor
was principally indebted to "Memorials of Bishop Coverdale," London,
1838.

ecclesiæ Danicæ in sermonem Anglicanum transtulit. *Longam epistolam* lectori præfixit: Pr. "As the author of this little book." Pr. Lib. "For as muche as the holi." Lond. . . 12mo. Baleus tractatum hunc h. t. insignivit: *Ordinem rectum cœnæ Domini*, Lib. I. *Defensionem pauperis cujusdam Christiani, qui lege pontificia damnari debuit*, transtulit in Anglic. Noribergæ MDXLV. 8vo. *Novi Testamenti concordantias*, Lib. I. *Catechismum Christianum*, Lib. I. *De Christiano matrimonii statu*, Lib. I. c. 25. "Whan our Lorde Jesus Christ." MDXLI. 8vo. . . MDXLIII. 24to. et Lond. MDLII. 24to. Pr. pr. edit. Lond. MDLXXV. 24to. "Among other grieveous syns and." *Original of wedlock or matrimony* [a Baleo liber hic Bullingero attribuitur, et a Coverdalio versus fuisse in linguam Anglicam dicitur] Lond. MDLII. 8vo. *An exhortation to accustomable swearers; also what a right and lawful oath is.* Pr. pr. "In the Lord's vineyard, dear friend." Lond. MDLXXV. 8vo. 2 edit. . . MDXLIII. 24to. *A short instruction to all estates of men in the world.* Pr. "Be learned, ye kings, and understand." Ad finem libri, *An exhortation to accustomable swearers.* *The manner of saying grace after the doctryne of the holy Scripture.* Pr. "The eyes of all loke." Ibidem. *Fruitful lessons upon the passion, burial, resurrection, ascension, and of the sending the Holy Ghost; gathered out of the four evangelists, with a plain exposition of the same.* Pr. pr. "Since our human imperfections." Marp. MDXL. . . MDXLVII. 8vo. Lond. MDXCIII. 4to. *Christian rule of the world for every one to please God in his calling.* Printed with the christian state of matrimony. . . MDXLI. 8vo. *An evident declaration out of the holy Scriptures, that the christian faith hath endured since the beginning of the world, and that through it all virtuous men pleased God, and were saved*, c. 11. Pr. pr. "Like as the almighty eternal God." Pr. Lib. "I suppose plainly that many simple." Lond. MDXLVII. 8vo. et MDCXXIV. 4to. *Epistolam tempore Mariæ reg. Anglicam.* Pr. "It moch rejoyceth my poore heart." MS. Eman. coll. Cantabr. inter epist. martyrum. *A faithful and true prognostication upon the year* MDXXXVI. *translated out of high German.* Inter libros prohibitos memoratur a Foxio 1 edit. p. 573. *Confutationem concionis doct. Weston apud crucem Paulinam* 20 Octob. MDLIII. MS. olim penes Jo. Fox. p. 1466. Edidit

*Certain most godly letters of the protestant martyrs here
written in the tyme of their imprisonment.* Pr. pr. "The
more nigh that men's wordes and workes." Lond. MDLXIV.
4to. Transtulit in sermonem Anglicum *Biblia tota;* cum
præfatione ad Henr. VIII. extant MDXXXV. et MDXXXVII.
Vetus Testamentum hujus translationis. Pr. epist. ad Edw.
VI. "Caiaphas being byshop that yeare." In fine hujus
epistolæ ait se translationem hanc ante annos 16 patri Henr.
VIII. dicasse. Pr. pr. lectori. "Consydering how excellent."
In præf. ait se hanc translationem A. MDXXXIV. inchoasse
rogatu doctorum amicorum. Pr. transl. "In the beginning,"
&c. Lond. MDL. MDLIII. 4to. Principium epistolæ dedicatoriæ
et præfationis hujus impressionis idem est cum epist. et præfat.
principio editionis Southwark. MDXXXVII. fol. *Novum Testamentum.* Pr. ded. dom. Cromwell. "I was never so wyl-
linge to labour." Lond. MDXXXVIII. 8vo. Hæc editio anni
MDXXXVIII. accurata est ; in præfatione de erroribus in alia
editione conqueritur. Impr. Lat. et Anglice Lond. MDXXXIX.
8vo. Translatio hæc collata cum versione Gul. Tindalli.
Lond. MDL. 8vo. *Bullingerum de antiqua fide,* Lib. I. "An
old book called the old faith by Miles Coverdale." Fox, 1
edit. 573. Reprinted MDLXXX. *Eundem de matrimonio
Christi,* Lib. I. *Lutheri expositionem in psalmum* xxii. vel
xxiii. Pr. "The Lord is my shepherd." Pr. "In this
psalme doth David," Southwark. MDXXXVII. 12mo. ex Germanico. *Osiandrum super qui habitat,* Lib. I. *Psalterium
Joannis Campensis,* Lib. I. *Psalms and songs drawn as is
pictended out of the Holy Scripture* by Miles Coverdale. Inter
Libros prohibitos, Fox. 1 edit. 573. *Apologiam adversus
concilium Mantuæ,* Lib. I. *Erasmi paraphrases in Paulum
ad Romanos, Corinthios et Galatas,* Lib. IV. Lond. MDXLIX.
fol. Secundum earum volumen, nomine translatoris et typo-
graphi dicavit regi Edwardo VI. Pr. "So mercifully did
almighty God." *Supplicationem plebis Austriacensis ad
regem Ferdinandum in causa religionis cum regis responso...*
8vo. *Epitomen enchiridii Erasmi,* Ausborough, MDXLV. 8vo.
Prognosticationem in A. MDXLIX. c. 17, *et kalendarium spirituale,* Lond. MDXLIX. 8vo. *Gemmam pretiosam* (Calvini)
docentem omnes crucem amare et amplecti, c. 31. Pr. "I call
that trouble and affliction." Lond. MDLXIX. 16mo. *Mortis
librum, quomodo in mortis periculo Christianus se gerere*

debet, Lond. MDLXXIX. 16mo. ex Germanico.   *M. Buceri et*
Phil. Melanchtonis acta disputationis in concilio Ravens-
purgensi...MDXLII. 8vo.   Pr. ded. M. Buceri, "Whansoever
any councell or." *Spem fidelium, sc. de resurrectione tum*
Christi, tum corporum nostrorum...MDLXXIX. 16mo....24to.
ex Germ.   Pr. pr. transl. "Every man must nedes confess."
Justificationem esse ex libera Dei misericordia, non ex bonis
operibus, MDLXXIX. 16mo. ex German.   *Ordinem baptismi*
et cœnæ Dominicæ in Dania et quibusdam Germaniæ ec-
clesiis...12mo.   *Concionem in psalm.* xci. *de fuga a peste,*
Lond....8vo. Southwark. MDXXXVII. 12mo. ex Germ.   *An*
exposition upon Magnificat ex Lat. tempore Henr. VIII.
Fox. 1 edit. 574.   *The original and spring of all sects;*
ex Germ. Ibidem.   *The old God and the new;* ex Germ.
Ibidem.   Londini grandævus ætatis 80, vel 81, obiit Jan. 20,
MDLXXX. Fuller, *Eccl. Hist.* ix. 64, 65. A. MDLXV. juxta
Strype in *Vita Parker,* p. 149. attamen juxta pag. 241 ejus-
dem libri in vivis adhuc erat A. MDLXVII.   Et in ecclesia S.
Bartholomæi humatus jacet. Godwin. I. 476. Bal. IX. 61.

To this may be added the account given by Bale, his
contemporary and friend, in his *Scriptores illustres majoris*
Britanniæ :

Milo Coverdalus, patria Eboracensis, ex Augustiniano fra-
terculo Christianus minister factus, ex primis unus erat, qui
renascente Anglorum ecclesia, cum Roberto Barnso, suæ pro-
fessionis doctore, Christum pure docuit.   Alii partim, hic se
totum dedidit ad propagandam Evangelii regni Dei gloriam, ut
patet in utriusque Testamenti laboriosissima versione.   Ex-
aravit etiam vir pius et doctus, in nativo sermone, *Confuta-*
tionem Joann. Standicii, Lib. I. *Septimo die Decembris trad.*
Ordinem rectum cœnæ Do. Lib. I. *Omnibus qui esuriunt et*
sit. Defensionem cujusdam Christiani, Lib. I. *Cogit amor*
æqui judices.   Novi Testamenti concordantias, Lib. I. *Ca-*
techismum Christianum, Lib. I.   Transtulit in Anglicum
sermonem, præter Biblia tota, *Bullingerum de antiqua fide,*
Lib. I.   *Eundem de matrimonio Christiano,* Lib. I.   *Lu-*
therum super Dominus regit, Lib. I.   *Osiandrum super qui*
habitat, Lib. I.   *Psalterium Joannis Campensis,* Lib. I.
Cantiones Witenbergensium, Lib. I.   *Apologiam adversus*
concilium Mantuæ, Lib. I.   *Erasmi paraphrases in Paulum,*

Lib. iv. *Aliaque plura fecit.* Claruit episcopus Excestri-ensis sub rege Edwardo sexto, anno Domini 1552, nunc autem in Germania pauper ac peregrinus manet.

In concluding this portion of the works of bishop Coverdale, the editor is desirous of acknowledging his obligations to different persons for the use of scarce copies of his works; to the Very Reverend the Dean and Chapter of Peterborough; the Reverend the Warden and Fellows of All Souls College, and the Provost and Fellows of Queen's College, Oxford; to the Reverend the Master and Fellows of St John's College, Cambridge; to the Reverend Dr Thackeray, Provost of King's College; to the Very Reverend the Dean of Bristol, Master, and the Reverend H. Goodwin, Fellow of Corpus Christi College, Cambridge, for the privilege of access to the MS. Library of that college; to George Offor, Esq. of Hackney; to John Matthew Gutch, Esq. of Claines, Worcestershire; and to the Reverend S. R. Maitland, for valuable assistance derived from the archiepiscopal Library at Lambeth.

ADDENDA ET CORRIGENDA.

4. l. 11. For *throughout*, read *thoroughout*.
   l. 9 and 20. *Your grace*. Note (4) is here transposed.
6. l. 11. For *the*, A. B. read *this*.
12. l. 18, 19. For, *I have been the more glad to follow for the most part*, C. D. read, *I have been glad to follow*.
— l. 23. After *we*, C. D. read, *in ours*.
— l. 24. *And that with a good will*, omitted C. D.
13. l. 2. *Vulgarius*, i. e. *Theophylact*, as he was called by Erasmus, by a singular mistake, in the first and second editions of his New Testament; from whom it appears to have been borrowed by bishop Coverdale. It was corrected by Erasmus in the subsequent editions. For an account of the origin of this mistake, see Wetstein Proleg. ad N. T., and Jortin's Life of Erasmus, Vol. II. pp. 230—5. Ed. 1560.
14. *n*. 3. *did:* so also A. B.
25. l. 5. for *sinisterly*, read *sinistrally*.
— l. 25. dele *a*.
40. *n*. l. 1. for *philosopher*, read *philosophers*.
276. l. 7. for *him*, read *us*.
281. l. 1, 2. for *paraphrase*, read *exposition*.
348. l. 21. for *Lutice's error*, read *Eutyches' error*, the reading of the old edition being *Eutice's error;* and for *n*. 2. substitute the following: "The opinions of Eutyches on this subject are alluded to in the note of Dr Grabe on Irenæus, Lib. I. cap. 13, which is referred to in the preceding note. In this note the learned writer refers to Vigilius Tapsensis, who in his work *Adversus Nestorium et Eutychem pro defensione Synodi Chalcedonensis*, Lib. III., has especially noticed the errors of Eutyches on this subject: and he also corrects an error committed by some writers, (and amongst them by our author, *Hope of the Faithful*, p. 154,) who speak of him as Vigilius, *the martyr;* a title which belongs to another person. See Cave, Hist. Lit. Vol. I. p. 370. For some further account of the opinions of Eutyches, see August. de Hæresibus, Opera, Tom. X. p. 8. A. 1541, and bishop Pearson ON THE CREED, Art. III.
520. *n*. 5. Fagius was not Professor of *Divinity* at Cambridge, but of *Hebrew*, the Divinity chair being filled at the same time by Bucer.
528. l. 28. for *relating to*, read *from*.

DEDICATIONS AND PROLOGUES

TO

THE TRANSLATIONS

OF THE

BIBLE AND NEW TESTAMENT.

[DEDICATION AND PROLOGUE TO THE BIBLE.

The Dedication and Prologue to the Bible are taken from the first edition of Bishop Coverdale's Bible of the year 1535. They are here printed from a copy in the University Library, Cambridge, and have been collated with the following editions, viz.:

1. The folio edition of 1537, published by James Nycolson of Southwark, in the Cathedral Library at Lincoln. Another copy of this edition is in the Baptist College Library at Bristol. A.

2. The quarto edition, published by Nycolson in the same year, in the library of Earl Spencer at Althorp. B.

3. The edition of 1550, published by Andrew Hester, in the University Library, Cambridge. C.

4. The edition of 1553, published by Richard Jugge, also in the University Library, Cambridge. D.

These last two are in fact the same edition; the last edition consisting of copies of the original edition, which was printed by Christopher Froschover at Zurich in 1550, and re-issued in London, with a new Title and Calendar, and with the Dedication and Prologue reprinted, by Richard Jugge, in 1553.]

DEDICATION AND PROLOGUE

TO THE

TRANSLATION OF THE BIBLE.

UNTO THE MOST VICTORIOUS PRINCE AND OUR MOST GRACIOUS SOVEREIGN LORD

KING HENRY THE EIGHTH,

KING OF ENGLAND AND OF FRANCE, LORD OF IRELAND, &c.[1],
DEFENDER OF THE FAITH, AND UNDER GOD THE CHIEF
AND SUPREME HEAD OF THE CHURCH OF ENGLAND.

¶ *The right and just administration of the laws that God gave unto Moses and unto Josua: the testimony of faithfulness that God gave of David: the plenteous abundance of wisdom that God gave unto Salomon: the lucky and prosperous age, with the multiplication of seed, which God gave unto Abraham and Sara his wife: be given unto you, most gracious prince[2], with your dearest just wife, and most virtuous princess, queen Anne[3].* Amen.

CAIPHAS, being bishop of that year, like a blind prophet, not understanding what he said, prophesied that Joh. xi. it was better to put Christ unto death, than that all the people should perish : he meaning that Christ was an heretic, a deceiver of the people, and a destroyer of the law, and that it was better therefore to put Christ unto death, than to suffer him for to live, and to deceive the people, &c. ; where in very deed Christ was the true prophet[4], the true Messias, and the only true Saviour of the world, sent of his heavenly Father to suffer the most cruel, most shameful, and most necessary death for our redemption, according to the meaning of the prophecy truly understand.

[1 King Edward VI, king of England, France, and of Ireland, C.D.]
[2 C. D. omit all after "most gracious prince."]
[3 Queen Jane, A. B.]   [4 Omitted, C. D.]

1—2

Even after the same manner the blind bishop of Rome, (that blind Baalam, I say,) not understanding what he did, gave unto your grace[1] this title, *Defender of the faith*, only because your highness[2] suffered your[3] bishops to burn God's word, the root of faith, and to persecute the lovers and ministers of the same: where in very deed the blind bishop (though he knew not what he did) prophesied, that by the righteous administration and continual diligence of your grace[4] the faith should so be defended, that God's word, the mother of faith, with the fruits thereof, should have his free course throughout all christendom, but specially in your realm.

If your highness now, of your princely benignity, will pardon me to compare these two bishops (I mean bishop Caiphas and the bishop of Rome) and their prophecies together, I doubt not but we shall find them agree like brethren, though the one be a Jew, and the other a counterfeit Christian. First, Caiphas prophesied that it was better to put Christ unto death than that the people should perish. The bishop of Rome also, not knowing what he prophesied, gave your grace this title, *Defender of the faith*. The truth of both these prophecies is of the Holy Ghost (as was Baalam's prophecy), though they that spake them knew not what they said. The truth of Caiphas's prophecy is, that it was necessary for man's salvation that Christ by his death should overcome death, and redeem us. And the truth of our Baalam's prophecy is, that your grace in very deed should defend the faith, yea, even the true faith of Christ; no dreams, no fables, no heresy, no papistical inventions, but the uncorrupt faith of God's most holy word; which to set forth (praised be the goodness of God, and increase your gracious purpose!) your highness, with your most honourable council, applieth all his study[5] and endeavour.

Num. xxiv.

These two blind bishops now agree in the understanding of their prophecies: for Caiphas taketh Christ for an heretic, our Baalam taketh the word of Christ for heresy. Caiphas judgeth it to be a good deed to put Christ unto[6] death, that

[1 your grace's most noble progenitors, C. D.]
[2 they, C. D.]   [3 the, C. D.]
[4 your grace's most noble father, C. D.]
[5 all study, A. B.]   [6 to, A. B.]

he should not deceive the people: our Baalam calleth defending of the faith the suppressing, keeping secret, and burning of the word of faith, lest the light thereof should utter his darkness; lest his own decretals and decrees, his own laws and constitutions, his own statutes and inventions, should come to none effect; lest his intolerable exactions and usurpations should lose their strength; lest it should be known what a thief and murtherer he is in the cause of Christ, and how heinous a traitor to God and man, in defrauding all christian kings and princes of their due obedience; lest we, your grace's subjects, should have eyes in the word of God, at the last to spy out his crafty conveyance and jugglings; and lest men should see, how sore he and his false apostles have deceived all christendom, specially your noble realm of England.

Thus your grace seeth how brotherly the Jewish bishop and our Baalam agree together, not only in mitre and outward appearance; but, as the one persecuted the Lord Jesus in his own person, so doth the other persecute his word, and resisteth his holy ordinance in the authority of his anointed kings. Forsomuch now as the word of God is the only truth that driveth away all lies, and discloseth all juggling and deceit, therefore is our Baalam of Rome so loath that the scripture should be known in the mothertongue; lest, if kings and princes, specially above all other, were exercised therein, they should reclaim[7] and challenge again their due authority, which he falsely hath usurped so many years, and so to tie him shorter; and lest the people, being taught by the word of God, should fall from the false feigned obedience of him and his disguised apostles unto the true obedience commanded by God's own mouth; as namely, to obey their prince, to obey father and mother, &c., and not to step over father and mother's belly to enter into his painted religions, as his hypocrites teach. For he knoweth well enough, that if the clear sun of God's word come once to the heat of the day, it shall drive away all the foul mist of his devilish doctrines. Therefore were it more to the maintenance of antichrist's kingdom, that the world were still in ignorance and blindness, and that the scripture should never come to light. For tho scripture,

[7 claim, C. D.]

both in the old testament and in the new, declareth most abundantly, that the office, authority, and power given of God unto kings is in earth above all other powers: let them call themselves popes, cardinals, or whatsoever they will, the word of God declareth them (yea, and commandeth them under pain of damnation), to be obedient unto the temporal sword, as in the old testament all the prophets, priests, and Levites were. And in the new testament Christ and his apostles both were obedient themselves, and taught obedience of all men unto their princes and temporal rulers; which here unto us in the world present the person of God, and are called gods in the scripture, because of the excellency of their office. And though there were no more authorities but the same, to prove the pre-eminence of the temporal sword; yet by this the scripture declareth plainly, that as there is nothing above God, so is there no man above the king in his realm, but that he only under God is the chief head of all the congregation and church of the same. And in token that this is true, there hath been of old[1] antiquity, and is yet unto this day, a loving ceremony used in your realm of England, that when your grace's subjects read your letters, or begin to talk or commune of your highness, they move their bonnets for a sign and token of reverence unto your grace, as to their most sovereign lord and head under God: which thing no man useth to do to any bishop; whereby (if our understanding were not blinded) we might evidently perceive, that even very nature teacheth us the same that scripture commandeth us; and that, like as it is against God's word that a king should not be the chief head of his people, even so, I say, is it against kind, that we should know any other head above him under God.

And that no priest nor bishop is exempt, nor can be lawfully, from the obedience of his prince, the scripture is full both of strait commandments and practices of the holiest men. Aaron was obedient unto Moses, and called him his lord, though he was his own brother. Eleasar and Phineas were under the obedience of Josua. Nathan the prophet fell down to the ground before king David; he had his prince in such reverence: he made not the king for to kiss his foot, as the bishop of Rome maketh empe-

Rom. xiii.

Matt. xvii.
Tit. iii.

Exod. xxii.
Psal. lxxxii.

1 Pet. ii.

Numb. xii.

Josh. iv.

1 Kings i.

[1 all, C. D.]

rors to do ; notwithstanding he spared not to rebuke him, 2 Sam. xii.
and that right sharply, when he fell from the word of God
to adultery and manslaughter. For he was not afraid to
reprove him of his sins, no more than Helias the prophet
stood in fear to say unto king Achab, " It is thou and thy 1 Kings xviii.
father's house that trouble Israel, because ye have forsaken
the commandments of the Lord, and walk after Baal;" and
as John Baptist durst say unto king Herode, " It is not Levit. xviii.
lawful for thee to take thy brother's wife." But to my pur- Matt. xiv.
pose. I pass over innumerable more ensamples both of the
old testament and of the new, for fear lest I be too tedious
unto your grace. Summa, In all godly regiments of old
time the king and temporal judge was obeyed of every
man, and was alway under God the chief and supreme
head of the whole congregation, and deposed even priests 1 Kings ii,
when he saw an urgent cause, as Salomon did unto Abia-
thar. Who could then stand against the godly obedience
of his prince, except he would be at defiance with God and
all his holy ordinances, that were well acquainted with the
holy scripture, which so earnestly commendeth unto every
one of us the authority and power given of God unto kings
and temporal rulers ? Therefore doth Moses so straitly
forbid the Israelites to speak so much as an evil word Exod. xxii.
against the prince of the people, much less then to disobey him, or to withstand him. Doth not Jeremy the Jer. xxix.
prophet, and Baruc also, exhort the people in captivity, Bar. ii.
to pray for the prosperous welfare of the king of Babylon,
and to obey him, though he was an infidel ? In the new
testament, when our Saviour Christ, being yet free and
Lord of all kings and princes, shewed his obedience in
paying the tribute to our ensample, did he not a miracle Matt. xvii.
there in putting the piece of money in the fish's mouth,
that Peter might pay the customer therewith ; and all to
stablish the obedience due unto princes ? Did not Joseph, Luke ii.
and Mary, the mother of our Saviour Christ, depart from
Nazareth unto Bethleem, so far from home, to shew their
obedience in paying the tax to the prince ? And would
not our Saviour be born in the same obedience ? Doth
not Paul pronounce him to resist God himself, that resisteth Rom. xiii.
the authority of his prince ? And to be short, the apostle
Peter doth not only stablish the obedience unto princes 1 Pet. ii.

and temporal rulers, but affirmeth plainly the king, and
no bishop, to be the chief head.   Innumerable places more
are there[1] in scripture, which bind us to the obedience of
our prince, and declare unto us, that no man is nor can
be, lawfully except from the same; but that all the ministers
of God's word are under the temporal sword, and princes
only to owe obedience unto God and his word.

And whereas antichrist unto your grace's[2] time did thrust
his head into the imperial crown of your highness, (as he
doth yet with other noble princes more[3],) that learned he
of Sathan, the author of pride; and therein doth he both
against the doctrine, and also[4] against the ensample of Christ;
which, because his kingdom was not of this world, meddled
with no temporal matters, as it is evident both by his words
and practice, Luke xii., Matt. xxvi., John vi. xviii.; where
he that hath eyes to see may see, and he that hath ears
to hear may hear, that Christ's administration was nothing
temporal, but plain spiritual, as he himself affirmeth and
proveth in the fourth chapter of St Luke out of the prophet
Esay: where all bishops and priests may see, how far their
binding and loosing extendeth, and wherein their office consisteth, namely[5], in preaching the gospel, &c.

Wherefore, most gracious prince, there is no tongue, I
think, that can fully express and declare the intolerable
injuries, which have been done unto God, to all princes, and
to the commonalties of all christian realms, since they which
should be only the ministers of God's word became lords
of the world, and thrust the true and just princes out of
their rowmes[6].   Whose heart would not pity it, (yea, even with
lamentation,) to remember but only the untolerable wrong
done by that antichrist of Rome unto your grace's most
noble predecessor king John?   I pass over his pestilent
picking of Peter-pence out of your realm; his stealing away
of your money for pardons, benefices, and bishopricks; his
deceiving of your subjects' souls with his devilish doctrines and
sects of his false religious; his blood-shedding of so many
of your grace's people for books of the scripture: whose heart
would not be grieved, (yea, and that out of measure,) to call

[1 there be, C. D.]   [2 grace's most noble father's, C. D.]
[3 omitted, C. D.]   [4 omitted, A. B.]
[5 namely, &c. omitted, C. D.]   [6 rowmes: i. e. realms.]

to remembrance, how obstinate and disobedient, how presumptuous and stubborn that antichrist made the bishops of your realm against your grace's noble predecessors in times past, as it is manifest in the chronicles? I trust, verily, there be no such now within your realm: if there be, let them remember these words of scripture: Presumptuousness Prov. xvi. goeth before destruction, and after a proud stomach there followeth a fall.

What is now the cause of all these untolerable and no more to be suffered abominations? Truly, even the ignorance of the scripture of God. For how had it else been possible, that such blindness should have come into the world, had not the light of God's word been extinct? How could men, I say, have been so far from the true service of God and from the due obedience of their prince, had not the law of God been clean shut up, depressed, cast aside, and put out of remembrance? as it was afore the time of that noble king Josias, and as it hath been also[7] among us unto your grace's time[8], by whose[9] most righteous administration, through the merciful goodness of God, it is now found again, as it was in the days of that most virtuous king Josias. 2 Kings xxii.
And praised be the Father, the Son, and the Holy Ghost, 2 Chron.
xxiv.
world without end, which so excellently hath endued your princely heart with such ferventness to his honour, and to the wealth of your loving subjects, that I may righteously, by just occasions in your person, compare your highness unto that noble and gracious king, that lantern of light among princes, that fervent protector and defender of the laws of God; which commanded straitly, as your grace doth, that the law of God should be read and taught unto all the people; set the priests to their office in the word of God; destroyed idolatry and false idols[10]; put down all evil customs and abusions; set up the true honour of God; applied all his study and endeavour to the righteous administration of the most uncorrupt law of God, &c. O what felicity was among the people of Jerusalem in his days! And what prosperous health, both of soul and body, followeth the like ministration in your highness, we begin now (praised be God!) to have experience. For as false doc- Jer. xliv.

[7 omitted, C. D.]　[8 your grace's most noble father's time, C. D.]
[9 by whose and by your majesty's, C. D.]
[10 the mountains of idolatry, superstition, and hypocrisy, C. D.]

trine is the original cause of all evil plagues and destruction, so is the true executing of the law of God, and the preaching of the same, the mother of all godly prosperity. The

Wisd. vii.
only word of God, I say, is the cause of all felicity : it bringeth all goodness with it, it bringeth learning, it gendereth understanding, it causeth good works, it maketh children of obedience; briefly, it teacheth all estates their office and duty. Seeing then that the scripture of God teacheth us everything sufficiently, both what we ought to do, and what we ought to leave undone, whom we are bound to obey, and whom we should not obey; therefore, I say, it causeth all prosperity, and setteth everything in frame; and where it is taught and known[1], it lighteneth all darknesses, comforteth all sorry hearts, leaveth no poor man unhelped, suffereth nothing amiss unamended, letteth no prince be disobeyed, permitteth no heresy to be preached; but reformeth all things, amendeth that is amiss, and setteth everything in order. And why? because it is given by the inspiration of God, therefore is it ever bringing profit and fruit, by teaching, by improving, by amending and

2 Tim. iii.
reforming all them that will receive it, to make them perfect and meet unto all good works.

Considering now, most gracious prince, the inestimable treasure, fruit, and prosperity everlasting, that God giveth with his word, and trusting in his infinite goodness, that he would bring my simple and rude labour herein to good effect; therefore[2], as the Holy Ghost moved other men to do the cost hereof, so was I boldened in God to labour in the same. Again, considering your imperial majesty not

[1 truly taught and thankfully received, C. D.]

[2 The remainder of this paragraph stands thus in C.D: "Therefore was I boldened in God sixteen years ago, not only to labour faithfully in the same, but also in most humble wise to dedicate this my poor translation to your grace's most noble father; as I do now submit this and all other my poor corrections, labours, and enterprises, to the gracious spirit of true knowledge, understanding, and judgment, which is in your highness; most humbly beseeching the same, that though this volume be small, and not wholly the text appointed for the churches, it may yet be exercised in all other places, so long as it is used within the compass of the fear of God, and due obedience to your most excellent majesty; whom the same eternal God save and preserve evermore! Amen. Your grace's most humble and faithful subject, MYLES COVERDALE."]

only to be my natural sovereign liege lord, and chief head of the church of England, but also the true defender and maintainer of God's laws, I thought it my duty, and to belong unto my allegiance, when I had translated this Bible, not only to dedicate this translation unto your highness, but wholly to commit it unto the same; to the intent, that if anything therein be translated amiss, (for in many things we fail, even when we think to be sure,) it may stand in your grace's hands to correct it, to amend it, to improve it, yea, and clean to reject it, if your godly wisdom shall think it necessary. And as I do with all humbleness submit mine understanding and my poor translation unto the spirit of truth in your grace; so make I this protestation, having God to record in my conscience, that I have neither wrested nor altered so much as one word for the maintenance of any manner of sect, but have with a clear conscience purely and faithfully translated this out of five sundry interpreters, having only the manifest truth of the scripture before mine eyes, trusting in the goodness of God, that it shall be unto his worship, quietness and tranquillity unto your highness, a perfect stablishment of all God's ordinances within your grace's dominion, a general comfort to all christian hearts, and a continual thankfulness both of old and young unto God and to your grace, for being our Moses, and for bringing us out of this old Egypt from the cruel hands of our spiritual Pharao. For where were the Jews, by ten thousand parts, so much bound unto king David for 1 Sam. xvii. subduing of great Goliath and all their enemies, as we are to your grace for delivering us out of our old Babylonical captivity? For the which deliverance and victory I beseech our only Mediator Jesus Christ to make such means for us unto his heavenly Father, that we never be unthankful unto him, nor unto your grace; but that we ever increase in the fear of him, in obedience unto your highness, in love unfeigned unto our neighbours, and in all virtue that cometh of God. To whom, for the defending of his blessed word by your grace's most rightful administration, be honour and thanks, glory and dominion, world without end! Amen.

Your grace's humble subject and daily orator,

MYLES COVERDALE.

A PROLOGUE.

MYLES COVERDALE UNTO THE CHRISTIAN READER.

CONSIDERING how excellent knowledge and learning an interpreter of scripture ought to have in the tongues, and pondering also mine own insufficiency therein, and how weak I am to perform the office of a translator, I was the more loath to meddle with this work. Notwithstanding, when I considered how great pity it was that we should want it so long, and called to my remembrance the adversity of them which were not only of ripe knowledge, but would also with all their hearts have performed that they began, if they had not had impediment[1]; considering, I say, that by reason of their adversity it could not so soon have been brought to an end, as our most prosperous nation would fain have had it; these and other reasonable causes considered, I was the more bold to take it in hand. And to help me herein, I have had sundry translations, not only in Latin, but also of the Dutch[2] interpreters[3], whom, because of their singular gifts and special diligence in the Bible, I have been the more glad to follow for the most part, according as I was required. But, to say the truth before God, it was neither my labour nor desire to have this work put in my hand: nevertheless it grieved me that other nations should be more plenteously provided for with the scripture in their mother-tongue, than we: therefore, when I was instantly required, though I could not do so well as I would, I thought it yet my duty to do my best, and that with a good will[4].

Whereas some men think now that many translations make division in the faith and in the people of God, that is not so: for it was never better with the congregation of God, than when every church almost had the Bible of a

[1 impediments, C. D.]   [2 Dutch, i. e. German.]
[3 in other languages, C. D.]
[4 that the scripture might wholly come forth in English, C. D.]

sundry translation.   Among the Greeks had not Origen a
special translation?   Had not Vulgarius one peculiar, and likewise Chrysostom?   Beside the 'seventy interpreters, is there
not the translation of Aquila, of Theodotio, of Symmachus,
and of sundry other?   Again, among the Latin men, thou
findest that every one almost used a special and sundry translation; for insomuch as every bishop had the knowledge of
the tongues, he gave his diligence to have the Bible of his own
translation.   The doctors, as Hireneus, Cyprianus, Tertullian,
St Hierome, St Augustine, Hilarius, and St Ambrose, upon
divers places of the scripture, read not the text all alike.

Therefore ought it not to be taken as evil, that such
men as have understanding now in our time, exercise themselves in the tongues, and give their diligence to translate
out of one language into another.   Yea, we ought rather
to give God high thanks therefore, which through his Spirit
stirreth up men's minds so to exercise themselves therein.
Would God it had never been left off after the time of St
Augustine! then should we never have come into such blindness and ignorance, into such errors and delusions.   For as
soon as the Bible was cast aside, and no more put in exercise,
then began every one of his own head to write whatsoever
came into his brain, and that seemed to be good in his own
eyes; and so grew the darkness of men's traditions.   And
this same is the cause that we have had so many writers,
which seldom made mention of the scripture of the Bible;
and though they sometime alleged it, yet was it done so
far out of season, and so wide from the purpose, that a man
may well perceive, how that they never saw the original.

Seeing then that this diligent exercise of translating doth
so much good and edifieth in other languages, why should it
do evil in ours?   Doubtless, like as all nations in the diversity
of speeches may know one God in the unity of faith, and be
one in love; even so may divers translations understand one
another, and that in the head articles and ground of our most
blessed faith, though they use sundry words.   Wherefore
methink we have great occasion to give thanks unto God,
that he hath opened unto his church the gift of interpretation
and of printing, and that there are now at this time so many,
which with such diligence and faithfulness interpret the scripture, to the honour of God and edifying of his people: whereas,

like as when many are shooting together, every one doth his best to be nighest the mark ; and though they cannot all attain thereto, yet shooteth one nigher than another, and hitteth it better than another ; yea, one can do it better than another.   Who is now then so unreasonable, so despiteful, or envious, as to abhor him that doth all his diligence to hit the prick, and to shoot nighest it, though he miss and come not nighest the mark ?   Ought not such one rather to be commended, and to be helped forward, that he may exercise himself the more therein ?

For the which cause, according as I was desired[1], I took the more upon me to set forth this special translation, not as a checker, not as a reprover, or despiser of other men's translations, (for among many as yet I have found none without occasion of great thanksgiving unto God;) but lowly and faithfully have I followed mine interpreters, and that under correction ; and though I have failed anywhere (as there is no man but he misseth in some thing), love[2] shall construe all to the best, without any perverse judgment.   There is no man living that can see all things, neither hath God given any man to know everything.   One seeth more clearly than another, one hath more understanding than another, one can utter a thing better than another; but no man ought to envy or despise another.   He that can do better than another, should not set him at nought that understandeth less.   Yea, he that hath the more understanding ought to remember, that the same gift is not his, but God's, and that God hath given it him to teach and inform the ignorant. If thou hast knowledge therefore to judge where any fault is made, I doubt not but thou wilt help to amend it, if love be joined with thy knowledge. Howbeit, whereinsoever I can[3] perceive by myself, or by the information of other, that I have failed (as it is no wonder), I shall now by the help of God overlook it better, and amend it[4].

Now will I exhort thee, whosoever thou be that readest scripture, if thou find ought therein that thou understandest not, or that appeareth to be repugnant, give no temerarious nor hasty judgment thereof; but ascribe it to thine own ignorance, not to the scripture: think that thou understandest

[1 Anno, 1534, C. D.]   [2 christian love, C. D.]
[3 did, C. D.]
[4 I have now ... overlooked and amended it, A. B. C. D.]

it not, or that it hath some other meaning, or that it is haply overseen of the interpreters, or wrong printed. Again, it shall greatly help thee to understand scripture, if thou mark not only what is spoken or written, but of whom, and unto whom, with what words, at what time, where, to what intent, with what circumstance, considering what goeth before, and what followeth after. For there be some things which are done and written, to the intent that we should do likewise; as when Abraham believeth God, is obedient unto his word, and defendeth Loth his kinsman from violent wrong. There be some things also which are written, to the intent that we should eschew such like; as when David lieth with Urias' wife, and causeth him to be slain. Therefore, I say, when thou readest scripture, be wise and circumspect; and when thou comest to such strange manners of speaking and dark sentences, to such parables and similitudes, to such dreams or visions, as are hid from thy understanding, commit them unto God, or to the gift of his Holy Spirit in them that are better learned than thou.

As for the commendation of God's holy scripture, I would fain magnify it, as it is worthy, but I am far unsufficient thereto: and therefore I thought it better for me to hold my tongue, than with few words to praise or commend it; exhorting thee, most dear reader, so to love it, so to cleave unto it, and so to follow it in thy daily conversation, that other men, seeing thy good works and the fruits of the Holy Ghost in thee, may praise the Father of heaven, and give his word a good report: for to live after the law of God, and to lead a virtuous conversation, is the greatest praise that thou canst give unto his doctrine.

But as touching the evil report and dispraise that the good word of God hath by the corrupt and evil conversation of some that daily hear it and profess it outwardly with their mouths, I exhort thee, most dear reader, let not that offend thee, nor withdraw thy mind from the love of the truth, neither move thee to be partaker in like unthankfulness; but seeing the light is come into the world, love no more the works of darkness, receive not the grace of God in vain. Call to thy remembrance, how loving and merciful God is unto thee, how kindly and fatherly he helpeth thee in all trouble, teacheth thine ignorance, healeth thee in all thy sickness,

forgiveth thee all thy sins, feedeth thee, giveth thee drink,
helpeth thee out of prison, nourisheth thee in strange countries,
careth for thee, and seeth that thou want nothing. Call this
to mind, I say, and that earnestly, and consider how thou
hast received of God all these benefits, yea, and many more
than thou canst desire; how thou art bound likewise to shew
thyself unto thy neighbour, as far as thou canst, to teach him,
if he be ignorant, to help him in all his trouble, to heal his
sickness, to forgive him his offences, and that heartily, to feed
him, to cherish him, to care for him, and to see that he want
nothing. And on this behalf I beseek thee, thou that hast
the riches of this world, and lovest God with thy heart, to
lift up thine eyes, and see how great a multitude of poor
people run through every town; have pity on thine own
flesh, help them with a good heart, and do with thy counsel all
that ever thou canst, that this unshamefaced begging may be
put down, that these idle folks may be set to labour, and that
such as are not able to get their living may be provided for.
At the least, thou that art of counsel[1] with such as are in
authority, give them some occasion to cast their heads together,
and to make provision for the poor. Put them in remembrance of those noble cities in other countries, that by the
authority of their princes have so richly and well provided
for their poor people, to the great shame and dishonesty of
us, if we likewise, receiving the word of God, shew not such
like fruits thereof. Would God that those men, whose office is
to maintain the commonwealth, were as diligent in this cause,
as they are in other! Let us beware bytimes, for after unthankfulness there followeth ever a plague. The merciful
hand of God be with us, and defend us, that we be not partakers thereof!

Deut. vi. Go to now, most dear reader, and sit thee down at the
Lord's feet, and read his words, and, as Moses teacheth the
Jews, take them into thine heart, and let thy talking and communication be of them, when thou sittest in thine house, or goest
by the way, when thou liest down, and when thou risest up.
And, above all things, fashion thy life and conversation according to the doctrine of the Holy Ghost therein, that thou
mayest be partaker of the good promises of God in the Bible,
and be heir of his blessing in Christ: in whom if thou put

[1 of the council, A. B.]

thy trust, and be an unfeigned reader or hearer of his word with thy heart, thou shalt find sweetness therein, and spy wondrous things, to thy understanding, to the avoiding of all seditious sects, to the abhorring of thy old sinful life, and to the stablishing of thy godly conversation.

In the first book of Moses, called Genesis, thou mayest learn to know the almighty power of God in creating all of nought, his infinite wisdom in ordering the same, his righteousness in punishing the ungodly, his love and fatherly mercy in comforting the righteous with his promise, &c.

In the second book, called Exodus, we see the mighty arm of God in delivering his people from so great bondage out of Egypt, and what provision he maketh for them in the wilderness; how he teacheth them with his wholesome word, and how the tabernacle was made and set up.

In the third book, called Leviticus, is declared, what sacrifices the priests and Levites used, and what their office and ministration was.

In the fourth book, called Numerus, is declared, how the people are numbered and mustered, how the captains are chosen after the tribes and kindreds, how they went forth to the battle, how they pitched their tents, and how they brake up.

The fifth book, called Deuteronomium, sheweth how that Moses, now being old, rehearseth the law of God unto the people, putteth them in remembrance again of all the wonders and benefices that God had shewed for them, and exhorteth them earnestly to love the Lord their God, to cleave unto him, to put their trust in him, and to hearken unto his voice.

After the death of Moses doth Josua bring the people into the land of promise, where God doth wonderous things for his people by Josua, which distributeth the land unto them, unto every tribe their possession. But in their wealth they forgat the goodness of God, so that ofttimes he gave them over into the hand of their enemies. Nevertheless, whensoever they called faithfully upon him, and converted, he delivered them again, as the book of Judges declareth.

In the books of the Kings is described the regiment of good and evil princes, and how the decay of all nations cometh by evil kings. For in Jeroboam thou seest what mischief, what idolatry, and such like abomination followeth, when the king is a maintainer of false doctrine, and causeth the people to sin against God; which falling away from God's word increased so sore among them, that it was the cause of all their sorrow and misery, and the very occasion why Israel first, 2 Chron. xvii. and then Juda, were carried away into captivity. Again, in Josaphat, in Ezechias, and in Josias, thou seest the nature of a virtuous king. He putteth down the houses of idolatry, seeth that his priests teach nothing but the law of God, commandeth his lords to go with them, and to see that they teach the people. In these kings, I say, thou seest the condition of a true defender of the faith; for he spareth neither cost nor labour to maintain the laws of God, to seek the wealth and prosperity of his people, and to root out the wicked. And where such a prince is, thou seest again, how God defendeth him and his people, though he have never so many enemies. Thus went it with them in the old time, and even after the same manner goeth it now with us. God be praised therefore, and grant us of his fatherly mercy that we be not unthankful; lest where he now giveth us a Josaphat, an Ezechias, yea, a very Josias, he send us a Pharao, a Jeroboam, or an Achab!

In the two first books of Esdras, and in Hester, thou seest the deliverance of the people, which though they were but few, yet is it unto us all a special comfort; forsomuch as God is not forgetful of his promise, but bringeth them out of captivity, according as he had told them before.

In the book of Job we learn comfort and patience, in that God not only punisheth the wicked, but proveth and trieth the just and righteous (howbeit there is no man innocent in his sight,) by divers troubles in this life; declaring thereby, that they are not his bastards, but his dear sons, and that he loveth them.

In the Psalms we learn how to resort only unto God in all our troubles, to seek help at him, to call only upon him, to settle our minds by patience, and how we ought in prosperity to be thankful unto him.

The Proverbs and the Preacher of Salomon teach us wisdom, to know God, our own selves, and the world, and how vain all things are, save only to cleave unto God.

As for the doctrine of the Prophets, what is it else, but an earnest exhortation to eschew sin, and to turn unto

God; a faithful promise of the mercy and pardon of God unto all them that turn unto him, and a threatening of his wrath to the ungodly? saving that here and there they prophesy also manifestly of Christ, of the expulsion of the Jews, and calling of the heathen.

[1] Thus much thought I to speak of the old Testament, wherein Almighty God openeth unto us his mighty power, his wisdom, his loving mercy and righteousness: for the which cause it ought of no man to be abhorred, despised, or lightly regarded, as though it were an old scripture that nothing belonged unto us, or that now were to be refused. For it is God's true scripture and testimony, which the Lord Jesus commandeth the Jews to search.   Whosoever believeth John v. not the scripture, believeth not Christ; and whoso refuseth it, refuseth God also.

The new Testament, or Gospel, is a manifest and clear testimony of Christ, how God performeth his oath and promise made in the old Testament, how the new is declared and included in the old, and the old fulfilled and verified in the new.

Now whereas the most famous interpreters of all give sundry judgments of the text; so far as it is done by the spirit of knowledge in the Holy Ghost, methink no man should be offended thereat, for they refer their doings in meekness to the spirit of truth in the congregation of God: and sure I am, that there cometh more knowledge and understanding of the scripture by their sundry translations, than by all the glosses of our sophistical doctors.   For that one interpreteth something obscurely in one place, the same translateth another, or else he himself, more manifestly by a more plain vocable of the same meaning in another place. Be not thou offended, therefore, good reader, though one call a scribe that another calleth a lawyer; or elders, that another calleth father and mother; or repentance, that another calleth penance or amendment.   For if thou be not deceived by men's traditions, thou shalt find no more diversity between these terms, than between fourpence and a groat. And this manner have I used in my translation, calling it in some place *penance*, that in another place I call *repentance;* and that not only because the interpreters have done

[1 This paragraph is omitted, A. B. C. D.]

2—2

so before me, but that the adversaries of the truth may see, how that we abhor not this word penance, as they untruly report of us, no more than the interpreters of Latin abhor *pœnitere*, when they read *resipiscere*. Only our heart's desire unto God is, that his people be not blinded in their understanding, lest they believe penance to be ought save a very repentance, amendment, or conversion unto God, and to be an unfeigned new creature in Christ, and to live according to his law. For else shall they fall into the old blasphemy of Christ's blood, and believe that they themselves are able to make satisfaction unto God for their own sins: from the which error God of his mercy and plenteous goodness preserve all his!

Now to conclude: forsomuch as all the scripture is written for thy doctrine and ensample, it shall be necessary for thee to take hold upon it while it is offered thee, yea, and with ten hands thankfully to receive it. And though it be not worthily ministered unto thee in this translation, by reason of my rudeness; yet if thou be fervent in thy prayer, God shall[1] not only send it thee in a better shape by the ministration of other that began it afore, but shall also move the hearts of them which as yet meddled not withal, to take it in hand, and to bestow the gift of their understanding thereon, as well in our language, as other famous interpreters do in other languages[2]. And I pray God, that through my poor ministration herein I may give them that can do better some occasion so to do; exhorting thee, most dear reader, in the mean while on God's behalf, if thou be a head, a judge, or ruler of the people, that thou

Josh. i.
Deut. xvii.

let not the book of this law depart out of thy mouth, but exercise thyself therein both day and night, and be ever reading in it as long as thou livest: that thou mayest learn to fear the Lord thy God, and not to turn aside from the commandment, neither to the right hand nor to the left;

Deut. xxiv.

lest thou be a knower of persons in judgment, and wrest the right of the stranger, of the fatherless, or of the widow, and so the curse to come upon thee. But what office so ever

Rom. xii.
1 Pet. iv.

thou hast, wait upon it, and execute it to the maintenance of peace, to the wealth of thy people, defending the laws

[1 God shall move the hearts of them which, &c. C. D.]
[2 tongues, C. D.]

of God and the lovers thereof, and to the destruction of the wicked.

If thou be a preacher, and hast the oversight of the ^{Acts xx. 1 Pet. v.} flock of Christ, awake and feed Christ's sheep with a good heart, and spare no labour to do them good : seek not thyself, and beware of filthy lucre; but be unto the flock an ^{1 Tim. iv. Tit. ii.} ensample in the word, in conversation, in love, in ferventness of the spirit, and be ever reading, exhorting, and teaching in God's word, that the people of God run not unto other doctrines, and lest thou thyself, when thou shouldest teach other, be found ignorant therein. And rather than thou wouldest teach the people any other thing than God's word, take the book in thine hand, and read the words, even as they stand therein; for it is no shame so to do, it is more shame to make a lie. This I say for such as are not yet expert in the scripture; for I reprove no preaching without the book, as long as they say the truth.

If thou be a man that hast wife and children, first love ^{Eph. v.} thy wife, according to the ensample of the love wherewith Christ loved the congregation; and remember that so doing thou lovest even thyself: if thou hate her, thou hatest thine own flesh; if thou cherish her and make much of her, thou cherishest and makest much of thyself; for she is bone of thy bones, and flesh of thy flesh. And whosoever thou be that hast children, bring them up in the nurture and ^{Eph. vi.} information of the Lord. And if thou be ignorant, or art otherwise occupied lawfully, that thou canst not teach them thyself, then be even as diligent to seek a good master for thy children, as thou wast to seek a mother to bear them; for there lieth as great weight in the one, as in the other. Yea, better it were for them to be unborn, than not to fear God, or to be evil brought up: which thing (I mean bringing up well of children) if it be diligently looked to, it is the upholding of all commonwealths; and the negligence of the same, the very decay of all realms.

Finally, whosoever thou be, take these words of scripture into thy heart, and be not only an outward hearer, but a doer thereafter, and practise thyself therein; that thou mayest feel in thine heart the sweet promises thereof for thy consolation in all trouble, and for the sure stablishing of thy hope in Christ; and have ever an eye to the words of scripture, that if thou be a teacher of other, thou mayest be within the bounds of the truth; or at the least, though thou be but an hearer or reader of another man's doings[1], thou mayest yet have knowledge to judge all spirits, and be free from every error, to the utter destruction of all seditious sects and strange doctrines; that the holy scripture may have free passage, and be had in reputation, to the worship of the author thereof, which is even God himself; to whom for his most blessed word be glory and dominion now and ever! Amen.

[1 doing, C. D.]

[DEDICATIONS AND PROLOGUES TO THE NEW TESTAMENT.

Three editions of Bishop Coverdale's translation of the New Testament were published in 1538:

1. That by James Nycolson, with a Dedication to Henry VIII. and a Preface to the reader. These are here presented from a copy of this edition in the British Museum.

2. Another edition of the same year, with a Dedication to Lord Cromwell, and an Address to the reader, printed by Francis Regnault at Paris, under the immediate direction of Bishop Coverdale, and published in London by Grafton and Whitchurch, which are here presented to the reader from a copy in the Library of St John's College, Cambridge. This edition was afterwards re-issued in London in the following year, with a new title, by Grafton and Whitchurch.

3. Another edition of the same year, published by Nycolson, and said to be translated by John Hollybushe, which however was published without the concurrence of Coverdale[2], and therefore does not call for any notice in the present work.

[2] Anderson's Annals of the English Bible, Vol. II. p. 38.]

DEDICATION AND PROLOGUE

THE NEW TESTAMENT.

Printed by Nycolson, A D. 1538.

DEDICATION TO HENRY VIII.

TO THE MOST NOBLE, MOST GRACIOUS, AND OUR MOST DREAD SOVEREIGN
LORD, KING HENRY THE EIGHTH, KING OF ENGLAND AND OF
FRANCE, &C., DEFENDER OF CHRIST'S TRUE FAITH, AND
UNDER GOD THE CHIEF AND SUPREME HEAD OF
THE CHURCH OF ENGLAND, IRELAND, &C.

CONSIDERING, most gracious sovereign, how lovingly, how favourably, and how tenderly your highness hath taken mine infancy and rudeness in dedicating the whole bible in English to your most noble grace; and having sure experience also, how benign and gracious a mind your highness doth ever bear to all them that in their calling are willing to do their best; it doth even animate and encourage me now likewise to use the same audacity toward your grace, never intending nor purposing to have been thus bold, if your most noble kindness and princely benignity had not forced me hereunto. This, doubtless, is one of the chiefest causes, why I do now, with most humble obedience, dedicate and offer this translation of the New Testament unto your most royal majesty. And, to say the truth, I cannot perceive the contrary, but as many of us as intend the glory of God have all need to commit unto your gracious protection and defence, as well our good doings, as ourselves: our good doings I mean, and not our evil works. For if we went about evil, God forbid that we should seek defence at your grace! But even our well-doings, our good-wills, and godly purposes, those with all humble obedience must we, and do, submit to your grace's most sure protection. For as our adversary the devil walketh about like a roaring lion, and seeketh whom he may devour;

and as the enemies of Christ went about to tangle himself in
his words, and to hunt somewhat out of his own mouth; even so
do not the enemies of God's words cease yet to pick quarrels,
and to seek out new occasions, how they may deprave and
sinisterly interpret our well-doings. And whereas with all
faithfulness we go about to make our brethren, your grace's
loving subjects, participant of the fruits of our good-wills; they
yet, not regarding what profit we would be glad to do them,
report evil of us, slander us, and say the worst of us: yea,
they are not ashamed to affirm, that we intend to pervert the
scripture, and to condemn the common translation in Latin,
which customably is read in the church; whereas we purpose
the clean contrary. And because it grieveth them that your
subjects be grown so far in knowledge of their duty to God,
to your grace, and to their neighbours, their inward malice
doth break out into blasphemous and uncomely words; insomuch that they call your loving and faithful people heretics,
new-fangled fellows, English biblers, coblers of divinity, fellows of the new faith, &c., with such other ungodly sayings.

How needful a thing is it then for us to resort unto the
most lawful protection of God, in your grace's supreme and
imperial authority under him! without the which most lawful defence, now in these turbulent and stormy assaults of the
wicked, we should be but even orphans, and utterly desolate
of comfort. But God, whom the scripture calleth a father of
the comfortless and defender of widows, did otherwise pro- Psal. lxviii.
vide for us, when he made your grace his high and supreme
minister over us.

To come now to the original and first occasion of this my
humble labour, and to declare how little I have or do intend
to despise this present translation in Latin, or any other in
what language soever it be, I have here set it forth, and the
English also thereof,—I mean the text which commonly is
called St Hierome's, and is customably read in the church.
And this, my most gracious sovereign, have I done, not so
much for the clamorous importunity of evil speakers, as to
satisfy the just request of certain your grace's faithful subjects; and specially to induce and instruct such as can but
English, and are not learned in the Latin, that in comparing
these two texts together, they may the better understand the
one by the other. And I doubt not but such ignorant bodies

as, having cure and charge of souls, are very unlearned in
the Latin tongue, shall through this small labour be occasioned to attain unto more knowledge, and at the least be constrained to say well of the thing which heretofore they have
blasphemed. The ignorance of which men, if it were not so
exceeding great, a man would wonder what should move them
to make such importune cavillations against us. It is to be
feared, that frowardness and malice is mixed with their ignorance. For, inasmuch as in our other translations we do not
follow this old Latin text word for word, they cry out upon
us, as though all were not as nigh the truth to translate the
scripture out of other languages, as to turn it out of the Latin;
or as though the Holy Ghost were not the author of his
scripture as well in the Hebrew, Greek, French, Dutch, and
in English, as in Latin. The scripture and word of God is
truly to every christian man of like worthiness and authority,
in what language soever the Holy Ghost speaketh it. And
therefore am I, and will be while I live, under your most
gracious favour and correction, alway willing and ready to
do my best as well in one translation as in another.

Now as concerning this present text in Latin, forasmuch
as it hath been and is yet so greatly corrupt, as I think none
other translation is; it were a godly and a gracious deed, if
they that have authority, knowledge, and time, would, under
your grace's correction, examine it better after the most ancient interpreters and most true texts of other languages.
For certainly, in comparing divers examples together, we see
that in many places one copy hath either more or less than
another, or else the text is altered from other languages.

To give other men occasion now to do their best, and to
express my good-will, if I could do better, I have, for the
causes above rehearsed, attempted this small labour, submit-
ting, with all humbleness and subjection, it and all other my
like doings to your grace's most noble majesty : not only
because I am bound so to do, but to the intent also, that
through your most gracious defence it may have the more
freedom among your obedient subjects, to the glory of the
everlasting God. To whom only for your grace, for your
most noble and dear son prince Edward, for your most ho-
norable council, and for all other his singular gifts, that we
daily receive in your grace; to him, I say, which is the only

giver and granter of all this our wealth, be honour and praise for evermore; to your grace, continual thankfulness and due obedience, with long life and prosperity; finally, to us, the receivers of God's good gifts, be daily increase of grace and virtue more and more! Amen.

Your grace's humble

and faithful subject,

MYLES COVERDALE.

PROLOGUE.

TO THE READER.

I must needs advertise thee, most gentle reader, that this present text in Latin, which thou seest set here with the English, is the same that customably is read in the church, and commonly is called St Hierome's translation. Wherein though in some places I use the honest and just liberty of a grammarian, as needful is for thy better understanding; yet, because I am loath to swerve from the text, I so temper my pen, that, if thou wilt, thou mayest make plain construction of it by the English that standeth on the other side. This is done now for thee that art not exactly learned in the Latin tongue, and wouldest fain understand it. As for those that be learned in the Latin already, this our small labour is not taken for them, save only to move and exhort them, that they likewise, knowing of whom they have received their talent of learning, will be no less grieved in their calling to serve their brethren therewith, than we are ashamed here with this our small ministration to do them good. I beseech thee therefore, take it in good worth : for so well done as it should and might be, it is not ;. but as it is, thou hast it with a good-will.

Whereas by the authority of the text I sometime make it clear for thy more understanding, there shalt thou find this mark [ ], which we have set for thy warning, the text nevertheless neither wrested nor perverted. The cause whereof is partly the figure called eclipsis, divers times used in the scriptures, the which though she do garnish the sentence in Latin, yet will not so be admitted in other tongues ; wherefore of necessity we are constrained to inclose such words in this mark : partly, because that sundry, and sometime too rash writers out of books have not given so great diligence as is due in the holy scripture, and have left out, and sometime altered, some word or words, and another, using the same book for a copy, hath committed like fault. Let not therefore this our diligence seem more temerarious unto thee, gen-

tle reader, than was the diligence of St Jerome and Origen
unto learned men of their time; which, using sundry marks in
their books, shewed their judgment, what were to be abated
or added unto the books of scripture, that so they might be
restored to the pure and very original text. Thy knowledge
and understanding in the word of God shall judge the same of
us also, if it be joined with love to the truth. And though I
seem to be all too scrupulous, calling it in one place *penance*
that in another I call *repentance,* and *gelded,* that another
calleth *chaste;* this methink ought not to offend thee, seeing
that the Holy Ghost, I trust, is the author of both our doings.
If I of mine own head had put into the new Testament these
words, *Nisi pœnitueritis, pœnitemini, sunt enim eunuchi,
pœnitentiam agite, etc.;* then, as I were worthy to be reproved, so should it be right necessary to redress the same.
But it is the Holy Ghost that hath put them in, and therefore I heartily require thee think no more harm in me for
calling it in one place *penance* that in another I call *repentance,* than I think harm in him that calleth it *chaste,* which
I by the nature of this word *eunuchus* call *gelded.* Let
every man be glad to submit his understanding to the Holy
Ghost in them that be learned; and no doubt we shall think
the best one by another, and find no less occasion to praise
God in another man than in ourselves. As the Holy Ghost
then is one, working in thee and me as he will ; so let us not
swerve from that unity, but be one in him. And for my
part, I ensure thee, I am indifferent to call it as well with the
one term as with the other, so long as I know that it is no
prejudice nor injury to the meaning of the Holy Ghost:
nevertheless I am very scrupulous to go from the vocable of
the text.

And of truth so had we all need to be : for the world is
captious, and many there be that had rather find twenty
faults, than to amend one. And ofttimes the more labour a
man taketh for their commodity, the less thank he hath.
But if they that be learned, and have wherewith to maintain
the charges, did their duty, they themselves should perform
these things, and not only to look for it at other men's
hands. At the least, if they would neither take the pain
of translating themselves, nor to bear the expenses thereof,
nor of the printing; they should yet have a good tongue,

and help one way that they cannot do another.   God grant
this world once to spy their unthankfulness!   This do not I
say for any lucre or vantage that I look for at your hands,
ye rich and wealthy bellies of the world: for he that never
failed me at my need, hath taught me to be content with
such provision as he hath, and will make for me.   Of you
therefore, that be servants to your own riches, require I
nothing at all, save only that which St James saith unto you
in the beginning of his fifth chapter; namely, that ye weep
and howl on your wretchedness that shall come upon you.
For certainly ye have great cause so to do; neither is it unlike but great misery shall come upon you, considering the
gorgeous fare and apparel that ye have every day for the
proud pomp and appetite of your stinking carcases, and ye
be not ashamed to suffer your own flesh and blood to die
at your doors for lack of your help.   O sinful belly-gods!
O unthankful wretches!   O uncharitable idolaters!   With
what conscience dare ye put one morsel of meat into your
mouths?   O abominable hell-hounds, what shall be worth of
you?   I speak to you, ye rich niggards of the world, which
as ye have no favour to God's holy word, so love ye to do
nothing that it commandeth.   Our Lord send you worthy
repentance!

But now will I turn my pen unto you that be lords and
rulers of your riches.   For of you, whom God hath made
stewards of those worldly goods; of you, whom God hath
made plenteous, as well in his knowledge, as in other riches;
of you, I say, would I fain require and beg, even for his
sake that is the giver of all good things, that at the last
ye would do but your duty, and help, as well with your
good counsel, as with your temporal substance, that a perfect
provision may be made for the poor, and for the virtuous
bringing up of youth: that as we now already have cause
plentiful to give God thanks for his word, and for sending
us a prince, with thousands of other benefits; even so we,
seeing the poor, aged, lame, sore, and sick provided for,
and our youth brought up as well in God's knowledge, as in
other virtuous occupations, may have likewise occasion sufficient to praise God for the same.   Our Lord grant that this
our long begging and most needful request may once be
heard!   In the mean time, till God bring it to pass by his

ministers, let not thy counsel nor help be behind, most gentle
reader, for the furtherance of the same.   And for that thou
hast received at the merciful hand of God already, be
thankful alway unto him, loving and obedient unto
thy prince. And live so continually in helping
and edifying of thy neighbour, that
it may redound to the praise
and glory of God
for ever.
Amen.

DEDICATION AND PROLOGUE

TO

THE NEW TESTAMENT.

Printed by Francis Regnault, and published by
Grafton and Whitchurch, A.D. 1538.

DEDICATION TO LORD CROMWELL.

TO THE RIGHT HONOURABLE LORD CROMWELL, LORD PRIVY SEAL, VICE-
GERENT TO THE KING'S HIGHNESS, CONCERNING ALL HIS
JURISDICTION ECCLESIASTICAL WITHIN THE
REALM OF ENGLAND.

I WAS never so willing to labour and travail for the edifying of my brethren, right honourable, and my singular good
lord, but I am, and purpose to be while I live, by God's
grace, even as ready to amend and redress any manner of
thing, that I can espy to be either sinistrally printed, or
negligently correct. And no less do I esteem it my duty to
amend other men's faults, than if they were my own. Truth
it is, that this last Lent I did with all humbleness direct an
epistle unto the king's most noble grace; trusting that the
book, whereunto it was prefixed, should afterward have been
as well correct as other books be. And because I could not
be present myself, by the reason of sundry notable impediments; therefore inasmuch as the new Testament, which I
had set forth in English before, doth so agree with the
Latin, I was heartily well content, that the Latin and it
should be set together; provided alway, that the corrector
should follow the true copy of the Latin in any wise, and
to keep the true and right English of the same. And so
doing, I was content to set my name to it. And even so
I did, trusting, that though I were absent and out of the
land, yet all should be well; and, as God is my record, I
knew none other, till this last July, that it was my chance
here in these parts at a stranger's hand to come by a copy

of the said print : which when I had perused, I found that as it was disagreeable to my former translation in English, so was not the true copy of the Latin text observed, neither the English so correspondent to the same as it ought to be ; but in many places, both base, insensible, and clean contrary, not only to the phrase of our language, but also from the understanding of the text in Latin. Whereof though no man to this hour did write nor speak to me, yet, forasmuch as I am sworn to the truth, I will favour no man to the hinderance thereof, nor to the maintaining of anything that is contrary to the right and just furtherance of the same. And therefore as my duty is to be faithful, to edify, and with the utmost of my power to put away all occasion of evil, so have I, though my business be great enough beside, endeavoured myself to weed out the faults that were in the Latin and English before; trusting that this present correction may be unto them that shall print it hereafter a copy sufficient. But because I may not be mine own judge, nor lean to mine own private opinion in this or any like work of the scripture ; therefore, according to the duty that I owe unto your lord-ship's office in the jurisdiction ecclesiastical of our most noble king, I humbly offer it unto the same, beseeching you that, whereas this copy hath not been exactly followed before, the good heart and will of the doers may be considered, and not the negligence of the work : specially, seeing they be such men, which as they are glad to print and set forth any good thing, so will they be heartily well content to have it truly correct, that they themselves of no malice nor set pur-pose have overseen. And for my part, though it hath been damage to my poor name, I heartily remit it, as I do also the ignorance of those which not long ago reported, that at the printing of a right famous man's sermon I had depraved the same; at the doing whereof I was thirty miles from thence, neither did I ever set pen to it, though I was de-sired.

Now as concerning this text of Latin, because it is the same that is read in the church, and therefore commonly the more desired of all men, I do not doubt but after that it is examined of the learned, to whom I most heartily refer it, it shall instruct the ignorant, stop the mouths of evil speakers, and induce both the hearers and readers to faith and good

3

works; which thing as it is most acceptable to God, so shall it please right well not only the king's highness, but your lordship also, and all other members of godliness. And if it so come to pass, (as I doubt not but it shall,) then have I my whole desire, and all the gains that I seek therein.

To be short, I might have dedicate unto your lordship some other little treatise touching some part of the administration of the commonwealth, as prudence, policy, or some other private virtue. But forasmuch as in the New Testament is contained the very pith and substance of all virtue, and the pattern of all good governance; considering also that your lordship doth advance nothing so much as the true worship of God, the king's honour, the wealth of his realm, and increase of all virtue, which this New Testament doth teach; I thought nothing meeter to send unto you than that which ye be daily occupied withal, and that all your chief study and pleasure is in. In the which estate Almighty God, that brought you thereto, grant your lordship long to endure! Amen.

Your lordship's humble

and faithful servitor,

MYLES COVERDALE.

PROLOGUE.

TO THE READER.

This translation, most dear reader, have I with a right good-will set forth for thy edifying, trusting that if thou use it well, it shall move thee to increase and grow in all such virtuous ways, as Almighty God hath begun in thee. And whereas it hath not been set forth unto thee heretofore so exactly, and in all points so perfectly, as might have been, I pray thee conster[1] all to the best, and blame neither the printer nor me, considering that we bear no worse mind unto thee than thou dost to thyself. Let christian love have some governance in thy judgment, and think not the contrary in us; but as we see peradventure to-day that we did not yesterday, so will we be right glad to do for thee to-morrow that we cannot do to-day.

And for my part, I will desire nothing of thee again, but that (as thou art graciously licensed, by the goodness of God in our prince, to read and enjoy this and all the other parts of the lively word of God) thou wilt so embrace it, follow it, and practise it in thy daily living, that thou even marry thyself to the fruits of the Holy Ghost therein; and so to use it, that thou be sober in the knowledge thereof; not only avoiding all contention and strife, but also with all humbleness, and under correction, to require of them that be learned in scripture the true sense and understanding of such places as unto thee be yet dark and obscure.

As touching this text in Latin, and the style thereof, which is read in the church, and is commonly called St Jerome's translation, though there be in it many and sundry sentences, whereof some be more than the Greek, some less than the Greek, some in manner repugnant to the Greek, some contrary to the rules of the Latin tongue and to the right order thereof, (as thou mayest easily perceive, if thou compare the diversity of the interpreters together;) yet for-

[1 Conster: construe, interpret.]

3—2

asmuch as I am but a private man, and owe obedience unto the higher powers, I refer the amendment and reformation hereof unto the same, and to such as excel in authority and knowledge. Only in this one thing thus bold I am, under correction, that whereas the Greek and the old ancient authors read the prayer of our Lord in the eleventh chapter of Luke after one manner, leaving out no petition of the same, I follow their lecture, though sundry copies of the vulgar translation do the contrary, omitting two petitions thereof[1].

Now for thy part, most gentle reader, take in good worth that I here offer thee with a good-will, and let this present translation be no prejudice to the other that out of the Greek have been translated before, or shall be hereafter. For if thou open thine eyes and consider well the gift of the Holy Ghost therein, thou shalt see that one translation declareth, openeth, and illustrateth another, and that in many places one is a plain commentary unto another. I pray God, whose Spirit is the author of all good doing, that as his scripture is written and set forth unto thee, thou mayest have a true understanding therein, and be thankful unto him therefore, loving and obedient unto thy prince, and shew no less favour and charity to thy neighbour, than thou thyself art glad to receive. And shortly to conclude : if when thou readest this or any other like book, thou chance to find any letter altered or changed, either in the Latin or English (for the turning of a letter is a fault soon committed in the print), then take thy pen and mend it, considering that thou art as much bound so to do, as I am to correct all the rest. And what edifying soever thou receivest at any man's hand, consider that it is no man's doing, but cometh even of the goodness of God. To whom only be praise and glory, thanks and dominion, now and ever! Amen.

[1 The passages alluded to are (1) that in the second verse, Γενη-θήτω τὸ θέλημά σου ὡς ἐν οὐρανῷ καὶ ἐπὶ τῆς γῆς, and (2) that in the fourth verse, ἀλλὰ ῥῦσαι ἡμᾶς ἀπὸ τοῦ πονηροῦ. With regard to the authorities which have been alleged for the omission of these passages, compare Griesbach ad locum.]

TREATISE ON DEATH.

⅔ A most

frutefull píththye

and learned treatyse, how a chri

sten man oughte to behaue hym=

selfe in the dauger of death: and

how they are to bee releued and

comforted, whose deare frendes

are departed oute of this

worlde, moste necessary

for this our vnfortu=

nate age and sor=

rowefull

dayes.

۞Iohn. 6.

Verely verely, J saye vnto you,
he that beleueth in me, hath e=
uerlastynge lyfe.

[THE TREATISE ON DEATH.

This is the second of the four treatises of Otho Wermullerus [1], or Vierdmullerus, which were translated by Bishop Coverdale, and of which an account is given in the preface to the Spiritual Pearl. This treatise was reprinted by Hugh Singleton: but of this edition no copy has been met with. Of the old edition in the Swiss angular type there are copies in the Bodleian library at Oxford, and in the library of St John's college, Cambridge; which latter copy formerly belonged to the learned Thomas Baker, B.D., fellow of the college, and contains his autograph. This copy however wants the last page of the preface. The present edition has been printed from the copy in the library of St John's college, by permission of the Master and Fellows of that society; the deficiency in the preface having been supplied from the Bodleian copy.]

[1 Mention is made of this learned person in a letter of Caspar Thoman to Caspar Waser. Zurich Letters, Second Series. Letter CXXXVIII. p. 328.]

PREFACE.

UNTO ALL THOSE THAT UNFEIGNEDLY DESIRE
TO LIVE UNDER THE FEAR OF GOD, AND WITH
PATIENCE ABIDE THE COMING OF OUR LORD
AND SAVIOUR JESUS CHRIST, THROUGH
THE WORKING OF THE HOLY
GHOST, GRACE AND PEACE
BE MULTIPLIED.

THOUGH all kinds of beasts have some things in common
one with another, as in that they see, hear, feel, desire, move
from one place to another; yet hath every beast also his own
special property, as the bird hath another nature than the
fish, the lion another disposition than the wolf. Even so in
other my books, heretofore by me published, I have set forth
a general comfort concerning trouble, sickness, poverty, displeasure, dearth, war, imprisonment, and death, under which
I have comprehended all the cross and affliction of man.
Nevertheless every mischance or adversity hath also his own
special consideration: and forasmuch as among terrible things
upon earth death is esteemed the most cruel of all, and it
can yet with no wisdom of man be rightfully judged, how it
goeth with a Christian in and after death; therefore the
greatest necessity requireth, that we Christians be diligently
instructed by the infallible word of God in especial, touching
the end and conclusion of our life. For when the last hour
draweth nigh, which we every day, yea, every twinkling of
an eye look for; whether the soul after it be departed do
live, whether the corrupted body shall rise again, whether
eternal joy and salvation be at hand, and which way conducteth and leadeth to salvation; thereof hath the most subtle
worldly-wise man by his own natural reason no knowledge
at all. Plato, Aristotle, Cicero, the greatest-learned and
wisest, write of these high weighty matters very childishly
and foolishly[1]; and as for consolation that they give, it is in

[1 With respect to the opinions of the ancient philosopher on the
immortality of the soul and a future state, those who wish to ex-

no sort nor wise to be compared unto the holy divine scripture, which only ministereth the true christian comfort in life and death. And though every man ought daily to consider his end, and at all times to make himself ready for death, seeing that he knoweth not how, where, and when God shall lay his hand upon him; yet nevertheless at this present time we have more occasions to talk and treat thereof, now that Almighty God doth with diverse and sundry plagues, more grievously than heretofore, visit our unrepentant life, for that he all this while hath perceived in us but little amendment; neither need we to think, that these, that rain, and other plagues shall over-leap us. Considering now that I, though unworthy and unmete, was called by authority, but specially of God, to teach, to exhort, and to comfort; I have, with great labour, out of the holy scripture and out of old and new authors collected, how a man should prepare himself unto death, how he is to be used that lieth a dying, and how they[2] ought to be comforted, whose dear friends are departed. Which things, as they be orderly set in this book, right dearly beloved and loving reader, I do present, dedicate, and offer unto thee. And though I can consider, that this little book is so small and slender a gift, because of my person; yet is it neither little, nor to be despised, for the fountain's sake that it floweth out of, and by reason of the matter whereof it is written. For herein out of the unchangeable word of God are noted the head articles of our last conflict and battery, whereupon dependeth either eternal victory, honour, and joy, or else everlasting loss and endless pain; of the which things we can never think, talk, nor treat sufficiently. Wherefore, whereas this little book goeth forth unto thy use, that art an unfeigned Christian, and to the comfort of all such as are afraid of death; I pray thee, for Christ's sake, not only to accept it as the testimony of a willing and loving mind toward thee, but also to have still an earnest desire to that that it hath pleased God by me at this time to communicate unto thee; that with thy thankfulness thou

amine the subject may consult Bishop Warburton's Divine Legation, Book III., where the opinions of the ancient philosophers are investigated.]

[2 From this place to the end of the preface is supplied from the Bodleian copy.]

mayest move other to the like, that can do better, and by thy
profit stir the harvest-lord to send more harvest-men into his
harvest. Which he cannot but do, except he could deny
himself, that came into the world, neither to
put out the flax that smoketh, nor to
break the reed that is but bruised,
but to open to them that knock
to him. Vale. Love God,
leave vanity, and
live in Christ.

THE TABLE.

THE CONTENTS OF THE FIRST PART.

THE CONTENTS OF THE SECOND PART.

THE CONTENTS OF THE THIRD PART.

FIRST BOOK OF DEATH.

CHAPTER I.

DECLARING WHAT DEATH IS.

HOLY scripture maketh mention of four manner of deaths and lives.

1. The first is called a natural life, so long as the soul remaineth with the body upon earth. The natural death is it that separateth the soul from the body.

2. The second is a spiritual unhappy death here in time of life, when the grace of God, for our wickedness' sake, is departed from us; by means whereof we were dead from the Lord our God and from all goodness, although as yet we have the life natural. Contrary unto this there is a ghostly blessed life, when we, through the grace of the Lord our God, live unto him and to all goodness. Hereof writeth St Paul after this manner: " God, which is rich in mercy, through his Eph. ii. great love wherewith he loved us, even when we were dead in sins, hath quickened us together in Christ."

3. The third is a ghostly blessed death here in time, when the flesh being ever, the longer the more, separated from the spirit, dieth away from his own wicked nature. Contrary hereunto is there a ghostly unhappy life, when the flesh with his wicked disposition continually breaketh forth, and liveth in all wilfulness. Against this doth Paul exhort us, saying: " Mortify therefore your members which are upon earth, for- Coloss. iii. nication, uncleanness, unnatural lust, evil concupiscence, covetousness, &c."

4. The fourth that the scripture maketh mention of, is an everlasting life, and an everlasting death. Not that the body and soul of man shall after this time lose their substance, and be utterly no more. For we believe undoubtedly, that our soul is immortal, and that even this present body

shall rise again. But forasmuch as we ourselves grant that life is sweet, and death a bitter herb, this word life by a figurative speech is used for mirth and joy; this word death, for heaviness and sorrow. Therefore eternal life is called eternal joy ; and eternal death eternal damnation.

Of these manifold deaths have we commonly a perverse judgment. We abhor the death of the body, and haste on apace to the unhappy ghostly death, which yet in itself is a thousand times more terrible than any death corporal. For when a man delighteth in his own wickedness, though as yet he live upon the earth, he is nevertheless dead before God, and the soul must continue still damned for evermore.

In this book my handling is of natural death, which before our eyes seemeth to be an utter destruction, and that there is no remedy with the dead, even as when a dog or horse dieth ; and that God hath no more respect unto them. Yea, the world swimmeth full of such ungodly people, as have none other meaning. Else, doubtless, would they behave themselves otherwise towards God. Death verily is not a destruction of man, but a deliverance of body and soul. Wherefore as the soul, being of itself immortal, doeth either out of the mouth ascend up into heaven, or else from the mouth descendeth into the pit of hell; the body, losing his substance till doomsday, shall then by the power of God be raised from death, and joined again to the soul; that afterward the whole man with body and soul may eternally inherit either salvation, or else damnation.

CHAPTER II.

THAT THE TIME OF DEATH IS UNCERTAIN.

THE body of man is a very frail thing. Sickness may consume it, wild beasts may devour it, the fire may burn it, the water may drown it, the air may infect it, a snare may choke it, the pricking of a pin may destroy it. Therefore when his temporal life shall end, he cannot tell.

The principal cause why we know not the time of death,

is even the grace of God; to the intent that we by no occa- Luke xii. sion should linger the amendment of our lives until age, but alway fear God, as though we should die to-morrow.

But as soon as the hour cometh, no man shall overleap it. Hereof speaketh Job, when he saith, that "God hath Job xiv. appointed unto man his bounds which he cannot go beyond."

CHAPTER III.

THAT IT IS GOD WHICH HATH LAID THE BURDEN OF DEATH UPON US.

IT becometh all Christians not only to suffer, but also to commend and praise, the will of the heavenly Lord and King. Now is it his will that we die. For if the sparrows, whereof two are bought for a farthing, fall not on the ground without God the Father, much less we men, whom God himself esteemeth to be of more value than many sparrows, yea, for whose sakes other things were created, do fall to the ground through death without the will of God: like as the soldier tarrieth in the place wherein he is appointed of the chief captain to fight against the enemies, and if he call him from thence, he willingly obeyeth; even so hath the heavenly Captain set us upon earth, where we have to fight, not with Ephes. vi. flesh and blood, but with wicked spirits. Therefore if he give us leave, and call us from hence, we ought by reason to obey him. Like as one should not withdraw himself from paying what he oweth, but gently to restore the money; so hath God lent us this life, and not promised that we may alway enjoy it. Therefore is death described to be the payment of natural debt.

CHAPTER IV.

THAT GOD SENDETH DEATH BECAUSE OF SIN.

ACCORDING hereunto ponder thou the just judgment of God; for out of the third chapter of the first book of Moses it is evidently perceived, that death is a penalty deserved, laid upon us all for the punishment of sin. As the little worm that groweth out of the tree gnaweth and consumeth the tree of whom it hath his beginning; so death groweth, waxeth out of sin, and sin with the body it consumeth: and specially the venomous sickness which they call the pestilence, is sent of God as a scourge for the punishment of our naughtiness. Hereof speaketh the word of God in the fifth book of Moses Deut. xxviii. after this manner: " If thou wilt not hearken unto the voice of the Lord thy God, to keep and to do all his commandments and ordinances, which I command thee this day, then shall all these curses come upon thee, and overtake thee: the Lord shall make the pestilence to cleave unto thee, until he have consumed thee from the land, whither thou goest to enjoy it. The Lord shall smite thee with swelling, with fevers, heat, burning, withering, with smiting and blasting. And they shall follow thee till thou perish."

2 Sam. xxiv. Yet among the most gracious chastenings is the pestilence reckoned of the holy prophet, and king David; who, after that he of a pride had caused the people to be numbered, when the election was given him, whether he would rather have seven years' dearth, three months' overthrow in war, or 1 Chron. xxii. three days' pestilence in the land, made this answer: " I am in a marvellous strait. But let me fall, I pray thee, into the hands of the Lord, for much is his mercy; and let me not 2 Sam. xxiv. fall into the hands of men. Then sent the Lord a pestilence 1 Chron. xxii. into Israel, that there died of them seventy thousand men." Wherefore, if God overtake thee with this horrible disease, be not thou angry with Saturnus and Mars, nor with the corrupt air and other means appointed of God; but be displeased with thine own sinful life. And when any fearful image of death cometh before thee, remember that thou with thy sins hast deserved much more horrible things, which God nevertheless hath not sent unto thee.

CHAPTER V.

THAT GOD TURNETH DEATH INTO GOOD.

ALTHOUGH thou hast deserved an hundred thousand greater plagues, yet shalt thou comfort thyself beforehand after this manner: A father doth his children good, and not evil. Now is my belief in God, as in my gracious Father, through Jesus Christ; and sure I am, that Christ upon the cross hath made a perfect payment for all my sins, and with his death hath taken away the strength of my death; yea, for me hath he deserved and brought to pass eternal life. Wherefore though death in the sight of my eyes and of natural reason be bitter and heavy; yet by means of the passion and death of Jesus Christ it is not evil or hurtful, but a benefit, a profitable and wholesome thing, even an entrance into everlasting joy.

CHAPTER VI.

THAT DEATH IN ITSELF IS GRIEVOUS TO THE BODY AND SOUL.

WHAT grief and hurt death doth bring with it, I will now declare, to the intent that when we have considered the same, before trouble come, we may in our distress be the less afraid, holding against it the great commodities of death that Christ hath obtained for all faithful. It grieveth a man at his death to leave the pleasant beholding of heaven and earth, his own young body and cheerful stomach, his wife and children, house and lands, fields and meadows, silver and gold, honour and authority, good friends and old companions, his minstrelsy, pastime, joy, and pleasure, that he hath had upon earth.

Afterward, when death knocketh at the door, then beginneth the greatest trouble to work. When the diseases be fallen upon the body of man in greater number, they are against all the members in the whole body, breaking in by heaps with notable griefs; so that the power of the body is weakened, the mind cumbered, the remembrance

astonished, reason blinded, sleep hindered, the senses all-to
broken : by means whereof the eyes are darkened, the face
is pale, the feet are cold, the hands black, the members out
of course, the brow hardened, the chin falleth down, the
breath diminisheth, the deadly sweat breaketh out; yea,
the whole man is taken in and disturbed, in such sort that
he is now past minding any other thing.   Death also is so
much the more bitter and terrible, because that the feeble
discomfited nature doth print the horrible image of death too
deep in itself, and feareth it too sore.   And hereunto is the
devil likewise busy, to set before us a more terrible evil death
than ever we saw, heard, or read of; to the intent that we,
being oppressed with such imaginations or thoughts, should
fly and hate death, and be driven to the love and carefulness
of this life, forgetting the goodness of God, and to be found
disobedient at our last end.   Moreover, whoso of himself is
not thoroughly assured, and knoweth yet sin by himself, he
is not astonished for nought; forasmuch as sin carrieth with
it the wrath of God and eternal damnation.   Now not only
the evil, but also the good, have grievous and manifold sins,
(yea, more than they themselves can think upon,) with the
which, in dangers of body and life, their mind is oppressed,
as it were, with a violent water that fiercely rageth and
gusheth out; yea, even the same praiseworthy and commendable thing which the godly have practised already, that do
they yet perceive not to be perfect, but mixed with unclean-
Isai. lxiv.   ness.   Hereof speaketh Isaiah in this wise: "We offend and
have been ever in sin, and there is not one whole.   We are
all as an unclean thing, and all our righteousnesses are as
filthy rags."

Psal. cxliii.   David prayed: "Lord, enter not into judgment with thy
servant; for in thy sight shall no man living be justified."

Gregory writeth: "Woe unto the commendable life of
men, if it be led without mercy !"

1 Pet. v.   *Item*, the apostle Peter giveth warning: "Your adversary, the devil, goeth about as a roaring lion, seeking whom
he may devour."

If one that is about to shoot a gun be unsteady at the
letting of it go, he misseth altogether, and all that he prepared
for it before is in vain : even so, at the end of this life, are
devils most busy to turn us from the right mark, that our

former travail and labour may be lost; forasmuch as they
know that there remaineth but a very small time of life; so
that if the soul escape them now, they shall afterward go
without it for evermore.

Even as mighty enemies do besiege and lay assault to a
city, so the devils compass the soul of man with violence and
subtlety, to take possession of the poor soul, to apprehend it,
and bring it to hell.   When we are yet in prosperity, the
devils would have us to make but a small matter of it, as
though we were in no danger to God-ward, albeit we blaspheme, be drunken, and commit whoredom, break wedlock,
&c.   But in the danger of death they bring forth those
wicked sins in most terrible wise, putting us in mind of the
wrath of God, how he in times past here and there did
punish and destroy wicked doers,—to the intent that our souls
might be hindered, snared, shut up, bound, and kept in prison
from repentance and faith, and never to perceive any way
how to escape and to be delivered; and by reason thereof
wholly to despair, and to become the devil's portion.

Furthermore, good friends and companions are loth to
depart asunder, specially such as are new knit and bound
together one to another, as two married persons.   Now is
the body and soul nearest of all bound and coupled one to
the other; but in the distress of death the pain is so great,
that it breaketh this unity, and parteth the soul from the
body : for the which cause a man at his death doth naturally
sigh in himself.   Good companions upon earth, though they
depart one from another, have an hope to come together
again; but when the soul once departeth from the body, it
hath no power to return again to the body here in this time.
Whereof Job giveth two similitudes : "A tree, if it be cut _{Job xiv.}
down, there is some hope yet, and it will bud and shoot forth
the branches again.   Likewise the floods, when they be dried
up, and the rivers, when they be empty, are filled again
through the flowing waters of the sea.   But when man sleepeth, he riseth not again, until the heaven perish."   This understand, that after the common course one cometh not again
in this present life; one cannot die twice, and after death
cannot a man accomplish any more that he neglected aforetime.

How goeth it now both with the body and soul after

death? As soon as the soul from the body is departed, the
body is spoiled of all his powers, beauty, and senses, and become a miserable thing to look upon. Augustine saith : "A
man that in his lifetime was exceeding beautiful and pleasant
to embrace, is in death a terrible thing to behold[1]." How
nobly and preciously soever a man hath lived upon earth, his
body yet beginneth to corrupt and stink, and becometh worms'
meat : by means whereof the world is of this opinion, that
the body cometh utterly to nought for ever. The world also
knoweth nothing concerning the immortality of the soul ; and
they which already believe that the soul is immortal, doubt
yet whether it shall be saved ; yea, they say plainly, it were
good to die, if one wist what cheer he should have in yonder
world. To them is death like unto a misty and dark hole,
where one woteth not what will become upon him.

CHAPTER VII.

THAT WE ALL COMMONLY ARE AFRAID OF DEATH.

By means of the occasions aforesaid, certain heathen men
have given uncomfortable and desperate judgments concerning
the passage of death. In the poet Euripides, in *Orestes*[2], one

[1 The author appears to refer to the treatise entitled, *Exhortatio
de salutaribus documentis;* which is falsely attributed to Augustine,
and is given by the Benedictine editors on the authority of MSS.
to Paulinus, bishop of Aquileia, A.D. 776; with whom Cave agrees.
Hist. Lit. Vol. I. pp. 250, 495. "Dic mihi, quæso, frater mi, qualis
profectus est in pulchritudine carnis? Nonne, sicut fœnum æstatis
ardore percussum arescit, et paulatim decorem pristinum amittit?
Et cum mors venerit, dic mihi, quæso, quanta remanebit in corpore pulchritudo? Tunc recognosces, quia vanum est, quod antea
inaniter diligebas. Cum videris totum corpus intumescere, et in
fœtorem esse conversum, nonne claudes nares tuas, ne sustineas
fœtorem fœtidissimum? . . . . Ille est finis pulchritudinis carnis et
oblectationis."—Augustin. Vol. IV. 254 D. Ed. 1541.]

[2 The passage is in the Iphigenia in Aulide, vv. 1250—2:

τὸ φῶς τόδ' ἀνθρώποισιν ἥδιστον βλέπειν·
τὰ νέρθε δ' οὐδέν. μαίνεται δ' ὃς εὔχεται
θανεῖν. κακῶς ζῆν κρεῖσσον ἢ θανεῖν καλῶς.]

saith: "It is better to live ill, than to die well." Which words are very unchristianly spoken. Yet are there found examples, even of holy men, that they had a natural fear of death. The holy patriarch Abraham, thinking that he stood in danger of death by reason of his wife's beauty, would rather suffer all that else was exceeding heavy and bitter. He judged it a smaller matter to call his wife his sister, than to be destroyed himself.

Hezekiah, an upright valiant king, when the prophet told him he should not live, was afraid of death, and prayed earnestly that his life might be prolonged. In the new Testament, when the Lord Jesus drew near to his passion and death, he sweat blood for very anguish, and said: "My soul is heavy even unto the death." And thus he prayed: "Father, if it be possible, take this cup from me." *Isai. xxxviii.* *Matth. xxvi.*

The Lord saith unto Peter: "Verily, verily, I say unto thee, When thou wast young thou girdedst thyself, and walked whither thou wouldest: but when thou art old, thou shalt stretch forth thine hands, and another shall gird thee, and lead thee whither thou wouldest not." Lo, Peter being excellently endowed with the Spirit of God, and stedfast in faith, had yet in his age a natural fear of death; for the Lord said unto him before, that another should lead him whither he would not. Therefore writeth Gregory not upright, when he saith: "If the pillars tremble, what shall the boards do? Or if the heavens shake for such fear, how will that be unmoved which is under?" That is, if famous saints did fear to die, it is much less to be marvelled at, when we poor Christians are afraid. *John xxi.*

Experience witnesseth how feebly we set ourselves against death. Many an old, or otherwise vexed man, can neither live nor die: for in his adversity he ofttimes wisheth death; and when death approacheth, he would rather suffer whatsoever else upon earth, if he might thereby escape death. Many of us have heard the gospel a long season, and studied it thoroughly, so to say; yet are we so afraid of the death of ourselves and of our friends, as though there were none other life more to look for; even like as they that be of Sardanapalus' sort do imagine, or else mistrust the promise, comfort, and help of God, as though he were not able, or would not succour and deliver us. Yea, some there be, that if death be but spoken of, they are afraid at it.

CHAPTER VIII.

THE COMMODITY OF DEATH, WHEN IT DELIVERETH US FROM THIS SHORT TRANSITORY TIME.

ALL the aforesaid disprofits and griefs do justly vanish, and are nothing esteemed, in comparison of these commodities, when death delivereth us from this ruinous miserable life, from all enormities and vicious people, and conducteth us to eternal joy and salvation : which thing shall hereafter be plainly declared.

First, a short, transitory, and shifting life ought not to make us sorry. Though this life had nothing else but pleasure, what is yet shorter and more in decay than the life of man ? Half the time do we sleep out; childhood is not perceived; youth flieth away so, that a man doth little consider it; age creepeth on unawares, before it is looked for. We can reckon well, that when children grow, they increase in years and days; but properly to speak, in their growing are their days diminished. For let a man live threescore or fourscore years, look now, how much he hath lived of the same days or years, so much is abated of the time appointed.

A lively similitude. Is it not now a folly, that a man can consider how his wine diminisheth in the vessel, and yet regardeth not how his life doth daily vanish away ?

Among all things most undurable and most frail is man's life, which innumerable ways may be destroyed. It is compared unto a candle-light, that of the wind is soon and easily *Psal. ciii.* blown out. A man in his time is as the grass, and flourisheth as a flower of the field; for as soon as the wind goeth over it, it is gone.

The heathen poet Euripides called the life of mortal men *Dieculam,* that is, *a little day.* But the opinion of Phalerius Demetrius is, that it ought rather to be called one point of this time. This similitude soundeth not evil among Christians. For what is the whole sum of our life, but even one point, in comparison of the eternity that undoubtedly *Psal. xc.* followeth hereafter? David himself saith, "that our years *Psal. cxliv.* pass away suddenly." "Man is like unto a thing of nought: his time goeth away as doth a shadow."

CHAPTER IX.

ANOTHER COMMODITY, WHEN DEATH DELIVERETH US FROM THIS MISERABLE LIFE-TIME.

OUR desire is to be free from all weariness and misery; yea, the more we consider this present wretched life, the less fear shall we have of death, which delivereth us from all mischances and griefs of this time: heaps of troubles happen unto us and unto other men, yea, to special persons and whole nations, in body, soul, estimation, goods, wives, children, friends, and native countries.

Bodily health is soon lost, but hard to obtain again; and when it is already gotten, the doubt is, how long it will continue. There be more kinds of diseases than the best learned physicians do know: among the same some are so horrible and painful, that if one do but hear them named, it maketh him afraid; as the falling sickness, the gout, frenzy, the sudden stroke, and such like. Besides sickness, a man throughout his whole life cometh into danger by a thousand means and ways. Consider, with how great carefulness the child is carried in the mother's womb; how dangerously it is brought forth into the world. The whole childhood, what is it else but a continual weeping and wailing? After seven years the child has his tutors and schoolmasters to rule him, and beat him with rods. When he is come to man's stature, all that he suffered in his youth doth he count but a small travail, in comparison of it that he now from henceforth must endure. The old man thinketh that he carrieth an heavy burden or mountain upon his neck. Therefore weigh well the miserable body and the miry sack of thy flesh towards thy helper, and be not so sore afraid of death, that easeth thee of this wretched carcase. According hereunto is the mind cumbered and vexed, through sickness and griefs of the body, by reason that the body and soul are joined together. And how precious a thing, I pray you, is our natural reason! Childhood knoweth nothing concerning itself. Young folks take vain and unprofitable things in hand, supposing all shall be gold, and consider neither age to come, neither yet death;

Man's whole life.

and, even as the common saying is, thus will the world be beguiled. Whereas a man, the longer he liveth, should ever be the more and more wise, it cometh oft to pass that the more he groweth in years, the more he doteth, and afterward becometh even a very child, yea, twice a child.

The disquietness of man's life. The mind is tempted, the lust rageth, the hope deceiveth, heaviness vexeth, carefulness is full of distress, fear disquieteth; yea, the terror of death is more grievous than death itself. It cannot be expressed, how a man is sometimes plagued with worldly favour; afterward vexeth he himself with care of temporal things. Many one marreth himself with vice and wickedness, getteth him an evil conscience and a gnawing heart.

The virtuous also have their blemishes and temptations, which unto them are heavier and more hurtful than the blemishes of the body. Wherefore in the misery of this time this must not be esteemed the least portion, that we and other folks do daily commit grievous sins against God. Which thing thoroughly to consider maketh a good-hearted person the more desirous of death, which delivereth us from this *The griefs of all estates.* sinful life. Moreover, all conditions and estates of men have their griefs. Riches, that with great care and travail are gathered together and possessed, be sometimes lost by storm, fire, water, robbery, or theft. He that is in honour and prosperity hath enemies and evil willers. Whoso hath the governance and rule of many must also stand in fear of many things. And what occupation or handicraft can a man use, but he hath in it whereof to complain?

Not only hath a man trouble on his own behalf, but a very stony stomach and an iron heart must it be, that is not sorry when hurt doth happen to his father and mother, to his own wife, children, friends, or kinsfolk.

Furthermore, the universal trouble is manifold and piteous, specially now at this present, with noisome diseases, divisions, wars, seditions, uproars: like as one water-wave followeth upon another, and one can scarce avoid another; even so oft-times cometh one mischance in another's neck: and in this short life upon one only day to have no trouble, is a great advantage. Therefore ought we to be the less sorry, when the time of our deliverance approacheth.

Now might one object against this, and say, that this Our troubles more than joys. present life hath many pleasures and pastimes withal. Never-theless a man must open the other eye also, and behold, that in this life there is ever more sorrow than joy behind. Worldly joy is mixed, defiled, spotted, and perverted with sorrow and bitterness.   It may well begin in a sorrowful matter, to bring a short fugitive pleasure; but suddenly it endeth to a man's greater heaviness.   Not in vain doth the wise man say: "The Prov. xiv. heart is sorrowful even in laughter, and the end of mirth is heaviness."

Philip, the king of the Macedonians, when he upon one day had received three glad messages; one that the victory was his in the stage-play of Olympus; the second, that his captain Parmenio had with one battle overcome the Dardanes; the third, that the queen his wife was delivered of a son; he held up his hands to heaven and said: "O ye Gods, I be-seech you, that for so great and manifold prosperity ye will appoint me a competent misfortune."   The wise prudent king feared the inconstancy of fortune, which, as the heathen talk thereof, envieth great prosperity.   And therefore his desire was, that his exceeding welfare might be sauced with a little trouble.

Experience itself teacheth us.   Where did ever one live the space of a month, or one whole day, in pleasure and ease so thoroughly, but somewhat hath offended or hindered him? Therefore earthly joy is not so great, so durable, nor so pure, but that the whole life of man may well be called a vale of misery.

CHAPTER X.

WITNESS THAT THIS LIFE IS MISERABLE.

TESTIMONY of the scripture: "Man is born to misery as Job v. the bird is to fly[1]."   "The days of man are like the days of Job vii.

[1 So also Cov. Bible, following the LXX. Syr. Vulg.   The autho-rised version, following, as appears, the Chaldee paraphrase and some of the Hebrew commentators: "Man is born to trouble, as the sparks fly upwards."]

an hired servant, even a breath, and nothing but vain." Look through the whole book of Ecclesiastes, the Preacher. Augustine writeth : " If a man were put to the choice, that either he must die, or else live again afresh, and suffer like things as he had suffered already before, he would rather die, specially if he thoroughly consider how many dangers and mischances he scarce yet hath escaped."

Whoso now knoweth likewise, that God through death doth make an end of misery upon earth, it bringeth him great comfort and ease. Yea, he shall rather desire death than fear it. For even holy Job himself also, when he was robbed of his health, riches, and children, and rebuked of his wife and friends, wished rather to die than to live.

1 Kings xix.

[Tobit iii.]

Elias, being sure in no place, desired to die. Tobias, being stricken with blindness, and misentreated of his wife, prayed thus : " O Lord, deal with me according to thy will, and command my spirit to be received in peace ; for more expedient were it for me to die than to live." If holy men now by reason of their great troubles desired death ; it is no marvel if we, that are weaker and of more imperfection, be weary of this life. Yea, an unspeakable folly is it, a man to wish for to continue still in the life of misery, and not to prepare himself to another and better life.

CHAPTER XI.

THAT THE CONSIDERATION OF DEATH BEFOREHAND IS PROFITABLE TO ALL VIRTUES.

A VERY mad and unhappy man must he needs be, which thoroughly considereth, that undoubtedly he must depart hence, he knoweth not how nor when ; and whether he shall then have his right mind, directing himself to God and desiring grace, he cannot tell ; and will not even now out of hand begin to fear God, and serve him more diligently.

As the peacock, when he looketh upon his own feathers, is proud, but when he beholdeth his feet, letteth the feathers down; even so doth man cease from pride, when he considereth his end. For in the end he shall be spoiled of all temporal beauty, strength, power, honour, and goods. " Naked ^{Job i.} came I out of my mother's womb, and naked shall I turn thither again."

Through the consideration of death may a man despise all fleshly lust and worldly joy. For even the same flesh that thou so pamperest with costly dainties and vain ornaments, must shortly be a portion for worms: neither is there a more horrible carrion than of man.

Many one through fear of death giveth alms, exerciseth charity, doth his business circumspectly. To be short; the consideration of death is even as a scourge or spur that provoketh forward, and giveth a man sufficient occasion to avoid eternal death, whereof the death of the body is a shadow. Therefore the Ninevites, fearing their own overthrow and ^{Jonas il.} destruction, repented and fell to a perfect amendment.

CHAPTER XII.

IN DEATH WE LEARN THE RIGHT KNOWLEDGE OF OURSELVES AND OF GOD, AND ARE OCCASIONED TO GIVE OURSELVES UNTO GOD.

MANY a man in his lifetime can dissemble and shew a fair countenance; but at the point of death no hypocrisy or dissimulation hath place. There verily shall we be proved and tried, what manner of faith, love, conscience, and comfort we have, and how much we have comprehended out of the doctrine of Christ.

Then doth God let us see our own strength, how that all worldly strength is a thousand times less than we ever would have thought all the days of our life. Then perceive we seeingly and feelingly (so to say), that we stand in the only hand and power of God, and that he alone endureth still Lord and Master over death and life. Then learn we right to feel the worthiness of the passion and death of Christ, and in ourselves to have experience of the things, whereof we never took so diligent heed before in our lifetime.

Then come the fits of repentance for sins committed, that we think: "O, if I had known that God would have been so earnest, I would have left many things undone, which I (alas therefore!) have committed." Then are we forced to receive and love the gospel, which else heretofore might not come to such stout and jolly youngsters. Then begin we to run to God, to call upon him, to magnify and praise him, faithfully to cleave unto him, and uprightly to serve him.

CHAPTER XIII.

THAT THE DEAD CEASETH FROM SIN.

ALL Christians desire to be free from sin: for sin and vice doth far far vex the faithful, more than all misfortunes of the body. Now though one do keep himself from sin, yet standeth he in a slippery place; the flesh is weak, strong is the devil, of whom it is easily overcome: "Whoso standeth, let him look that he fall not."

1 Cor. x.

While the captain yet fighteth, it is uncertain whether he shall have the victory and triumph: even so, though a man do valiantly defend himself against the lusts of the flesh and temptations of the devil, he may yet fall and lose the victory. Yea, if we always lived, we should do more evil: sin ceaseth not, till we come to be blessed with a shovel. Death cutteth away sin from us, and delivereth us from unclean senses, thoughts, words, and deeds. For though death in Paradise was enjoined unto man for a penalty of sin; yet through the grace of God, in the merits of Christ, it is become unhurtful; yea, a medicine to purge out sin, and a very workhouse, wherein we are made ready to everlasting righteousness.

Like as terrible Goliath with his own sword was destroyed of David; even so with death, that came by the means of sin, is sin overcome and vanquished of Christ. If it grieved us from our hearts, that we daily see and find how we continually use ourselves against the most sweet will of our most dear Father, and were assured withal, that in death we cease from sin, and begin to be perfect and righteous; how were it possible, that we should not set little by death, and patiently take it upon us? Out of such a fervent jealousy and godly displeasure Paul, after he had earnestly complained that he found another law, which strove against the law of God, sighed and cried: "Oh wretched man that I am! who shall Rom. vii. deliver me from the body of this death?" Again, so long as death hath so evil a taste in us, and we will perforce continue still in the life of the flesh; we bewray ourselves, that we do not well, nor sufficiently understand our own defaults, neither feel them deep enough, nor abhor them so much as we should; yea, that we be not earnest desirers of innocency, nor fervent lovers of our heavenly Father.

CHAPTER XIV.

THAT THE DEAD IS DELIVERED FROM THIS VICIOUS WORLD, HAVING NOT ONLY THIS ADVANTAGE, THAT HE SINNETH NO MORE, BUT ALSO IS DISCHARGED FROM OTHER SINS.

WHOSO leaveth nothing else worthy behind him, but that he is quiet from vicious people, may well be the gladder to depart hence; partly, for that he can be no more tempted of them, nor enticed by their evil examples; partly, for that, though he could not be deceived by others, yet it grieveth him at the heart to see other folks practise their wilfulness. Now hath vice and sin everywhere gotten the upper hand; the truth is despised, God himself dishonoured, the poor oppressed, the good persecuted, the ungodly promoted to authority, antichrist triumphing. Great complaining there is, that the world is ever the longer the worse. Forasmuch then as through death we be discharged of so vicious a world, whom should it delight to live here any more? This meaning doth the preacher set forth in the fourth chapter of Ecclesiastes, saying: "So I turned me, and considered all the violent wrong that is done under the sun. And behold, the tears of such as were oppressed, there was no man to comfort them, or that would deliver and defend them from the violence of

their oppressors." There is at this day, by the grace of
God, many a worthy Christian that desireth rather to die,
than to be a looker upon such devilish wilfulness as commonly
goeth forward.

CHAPTER XV.

THAT THE DEAD OBTAINETH SALVATION.

As for vicious unrepentant people, when they die, I know
no comfort for them. Their bodies indeed shall rise at the
last day, but foul and marked to eternal pain. Their souls
shall be delivered unto the devil, to whom they have done
Luke xvi.   service. An example hereof standeth of the rich man : again,
there is the example of good Lazarus, that all Christians are
taken up of the angels into eternal joy and salvation. We
must not first be purged in purgatory ; but through death we
escape the devil, the world, and all misfortunes that this time
is oppressed withal.

If we now should lose our bodies, and not have them
again, then were death indeed a terrible thing, neither precious nor much worth. But our body is not so little regarded
before God : for even unto the body also hath he already
prepared salvation. Yea, even for this intent hath he laid
upon our necks the burden of natural death, that he might
afterward clothe us with a pure, renewed, and clear body,
and to make us glorious in eternal life. Therefore death
also, which is a beginning of the joyful resurrection, ought
to be esteemed dear and precious in our eyes. After death
verily is the soul in itself cleansed from all sins, and endowed
with perfect holiness, wisdom, joy, honour, and glory for
evermore.

CHAPTER XVI.

SIMILITUDES THAT DEATH IS WHOLESOME.

If an old silver goblet be melted, and new-fashioned after
a beautiful manner, then is it better than before, and neither

spilt nor destroyed.   Even so have we no just cause to complain of death, whereby the body being delivered from all filthiness, shall in his due time be perfectly renewed.

The egg-shell, though it be goodly and fair-fashioned, must be opened and broken, that the young chick may slip out of it.   None otherwise doth death dissolve and break up our body, but to the intent that we may attain unto the life of heaven.

The mother's womb carrieth the child seven or nine months, and prepareth it not for itself, but for the world wherein we are born.   Even so this present time over all upon earth serveth not to this end, that we must ever be here, but that we should be brought forth and born out of the body of the world into another and everlasting life.   Hereunto behold the words of Christ: "A woman, when she *John xvi.* travaileth, hath sorrow because her hour is come: but as soon as she is delivered of the child, she remembereth no more the anguish, for joy that a man is born into the world." Namely, like as a child out of the small habitation of his mother's womb, with danger and anguish is born into this wide world ; even so goeth a man through the narrow gate of death with distress and trouble, out of the earth into the heavenly life.

For this cause did the old Christians call the death of the saints a new birth.   Therefore ought we to note well this comfort, that to die is not to perish, but to be first of all born aright.

The death of the faithful seemeth indeed to be like unto the death of the unbelievers : but verily this is as great a difference as between heaven and earth.   Our death is even as a death-image made of wood, which grinneth with the teeth, and feareth, but cannot devour.   Our death should be esteemed even as Moses' brasen serpent ; which, having the form and proportion of a serpent, was yet without biting, without moving, without poisoning.   Even so, though death be not utterly taken away, yet through the grace of God it is so weakened and made void, that the only bare proportion remaineth.   When the master of the ship thinketh he is not wide from the place where he must land and discharge, he saileth on forth the more cheerfully and gladly : even so, the nearer we draw unto death, where we must land, the more

stoutly ought we to fight against the ghostly perils. Like as
he that goeth a far journey hath uncertain lodging, travail,
and labour, and desireth to return home to his own country,
to his father and mother, wife, children and friends, among
whom he is surest, and at most quiet ; by means whereof he
forceth[1] the less for any rough careful path or way homeward:
even so all we are strangers and pilgrims upon earth.   Our
home is paradise in heaven ; our heavenly father is God, the
earthly father of all men is Adam; our spiritual fathers are
the patriarchs, prophets, and apostles, which altogether wait
and long for us.   Seeing now that death is the path and way
unto them, we ought the less to fly it, to the intent that we
may come to our right home, salute our fathers and friends,
embrace them, and dwell with them for ever.   We have here
no remaining city, but we seek one to come.   Our conversation and burghership is in heaven.

But if any man be afraid of death, and force not for
the country of heaven, only because of temporal pleasures,
the same dealeth unhonestly ; even as do they, that whereas
they ought to go the next way home, set them down in a
pleasant place, or among companions at the tavern : where
they lying still, forget their own country, and pass not upon
their friends and kinsfolks.   How evil this becometh them,
every man may well consider by himself.

The Lord Jesus giveth this similitude : " Except the wheat
corn fall into the ground and die, it bideth alone: but if it die,
it bringeth forth much fruit."   Likewise Paul compareth us
men unto grains of corn, the churchyard to a field.   To die,
he saith, is to be sown upon God's field.   The resurrection,
with the life that followeth after, resembleth he to the pleasant
green corn in summer.

If a man lie in a dark miserable prison, with this condition
that he should not come forth, till the walls of the tower were
fallen down, undoubtedly he would be right glad to see the
walls begin to fall : our soul is kept in within the body upon
earth, as in captivity and bonds.   Now as soon as the body
is at a point that it must needs fall, why would we be sorry ?
For by this approacheth the deliverance, when we out of the
prison of misery shall be brought before the most amiable
countenance of God, into the joyful freedom of heaven.   Ac-

Marginal notes: 1 Chron. xxix. Psal. xxxix. cxix. 1 Pet. ii. 2 Cor. v. Phil. iii. Heb. xi. xiii. 1 Cor. xv.   Heb. xiii. Phil. iii.   1 Cor. xv.

[1 To force : to lay stress upon.   Johnson.]

cording to this did David pray: "Bring my soul out of Psal. cxlii.
prison, O Lord, that I may give thanks unto thy name."
Item, in many places of scripture, *to die* is called *to sleep*;
death itself, a sleep.   Like as it is no grief for a man to go
to sleep, nor when he seeth his parents and friends lay them
down to rest; (for he knoweth that such as are asleep do
soon awake and rise again;) so when we or our friends depart 1 Cor. xv.
away by death, we ought to erect and comfort ourselves with 1 Thess. iv.
the resurrection.

CHAPTER XVII.

WITNESS THAT DEATH IS WHOLESOME.

FOR the strengthening of our faith, I will allege evident
testimony of God's word.   The preacher saith: "The day Eccl. vii.
of death is better than the day of birth."   As if he would
say: In the day of thy birth thou art sent into the cold,
into the heat, into hunger and thirst, wherein is sin and
wretchedness: in the day of thy death thou shalt be delivered from all evil.   Again we read: "Though the righteous Wisd. iv.
be overtaken with death, yet shall he be in rest."

"Verily, verily, I say unto you, he that heareth my John v.
words, and believeth on him that sent me, hath everlasting
life, and shall not come into damnation, but is escaped from
death into life."   "If we live, we live unto the Lord: if we Rom. xiv.
die, we die unto the Lord.   Therefore whether we live or die, 2 Cor. iv.
we are the Lord's."   Behold, how comfortably this is spoken
of all Christians.

CHAPTER XVIII.

THAT DEATH CANNOT BE AVOIDED.   ITEM, OF COMPANIONS OF THEM THAT DIE.

UPON this condition are we born into the world, into this
light, not to continue alway therein; but when God will,
through temporal death to lay aside and put off the travail of

5—2

this miserable life. Witty men have found out, how hard stones may be broken and mollified, and how wild beasts may be tamed: but nothing could they invent, whereby death might be avoided. It is not unwisely said: "God's hand may a man escape, but not death."

Metrodorus writeth, that against bodily enemies there may be made fortresses, castles, and bulwarks; but so far as concerneth death, all men have an unfenced city. In other dangers, power, money, flight, counsel, and policy may help: but as for death, it can neither be banished with power, nor bought with money, nor avoided with flying away, nor prevented with counsel, nor turned back with policy. And though thou be now delivered from sickness, yet within a little while thou must, whether thou wilt or no, depart hence to death's home; for the highest lawgiver of all told our first father so before: "In what day soever thou eatest thereof, thou shalt die the death." Understand, that the death of the soul bringeth with it the death of the body.

Gen. ii.

Whoso now grudgeth, and is not content to die, what is that else, but that he, forgetting himself and his own nature, complaineth of God in heaven, that he suffered him to be born, and made him not an angel?

Why should we refuse the thing that we have common with other men? Now doth death touch not only us, but high and low estate, young and old, man and woman, master and servant.

As many as came of the first man must lay down their necks. Death is an indifferent judge, regardeth no person, hath no pity on the fatherless, careth not for the poor, dispenseth not with the rich, feareth not the mighty, passeth not for the noble, honoureth not the aged, spareth not the wise, pardoneth not the foolish.

For like as a river is poisoned in the well-spring, or fountain, so was the nature of man altogether in our first parents. And forasmuch as they themselves were maimed through sin, they have begotten unright and mortal children. Touching this saith Paul: "By one man came death upon all men."

Rom. v.

Now let us consider, what excellent companions and holy fellowship they also have that are dead. Paul writeth, that "we must be like shapen unto the image of the Son of God."

If he now that of nature was immortal and innocent, became
mortal for our sakes, even Jesus Christ our Saviour ; why
would we then, that many and sundry ways have deserved
death, continue here still, and not die ? Abraham the faithful,
Sampson the strong, Solomon the wise, Absolom the fair one,
yea, all the prophets and apostles, kings and emperors, through
death departed out of this life. A very dainty and tender
body must that be, which, considering so great multitudes of
corpses, doth yet out of measure vex himself, because the
like shall happen unto him. That were even like as if one
would take upon himself to be better than all righteous and
holy men, that ever were since the beginning of the world.

CHAPTER XIX.

OF NATURAL HELP IN DANGER OF DEATH.

WHOSO will help himself from the pestilence with flying
away, leaving his own wife, friends, and neighbours ; he declareth unperfectness of faith, and standeth not with christian
charity, where we owe unto others the same that we in like
case would gladly have at their hands.

Grant that the pestilence is such an infectious sickness, as
one taketh of another. What then ? If one stand in battle
array to fight for his country, must not he also look for a
gun-stone to be sent him into his bosom to carry home ? doth
it therefore beseem him to break the array and to fly ? Like
as there the enemies of the body are at hand ; so here do
the ghostly adversaries besiege the soul of him that is a
dying, where one Christian should help another with worthy
talk. Therefore is that a foolish unadvised counsel, when we
with neglecting of our own members will flee from the wrath
of God, thinking through sin to escape the punishment of sin.
Experience also doth shew, that such folks do oft perish, as
well as other ; yea, sooner than they that fled not at all.
But physic is permitted of God, as in the time of pestilence
with fires and perfumes to make the air more wholesome from
poison, and to receive somewhat into the body, for the consuming of evil humours, and to hinder the infection. Item,
when one is taken with a disease, to be let blood, to sweat, to

follow the physician's instruction; such things are in no wise to be reprehended, so that, whether it turn to death or life, the heart only and hope hang upon God. The physician should neither be despised nor worshipped. For to think scorn to use medicine in sickness, what were that else but even to tempt God?

CHAPTER XX.

THAT GOD IS ABLE AND WILL HELP FOR CHRIST'S SAKE.

SPECIALLY when death is at hand, a man findeth no help in any creature of heaven and earth, whereby he might fortunately suppress the exceeding great fear of death, but only in God the Father, in Christ his Son, and in the Holy Spirit of them both.

It is God that knoweth the perils of thy death, and can meddle withal. Through his power shalt thou get through, and drink the bitter draught. Though we die, yet liveth God before us, with us, after us, and is able to preserve us for ever. Christ sayeth: "Weep not, the damsel is not dead, but sleepeth." Faithless reason understandeth not the mystery of God, and laugheth: but Christ, the true God, hath both the word and work together, and saith no more but "Arise;" and the soul came again to the body, and she arose. Out of this, and such like examples, oughtest thou, faint-hearted man, to understand the infinite power of God, who can receive thy soul also and preserve it.

Not only is God able, but will also help graciously. Why should not he lay upon thee some great thing, as death is, seeing he addeth so great advantage, help, and strength thereto, to prove what his grace and power may do? For *Matt. x.* *Luke xii.* *Psal. xxxiv.* *Psal. lx.* *1 Pet. v.* he hath numbered all the hairs of our head: that is, he alway hath his eyes upon us, and careth ever for us.

Yea, that he loveth us more than we love ourselves, and maketh better provision for us than we can wish, he hath openly and evidently testified in his own dear Son; whom he *Mark xvi.* *Luke xxii.* *Acts vii.* *Rom. viii.* *Eph. i. iv.* *Philip. ii.* caused to take our miserable nature upon him, and therein for the sins of all the world to suffer, to die, to rise again, to ascend up to heaven, where he sitteth at the right hand of

God the Father Almighty. Among the which articles, every Col. iii.
1 Pet. iii.
Heb. i. ii. x.
xii.
one doth help and comfort such as are a dying.

The natural Son of God himself from heaven became a Psal. cx.
The
humanity
of Christ.
mortal man, to the intent that man's mortal nature, through
the uniting thereof with the immortal nature of the Godhead
in his own only person, might be exalted to an immortal life.

He, having a natural fear of death, said: "My soul is The passion
of Christ.
Matt. xxvi.
Mark xiv.
John xii.
Luke xxii.
heavy, even unto death." He prayed also: "Father, if it be
possible, take this cup from me." But this fear and terror
did he overcome; for he added thereto and saith: "Father,
not my will, but thine be fulfilled." Through this victory of
Christ, may all Christians also overcome such terror and fear
as they be in.

Item, though the Jews blaspheme never so much, and
say, "Let him come down from the cross: he hath helped
other, let him now help himself;" as though they would say,
"There, there, seest thou death, like a wretch must thou die,"
and no man is able to help thee; yet did the Lord Jesus
hold his peace there-to, as if he heard and saw them not.
He made no answer again, but only regarded the good will
and pleasure of his Father. Therefore though we have an
horrible temptation of death, as though there were neither
comfort nor help for us any more, yet in Christ and with
Christ we may endure all, and wait still upon the gracious
good will of God. He did not only suffer the horror and
temptation of death, but death itself; yea, the most horrible
death, whereby he took from us the death eternal, and some
deal mollified and assuaged our temporal death: yea, besides
this, he made it profitable and wholesome; so that death,
which of itself should else be a beginning of everlasting sorrow, is become an entrance into eternal salvation. According
to this meaning are the words of Paul, when he saith, that
"Christ, by the grace of God, tasted death for all men." 2 Cor. v.
Phil. i.
Rom. vii.
Heb. ii.

Item, "He became partaker of flesh and blood, to put
down through death him that had the lordship over death,
that is to say, the devil; and that he might deliver them,
which through fear of death, were all their life-time in danger
of bondage."

Moreover, that Christ is the living and immortal image
against death, yea, the very power of our resurrection and
of life everlasting, he himself hath testified with his own joy- Christ's re-
surrection.

ful and victorious resurrection; and also with that, that in
his resurrection many other saints that were dead rose from
death again.

Again, how full is it of comfort and pure treasure, that
St Paul joineth our resurrection unseparably to the resurrection of Jesus Christ! Likewise doth St Paul comfort his
disciple Timothy with the resurrection, and saith: "If we
die with Christ, we shall live with him; if we be patient, we
shall also reign with him."

No less must the fruit of the ascension of Christ be considered. For the Son of God hath promised and said:
"Father I will, that where I am, they also be whom thou
hast given me." Seeing that Christ now with body and soul
is gone up to heaven, what can be thought more comfortable
for a man at his death, than that we Christians shall also
after death be taken up into the joy of heaven?

In heaven sitteth Christ at the right hand of God, Lord
and King over sin, devil, death, and hell. Him we have in
that heavenly life with God an assured faithful mediator and
helper. Though we must fight in extremity of death, yet
are we not alone in this conflict or battle; even the valiant
heavenly captain himself, who upon the cross overcame death
and all misfortune for our sakes, hath respect unto us from
time to time, goeth before us in our battle, and fighteth for
us, keepeth us from all mischances in the way to salvation;
so that we need not care nor fear, that we shall sink or fall
down to the bottom.

He shall cause us with our own bodily eyes to see the
glorious victory and triumph in the resurrection of the dead,
and to have experience thereof in our own body and soul.
Death is even as a dark cave in the ground: but whoso
taketh Christ's light candle, putteth his trust in him, and
goeth into the dim dark hole, the mist flieth before him, and
the darkness vanisheth away.

In Christ have we a mighty effectuous image of grace, of
life, and of salvation, in such sort, that we Christians should
fear neither death nor other misfortune. Summa, he is our
hope, our safeguard, our triumph, our crown.

Witness of scripture: "I am the resurrection and the
life: he that believeth on me, yea, though he were dead, yet
shall he live; and whosoever liveth and believeth in me shall

Margin notes:
Matt. xxvii.

2 Tim. ii.
Rom. vi.

[John xvii.]

Deut. i. xx.
Exod. xiv.
Jos. xxiii.
1 Chron. vi.
2 Chron. xx.
xxxii.
2 Kings vi.
Zech. x.

John xi.

never die." Forthwith, after he had spoken these words,
raised he up Lazarus, who had lain four days in the grave,
and began to corrupt and stink.

"As by Adam all die, so by Christ shall all be made 1 Cor. xv.
alive, every one in his order." Item, "Our burghership is in Phil. iii.
heaven: from whence we look for a Saviour, even Jesus
Christ; which shall change our vile bodies, that they may
be fashioned like unto his glorious body, according to the
working whereby he is able to subdue all things unto himself." Also: "Ye are dead, and your life is hid with Christ Col. iii.
in God. But when Christ your life shall shew himself, then
shall ye also appear with him in glory." Here doth Paul
declare, that our life is not in this world, but hid with Christ
in God, and shall through Christ in his time be gloriously
opened. After this manner should Christ be printed into the
feeble, troubled, and doubtful consciences of the sick. And
with all diligence ought the office of Christ to be considered,
how that he, according unto the scripture, coming into this
world for our wealth, did also for our wealth preach, wrought
miracles, suffered, and died, to deliver us out of this false unhappy world, to open unto us the right door into eternal life,
and to bring us with body and soul into heaven; wherein
neither sin, death, nor devil shall be able to hinder us for
evermore.

Who shall ever be able sufficiently to praise and magnify
the infinite glory of the grace of God? What would we have
the Lord our God to do more for us, to make us lustily step
forth before the face of death, manfully to fight in all trouble,
and willingly to wait for the deliverance?

CHAPTER XXI.

THAT GOD HATH PROMISED HIS HELP AND COMFORT.

OUT of this exceeding grace of God, for the blessed Seed's
sake, proceed God's comfortable promises in the old and
new Testament. "Mine eyes shall still be upon thee, that Psal. xci.
thou perish not. The Lord shall deliver thee from the snare
of the hunter, and from the most noisome death. With his

own wings shall he cover thee ; so that under his feathers thou shalt be safe. His truth and faithfulness shall be thy shield and buckler : so that thou shalt neither need to fear any inconvenience by night, neither swift arrow in the day-season ; neither the pestilence that creepeth in darkness, nor yet any hurt that destroyeth by day-time. Though a thousand fall on thy left hand, and ten thousand on thy right, yet shall it not touch thee."

Here doth God evidently promise, that he will graciously preserve his own children, first, from such temptation, phantasy, and deceivableness, as come upon a man by night in the dark : secondly, from the violence of wicked unthrifts, and all mischances that overtake men openly in the day-season, yea, sometimes suddenly and unawares : thirdly, from the pestilence, that we need not to fear it, though there die of it a thousand on the left hand and ten thousand on the right : the pestilence shall either not take us, or not wound us unto death, or else serve to our everlasting welfare : fourthly, from hot feverish sicknesses, such as commonly grow in hot countries, when the sun shineth most strongly. Under these four plagues are all mischances comprehended.

In the end of this psalm stand these words : " I am with him in trouble, I will deliver him, and bring him to honour." When God saith, " I am with him," consider not thou thine own powers ; for they help nothing at all : behold much more the power of him that is with thee in trouble. When thou hearest, " I will deliver him," thou must not be faint-hearted, though the trouble do seem long to continue. When thou hearest, " I will bring him unto honour," be thou sure, that as thou art partaker of the death of Christ, so shalt thou be also of his glory.

Matt. xi.   Christ calleth thee to him, and crieth yet still : " Come to me, all ye that labour and are laden, and I will ease you. Take my yoke on you, and learn of me, that I am meek and lowly in heart, and ye shall find rest unto your souls." Again:
[John viii.]   " Verily, verily, I say unto you ; If any man keep my sayings, he shall never see death." Understand, that the light of life doth shine clearer, than the darkness of death can blind. For the faithful, through his belief, is after such sort incorporated and joined unto the Lord Christ, the true life, that he shall not be separated from him. Though body and

soul depart asunder now for a season; yet is that done in an assured undoubted hope of the blessed resurrection, that very shortly both body and soul shall come together again to eternal joy.   And thus the christian believer neither seeth, feeleth, nor tasteth the everlasting death of his body and soul, that is to say, eternal damnation.

CHAPTER XXII.

GOD SETTETH TO HIS OWN HELPING HAND IN SUCH WISE AND AT SUCH TIME AS IS BEST OF ALL.

GOD now, through Christ, doth not only promise most graciously his comfort and help, but faithfully performeth he the same in due season, so far, and after such sort as is expedient.   The very right time undoubtedly doth not he omit.   Death indeed is a narrow way; but God shorteneth it. The bitterness of death passeth all the pains that we have felt upon earth; but it endureth not long.   Death must make quick speed with us, as Hezekiah the king of Judah saith : "He shall cut off my life, as a weaver doth his web."   And Isai. xxxviii. when the pain is greatest of all, then is it near the end. Hereunto may be applied that Christ said, "It is but a John xiv. modicum, a very little while."   Though it were so that the troubles of death did long endure, yet towards the eternity that followeth after is the same scarce as one point or prick in comparison of a whole circle.   In the mean season, God can more comfort and help, than the most horrible death of all is able to disturb or grieve.   Sometime taketh he from us the grievous enemy or mortal sickness, and so delivereth us out of the perils of death.   Else giveth he some ease or refreshing outwardly : or if the trouble go on still, he sendeth his sweet gracious comfort inwardly, so as the patient through the working of the Holy Ghost doth feel a taste, a proof and beginning of the heavenly joy; by means whereof he is able willingly to forsake all that earthly is, and to endure all manner of pain and smart until the ond.

"The Spirit of God certifieth our spirit, that we are the Rom. viii.

children of God. If we be children, we are also heirs, the heirs, I mean, of God, and heirs annexed with Christ, if so be that we suffer with him, that we may also be glorified with him." God commandeth his angels, that they with him do look unto thee, O man, when thou diest, and to take heed unto thy soul, to keep it, and to receive it, when it shall depart out of the body. Witness this is : "The angel of the Lord pitcheth round about them that fear him, and delivereth them." And : "He hath given his angels charge concerning thee, that they keep thee in all thy ways, and bear thee in their hands, that thou hurt not thy foot against a stone."

The angels, which are many without number, be ministering spirits, sent to do service for their sakes, which shall be heirs of salvation. Therefore a Christian at his last end must be thoroughly assured, that in his death he is not alone, but that very many eyes look unto him : first, the eyes of God the Father himself, and of his Son Jesus Christ; then the worthy angels, and all Christians upon earth.

Then, according to the contents of the sacrament of baptism and of the supper of the Lord, all Christians, as a whole body to a member thereof, resort unto him that is a dying, by having compassion and prayer to help him by, that at his death he may overcome death, sin, and hell.

Psal. xxxiv.

Psal. xci.

Heb. i.

CHAPTER XXIII.

EXAMPLES OF GOD'S HELP.

In the time of the prophets and apostles God raised certain from death ; to the intent that our weak feeble nature might have the more help to believe the resurrection and eternal life. For the dead could not have been raised, if death did bring man utterly to nought. Abraham fell sick, and died in a good age, when he was old, and had lived enough, and was put unto his people ; that is, his soul came to the soul of the other saints, which died before. So is it also of Isaac. Word was brought to king Hezekiah, that he should live no longer; but after he had made his earnest prayer unto God, there were added fifteen years unto life.

Gen. xxxv.

When Lazarus died, his soul was carried of the angels into Luke xvi.
Abraham's bosom.   The murderer upon the cross heard in
his extreme trouble that Christ said unto him : " This day Luke xxiii.
shalt thou be with me in paradise."

Daily experience testifieth, that God forsaketh not his
own.   Therefore undoubtedly he that hath begun his kingdom in us, shall graciously perform and finish it.

CHAPTER XXIV.

THAT IT IS NECESSARY TO PREPARE FOR THIS JOURNEY.

IF we could find in our hearts gladly for to hear, how
unhurtful, yea, wholesome and vincible death is become
through Christ, we would not be idle, and linger still till the
time came that we must needs die.

A good householder maketh provision for himself and his
family, and buyeth beforehand fuel and victuals, and such
things as he hath need of for a whole year, or for a month,
&c., according as he is able.   Much more ought a Christian
to provide that, which concerneth not only one month or one
year, but an eternity that hath no end.   Like as faithful
servants wait for their master, so ought we to look for the
coming of Christ, when he shall call us out of this time.   " If Luke xii.
the householder knew what hour the thief would come, he
would watch, and not suffer his house to be broken up.
Therefore be ye also ready : for in the hour that ye think Matt. xxiv
not, will the Son of man come."

Whoso hath perfect knowledge of death, as it is hitherto
described and set forth, he in making provision beforehand
hath first this advantage, that it is good fighting with a
known enemy.   Contrariwise, on the other side, what shall
an unmeet warrior do, that knoweth not the nature, subtlety,
weapons, and policy of the enemy ?

CHAPTER XXV.

PROVISION CONCERNING TEMPORAL GOODS, CHILDREN, AND FRIENDS, WHICH MUST BE LEFT BEHIND.

AGAIN, concerning temporal goods: Let the rich who hath wife and children, or other heirs, make provision for them in good order under writing, according as in every place the custom is. But if honour and authority, substance or goods, go too near thy stomach, then consider that they be not true, but uncertain, transitory, and vain goods, which bring more unquietness than rest. Consider also, that many more rich mighty princes, kings, and lords must be spoiled of all their glory, and be fain to content themselves with a short narrow place of the grave.

Though we here lose all, yet do we scarce lose one farthing. And in the other life we have not kingdoms, nor empires, but God himself and everlasting goods; in comparison whereof, all minstrelsy, pastime, pomp, mirth, and cheer upon earth is scarce to be esteemed as casting counters towards the finest coins of gold. Therefore ought we to learn, specially in sickness, to give all temporal goods their leave, and to bid them farewell. And if any man will furthermore disquiet and trouble us in telling us still of them, then must we require him to depart and let us alone. Whoso hath a train hanging upon him, as father, mother, sisters, brothers, wife, children, and friends, the same is the sorer laid at: for naturally we all are loth to depart from them. Here must
Matt. x. we remember the words of Christ: "He that loveth father or mother more than me, is not worthy of me. And he that loveth son or daughter more than me, is not meet for me. And whoso taketh not up his cross and followeth me, is unapt for me." Therefore must thou break thine own will, take up thy cross, and give over thyself unto the will of God; specially, forasmuch as even they whom thou art loth to leave behind thee upon earth, shall shortly come to thee. And in the mean season, when thou departest from thy friends, thou goest the next way, and speedest thee unto better and more loving friends. And therefore the holy patriarch Jacob said,
Gen. xlix. when he should die: "I shall be gathered unto my people."

Item, unto Moses and Aaron said God: "Thou shalt go to [Numb. xxvii. xx.] thy people and unto thy fathers." Hereby is it declared, that death is a passage to many more folks and better friends than we leave here. There is God our Father, his Son our Brother, his heaven our inheritance, and all angels and saints our brethren, sisters, and kinsfolks, with whom we shall enjoy eternal goods for ever.

Again, whoso leaveth behind him a poor wife, children not brought up, and friends that are in necessity, must also do his best, committing them to the protection, help, and comfort of God, with an earnest prayer that he will graciously take the governance of them. For our wives, children, and posterity doth the second commandment set in God's tuition, when it saith: "Mercy and kindness shew I unto [Exod. xx.] thousands of them that love me, and keep my commandments."

Item, God writeth himself a father of the widows and [Exod. xxii. Psal. cxlv.] fatherless, and taketh them into his own protection.

Now if thou receive not this godly consolation and comfort, then, to thine own great notable hurt, thou disquietest thyself so grievously, that thou canst consider nothing that is right and just, eternal or heavenly.

CHAPTER XXVI.

PREPARATION CONCERNING GHOSTLY MATTERS, WITH WHAT COGITATIONS THE MIND OUGHT MOST TO BE EXERCISED.

MOREOVER, the sick must give all other worldly matters their leave, that the soul be not tangled with any earthly business, but directed upward into heaven, where it desireth everlastingly to live.

Here shall it be needful, that our mind have an assured understanding of the holy gospel. In this consideration endure thou still; hang thou thereupon with stedfast faith, whereout grow these fruits, prayer, righteousness, patience, and all goodness.

After the doctrine of the true gospel, without thine own

and religious men's works, without the merits of saints, art thou justified, made righteous, and saved only through Christ, who alone is thy mediator, advocate, helper, satisfaction, hope, comfort, and life. It is Christ's will to convey thee away from sin, from the world, from the devil, and from hell, and to take thee to his grace into the eternal paradise, though all creatures were against thee.

John xvii.   Probation out of the scripture : " This is the life eternal, that they know thee to be the only true God, and whom thou hast sent, Jesus Christ." With this evangelical doctrine, and with nothing else, must our hearts be occupied, what temptations soever happen, which undoubtedly will not tarry behind.

While we go about yet merry and in health, it bringeth exceeding great profit, if we exercise ourselves with the cogitations of death. But in sickness, and when we must die, that is, when the horrible image of death would make us afraid, we must not unquiet ourselves with heavy remembrance of death. We should not behold or consider death in itself, nor in our own nature, neither in them that are slain through the wrath of God; but principally in Christ Jesu, and then in his saints, which through him overcame death, and died in the grace of God. From this fight may not we suffer ourselves to be driven, though all angels and all creatures, yea, though God himself, in our opinion, would lay other things before our eyes, which they do not : howbeit, the evil spirit maketh such an appearance. For Christ Jesus is nothing else but life and salvation. Yea, the more deeply and stedfastly we do set, print, and behold Christ before us, the more shall death be despised and devoured in life ; the heart also hath the more rest, and may quietly die in Christ.

John xvi.   Therefore saith Christ: " In the world, that is, also, in yourselves, ye shall have trouble; but in me peace. Be ye of good comfort, I have overcome the world."

Rev. xiv.
Numb. xxi.   " Blessed are they that die in the Lord." This aforetime was figured and signified, when the children of Israel, being bitten of fiery serpents, might not struggle with them, but behold the brasen serpent, namely Christ. So the quick serpents fell away of themselves, and vanished.

When we now behold death and the pangs of death in itself with our own feeble reason, without Christ, without

God's word, specially out of season, that is to say, in the danger of death; then hath death his whole power and strength in our feeble nature, and killeth us with the greater pain, so that we forget God, and are lost for ever.

CHAPTER XXVII.

OF REPENTANCE AND SORROW FOR SIN.

To the intent that our will, heart, and mind may right and truly receive and apprehend the Lord Christ, we must first be thoroughly sorrowful for our sinful life, and confess that there was no remedy, but of ourselves we should have been damned for ever. This shrift or confession of sins must not forthwith be done to the priest, but unto God, with hearty sorrow and repentance, after the example of the poor sinner and of the publican. Therefore must we also acknowledge, that with all our own power and works we are able to prevail neither against death, nor other mischance. For how were it possible, that we, poor silly worms, feeble and weak in body and soul, should be able to endure the stormy waves and intolerable burden of death, if the right hand of God himself were not present to help our infirmity? Full truly spake a certain king in France, when he lay on his deathbed: "I have been very rich, I have had exceeding much honour, my power was passing great; and yet for all my riches, power, and friends, I am not able to obtain of death so much as one hour's respite."

CHAPTER XXVIII.

OF TRUE FAITH.

To such a confession belongeth the christian belief, that we turn ourselves away from all comfort of man, yea, from all creatures, to the only Creator through Jesus Christ, and to give ourselves over wholly unto him. With all our natural reason and wisdom shall we never be able to comprehend, how

6

it cometh to pass, that the soul must depart out, and yet be preserved; that worms consume the body, and that the same yet shall rise again and live for ever. Therefore is there required faith in Christ and in his word. The sum hereof have we in the twelve articles of the old ancient undoubted christian belief.

And though it be our duty alway, specially at the time of death, earnestly to consider all the articles, yet principally, when we die, we ought to exercise the four last articles; "the communion of saints, the forgiveness of sins, the resurrection of the body, and the life everlasting." For these four in themselves comprehend all the power, commodity, and fruit of faith: namely, whosoever doth stedfastly look for all grace and help at God's hand through the conception and birth, death and passion, resurrection and ascension, intercession and merits of Jesus Christ, and standeth, liveth, and dieth in the same faith; though all sins, devils, death, and hell would fall upon him and oppress him, yet can they not hurt him.

The fruits of faith.

To be short, it is not otherwise possible: he must needs have fellowship with God and the elect, and be quite discharged from all sins, and joyfully rise again to eternal life. Yea, whatsoever the Son of God himself hath, can do, and is able, that same hath this believer also obtained; neither can it go otherwise with him but prosperously in life and death, here and in the world to come, temporally and eternally.

Witness: whoso hath Christ, hath already the true life and all blessing; for Christ is the life, the resurrection, and a plentiful sufficiency of all good things. Through faith doth Christ dwell in our hearts. Therefore through faith we obtain all consolation and blessing.

Eph. iii.

That faith is the true absolution, it may be perceived by the words of Christ, when he saith so oft in the gospel: "Be it unto thee according to thy belief."

Item, God will constantly stand to his word and promise; he is of nature the truth itself. Heaven and earth shall pass, but his words shall not pass.

Luke xxi.

What are now the promises of God? "So God loved the world, that he gave his only-begotten Son, that whosoever believeth on him, should not perish, but have everlasting life." O how blessed a promise is this, that if we believe in Christ the Son of God, we shall through him inherit eternal life!

John iii.

Item: "Verily, verily, I say unto you, he that heareth my words, and believeth on him that sent me, hath everlasting life, and shall not come into damnation, but is escaped from death unto life." Lord, how comfortable a thing is this, that a faithful believer by temporal death escapeth through, yea, is already escaped into everlasting life!

Again: "This is the will of my Father, which hath sent John vi. me, that every one which seeth the Son and believeth on him, have eternal life; and I shall raise him up at the last day." As though he said: "This is the most gentle good-will of God the Father, and of God the Son, that such a man as still endureth in stedfast confidence upon the grace and word of God, shall be preserved and saved for ever. And even as little shall sin, hell, and the devil be able to hurt him, as they could hurt Christ himself. When the darkness of the *A pithy* night falleth down, it covereth the whole world, dimmeth the *similitude.* colour and fashion of all creatures, feareth and discomforteth them; yet is it not of such power, as to darken, suppress, and quench the least light of all that is found in the world. For the darker the night is, the clearer do the stars shine; yea, the least light of a candle withstandeth the whole night, and giveth light round about in the midst of darkness. A little spark also of a coal cannot the darkness cover, much less is it able to quench it. Now is God the true, everlasting, *i John i.* and heavenly light. And all they that put their trust in him are as a burning candle. For through faith doth God dwell in our hearts, and we are the living temple of God, and Christ's disciples are called the lights of the world. Hereout followeth it, that though the prince of spiritual darkness thrust in with his noisome poison and plagues; yet shall we behold in faith, that he with his poison and plagues can neither apprehend nor destroy any true faithful man or woman, but shall be smitten back and driven away perforce.

A little vein of water breaketh forth out of the ground *An apt* sometime scarce a finger big; and when the water is gathered *similitude.* into a ditch or pond, it springeth nevertheless. And though the water become heavy of certain hundred weight, and move about the fountain, yet can it not drive back the fountain, but it driveth the whole weight of the water backward and forward, and springeth still continually, till the ditch be so full that it go over. And if the other water be foul and troubled, it cannot mingle itself among the fresh clear water of the fountain; but the same remaineth pure and fair, till in time it come far from the head spring.

Now is God the only plentiful fountain of all life. And the faithful are very flowing wells. For Christ saith : "Whoso believeth on me, out of his body, as saith the scripture, shall flow streams of the water of life." Which words "he spake of the Spirit, that they which believe on him should receive." Thus no mischance of this world can spoil any faithful man of his comfort and life ; forasmuch as God, the eternal well-spring of life, dwelleth and floweth in his heart, and driveth all noisome things far away from it.

To the intent now that thou mayest be partaker of all the fruits of faith, thou must manfully strive and exercise thy belief after this manner. If any imagination or thought concerning sin or death will fear thee, though flesh and blood tell thee otherwise, and though thine own natural reason would make thee to believe none other, and thou thyself feelest not the contrary, but that God of very wrath will kill thee and damn thee for ever ; yet let no despair pluck the noble comfort of the Saviour out of thine heart ; let not thy heart waver in the loving and fatherly promises of God; let the terrible cogitations pass, as much as is possible. Remember the comfortable gracious word of the Lord Jesu. Comprehend and keep it sure in a stedfast belief, confidence, and hope. Pluck up thine heart, and say : O death, thy false fear would fain deceive me, and with lying cogitations pull me away from Christ, the worthy. I may not hearken to thy fear, neither accept it. I know of a dear, valiant, worthy, and victorious man, that said : "Be of good comfort, I have overcome the world ; " that is to say, sin, death, devil, hell, and whatsoever cleaveth to the world; and, "Verily, verily, he that believeth and putteth his trust in me, hath eternal life." With the which words the same dear, valiant, worthy, and victorious man doth apply also unto me his victory and power. With him will I continue, and keep me to his word and comfort, whether I live longer, or must die. Here ought we perfectly to be sure, that the greater the battle of death is, the nearer is Jesus Christ, to crown us with mercy and loving-kindness.

Evident examples out of the new and old Testament.

Jer. ii.
Psal. xxxvi.
John vii.

The exercise
of faith.

Blessed of
God is he that
hath this
mind.

John vi.

Paul rejoiceth, and boasteth against the terror of death: "Death is swallowed up in victory. Death, where is thy victory? Hell, where is thy sting?" As though he would say: O death, thou mayest well make one afraid, as a death-image of wood may do; but to devour thou hast no might. For thy victory, sting, and power is swallowed up in the victory of Christ. And through Jesus Christ our Lord hath God given us the victory against thee, so that all true faithful Christians are become lords over death and hell. But of such a faith is Paul not afraid to say: "Whether we live or die, we are the Lord's." 1 Cor. xv. To the faithful death is a comfort. Rom. xiv.

And again thus he speaketh exceeding comfortably: "Christ is to me life, and death is to me advantage." For hereby go we from labour to rest, from shame to honour, from heaviness to joy, from death to life. "We know that we are translated from death unto life." "Though I walk in the valley of the shadow of death, yet fear I no evil; for thou, Lord, art with me." Phil. i. Oh that these words were printed in our hearts. 1 John v. Psal. xxiii.

Therefore let them fear death, that know not Christ, neither believe in him; even such as from temporal death pass unto death everlasting. For God giveth charge and commandment, that we should receive comfort in the Lord Jesu, as the words sound: "Be of good comfort, I have overcome the world." Whoso now will not be comforted with the Lord Jesu, doth unto God the Father and the Son the greatest dishonour; as though it were false that he biddeth us, "Be of a good comfort;" and as though it were not true, that he "hath overcome the world." And by this, whereas the devil, sin, and death is overcome already, we strengthen them to be our own tyrants against the faithful true Saviour. Hereof proceed such words as these: "I wot not how to endure and abide it: alas! what shall become of me?" What is that else, but to have respect unto our own strength, as though Christ were not at hand to take our part, and to finish the matter? Item, through unbelief a man desireth to remain here longer, whether God be content withal, or no. In the sight of the world he is taken to be no honest man, that vilely forsaketh his bodily master: doth not he then procure unto himself everlasting shame, that in trouble of death picketh himself away from Christ, the heavenly master? Witness: "He that be- Unbelief. How God is blasphemed by our fear of death. The fearer of death armeth the devil against himself. Trust in our own strength is the way to desperation. Mark xvi.

John iii. lieveth not shall be damned. He that believeth not on the Son of God, shall not see life, but the wrath of God abideth on him."

CHAPTER XXIX.

OF HOPE.

The work and strength of the lively faith.

Psal. xxxvii.

FAITH, though it be no greater than a little spark, gendereth hope, which looketh and waiteth for the deliverance to come, and shall undoubtedly not come to confusion. "Commit thy cause unto the Lord, hope upon him; and he full well shall bring it to pass." *Ipse faciet*, he himself will be the doer.

The good patriarch Abraham is set forth unto us for an example of faith and hope. Like as he hoped against hope, that is to say, there as nothing was to hope; even so must our hope stand fast and sure against all, that our own natural reason or the wicked enemy can object or cast in our way.

CHAPTER XXX.

OF THE SACRAMENTS.

To the confirmation of faith and hope serve the holy sacraments of Baptism and of the Supper of the Lord. Baptism is an undoubted true token and evidence of the grace of God, fastened even upon the body; with the which God promiseth and bindeth himself, that he will be thy God and Father for his Son's sake, and will also preserve thee with his own Spirit in thy greatest perils for evermore.

The place of the supper, and persons.

The sacrament of the body and blood of Christ must be exercised and practised only in the coming together of the whole congregation and church, according to the example of the apostles. Therefore let the sick satisfy himself with the general breaking of bread, whereof he was partaker with the whole congregation[1]. But let him diligently consider the

[1 The same opinion is maintained by *Bishop Hooper* in his *Answer to the Bishop of Winchester's Book*. *Early Writings of Bishop*

fruit thereof, after this manner: God hath promised me his *The fruit of the supper.* grace in Christ, and given me an assured token from heaven in this sacrament, that Christ's life hath in his death overcome my death, and that his obedience in his passion hath destroyed my sins. This godly promise, token, and evidence of my salvation shall not deceive me. I will not suffer this to be taken from me, to die for it. I will rather deny all the world and myself also, than to doubt in God's token and promise. Here the devil tempteth a man to say: "Yea, but through my unworthiness I may spill the gifts of God that are offered me by the word and token, and so be spoiled of the same for ever." Answer: God giveth thee nothing for thine own *Our worthiness to communicate.* worthiness' sake; yea, he buildeth thee unworthy upon the worthiness of his own Son: if thou believe on the Son of God, thou art and continuest worthy before the face of God.

Item: Forasmuch as thou hast gone heretofore unto the Supper of the Lord, thou art through the same sacrament incorporated and conjoined with all them that are sanctified in God, and art already come into the fellowship of the saints, so that they with thee in Christ die and overcome.

CHAPTER XXXI.

OF PRAYER.

No man should presume to exercise faith, and hope, or other spiritual gifts, out of his own power; but humbly to pray unto God for all such things as are needful. And seeing we have need of one mediator and advocate, God hath given *Our sufficiency is from God.* us his Son Jesus Christ. Neither is any of our prayers acceptable unto God, but such as we offer through Jesus Christ. *Heb. xiii.* Therefore must we withdraw ourselves from all creatures, praying and desiring all things at God's hand only through the name of Jesu.

How ought a man to call upon God through Christ? *What is to call upon God in Christ.* With belief that we doubt not but our prayer is heard already.

Hooper, pp. 170—173. Parker Soc. Ed. The objection to the private celebration of the Lord's Supper prevailed at a very early period, as we learn from the second Apology of Justin Martyr, c. 98.]

To such a faith and confidence are we occasioned, in that God hath commanded us to pray, and promised that he will graciously hear us: " Knock, and it shall be opened unto you, &c."

For what thing ought we to make our prayer unto God? For the understanding of his word, for remission of sins, for increase of faith, for love even towards our enemies, for help, patience, comfort, and all spiritual gifts. To pray for health and long life, is not unright, so far as we commit and refer it unto the holy will of God. For we cannot make it better than the faithful Father, that knoweth best of all. And to pray for a long life is ofttimes nothing else than to desire to be kept long in misery. Good Hezekiah yet prayed with tears, that he might live for a season.

Christ, the most perfect example of all, did pray: " Father, if it be possible, take this bitter draught from me; nevertheless, not my will, but thine be done." Like as he now prayed, as the second and third time most earnestly ; so ought we also without ceasing to call upon God. Some appoint God beforehand, what death he must suffer them to die. But they do best of all, that prescribe unto the Lord their God neither fashion of death, nor time, neither other circumstance ; but refer all unto him, who knoweth what is profitable and good, better than we ourselves.

Moreover, we must pray for wife and child, for friend and enemy, and for the whole congregation of the Christians, that God may graciously take them all into his own protection. Unto prayer belongeth it also, cheerfully to give God thanks for all bodily and ghostly benefits.

The moderation of prayer for temporal things.

Isai. xxxviii.

CHAPTER XXXII.

THE FORM OF PRAYER.

Prayer to God the Father.

O ALMIGHTY everlasting God, merciful Father of heaven, thou hast created me after thine own image, and endowed me with exceeding plentiful gifts. Yet notwithstanding all thy benefits, I have many and sundry ways contemned and transgressed thy commandments. All my days are passed forth

with grievous sins. I fear and flee from thee, as from a Confession.
righteous judge. All this, whatsoever it be, I freely acknowledge and confess, and am sorry for it from the ground of
my heart. But, O heavenly Father, I cry and call for thy Desire of grace.
large and great mercy : O enter not with me into judgment;
remember not the sins of my youth. O think upon me according to thy mercy, for thy name's sake, and for thy goodness, which hath been from everlasting. Vouchsafe to grant
me thy mercy, which thou according to the contents of the
gospel hast promised and opened through thy beloved Son, in
such sort, that whoso believeth on him shall have everlasting
life. Now is my belief in Jesu Christ, even in the only
Redeemer of the whole world. I utterly refuse all other
comfort, help, and assistance; and my hope is only through
Christ to have pardon of my sins and eternal life. Thy
words are true; be it unto me according to thy words : O let
me enjoy the passion and death of thine only-begotten Son.
Take for my sins the satisfaction and payment of our Lord
Jesus Christ, according to the tenor of my belief. Of this
my faith thou shalt thyself, O Lord, be witness, and all thine
elect. My last will also shall it be, upon thy mercy to die in
this faith. Though I now, by occasion of pain, lack of reason,
or through temptation should happen or would fall away;
suffer me not yet, O Lord, to stick fast in unbelief and blasphemy; but help mine unbelief, strengthen and increase my
faith, that sin, death, the devil, and hell do me no harm.
Thou art stronger and mightier than they : that is only my
trust and confidence.

O Lord, the flesh is feeble and impatient: lay not thou Patience and lowliness is
my weakness to my charge, but burn, smite, prick, and the sign of a Christian.
plague, as thou wilt thyself; only, I beseech thee, grant me
patience and lowliness of mind. Be thou the strength of my
soul in this far journey, which I have now to go in an unknown land. Now shew thyself unto my poor soul, so as it
may feel that thou art my refuge, my help, protection, defence, comfort, castle, my sure stony rock, my safeguard, my
treasure, prosperity, health, and welfare. I yield myself
wholly unto thee with soul and body; let me never be con-
founded. Help also, O heavenly Father, that according unto Prayer for the enemy.
thy commandment I may love mine enemies, and pray for Matt. v. Rom. xii.
them that have hurt me; and bring to pass, through thy holy

Spirit, that all they whom I have done harm unto, may also forgive me, to the commodity and health of their own souls. For it rueth me, and sorry I am, that at any time I have broken christian love and charity, and beguiled, deceived, or offended any man with evil example, or with too few benefits. I beseech thee, O Lord, through Jesus Christ, forgive thou all them that ever have hurt me in thought, word, or deed.

Prayer for every man.

To thy faithfulness and protection, O dearest Father, I commit all that concerneth me, especially wife, children, friends, and all such as thou hast put under my governance. Comfort and help thou all those that lie in bonds, and are persecuted for thy word's sake.

Have mercy upon all such as are in prison, poverty, sickness, and heaviness. O bring thou the whole world to the knowledge of thy holy word, that they may live according to thy godly will, and throughout all troubles to endure and continue still in the christian faith.

Prayer to God the Son.

O Lord Jesu Christ, I beseech thee, through thine own merits, have mercy upon me. Seeing I myself cannot make satisfaction or sufficient amends towards the Father for my sins, I lay them upon thee, in hope that thou hast already taken them away. For thou hast paid that we ought, and our wounds hast thou healed. O increase thou in me and other men faith, patience, and consolation, what adversity or trouble soever we be in. Thou, Lord Jesu, in thy passion didst pray: "Father, if it be possible, let this cup pass from me: nevertheless, not my will, but thine be done:" and that is my prayer also. Upon the cross thou didst pray: "Father, forgive them." Even so, Lord, forgive I all those that ever have done any thing against me. Thou didst cry: "My God, my God, why hast thou forsaken me?" O Lord, forsake not thou me then in my deadly trouble. Upon the cross thou saidst: "Into thy hands I commend my spirit." Even so now, Lord, commend I my poor soul into thy hands.

Prayer to God the Holy Ghost.

O thou Holy Spirit, great is the anguish and distress of my heart; have mercy upon me for Jesus Christ's sake. I am afflicted, and so are many more: O vouchsafe thou to illuminate, comfort, and strengthen me and them unto all goodness; convey thou and bring us out of all trouble, and fail us not, neither forsake us for evermore. Amen.

CHAPTER XXXIII.

A FORM OF PRAYER AND THANKSGIVING.

O ALMIGHTY, eternal, merciful God and Father, I laud and praise thee, that thou hast created me a reasonable man, and as a Father hast preserved me to this hour; keeping me from great dangers ever since I was born, and doing me more good than ever I was or am worthy. Especially I give thee thanks for thy endless grace, which thou shewest unto me and all faithful, through thy most dear beloved Son; in that he for my sins would be tempted so many ways, and suffer so vile a death, to the intent that I from henceforth might be assured of faithful assistance. *Thanksgiving to God the Father.*

Magnified and blessed be thy name, that thou sufferest me not to die without knowledge of the Holy Ghost. I thank thee also, dearest Father, that thou, visiting me with this sickness and danger, dost not forget me. For in the mean season also thou comfortest and helpest, and full graciously shalt thou bring the matter to an end.

Honour, praise and thanks be unto thee, my most dear Lord Jesu Christ, for thy holy incarnation, for thy martyrdom and bitter passion; whereby I am perfectly assured, that thou art my Redeemer and Saviour. Upon that only set I my building; thitherward standeth my hope; there will I be found cheerfully and gladly; with thy help will I depart hence; trusting that as I am partaker of thy troubles, so shall I also have my part in thy everlasting glory; namely, that at the last day thou shalt raise up this my poor mortal body, taking my soul unto thee immediately at my departing hence. O thou Holy Spirit, I render unto thee praise and thanks for the true understanding, belief, comfort, patience, and all gifts, which thou graciously dost minister and give by the grace of our Lord Jesus Christ. *Thanksgiving to the Son.* *Rom. vi. Rom. viii. 2 Tim. ii.* *Thanksgiving to the Holy Ghost.*

CHAPTER XXXIV.

THAT THE PRAYER IS HEARD.

HEREUNTO serve all psalms of prayer and thanksgiving. Howbeit, whatsoever concerneth prayer, it is all comprehended with few words in the holy *Pater-noster*, if it be diligently and earnestly considered. Notwithstanding no christian prayer can be done in vain, that it should not be faithfully heard. God saith : " He hath a desire unto me, and I will deliver him : when he calleth upon me, I shall hear him ; yea, I am with him in his trouble, whereout I will deliver him, and bring him to honour. He knoweth my name, therefore will I defend him ; with long life will I satisfy him, and shew him my salvation." Yea, the whole Psalter is full of such comfortable promises. Example : if thou pray with the murderer upon the cross, that Christ will " remember thee in his kingdom," thou shalt also in thy heart hear the gracious comfort, " This day shalt thou be with me in paradise." Nevertheless, whosoever is in trouble, heaviness, or adversity, ought earnestly to desire the intercessions and prayers of faithful believers.

Psal. xci.

Luke xxiii.

CHAPTER XXXV.

THAT THE WORD OF GOD OUGHT TO BE PRACTISED AND USED.

FURTHERMORE he ought always to have God's word before his eyes, and fervently to exercise himself therein. For whereas he faithfully calleth unto God, he doeth it upon his word ; and in the word of God he is taught how to behave himself towards all, whatsoever cometh in his way. If a man now cannot give himself true information out of the holy scripture, whether it be concerning sins committed, or other temptations ; then ought he to ask counsel of his learned soul-shepherd, or of some other men of godly understanding. The Lord sayeth not for nought : " My sheep hear my voice, and I know them, and they follow me, and I give them eternal life, and they shall never perish."

John x.

CHAPTER XXXVI.

AMENDMENT OF LIFE NECESSARY.

THE true faith bringeth with it naturally a stedfast purpose to live from henceforth according unto all the commandments of God.

Christ also exhorteth every man rightly to exercise and well to use the gifts of God. Hereof bringeth he in a parable : " A certain man, taking a journey into a strange country, [Matt. xxv.] called his servants, and delivered unto them his goods. And unto one he gave five talents, to another two, and to the third one, &c." Upon the same doth the Lord appoint the faithful servant his reward, and punisheth the sluggish and evil servant. The righteousness of faith comprehendeth the fear of God, love of thy neighbour, patience, and all virtue. Of this fear it is written : " The fear of God is a fountain of [Prov. xiv.] life, to avoid the snares of death." Neighbourly love doth first and principally require, that we friendly and unfeignedly, for God's sake, forgive all them that ever have offended us ; and again to undertake, as much as lieth in us, to reconcile all our enemies. Then doth charity require to give alms, to comfort the heavy-hearted, and to practise all works of mercy : and look, who hath done thee good in thy sickness, it is requisite that thou give them thanks. Among benefits this is not the least, when one moveth and exhorteth another to keep himself from all filthiness. As for bodily things, the sick should dispatch them with few words ; but such as concern our honesty, the fear of God, safeguard in him, and the homage which is due unto him, that ought to be done with more deliberation. For look, what one speaketh at the point of death, the same goeth deeper to the heart of such as hear it ; partly, because it cannot be thought, that a man on his death bed, being in greatest trouble, will use hypocrisy, or dissemble ; partly, for that when the soul beginneth to be discharged of the body, it ofttimes sheweth some token of the freedom and joy, with the which it shall, even now forthwith, be perfectly endowed. Example : the dear worthy patriarchs in the old Testament, before their departing out of this life, sent and called for their children and other folks, instructing and exhorting them to submit themselves unto the

[1 Macc. ii.] law of God, and diligently to walk therein. How faithfully did Mattathias at his death speak to his noble sons, comforting them out of God's word against all their enemies.

CHAPTER XXXVII.

EXHORTATION UNTO PATIENCE.

FINALLY, we cannot do better than with God's help, being patient in all adversity, and stedfast in all temptations, most gently and meekly to give over our wills into the will of God. I speak not of such a patience and valiantness, as utterly to feel no more terror of death; for that is a very blockish unsensibleness of wild, mad, barbarous people : but all such feebleness as is felt, must a christian man overcome, and with faithful confidence upon the grace of God cheerfully step forth before the eyes of death.

In the passion and death of Christ we have a perfect example, not only of patience, but also of every other thing, that hitherto is written concerning preparation unto death.

For he is given unto us of God not only to be our re-
1 Cor. i.
Coloss. ii. demption; but also to be unto us wisdom, whereby we must learn all that is necessary for our health.

The seven words that the Lord spake upon the cross, are specially to be pondered, weighed, and considered.

The first : " Father, forgive them, for they wot not what they do."

The second : " Woman, lo! there is thy son."

The third : "This day shalt thou be with me in paradise."

The fourth : " My God, my God, why hast thou forsaken me ? "

The fifth : " I am athirst."

The sixth : " It is finished."

The seventh : " Father, into thy hands I commend my spirit."

Examples of
saints. Through the knowledge of Jesus Christ did all holy fathers and servants of God in the old and new Testament give over themselves willingly unto death, the way of all Luke ii. flesh. Holy Simeon saith : " Lord, now lettest thou thy servant depart in peace, according to thy word : for mine eyes have seen thy salvation, which thou hast prepared before the face of all people, &c."

Seeing then that every faithful Christian doth no less see *A lesson to learn to die.* Christ with the eyes of his heart; he ought with praise and thanks to say: "Forasmuch as I am assured and do constantly believe, that I am redeemed and delivered by Jesus Christ, and not destroyed, but only changed through the death of the body; I am right willing and well content to depart hence and to die, whensoever now it shall please the Lord my God."

The murderer upon the cross did willingly suffer the death that he had deserved; and so he obtained the everlasting triumph of a martyr.

Holy Steven was content to suffer the fierce cruelty of the enemies; for in his last trouble he knelt down and cried with a loud voice: "Lord Jesu, receive my spirit; Lord, lay *Acts vii.* not this sin to their charge."

Paul, the chosen vessel of God, speaketh thus very comfortable: "My desire is to be loosed, to depart hence out of *Phil. i.* misery, and to be with Christ, which thing is best of all: for Christ is to me life, and death is to me advantage."

These and such noble examples of other holy martyrs should by reason provoke us feeble sluggish Christians to be the more hardy and stout, and to think thus: Well, go to, thou hast as yet suffered no great thing for the Lord Christ's sake; therefore now, even as a lamb, give over thyself cheerfully unto death for his name's sake.

Thou hast daily made thy prayer, as Christ hath taught *Prayer requireth* thee, that God will take thee out of this wicked world into *patience.* his kingdom, and that his will be done. Now if he will *Matt. vi.* graciously convey thee into his kingdom, thou oughtest from the bottom of thy heart to rejoice, and as his own child, willingly to obey them.

Forasmuch as the famous heathen man, Socrates, being before the seat of judgment, where the matter touched his body and life, desired no advocate, neither submitted himself to the judges, but valiantly disputed before them, and proved that there is no evil in death; it should sound very evil, if we (which out of the infallible word of God are instructed concerning a better life) should forsake this life of misery with less patience, and with more unquietness of mind, than died the heathen man.

CHAPTER XXXVIII.

THE ORIGINAL AND FRUIT OF PATIENCE.

To the intent that the feebleness of our nature, which quaketh at death as at a thing terrible, may shew christian patience, we must cleave unto Jesus Christ with true faith, which shall warm our hearts to have a love and desire after the heavenly glory and everlasting salvation; yea, rather to lose an hundred bodies, if it were possible, than to be destitute of the holy gospel, whereby we are assured of deliverance from sin, devil, and hell, by means of the blood-shedding of Jesus Christ.

Impatient folks grudge against God, pouring out all unthankfulness, for that they were not created immortal; and so imagine they in themselves a terrible cruel God; yea, all manner of vices grow out of impatiency. Abraham, who otherwise is set forth for an example of faith and righteousness, fearing death too sore, sinned grievously, denying Sara to be his wife.

Gen. xv.
Rom. iv.
Gal. iii.
Gen. xii. xx.
and xxvi.

Note this
well. What
christian
heart can
read this
without
tears?

In these latter days (the more pity, God be merciful unto us!) it is become a common thing, for fear of death, to carry the true belief only in heart secret, outwardly to deny the holy gospel, and with mouth, behaviour, and gesture to serve antichrist.

CHAPTER XXXIX.

THAT A MAN, WHILE HE IS YET IN HEALTH, OUGHT TO PREPARE HIMSELF BEFOREHAND.

This preparation ought no man to linger or defer till another time, though he be never so whole and sound; but every one forthwith and daily to begin to make himself for death, to the intent that at all hours he may be found ready. Like as a stout and valiant soldier, when he must be up and fight with the enemies, oversleepeth not himself, but keepeth his standing, and hath his weapons and harness already upon him; so much more ought we Christians at all times to wait

upon our heavenly Captain, when he bloweth the trump, that
we may be ready to pass forth with him.   " Let your loins Luke xii.
be girded about and your lights burning, and ye yourselves
like unto men that wait for their master, when he will return
from the wedding; that as soon as he cometh and knocketh, they may open unto him immediately.   Happy are
those servants, whom the Lord, when he cometh, shall find
waking."

With this similitude doth Christ exhort every man, that
at all times we prepare ourselves against his coming, when he
knocketh through sickness and other dangers; when he calleth
us out of this life; and when he shall come again out of his
heavenly palace to judge the living and the dead.   The right
preparation is true faith, fervent love and charity, the clear
shine of all virtues, and specially a gentle willing mind to
open unto the Lord, to let him in, and with him to pass into
his royal and matrimonial palace of the everlasting joyful
kingdom.

The preacher saith: "Remember thy Maker in thy youth, Eccl. xii.
or ever the days of adversity come, and before the years
draw nigh, when thou shalt say, I am weary of my life."
Again we read: " Examine and correct thyself, before the Wisd. xviii.
judgment come : so shalt thou find grace in the sight of God.
Humble thyself before thou be sick, and declare in season
that thou wilt cease from sin.   Be not hindered to pray in
due time, and defer not thy amendment until death."   No man
knoweth the time, place, or manner, how he shall end this
life.   Many one hopeth yet long to live, and thinketh, "I am
yet young, I will follow the world.   When I am old, or have
a wife and keep house, then will I begin to frame myself."
But, O thou fool! who hath promised thee that thou shalt be
an old man, yea, that thou shalt live to-morrow ?   As nothing
is more certain than death, so is nothing more uncertain than
the hour of death, which the Lord hath not opened to his
best friends.   Therefore every day think thou none other A friendly
in thy mind, but that thy glass is run out: let every day be warning.
unto thee the last day, seeing thou wotest not whether thou
shalt live till to-morrow.   Learn to beware by the example of
other men, upon whom stretch-leg came suddenly, and slew
them, even when they thought nothing less than to die.

Yea, of death ought we to think, as of that which is

present : for wo have death by the foot, and carry him about with us in our whole body.

Like as one in a ship, whether he sit, stand, awake or asleep, is ever still borne and carried forward, although he mark it not greatly, neither feel it; so our life in a continual motion doth every twinkling of an eye steal forth, and privily creep to the end, though we mark not how the time passeth.

David saith: "Our time goeth forth swiftly, as though we did fly." As if he would say, there can nothing run or fly away more swiftly. And Sirac saith: "Remember that death tarrieth not."

Paul saith: "I die daily." For even "in the midst of life are we in death:" yea, death daily, as soon as we are born, taketh away somewhat of our life. After this meaning writeth Augustine: "The time of this life is nothing else but a rounding unto death[1]."

Moreover, death is daily set before our eyes: we hear the sighing and lamentable voices of them that die; we see the corses carried to the burial; we go by the graves of the dead; we be still talking of those that are dead and buried.

If the example of others touch us but a little, then let us consider ourselves. Where is there one of us, that hath not sometime been in danger of life, either through tempest, sickness, pestilence, murder, war, or other misfortune? Therefore seeing death waiteth for us on every side; we do wisely, when we also on every side wait for him, that he take us not unprepared, or catch us suddenly. Though a man perfectly knew, (as no man doth indeed,) that it should be long before he died; yet were it exceeding dangerous to defer the preparation till then. And more profitably could not one handle the matter, than by time and in due season to direct himself unto that place, where he desireth everlastingly to remain. For uncertain he is, when the last hour cometh, whether he shall convert himself to God, and whether he shall have his right mind, or not.

Though he be not robbed of his right mind, yet in deadly sickness he hath so much to do with the trouble, that it is hard then for him to learn that he hath not comprehended and learned before. The unspeakable pain of the body, the

[1 Præsens vita fragilis est, et in mortem proclivis.—Augustin. *De verbis Domini.* Sermo xxv. Opera, Vol. x. 24. E. Ed. 1541.]

horrible sight of thine own sins, the terrible fear of God's judgment, and the cruel temptation of the devil, come altogether upon one heap in the perturbance and cumbrance of death, and hinder exceeding much in every thing that one ought to think, speak, or do.   If thou now hast lightly regarded all warning, and so diest in thy sins, thou shalt not be able after death to amend any more.   All repentance and sorrowing from that time forth shall be in vain.   When the ungodly dieth, his hope is gone.   Forasmuch then as it is so, that in death we must abide the sorest and most dangerous conflict and battle; every reasonable man may well perceive, that we ought by time and season, yea, all our life-time, to prepare beforehand against the said battle.

CHAPTER XL.

THAT THE FORESAID THINGS OUGHT BY TIME AND IN DUE SEASON TO BE TAKEN IN HAND.

THY last will and testament being made, while thy body is whole and sound, causeth not thee to die the sooner, as our feeble understanding imagineth; but is an occasion that thou diest the more quietly, and that thou then goest not first about such thorns, when thou liest upon thy death-bed. Well done is it, when one that dieth doth restore evil-gotten goods: but unto God it is a hundred times more acceptable, if thou restore it thyself, while thou art whole and sound in body.   It is well done to bestow one portion of goods for the relief of the poor: but yet it is a much more acceptable offering unto God, when one himself in his lifetime giveth unto the poor.   For that which thou upon thy death-bed appointest for them, is not always distributed; and though it be, yet is it no more thine.   Some do even as the wife, that would give none of her pottage to any body, till her pot was overthrown; then called she the poor unto it.

It is well done in the end to forgive all men, and to pray unto God that he also will forgive all thine enemies:

The fruit of making thy testament in time of health.

but much more commendable is it to forgive them before, while thou hast thy health, and not do it for fear of death, but for the very love of Christ. As for other weighty matters wherewith thou art wrapped, concerning wife, children, neighbours, debts, friends, or enemies, those likewise oughtest not thou to defer till the last day, wherein thou hast enough to do with the world, which thou art loath to forsake; with death, whom naturally thou hatest; with the devil, who practiseth all his crafty falsehood and subtlety; with the fear of hell, the terror whereof is horrible. By means of such things an unprepared man doth oft forget the grace of God and the soul's health. For if thou, having alway a loving friend in estimation, doest contrariwise little regard a poor neighbour; it were no wonder, if thou shouldst forget the same neighbour in the mean season, when thy dear friend is departed. Even so, when one now hath alway cast what may do the body good, howsoever it goeth with the soul, no marvel that the soul's health is neglected, when the body faileth.

After this meaning doth holy Augustine earnestly threaten, saying: "With this penalty is a sinner punished, that when he dieth he forgetteth himself, who in his life-time thought not upon God." Therefore while a man is in his flowers of health, he ought in such sort to learn the comfortable sayings of the gospel, that in his trouble they may of themselves fall into his mind; or if other men advertise him of them, he may be the better acquainted with them, and have them on his finger's end, as them that he hath known, exercised, and used before.

Moreover faith, whereby we overcome death and hell, hath her beginning, increase, and strength, and is direct not only above, but also against all the natural reason of man, that the infinite eternal God should freely, of a very gracious favour through his dear Son, take our part that are most grievous sinners. Therefore by times and in due season, through the preaching of the word, through the prayer and sacrament, should faith in us be planted, increased, practised, and made perfect.

In the mean time, as long as we live, ought we to pray and beseech God of a gracious hour and blessed end; and when the end draweth nigh, to put God in remembrance of the same prayer, as well as of his commandment and promise, in that he hath not only charged us to pray, but promised also that he will graciously hear us.

Daily ought we to have remorse of conscience, where as we have failed, to repent and be sorry, to crave of God forgiveness, and to take upon us immediately to amend all such things as are amiss. For in the sight of God it is a thousand times more acceptable to cease from evil by time in due season, before trouble come, than that present danger and fear should force us to amendment.

Oh most gracious God, give us grace to do this, and with unfeigned hearts to put it in practice.

He that is fallen into a deep foggy well, and sticketh fast in it, will he not straightway call unto every man to help him out one way or another? Will he not make a sore moan, howsoever men haste to deliver him? Out of doubt he that goeth above with sin and vice, hangeth by a bare weak thread, so to say, above the pit of hell; yea, he is now in hell already, forasmuch as he turneth not from sin to the grace of God.

Then must it needs be an horrible, devilish, and obstinate blindness, when one sticketh fast in such a state of life, as is altogether cursed, and yet will appoint a day a great while hence for to come, and therein think to begin to give the devil his leave; when he knoweth not himself, whether he shall live till that day, and whether he shall then have a mind to convert.

For to have a will unto true repentance, is a free gift of God, which ought of him daily to be desired, that the common proverb be not verified in us: "Vicious life, unhappy death." He that will lie well and soft, must make his bed hereafter. Yet for all this it is not my mind to shut up the grace of God into a narrow strait, or to bid any man despair. When an evil-disposed man, that feareth not God, lieth upon his death-bed, being afraid of hell and damnation, he may happen to desire of God longer life, for this intent that he may afterward amend, become a better man, and more directed to die. But let not such vain thoughts trouble thee. For though thou shouldst live yet an hundred years longer, thou mightest through thine own perfectness deserve nothing toward God. But be thou of this assured without all doubt,

that there can no true repentance come too late. Turn thee
yet, even this present day, unto God; be heartily and unfeignedly sorry for thy sins; be of a good mind and whole
purpose, that if God help thee up again, thou wilt amend
all things. Nevertheless comfort thyself by that only mean
which God hath prescribed; namely, the Lord Jesus. So
shalt thou be sure, with the murderer upon the cross, to have
gracious favour for ever.

SECOND BOOK OF DEATH.

CHAPTER I.

HOW THE SICK OUGHT TO BE SPOKEN UNTO, IF NEED SHALL REQUIRE.

HITHERTO have we declared, how one ought to use himself in the dangers of body and life.

Now followeth, how we should behave ourselves towards them that be in like case. Hereof did David sing these words in the 41st Psalm: "Blessed is he that considereth or thinketh upon the poor; for in the time of trouble the Lord shall deliver him. The Lord shall preserve him and save his life; he shall make him prosper upon earth, and shall not deliver him into the will of his enemies. When he himself lieth sick upon his bed, the Lord shall refresh him; yea, thou, Lord, makest his bed in all his sickness." Item, he that is judge of us all shall at the latter day pronounce this sentence: "Come, ye blessed of my Father, possess the kingdom that hath been prepared for you from the beginning of the world. For I was sick, and ye visited me." O what a wicked unbelief is this, that we are more afraid at a little adversity and uncertain danger, than encouraged by such a godly, sure, and faithful promise!

Therefore among the greatest works of mercy this is reckoned, to visit the sick, to have compassion on them, to give them good counsel, and to comfort them. Which thing must be done with reason and discretion, to the intent that neither too little nor too much be meddled withal. Too little were it, to cause the sick still to believe, that he shall shortly come up again and recover. For such fond hope have men already of their own nature, and thereby sometime they oversee themselves.

Again, it were too much to deal roughly with one that is weak of faith, and suddenly to fear him with death: that were even as much as to break the bruised reed, and utterly to quench the smoking flax, contrary to the example of Christ our Lord.

A whole instruction ought to be given unto such sick persons as have need thereof, to make them strong and willing unto the cross and death. And so should they also be put in mind, what death is, whence it came, and wherefore, what it doeth through the grace of God for Christ's sake, by whose Spirit and power the most horrible death of all is overcome. Hereof is spoken sufficiently in the chapters going before.

Out of the which foundation, it may thus be spoken unto the sick: "Thou hast the Almighty God thy dear Father, and Jesus Christ thine intercessor and Saviour, who hath taken all thy cause in hand; let him alone withal; he will not suffer thee to perish, but give thee his holy Spirit, which shall conduct thee into eternal joy and salvation. Only direct thou thyself even now at this present, and prepare thee to depart, giving all temporal things their leave, having a right understanding of the holy gospel, and exercising the true belief thereof by fervent prayer, charitable love, and patience.

"Turn thee, for God's sake, from all creatures to the Creator and Maker; turn thee from wife and child, turn thee from temporal goods and honour, considering that none of them can help thee, neither from sin, nor from death. All that thou leavest behind thee, the Lord according to his almighty providence shall well and fatherly take care for them. He that hath created thy wife and children, shall also provide them a living, as he hath sent unto thee all things necessary, even unto this hour."

Afterward ought not the mind of the sick to be disturbed or pointed hither and thither, up and down, as (the more pity!) they use to do in the papistry; but only unto God the Father through Jesus Christ, according to the contents of the whole gospel, after this meaning: "Dost thou believe and confess from the ground of thy heart, that there is but one only God, who hath given thee body and soul, meat and drink, lodging and clothing, with all other necessaries,

The spiritual comforter.

and graciously helped thee out of many grievous mischances and miseries?" Then let the sick say: "Yea, that I acknowledge and confess." *The sick.*

"Dost thou also confess that thou oughtest, above all things, to have feared and worshipped this thy gracious Maker and Father, and to have loved him with all thy heart, with all thy soul, with all thy strength, and, for his sake, thy neighbour as thyself? Hath not God deserved that at thy hand?" Then let him say: "O Lord God, I should indeed have done so." *The comforter.* *The sick.*

"Acknowledge thou likewise, that thou oft and many a time hast wittingly and willingly, of very ungraciousness, done against God and thy neighbour; by means whereof thou hast justly deserved the everlasting wrath, plague, and indignation of God in body and soul." Then let him say: "O sir, it is all too true; I yield myself guilty, and confess it before God." "Well, greater and more horrible sins than these couldst not thou do, if thou wouldst still not regard the wrath and rigorous judgment of God, as thou hast done heretofore. How art thou minded? Dost thou desire and pray from the ground of thy heart, that God will preserve thee from such slender regarding of thine own sins, and of his just wrath and judgment? Desirest thou also with thy whole heart, that God will not deal with thee after his divine judgment and justice, but according to his fatherly mercy, and that he will remit and forgive thy sins and trespasses?" Then let him say: "Yea, that is my desire from the bottom of my heart." *The comforter.* *The sick.* *The comforter.* *The sick.*

"God from heaven did send unto thee his dear and only-begotten Son, who took upon him the nature of man, and in his death upon the cross he bare not only our trespass, but the pain also and punishment due for the same, making full payment and satisfaction for us. John the Baptist with his finger pointeth unto Christ, and sayeth: 'Lo, this is God's Lamb, that taketh away the sin of the world.' And John the evangelist saith: 'The blood of Jesus Christ cleanseth us from all sin.' Dost thou now confess, that Jesus Christ, the Son of God, died and rose again for thee also? And wilt thou, as one parcel of the world, one broken reed, one piece of smoking flax, and one lost sheep, cast all thy sins upon him; embracing this comfort *The comforter.* 1 John i.

of the gospel in thy heart, and comprehending it with a
The sick. strong stedfast belief?" Then let him say: "O Lord Jesu,
my heart's desire is of thee to be healed, comforted, and
refreshed. And thanks be unto God for evermore, that I
may have him my mediator and redeemer! I will wholly
commit and yield myself unto him."

The comforter. "Then, upon this, the Lord Jesus Christ by his godly
word and gospel sendeth thee this message: 'Thy sins are
forgiven thee, and in his sight are all taken away: not only
the sin, but the pain also due for the same; namely, everlasting death, hell, and damnation: so that thou shalt be
received again as a dear acceptable child, and heir of eternal
life.' Believest thou this comfortable promise of Jesu Christ?"
The sick. Then let him say: "Yea, but, O merciful God, strengthen
thou my weak belief."

The sum of all this is contained in the articles of the
christian belief, which, with the aforesaid interpretation, may
be rehearsed unto the sick.

The comforter. "And to the intent that thy heart may be set at rest,
and thou assured in thy faith, therefore hath Christ instituted
his holy Supper and sacrament of his body and blood; wherein
he doth signify, witness, and put to his seal, that even thou also
art one of those many, for whom he gave his body and shed
his blood. Now when sin, death, hell, devil, and God's wrath
tempteth and turmoileth thy conscience, thou must with the
same sacrament, as with the word of God, comfort thy conscience, that Christ Jesus with his body and life is thy surety;
and that his soul and blood, and all that he is, standeth for thee
and on thy side, against all bodily and ghostly enemies."

Moreover, thou must bid the sick call upon God for faith,
patience, and other spiritual gifts.

Some time recite before him the Lord's Prayer, with a
short exposition, that he may direct his prayer the better.

Exhort also all such as stand about the sick to pray for
him, considering that our Lord hath made a rich and faithful
promise: "Where two or three are assembled in his name, he
himself will be in the midst among them, and grant them
their desire."

And forasmuch as all instructions must be taken of the
word of God, therefore before the sick these parcels following
may be read.

The vi. Psalm, which beginneth: "Lord, rebuke me not in thine anger," &c.

The xxii. "My God, my God," &c.

The xxv. "Unto thee, O Lord," &c.

The xxvii. "The Lord is my light," &c.

The xlii. "Like as the hart longeth," &c.

The li. "Have mercy upon me," &c.

The xci. "Whoso dwelleth," &c.

The cxvi. "I am well pleased," &c.

The cxxxix. "O Lord, thou searchest me," &c.

The cxliii. "Hear my prayer, O Lord," &c.

The Prayer of King Hezekiah: Isaiah xxxviii.

The Psalm of Simeon: "Nunc dimittis."   Luke ii.

The xi. chapter of John; of Lazarus.

The xiv. and xvii. of St John's gospel.

The Passion of Christ, and specially concerning the one of the two murderers.

The viii. chapter to the Romans.

The 1 Corinthians xv.   All which places serve to make the prayer fervent, and to strengthen true belief.

Furthermore, the sick ought to be told of the fruits of faith, because of provoking thankfulness for the unspeakable grace of God; with exhortation to forgive his enemies, to do every man good according to his power, and in every point to amend his own life and conversation; but especially with a patient, gentle, quiet, and good willing mind to wait for deliverance.

Namely thou mayest say thus: "Take up thy cross upon thy neck patiently, and follow Christ thy Lord. Remember, and behold Christ hanging in great martyrdom upon the cross. He suffered patiently until his Father's will was fulfilled in him. Even so thou also hold still unto the Lord thy God, that he may perform his will in thee: if it be his good pleasure now to take the stinking transitory flesh from thee, to purify it, and to make an eternal glorified body of it, thou hast great cause to rejoice."

When the sick is drawing away, and speechless, having yet understanding, thou mayest speak unto him these words: "Fight valiantly, as a worthy Christian, and despair not; be not afraid of the rigorous judgment of God; hold thee fast to the comfortable promise of Christ, thereas he saith: 'I

At the point of death.

am the Resurrection and the Life. He that believeth on me
shall live, though he were dead; and whoso liveth and believeth on me, shall never die.' In him is thy belief; therefore shalt thou live with him for ever. Christ thy Saviour
John x. shall never forsake thee. There can no man pluck thee out
Luke xxi. of his hand. Heaven and earth shall pass, but God's word
endureth for ever. Have thou therefore no doubt, thou shalt
after this battle receive the crown of everlasting life."

Ask now the man, whether he understand and believe;
desire a token of him, and cry unto him fair and softly:
" Good brother, upon thy soul's health depart not, shrink not
away from Jesus Christ; commit thy soul unto thy faithful
God and loving Father. Speak from thy heart-root with
Christ thy brother upon the cross: 'Father, into thy hands,
into thy protection and defence, I commit my spirit.'"

When his understanding is past, commit him unto God.
Make thy prayer alone, or with others, that God will take
this sick man into eternal life, and grant him a joyful resurrection at the last day, only for the Lord Jesus Christ's
sake. Amen.

CHAPTER II.

OF THE BURIAL, AND WHAT IS TO BE DONE TOWARDS THOSE THAT ARE DEPARTED HENCE.

THE soul of the dead, as soon as it is departed from
hence, cometh into a state there, as prayers (if one would
make them for him afterward) have no place, and are either
unprofitable, or else vain; yea, offensive also, and hindrance
to our christian belief.

The body of him that is departed ought reverently and
soberly to be conducted unto the earth, and buried. For that
is the last service that we can do for such as are departed,
and thereby may we declare our charitable love towards them.
In the mean season, when we reverently commit the body,
as the wheat corn, unto the earth, we testify our belief of
the resurrection for to come. The scripture also commendeth
those that faithfully will have to do with burying of the dead,

after the example of Tobias.   Of misordering the bodies of
the dead writeth Plato, the heathen philosopher : "Is it not
a bond, greedy and voluptuous thing, to spoil the dead corpse,
and to rage against the body as an enemy, when the enemy
that fought in the body is departed away ?   What differ
they from dogs, which bite the stone that is cast at them,
and let him go free that cast it ?   There is no difference.
Of such points ought we to beware, for they bring hurt unto
victory."

Of gorgeous graves and sepulchres, it is written in the
poet Euripides : "Men's minds are mad, when they bestow
vain cost upon dead bodies[1]."   For if we consider the matter
right, we must needs greatly marvel, that ever a man should
fall into such a frensy, as to use pride after death.

Touching the place of burial, it is to be noted, that by
such ordinary means as be permitted us we are bound to
avoid sickness and all hurt.   Now out of graves there come
naturally evil savours or vapours, which alter and change
the air, and increase the disease of the pestilence, when the
church-yard or place of burial standeth in the midst of cities
or towns.   Therefore both the Jews, heathen, and Christians,
were wont to have their burials without the cities.   For what
time as Christ raised the widow's son from death, the evangelist saith : "When he came nigh unto the gate of the city, Luke vii.
behold, there was carried out one dead, who was the only
son of his mother, she being a widow, and much people of
the city with her."   Moreover the sepulchre of our Lord
Jesus Christ was without the city.   But the pope and his
adherents with their money market found here a treasure
bag, otherwise persuading the people ; as though to lie here
or there did further or hinder salvation.

Afterward let the dead rest quietly, no evil being spoken Good
of them of malice, but good, though they were our enemies : counsel.
of malice, I say ; for otherwise must vice and sin, as well of
the dead as of the living, be declared and rebuked, that others
may beware.   The old poet Mimnermus writeth : "We are
all inclined to envy an excellent famous man, but after death

[1 Ἀνθρώπων δὲ μαίνονται φρένες,
δαπάνας ὅταν θανοῦσι πέμπωσιν κενάς.
Euripides, Polyid. Fragm. v.]

to praise him[1]." Therefore do they not only against christian charity, but also against man's nature, that disdain to give unto the dead their due praise and commendation.

Especially when one that hath shewed us friendship and kindness is departed, we ought never to forget his benefits, but to declare our thankfulness to his kinsfolks or friends. But if we carry the remembrance of them to the grave, and bury it with the corpse, thinking no more upon their gentleness; then are we like unto wild beasts, that are hot and burning in desire, but as soon as the thing desired is out of sight, the love is quenched. Hereof complaineth the poet Euripides: "Seldom are there found faithful constant friends after death, though aforetime they were joined never so near together." The thankfulness that is shewed to him that is present passeth away and vanisheth, when one is carried out of the house.

[1 Δεινοὶ γὰρ ἀνδρὶ πάντες ἐσμὲν εὐκλεεῖ
ζῶντι φθονῆσαι, κατθανόντα δ᾽ αἰνέσαι.
                    Mimnermus apud Brunck. Analecta.]

THIRD BOOK OF DEATH.

CHAPTER I.

HOW THEY OUGHT TO BE COMFORTED, WHOSE DEAR FRIENDS ARE DEAD.

NATURALLY we mourn, weep, and lament, when our kins-folk and friends depart. When father and mother dieth, the son and the daughter remembereth, how many a footstep the elders went faithfully and worthily to provide them their living: yea, if it had been possible, they would have shewed the child their own soul, and given them the heart in their body.

Again, the parents consider how good obedient children they have had of their sons or daughters; and what honour and joyfulness more they might have had of their children, if they should have lived longer.

The sisters and brothers remember, that they came of one father, being born under one motherly heart, brought up in one house, eating and drinking at one table. If it were else a man's companion, he thinketh, he was my faithful dear friend, he did no man hurt nor harm, but desired to do every man service, and that so honestly, that a man might have trusted him with his own soul.

If he were a good ruler, we think he was to his own native country true and faithful, and excellently well inclined to the welfare thereof; who hath not then good cause to be sorry for his departing? This is the cause, that the blood naturally gathereth together, so that we are sorrier for the death of such one than of another private man.

Such heaviness, pity, and compassion doth God allow. For he hath not created us to be stones and blocks, but hath given us five senses, and made us an heart of flesh, that we might have feeling, and love our friends, being sorry when they suffer trouble and die : yea, God hateth unfriendly and unmerciful people, and whose hearts are not moved, when their friends are vexed and taken away from them.   There-

Gen. xxiii.

fore the holy patriarch Abraham lamented and mourned for Sarah his wife, when she was dead.

Gen l.

Good Joseph made great lamentation for Jacob his father.

Phil. ii.

Paul likewise writeth thus: "My helper and fellow-soldier Epaphroditus was deadly sick: but God had mercy upon him, and not only upon him, but also upon me, that I should not have one heaviness upon another."   But as in all things, so in this there ought a measure to be kept, that we continue not in fleshly inordinate heaviness, but still resist the sorrow, and comfort ourselves with this account following: What do we mean thus to mourn and lament?   What will we do?   The Lord is great, and doeth no man wrong.   And the same is an honest good will, that conformeth itself to the will of God.

A notable saying.

For the good heathen man Seneca wrote unto his scholar Lucillus after this manner: "A man ought to be content with every thing that God is pleased withal, only because it pleased God."

Lib. v. cap. 2.

Now in every thing ordered by the providence of God, as holy Augustine, *De Civitate Dei*, saith, "Without an orderly division and convenient joining together of the parts hath not God left so much as the bowels of any beast, how vile or small so ever the same be, nor the feathers of a bird, nor the flower of the herb, neither the leaf of the tree: so that there can nothing be found, that is not subject to the providence of God[1]; neither can there any little bird die, without his device, charge, and commandment."

[1 The author, according to his custom, has applied the passage of Augustine, to which reference is made by him, to the purposes of his argument: Deus summus et verus cum Verbo suo et Spiritu sancto, quæ tria unum sunt, Deus unus et omnipotens, creator et factor omnis animæ atque omnis corporis, ... qui non solum cœlum et terram, nec solum angelum et hominem, sed nec exigui et contemptibilis animantis viscera, nec avis pennulam, nec herbæ flosculum, nec arboris folium sine suarum partium convenientia et quadam veluti pace dereliquit, nullo modo est credendus regna hominum eorumque dominationes et servitutes a suæ providentiæ legibus alienas esse voluisse.   Augustin. *De Civitate Dei*. Lib. v. cap. 11. Oper. Vol. v. p. 44. D.   Ed. Par. 1541.]

If God now have so diligent respect to such small things, how then could thy friend, whom thou mournest for, depart away by death without the providence of God? Therefore if we speak against the Lord's works, and cry against his will, what is that else, but even as though we therefore lived upon earth, that we as lords and rulers should prescribe laws for the Almighty? Which thing to think, I will not say to speak, were yet horrible.

When thou givest forth thy child to a nurse, and she hath kept it long enough, thou takest it home again; the nurse having no reasonable cause to complain upon thee, for taking again thine own. Yet much less cause have we to grudge against God our creditor, when he by death taketh his own again. For as for father and mother, brother and sister, wife and child, friend and lover, yea, and all other things that we have, what are they else but lent goods and free gifts of God, which he hath committed unto us, and which we, as long as he lendeth us them, ought to esteem as advantage?

When a lord hath lent us a fair costly table, whether should we gladly with thanks restore it him again when he requireth it, or brawl with him after this manner: O thou terrible lord, how happeneth it that thou hast robbed us of so costly a table? How cometh it that thou hast taken it from us again so suddenly? Upon such a complaint might he not with good right answer: Is that now my reward for lending you so costly a table, which I did of love, undeserved on your part, that ye might have commodity and pleasure thereof for a while? Yea, the more worthy the gift was that I lent you to use, the more thankful should you be unto me. Yea, with rougher words might God justly rebuke us that be so impatient. When the house fell upon Job's ten living children, seven sons and three daughters, and when his seven thousand sheep were burned with fire from heaven, and his enemies carried away his five hundred yoke of oxen and five hundred asses, as the other enemies drove away three hundred camels, and slew also his servants; in all this misery and hurt Job comforteth himself, and thanketh God, who had lent him such things, and taken them away again. "The Lord," saith he, "hath given them, the Lord hath taken them; even as it hath pleased the Lord, so is it come ^{Job i.}

to pass: blessed be the name of the Lord." Let us therefore also say with Job: "The Lord gave us this father, that child, such a friend; the Lord hath taken him again; blessed be his name."

But when thou shouldst laud and praise God, it hindereth thee exceedingly, if thou fear that God of a wrath and enmity against thee hath taken away from thee thy son or thy wife, &c. Such an opinion cometh not of God, but is even a practice of the devil. And herewith agreeth our feeble nature: whatsoever is sung or said, we think in trouble, that God is angry, and that our will is good and profitable, and not God's will.

Contrary hereunto are we instructed by holy scripture, that though we know not perfectly for what cause God sendeth us this or that punishment, yet ought we to be satisfied in this, that God is gracious and favourable unto us for his beloved Son our Lord Jesus Christ's sake. Nevertheless, to the intent that we may both the better understand, and be the more glad to receive, the good-will of God, I will declare what profit such a death bringeth to him that departeth and to those that remain.

CHAPTER II.

THAT UNTO SUCH AS DIE, IT IS PROFITABLE TO DEPART OUT OF THIS LIFE.

IF they that be dead from hence had not suffered trouble in this world when they were alive, it were no marvel to see us mourn out of measure for their departing. As for all their joy and pastime upon earth, they are scarce to be accounted dreams, in comparison of the true joys and treasures above. Again: who will undertake to number the adversities that all men, of what estate soever they be, must be possessors [Job xiv.] of? We may well say with Job: "Man that is born of a woman, liveth but a short time, and is replenished with many miseries." Against the which there helpeth neither gold nor silver, neither power nor nobility, neither policy nor natural wit. To-day we are whole and sound, to-morrow sick; to-day merry, to-morrow sorry; to-day rich, to-morrow poor;

to-day honoured, to-morrow despised; to-day alive, to-morrow dead.

Moreover, vice commonly hath so the upper hand, that none can live upon earth, but he must displease either God or man, or else them both.   Therefore seeing thy loving friend is gotten out of the mire, and gone out of the sweat-bath that thou yet sittest in; art thou sorry now that he is released and unburdened of so much misery?   Thou shouldst rather give thanks and praise unto God for it; specially forasmuch as death doth utterly destroy neither body nor soul, neither honesty nor virtue, wherein he that is now departed did here exercise himself in time.   For look, what good thing one hath done, it shall not be quenched out through death; but the praise and commendation thereof, among all such as are good, doth rather increase than diminish after death. The soul departing in true faith, passeth straight to the joy of heaven.

The least parcel of the body doth not utterly perish, but the whole body shall at the last day be called to immortality, where our friends shall be a thousand times better, richer, more pleasant, and more blessed, than ever they were upon earth; when we all shall come to them again, see them, know them, and have perpetual company with them and all saints.   After this sort did Adam and Eve trust that Abel, who was slain, should be restored again unto them, because of the Seed that was promised.

A similitude: if a great lord had called thee and thy son, and promised you much wealth and good, shouldst thou weep when thy son goeth to him, and thou thyself wilt shortly follow after? No, verily; but thou wouldst order thy matter so that thou mightest be there out of hand.   Why unquietest thou thyself then so sore for the death of thy son or friend?   The Almighty Lord hath called him and thee to his eternal kingdom, to place thee and him among the princes of heaven.   Thy son passeth hence through the gates of death; he shall rise again to honour.   Why vexest thou then thyself?   Why orderest not thou thyself, joyfully to follow him? for thou hast not lost him, but only sent him before.

If it were possible that thy son knew of thy unmeasurable wailing and howling, and could speak unto thee, without all doubt he himself would rebuke it, and say:

"Why will you vex your age with unprofitable, yea, with unreasonable mourning? Wherefore will you blame God, his ordinance, and providence? Will ye envy me the great honour and joy that I am promoted unto? Think ye it is a thing to be bewailed and lamented, that I am brought out of danger into safeguard, out of misery into welfare, and out of the wicked world into the company of angels? I will go somewhat nearer unto you: I pray you, if it lay in your strength and power to send for me into the temporal life again, would ye call me down again into the misery of yours? With what great fault have I deserved such unfaithfulness at your hands? And if ye should not call me again, why mourn ye then so and lament?" Upon such words, we must needs be ashamed of our unmeasurable sorrow and heaviness. That we ought thus to judge of faithful christian men that are departed, we may learn by the words

John xi.

of Christ, who testifieth unto Martha: "I am the resurrection and the life. He that believeth on me shall live, although he die; and he that liveth and believeth on me, shall never

Psal. cxvi.

die." "How dear and precious in the sight of the Lord is the death of his saints!" Understand, that God doth faithfully take them into his protection, and hath respect unto their souls, to receive them into eternal life.

Now sayest thou: Alas! if I knew that my wife, child, or friend were saved, I could then better away with his death. As for a thief, he need not to be glad, when he is carried from prison to the gallows. This man hath been all his life a child of the world; he never feared God, but died in sin, haply without repentance, and peradventure from the cart of this misery he is yoked in the chariot of eternal fire.

Answer: no man can tell, how he behaved himself at his last end: happily he repented, and is pardoned. We ought ever to hope the best, till we have sufficient evidences that the man is lost.

Secondly: though his damnation were open and manifest, yet ought a faithful man to rejoice in the righteousness of God. The ravens must have dog's garbage; partridges must be set upon the board before lords; a murderer must be laid upon a wheel. It is as meet for Judas to sit in hell, as for St Peter to be in heaven.

Thirdly, thou sayest: if he had lived longer, he would peradventure have amended. Whereupon take this answer: he might have happened as soon to be worse. A prudent man looketh for no better, but feareth the worse in this blasphemous world.

St John Chrysostom testifieth plainly, that "as soon as God taketh away a man through death, the same man from thenceforth should never have been better[1]."

Verily, God is to be praised and thanked, when he taketh away the ungodly. For the more a man heapeth up sin upon sin, the greater punishment must he suffer afterward, for God's righteous justice sake. The ungodly sinneth ever the longer, the more upon earth: but by death doth God pluck him down from his sinful life; though not spiritually and inwardly, yet with external members, the same must cease from sin. Therefore to such as are hard-hearted and disordered, there is nothing better than to die the sooner.

CHAPTER III.

WHAT PROFIT THE DEATH OF FRIENDS BRINGETH TO SUCH AS ARE LEFT BEHIND ALIVE.

THAT the death of the ungodly doth profit other men, it is easy to perceive; for thereby are the wicked upon earth somewhat diminished and swept out, and other poor wretches fare the better.

But that the death of the righteous should bring any commodity to such as remain alive, it soundeth strange in our ears: therefore shall it be declared.

When a man endowed with excellent gifts is made an idol, Almighty God cannot suffer it. For God himself will be he, of whom all good things undoubtedly must be hoped and looked for; and unto his dishonour it serveth, if the heart cleave not only unto him. And blessed is the man, that setteth his love, comfort, and hope upon the Lord. Again, "Cursed be the man," as the prophet saith, "that [Jer. xvii.] upon man doth put his trust." Now cometh it lightly to

[1 The sentiment is found in Chrysostom, Homil. ad Matthæum XXXI. in fine. Opera, Tom. VII. p. 364. B. Ed. Paris. 1727.]

pass, that we set too much by rich parents, by fair children, honourable friends, and men of good properties. Therefore God plucketh them away from us, to draw us away from creatures, and that we might perceive his fervent love towards us, in that he is jealous over us, that he taketh out of our sight whatsoever we gape upon besides himself; and also to the intent that we might perceive, that whatsoever is in the world, it is but temporal, and lasteth but the twinkling of an eye; and that only the Father of heaven will, can, and may help in all troubles.

Moreover, what a number is there of them, that of an inordinate love toward their children, parents, and friends, to make provision for them, and to bring them aloft, jeopard their souls for them, fall into great unquietness, being unmerciful, covetous, bribers, usurers, liars, deceivers! Franciscus Petrarcha writeth: "Thou hast lost thy son; yea, but thou hast lost with him also much fear, and an infinite matter of careful sorrows: by reason of the which cares, that thou mightest be delivered from them, it behoved either thee or thy son to die."

Therefore give God thanks for his grace, when he dischargeth thee of those things that hinder thee in his free service; and when he taketh from thee thy wife, child, friend, or others upon whom thou hast hanged too much, and for whose sakes thou hast done wrong many a time.

That thou mayest understand this thing the better, take for example mercy towards the poor. We see that they whose children and friends are departed give alms richly, which while their wives, children, and friends were alive, would not have given one penny, for fear that their friends after their death should have had need, and been destitute of money themselves. Yea, rich folks, which, as God sometime appointeth, have no children, nor heirs of their own bodies, become fathers and upholders of many poor men. Which thing unto them and unto all Christendom is more profitable and more worthy of commendation, than ten sons of a naughty life, such as commonly there be many: among whom scarce one of ten speedeth well, I mean of those that inherit their father's riches and goods; for shamefully they waste and consume them, to the hurt of themselves and of others.

Item, though one know that he ought to love no man in such sort, as to displease God for his sake; yet many a time is one moved through his friends to do against his own conscience, if he will not displease them. Therefore graciously doth God pluck away those friends, whose presence serveth unto thy destruction.

Moreover thou sayest: How should not I mourn, seeing I am now robbed of such help and succour, as I should still have, if he were yet alive? Answer: such complaining cometh not of a free love towards the dead, but of a servile and bond stomach, that looketh and hath respect to itself, and desireth to work his own profit with another man's hurt. Now if thy son or friend, that might have been thy comfort in thine age, be departed, God may send thee others in their place; yea, there be some at hand already, that offer their help and counsel to thee and thine, and will not fail thee at thy need. And though it were so, that thou hadst none other child nor friend in their stead, but were destitute of all bodily help; yet hast thou a gracious God through Jesus Christ, with the spiritual gifts which shall continue with thee for ever.

But some say, and especially great youngsters, My mourning and sorrow is because my kindred, name, and stock, mine arms and badge perisheth, now that I leave no heirs of my body behind me. O thou great idiot! thou lamentest that thy name and honour perisheth in this transitory world, and forcest little, how thy name and honour may continue for evermore in the kingdom of heaven.

What is become of the mighty kings and emperors, which fought for the greatest honour and magnificence, that they might never be forgotten upon earth? The memorial of them is past long ago; they have their reward already, as our Lord sayeth. Contrariwise, the dear worthy saints, which despised all glory of this mortal life, have at this day greater honour, praise, and commendation, than they that travailed to obtain the glory of this world. Now therefore will God help thee, not to pass upon temporal honour and pomp; but most of all to care, how thy name may remain in remembrance before God, with those that unto him have done faithful service.

CHAPTER IV.

COMPANIONS THAT SUFFER LIKE HEAVINESS OF HEART.

IF any thing were practised against thy child or friend, that necessarily must not come to pass, so that he might well have escaped it, then hadst thou just cause to howl and lament. But now behoved it him, as a mortal man, to end this life even according to the first ordinance of God. Thou hast thousands and thousands of companions, whose dear friends departed hence by death: why wilt thou then disquiet thyself? What time as Abraham was commanded of God to sacrifice his own only beloved son, what mind had he, thinkest thou, when he now drew the sword, and thought to slay his son? Greater sorrow had he for his son that yet was alive, than thou for thy son that is dead. In what case was the holy patriarch Jacob's heart, when tidings came to him, that his dear son Joseph was torn of wild beasts? Where was there ever father in greater heaviness than even David, when by his own son Absalom, whom he yet exceedingly loved, he was expelled from his kingdom? Doubtless he was in none other case, than as though the heart in his body shrunk and melted like wax. These and such like examples oughtest thou to set before thine eyes; whereby thou shalt perceive, that thy sorrow is to be esteemed but small towards these; and therefore through the contemplation thereof undoubtedly it shall be assuaged.

CHAPTER V.

THROUGH GOD'S HELP ALL HEART-SORROW IS EASED.

UNHANDSOME physicians are they, that well can see the greatness of the sickness, and brawl with the patient for his excess, but cannot shew a remedy whereby the blemish may be healed. Therefore now that I have hitherto reproved unmeasurable sorrow and heaviness, I will not leave the matter so bare; but declare now also a medicine, whereby unreasonable mourning, if it be not clean taken away, may yet be eased and diminished.

The time of itself maketh all cumbrance lighter. For there be many men and women which in times past have set finger in the eye, knocked upon their breasts, pulled the hair out of their own heads, ran against the wall, disfigured their whole bodies, and horribly howled for the dead. But now they have their pastime in all kinds of minstrelsy, as though they never had ailed anything. Notwithstanding to wait still till heaviness forget itself, is a womanish thing: and again, to bridle it betimes, beseemeth the natural reason and soberness of a man. What is then to be done? It lieth not in thy power, without the special help of God, to expel sorrowful mourning. First and principally, ponder thou the power and grace of God: the power, in that the Almighty is able many hundred ways faithfully to ease thee of thy sorrow; the grace, in that he is willing and ready, for the worthiness of his Son, to make thee joyful again here and in the world to come, so as is most for thy profit and wealth. Adam and Eve had unspeakable sorrow, when their obedient and righteous son Abel was murdered: God then did well put them in remembrance of their sin. But they being also mindful of the promise of the blessed Seed, were thereby erected and comforted again: howbeit in such an exceeding heaviness it was very hard to withstand desperation, and to overcome all mischance. Therefore let us consider, that though we Christians be not altogether called to the pleasures of this time, but stoutly to strive and valiantly to fight against them; yet shall not Christ leave us comfortless, but, according to his promise, he shall faithfully be with us unto the end of the world.

CHAPTER VI.

WE MUST FURNISH OURSELVES WITH PRAYER AND PATIENCE.

To the intent that God may assist us with his might and grace, we must earnestly pray unto him, that with his holy Spirit through his godly word he will comfort us, that we may render thanks unto him when he hath delivered our

friends from the daily battle of the soul against the flesh,
the devil, and the world, and from all discommodities of this
vale of misery.

For like as one that hath fared well at a dinner, doth
thank his host, though the host let him depart again, yea,
the guest rejoiceth afterwards to remember it; even so, forasmuch as God for a season hath lent us wife, child, and friends
(which is more than he owed us), though he suffer them to
depart, we ought nevertheless to give him most high thanks.

Especially there is required a willing and stout mind:
whereof holy St Paul hath written this very comfortably:
1 Thess. iv. "I would not, brethren, that ye should be ignorant concerning them which are fallen asleep, that ye sorrow not as
other do which have no hope. For if we believe that Jesus
died and rose again, even so them also which sleep by Jesus
will God bring again with him."

By these words may we perceive, that there be two
manner of mourners for the dead. The heathen and unbelievers mourn without hope of the resurrection: their opinion
is, that seeing their near friends are dead, there is no more
of them, but that they have utterly lost them for ever. This
heathenish sorrow will not St Paul have of Christians.

The Christians mourn also, but with a living hope of the
joyful resurrection. For like as God the Father left not
Christ the Lord in death, but raised him up again, and
placed him in eternal life; even so us that believe shall not
he leave in death, but bring us out into everlasting life. For
this cause doth the Apostle speak of the dead, as of those
that sleep, which rest from all travail and labour, that they
may rise again in better case.

Like as the flowers with all their virtue, smell, and
beauty, lieth all the winter in the root, sleeping and resting
till they be awaked with the pleasant time of May, when
they come forth with all their beauty, smell, and virtue;
even so ought not we to think that our friends which be departed are in any cumbrance or sorrow, but their strength
and virtue being drawn in, liveth in God and with God.
They lie and rest till the last day, when they shall awake
again, fair, beautiful, and glorious, in soul and body. Who
will not now rejoice at this comfort of Paul, and set aside
all unprofitable sorrow, for this exceeding joy's sake?

Faith that is confessed with the mouth, must not be destroyed with a contrary deed.   Now is our belief set thus: " I believe forgiveness of sins, the resurrection of the body, and the life everlasting."   Therefore remaineth there nothing behind, for the which the soul of the faithful should be tormented in the world to come, or shut out from everlasting joy.   In the law xiii. 9, 2, *Ubicunque*, it is noted: " Unseemly heaviness for the dead springeth out of despair of the resurrection for to come ; and rather of faintness of mind, than of mercy or godliness[1]."

CHAPTER VII.

ENSAMPLES OF PATIENCE IN LIKE CASE.

IF the wise famous heathen could be numbered, which took the death of their friends and children in good part and with a stout stomach, should it not be counted a shame unto us christian men, that declare less constancy in that behalf?

Pericles, the captain of the Athenians (who for his wisdom and virtue was called Olympius, one of heaven), when he had lost his two sons, Paralius and Zantippus, within the space of four days, was no more sorry nor unquieted in the same sudden chance, but that on the day following he came clothed in white before the whole multitude, and consulted of the present wars so discreetly and manfully, that every man wondered at him and honoured him[2].

Xenophon, a disciple of Socrates, when he understood that his only son Gryllus had fought valiantly, and upon the same was slain of the enemies, he said unto those that brought him the message: " I made my prayer unto the gods, not that they should give me an immortal son, or that he might be a long liver, (for I knew not whether that were profitable for him,) but that of my son they would make a good man, and a lover of his own native country; which

[1 Lugere autem et deplorare et lamentari eos, qui de hac vita decedunt, ex pusillanimitate contingit. Hoc autem ex desperatione futuræ resurrectionis intelligitur. Corpus Juris Canon. Tom I. p. 1042. Ed. Lugd. 1661.]

[2 Valerius Maximus, Lib. v. cap. 10.]

prayer, as I perceive, they have granted; and therefore I thank them [1]."

If thou hadst rather hear examples of the Romans, then consider Paulus Emilius, who overcame the Macedonians, and triumphed gloriously over them. When he within seven days had lost both his sons, he was not therefore broken-minded; but as he went forth to the multitude without both his sons, (which beforetime always led him and stayed him, the one on the right hand, the other on the left,) the people of Rome, having pity on the old honourable man, began to lament and weep. But he, being nothing moved, stood there and said: " I besought the gods, if our commonwealth, for the great prosperity thereof, have any evil will among those which be in heaven, that I myself, and not the whole multitude, might recompense and bear it: and seeing it is so, I give God great thanks [2]." M. Fabius Maximus also, not without just cause, belongeth unto the number of dear worthy men. When he upon a time had to do with the office of the master of works, there came unto him a message, first, that his house was fallen down, and had also bruised his wife, a virtuous honourable woman; secondly, slain his mother, who in weighty affairs had oft given him good counsel, which he followed to the great commodity of the commonwealth: thirdly, it was told him the same day, that his young son, of whom he had an expectation and hope of all goodness, was dead in Umbria. The friends and lovers of this Fabius, that stood about him, when they heard this, wept very sore: but he alone being unmoved, went forward stoutly in the business that concerned the commonwealth [3].

[1 Valer. Max. Ibid.]

[2 The circumstances of this history are related by Livy, Lib. XLV. c. xl. xli. Postquam omnia secundo navium cursu in Italiam pervenerant, neque erat quod ultra precarer; illud optavi, ut quum ex summo retro volvi fortuna consuesset, mutationem ejus domus mea potius quam respublica sentiret. Itaque defunctam esse fortunam publicam mea tam insigni calamitate spero. Compare also Valer. Max. Lib. v. cap. 10.]

[3 It does not appear from what source the learned writer has borrowed this history. Plutarch, in his life of Fabius Maximus, (ed. Bryan. 1729. Vol. I. p. 407), relates the account of the fortitude of Fabius on the death of his son; but omits all mention of the other circumstances of the history.]

Here, because of shortness, I leave out a multitude of examples of sundry men, named Galli, Pisones, Scævolæ, Metelli, Scauri, Marcelli; whom in such points to follow, it is laudable and worthy of commendation.

I will yet shew one example, of the virtuous woman Cornelia, which was daughter unto Scipio Africanus. When she understood that her two sons, Tiberius Gracchus and C. Gracchus (who, being magistrates, had honourably and well behaved themselves), were slain, and she of her friends was called miserable, she said : " I will never think myself a miserable woman, forasmuch as I have brought forth such men[4]."

This woman now overcame her own natural feebleness and motherly heart : should not then a man (which word noteth the stronger kind and more valiant stomach) declare himself even as stout? That an heathenish unbelieving woman could despise, should that make a faithful christian man so utterly faint-hearted? That she willingly gave again unto nature, wilt not thou suffer God to have it, when he requireth it of thee? She took upon her, with an unbroken mind, the death of many children; and wilt not thou, that foregoest but one child, be comforted again? The heathenish woman knew none other, but that after death there remaineth nothing behind; yet made not she an unmeasurable howling. Thou knowest that after this time there remaineth an ever-lasting life : so much the worse then beseemeth it a christian man to unquiet himself with excess of heaviness.

CHAPTER VIII.

THE COMMODITY OF PATIENCE.

UNSEEMLY sorrow for their sakes that are dead is un-profitable and hurtful. Unprofitable : for as soon as the soul is once departed out of the body, it cometh either into heaven or into hell, and with no crying shall it be called back again, or altered. Neither canst thou serve the dead with any thing more, than that his remembrance be dear

[4 See Plutarch, Vit. C. Gracchi. Vol. IV. p. 400. ed. Bryan.]

and had in honour with thee. The heathenish poet Sophocles
writeth : "If the dead might with tears be called again,
then should weeping be counted more worthy than gold.
But, O my good old man, it may not be, that he which once
is buried should come again to the light. For if weeping
might help, my father had been alive again[1]." Hurtful:
hereof hath the heathenish poet Philemon written right
wisely : "Many of them through their own fault increase
misfortune to themselves, and make the same more grievous
than it is of nature. Example : when one hath his mother,
child, or friend dead, if he thought thus, He was a man, and
therefore he died ; this adversity should be no greater, than
nature bringeth with it. But if he cry, 'I am undone, I
shall see him no more, he is gone and lost for ever;' such
one heapeth up yet more sorrow to that he hath already.
But whoso considereth everything with discretion, maketh
the adversity to be less unto himself, and obtaineth the more
quietness[2]."

It were a very scornful thing, if when a man hath hurt
one foot, he would therefore mar the other also ; or if, when
one part of his goods is stolen away, he would cast the rest

[1 This passage is found amongst the Fragments of Sophocles,
and is taken from the lost play of the ΣΚΥΡΙΑΙ :

Ἀλλ' εἰ μὲν ἦν κλαίουσιν ἰᾶσθαι κακὰ,
καὶ τὸν θανόντα δακρύοις ἀνιστάναι,
ὁ χρυσὸς ἧσσον κτῆμα τοῦ κλαίειν ἂν ἦν.
νῦν δ', ὦ γεραιὲ, ταῦτ' ἀνηνύτως ἔχει,
τὸν μὲν τάφῳ κρυφθέντα πρὸς τὸ φῶς ἄγειν·
κἀμοὶ γὰρ ἂν πατήρ γε δακρύων χάριν
ἀνῆκτ' ἂν εἰς φῶς.

Sophocl. ed. Brunck. Vol. ii. pp. 51, 52.]

[2
Μείζω τὰ κακὰ ποιοῦσι πολλοὶ, δέσποτα,
αὐτοὶ δι' αὑτοὺς, ἢ πέφυκε τῇ φύσει.
οἷον, τέθνηκεν υἱὸς ἢ μήτηρ τινὶ,
ἢ νὴ Δί' ἄλλων τῶν ἀναγκαίων γέ τις·
εἰ μὲν λάβῃ τοῦτ', Ἀπέθαν', ἄνθρωπος γὰρ ἦν,
τοσοῦτο γέγονε τὸ κακὸν, ἡλίκον περ ἦν.
ἐὰν δ', Ἀβίωτος ὁ βίος, οὐκ ἔτ' ὄψομαι,
ἀπόλωλ',—ἐν ἑαυτῷ τοῦτ' ἐὰν σκοπῇ, κακὰ
πρὸς τοῖς κακοῖσιν οὗτος ἕτερα συλλέγει.
ὁ δὲ τῷ λογισμῷ πάντα παρ' ἑαυτῷ σκοπῶν
τὸ κακὸν ἀφαιρεῖ, τἀγαθὸν δὲ λαμβάνει.

Philemon ap. Stobæi Florileg. Tom. III. p. 379, ed. Gaisford.]

into the sea, and say that he so bewaileth his adversity. No
less foolishly do they, that enjoy not such goods as are
present, and regard not their friends that be alive; but spoil
and mar themselves, because their wives, children, or friends,
be departed.

Though one of the husbandman's trees doth wither away,
he heweth not down therefore all the other trees; but
regardeth the other so much the more, that they may win
the thing again, which the other lost. Even so learn thou
in adversity, with such goods as are left thee to comfort
and refresh thyself again.

CHAPTER IX.

WE OUGHT SO TO LOVE OUR CHILDREN AND FRIENDS, THAT WE MAY FORSAKE THEM.

ALL such things ought of us to be considered, taken in
hand, and exercised, while our wives and friends are still
alive. Namely, if thou have father or mother, husband or
wife, child or friends, lay not thine heart, love, and affection
too much upon them, how good, profitable, and honest *Love thy
friends, be-*
soever they be; but remember alway that they are tran- *cause God
hath com-*
sitory things, which thou mayest lose and forego, when time *manded thee
to love them,*
requireth. Love him most of all, whom thou canst not lose, *and not for
affection to*
even thy Redeemer; who, to draw thee unto his love, and *them, and
then wilt*
to deliver thee from the love of the world, stretched out *thou be
contented*
his arms, and suffered the most vile death for thee upon the *with God's
good will and
pleasure.*
cross.

Seneca saith not unwisely : " I lend myself unto the *Note the saying of an hea-*
things of the world, but I do not give myself to them." He *then man
greatly to*
saith moreover, that " nothing is possessed as it ought to be, *our shame.*
except one be ready at all times to lose it."

But if we fasten our hearts (so to say) upon our children and friends; that is, if we love them too much, and
not God above all things; then hath our sorrow no measure
as ought, as they are altered or taken away. Therefore if
thou hast not prepared thyself to adversity by times, and
art once overtaken with indiscreet heaviness, then let it be
unto thee a warning from henceforth to keep thee from the

greater love of transitory things, which hath brought thee into such heart-sorrow; to the intent that at other times thou mayest take the death of thy wife and children in good part, and with more constancy of mind.

CHAPTER X.

OF THE DEATH OF YOUNG PERSONS IN ESPECIAL.

AFTER the general instruction concerning death, must certain objections be answered that hitherto are not resolved. If a young man, or if a young daughter die, Lord, what a great mourning beginneth there to be! 'Alas! he is taken away in his young days before his time; he should first have been married, and had a good wife upon earth, and in his last age have died in peace and rest.' Hereof cometh it that we think the death of children to be unnatural, even as when the flame of fire through water is violently quenched. The death of the aged we think to be natural, as when the fire quencheth of itself, according to the saying of Cicero[1].

Item, the death of young persons is compared to unripe apples, that with violence are plucked off from the tree: the death of the aged is thought to be, as when ripe apples fall down of themselves.

Item, as it is hard to undo two boards newly glued together, but old joinings are lightly broken asunder; so we complain that young folks die with greater pain than the old: yea, it grieveth the father's and mother's heart, when, as they count it, that matter is turned upside down, that children depart out of this world before old folks. The answer is taken out of the before rehearsed ground. If God,

The will of God. who hath all in his own power, had promised every one a long life, then mightest thou complain at the shortening of the life of thyself or of thy friends against God's promise. Now hath God compared and clothed the soul with the body, that what day or what twinkling of an eye soever he commandeth it to depart, it keepeth the same time wherein one finisheth his course. Therefore hath no man cause to complain of an untimely death; but look, whatsoever one hath lived

The shortness of this time. over and beside the first day of his birth, it is an increase.

[1 De Senectute. c. 19.]

Moreover, God knoweth much better than thou and we all, when it is best for every one to die. And so faithful is he for the Lord Jesus Christ's sake, that he in no wise will be too hasty upon us.

Secondly, though we remain a long season in this fickle transitory life, yet is all our time but short, specially towards the endless eternity. Therefore it hath but a slender difference, to depart hence in youth, or in age.

Thirdly, through death is a young person withdrawn away from many troubles, which else were at his door. For commonly, the longer a man liveth, the more miserable is he.

Take examples out of old stories. If Themistocles, after the most glorious victory against Xerxes, when all the Greeks acknowledged and commended him for their redeemer and deliverer, had died, should it not have served him to a perpetual praise and honour? Then should not he afterward have been rated as a betrayer of Greece; then needed not he to have been in bondage, nor to have fallen down at the foot of the king of Barbary, as before a God, whom he before had driven out of Greece. How thrall and vile a thing was it to be esteemed before the world, that Themistocles must needs come before king Xerxes!

What is to be said of Marcus Cicero, who confesseth himself, that if he had died sooner, he had escaped exceeding great troubles? And forasmuch as he so said, while the matter was yet tolerable; how would he first have thought and lamented in his age, to see with his eyes the drawn swords over the senators' and citizens' heads, and when the most principal men's goods were parted among murderers; yea, when, whereas beforetime there was one Catiline, the city was now become full of such seditious persons! _{Catiline was a seditious man.}

The examples of daily experience declare sufficiently before our eyes, whereby we may evidently perceive, that death, though they call it untimely, delivereth yet from great misfortune and adversity.

Fourthly, the innocency and cleanness of youth is of their own nature, and through evil example, defiled and stained with the life and conversation that followeth after. Augustine saith, " The older the worse[2]."

[2 The following passage appears to contain the sentiment of Augustine, which is here referred to: Quisquis igitur es amator vitæ

Therefore when a young man falleth on sleep, know thou that God sheweth great grace unto him, in that he suffereth him not, as many other, to remain long in this blasphemous world, to the intent he should no more be hindered and defiled with it; but hath called him from hence to a right good state, that with himself and all the elect he might possess the kingdom of heaven. Witness of the scripture: "Suddenly was he taken away, to the intent that wickedness should not alter his understanding. His soul pleased God, therefore hasted he to take him away from among the wicked."

He speaketh of Henoch. Wisd. iv.

Similitudes. He that is upon the sea, and with a good strong wind is carried soon to the haven or land where he would be, is happier than he, that for lack of wind is fain to sail still many years and days upon the sea with much trouble and weariness. Even so the more happy is he, whom death taketh away from the stormy and raging sea of this world. Seeing there is set before us an universal native country, and he that is long in going thither, obtaineth no more than he that is speedily gone thither before-hand; should not one wish, that he had soon overcome the foul dangerous way that leadeth to the heavenly harbour?

The sooner one payeth his debt, the better it is. If there were none other remedy, but that with an hundred more thou must needs be beheaded, and thou art the first that is put to execution, art thou not then the first that is despatched of the pain?

Finally, if thou consider the mischances of other folks, thou hast the less cause to complain. One dieth in the mother's womb, before he be born. Another dieth in the very birth. The third in his flourishing youth, when he first delighteth to live, falleth away as a beautiful rose. Among a thousand is there not one that cometh to the perfect age.

longæ, esto potius bonæ vitæ. Nam si male vivere volueris, longa vita non erit verum bonum, sed erit longum malum. August. de Verbis Apostol. Homil. I. Opera, Vol. x. p. 90. G. Ed. 1541.]

CHAPTER XI.

OF THE DEATH OF THE AGED.

WHEN old aged folks are greedy of this wretched life, they do even as those that, when the wine is all spent, will needs drink out the wine-lees also. Whoso dwelleth in an old rotten house that sinketh down, needeth not long to seek props to underset it, but should rather be glad to get him out of it : even so old aged folks, by reason of their decayed body, should rather be content to depart from it. And this advantage they have, that their death is not so fierce and painful as the death of young folks.

This is chiefly to be considered, that the Lord our God will not have us careful, (which thing belongeth unto him alone,) but to be faithful and true, and diligently to labour. Old fathers and mothers are not able to travail any more; and yet with earnest carefulness they think to bring all things to pass. This special fault they have, that they think they shall ever lack. Therefore unto them verily it is best, that God take them away from all care, sorrow, and trouble, and place them in quiet rest with other faithful christian folks.

CHAPTER XII.

OF STRANGE DEATH.

WHOSO is taken with the pestilence, or dieth else of sickness in his bed, ought gladly to suffer the hand of God; for everybody hath deserved a far worse death. And a very small rod is this towards it that God sendeth over the ungodly, yea, ofttimes over his own dear children, when one is beheaded, another burned, the third drowned, &c. ; where they altogether may sing with David : " For thy sake are we killed every day, and counted as sheep appointed to be slain." But if one die an unwonted death, (as one is destroyed by the hangman, another dieth a sudden death, the third, as happily a man's child falleth down dead from an

Ps. xliv.
Rom. viii.
2 Cor. iv.

9—2

high place,) this take we for a terrible death, and cannot tell else what to say of it; as though every kind of death in itself were not terrible unto the nature of man. Though one dieth upon the wheel for murder, there is sometime more hope of him, that he hath found grace at God's hand, than of many one that dieth at home in his bed. Examples also are to be considered: for a great sort of God's elect died not a right death, as we use to term it. Abel was murdered of his own natural brother. The prophet, being sent to Jeroboam, was destroyed of a lion. Isaiah was sawn asunder through the middle. Jeremiah, like as Steven also, was stoned to death. James, being thrown down from the pulpit, was slain of a fuller[1]. Peter at Rome was fastened to a cross. Upon Paul was execution done with the sword[2]. Such like examples hast thou.

Item, the most excellent heathen men came miserably out of this world. The good Socrates was poisoned; Euripides was all-to torn of dogs; Sophocles was choked with a little stone of a grape berry; very sorrowful cumbrance did fret out the heart of Homer. Innumerable examples declare, that there happeneth no new thing unto us, what death soever we or our friends die.

Especially let us observe this rule: death is terrible to them that have no God; but of us that are God's children ought not the horrible image of death to be feared, but to be welcome unto us. For God himself comforteth us with these words following: "I live, and ye also shall live." Of this are we assured in Christ Jesu, who upon the cross died the most horrible death for our sakes: to whom with the Father, and the Holy Ghost, be all honour and glory for ever and ever. Amen.

Heb. xi.

John xiv.

Only unto God give the praise.

[1 Euseb. Hist. Eccles. Lib. II. c. 23. p. 30. ed. Reading, 1720; and Hegesippi Fragmenta apud Routh. Rel. Sacr. Vol. I. p. 195.]

[2 With respect to the martyrdom of St Peter and St Paul, compare Euseb. Hist. Eccles. Lib. II. c. 25. p. 83. S. Petri Alexandrini Fragmenta apud Routh. Rel. Sacr. Vol. III. p. 332; and Pearson. Annales Paulini ad annum Christi 68, Neronis 14.]

AN EXHORTATION WRITTEN BY THE LADY JANE, THE NIGHT BEFORE SHE SUFFERED, IN THE END OF THE NEW TESTAMENT IN GREEK, WHICH SHE SENT TO HER SISTER, LADY KATHARINE.

I HAVE here sent you, good sister Katherine, a book; which although it be not outwardly trimmed with gold, yet inwardly it is more worth than precious stones. It is the book, dear sister, of the law of the Lord; it is his testament and last will, which he bequeathed to us wretches, which shall lead you to the path of eternal joy. And if you with a good mind read it, and with an earnest desire follow it, it shall bring you to an immortal and everlasting life. It will teach you to live, and learn you to die; it shall win you more than you should have gained by the possessions of your woeful father's lands. For as, if God had prospered him, you should have inherited his lands; so if you apply diligently this book, seeking to direct your life after it, you shall be an inheritor of such riches, as neither the covetous shall withdraw from you, neither the thief shall steal, neither yet the moths corrupt.

Desire with David, good sister, to understand the law of the Lord your God. Live still to die; that you by death may purchase eternal life, or after your death enjoy the life purchased you by Christ's death. And trust not, that the tenderness of your age shall lengthen your life: for as soon, if God call, goeth the young as the old. And labour alway to learn to die, deny the world, defy the devil, and despise the flesh, and delight yourself only in the Lord. Be penitent for your sins, and yet despair not. Be strong in faith, and yet presume not. And desire with St Paul to be dissolved and to be with Christ, with whom even in death there is life. Be like the good servant, and even at midnight be waking; lest when death cometh and stealeth upon you, like a thief in the night, you be with the evil servant found sleeping; and lest for lack of oil ye be found like the five foolish women, and like him that had not on the wedding-garment; and then be cast out from the marriage. Rejoice in Christ, as I trust ye do. And seeing ye have the name of a Christian, as near as ye can, follow the steps of your master Christ, and take up your cross, lay your sins on his back, and always embrace him. And as touching my death, rejoice as I do, good sister, that I shall be delivered of this corruption, and put on incorruption. For I am assured that I shall, for losing of a mortal life, win an immortal life. The which I pray God grant you; send you of his grace to live in his fear, and to die in the true christian faith: from the which, in God's name, I exhort you that you neither swerve, neither for hope of life, nor fear of death. For if ye will deny his truth to lengthen your life, God will deny you, and yet shorten your days. And if ye will cleave to him, he will prolong your days to your comfort and his glory. To the which glory God bring me now, and you hereafter, when it shall please God to call you! Farewell, good sister, and put your only trust in God, who only must help you.

Your loving sister,
JANE DUDLEY.

THE

HOPE OF THE FAITHFUL.

The Hope of the Faythfull,

declaringe breefely and clearely the Resurrection of
our Lord Jesus Christ past, and of our true
essentiall bodies to come: and playnely confuting the chiefe errors that habe sprong
thereof out of the Scripture and Doctors. With an ebident probatiō
that there is an eternall life of
the faithful, and eberlasting
damnation of the
wicked.

[THE HOPE OF THE FAITHFUL.

This is the third of the treatises of Otho Wermullerus, or Vierd-mullerus, translated by Bishop Coverdale; for an account of which the reader is referred to the preface to the Spiritual Pearl. Of this work there are copies of the edition printed by Hugh Singleton in 1579 in the libraries of Christ Church, Oxford, and of Trinity college, Dublin. The present edition is printed from a copy of the old edition without date in the Swiss angular type, (exactly resembling that in which the preceding treatise is printed, and both of them probably under the immediate superintendence of Coverdale himself,) in the possession of George Offor, Esq.]

PREFACE.

_____

TO THE CHRISTIAN READER,

GRACE AND PEACE.

EVERY man must needs confess, that this is now a lamentable time, in the which the world is not only unquieted with wars, dearth, sickness, and such like; but also standeth ever more and more in greater peril, through vices every where bearing the sway: so that it is to be feared, if we banish them not the sooner, we and our posterity shall yet come into far greater sorrow, than we are already wrapped in. For if one should barely, and without all rhetorical amplifications, rehearse only the great pomp, vain glory, riot, fornication, open idolatry, perjury, &c. of mighty men and rulers, which waste the world miserably, the space even of many days would scarce be any thing sufficient thereunto.

And what heaps of wickedness private persons do add unto the same, all wise men can ponder by themselves. For if we go into our own bosoms, we find that we altogether will wholly fashion and frame our lives after the world; seeking vain pomp and private commodity for our own lust, with sure shame and public discommodity to others' loss.

Which all are undoubted tokens, that the law and love of God is little esteemed among us; which with grievous threats forbiddeth the aforesaid and other vices, by strait commandment forcing, and sure rewards alluring us to the contrary dealing. Neither may we think, but that such vices daily will increase, until the time they overwhelm us, except, the contempt of God's law set apart, (being the only sufficient well-spring of all wickedness, for which the wrath of God is enkindled and his bitter curses fall upon us,) the same would be had in greater price and reverence. For why? what godliness can be hoped for of them which hold

nothing of God, the only fountain of goodness, and laugh his
word to scorn, of whom we can know nothing but is there
shewed us, save the small knowledge there is of beholding of
the creatures; which nevertheless declareth rather, that there
is a God, than what he is, and how he will be pleased? And
though all the scriptures serve us to enjoy God's blessings,
yet as in a compound medicine all the simples being wholesome, some one may less be spared than the other; so the
article of resurrection, clear and oft inculcated in scripture,
is most available, so that it is known all vices swarm and
roost in us. For we not considering our end, wherein salvation and life standeth, or pains prepared for the accursed,
will but stain ourselves in voluptuousness. For who knoweth
but the flesh in this life, why should he not think as good
take it, as leave it, and best to make the most of that which
at last ceaseth? In this case the Ethnics being, said:
" Live merrily while ye be in the world, and eat we and
drink we lustily; to-morrow we shall die:" which all the
epicures protest openly, and the Italian *atheoi* in like
practice; and no worse man than a pope in our days hath
given the like definitive sentence among his court divines of
the soul's immortality[1]: the story is known. Contrariwise
the learned in God's word, knowing that this life is a death
from sin, and a way to the life to come, which Christ with
his cross hath opened unto them, for desire thereof run forth
in the race of godliness, assured of the reward; since Christ
therefore, by doing death battle, that we might live, hath
broken her bonds, and risen again. For goods are not the
possessor's, as the philosopher saith, and Christ alludeth in

[1 Allusion is probably made to Leo X.; who has often been
charged not only with holding infidel opinions, but also with giving
utterance to them. Compare with what is here stated, what is written
concerning Leo by Waterland, in his Charge on *Christianity defended
against Infidelity;* Works, Vol. VIII. p. 77. Ed. 1823: also the remarks
which are made on his character by Seckendorf, *Commentarius de
Lutheranismo,* (Lib. I. sect. 47. § CXVIII. Vol. I. p. 190,) who thus
gives his opinion of Leo: Hæc et alia ad mores Leonis pertinentia
Varillasius nuper in *Arcana historia Florentina* prodidit, ex quibus et
ex silentio *Pallavicini* judicium *Pauli Veneti* de Pontifice hoc con-
firmatur, quod duobus maximis vitiis laboraverit ignorantia religionis,
et impietate, sive atheismo. See Illyr. Flac. Catalog. Test. Genev.
1608. col. 2103. Also Bale, Pageant of Popes, Lond. 1574. fol. 179.]

the parable of the two strong men, but the more valiant man's. Wherefore, gentle reader, I having this little, but absolute work of Christ's and our resurrection, and that there is an eternal life and damnation, wherein the devil hath sore assaulted the church by men (this only excepted) of great authority and learning, thought it my duty to put it in print, not keeping that private, which might do such good common. The matter is plain in scripture; yet learn we better things called in question, and forced to us by reason : wherefore not to stir up God's grace in us by embracing such treatises, were to tempt God, and extinct the Spirit.

For the scholar learneth of his schoolfellow, what he perceived not by his more learned master, and understandeth him ever after the better; and so men further one another in scripture: which, as I mean in printing, if thou desire in reading, the Lord, no nay, shall grant our request, which giveth blessings plenteously to all such as ask it constantly. To whom give honour and thanks from heart, for the good that thou reapest in his crea- tures. Farewell.

FIRST PART OF THIS BOOK,

ENTITLED

THE HOPE OF THE FAITHFUL,

WHICH ENTREATETH OF THE RESURRECTION AND
ASCENSION OF CHRIST, WITH THE FRUIT
AND COMMODITY THEREOF.

CHAPTER I.

THE CONTENTS OF THIS BOOK, AND THE AUTHOR'S
PURPOSE.

CONSIDERING that by the evangelists and by all the
apostles there is nothing written more diligently, than touching the resurrection of our Lord Jesus Christ, my purpose is
somewhat more largely to talk of the same, and of the
glorious ascension of his body into heaven : item, of the
resurrection and ascension of our own bodies, of the damnation of unbelievers, of the hope and eternal life of the
blessed. And this I mind to do only unto the honour, laud,
and praise of our Lord Jesus Christ; that the mystery of the
holy gospel may be set forth and opened to the commodity
and edifying of the faithful, and that of every man it may
be plainly understanded, how great things are prepared and
given us of Christ. This matter also doth specially belong
to the declaration of the holy gospel; forasmuch as the best
state of the gospel is contained and taught therein. Therefore if I write aught herein more largely, I do nothing that
concerneth not my purpose. Yet I intend also to keep a
measure, and not to open every thing that hereof might be
written, but only that which is chiefest and most necessary
of all.

CHAPTER II.

THAT THE LORD VERILY AROSE WITH HIS BODY.

THAT our Lord Jesus Christ with his own very true body did verily arise from the dead, it shall be expedient before all things to testify and prove. Therefore let the first witness, even the Lord Jesus Christ himself, come forth now, and bear us record out of the prophets concerning his true re

Matt. xii. surrection : " Like as Jonas," saith he, " was three days and three nights in the whale's belly, so shall the Son of man be three days and three nights in the heart of the earth." Now did not the fish cast up to the dry land any other for Jonas, but even the same Jonas himself, whom he had swallowed. Therefore the very same true body of the Lord also, that was buried, arose again. Which thing the holy apostle Paul

1 Cor. xv. minding perfectly to express, said : " First of all I delivered unto you, or taught you, that which I received ; how that Christ died for our sins according to the scriptures ; and that he was buried, and that he rose again the third day according to the scriptures."

Lo, what can be spoken more evident and plain ? He that died for our sins, and was buried, even he himself the very same rose also again. Of this now it followeth, that the very true substantial body of our Lord did rise again ; for even the same died, and was buried. But to the intent that it might the sooner be believed, Paul, the holy teacher, declareth furthermore, that he speaketh thus according to the contents of scripture, and that the same was taught in the scriptures afore, meaning undoubtedly the law and the prophets.

Nevertheless we will now bring forth the true and evident

Matt. xxviii.
Mark xvi.
Luke xxiv. testimonies of the angels, who in Mark, Luke, and Matthew, speak unto the women that came to the sepulchre : " Ye seek Jesus of Nazareth, him that was crucified. Why seek ye the living among the dead ? He is risen, he is not here. Behold the place where they had laid him. Remember, how he spake unto you, while he was yet in Galilee, saying, that the Son of man must be delivered into the hands of sinful men, and be crucified, and the third day rise again. There-

fore go quickly and tell this to his disciples, that he is risen
from the dead. And behold, he shall go before you into
Galilee; there shall ye see him, as he himself told you."

These are the words of the angels, which, if all circumstances be thoroughly well considered, do plainly declare,
that the very true body of the Lord did verily arise from
the dead. The women come and seek the body of the Lord,
desiring to anoint it; therefore the question is touching the
body of Christ. The angels also speak of the true body of
Christ, and make answer, saying, "Ye seek Jesus of Nazareth;" whereunto they add distinctly, "him that was crucified." Now are we sure, that his very true body was
crucified, and died. He, say they namely, that died, even
Jesus of Nazareth, the same is become alive again. "Why
seek ye the living among the dead?" The Lord died of a
truth; but death must not have dominion over him, neither
must his body putrefy or corrupt, as other men's bodies do;
according as holy David said before: "Aforehand I saw God Psal. xvi.
always before me; for he is on my right hand, that I should
not be moved. Therefore did my heart rejoice, and my
tongue was glad; moreover my flesh also shall rest in hope;
because thou wilt not leave my soul in hell, neither wilt thou
suffer thy Holy One to see corruption. Thou hast shewed me
the ways of life, thou shalt make me full of joy with thy
countenance; and at thy right hand there is pleasure for
evermore." These words extend wholly unto Christ, ac-
cording as the two excellent apostles, namely, Peter in the Acts ii. xiii.
second, and Paul in the thirteenth of the Acts, do declare.
Out of the angels' words also is it come into the articles of
the Creed, as we all confess with these words, "HE ROSE
AGAIN FROM THE DEAD." This word, "from the dead,"
doth truly express the death and resurrection after this sense:
He died, as other men also do, according to the law of
nature; and even in the same flesh, which he therefore took
upon him that he might die, received the immortality, and
took it unto him again. Therefore, say the angels, "he is
risen again." But that thing riseth not up, which fell not
afore; therefore even the same body of Christ, that fell to
death, is from death risen up again.

Moreover, they name also the place where he was laid,
to express perfectly, that the very true body was risen, saying:

"Behold the place where they laid him." The mortal body of the Lord hath his certain place, yea, his own place, (that the logicians call *ubi*, that is to say, where,) in the which he was laid; and as he now is become immortal, he hath his own place again. For if the body that was raised up were every where, then had not the angels said: "Behold the place where they laid him." Yea, they had not been able to shew any one place, where he was not; for the immortal body must be every where. But now they shew a place, in which the immortal body was not, and that with plain express words, saying: "He is not here." Of this now it followeth, that the body of Christ, which is but in one place, did verily rise again. In the gospel of St John also the sepulchre-clothes wherein the Lord was wrapped (as the head-cloth and that which was about his body) are mentioned as strong testimonies of the body risen up; which clothes Peter and John did perfectly see.

Furthermore, the angels prove his very true resurrection out of the word of God, and say: "Remember what he said unto you, while he was yet in Galilee: The Son of man must be delivered into the hands of sinful men," &c. With these words will they instruct us, that the Son of man, in a very true body, is truly risen again. They say moreover: "Go quickly, tell the disciples, that he is risen from death." Now was the body dead, and, as all men's bodies that die, laid in the grave. And even the same body was made immortal, and rose again from the dead. "He shall go before you into Galilee," yea, before you shall he go with a true body, that moveth from one place unto another; "there," as in a certain place, "shall ye see him." "Ye shall see him," I say; for with a visible and palpable body is he risen, as ye are told by the Lord himself, who can neither lie nor deceive.

CHAPTER III.

APPEARINGS OF THE BODY RAISED UP.

HEREUNTO extend the manifold appearings, or open-shewings of Christ, mentioned by the evangelists. In Mark it is written thus: "When Jesus was risen early the first *Mark xvi.* day after the Sabbath, he appeared first to Mary Magdalen;" to whom in the gospel of St John he saith: "Go to my *John xx.* brethren, and tell them, I go up to my Father and your Father, to my God and your God. Now when she came to the disciples, she told them that she had seen the Lord, and that he had spoken such things unto her." In Matthew he meeteth the women, and saith: "All hail. Fear not: go *Matt. xxviii.* and tell my brethren, that they go into Galilee; there shall they see me." In holy St Luke is mention made of two appearings: the first, when he shewed himself to the two that went to Emaus, and opened unto them the true re- *Luke xxiv.* surrection of his body; the second, when they were gone again from Jerusalem, they came to the disciples, minding to shew them, and to give them to understand, what they had seen and heard. Then prevented they them, and said: "The *Luke xxiv.* Lord is truly risen indeed, and hath appeared unto Simon." "Now while they were talking of such things among them- selves, Jesus stood in the midst of them, and said, Peace be unto you. But when they saw him, they were sore afraid, thinking that they had seen a spirit, or some other vision. Then said the Lord unto them, Why are ye troubled, and why do thoughts arise in your hearts? behold my hands and my feet."

CHAPTER IV.

THE BODY OF CHRIST ROSE AGAIN, NOT A SPIRIT, BUT A TRUE BODY.

Now, that no man should think it to be another body, which he had not afore his resurrection, he addeth thereto immediately: "It is even I myself; handle me, and see; a spirit hath not flesh and bones, as ye see me have. And with that he shewed them his hands and his feet."

With this evident testimony of the Lord was St Augus- *De Agone* tine moved boldly to say, that "they ought not to be heard, *Christiano.* *cap. 24.* which deny the body of the Lord to have risen again, as it was laid in the sepulchre. For if it were not so, he would not have said to his disciples after the resurrection : 'Handle me and see; for a spirit hath not flesh and bones, as ye see me have.'   Now is it as much as to rob God of his honour, if any man would think that the Lord, who is the truth itself, had, in anything that he spake, not said the truth[1]."

Thomas was not there, when the Lord shewed himself alive unto his disciples; but when he came again, they told him with great joy what they had seen and heard.   Nevertheless he

John xx. thought it had not been as they spake, and he said: "Except I see in his hands the print of the nails, and put my fingers into the holes of them, and my hand into his side, I will not believe it.   Therefore after eight days, when the disciples were assembled together again, and Thomas with them, Jesus cometh in, while the doors were shut, and standeth in the midst among them, and saith, Peace be unto you.   Afterwards said he unto Thomas, Reach hither thy finger, and behold my hands ; put thy hand here also, and lay it in my side ; and be not faithless but believing.   Thomas answered and said unto him, My Lord, and my God."   For St Paul also, in the first chapter of the epistle to the Romans, doth out of the resurrection of the Lord prove the Godhead thus :

Rom i. "Which was born of the seed of David after the flesh, and evidently declared to be the Son of God after the Spirit that sanctifieth, and by that he rose again from the dead;" namely, Jesus Christ our Lord.   What can be spoken more plain, more evident, or more certain?   For freely did the Lord set before their eyes his body which was hanged upon the cross, that they might see it and handle it.   For the body was pierced with nails, and marred with the prints thereof.   Out of this now it followeth, that the Lord with his true body did verily rise again, and was not a spirit.   And further, the Lord also sheweth himself unto the seven, which then were

John xxi. in Galilee, fishing at the Sea of Tiberias.   The evangelist addeth likewise thereunto, that it was not expedient for any

---

[1 Nec eos audiamus, qui negant tale corpus Domini resurrexisse, quale positum est in monumento. Si enim tale non fuisset, non ipse dixisset post resurrectionem discipulis, Palpate et videte, quoniam spiritus ossa et carnem non habet, sicut me videtis habere. Sacrilegum est enim credere, Dominum nostrum, cum ipse sit veritas, in aliquo fuisse mentitum. August. De Agone Christiano. cap. 24. Opera, Tom. III. p. 74. F. ed. Paris. 1541.]

of the disciples to ask him who he was; for they knew that it was the Lord. In the twenty-eighth chapter of Matthew, the eleven apostles "saw the Lord, and worshipped him," as Matt. xxviii. it is declared afore. Some think, that the same was the excellent appearing that Paul speaketh of, saying: "Afterwards 1 Cor. xv. was he seen of more than five hundred brethren at once, of whom many are alive this day, but some are asleep," or dead. And in the same place doth the apostle make mention yet of two more appearings, saying: "After this was he seen of James, then of all the apostles, and last of all he was seen of me, as of one that was born out of due time."

Luke the Evangelist, in the beginning of the Acts of the Apostles, hath in manner collected all the probations together. "The Lord," saith he, "shewed himself alive unto Acts 1. his apostles after his passion; and that by many tokens, appearing unto them forty days, and speaking of the kingdom of God." St Peter also, instructing Cornelius in the faith of Christ, said: "We are witnesses of all things which Matt. x. he did in the land of the Jews, and at Jerusalem; whom they slew and hanged on a tree: him God raised up the third day, and shewed him openly, not to all the people, but unto us witnesses chosen before of God, for that intent, which did eat and drink with him after he arose from death." With these plain probations and testimonies, as I suppose it, it is evidently declared and sufficiently shewed, that our Lord Jesus Christ, with his own very true body which hanged on the cross, did verily rise from the dead. As touching the glorification, I shall speak thereof, when I come to the resurrection of the bodies; and there will I shew more, that the glorification doth nothing minish the verity or truth of the body. Read the sixth chapter.

CHAPTER V.

THE FRUIT OF THE RESURRECTION OF CHRIST.

Now will I declare the occasion, why I have with such diligence and so earnestly pressed on to this, that Jesus Christ with his true body did truly rise again: that is, how profitable and necessary it is so to believe, and what fruit the true resurrection of Christ doth bring and engender unto us.   And albeit that hereof, as of a plentiful treasure, much might be spoken, yet will I comprehend it all in a short sum.   Though we be complete and made perfect through the death of Christ, while the just judgment of God is satisfied, the curse taken away, and the penalty recompensed and paid; yet saith Peter, that " we are born again through the resurrection of Jesus Christ unto a living hope." For like as Christ with his resurrection overcame death, so standeth also the triumph and victory of our faith in the resurrection of Christ.   Therefore through his death is sin taken away, by his resurrection is righteousness brought again.   For how could he with his death have delivered us from death, if he himself had of death been overcome?   or how could he have obtained the victory for us, if he had been destroyed in the battle himself?   Therefore through death is death discomfited, and with the resurrection is life to us restored.

1 Peter i.

Hereof cometh it that Paul saith : "If Christ be not risen, then is your faith in vain, and ye are yet still in your sins ; and so they that be asleep in Christ are lost ;" and to the Romans : " Christ," saith he, "was delivered up for our sins, and rose again for our justification."

1 Cor. xv.

Rom. iv.

Hereunto cometh it also that he writeth in the tenth chapter : "If ye confess the Lord Jesus with thy mouth, and believe in thine heart, that God raised him from the dead, thou shalt be saved."

Rom. x.

To the Philippians he saith moreover : " I count all things but loss for the excellent knowledge sake of Jesus Christ."

Phil. iii.

Out of all this is there yet another thing concluded, namely, that not only life is restored unto us, but also that in the resurrection of the Lord the immortality of the soul is grounded fast and sure.   For so saith the Lord himself in the Gospel : " I am the resurrection and the life : he that believeth on me, though he were dead, he shall live; and whosoever liveth and believeth on me shall never die."

John xi.

Yet another fruit also receive we out of the resurrection of the Lord, namely, that we are assured and out of doubt, even as if we had received writing and seal thereof, that our own bodies likewise shall rise from death ; forasmuch as in the true resurrection of the body of Christ our resurrection hath a fast and immoveable ground.   For Paul saith : " Christ 1 Cor. xv. rose from the dead, and is become the first-fruits of them that sleep.   For by one man came death, and by one man came the resurrection of the dead.   For as by Adam all die, so by Christ shall all be made alive.   But every one in his own order : the first is Christ, then they that are Christ's."   Now he that is the first cannot be alone ; the head also shall not forsake the members.   Seeing then that Christ the head is risen, it must needs follow, that we also as members must rise again.   For even in the same place doth Paul conclude : " If the dead rise not again, then is not Christ risen again."

And finally, out of the words of the holy apostle Paul we learn, that through the ensample of Christ that was raised up, we are not only provoked to take upon us a new life ; Rom. vi. but that we also, through the power of Christ, are renewed, Coloss. iii. that we might lead an innocent and holy life.   And thus have I briefly comprehended and declared the principal fruits of the resurrection of the Lord.

CHAPTER VI.

OF THE TRUE ASCENSION OF THE LORD'S BODY, THAT AROSE A BODY, AND NO SPIRIT ; AND OF HIS PLACE WHITHER HE WENT TO BE IN.

MOREOVER it shall be expedient to know, to what place the true body of the Lord was carried, or came ; whether it was laid in the earth again, or vanished away, or turned into the nature of the Godhead, or otherwise changed into a spirit.   In this point we affirm thus.   The right old christian faith, the upright holy scripture, and the ancient doctrine of the christian church, doth teach, hold, and confess, that Jesus Christ, very God and man, hath not laid away, nor mixed together, nor yet put off his natures, the Godhead and the manhood ; but that he keepeth still both the natures in their properties unblemished, and that he ascended up to heaven very true God and man.   For so we acknowledge and confess in the Creed : " HE ASCENDED UP TO HEAVEN."

Mark xvi. We find also in the Gospel of Mark: "So then when the Lord had spoken unto them, he was received into heaven, Ruffinus. and sitteth at the right hand of God." Item, Ruffinus, an old writer, who hath declared the articles of the faith, saith: "He ascended into the heavens, not thither where the Word that is God was not afore, (for he was ever still in heaven, and continued in his Father;) but thither where the Word that became man sat not afore[1]." Yet will we declare this more plainly out of the Gospel of Luke, where it is written Luke xxiv. thus: "And he led them out into Bethany, and lift up his hands, and blessed them: and it came to pass, as he blessed them, he departed from them, and was carried up into heaven."

Now if thou ponder everything here thoroughly, thou must needs acknowledge, and being overcome with the truth thou must needs confess, that the very true body of the Lord was not laid away, neither turned into the nature of the Godhead[2]; but he a very true man, who at one time is but in one place, ascended and was taken up into heaven, as into one place: "He led them out," saith he. Who, I pray thee? Even the Lord Jesus Christ, which until then, by the space of forty days had in very deed truly shewed himself unto his disciples, that he was risen from the dead with a very true essential body,—even he, the very same that had taken unto him a true body, led his disciples out unto Bethany, and from thence brought he them further to mount Olivet; and in the same place lifting up his hands, (no doubt bodily and human hands, yea, with the prints and tokens of the wounds,) he blessed them, namely, his disciples, that is, he saluted them, as the manner is of those that take their leave of us; and so departed he from them, and set his body corporally in heaven, as in one place. For afterwards it followeth yet more plain: "he departed from them," that is,

[1 Ascendit ergo ad cœlos, non ubi Verbum Deus ante non fuerat; quippe qui erat semper in cœlis, et manebat in Patre; sed ubi Verbum caro factum ante non fuerat. Ruffini Expositio in Symbolum Apostolicum apud Cypriani Opera, edit. Fell; also Opuscula, p. 185, ed. 1580.]

[2 Some account of the Apellitæ, and of other persons who held heretical opinions on our Lord's ascension, are found in bishop Pearson, On the Creed. Art. VI.]

he was carried into heaven.　For to be carried may here be spoken only of the body; and in such sort departed he from them, that his body was from the earth taken up into heaven.

And though all this be evident and plain in itself, yet by the Evangelist Luke in the Acts of the Apostles is it set <sub/>forth and opened more manifestly.　So afore all things he testifieth, that the Lord arose with his own true body, and that by the space of forty days with many tokens and evidences he plainly proved and declared his resurrection unto the disciples; and immediately he addeth thereunto, and even the very same body was taken up into heaven: "for when he had spoke these things," saith he, "while they beheld him, he was taken up on high, and a cloud received him up out of their sight."　So the Lord was taken up, yea, even in their eye-sight was he taken up on high; so that a cloud received his very true body away from the sight of their eyes.　I beseech you, what can be more aptly or more conveniently spoken of an essential body?

It followeth further in the evangelist Luke: "And while they looked stedfastly up towards heaven, as he went, (mark that well), behold, two men stood by them in white apparel, which also said, Ye men of Galilee, why stand ye gazing up into heaven?　This same Jesus, who is taken up from you into heaven, shall so come, even as ye have seen him go into heaven."　Wherefore our Lord Jesus is departed up into heaven with his own true essential body, yea, even with the same which he raised up from death.　For even with the same very true human body shall he come again unto judgment, according as the Lord himself said, and the prophet Zachary, whose words St John allegeth: "They shall look on him whom they have pierced."

Thus, I trust, is sufficiently proved and declared, that the Lord Jesus with his own very true body, which he raised from death, is gone up into heaven.　But to the intent that no man mistake this word, *heaven,* or otherwise imagine anything that is dark or not understood, whereby the simple, being in error, may scarce know at the last where heaven is, or where Christ hath his dwelling; it shall therefore be needful briefly to declare, what the heaven is, and that the Lord with his own true body doth dwell in heaven, as in one place: for heaven is a certain assured place, and not only

Acts i.

Matt. xxvi.
Zech. xii.
John xix.

a name and declaration of the estate and being in heaven. Therefore when it is said, " Christ is gone up into heaven," it is not so much as only to say, he hath taken upon him an heavenly estate or being; but also, he dwelleth bodily in heaven, as in one place.

CHAPTER VII.

THE DIVERS SIGNIFICATIONS OF THIS WORD HEAVEN, AS IT IS USED IN SCRIPTURE.

THIS word, *heaven,* in the scripture is used divers and sundry ways. First, for the whole firmament, which is called the heavenly host, or beautiful apparel of the heavens. Psalm viii. xix. Hereof hast thou record in the eighth and nineteenth Psalms. It is taken also for the air, which is above us, as the prophet Psalm cxlvi. cxlvii. saith : " He covereth the heaven with clouds, to prepare rain for the earth." Hereof cometh it, that the fowls which fly in the air are called fowls or birds of heaven, that is to say, birds in the air. The heaven also is used for a seat, habita-Psalm ciii. civ. tion, or dwelling, as: " The Lord hath prepared his seat in Matt. v. heaven;" and, " Ye shall not swear by heaven, for it is God's seat :" and though God be infinite, and cannot be compassed about with any place, as the most wise Salomon 1 Kings viii. said : " The heavens and the heavens of all heavens are not able to contain thee, and how should then this house do it, that I have builded?" yet the scripture calleth the heaven that is above us a dwelling of God; which dwelling is ordained for all faithful and virtuous believers, and is named 2 Cor. v. the heaven. This doth Paul witness, saying : " We know that if our earthly mansion of this dwelling were destroyed, we have a building of God, an habitation not made with hands, but eternal in heaven." There is now heaven taken for the kingdom of God, for the kingdom of the Father, or joy and eternal life, which is peace and rest. The heaven, I say, is a seat and dwelling of the faithful, or blessed be-lievers ; a determinate place also, into which the Lord Jesus was received, when he was taken up into the heaven. And this doth the scripture plainly declare unto us, namely, that

above us there is a certain determinate place prepared for
us. For Luke saith : " He was received up on high, and a Acts i.
cloud took him up away out of their sight." Item : " And
while they looked stedfastly up towards heaven, the angels
said, This same Jesus, which is taken away from you into
heaven, shall so come, even as ye have seen him go into
heaven." Who is so ignorant now, that he wotteth not
where heaven is, or the clouds, or into which heaven the
apostles looked so stedfastly ? Besides this, the holy apostle
Paul saith : " Also our conversation, free burghership, or Phil. iii.
dwelling, is in heaven, from whence we look for the Saviour,
even the Lord Jesus." Lo, " in heaven," saith the apostle,
" is our dwelling." In which heaven, I pray you ? Even in
the same, whence we look for the Saviour. Now is it
evident, from whence we wait and look, seeing that the
apostle saith again : " We which shall live and remain, shall 1 Thess. iv.
be caught up with him also in the clouds to meet the Lord
in the air, and so shall we ever be with the Lord." He
saith also in another place : " If ye be risen again with Col. iii.
Christ, then seek those things which are above, where Christ
sitteth at the right hand of God." And therefore is the
Lord Jesus gone up into the heaven that is above us, namely,
into that sure certain place, which is prepared for the blessed.

And in the same heaven, as in a sure certain place, doth
Christ now dwell bodily.

Of this opinion also was holy Augustine, as indeed it is
right and agreeable unto holy scripture. His words are
found in the book *Ad Dardanum de præsentia Dei*[1]. Holy
Fulgentius, in the second book that he wrote unto king Tra- Fulgentius.
simundus, is earnest to bring every man unto this understanding, that the human kind and nature of Christ, which
now dwelleth in heaven, is circumscribed and in one place[2].

[1 Noli itaque dubitare, ibi nunc esse hominem Jesum Christum,
unde venturus est; memoriterque recole, et fideliter tene Christianam
confessionem ; quoniam resurrexit a mortuis, ascendit in cœlum, sedet
ad dexteram Patris, nec aliunde quam inde venturus est ad vivos
mortuosque judicandos. Et sic venturus est, illa angelica voce testante,
quemadmodum ire visus est in cœlum ; id est, in eadem carnis forma
et substantia, cui profecto immortalitatem dedit, naturam non abstulit. August. Epistolæ. Ad Dardan. Epist. lvii. Opera, Tom. II. p. 56.
M. ed. Par. 1541.]

[2 Fulgentii Opera. pp. 88, &c. ed. 1684, particularly cap. xviii.]

Vigilius.

With him also accordeth uniformly the holy martyr Vigilius[1]; whose testimony I will now omit, and come again to the holy scripture.

The scripture, minding to shew what is become of the body that rose again from death and ascended up, and where he hath his dwelling, saith simply and plainly : "He sitteth at the right hand of God, the Father Almighty." Thus now is the body of Christ come to the right hand of God; there sitteth he. But here it shall be expedient to declare what the right hand of God is, and what it is to sit at God's right hand.

CHAPTER VIII.

WHAT GOD'S RIGHT HAND IS, AND TO WHOM IT IS REFERRED.

FIRST, the right hand of God is not referred unto God himself, but unto men that are on the right hand. So that first the right hand of God doth signify the eternal salvation, and the place of those that be saved. This did holy Augustine teach, whose words I may well allege; forasmuch as he also doth confirm and prove his opinion by the divine and holy scriptures. In his book *De Agone Christiano* he saith :

Augustinus De Agone Christiano. cap. 26.

"We ought not to hear them that deny the Son to sit at the right hand of God. For they say, Hath God the Father also a right or left side, as bodies have? Neither do we understand that of the Father. For with no bodily proportion can God be described or comprehended. As for the right hand of the Father, it is nothing else but the eternal salvation, which he shall give to all godly and faithful believers. In like manner is the left hand rightly taken for the everlasting damnation that shall come upon the unbelievers. So that not of God, but of the creatures, it must be expounded what is written of the right or left hand. For even the body of Christ also, which is the church, shall come to the right hand, that is, unto salvation, as the apostle

Ephes. ii.

saith to the Ephesians : 'He hath raised us up together with him, and made us sit together with him among them of

[1 Vigilii Opera. Contra Varimadum, Lib. I. cap. 37. ed. 1564.]

heaven.' For though our bodies as yet be not there, our
hope nevertheless is there already[2]."

The same holy Augustine saith also further in the book
De Fide et Symbolo: " By the right hand," saith he, De Fide et
" must be understood the highest salvation, where righteous- cap. 7 Symbolo.
ness, peace, and joy is: like as the goats also shall be set on
the left hand; that is, by reason of their sins and wickedness,
they shall come into great calamity, trouble, and misery[3]."
All these are the words of holy Augustine.

CHAPTER IX.

WHAT IT IS TO SIT AT THE RIGHT HAND OF GOD. HOW CHRIST SITTETH THERE, AND WHAT HE DOETH.

AND thus now to sit at the right hand of God, is even
as much as to be in rest, that is to say, all wickedness and
misery set aside, to live in a godly life, and to be partaker
of eternal joy.

Now that this word, *to sit,* is used in scripture for rest,
these places declare. In the fourth book of Moses it is
written thus: " Shall your brethren go to war, and would Num. xxxii.

[2 Nec eos audiamus, qui negant ad dexteram Patris sedere
Filium. Dicunt enim, Numquid Deus Pater habet latus dexterum
aut sinistrum, sicut corpora? Nec nos hoc de Deo sentimus: nulla
enim forma corporis Deus definitur et concluditur. Sed dextera
Patris est beatitudo perpetua, quæ sanctis datur; sicut sinistra ejus
rectissime dicitur miseria perpetua, quæ impiis datur: ut non in
ipso Deo, sed in creaturis, hoc modo quo diximus intelligatur dextera
et sinistra; quia et corpus Christi, quod est ecclesia, in ipsa dextera,
hoc est, in ipsa beatitudine futurum est, sicut apostolus dixit, Quia et
simul nos suscitavit, et simul nos sedere fecit in cœlestibus. Quamvis
enim corpus nostrum nondum ibi sit, tamen spes nostra ibi jam est.
August. De Agon. Christian. cap. 26. Opera, Tom. III. p. 174. G.]

[3 Credimus etiam, quod sedet ad dexteram Patris: nec ideo tamen
quasi humana forma circumscriptum esse Deum Patrem arbitrandum
est, ut de illo cogitantibus dexterum aut sinistrum latus animo oc-
currat......Ad dexteram igitur intelligendum est dictum esse in
summa beatitudine, ubi et justitia, et pax, et gaudium est: sicut ad
sinistram hædi constituuntur, id est, in miseria, propter iniquitates et
labores et cruciatus. Id. de Fide et Symbolo. cap. 7. Opera, Tom. III.
p. 33. F.]

Micah iv. ye sit here?" and in Micah, "Every one shall sit under his vine and fig-tree." Many more such places there be. Wherefore now, when the scripture saith, that the Lord Jesus sitteth at the right hand of his Father, it understandeth it chiefly of his human nature which he took upon him, that the same, being discharged and free from all travail and misery of man, is now all in joy, and partaker of the kingdom everlasting.

Ruffinus. Thus saith also Ruffinus in his exposition of the Creed: "To sit at the right hand of the Father is convenient for the manhood received, which is received through a mystery. For to ascribe it to the divine nature is unseemly, as though it had a seat in heaven; but of the human nature it is properly understood and spoken[1]."

And the like yet did holy Saint Peter teach afore Ruffi-
Acts ii. iii. nus's time, as it is to see in the Acts of the Apostles.

But now might one ask, What doeth the Son at the right hand of the Father? must he always sit there, and be as much as made fast and bound unto it?

Answer. The Lord Jesus, after his human nature that he took upon him, and which he put not from him in heaven, hath now eternal joy with his elect; he, as the head with his members, ruling and reigning with all faithful believers for evermore. Whereof we shall speak more afterward.

A very superfluous and unprofitable question also is it, when one will so curiously inquire and know, what God doeth in heaven.

For God will only teach us with his holy word, that he liveth and ruleth eternally in the glory of his heavenly
De Fide et Father. Holy Augustine saith also in the book *De Fide et*
Symbolo. *Symbolo:* "To go about for to seek and inquire, where and
cap. 6. how the body of our Lord is in heaven, it is a point of nice people, and bringeth no profit. Only we ought to believe, that he is verily in heaven. For truly it standeth not with our weakness to comprehend and discern the privity of the heavens; but it beseemeth our faith to have the worthy and

---

[1 Sedere quoque ad dexteram Patris carnis assumtæ mysterium est; neque enim incorporeæ illi naturæ convenienter ista absque assumtione carnis aptantur; neque sedis cœlestis profectum divina natura, sed humana conquirit. Ruffini Expos. in Symbolum apud Cyprian. p. 163. ed. Fell. Oxon. 1700.]

glorious body of the Lord in high and worthy estimation[2]."
Hitherto Augustine.

CHAPTER X.

THAT CHRIST SITTETH AT THE RIGHT HAND OF GOD BY HIS HUMANITY, BUT CIRCUMSCRIBED IN PLACE, AND IS NOT EVERY WHERE.

Now, though the heavenly honour and glory be high,
and may not be expressed; yet the place where he dwelleth
is certain, and the body that is in heaven cannot be every
where. For the right hand of God, in and after this first
signification thereof, is not infinite. Else must all faithful believers also, and they that are saved, be every where, seeing
they are with the Son of God, who is taken up into heaven.
For the Lord himself saith: "Now from henceforth shall I John xvii.
be no more in the world; but they are in the world: and I
come unto thee." Upon this he saith: "Father, whom thou
hast given unto me, I will that where I am they also be
with me, that they may see my glory which thou hast given
me." Item, "He that doth me service, let him follow me : John xii.
and where I am, there also shall my servants be." Seeing
now that our souls, and our bodies also, after the resurrection
of the flesh shall be in heaven, as in a place certain; it followeth, that the body of the Lord, which into heaven is taken
up, hath also a place certain in heaven, and that the right
hand of God in this signification cannot be every where.

In this upright matter let it trouble no man that is read
in St Paul, how that "Christ ascended up above all the Ephes. iv.
heavens:" by means whereof a curious body might peradventure conclude, if Christ our Lord be taken up above the
heavens, then can there no place certain be ascribed unto
him; seeing there is no place about or without the heaven.

[2 Sed ubi et quomodo sit in cœlo corpus Dominicum, curiosissimum
et supervacaneum est quærere: tantummodo in cœlo esse credendum
est. Non enim est fragilitatis nostræ cœlorum secreta discutere, sed
est nostræ fidei de Dominici corporis dignitate sublimia et honesta
sapere. August. De Fide et Symbolo cap. 6. Opera, Tom. III. p. 33.
E. ed. 1541.]

Neither ought it to offend any man that is written, how that
[Phil. ii.] "unto Christ there is given a name, which is above all
1 Cor. ii. names;" and that Paul saith: "Neither eye hath seen,
neither ear heard, nor is come into the heart of man, what
God hath prepared unto them that love him." For the
scripture of God throughout doth witness constantly and
sure, that Jesus Christ is taken up into heaven, and sitteth
at the right hand of his Father. Whereby it is out of doubt,
that the Apostle thought not to set Christ without heaven;
but therefore proponeth he the matter with so high and excellent words, to shew and declare unto us, that the body of
our Lord, which afore was despised and shamefully defaced,
is now in the supreme and brightest glory; and that meaneth
he, when he saith, "above all heavens." For [whoso] doth
thoroughly cons[ider the] place of Paul to the [Ephesians],
findeth that Paul [doth set the] two parts of his oration,
[the] one against the other. For he saith thus: "That
he ascended, what meaneth it, but that he also descended
first into the lowest parts of the earth?" Against this
setteth he now: "He that descended, is even the same
also that ascendeth up, even above all heavens." Therefore
is here the one set against the other; namely, to descend
into the lowest parts of the earth, and to ascend above all
heavens. But who would here conclude, Christ descended
into the lowest parts of the earth; ergo, he had no place
upon earth? For every man understandeth well, that Paul
with these words minded to declare the true coming of the
Lord upon earth, and the great humility and meekness of
our Lord Jesus Christ. Therefore who would then in the
other part of the oration conclude, Christ ascended up above
all heavens; ergo, he is not in heaven, or in any other
place? For is there also any one place without the heaven?
Who understandeth not now, that Paul here minded to say
nothing else, than that which he uttereth more plainly to
Phil. ii. the Philippians, "He hath exalted him on high?" And though
this height of heavenly honour be greater and more glorious,
than any man's tongue can or may express, yet the heaven
is and doth contain still the dwelling of the faithful; and
therefore is it a place certain. Wherefore after my plain
and simple understanding, which is not curious, I believe
constantly, that the glorified body of Christ is ascended up

above all heavens, that is, above all compass, or sphere, or height of heaven; and so even in heaven, that is, in the dwelling of the faithful; and there remaineth, and is not, as they say, passed by on the outside of heaven.

For the truth witnesseth evidently : " Where I am, there John xii. shall also my servants be." Now shall the servants of God be in heaven, and not without, or above the heaven, that is to say, in no place. For Paul, the chosen man of God, saith to the Philippians : " Our dwelling is in heaven, from whence Phil. iii. we look for the Saviour Jesus Christ." Plainly also and Jesus Christ. evidently doth the true word of God declare, that the heaven, into the which Christ ascended, is a place certain; for the Lord saith : " In my Father's house are many John xiv. dwellings : if it were not so, I would have told you : I go to prepare a place for you. And if I go to prepare a place for you, I will come to you again, and receive you even unto myself; that where I am, there you may be also."

There indeed could nothing be brought forth more meet and convenient to our purpose. For the thing that we now treat of is the heaven, which is the dwelling and native country of the blessed, and which here is called a dwelling, or mansion, or place; yea, a dwelling and place in the house of God the Father.

Who is now any more so malapert or arrogant, as to undertake to deny that heaven is a place? For thus saith the Lord : ' In my Father's house already there are many mansions, that not only I, but all mine also have a place and dwelling. If it were not so, then had I told you, that I would go to prepare the same for you. But now it is not needful; seeing they be prepared already, and wait for you. Whereas I now go away, and must be from you a little season, it is not that I would prepare mansions for you, for they are prepared already; but that I through my death may make the way for you into heaven, and open the street to the said dwelling.'

Now to the intent no man shall say, that we haply have a place in heaven, as men, but Christ hath not so a place; therefore doth the truth of God plainly express, that the place where Christ is is a place indeed. For he saith : " I will take you unto me ;" yea, not only unto me, but unto myself : for immediately upon the same doth he yet add it more plain, " that where I am, there you may be also."

Christ then, as a very true man, is in heaven, as in one place: wherefore it followeth, that we also shall be in heaven, as in one place certain. This the Truth saith: therefore must it needs be even so, and can be none otherwise.

The same also doth the human kind and nature require; "which God," as Augustine saith, "did endue with immortality, but took not away the nature and kind[1]."

The Seleucians' error.

The Seleuciani, or Hermiani, denied our Saviour Christ after the flesh to sit at the right hand of the Father[2]. But the true faithful believers have ever still confessed and taught, that the very true body or flesh of our Lord doth sit at the Father's right hand. For verily, if the body and flesh of our Lord have not his place given him, or if that be withdrawn from him, then is this the plain meaning, that our Lord had no true body.

For holy Augustine saith, and saith right: "Take all room and place from the bodies, that they have no place to be in, and they are no where; if they be no where, then are they nothing at all[3]." As for the place of Paul to the Philippians in the second chapter, it teacheth nothing at all, that with the exaltation and ascension of Christ any thing is withdrawn from the nature human, or that we ought to speak nothing more of it, or we should or might ascribe no name and place unto it; but like as with the words going before, which serve much to the matter, he thought to express the lowest humility of Christ, even so is it now his mind, with very honourable and high excellent words to set forth his glory.

[1 Carnis forma et substantia...cui profecto immortalitatem dedit, naturam non abstulit. August. Epistolæ. Ad Dardanum Epist. lvii. Opera, Tom. II. p. 56. M.   See above, p. 154, note 1.]

[2 The Seleuciani and Hermiani taught that the body of Christ ascended no farther than the sun, in which it was deposited, as we are informed by Augustine: Seleuciani vel Hermiani ab auctoribus Seleuco et Hermia...negant Salvatorem in carne sedere ad dextram Patris; sed ea se exuisse perhibent, eamque in sole posuisse, accipientes occasionem de Psalmo, ubi legitur, *In sole posuit tabernaculum suum.* De Hær. Opera, Tom. VI. p. 6. I. ed. 1541. See bishop Pearson on the Creed, Art. VI., who mentions that the same heresy was held by the Manichees, and also by Hermogenes.]

[3 Nam spatia locorum tolle corporibus, nusquam erunt; et quia nusquam erunt, nec erunt. August. Epist. lvii. ad Dardanum. Opera, Tom. II. p. 57. G. ed. 1541.]

Yea, he declareth himself in the words following, and saith: "In the name of Jesus shall all knees bow, both of things Phil. ii. that are in heaven, of things that are on the earth, and things that are under the earth."

And thus hath the Father exalted the name of Jesus The name of Christ is above all names. above all names, even in shewing and declaring that Jesus is the same, whom all they that are in heaven, upon earth, and under the earth, ought by right to know, worship, and fear, as Lord of all things and creatures; yea, and that all things should confess that Jesus is the Lord, to the praise of God the Father. For verily we must needs acknowledge that Jesus Christ is Lord, yea, Lord of all things, King, Defender, and Redeemer, of like power and honour with the Father: which thing extendeth not to the Father's derogation or dishonour, as the Arians foolishly thought, but to the greater Ariani. glory of the Father.

The Lord saith himself in the gospel: "The Father hath John v. committed all judgment unto the Son; because that all men should honour the Son even as they honour the Father. He that honoureth not the Son, the same honoureth not the Father which hath sent him." Moreover there he saith: "And now glorify thou me, O Father, with thine own self, John xvii. with the glory which I had with thee or ever the world was." From the beginning had he the honourable name of God, which is glorious and far excellent above all names.

Now through the incarnation, and by reason of the contemned and despised cross of Christ, the godly honour in Christ was thought to be somewhat darkened. But that did the Father restore and bring to glory, in that he raised up his Son from death, and took him up into heaven. And thus gave he him a name which is above all names; for so he declared that he is Lord of all things.

Holy Peter also, a fellow-helper of St Paul, in the second Acts ii. chapter of the Acts of the Apostles, did in like manner utter the same. For after he hath opened and declared the true resurrection of our Lord Jesus Christ from death, and his glorious ascension into heaven, he saith: "Lo, therefore let all the house of Israel know for a surety, that God hath made this same Jesus, whom ye have crucified, Lord and Christ." And to be short, Paul by the name of Christ that is above all names understood the blessed name of

God the Lord, which cannot be altered, and is above all names.

But seeing our Lord is a true man, like as he is also very God, both together, and hath with the glorification not put off the kind and nature of man, neither consumed it through the Godhead; therefore remaineth he still a true creature, that is, a very true man, and therefore may he also right well be named after the same nature, and hath likewise a place certain.

1 Cor. ii. Finally, as for the words of the apostle Paul, "The eye hath not seen, the ear hath not heard, neither have entered into the heart of man, the things which God hath prepared for them that love him;" these matters, I say, must not be referred to the place of those that are saved. For they are written of the unoutspeakable greatness of the joy, as the whole text of the words sufficiently doth declare.

Briefly, forasmuch as it is open and manifest to us, that the Lord Jesus Christ, after his nature that he took upon him, is a very true man in glory; it followeth that the true human body of Christ hath his own place: whereof I have hitherto spoken so much not without cause, namely, to the intent all godly persons may know that this is a place certain, prepared for them in heaven, and that they may constantly believe, that in heaven they have a brother, namely, the Lord Jesus Christ. Touching the fruit of the ascension of our Lord, I shall more largely speak of it afterward.

CHAPTER XI.

ANOTHER SIGNIFICATION OF SITTING AT THE RIGHT HAND OF GOD, BY WHICH MANNER OF SITTING CHRIST IS EVERY WHERE, SITTING THERE IN SUCH SORT AFTER HIS GOD-HEAD.

THUS come I again to the former part, what the right hand of God signifieth and is called. It is taken in the scripture for strength, protection, power, and for the incomprehensible honour or glory. And therefore it is written: "Thy right hand, Lord, is become glorious in power; thy right hand

Exod. xv.

also hath dashed the enemy." Item, in the Psalm: "Thou _{Psal. xviii.} hast given me the defence of thy salvation; thy right hand also shall hold me up." Moreover: "The right hand of the _{Psal. cxviii.} Lord hath the pre-eminence; the right hand of the Lord bringeth mighty things to pass." After this signification of the right hand soundeth the name, *to sit, to rule, to govern, to defend, to behave himself as a prince or regent diligently in his office, and faithfully to execute the same.* For in the third book of Kings saith David: "Solomon shall sit upon _{1 Kings i.} my seat, and shall reign after me." And so in the Psalm he saith: "The Lord said unto my Lord, Sit thou at my right _{Psal. cx.} hand, till I make thine enemies thy footstool." And Paul saith: "Christ must reign, till he hath put all his enemies _{1 Cor. xv.} under his feet." Item, in the prophet Zachary: "Behold _{Zech. vi.} the man, whose name is the Branch, and he that shall spring up after him shall build up the temple of the Lord; yea, even he shall build up the temple of the Lord, he shall bear the praise, he shall sit upon the Lord's throne, and have the domination; a priest shall he be also on his throne." This kind of speech is taken of the use and custom of kings and princes, which have their deputies, to whom they freely give all authority to rule and govern. Even so is Christ, in whom the Father will be honoured; and through his authority and power it is his pleasure to rule. He is taken up to the right hand of the Father, that is to say, to have the dominion or governance in heaven and in earth; and this commission is given him faithfully to execute, and to be Lord and Governor of all things.

Thus the right hand of God is infinite, neither may it be shut in; for God's might and power is incomprehensible. The kingdom of Christ also, which is everlasting, is a kingdom of all worlds; and so is he of one substance, of one power and honour, with the Father, not bound to one place, but is every where; who in all things ruleth and worketh, seeing he is not only a very true man, but also the very true God; after the manhood finite, but after his Godhead infinite and incomprehensible; and that in one undivided person he containeth very true God and man, King and Lord of all things. For St Peter saith: "Christ is at the right hand _{1 Pet. iii.} of God, gone up into heaven, angels, might, and power being subdued unto him." Item, Paul to the Ephesians: "God the

Father raised up Christ from the dead, and hath set him on his right hand in heavenly things, above all rule, power, might, and domination, and above all names that are named, not in this world only, but also in the world to come; and hath put all things under his feet, and hath made him above all things, and head of the congregation, which is his body, and the fulness of him that filleth all in all things." Thus much concerning the right hand of God, and concerning heaven, that is, the place certain or dwelling of the blessed; in the which also our Lord Jesus with his body hath his mansion and seat.

CHAPTER XII.

THE FRUIT AND COMMODITY OF THE CORPORAL ASCENSION OF CHRIST, BOTH IN THAT HE DOTH NOW FOR US, AND IN THAT WE LEARN BY IT.

AFTER this from henceforth will I speak of the fruit and profit of the corporal ascension of our Lord Jesus Christ, and of his seat and place at the right hand of his Father. Afore all things we must know, that our Lord ascended up with his very true body, that he, as mediator between God and man, being very God and man himself, and high priest in his own temple, might before his heavenly Father make intercession for us, and wholly take upon himself our necessities and griefs. For Paul saith to the Hebrews: " Christ is not entered into the holy places that are made with hands, which are similitudes of true things, but is entered into the new heaven, to appear now in the sight of God for us." Thereto also pertain other sentences and testimonies of John in his first epistle.

Item, of Paul to the Romans, wherein he saith: According to the same did our Lord ascend up bodily, that he with his flesh taken up into heaven might stay and direct upon the Holy Ghost all worshipping and God's service of those that are his. For no corporal worshipping doth from henceforth please him, but such as is done to his spiritual body.

Heb. ix.

1 John i. ii.

Rom. viii.

He saith in the gospel of John: "The poor have ye John xii.
Mark ·xiv.
alway with you, and when ye will, ye may do them good;
but me have ye not alway." Thereunto also serveth the
saying of Paul: "Although we have known Christ after the 2 Cor. v.
flesh, yet know we him so no more."

Moreover the Lord with his resurrection hath taught us,
that we also should lift up our minds unto heaven, seeking
no salvation at all upon earth, seeing that heaven is our right
native country. Therefore ought we to use the world as 1 Cor. vii.
though we used it not, and to direct all our care and thought
unto heavenly things. For Paul saith to the Colossians:
"Set your affection on things which are above, and not on Coloss. iii.
things which are on earth. For ye are dead, and your life
is hid with Christ in God." Item, to the Philippians: "Our Philip. iii.
dwelling is in heaven, from whence we look for the Saviour,
even Jesus Christ our Lord."

Christ also with his ascension into heaven thought to
declare unto us his power and might, wherein consisteth our
strength, our power, riches, triumph against sin, death, world,
devil, and hell.

For he ascending up on high led captivity captive, and Ephes. iv.
when he had spoiled the enemies, he gave gifts unto his
people, and endueth them yet daily with spiritual riches.
Therefore sitteth he now on high, to the intent that with
his own strength, which he daily bestoweth upon us, he may
regenerate us unto a spiritual life, and quicken us with his
holy Spirit, garnishing the church, that is to say, the faithful, with manifold gifts of thanks, defending them against
all evil, suppressing the terror of his enemies, but preserving
and saving us, as those that do truly honour and worship
him. For he, as having the victorious triumph, is the King,
Saviour, and head of all faithful believers.

Finally, also with his resurrection he hath prepared us a
place, and made the way and opened it into heaven. Thus
in heaven hath he placed the true man, that we might have
an assured true testimony, that our flesh also shall rise again,
and that the whole perfect man, the body and soul, shall be
carried into heaven. For the members shall be like unto
the head. Therefore as the cloud took up the very true
body of the Lord, yea, even the whole perfect man, Christ;
so shall all godly persons be taken up into the air to meet

1 Thess. iv.
the Lord, that they may live in Christ their Lord and head for evermore. For Paul saith: "The dead in Christ shall arise first. Then we which live and remain shall be caught up with them also in the clouds, to meet the Lord in the air, and so shall we ever be with the Lord." Item, to the Heb. x. Hebrews: "By the means of the blood of Jesu we have free entrance into the holy place, by the new and living way, which he hath prepared for us through the veil, that is to say, by his flesh." Unto this meaning agreeth very well the godly and excellent sentence of the old writer Tertullian, who in the book of *The resurrection of the flesh* saith thus: Tertullian. "Christ, which is called the arbiter and mediator between God and man, hath of the same that is set and committed unto him of both, reserved also unto himself the adding to of the flesh, for an earnest-penny of the whole sum. For like as he hath left us the pledge of the Spirit, even so contrariwise hath he received of us the earnest-penny of the flesh, and carried it up with him into heaven; a true evidence or pledge, that he will bring thither also the whole sum, body and soul[1]." For this great and high benefit, declared unto us by his own mercy without our deserving, be laud and praise, honour and thanks unto our King, our victorious triumpher, head, and Redeemer, even our Lord Jesus Christ, from henceforth, now, for evermore. Amen.

[1 Hic sequester Dei atque hominum appellatus, ex utriusque partis commisso deposito sibi, carnis quoque depositum servat in semetipso, arrhabonem summæ totius. Quemadmodum enim nobis arrhabonem Spiritus reliquit, ita et a nobis arrhabonem carnis accepit, et vexit in cœlum, pignus totius summæ illuc quandoque redigendæ. Tertull. De Resurr. Carn. cap. 51, p. 357. Ed. Rigalt. 1564.]

SECOND PART OF THIS BOOK,

ENTITLED

THE HOPE OF THE FAITHFUL,

ENTREATING OF OUR BODIES.

CHAPTER XIII.

OF THE TRUE RESURRECTION OF OUR FLESH.

Now cometh it to the point, that we must also speak of
the true raising up of our bodies, or resurrection of this our
flesh; for the same followeth out of the resurrection and
ascension of our Lord Jesus Christ. This word, *to rise up*,
as Tertullian *De resurrectione carnis* declareth, extendeth to
nothing more, than unto that which was fallen[2]. For nothing
can arise, save only it that fell. For when a thing was fallen
and standeth up again, we say, it is risen. Forasmuch as
this term, *to rise up*, hath a relation, St Paul useth the
word *Anistemi* (ἀνίστημι), which signifieth *to erect, to rise
up, to set up again,* and *to stand. Egeiromai ex hypnou*
(᾿Εγείρομαι ἐξ ὕπνου), *I arise up and awake from sleep.* The
Hebrews use the word *Kum* (קוּם), which signifieth not only
to rise up, but also *to endure, to continue,* and *to remain
upright.* For in the book of Joshua we read: "The children Josh. vii.
of Israel could not stand before their enemies," that is, they
might not endure and continue before them. Furthermore,
in the book of Genesis: "Every thing was destroyed, that Gen. vii.
remained (that is, whatsoever there was that stood upright,
or erected itself) upon the face of the earth." Thereof it
cometh, that to stand up, and to raise up, is called the immortality, or the everlasting and perpetual continuance of the

---

[2 De Resurr. Carn. cap. 18, p. 336; also Adv. Marcion. Lib. v.
cap. 9, p. 471.]

soul. As when the Lord saith in the Gospel of John: "I will raise him up at the last day." For if by the last day the hour of every man's death be understood, then doth the Lord raise up, that is, he preserveth, the soul in the state that it dieth not, neither perisheth in death. Now if by the last day be understood doomsday, then raiseth he up the body from the earth at the last day in the general judgment. Therefore the words, *to stand up, and rise up,* signify either the conservation of a thing which is, that it be not destroyed and perish, or else the restoring of a thing that was fallen to his right case and estate again.

CHAPTER XIV.

OUR FLESH OR BODY ITSELF SHALL RISE AGAIN, THOUGH IT BE HARD TO BELIEVE, AND WHAT THE FLESH OR BODY IS.

Now will we speak also of these terms, flesh and body, or corpse. We believe the resurrection of the body or flesh.

The scripture commonly calleth it the resurrection of the dead, to declare evidently, that the resurrection must not be referred to the soul nor to the spirit, but directly unto the body and to the flesh. Cyprianus, or Ruffinus, saith, that the church towards the west did express and acknowledge the article in the holy apostolical creed after this manner: "I believe the resurrection of the flesh:" and so they added thereunto manifestly this term, *the,* to the intent that no man should understand any other flesh, save only the same natural and essential flesh which we carry about[1]." So saith Augustine

[1 Satis provida et cauta adjectione fidem symboli ecclesia nostra docet, quæ in eo quod a ceteris traditur, *carnis resurrectionem,* uno addito pronomine tradit, *hujus carnis resurrectionem; hujus* sine dubio, quam is, qui profertur, signaculo crucis fronti imposito contingit; quo sciat unusquisque fidelium, carnem suam, si mundam servaverit a peccato, futuram esse vas honoris, utile Domino, ad omne opus bonum paratum; si vero contaminata fuerit in peccatis, futuram esse vas iræ ad interitum. Ruffin. Expos. in Symbol. Apostol. apud Cyprian. Edit. Fell.]

also in the book of the articles of the creed: "The same visible, which properly is called flesh, shall without doubt and assuredly rise up again[2]."

Methinketh that Paul the apostle minded to point unto 1 Cor. xv. the flesh, as with a finger; and therefore said: "This corruptible must put on incorruption." With the term, *this*, pointeth he, as with a finger, to our flesh.

Holy Jerome forceth and compelleth John, the bishop of Jerusalem, to confess and acknowledge the resurrection, not only of the body, but also of the flesh, and saith: "The flesh and the body are two things. Every flesh is a body, but every body is not flesh; namely, a wall is a body, but flesh it is not. For flesh is properly called a substance of *What the* blood, sinews, bones, and veins set together. As for a body, *body or* *corpse is* though the name thereof also be used for flesh, and most *called of the* *Latinists.* part for a substance that may be seen or handled; yet it betokeneth sometimes a subtle state, that can neither be handled nor seen, as namely the air[3]." But at all times it hath been a hard thing for man to believe, that bodies which are buried and resolved to corruption, should wholly, without imperfection or blemish, be brought again and restored. Therefore the Athenians, when they heard of the holy apostle the resurrection of the dead, they mocked and laughed his doctrine to scorn. For who would lightly credit, that the bodies which now are corrupt and returned to earth, or otherwise torn and devoured of wild beasts and fowls, yea, sometimes burnt and brought to ashes, or drowned with water, should perfectly be brought again, and wholly restored?

[2 Et ideo credimus et carnis resurrectionem, non tantum quia reparatur anima, quæ nunc propter carnales affectiones caro nostra nominatur; sed etiam hæc visibilis caro, quæ naturaliter est caro, cujus nomen anima non propter naturam, sed propter affectiones carnales accepit. Hæc ergo visibilis, quæ proprie caro dicitur, sine dubitatione credenda est resurgere. August. de Fid. et Symb. cap. 10. Opera, Tom. iii. p. 34. G. Ed. 1541.]

[3 Alia carnis, alia corporis definitio est: omnis enim caro corpus est, non omne corpus est caro. Caro est proprie, quæ sanguine, venis, ossibus, nervisque constringitur. Corpus, quanquam et caro dicatur, interdum tamen ætherium aut aereum nominatur, quod tactui visuique subjacet, et plerumque visibile est et tangibile. Hieron. Epist. xxxviii. ad Pammach. adversus errores Joannis Hierosolymitani. Opera, Tom. iv. p. 322. Ed. 1706.]

But God, willing to make that easy and light, which is hard unto us, hath in the resurrection of our Lord Jesus Christ set before our eyes an open, plain, and sure trial, declaration, or evidence of the true undoubted resurrection : whereunto, as to an ensample and sure strength of the resurrection, we ought to have respect, as much and as oft as we think upon it, and wonder how our bodies should rise again.

Therefore with so many testimonies and arguments have I declared afore, that Christ our Lord with his own body rose truly again from death. He carried up Elias also living, body and soul, into heaven, and many one raised he up from the dead; that we, concerning the resurrection of the dead, should have utterly no doubt at all. Finally, with plain and evident testimonies of the scripture hath he opened and shewed, as I now will declare : which testimonies and arguments truly do teach, that the flesh of men shall rise again from the dead, that is, that our bodies shall at the last day be truly raised up unto judgment. Holy Job saith thus in chapter xix. : "O that my words now were written! O that they were put into a book! would God they were graven with an iron pen in lead or in stone to continue! For I am sure that my Redeemer liveth; and that he shall stand over the dust, or earth, in the latter day; that I shall be clothed again with this skin, and see God in my flesh. Yea, I myself, or for myself, shall behold him, not another, but with these same eyes. My reins are consumed within me." Job's adversaries complained of him, as though he knew not God, and as though he set nothing by him. Upon this great slander and blasphemy, he answereth and declareth his faith, desiring that his belief were written in lead and in hard stone, that is, he wisheth his faith to be known to those that come after, which he also declareth with few words after this manner : 'I am of you complained upon and accused, as though I knew not God; now do I know right well in my heart, yea, I believe and am certified assuredly, that my Redeemer, or Avenger, liveth.' The holy Job useth an Hebrew word called *Goel*[1], which some have expounded a *Redeemer* : it signifieth a *rescuer*, and an *avenger;* such one as is more friend of ours, such as were they, to whom in the law of the Jews

The true resurrection of the flesh proved.

Antagonistai Job.

[1 גֹּאֵל]

it appertained to redeem the goods, and to rescue them; as we may learn further out of Ruth, and of the fourth book of Moses: and with the aforesaid name, *Goel,* hath Job set forth and specified the Messias, our Lord Jesus Christ; that he liveth, namely, that he is the true living God, the life and resurrection of men; and that he is also the rescuer and avenger, doubtless even the same that is our very near friend; namely, a very true man, such one as hath taken our own flesh and blood upon him, suffered death, and with his death hath made us living. Moreover he saith: "At the last shall he stand over the dust." For our Lord Jesus Christ, with his very true body, shall come at the last day to judge, and then shall he stand over the dust. This saying declareth evidently, that he will undertake and do somewhat, namely, that he shall put to his mighty hand, so order and bring to pass, that the dust shall come to life again. The dust calleth he here our flesh, and that according to the scripture; and with this doth he wonderful well express the truth of our flesh, namely, that our own very true flesh shall rise again. For he will certify us, that even the very same body, which at the first was made of dust, and now into dust is sown, and through the corruption is become dust again, yea, even that same very body, and none other, shall be raised up.

But to the intent that no man should draw or refer the dust to any other thing, than to the body of man, it followeth moreover in holy Job, that after they, namely, the Father, the Son, and the Holy Ghost, have with my skin (not with a strange, but with mine own skin) clothed the body, even mine own body which I now have, called dust, (and thereby understandeth he the flesh, the sinews and the bones;) then shall I see God in my flesh, that is, fully and perfectly shall I be restored and made whole again. For to see God is nothing else but to be partaker of eternal joy and salvation; and to see God in or from out of the flesh, is to be taken up corporally into everlasting joy. Besides this, he doth yet more evidently express the perfectness of the resurrection of the flesh, and saith: "Whom I for myself shall see," that is, to my commodity and salvation, mine eyes shall see him, even I myself shall see him, and none other for me. In the which words it is principally to be noted, that he saith, "I

Ruth iv.
Num. xxxv.

Gen. iii.

shall see him," yea, even I myself. Then, "mine eyes shall
see him." Finally, "I, and else none other." As he would
say, 'Even I that now have true flesh and bone, and look
now upon you with mine eyes, shall with the very same eyes
behold God also.' Therefore in the resurrection of the dead
we shall with the essential substance and nature be even the
same that we were before death, namely, we shall have our
members, as head, eyes, bones, belly, arms, legs, hands, feet,
&c. Now where this distinction is, there must be also cir-
cumscription, there must the same have compass and limits.

It followeth yet further in Job: "My reins," namely,
my desire and lust, "are wasted away, and consumed within
me," that is, within me, namely, in my heart, or ceased all
other desires, lusts, and pleasures, in comparison of this my
hope towards the resurrection; yea, in comparison thereof
they all are nothing, neither worthy to be esteemed: for
in the only resurrection resteth all my hope and delight.

Phil. iii. So said Paul also: "I have counted all things but loss, and
do judge them but dung, that I might win Christ, to know
him and the virtue of his resurrection." And therefore the
old translator of the book of Job hath evil interpreted these
words after the sense, "this hope is laid up in my heart[1]."

After all this, doth holy Job add hereunto that maketh
the understanding perfect, and concludeth his saying thus:
"Seeing I thus acknowledge and confess, why hold ye me
for ungodly? Why do ye persecute and vex me thus with
spiteful words of reproach and slander? Yet is the root
of the word found in me." And he calleth the root of the
word the right foundation and ground of godliness: as if
he would say: "Forasmuch as the true head article of
salvation is found in me." For like as the root giveth all
virtue and sap unto the tree, even so is the matter of the
resurrection of the dead through Christ the chiefest, greatest, and true principal point of the word and affairs of God.
"Repent therefore," saith Job: "for wrath humbleth, and

[1 The original is: בָּלוּ כִלְיֹתַי בְּחֵקִי ; of which the meaning is
expressed in the Latin Vulgate by, *reposita est hæc spes in sinu meo;*
adopting, as Rosenmuller has observed, a meaning of the word בָּלָה,
which is found in different passages, "*de vehementissimo desiderio, quo
quis consumitur quasi et deficit.*" Comp. Psalm lxxxiv. 3, cxix. 81, 82,
123, cxliii. 7.]

doth nothing right, but rather provoketh God unto vengeance."

The prophet Isaiah doth testify the resurrection after this manner : "Thy dead shall live, even with my body *Isai. xxvi.* shall they arise. Stand up and be glad, ye that rest, or dwell, in the dust; for the dew of the herbs is thy dew, and the ground of tyrants shalt thou cast down." "Thy dead, O God," saith the prophet, "shall live;" namely, the souls that for thy sake are slain, and that have worshipped thee. Nevertheless their bodies shall not prevent my body in the resurrection; but at the last judgment, or upon doomsday, shall they arise again with my body. Likewise saith also St Peter, that the souls of such as died aforetime do *1 Pet. iv.* live with God; but with the flesh they shall be judged as other men.

Therefore did the holy prophet Isaiah believe and confess the general resurrection of all bodies at the last day. In the which resurrection, he openly acknowledgeth, that his own body also shall rise again. Afterward bringeth he in an archangel, blowing the trumpet, and saying : "Stand up, and be glad, ye that rest in the dust." To rest in dust is *To rest in* nothing else but a description of man's body. For the souls *dust.* and spirits do not rest or lie in dust; but the bodies are buried therein, and are become dust. Therefore men, according to the substance and state thereof wherein they rise again, are called inhabiters, or indwellers of dust, or such as rest in dust. Then declareth he with a similitude, how our bodies, that putrefy and corrupt, shall, through the power of God, from death and corruption be safely raised up again.

The power of God, that chargeth and commandeth us to rise up from death, doth he compare to the dew, which, when it falleth down, quickeneth and reviveth the dead herbs. Likewise also doth the power of God to our dead bodies, which it quickeneth and raiseth up again. Contrary to this he setteth another sentence, saying : "The earth of tyrants, that is, the bodies of tyrants, shalt thou raise up, O God; but thou shalt cast them down," that is, thou shalt overthrow them into hell and eternal pain. Moreover, touching the true resurrection of our bodies, the vision of the prophet Ezekiel is so evident and plain, that it is not needful to speak *Ezek. xxxvii.* aught thereof.

And of this have we many testimonies and witnesses in the prophets, which might here well have served; but seeing it is not necessary, I have because of shortness omitted them, and now will I come to the sentences of the new Testament.

John v.

The Lord saith: " Verily, verily, I say unto you, the hour shall come, and now it is, that the dead shall hear the voice of the Son of God, and they that hear it shall live." And immediately after he saith: " The hour shall come, in the which all they that are in the graves shall hear his voice, and shall come forth." Now is it manifest, that neither the souls, nor spirits, but the bodies are in the graves; and if other bodies should rise up for ours, what needed he alway to make mention of the graves, but to the intent that he immediately in the gospel might declare the evident, plain, and undoubted resurrection of our bodies? He forthwith, by

John xi.

his mighty and wonderful power, raised up Lazarus from death, who now did stink, and had lain four days in the grave. This marvellous act had the Lord himself declared unto Martha with these words: " Thy brother shall rise again. Then answered she, I know that he shall rise in the resurrection at the last day." Lo, how common, manifest, and known unto every man was the general resurrection of our bodies. The Lord saith more unto Martha: " I am the resurrection and the life: he that believeth on me, though he were dead, yet shall he live; and every one that liveth and believeth on me, shall never die." But what needeth me to collect so many testimonies of the resurrection of the dead, considering that the apostles were upon no article more fervent and earnest than upon this? He that will allege all the sentences and witnesses, must write out almost the whole new Testament.

Acts iv.

Luke saith in the Acts of the Apostles: " With great power did the apostles bear witness of the resurrection of the Lord

Acts xxiii.

Jesus Christ." And in the same book saith Paul: " For the hope and resurrection of the dead am I judged." And

Acts xxviii.

yet again: " For the hope sake of Israel am I bound with this chain." In many places hath the holy apostle Paul brought forth evident ensamples and testimonies of our resurrection; concerning the which we shall speak in due time.

2 Cor. iv.

He saith moreover: " We which live are always delivered unto death for Jesus' sake, that the life of Jesus might ap-

pear in our mortal bodies." What could he have spoken
more evident and plain? For immediately upon the same he
saith : " Thus we have believed : therefore have we spoken;
and know, that he which raised up the Lord Jesus, shall
through Jesus raise us up also." Wherefore our true bodies,
which now are mortal, shall verily rise again ; howbeit after
the resurrection they shall no more be mortal, but immortal.

To these witnesses out of God's word, and therefore invincible, I will also add the testimony of one man, namely,
out of the fourth book of John Damascen *De orthodoxa fide*, Johannes
Cap. 28. " The resurrection," saith he, " shall be nothing Damascenus.
else but a true conjunction of soul and body, and another
laudable restitution of it that was fallen away, and brought
to nought. Therefore the same body that perisheth is dissolved and fallen asunder, and the very same riseth up again
indissoluble. For he that in the beginning created man out
of the dust of the earth, and then brought him again to earth
and dust, that he was taken of, the same, I say, is mighty
and of power, according to his word, to raise up the selfsame
man again from death[1]." Thus much Damascenus. And
truly every man now may well think, that God principally
for this cause did not create the first man of nought, as he
did other things, but out of the dust of the earth ; that as
concerning the resurrection of our bodies, though they turn
to dust and earth again, we should have no doubt. Now,
as I suppose, I have sufficiently and plainly declared, that the
true flesh of all men, yea, even our own body, and else none
for it, yea, even the human true body shall rise again from
death, namely, formed and fashioned with his own right proportion, measure, and property, as a true body ; so that the
measure and property of the true body, which now is divided
and parted in his members and joints, remaineth, that is, he
shall have true flesh, blood, bones, sinews, joints, members, &c.

[1 Ἀνάστασίς ἐστι πάντως, συνάφεια πάλιν ψυχῆς τε καὶ σώματος,
καὶ δευτέρα τοῦ διαλυθέντος καὶ πεσόντος ζώου στάσις. αὐτὸ οὖν τὸ σῶμα
τὸ φθειρόμενον καὶ διαλυόμενον, αὐτὸ ἀναστήσεται ἄφθαρτον· οὐκ ἀδυνατεῖ
γὰρ ὁ ἐν ἀρχῇ ἐκ τοῦ χοὸς τῆς γῆς αὐτὸ συστήσαμενος, πάλιν ἀναλυθὲν καὶ
ἀποστραφὲν εἰς τὴν γῆν, ἐξ ἧς ἐλήφθη, κατὰ τὴν τοῦ δημιουργοῦ ἀπόφασιν,
πάλιν ἀναστῆσαι αὐτό. Joann. Damasc. De Orthod. Fide, Lib. IV.
cap. 27. Opera, Tom. I. p. 321. Ed. 1712.]

CHAPTER XV.

THE MANNER HOW THE BODIES SHALL RISE AGAIN, AND THE KIND THAT THEY SHALL BE OF.

But to the intent that this may yet be more plainly understood, I will now tell how our bodies shall rise, and what nature and kind they shall be of in the resurrection. At the end of the world shall the Lord come with great majesty and judgment, and shall declare and shew himself in and with a right true essential body. Hither also too shall he be brought, and shall stand in the clouds of heaven, that all flesh may see him; yea, all men that are upon earth shall behold him, and know him by his glory. In the mean season also shall he send his archangel to blow the trump. Then shall all the dead hear, and perceive the voice and power of the Son of God. And so all men that died, from the first Adam, shall immediately arise out of the earth.

And all they that live until the last day shall, in the twinkling of an eye, be changed. And thus all men, every one in his own flesh, shall stand before the judgment-seat of our Lord Jesus Christ, and shall wait for the last judgment and sentence of the Lord; which sentence being given, quickly, and without delay, (he) shall call one part into heaven, and thrust out the other into hell.

This fashion and manner of the resurrection have not I imagined of myself, but written it all out of the evangelists Matth. xxiv. and scriptures of the holy apostles. For thus we read: "The power of heaven shall move in the last time, and then shall appear the sign of the Son of man in heaven; and then shall all the kindreds of the earth mourn, and they shall see the Son of man come in the clouds of heaven with power and great glory. And he shall send his angels with the great voice of a trumpet, and they shall gather together his chosen from the four winds, and from the one end of the world to Matth. xxv. the other," &c. Thereunto add that he spake in Matthew John v. and John. And Paul in the first to the Thessalonians saith: 1 Thess. iv. "This say we unto you in the word of the Lord; that we which live and are remaining in the coming of the Lord, shall not come before them which sleep. For the Lord himself shall descend from heaven with a shout, and the voice of the archangel, and trump of God : and the dead in Christ shall rise first. Then shall we that live and remain be caught up with them also in the clouds, to meet the Lord in the air ; and so shall we ever be with the Lord." Furthermore to the Corinthians saith Paul : "Behold, I shew 1 Cor. xv. you a mystery : we shall not all sleep, but we shall all be changed, and that in a moment, in the twinkling of an eye, at the time of the last trump. For the trump shall blow, and the dead shall rise incorruptible, and we shall be changed. For this corruptible must put on incorruption, and this mortal must put on immortality." This is now the manner of the resurrection of our bodies, and in what nature and kind they shall rise again. But in the resurrection they shall, through the power of God, be made immortal and incorruptible. For the apostle saith expressly : "The dead shall rise again." After that he saith : "This corruptible and mortal must put on incorruption and immortality." In the which words the term "*this*" pointeth directly, as with a finger, to our living and human body.

And so Job said : "Even I myself shall see him, and Job xix. none other." Wherefore our bodies, after they be risen again from death, shall remain even in their own right state and substance, as afore. Yea, even the very same men shall keep still this nature and kind, as they did afore ; saving that they which aforetime were subject to frailty shall from thenceforth be pure, clean, perfect, immortal, of a sincere and purified nature, subject and obedient unto the spirit.

Such bodies raised from death did the old writers call What a glorified, purified, or glorious bodies ; and that according to body is. the doctrine of the holy apostles. Albeit there were some which abused that word, and therefore made the verity of the bodies void and of none effect, beginning to dispute of glorified bodies, as of the pure substance and estate of a spirit. Whereof we shall speak shortly, if God will.

CHAPTER XVI.

THAT PAUL SPAKE RIGHTLY OF A GLORIFIED BODY, AND WHAT A GLORIFIED BODY IS, AND WHAT A NATURAL.

BUT now will I declare, that Paul did rightly and well use this word glorious, or glorified body, even as it is truly in itself. For to the Philippians he saith: " Our dwelling is in heaven: from whence we look for the Saviour, even Jesus Christ the Lord; which shall change our vile earthy body, that it may be fashioned like unto his own glorious body, according to the working whereby he is able to subdue all things unto himself." In this sentence thou hast that term, *glorified body;* thou hast also of what nature and kind the glorified body shall be, namely, whole, and as the body of Christ that rose again from death. And thus shall it not be a body utterly made void or brought to nothing, or altogether turned into a spirit, and therefore having no room and place, incomprehensible and invisible; but it shall be an upright, very true human body, as it is sufficiently declared afore, where I spake of the true resurrection of the Lord. In the which place we understand, that when the Lord's disciples thought they had seen a spirit, when they saw the Lord, he said unto them: "A spirit hath not flesh and bones, as ye see me have. Handle me and see; for it is even I myself." The Lord also after his resurrection set before them some fashion or evidence of his glorification, namely, when he was transfigured before them; and at the time remained the right essential substance of the body; but in form and fashion it was altered, in that it became glorious. So standeth it plainly, "he was transfigured," and not that he was made void or brought to nothing, or altered into another substance. Thus saith Paul also: "He shall change our body," &c. Wherefore even the right true substance of the glorified body shall remain still. As for the change or alteration, it shall be in the infirmities that happen unto us; so that when the body taketh upon it the glorification and immortality, they shall be wholly removed and fall away.

Phil. iii.

Luke xxiv.

Phil. iii.

Howbeit this shall be more evident and plain to under-stand, if it be thoroughly and with diligence considered and declared, what this word *glory* or *glorification* meaneth.

For transfiguration, glory, and glorification, is one thing. So saith holy Augustine[1] in his book against the Arians: "To bring to glory, to make glorious, and to glorify, are three words, yet is it but one thing. The Greeks call it δοξάζειν, *doxazein;* but the translators in Latin have other-wise interpreted it." Thus much saith Augustine. But glory in scripture is taken for light, brightness, and shine, as St Paul speaketh to the Corinthians: "If the ministration that through the letter killeth, and was graven in stone, hath glory, so that the children of Israel could not behold the face of Moses for the glory of his countenance," &c. And hereunto serveth this sentence of Daniel the wise: "Such as have taught others shall shine as the brightness of heaven, and they that have instructed multitudes, or many, unto god-liness, shall be as the stars world without end." Much after the same wise doth the Lord himself also use it, saying: "Then shall the righteous shine as the sun in the kingdom of their Father."

Wherefore the glorified bodies shall be clear, bright, and shining bodies, even as the body of Christ was in his trans-figuration upon the mount of Thabor; of whom it is specified in the gospel, that "his face was as bright as the sun, and his clothes did shine as the light." After the resurrection did the Lord shew unto his disciples his palpable and visible, that is, his very true substantial body: but the brightness and shine he reserved, to teach and instruct the weak here beneath. Like as also after the resurrection he did eat and drink, not that he needed any such thing, but that he so would declare and prove the true resurrection of his body. The glorification also is set directly against the low estate and dishonour, as Paul evidently declareth, saying: "He shall change our vile body, that he may make it like unto his own glorious and glorified body." This word *humility,* *low estate,* or *dishonour,* comprehendeth all that is called

Contra Aria.
cap. 31.

2 Cor. iii.

Dan. xii.

Matth. xiii.

Matth. xvii.

[1 Glorificare, et honorificare, et clarificare, tria quidem verba, sed res una est, quod Græce dicitur δοξάζειν: interpretum autem varietate, aliter atque aliter positum est in Latino. August. Contr. Serm. Arian. cap. 31. Opera, Tom. vi. p. 146, E. Ed. 1541.]

earthy, frail, miserable, and mortal. For by means of our sins we are brought low and into misery; so that we must needs feel and suffer sickness, hunger, thirst, cold, heat, pain, vexation, manifold lusts and affections, fear, wrath, heaviness, and such like things innumerable, yea, and death also at the last.

Again, glorification comprehendeth deliverance, that is, the laying away and clear discharge of all these miseries and sorrows. So that now glorification is called (and so it is in very deed) pureness, perfect strength, immortality, and joy; yea, a sure, quiet, and everlasting life. For Paul saith: "We that are in this tabernacle sigh and are grieved; because we would not be unclothed, but we would be clothed upon, that mortality might be swallowed up of life." And to the Romans he saith thus: "I suppose that the afflictions of this life are not worthy of the glory which shall be shewed upon us. For the fervent desire of the creature abideth waiting for the appearing of the children of God."

2 Cor. v.

[Rom. viii.]

In all these words it is sufficiently declared, what glorification meaneth, and what is understood by it; namely, a freedom or discharge from this frail servitude and bondage, and a deliverance into the glorious and comfortable liberty of God's children. By the which freedom we are delivered from all sickness and frailty, and from all thraldom of weakness, that is, from all that which bringeth sickness, heaviness, and frailty. From all such are we free discharged and delivered, having now the perfect fruition of God, and made of like shape unto his Son Jesus Christ, as holy St John declareth. Hereunto serveth it well that Paul saith: "When this corruptible hath put on incorruption, and this mortal hath put on immortality, then shall be brought to pass the saying that is written, Death is swallowed up in the victory."

1 John iii.

1 Cor. xv.

Therefore the glorified body, after the signification of glory, shall be a purified body, which is purged and cleansed from all frailty and vileness, and now is clothed upon and apparelled with cleanness, pureness, joy, and rest, and finally, with the glory of eternal life. That this is now the kind and nature of the glorified body, the holy apostle Paul more largely and more perfectly declareth with these words: "It is sown in corruption, and riseth in incorruption; it is sown in dishonour, and riseth in glory; it is sown in weakness, and

riseth in power; it is sown a natural body, and riseth a spiritual body." Item, what he meaneth by the natural and
by the spiritual body, he declareth immediately upon the
same, and saith further: "If there be a natural body, there A natural
is also a spiritual body, as it is written: The first man Adam body.
is made into a natural life, and the last man Adam into a
spiritual life. Yet is not the spiritual body the first, but
the natural; and afterward the spiritual. The first man is
of the earth earthy, the second man is the Lord from heaven.
As is the earthy, such are they that are earthy; and as is
the heavenly, such are they that be heavenly. And as we
have borne the image of the earthy, so shall we bear also
the image of the heavenly." This the holy apostle declareth
yet more evidently, and saith: "By one man came death, 1 Cor. xv.
and by one man cometh the resurrection of the dead. For
like as in Adam they all die, so in Christ shall they all
revive." Thus Paul calleth *animale corpus* the soulish body, Animale et
which is interpreted, *the natural body*, the same that hath corpus.
his virtue, strength, power, and life of the soul; which body
we have of Adam; and it is earthy, frail, and mortal. The
spiritual body he calleth not it that is become or made a
spirit: but therefore nameth he the glorified body a spiritual
body, because it liveth of the Spirit of Christ; which spiritual
body, that is, incorruptible, indissoluble, and immortal, we
have received of Christ our Lord. Of all this is sufficiently
spoken in our expositions of the epistles of St Paul[1].

CHAPTER XVII.

THE CASE OF OUR MEMBERS IN THE BODY'S RESURRECTION, AND OF THEIR FUNCTIONS.

But here might some man say: If our very true bodies,
with their members, shall be in heaven, then it follows, that
the use and exercise of the members shall be in heaven also.

[1 The author alludes to the translation of Erasmus's paraphrase
of the epistles of St Paul, part of which was made by Bishop
Coverdale.]

To this I give like answer as now is said, namely, that we shall have even those members and this body, which we now carry; but seeing that through the glorification they shall be made heavenly, they shall not need earthy exercise, neither shall they use any frail thing at all. Hereof cometh it that

1 Cor. xv.

Paul saith: "Flesh and blood may not possess the kingdom of God, neither may corruption inherit incorruption." By flesh and blood he meaneth, not the true essential body, but bodily frail lusts and temptations, which he now calleth the earthy and frail body. Such temptations and lusts, saith he, shall not be in the glorified bodies, neither shall there any frail bodies be in heaven. For he saith immediately upon the same: "Corruption shall not inherit incorruption;" for in the kingdom of God there shall be no corruption nor frailty. For the heavenly joy is far of another kind and nature, than that it can receive or suffer such vile and unclean lusts and temptations, yea, such a stained and defiled flesh. For before the bodies of men come in heaven, they must be wholly and perfectly altered, that is, cleansed and purified from all filthiness and frailty.

Thus did our Saviour teach also, when he answered to

Matth. xxii.

the question of the Sadducees, who denied the resurrection of the dead. Upon which I have written much in the gospel of Matthew. Holy Augustine saith also: "This doth sore

Augustine, de fide et symbolo, cap. 6.

hinder the ethnics and heretics, that we believe that the earthy body is taken up into heaven; for they think, that into heaven can come no earthy thing. But they know not our scripture, neither understand how it is spoken of Paul: 'It is sown a natural body, and shall rise a spiritual body.' For this is not spoken, to the intent as though the body should become a spirit, or be changed into a spirit. For even now also our body, which is called natural, or soulish, and is natural indeed, is not changed into the soul, and become the soul. But therefore is the body called a spiritual body, that it may so be prepared to dwell in heaven. Which thing cometh to pass, when all feebleness and earthy blemish is changed into a heavenly pureness and stedfastness[1]." All these are the words of holy Augustine.

[1 Solet autem quosdam offendere vel impios gentiles vel hæreticos, quod credamus assumptum terrenum corpus in cœlum. At gentiles plerumque philosophorum argumentis nobiscum agere solent,

CHAPTER XVIII.

THE DIVERS ERRORS THAT SPRUNG ABOUT THE ARTICLE OF THE BODY'S RESURRECTION.

HITHERTO have I told what the scripture of the prophets and apostles doth hold and testify concerning the resurrection of the dead, and of our body, that is to say, of our own true flesh; namely, that our true flesh and body shall rise from death, and be glorified in the resurrection; and that the glorification doth not therefore take away the verity of the body, or make it nothing, but doth translate and bring it into a more upright and better state; so that nevertheless the true essential substance of the body remaineth still. Upon this now, to the commodity of the reader, and for a more evident declaration and understanding of the aforesaid words, I will shew what errors sprung up concerning the resurrection of the dead; that any good faithful Christian may the better avoid the same. That there have been many which denied the resurrection of our bodies, and had it utterly in derision, all histories declare. In the which register the philosophers for the most part are reckoned and esteemed; the Hymeneus and Philetus, of whom Paul maketh mention. In like manner are there many recited of Irenæus, Tertullian, Eusebius, Epiphanius, Philastrius, and Augustine; namely these, the Simonians[2], Valentinians[3], Marcionites[4],

Errors touching the resurrection of the flesh.

Philosoph.

2 Tim. ii.

ut dicant, terrenum aliquid in cœlo esse non posse: nostras enim scripturas non noverunt, nec sciunt quomodo dictum sit, Seminatur corpus animale, surget corpus spiritale. Non enim dictum est, quasi corpus vertatur in spiritum et spiritus fiat: quia et nunc corpus nostrum, quod animale dicitur, non in animam versum est et anima factum. Sed spiritale corpus intelligitur, quia ita coaptandum est, ut cœlesti habitationi conveniat, omni fragilitate ac labe terrena in cœlestem puritatem et stabilitatem mutata ac conversa. August. de Fid. et Symb. cap. 6. Opera, Vol. III. p. 33. E. Ed. 1541.]

[2 Simonians. August. De Hæres. Opera, Tom. VI. p. 3. K.]

[3 Valentinians. Id. Ibid. p. 4. C. Tertull. De Præscript. Hæret. cap. 33.]

[4 Marcionites. Tertull. De Præscript. Hæret. Ib.]

Cerdonians[1], Carpocratians[2], Caines[3], Archontici[4], Generians[5], Hierarchics[6], Seleucians[7], Apellysts[8], and Manichees[9]. Among the Greeks also and Latinists there were excellent men, that turned themselves to the golden and yet earthy Jerusalem, promising much, I know not what, of a kingdom of the world to come after the resurrection, ascribing unto us such bodies as, being partakers of the kingdom, should also behold with these earthy desires[10]. To these there is found yet the third part, which as touching the substance and state of the glorified bodies so said and taught, that they utterly took away and overthrew the bodily nature, and gave unto it no more nor other thing than a spirit. Against the second sort speaketh holy Jerome, that forasmuch as they were carnal, they have also loved only the flesh. Against the third speaketh the said Jerome, that they, being unthankful for the benefits of God, would not have and bear the flesh, wherein Christ yet was born and rose again. Whereupon he giveth very godly counsel, that we tarry in the mean

[1 Cerdonians. Tertull. De Præscript. Hæret. cap. 51. August. De Hæres. Opera, Tom. vi. p. 4. F.]

[2 Carpocratians. Tertull. De Præscript. Hæret. cap. 48. August. De Hæres. Ib. p. 4. B.]

[3 Caines. August. De Hæres. Ib. p. 4. E.]

[4 Archontici. Id. Ibid. p. 4. F.]

[5 Generians. The nature of their opinions does not appear.]

[6 Hierarchics. August. De Hæres. Ib. p. 6. C.]

[7 Seleucians. Id. Ibid. p. 6. I.]

[8 Apellysts. Tertull. De Præscript. Hæret. cap. 33.]

[9 Manichees. August. Contr. Faustum Manich. Lib. iv. cap. 2. Lib. v. cap. 10. Opera, Tom. vi.]

[10 Cerinthus appears to have been the leader and chief of the persons, who held these opinions concerning the earthly Jerusalem, as we learn from the fragments of Caius, (Euseb. Hist. Eccles. Lib. iii. cap. 28, and Caii Fragmenta apud Routh, Rel. Sacr. Vol. ii. p. 6, and the notes on this passage,) who thus explains the opinions propounded by Cerinthus, on the ground of a pretended divine revelation: μετὰ τὴν ἀνάστασιν ἐπίγειον εἶναι τὸ βασίλειον τοῦ Χριστοῦ, καὶ πάλιν ἐπιθυμίαις καὶ ἡδοναῖς ἐν Ἱερουσαλὴμ τὴν σάρκα πολιτευομένην δουλέυειν. Compare also Gennadius De ecclesiasticis dogmatibus, cap. 55. A learned account of the opinions of the ancients and moderns concerning the Millenium may be found in Mosheim De rebus Christianorum ante Constantinum Magnum, pp. 720—728; in Whitby, Treatise on the true Millenium; and in Mede's works, passim.]

way, namely, that we esteem and make the glorified bodies
no more spiritual, than the perfectness, property, and truth
of the bodies may permit and suffer : contrariwise, that we
make them not altogether so carnal and unghostly, that it
might be thought how that natural and frail bodies shall
be in the glory[11]. Old writers say also, that Origen did
not perfectly confess the resurrection of the flesh, but that
in the resurrection he fantasied and imagined such a body,
as hath little difference from a spirit. And therefore in
Definitionibus Ecclesiasticis there is a chapter against the
said Origen, in manner following : " If that which falleth do
stand up again, then shall our flesh truly rise again : for
the same falleth in very deed, and shall not come to nothing,
as Origen's opinion was, that there should be made a sifting
and change of the bodies, namely, that there should be given
us a new body for the flesh ; but even the same frail flesh
that falleth of the just, and vanisheth, shall with our feebleness rise again, that because of sin it may suffer pain, or
else, according to his deserts, continue in eternal honour
and glory[12]."

Defin. Eccles.
cap. 6.

[11 Jerome speaks strongly against these opinions in different parts
of his writings, and especially in those against Origen and John
bishop of Jerusalem. The allusion in the text appears to be to a
passage in his letter *Ad Pammachium et Oceanum de erroribus Origenis*,
Epist. LXV. where to the heretics who denied the resurrection of the
body, and who asked, Quid nobis prodest resurrectio, si fragile corpus resurget, et futuri angelorum similes habebimus et naturam? he
answers : Dedignantur videlicet cum carne et ossibus resurgere, cum
quibus resurrexit et Christus. In another letter (Epist. XXXVIII.)
against the errors of John bishop of Jerusalem, he writes : Hæc est
vera resurrectionis confessio, quæ sic gloriam carni tribuit, ut non
auferat veritatem. See below, Chap. XX. p. 190.]

[12 The work here referred to is a work of Gennadius, which has
been improperly ascribed to Augustine, entitled, *Liber de definitionibus
orthodoxæ fidei, sive ecclesiasticis dogmatibus*: Si id resurgere dicitur
quod cadit, caro ergo nostra in veritate resurgit, sicut in veritate
cadit. Et non secundum Origenem immutatio corporum erit, id est,
aliud novum corpus pro carne : sed eadem caro corruptibilis, quæ
cadit, tam justorum quam injustorum, incorruptibilis resurget, quæ
vel pœnam sufferre possit pro peccatis, vel in gloria æterna manere
pro meritis. August. Op. Tom. III. p. 45. D. Cave, Hist. Literaria.
Vol. I. p. 376. Ed. 1688.]

CHAPTER XIX.

THE ERRORS OF ORIGEN CONCERNING THE RESURRECTION CONFUTED BY JEROME.

BUT forasmuch as I have once recited Origen's opinion touching the resurrection of the body, and somewhat recited the errors of some that denied the resurrection, declaring the scornful opinion of those whom they call Chiliasts[1]; I will shew now more largely what holy Jerome held of the resurrection of the dead, and how he confessed the true upright belief. He speaketh to Pammachius concerning the errors of John bishop of Jerusalem, and in the same writing he comprehendeth the doctrine and opinion of Origen concerning the resurrection in manner following. Origen saith, that " in the church there be sprung up two errors, the one from us, the other from the heretics; namely, that we, as the simple and lovers of the flesh, say, that even these bones, this blood, and this flesh, that is, that our face, members, and all the proportions of the body, and the whole body itself, shall rise again at the last day, so that we shall also go with the feet, work with the hands, see with the eyes, and hear with the ears." " This," saith he, " we speak as simple, homely, gross, and ignorant people. But the heretics, as Marcion, Apelles, Valentinus[2], and mad Manes, deny wholly and utterly the resurrection of the flesh, or body, giving salvation only unto the soul; and saying, that our words are nothing, when we affirm that, according to the ensample and pattern of our Lord Jesus Christ, we shall rise again; saying, that the Lord himself rose in a fantasy, or spirit, and that not only his resurrection, but also his birth came to pass more in the imagination, than in very truth;

Hierome ad Pamma-chium.

[1 With respect to the heretics, who denied the resurrection of the body, see Irenæus adv. Hær. Lib. v. cap. 2, p. 395. col. 2, and Dr Grabe's note ad loc. Ed. Oxf. 1702.]

[2 Compare Tertullian, *De Carne Christi*, cap. 1, and *passim;* also his treatise *De Resurrectione Carnis:* and for the opinions of the Manichees, August. Contra Faustum Manicheum, Lib. IV. Opera, Tom. VI. p. 48. K. Ed. 1541, and his works, *passim.*]

that is, that he was not born in very deed, but supposed to be born."

"Now for the opinion and mind of both these parties," Origen saith, "it pleased him not; namely, that he abhorreth the flesh on our side, and the fantasy on the heretics' part; for each of them doth too much : and namely they of our side, for that they would be again the same they were afore; and for the other, that they utterly deny the resurrection of the bodies[3]."

And after certain words doth Jerome set forth Origen's opinion, what he held of the resurrection, and saith : "There is promised us another body, namely, a spiritual and heavenly, that cannot be comprehended nor seen with eyes, nor having any weight, and that, according to the circumstance and diversity of the place that it shall be in, shall be changed[4]." And after certain words doth Jerome set forth the opinion of Origen yet more plainly, saying : "O ye simple, the resurrection of our Lord Jesus Christ ought not to deceive you, in that he shewed his hands and feet, stood on the sea shore, went over the field with Cleophas, and said he had flesh and bones.   This body, that was not born of the seed of man, and of lust or pleasure of the flesh, is endued with greater

[3 Dicit ergo Origenes...duplicem errorem versari in ecclesia, nostrorum et hæreticorum.   Nos simplices et philosarcas dicere, quod eadem ossa et sanguis et caro, id est, vultus et membra totiusque compago corporis, resurgat in novissima die; scilicet ut pedibus ambulemus, operemur manibus, videamus oculis, auribus audiamus... Hæc nos innocentes et rusticos asserit dicere.   Hæreticos vero, in quorum parte sunt Marcion, Apelles, Valentinus, Manes, nomen insaniæ, penitus et carnis et corporis resurrectionem negare, et salutem tantum tribuere animæ.   Frustraque nos dicere ad similitudinem Domini resurrecturos, quum ipse quoque Dominus in phantasmate resurrexerit; et non solum resurrectio ejus, sed et ipsa nativitas τῷ δοκεῖν, id est, putative visa magis sit, quam fuerit.   Sibi autem displicere utramque sententiam, fugere se et nostrorum et hæreticorum phantasmata; quia utraque pars in contrarium nimia sit; aliis idem volentibus se esse quod fuerunt; aliis resurrectionem corporis omnino denegantibus.   Hieron. Epist. xxxviii. ad Pammach. adv. errores Joannis Hierosol. Opera, Tom. iv. Pars 2, p. 320. Edit. Paris. 1693—1706.]

[4 Aliud nobis spirituale et ætherium promittitur, quod nec tactui subjacet, nec oculis cernitur, nec pondere prægravatur, et pro locorum, in quibus futurum est, varietate mutabitur.   Ib. pp. 321, 322.]

freedom than another body, and with his nature is not unlike the spiritual and heavenly body. For when the doors were shut he entered, and in breaking of bread vanished he away from their sight[1]," &c. But at the last, Jerome answereth unto Origen's foundation, and saith: "Like as he shewed his true hands and his true sides, so did he truly eat with them, went truly with Cleophas, spake to them truly with his mouth, sat truly at the table with them at supper, took the bread with his true hands, gave thanks, brake it, and reached it them. And whereas he immediately vanished out of their sight, that is ascribed to the power of God, and to no fantasy, or false body. When he afore his resurrection was brought out from Nazareth, that they might throw him down from the top of the hill, he passed through the midst of them, that is, he escaped out of their hands. May we then talk with Marcion, that his birth was therefore but a fantasy, because that he against nature escaped those that had him? How sayest thou? did they not know him in the way, when he yet had the body that he had afore? Upon this hear the scripture: 'Their eyes were holden, that they should not know him.' But was he any other when they knew him not, or was he any other when they knew him? Verily he was always one and like himself. And therefore to know, and not to know, is given to the eyes, and not to him that is seen, although it be ascribed unto him also, that he held their eyes, lest they should know him[2]."

[1 Nec vos, O simplices, resurrectio Domini decipiat, quod latus et manus monstraverit, in litore steterit, in itinere cum Cleopha ambulaverit, et carnes et ossa habere se dixerit. Illud corpus aliis pollet privilegiis, quod de viri semine et carnis voluptate non natum est. Comedit post resurrectionem suam et bibit, et vestitus apparuit, tangendum se præbuit; ut dubitantibus apostolis fidem faceret resurrectionis. Sed tamen non dissimulat naturam aerei corporis et spiritualis. Clausis enim ingreditur ostiis, et in fractione panis ex oculis evanescit. Ib. p. 322.]

[2 Quomodo veras manus et verum ostendit latus; ita vere comedit cum apostolis et discipulis; vere ambulavit cum Cleopha; vere lingua locutus est cum hominibus; vero accubitu discubuit in cœna; veris manibus accepit panem, benedixit ac fregit, et porrigebat illis. Quod autem ab oculis repente evanuit, virtus Dei est, non umbræ et phantasmatis. Alioquin et ante resurrectionem, quum eduxissent eum

Afterward with many words giveth he answer to that, that the Lord entered when the doors were shut[3]. Yet doth he briefly answer thereunto in his commentaries on the last chapter of Isaiah, and saith : " I marvel that some after Christ's ascension will give and measure him a body made of the air, and soon returned to air again, because the Lord by the power of his majesty came in to the apostles, when the doors were shut ; considering that afore his resurrection also he went upon the water of the sea, permitting the same unto holy Peter, who at the first through faith walked upon the water, but afterward when he, being faint in faith, began to sink and go under, he said unto him, ' O thou of little faith, why hast thou doubted[4] ? ' " Thus much wrote Jerome against Origen, and many other more yet in this book written to Pammachius against John bishop of Jerusalem, which, because of greatness and length, I have omitted to put here in writing.

de Nazareth, ut præcipitarent de supercilio montis, transivit per medios, id est, elapsus est de manibus eorum. Numquid juxta Marcionem dicere possumus, quod ideo nativitas ejus in phantasmate fuerit, quia contra naturam qui tenebatur elapsus est?...Et quomodo, inquies, non cognoscebant eum in itinere, si ipsum habebat corpus quod ante habuit? Audi scripturam dicentem: *Oculi eorum tenebantur, ne eum agnoscerent.* Et rursum: *Aperti sunt oculi eorum*, inquit, *et cognoverunt eum.* Numquid alius fuit quando non agnoscebatur, et alius quando agnitus est? Certe unus atque idem erat. Cognoscere ergo et non cognoscere oculorum fuit, non ejus qui videbatur, licet et ipsius fuerit : oculos enim tenebat eorum, ne se cognoscerent. Ib. p. 328.]

[3 Ib. p. 329.]

[4 Miror quosdam aereum corpus, et paulatim in auras tenues dissolvendum, post resurrectionem introducere ; quia Dominus potentia sua clausis ingressus est januis. Qui certe et ante resurrectionem pendulo super mare ambulavit incessu, et hoc ipsum apostolo præbuit Petro; ut qui fide ambulavit, infidelitate postea mergeretur, cui dictum est : *Quare dubitasti, modicæ fidei?* Hieron. Comment. Lib. xviii. in Isai. Proph. cap. 66. Op. Tom. iii. p. 514. Ed. Paris. 1693—1706.]

CHAPTER XX.

SAINT JEROME'S OPINION OF THE RESURRECTION OF THE FLESH.

YET in the same book hath the said Jerome set his own opinion touching the resurrection of the flesh, directing the oration unto Bishop John, and saying: "If you will now confess the resurrection of the flesh after the truth, and not after fantasy, as thou sayest, then look that unto the words which thou hast spoken to content the simple, that even in the body, wherein we die and are buried, we shall rise again, thou add these words also, and say, *Seeing the spirit hath not flesh and bones, as ye see me have:* and forasmuch as it was so distinctly spoken unto Thomas, *Put thy finger in my hands, and thy hand in my side, and be not faithless, but believing;* therefore say thou, that we also after the resurrection shall have even the same members that we daily use, yea, the very same flesh, blood, and bone; the works whereof the holy scripture condemneth and rejecteth, and not their nature. And this is the right and true acknowledging of the resurrection; which so giveth honour unto the flesh, that therewith it minisheth nothing the verity of the flesh[1]."

Afterward speaketh he yet more evidently: "I will freely confess, though ye wry your mouths at it, scratch your head, and scrape with your feet, yea, and though ye should stone me to death forthwith, yet will I manifestly and plainly acknow-

[1 Vis resurrectionem carnis veritate et non putative, ut loqueris, confiteri? Post illa, quibus audientium blanditus es auribus, quod in ipsis corporibus, in quibus mortui sumus et sepulti, resurgamus; hoc potius adjunge, et dic, *Quoniam spiritus carnem et ossa non habet, sicut me videtis habere;* et proprie ad Thomam: *Infer digitum tuum in manus meas, et manum tuam in latus meum, et noli esse incredulus, sed fidelis.* Sic et nos post resurrectionem eadem habebimus membra, quibus nunc utimur, easdem carnes, et sanguinem, et ossa; quorum in scripturis sanctis opera, non natura damnatur....Hæc est vera resurrectionis confessio, quæ sic gloriam carni tribuit, ut non auferat veritatem. Hieron. Epist. XXXVIII. ad Pammach. adv. errores Joannis Hierosol. Opera, Tom. IV. p. 323. Ed. 1693—1706.]

ledge and confess the faith of the church or congregation of God; and boldly pronounce, that the right, profound, christian truth of the resurrection can utterly not be understood without flesh, bones, blood, and members. Where flesh, bones, blood, and members are, there must needs be a difference of kind, as of man and woman; and where these both are distinct the one from the other, there John must be John, and Mary must be Mary. But thou needest not be astonished at the matter, as though a wedding also were there to be kept in all the past, seeing that before they died they lived without the work of their kind, that is, without the act of marriage."

"It is promised us, that we shall be like unto the angels, that is, partakers of the salvation, in the which salvation the angels are without flesh and distinction of kind; and yet it is given unto us in our flesh and kind. Thus believeth my simplicity, and understandeth, that the kind must be understood, howbeit without the works of the kind; yea, that men must rise again, and so become like unto the angels of God."

"Neither ought the resurrection of members forthwith therefore to be esteemed unprofitable and superfluous, because they shall not do their office, but stand idle. For while we are yet in this life, we endeavour ourselves not to perform the works of our members. As for the comparison towards the angels, it is not a changing of men into angels, but it is an increasing of the immortality and glory[2]."

Thus much have I spoken of the confessions of holy Jerome.

[2 Ego libere dicam, et quamquam torqueatis ora, trahatis capillum, applaudatis pede, Judæorum lapides requiratis, fidem ecclesiæ apertissime confitebor. Resurrectionis veritas sine carne et ossibus, sine sanguine et membris, intelligi non potest. Ubi caro et ossa et sanguis et membra sunt, ibi necesse est ut sexus diversitas sit. Ubi sexus diversitas est, ibi Joannes Joannes, et Maria Maria. Noli timere eorum nuptias, qui etiam ante mortem in sexu suo sine sexus opere vixerunt....Angelorum nobis similitudo promittitur; id est, beatitudo illa, in qua sine carne et sexu sunt angeli, nobis in carne et sexu nostro donabitur. Mea rusticitas sic credit, et sic intelligit sexum confiteri sine sexuum operibus; homines resurgere, et sic eos angelis adæquari. Nec statim superflua videbitur membrorum resurrectio, quæ caritura sint officio suo; quum adhuc in hac vita positi, nitamur opera non

CHAPTER XXI.

SAINT AUGUSTINE'S MIND OF THE RESURRECTION OF THE FLESH.

TOUCHING the resurrection of our flesh, not only did holy Jerome believe thus, who yet testifieth that he acknowledgeth and confesseth the universal christian faith; but also St Austin wholly agreeth unto St Jerome, and namely, Lib. II. Retractat. cap. 3. For in repeating and correcting certain points out of the thirty-second chapter in the book *De Agone Christiano*[1], he saith: "I said it shall not be flesh and blood, but an heavenly body. This ought no man to understand, that therefore there shall be no true substance of the flesh; but with the names of flesh and blood must the infirmity of the flesh and blood be understood[2]." Item, Lib. I. Retractat. cap. 17, in repeating and correcting certain points which he had written long afore in the book [Cap. 10.] *De fide et symbolo*: "In the time of the angelical change," saith he, "it shall not be flesh and blood, but only a body, &c." This I spake of the changing of earthy bodies into heavenly, &c. But if one would understand it so, that the earthy body which we now have should so in the resurrection be altered and changed, that these members and the substance of this flesh shall not remain, no doubt he is not in the right way, but ought better to be instructed, considering that he

implere membrorum. Similitudo autem ad angelos non hominum in angelos demutatio, sed profectus immortalitatis et gloriæ est. Ib. p. 325.]

[1 Opera, Tom. III. p. 175. E. Ed. 1541.]

[2 In quo illud quod positum est,—"Nec eos audiamus qui carnis resurrectionem futuram negant, et commemorant quod ait apostolus Paulus, Caro et sanguis regnum Dei non possidebunt, non intelligentes quod ipse dicit Apostolus, Oportet corruptibile hoc induere incorruptionem, et mortale hoc induere immortalitatem: cum enim hoc factum fuerit, jam non erit caro et sanguis, sed cœleste corpus," —non sic accipiendum est, quasi carnis non sit futura substantia, sed carnis et sanguinis nomine ipsam corruptionem carnis et sanguinis intelligendus est apostolus nuncupasse, quæ utique in regno illo non erit, ubi caro incorruptibilis erit. August. Retractat. Lib. II. cap. 3. Opera, Tom. I. p. 10. D.]

is warned and monished through the body of our Lord,
which after the resurrection appeared even with the same
members, not only that he might be seen with eyes, but
handled also and touched with hands. Besides this he
testifieth, that he hath true flesh upon him, when he saith,
'Handle me, and see: for a spirit hath not flesh and bones
as ye see me have.' Therefore it is evident and plain, that
the holy apostle Paul denied not, that the true substance
of the flesh should be in the kingdom of God; but rather
with these words, *flesh* and *blood*, he understood, that either
men which live after the flesh should not have the inheritance
of heaven, else that there should be in heaven no infirmity
of the flesh at all. This is a grievous matter for unbelievers,
and hardly are they persuaded to believe the resurrection;
but most diligently, and after my power, have I treated
thereof in the last book *De Civitate Dei*[3]."

Yet handleth he of the resurrection not only in the last
book, but also in the thirteenth book *De Civitate Dei* he De Civitate
writeth thus: "The christian faith doubteth verily nothing Dei, Lib.
at all to confess of our Saviour, that also after the resur- XIII. cap. 22
rection, though now in the spiritual flesh, yet also in his et 23.
true flesh he did eat and drink with his disciples. Hereof
are they called also spiritual bodies; not that they therefore
cease to be bodies, but that through the spirit which giveth

[3 In hoc libro (scil. de Fide et Symbolo) cum de resurrectione
carnis ageretur, "Resurget," inquam, "corpus"...Quod cui videtur in-
credibile, qualis sit nunc caro attendit; qualis autem tunc futura sit
non considerat, quia illo tempore mutationis angelicæ non jam caro
erit et sanguis, sed tantum corpus...Sed quisquis ea sic accipit, ut
existimet ita corpus terrenum, quale nunc habemus, in corpus cœleste
resurrectione mutari, ut nec membra ista nec carnis sit futura substantia; proculdubio corrigendus est, commonitus de corpore Domini,
qui post resurrectionem in eisdem membris, non solum conspiciendus
oculis, verum etiam manibus tangendus (al. tractandus) apparuit.
Carnemque se habere etiam sermone firmavit, dicens: Palpate, et
videte; quia spiritus carnem et ossa non habet, sicut me videtis
habere.   Unde constat apostolum non carnis substantiam negasse in
Dei regno futuram; sed aut homines, qui secundum carnem vivunt,
carnis et sanguinis nomine nuncupasse, aut ipsam corruptionem, quæ
tunc utique nulla erit.....De qua re ad persuadendum infidelibus
difficili, diligenter quantum potui me disseruisse reperiet, quisquis *De
Civitate Dei* librum legerit novissimum. August. Retractat. Lib. I.
cap. 17, Tom. I. p. 6. I.]

And the same
is again, Re-
tractat. Lib.
I. cap. 13. life they shall be preserved and remain[1]." "For like as
these our bodies which have a living soul, and yet be not
named a spirit that giveth life, but natural or soulless bodies,
and therefore are not souls, but bodies; so shall the glorified
bodies be called spiritual. Yet God forbid we should therefore believe that they shall be spirits; but bodies shall they
be, which shall have the substance of the flesh. And forasmuch as they are preserved and made alive through the
spirit, they shall suffer no grief or infirmity. Then shall
not man be earthy, but heavenly; not that the body which
is made of the earth shall no more continue the same body,
but that through the heavenly gift and grace he shall be so
from henceforth, that being such a kind and nature as cannot perish, and altered from all infirmities, he shall be able
to dwell commodiously in heaven[2]."

Furthermore saith St Austin in the twenty-second book,
the thirtieth chapter: "How the bodies there shall move,
I dare not rashly define; for I cannot comprehend it, it
passeth my understanding. Yet shall their moving and state,
even as also their proportion, be altogether beautiful; and
howsoever it shall be, it shall be in the place where nothing
can be but that which is beautiful and holy; yea, where the
spirit will, there straight shall the body be also. Neither will
the spirit any thing, that is not very seemly and comely both
for him and it[3]." Thus have I hitherto recited St Augustine's
belief, to conclude this matter of the resurrection.

[1 Fides Christiana de ipso Salvatore non dubitat, quod etiam post
resurrectionem jam quidem in spiritali carne, sed tamen vera, cibum
ac potum cum discipulis sumpsit. Non enim potestas, sed egestas
edendi talibus corporibus auferetur. Unde et spiritalia erunt; non
quia corpora esse desistent, sed quia spiritu vivificante subsistent.
August. de Civ. Dei. Lib. XIII. cap. 22. Opera, Tom. v. p. 112. L.]

[2 Nam sicut ista, quæ habent animam viventem, nondum spiritum
vivificantem, animalia dicuntur corpora, nec tamen animæ sunt, sed
corpora: ita illa spiritalia vocantur corpora. Absit tamen ut spiritus
ea credamus futura, sed corpora carnis habitura substantiam, sed nullam tarditatem corruptionemque carnalem spiritu vivificante passura.
Tunc jam non terrenus, sed cœlestis homo erit; non quia corpus, quod
de terra factum est, non ipsum erit, sed quia dono cœlesti jam tale
erit, ut etiam cœlo incolendo, non amissa natura, sed mutata qualitate
conveniat. Ib. cap. 23. p. 113. A.]

[3 Qui motus illic talium corporum sint futuri, temere definire

CHAPTER XXII.

WHAT AURELIUS PRUDENTIUS THOUGHT OF THE SAME.

I WILL hereunto add the verses of the excellent and christian man, Aurelius Prudentius, which do wonderfully express unto us the resurrection of our flesh, and set it before our eyes:

My body in Christ
  Shall rise again:
I speak it earnest;
  For it is plain.

Why wouldst thou then
  I should despair,
O flesh, when I
  Do see so far?

The way that Jesus
  Christ my Lord,
Went after his death,
  As saith his word;

This is the ground
  And foundation,
My heart believeth
  With confession:

That I am sure,
  And know certain,
My body shall rise
  Wholly again.

Not one be less
  Than was before,
Neither in greatness
  Any more:

With strength and shape,
  As it lived here,
Afore they it
  To grave did bear.

There is no tooth,
  Nor nail so small,
No ear so little,
  But though it fall,

Yet perish it shall
  Not finally,
But out of grave
  Rise certainly.

God which afore,
  Created me,
With shape and strength
  Undoubtedly,

Wherewith I here
  On earth should live,
No feeble nor weak
  Thing me shall give.

For where any thing
  Shall perish at all,
It is old, feeble—
  So do not then call

non audeo, quod excogitare non valeo. Tamen et motus et status, sicut ipsa species, decens erit, quicumque erit, ubi quod non decebit non erit. Certe ubi volet spiritus, ibi protinus erit corpus; nec volet aliquid spiritus, quod nec spiritum possit decere nec corpus. Ibid. Lib. XXII. cap. 30. Opera, Tom. v. p. 217. K.]

Our bodies at
the resurrec-
tion shall not
be feeble nor
weak.

Of our bodies
   The renovation.
Therefore is this
   My expectation;

What sickness, pain,
   And adversity,
What death, in this,
   Vale of misery,

Out of this world
   Now taketh away,
Shall, when I rise
   At the last day,

From death to life
   Anew certain
Be given me all
   Together again.

Forseeing that death
   Is overcome,
It ever beseemeth
   Us all and some,

Quietly to trust
   With stedfastness,
Our God will keep
   With us promise;

Lest when we come
   Into the grave,
A man no hope
   Then after have;

When he to life
   Cometh eternal,
That he for his
   Body mortal,

Which here so full
   Of faultes was,
As brittle and frail
   As any glass,

Shall have a body
   Of perfectness,
That cold can not
   Nor hunger press;

Though weakness be
   At all season
The strength of death
   And operation.

Thereby in us
   What is consumed,
When it again
   Shall be restored;

Then through the power
   Whereby we rise,
We go to the Father
   In perfect wise.

This should right well
   Content our heart;
Therefore my body
   Regardeth no smart.

In Christ my trust
   Is constantly,
Who promiseth us
   Assuredly,

To raise us up
   From earth at last:
Therefore be thou
   Nothing aghast,

For sickness nor
   Adversity;
Nor yet let thou
   The grave fear thee.

Let this ever
   Thy comfort be,
That Christ prepareth
   The way for thee;

Wherein himself
Is gone before :
Follow thou, and live
For evermore[1].

CHAPTER XXIII.

THE BODIES OF UNBELIEVERS SHALL VERILY RISE AGAIN.

But to the intent that no man doubt touching the
resurrection of the flesh of the unbelievers, I will bring forth
certain testimonies of holy scripture, which do manifestly
declare that the unbelievers, or ungodly, shall with their
own true bodies rise again. The prophet Isaiah, in the last
chapter of his book, saith: "They shall go forth and look Isai. lxvi.
upon the bodies of them that have vilely behaved themselves
against me : for their worms shall not die, neither shall their
fire be quenched, and all flesh shall abhor them." With

[1 Nosco meum in Christo corpus consurgere : quid me
    Desperare jubes? veniam quibus ille revenit
    Calcata de morte viis. Quod credimus hoc est.
    Et totus veniam, nec enim minor aut alius quam
    Nunc sum, restituar: vultus, vigor, et color idem
    Qui modo vivit, erit; nec me vel dente vel ungue
    Fraudatum removet patefacti fossa sepulchri.
    Qui jubet ut redeam, non reddet debile quicquam;
    Nam si debilitas redit, instauratio non est.
    Quod casus rapuit, quod morbus, quod dolor hausit,
    Quod truncavit edax senium, populante veterno,
    Omne revertenti reparata in membra redibit.
    Debet enim mors victa fidem, ne fraude sepulchri
    Reddat curtum aliquid; quamvis jam curta voraris
    Corpora, debilitas tamen et violentia morbi
    Virtus mortis erat, reddet quod particulatim
    Sorbuerat quocunque modo, ne mortuus omnis
    Non redeat, si quid pleno de corpore desit.
    Pellite corde metum, mea membra, et credite vosmet
    Cum Christo reditura Deo; nam vos gerit ille
    Et secum revocat: morbos ridete minaces,
    Inflictos casus contemnite, tetra sepulchra
    Despuite; ersurgens quo Christus provocat, ite.
    Aurel. Prudent. Apotheosis. De resurrectione carnis humanæ.
Opera, p. 38. Ed. Paris. 1687.]

this sentence doth tho prophet play, after the manner and custom of those that have soon gotten the victory; which with great desire, after the battle is won, get them out of the city into the field, to view and look upon the bodies of such as are slain, and how fortunately they have fought. Forasmuch now as Christ also hath fought prosperously, overcome his enemies on dooms-day, and made them his footstool, the faithful shall go out to see the bodies of the ungodly.   The prophet doth for this cause call them bodies, even to declare, that the bodies raised up from death shall be very true flesh.   He continueth further also in the recited sentence, and saith, " Their worms shall not die :" for the bodies, or corpses, are full of worms, neither are they aught but worm's meat.

All this is spoken after the custom and property of man, and weakness of this time; and herewith is described unto us, and set before our eyes, eternal punishment, and how it shall go in the life to come.

Dan. xii.   In Daniel we read thus : " Many of them that sleep in the dust of the earth shall awake, some to everlasting life, some to perpetual shame and reproof."   The whole multitude of bodies, saith he, that are become dust, yea, all flesh shall through the power of God rise again, but not in like case and sort : for the good shall arise to eternal life, the evil to everlasting death.

John v.   After this manner spake the Lord also : " Verily, verily, I say unto you, the hour cometh, in the which all they that are in the graves shall hear his voice, and shall come forth ; they that have done good to life, and they that have done evil to death."   Who is so ignorant but he perceiveth, that to sleep in the earth, as the prophet Daniel said, and to be in the graves, as Christ said, is one manner of speech, and of like effect?   Now forasmuch as they that are in the dust of the earth, and in the graves, come forth and rise again, and only the bodies are in the graves wherein they corrupt ; it followeth that men's true bodies, not only of the good, but also of the evil, shall truly rise again.   And the same doth the Lord yet declare more evidently, Matth. x. : " Fear not ye them that kill the body, and are not able to kill the soul ; but rather fear him, which may destroy soul and body into hell."   Not only the souls, but also the bodies of unbelievers doth the Lord destroy. Out of the which it followeth, that they shall rise again: for if they should not rise again, they could not be tormented and plagued. Neither shall any other body rise again to pain and punishment, but even the same that with his vile works hath deserved the plague.

And hereunto serveth also the description of the last judgment, Matth. xxv. And St Paul saith, 2 Cor. v. "We must all appear before the judgment-seat of Christ, that every one may receive in his body according as he hath done, whether it be good or bad." See how manifestly and expressly the holy apostle testifieth, that the body shall rise again.

In the same terrible judgment of God, saith he, must every one take his body to him again. And why must he take the body upon him again? Even to the intent, that when any one hath received his body again, he may likewise receive the reward that he by and with his living body hath deserved. Now hath the body something to do with godliness and ungodliness, with virtue and vice: for the body is an instrument or vessel, wherewith somewhat is done, and therefore in the last judgment of God the body, according to the divine righteousness, shall not be omitted, neither forgotten at all. For if it have been obedient and subject unto the Spirit, if it have suffered much trouble for the name of Jesus Christ, if it hath been an earnest follower of righteousness, then shall it be worthy also to be glorified. Again, if it hath been given over to worldly voluptuous pleasures, or transitory things of this world, then with the soul that wrought with it shall it justly go to eternal damnation. Therefore the unbelievers shall truly rise again in their own flesh; yea, even in the same, which they here in this time have fed and pampered with all voluptuous pleasure and excess. And like as they in this time have with their body taken their own pleasure, joy, and delight; so in the life to come they shall be plagued and punished with everlasting pain and torment in the same body.

For St Paul witnesseth further in the Acts of the Apostles, and saith: "I worship the God of my fathers, believing Acts xxiv. all things which are written in the law and the prophets, and have hope towards God, that the same resurrection of the dead, which they themselves look for, shall bo of the just and unjust.

De Fide
ad Petrum,
cap. v.

Therefore holy Augustine, in the book *De fide ad Petrum Diaconum*, said well and christianly, according to the nature of the apostle's doctrine: "The unrighteous shall have a common resurrection of the flesh with the righteous; but the grace of the change, or glorification, they shall not have. For frailty and misery shall not be taken away from the bodies of the ungodly, neither the shame and reproach, sickness and feebleness, in the which they are sown; which therefore through death are not extinct and taken away, that they may belong to eternal death, pain, and punishment, everlastingly to be plagued, body and soul, with continual torment that never ceaseth[1]." These are Augustine's words. And after like

John v.

sort did the Lord also say in the gospel: "They that have done evil shall rise to the resurrection of judgment, or damnation." As if he would say, The ungodly that with their bodies shall rise again, shall rise with such property and proportion of their body, that their bodies may suffer the pain and torment, namely that they, now being made everlasting, may not be wasted and consumed away through any pain or trouble, how great and horrible soever it be. And so the bodies of the ungodly that rise again from death, shall after the said manner be altered and changed. For the bodies, that might afore through pain or trouble be broken and consumed, are now altogether as iron, yea, such as cannot be broken, and yet painful and passible; so that from henceforth the more they be tormented, the harder they become, and through God's vengeance more unapt to be destroyed, and yet made the more able to suffer misery.

[1 Habebunt ergo iniqui cum justis resurrectionem carnis communem; immutationis tamen gratiam non habebunt, quæ dabitur justis. Quoniam a corporibus impiorum non auferetur corruptio, et ignobilitas, et infirmitas in quibus seminantur; quæ ob mortem non extinguentur, ut illud juge tormentum corpori atque animæ sit mortis æternæ supplicium. August. de Fide ad Petrum Diac. cap. 3. Opera, Tom. III. p. 51. B. Ed. 1541.—This is not a genuine work of Augustine: it belongs to Fulgentius. See Cave, Hist. Lit. Vol. I. p. 385.]

THIRD PART OF THIS BOOK,

ENTITLED

THE HOPE OF THE FAITHFUL,

TOUCHING THE DAMNED'S PERDITION AND THE BLESSED'S SALVATION.

CHAPTER XXIV.

THE DEATH AND DAMNATION OF THE UNGODLY.

Now seeing the onset is given and the oration come so far, I must also speak somewhat of the eternal death and damnation of the unbelievers, that this matter may be wholly, uprightly, and perfectly brought to an end. I will therefore briefly declare, that the death and damnation of the unbelievers and ungodly is enjoined unto them of God. Item, that the souls are passible. Moreover, where the scripture declareth the place of damnation to be, and after what sort damnation shall torment the unbelievers. Finally, I will declare, whether the punishment of the ungodly be everlasting, or whether it shall cease at length.

Holy scripture doth oft and many times make mention of the death of the soul; which yet concerneth not the substance, but the state thereof. For holy Augustine in his book *De Fide et Symbolo* speaketh thereof very well and christianly: "Like as the soul," saith he, "by reason of vices and wicked manners is frail, so may it also be called mortal. For the death of the soul is to fall from God, and not to keep itself unto God: which is also the first sin committed in paradise, as it is contained in holy scripture[2]." Moreover the soul dieth, when it is verily

The death of the soul.

De Fide et Symbolo. cap. 10.

[2 Potest enim et anima, sicut corruptibilis propter morum vitia, ita etiam mortalis dici. Mors quippe animæ est apostatare a Deo, quod primum ejus peccatum in paradiso sacris literis continetur. August. de Fide et Symb. cap. 10. Opera, Tom. III. p. 34. H.]

spoiled of eternal life, and cast into everlasting sorrow, trouble, and misery; and therefore saith Augustine further: "The soul also hath her death, namely, when it lacketh and is destitute of the eternal and godly life, which truly and justly is called the life of the soul: but undeadly or immortal is it called, because it never ceaseth to live, how miserable soever the life of it be. What bodily death is, every man knoweth well; but eternal death, when a man dieth the second time, is this, when the flesh riseth again, and so is placed in everlasting torment. For after the last sentence or judgment of God the whole man, and not the half, shall be either saved or damned[1]." The eternal death

Rev. ii. 20.   also hath St John in his Revelation called the second death. This is appointed because of sin, and is not a resting or ceasing, but a continual pain. This death is called also damnation, that is, a judgment; because the ungodly is adjudged unto pain, and for that there is appointed him a torment, sorrow, and trouble that never ceaseth, and that, as touching the greatness thereof, can never be expressed with tongue.

CHAPTER XXV.

THAT THERE IS AN ETERNAL DEATH AND DAMNATION, AND THAT THE SOUL IS PASSIBLE.

Now that there is an eternal damnation, the truth and righteousness of God testifieth. For how could God be righteous, if he had no punishment wherewith to torment and plague the vicious and wicked? Therefore out of doubt an eternal death and damnation there is, though the ungodly do mock and laugh it to scorn, and pause not upon it.

The godly sacred bible, which is an assured witness of
Rom. vi.   the truth, saith evidently: "Death is the stipend, or reward of sin." And, "By one man came sin into the world,
Rom. vii.   and by sin death." Item, "Through the sin of one man is the evil fallen by inheritance, and come upon all men unto

[1 The substance of this passage is found in De Civ. Dei: Lib. XIII. cap. 2. Opera, Tom. v. p. 108. C—E.]

damnation:" for in the book of Genesis God saith: "In Gen. iii. what day soever thou eatest of this tree, thou shalt die the death." Now did he eat thereof, and therefore he also died, and was even condemned, appointed, and adjudged unto eternal death. The Lord saith also in the Gospel: "If ye believe not that it is I, ye shall die in your sins." John viii. Item, "He that believeth not is condemned already." Such John iii. like testimonies are found in holy scripture innumerable; out of the which we finally conclude, that death and damnation is enjoined, appointed, and adjudged of God unto all unbelievers and ungodly.

But forasmuch as there be some which think, that seeing the soul is a spirit, it cannot, neither may suffer, yea, that it is not subdued unto any passion at all; therefore against such curious teachers I will set now the soul of the gorgeous rich man in the Gospel, which expressly and plainly saith: "O send Lazarus, that he may dip the tip of his finger in water, and cool my tongue: for I am tormented in this flame." Lo, the rich man's soul is tormented in the fire. Hereon now it followeth, that the souls are passible, and subject to suffer. And though this be shewed us of the Lord as a parable, yet it is done for this intent, even to describe and to declare unto us the state and case of the souls that are separated from the bodies. And how pain and punishment is appointed unto the souls, it is found expressed, not only in the similitudes, but also in the holy Gospel of Matthew. The truth itself saith: "Fear ye him rather, which may destroy soul and [Matt. x.] body into hell." What the mouth of God speaketh must needs be true: yea, a shameful and strange thing were it for any man henceforth to doubt in this, that with so evident testimonies is witnessed. We ought rather to beware, that with our vicious life we deserve not to learn and feel by experience the righteous judgment of God, concerning the which we now doubt and demand so foolishly, as though there shall be nothing of it. Now what I have spoken of the souls already departed from the body, must be understood also of the bodies which come again to the souls in the resurrection.

CHAPTER XXVI.

THE BODIES OF THE UNBELIEVERS BEING RAISED ARE PASSIBLE.

FOR that the bodies, which come again to the souls, and are raised up, are passible, it may well be understood and perceived by that which is treated of already.

St Augustine, Lib. xxi. *De Civitate Dei*, cap. 4[1]. sheweth by many natural examples and evidences, that living bodies may well remain and continue in the fire. But touching the place of the punishment, or where the souls with their bodies shall be tormented, the scripture saith simply and plainly, that the unbelievers go down into hell. Hereof is it easy to perceive, that hell is under us in the earth: notwithstanding to go about to describe, to shew and compare precisely the place and the room where it lieth, and to print it, becometh not us verily, but is a foolish presumption. The testimonies of the scripture are simple and plain. For the prophet David saith: "Let death fall suddenly upon them, and let them go down quick into hell; for wickedness is in their houses and privy chambers." Item, "With all their substance went they down quick into hell, and the earth covered them, and they perished from out of the congregation." Hereunto serveth also right well the destruction of Sodom, and that which the prophet Ezekiel declareth, namely, that all cruel people are gone down and descended into hell; as the Elamites, which are the Persians, Edomites, and others: and therefore concludeth he farther, that even Pharao the king of Egypt, seeing that he also is a tyrant, must be thrust down into hell, and be gathered unto other uncircumcised, that is to say, unbelievers.

Item, in Luke is the hell placed beneath, downwards: for thus is it written in the evangelist: "Between us and you there is a great space set; so that they which would go down from hence to you cannot." The holy apostle Peter, speaking of the angels that fell, saith evidently, that they are cast down into hell, kept, and bound with the

Psalm lv.

Numb. xvi.

Gen. xix.

Ezek. xxxii.

Luke xvi.

2 Peter ii.

[1 August. Opera, Tom. iv. p. 198. B. G. Ed. 1541.]

chains of darkness for ever. Isaiah also speaketh of hell, and saith: "The Lord hath set hell in the deep, and Isai. xxx. made it wide." As for the manner, fashion, and measure of the damnation, and how great the torment of hell is upon unbelievers, I suppose no tongue is able to express the terrible and hugesome pain and punishment thereof; for Virgil the old poet, though he were an heathen man, yet Virgilius. when he had recited divers and sundry vices, and what punishment is ordained for them of God, he said, in the sixth book of his Æneid :

> An hundred tongues,
>   And mouths as many
> Although I had,
>   With eloquence high ;
> And though my voice
>   All iron were
> In strength ; yet could
>   I not declare
> The vices of men,
>   Nor yet can tell,
> What pains therefore
>   They suffer in hell[2].

CHAPTER XXVII.

THE PAINS OF HELL AND THE MATTER FOR THE CONTINUANCE
OF THE TORMENTS, WITH THE SPACE OF THE PLACE, AND
KINDS OF PUNISHMENTS.

YEA, though the holy scripture itself cannot with sufficient words express the pains of hell and punishment of the damned, yet doth it partly describe the same with outward and corporal things; giving us occasion thereby to consider far greater things, and, so to say, out of the small

[2 Virgil Æneid. Lib. VI. 624—626:
  Non, mihi si linguæ centum sint, oraque centum,
  Ferrea vox, omnes scelerum comprendere formas,
  Omnia pœnarum percurrere nomina possim.]

to ponder and weigh the greater. As when it calleth the
pains of hell the outward darkness, that is, most terrible
sorrow and trouble; calling the pain also weeping and
gnashing of teeth. Item, cold, and continual fire, that never
quencheth, and the perpetual gnawing worm; as every one
that hath read the gospel is well informed. The prophet
Ezek. xxxii. Ezekiel saith, that in hell there is a great multitude of
graves; and so by a figurative and borrowed speech he
declareth the horror, mourning, weeping, and lamentation of
the damned. The Greeks in their language named hell of
darkness, cold, trembling, and quaking. For Hades cometh
of *a* and εἴδειν, that is, *of not seeing;* or *Tartarus,* of the
ταράττω. word *tartarizein,* that is, *to shudder for cold,* or of *taratto,*
that is, *to be in heaviness, put in fear,* or *out of quiet.* But
for the opening of this matter we will take the testimonies of
Matth. xiii. the scripture in hand again. The Lord saith : " At the end
of the world shall the Son of man send forth his angels, and
they shall gather out of his kingdom all things that offend,
and them which do iniquity, and shall cast them into the
fiery oven; there shall be wailing and gnashing of teeth."
Matth. xxii. And even the said words doth the Lord use again in the
Isai. xxx. same evangelist. Item, Isaiah saith : " For he from the
beginning hath prepared Tophet, that is, hell, even for
kings; and hath made it deep and wide. The mansions
or chambers thereof are of fire and exceeding much wood,
which the breath of the Lord, as a river of brimstone, doth
kindle." The place of the prophet have I partly declared
in the exposition of the fifth chapter of Matthew, and here
will I now partly expound it.

The prophet truly with these words declareth an assured,
and a very wide and broad place of hell, when he saith :
" He hath made it deep and wide." Hereof then it followeth,
that hell is in the depth, and that the place itself is an horrible depth ; for that whoso doth once sink down into it,
shall come no more thereout : neither needeth any man to
think that the place is not great and wide enough ; for
touching wideness, it shall be able enough to hold all
damned persons. " For the wideness and greatness thereof,"
saith the prophet, " is exceeding horrible." The terrible
pain and torment, wherewith the ungodly are punished, hath
the prophet described with these words, and said : " The

mansions and chambers thereof are of fire." As if he would say: "The pain of hell is greater than can be expressed; for the fire noteth an unoutspeakable trouble." As for stuff to be tormented withal, it shall never lack, neither shall the pain have ever any end. Therefore saith he, that "there is much wood." It followeth moreover, that the Lord's breath, which is as a river of brimstone, doth kindle, and as a bellows blow the fire, quickening it, and ever renewing it to burn evermore. Therefore we ought not to think that that fire is kept in by natural causes; for by the power of God is it kindled and kept in. The same prophet saith also: "They shall go forth, and look upon the bodies or corses of [Isai. lxvi.] them that have vilely behaved themselves against me; for their worms shall not die, neither shall their fire be quenched, and all flesh shall abhor them." And unto these words hath the Lord respect, when he saith in the Gospel of Mark: "Better is it for thee to go halt or lame into life, than [Mark ix.] having two feet to be cast into hell, into the fire that never shall be quenched; where their worm never dieth, and their fire never goeth out."

Herein therefore consisteth the punishment and damnation, that the ungodly, which here upon earth would not know God and receive the light of the gospel, shall be cast out from the face of God, wherein only yet is the fulness and perfectness of all joy; and then shall they be shut up in the great thick and perpetual darkness. For the Judge commandeth them to depart from him, and to go into the eternal pain and damnation. Yea, the ungodly shall go into themselves, and shall know the equity of the Judge; and therefore fret and gnaw their own heart with sighing, with unspeakable pain, great sorrow, and trouble. This is called, and so it is indeed, the gnawing worm that in the hearts of the ungodly never dieth. For St Paul saith plainly, that "at the righteous judgment of God the consciences of all [Rom. ii.] men shall bear witness, and that the thoughts in themselves shall either accuse or excuse them." The same St Paul also, speaking of the judgment of God, saith: "Praise, honour, and immortality shall be given unto them that continue in good doing, and seek eternal life: but unto them that are rebellious, disobeying the truth, and follow iniquity, shall come indignation and wrath, trouble and anguish."

Besides all this shall the ungodly be in the fellowship of most foul spirits, with whom they had their lust in this life. There shall all be full of confusion, loathsome and great torment, and so shall all burn together for eternity. For thus shall the Judge give sentence with plain and express words: "Depart from me, ye cursed, into everlasting fire, which is prepared for the devil and his angels." The prophet Daniel saith also: "The wicked shall rise to perpetual shame and rebuke." Item, Isaiah: "All flesh shall abhor them." And holy scripture saith, that the ungodly are given over to the devil to burn perpetually.

Matth. xxv.

[Dan. xii.]

CHAPTER XXVIII.

THE REFUTATION OF THEM THAT DENIED THE PUNISHMENT OF THE UNGODLY TO BE ETERNAL.

MOREOVER St Augustine saith in the last book *De Civitate Dei*[1], that some heretofore have been so merciful, that they durst promise grace, deliverance, and life, even unto those that are damned, and adjudged unto eternal death. The same witnesseth also St Jerome in his writing upon the last chapter of Isaiah[2]. But no man ought to be moved by such a foolish and erroneous opinion of certain unbelievers; which opinion hath of all faithful men been ever still rejected and condemned. For the testimonies or witness of the scripture, which wholly without all contradiction are to be credited, speak simply and plainly, that the punishment and damnation of the ungodly or unbelievers is everlasting; and not only of long continuance, as some expound it, but so great, that it cannot be expressed, and so perpetual, that it is without end. Hereupon, for the opening of the matter, we will shew more testimonies. Isaiah saith: "Thy rivers

Isai. xxxiv.

[1 Lib. XXI. cap. 17. Opera, Tom. v. p. 202. I. K. Ed. 1541.]

[2 Hieron. Comment. Lib. XVIII. in Isai. Proph. cap. LXVI. Opera, Tom. III. p. 514. Ed. 1706.]

shall become resin, and the dust brimstone, the earth burning pitch, not able to be quenched day nor night. The smoke shall eternally go up; from generation to generation shall there be a destruction; neither shall any man be able to walk there in everlasting eternity." The prophet doubtless speaketh of hell, minding with many words to declare, that the punishment and pain of hell is eternal and without end. For first he saith: "Day and night shall it not quench:" then saith he further: "The smoke shall go up for evermore." Item, yet more plainly: "From generation to generation shall there be a destruction;" namely, a dwelling, wherein is nothing but pain and undoing. And at the end he addeth: "Neither shall any man be able to walk there in the everlasting eternity:" which is such a manner of speech, that scarce there can be any other found, that more distinctly, evidently, and plainly expresseth the eternity. For what is the everlasting eternity else, but a time without end? But to be able to dwell or walk there signifieth not, that no man shall dwell in hell; but that it is a loathsome horrible place, wherein every man desireth neither to dwell, nor walk.

Other prophets also, speaking of the destruction of lands and cities, have with such like manner of speech described a very foul and horrible subversion. Therefore would the holy prophet Isaiah also express here nothing else, but an everlasting loathsomeness, that never ceaseth.

In the holy prophet Daniel it is written thus: "They Dan. xii. that have instructed the multitude unto godliness, shall shine as the stars *in seculum et in perpetuum*, for ever and ever." Now lest by this word *seculum* any man understand a long season, as an hundred, or a thousand, or ten thousand years, he addeth thereto immediately, *in perpetuum*, that is, to the eternity, or for evermore. And like as the eternity is appointed for the righteous, so is there an everlasting eternity ordained for the wicked. For the Lord saith plainly: "They John v. that have done good shall come forth to the resurrection of life, and they that have done evil to the resurrection of judgment." Note here the manner of speech, "to the resurrection of life, and to the resurrection of judgment." Now have I shewed afore, that this saying, "to rise up unto the resurrection of judgment," is as much as to rise to a continual

14

and still remaining state, in the which the bodies raised up endure perpetually in torment. We find also the like in the
John iii. same gospel of John, that the Lord saith : " Whoso believeth on the Son hath eternal life ; but he that believeth not the Son shall not see life, but the wrath of God abideth upon him." Lo, what could be more evidently and pithily spoken ? " He shall not see life," saith the Lord. Item, " the wrath of God remaineth upon him." If he shall not see life, how shall he then, as yonder men say, be preserved or saved ? Item, if " the wrath of God abide upon him," then surely the vengeance, which is the pain and punishment, shall not be taken away from him. And note that he saith : " The wrath of God abideth, yea, abideth on him." As if he would say, the punishment hangeth upon him, sticketh fast, moveth not away, altereth not, but worketh in the unbelievers without ceasing for evermore.

Mark iii. The Lord saith : "All sins shall be forgiven the children of men, and also the blasphemies wherewith they blaspheme ; but whoso blasphemeth the Holy Ghost, hath no forgiveness for evermore, but is guilty of eternal judgment." " For evermore," saith he, " hath he no remission." And hereunto he addeth : " He is in danger of eternal judgment ;" that is, he shall be punished with everlasting continual punishment. The
Mark ix. Lord saith moreover in the same evangelist : " Better it is for thee to enter into life halt or lame, than having two feet to be cast into hell fire, the fire that never quencheth, where their worm dieth not and their fire goeth not out." Wherein he repeateth once again, " the fire never quencheth," and addeth thereto, that " the worm never dieth." Wherefore, as the bodies ever continue, so endureth their worm also perpetually. For the worm liveth and is sustained only of the body or carrion. St John also saith in his Revelation :
Rev. xiv. " If any man worship the beast and his image, and receive his mark in his forehead, or in his hand, the same shall drink the wine of the wrath of God, which is poured in the cup of his wrath ; and he shall be punished in fire and brimstone before the holy angels and before the Lamb. And the smoke of their torment ascendeth up for evermore, and they have no rest day nor night, &c." And the like is repeated in the twentieth chapter.

Thus much of eternal damnation.

CHAPTER XXIX.

OF ETERNAL LIFE AND SALVATION, AND THAT THERE IS AN ETERNAL LIFE.

Now resteth, that in the end of this book we collect somewhat out of the scripture concerning everlasting life and the most perfect salvation of all elect, which is our only expectation and only hope that we undoubtedly look for, and trust to inherit; and that through the benefits and merits of our Lord Jesus Christ.   That there is a blessed and eternal life, no man can deny, unless he be altogether an enemy of God, and except there be in him no life at all. For if there be no everlasting life and no everlasting salvation, then is there also no God; or, though there were one, yet were he neither true nor just, seeing that to all righteous and faithful he hath promised eternal life.   But a God there is, who is true and righteous : therefore is there also an eternal life and salvation, which he hath promised to faithful believers.   This doth holy scripture record with these witnesses.   David saith : " I believe and trust to see the riches Psalm xxvii. of the Lord."   And in the gospel the Lord saith : " Come, Matt. xxv. ye blessed of my Father, and possess the kingdom, which hath been prepared for you from the beginning of the world."   Item : " O thou good and faithful servant, that hast been faithful in a little, I will make thee ruler over much. Enter into the joy of thy Lord."   Paul also saith : " If 1 Cor. xv. we have a sure hope in Christ Jesus only in this life, then are we of all people the most wretched."   And in many words to the Hebrews treateth he of the everlasting rest. Heb. iv. But in the second chapter he speaketh of the hope of the Heb. xi. faithful : " They desire a better country, that is to say, an heavenly."   Item, Hebrews xiii : " We have here no remaining city, but we seek one for to come."   For holy scripture calleth eternal life the kingdom of God, the kingdom of the Father, the native country of heaven, the joy of the Lord, the blessed rest and everlasting life.   St Peter speaketh very evidently and plain : " Praised be God, the 1 Pet. i.

14—2

Father of our Lord Jesus Christ, which according to his abundant mercy hath begotten us again unto a lively hope, by the resurrection of Jesus Christ from death, to an inheritance immortal, undefiled, and that perisheth not, reserved in heaven for you, which are kept by the power of God through faith unto salvation," &c.

CHAPTER XXX.

WHERE THE PLACE OF THE FAITHFUL IS.

YET are there some that ask, where the region or place of the blessed and faithful believers is? Of this have all virtuous and godly men had ever one opinion, namely, that the dwelling of the living shall be with God, according to

Matth. v. that which the Lord saith in the gospel: " Blessed are they which be of a pure heart: for they shall see God." And though God be every where, yet will he not be seen in this time, but principally in the time to come, and in heaven,

[Exod. xxxiii.] according as Moses hath written: "No man shall be able to see God and live." Therefore is it necessary for us to depart out of this time, and to be brought elsewhere, namely,

1 Tim. vi. to the place that is above us; where "God dwelleth in a light that no man can attain unto," as Paul saith: for there will he be perfectly seen of his. In St Luke it is read, that Abraham's lap or bosom is above in the height, but the harbour or dwelling of the damned beneath in the depth. It is found also, that Elias was in a fiery chariot

2 Kings ii. taken hence, and carried upwards into heaven. And in

John xvii. John doth our Lord Jesus Christ pray, saying: " Father, those whom thou hast given me, I will that where I am, they also be there with me, that they may see mine honour and glory." But in this that I have treated of afore, it is manifestly declared, that the heaven is the same room and place of Jesus Christ, into the which he is bodily taken up in his glory. Whereof then it followeth of necessity, that the heaven, into which Christ ascended with his true body, is

even the same place and rest, that faithful believers are
taken up into. And into the same heaven desired Stephen
to be received, when he lift up his eyes into heaven, and
saw at the right hand of the Father Jesus standing; to
whom he committed his soul, and said, "O Lord Jesus,
receive my spirit."

CHAPTER XXXI.

HOW THE SALVATION SHALL BE.

BUT what the same life, and of what sort, fashion, and
manner the salvation of the faithful shall be, or what the
elect do or occupy in heaven, can of mortal men not perfectly
be spoken. For St Augustine also in his twenty-second book
De Civitate Dei, cap. 29, saith: "If I will say the truth, I   De Civitate
cannot tell after what manner the operation, rest, and quiet-   Dei, Lib.
ness of the blessed in heaven shall be. For the peace of   xxii. cap. 29.
God excelleth and passeth all understanding[1]." And likewise
speaketh also St Paul out of the prophet, concerning the   1 Cor. ii.
quality, fashion, and manner of eternal life: "The eye hath   Isai. lxiv.
not seen, and the ear hath not heard, neither have entered
into the heart of man, the things which God hath prepared
for them that love him." Wherefore touching the excellency
of eternal life, though all were spoken that the tongues of
men were able, yet should it be hard for them to attain, and
by words to express, the least and smallest portion thereof.
For albeit we hear that the kingdom of Christ be filled with
glory, joy, and salvation, yet the things that are named
continue still far from our understanding; yea, they remain
wrapped, as it were, in a dark speech and in a mist, until
the day come, wherein he will open and give unto us his
glory. Therefore when the holy prophets could with no
words express the spiritual salvation, as it is in itself, yet,

[1 Illa quidem actio, vel potius quies et otium, quale futurum sit,
si verum vellim dicere, nescio... Ibi enim est pax Dei, quæ, sicut ait
apostolus, superat omnem intellectum. August. de Civ. Dei, Lib. xxii.
cap. 29. Opera, Tom. v. p. 216. L. ed. 1541.]

as much as was possible they described, and set it forth by outward and bodily things. Therefore we may also, I suppose, by outward and corporal things get up, as it were, by steps to things invisible, and purchase unto ourselves an understanding of spiritual and everlasting good things. For

Rom. i.

St Paul to the Romans, speaking of the knowledge of the true, only, and eternal God, saith, that "God's invisible things, namely, his eternal power and Godhead, are understood, if his works be pondered and considered." And out of the good things that here upon earth are given unto men, hath the poet Marcellus very goodly and well concluded and counted, that the good things which for the blessed are prepared in the life to come, shall be such as now cannot be considered and expressed; and thus he saith:

Marcellus de Piscibus [1].

O heaven, that art
 The throne most high,
A beautiful crown,
 Fair and worthy;
How wonderful, pure,
 And excellent,
Art thou beset
In firmament
With stars, with sun,
 And moon doubtless,
Replete with joy,
 And much gladness;
Which God for us
 Hath prepared,

And cattle to give
 Hath not spared;
Waters and wood,
 With many a hill,
Vineyards, meadows,
 Fair fields to till,
Pleasant on earth,
 And commodious:
Thy dwelling, O Lord,
 How precious
Is it, all full of
 Honour and glory
For thy celestial
 Hast with thee.

Moreover holy scripture speaketh very simply and plainly, that eternal life consisteth herein, that we shall see God, and have the fruition of him, in whom is the fulness of all good, and without whom nothing can be desired or found

[1] The person who is here apparently referred to, is Marcellus Sidetes, a physician of Side in Pamphylia, who lived in the time of M. Antoninus, and the few remaining fragments of whose works have been edited by Fabricius in his Bibliotheca Græca, Lib. i. cap. 3. ed. 2da. Edit. Harles, Lib. xiii. But there is nothing in these fragments resembling these verses, nor in the fragments of a Latin poet of the same name contained in Maittaire's *Corpus Poetarum Latinorum*, Vol. ii.]

that is good, beautiful, or pleasant. For eternal life, or eternal salvation, is nothing else but man's everlasting and alway continuing state, which by means of the best things of all is fully perfect. This state is given us through the beholding or sight, through the fruition, and through the communion or fellowship, which we shall have with the blessed God in the world to come. Hereof is it that St Augustine saith, Lib. xxii. *De Civitate Dei*, cap. 29 : " If I be demanded, what the blessed shall do in this spiritual body, I shall not say that I now see, but that which I believe. Therefore I say, that even in this body they shall see God[2]." Thus also did holy Job hold thereof, and said : " I shall see him to myself, and mine own eyes shall see him, yea, I and none other." Even of this occasion spake St Augustine in the last chapter of this twenty-second book[3], that " the corporal eyes of the body raised up shall execute their office," that is, " they shall see." What he further treated of the beholding of God, it is penned at large in the 112th epistle which he wrote *Ad Paulinam*[4]. Our Lord Jesus saith also in the holy gospel : " This is the eternal life, that they know thee to be the only true God, and whom thou hast sent, Jesus Christ." This knowledge is not only belief and the knowledge of understanding, but also the present beholding and fruition of God, and the fellowship with God, which after this life shall happen unto all faithful believers. For Paul said : " We see now through a glass in a dark speaking, but then face to face." For faith is a stedfast substance of things that we hope for, and as a be-

(marginal notes: De Civitate Dei, Lib. xxii. Cap. 29. — Job xix. — Lib. xxii. — Epist. 112. ad Paulin. — John xvii. — 1 Cor. xiii.)

[2 Cum ex me quæritur, quid acturi sint sancti in illo corpore spiritali, non dico quod jam video, sed dico quod credo. Dico itaque, quod visuri sint Deum in ipso corpore. August. de Civ. Dei, Lib. xxv. cap. 29. Opera, Tom. v. p. 217. A. ed. 1541.]

[3 Augustine, in a long passage immediately following that which he had cited before, goes on to discuss the question,—"In what manner the righteous shall see God?" and he thus concludes: " Ita Deus erit nobis notus atque conspicuus, ut videatur spiritu a singulis nobis in singulis nobis, videatur ab altero in altero, videatur in seipso, videatur in cœlo novo et in terra nova, atque in omni quæ tunc fuerit creatura; videatur et per corpora in omni corpore, quocunque fuerint spiritalis corporis oculi acie perveniente directi. Ib. p. 217, H.]

[4 August. Opera, Tom. ii. pp. 109-114.]

holding or sight of God ; albeit somewhat more dark, and not
so evident and clear as shall be that, which, as a reward of
faith, shall be given to the faithful in the world to come. "To
see face to face," is nothing else but to use, enjoy, and have
the fruition of all things presently ; also to behold the promise, and perfectly to be partaker thereof. Therefore saith
the holy apostle John yet more evidently : " Dearly beloved,
we are now the children of God, and yet it doth not appear
what we shall be ; but we know that when he shall appear,
we shall be like him ; for we shall see him as he is." With
the which words St John will declare three things : namely,
that even now in this very present time we are God's children, and therefore also heirs. And though this be a great
foredeal, and an excellent jewel, yet the great and unspeakable glory, that in time to come shall be declared in us,
hath not yet appeared. " For we," saith he, " shall be like
him," namely, our Lord Jesu Christ, who, according to the
saying of Paul, " shall alter and change our vile body, that
he may make it like unto his own glorious body." Besides
this, " even as he is, shall we see him," namely, Christ the
Lord ; not only as man, but also as very God. Therefore
shall we see God as he is, namely, God as the chief and
brightest good in whom we have all good things. For
Paul saith : " When all things are subdued unto the Son,
then shall the Son also be subject unto him who unto him
hath subdued all things, that God may be all in all." And
therefore said he also in the gospel, that " they know thee
to be the only true God." Not that Christ is not very
God, but that the mystery and the entreating of the Son,
our mediator and reconciler, shall after the judgment be no
more so in heaven, as it hath been afore upon earth ; but
the only God in the holy Trinity shall be of all good the
full perfect sufficiency to all faithful. For all that we can
wish, think, and desire, shall only God give and be in all
things.

And that is also the meaning and understanding of Paul,
when he saith, " God shall be all in all." And hereunto
serveth now the goodly sentence of St Augustine, who saith
thus : " God shall be the end of all our longing and desire ;
him shall we perpetually see ; him shall we love without
tediousness and grief ; and him shall we praise without

Marginal notes:
John iii.

1 Cor. xv.

John xvii.

1 Cor. xv.

De Civitate
Dei, Lib.
xxii. Cap.
30.

ceasing[1]." For tediousness and grief runneth customably
with saturation or fulness. As for us, we shall with the
beholding of God be filled to the bodily satisfying; which
filling shall be as little tedious or grievous, as we are grieved
at the waters and rivers that still run into the sea, and yet
out of the ground of the earth spring forth again. For the
same cometh to pass without all men's tediousness, yea,
rather with great joy and commodity, seeing they water
and moisture all things, and make them fruitful. And hereunto serve now those testimonies of the scripture. The prophet
David saith: " In thy presence is the fulness of joy, and at Psalm xvi.
thy right hand there is pleasure for evermore:" that is, in
the beholding of thee is and consisteth all joy, and in
heaven shall everlasting pleasure be. Item: " In thy right- Psalm xvii.
eousness shall I behold thy face; and when I awake, with
thy righteousness shall I be satisfied." Unto the Lord
saith also the holy apostle Philip: " Lord, shew us the
Father, and it sufficeth us." Therefore the poet Marcellus[2]
spake very christianly and well in these his verses :

Hereof hath God	And what in the air
His name truly,	Is beautiful,
Because the highest	That may delight,
Good is he.	And be fruitful ;
For where he is,	There is in all that
There is present	Number not one,
Much honour and	Which is not seen
Glory excellent.	At all season
And therefore every	Within the circle
Pleasant thing,	Of heaven, I wis,
That water and earth	Where the highest
Doth here forth bring ;	Father's dwelling is.

The blessed also and elect shall, in the heavenly and
eternal country, with continual praise incessantly laud and

[1 Sic enim et illud recte intelligitur, quod ait apostolus, Ut Deus
sit omnia in omnibus. Ipse finis erit omnium desideriorum nostrorum, qui sine fine videbitur, sine fastidio amabitur, sine fatigatione
laudabitur. August. de Civ. Dei, Lib. xxii. cap. 3 Opera, Tom. v.
p. 218. L. ed. 1541.]

[2 Compare p. 214, and the note on that passage.]

Rev. v. xiv. magnify the name of God.   For what St John in his Revelation thought to signify and shew, thus he said : " I heard
the voice of many angels which were about the throne, and
about the beasts, and the elders.   And I heard many thousands that sung a new song, saying, Worthy is the Lamb
that was killed to receive power, and riches, wisdom and
strength, honour, glory, and blessing, &c."   Moreover, the
same eternal life shall be altogether free, and discharged
from all heaviness, sickness, and temptations, whereas temporal joy, rest, and welfare of men is mixed with sorrow;
as also the holy apostle John doth witness : "I John," saith
he, "saw that holy city new Jerusalem coming down from
God out of heaven, prepared as a bride garnished for her
husband.   And I heard a great voice out of heaven, saying,
Behold, the tabernacle of God is with men, and he will
dwell with them, and they shall be his people, and God
himself shall be with them, and shall be their God.   And
God shall wipe away all tears from their eyes, and there
shall be no more death, neither sorrow, neither crying,
neither shall there be any more pain ; for the old things are
gone.   And he that sat upon the seat said, Behold, I make
all things new : and he said unto me, Write, for these words
are faithful and true."   And hereunto in manner serveth all
that followeth after in the 21st chapter to the end of the
book.

CHAPTER XXXII.

THE SOULS DEPARTED WOT NOT WHAT THEY DO THAT ARE ALIVE, THEREBY ANY THING TO BE DISQUIETED.

De Cura pro
mortuis
agenda,
cap. 13. THEREFORE did holy Augustine also teach, that the souls
of those that are departed wot not what they do which are
alive.   Yet will I recite his words.   Thus saith Augustine :
" If the souls of those that are departed were among the
doings of such as are alive, they should, when we see them
in sleep, talk with us and them.   I will not speak of others
at all, lest my good and faithful mother, that by water and
land followed me so far to be with me, should now not for-

sake me.   For God forbid that he should have made that
blessed life more unfriendly or more terrible.   God forbid,
that when my heart doth any thing press and unquiet me,
she should not comfort me her son, whom she yet so entirely
loved, that she could never suffer or see me heavy.   Undoubtedly it must needs be true that the holy psalmist saith:
'My father and my mother have forsaken me; but the Psalm xxvii.
Lord hath taken the care to keep me.'   If our fathers now
and mothers have forsaken us, how can they be then in our
cares and doings? and if father and mother do nothing at
all in our business, how can we then think that the other
dead meddle ought with us, or know what we do or suffer?
The prophet Isaiah saith: 'Thou, O God, art our Father;
for Abraham wotteth not of us, and Israel knoweth us
not.'   Seeing then that such honourable patriarchs wist not
what was done concerning their people, which came of themselves, to whom yet, as to God's faithful believers, the same
people was promised out of their own stock; how can then
the dead open themselves the door, to know and further the
doings and not doings of them that are alive?   And how
shall we be able to say, that they which are dead were
helped and eased afore the evil came that followed upon
their death, when they after death feel all the calamity and
misery of man's life that here happeneth unto us?   Or be
we in error that speak such things, and count them to be in
rest; or doth he err, that maketh the unquiet way of the
living so careful and full of cumbrance?   I pray thee, what
great benefit is it then, that our Lord God promised the virtuous king Josiah, namely, that he should die, because he 2 Kings xxii.
should not see the great misery, which God threatened unto
all the land and people of Israel?   The words of the Lord
unto Josiah are these: 'Thus saith the Lord God of Israel,
Seeing that by reason of my words which thou hast heard,
thy heart hath melted, and thou hast humbled thyself before
the Lord, when thou heardest what I had threatened unto
this place, and to the inhabitants thereof, namely how they
shall be destroyed, destitute, and accursed; and thou thereupon hast rent thy garment, and wept before my sight;
behold, I have heard thee, saith the Lord God of hosts, the
plague shall not touch thee.   Behold, I will gather thee
unto thy fathers, and into thy grave shalt thou be laid in

peace, and thine eyes shall not see all the plagues that I will
bring upon this land, and upon those that dwell therein.'
Lo, this king, standing in awe at the threatening of God, did
weep and rend his clothes, and through death that came
aforehand was he in safety from all misery to come. For
he must afore depart in peace and take rest, lest he should
see the great calamity. Therefore the souls of those that
are departed must needs be in such a place, where they see
not all which is done and happeneth in the life of men[1]."
All this have we taken and written out of the 13th chapter.

[1 Si rebus viventium interessent animæ mortuorum, et ipsæ nos,
quando eas videmus, alloquerentur in somniis, ut de aliis taceam, me-
ipsum pia mater nulla nocte desereret, quæ terra marique secuta est,
ut mecum viveret. Absit enim, ut facta sit vita meliore crudelis
usque adeo, ut quando aliquid angit cor meum, nec tristem filium con-
soletur, quem dilexit unice, quem nunquam voluit mœstum videre.
Sed profecto quod sacer psalmus personat, verum est: *Quoniam pater
meus et mater mea dereliquerunt me, Dominus autem assumpsit me.* Si
ergo dereliquerunt nos patres nostri, quomodo nostris curis et rebus
intersunt? Si autem parentes non intersunt, qui sunt alii mortuorum,
qui noverunt quid agamus, quidve patiamur? Esaias propheta dixit:
*Tu es enim Pater noster; quia Abraham nos nescivit, et Israel non cog-
novit nos.* Si tanti patriarchæ quid erga populum ex his procreatum
ageretur, ignoraverunt, quibus Deo credentibus populus iste de eorum
stirpe promissus est; quomodo mortui vivorum rebus atque actibus
cognoscendis adjuvandisque miscentur? Quomodo dicimus eis fuisse
consultum, qui obierunt antequam venirent mala, quæ illorum obitum
consecuta sunt; si et post mortem sentiunt quæcunque in vitæ hu-
manæ calamitate contingunt? An forte nos errando ista dicimus, et hos
putamus quietos, quos inquieta vita vivorum sollicitat? Quid est ergo,
quod piissimo regi Josiæ pro magno beneficio promisit Deus, quod
esset ante moriturus, ne videret mala, quæ ventura illi loco et populo
minabatur? Quæ Dei verba hæc sunt: *Hæc dicit Dominus Israel,
Verba mea quæ audisti, et veritus es a facie mea cum audisti, quæ locutus
sum de isto loco, et qui commorantur in eo, ut deseratur, et in maledicto
sit; et concidisti vestimenta tua, et flevisti coram conspectu meo, et ego
audivi, dixit Dominus Deus Sabaoth; non sic (l. idcirco) ego apponam te
ad patres tuos, et apponeris cum pace; et non videbunt oculi tui omnia
mala, quæ ego induco in locum hunc, et qui commorantur in eo.* Ter-
ritus iste Dei comminationibus fleverat, et sua vestimenta considerat;
et fit omnium malorum futurorum de properatura morte securus, quod
ita requieturus esset in pace, ut illa omnia non videret. Ibi ergo sunt
spiritus defunctorum, ubi non vident quæcumque aguntur aut eveniunt
in ista vita hominibus. August. De Cura pro mortuis agenda. c. 13.
Opera, Tom. IV. p. 215, L. M. et 216, A. ed. 1541.]

of Augustine's book, *De cura pro mortuis agenda.* If the souls now in everlasting salvation have a perfect rest, yea, such a rest as their body which they have put off hath not received again; and seeing that they are yet alive, whom they specially loved, while they were with them in body; how much more perfect joy shall they then first have and possess, when their bodies shall come again, and when they shall see that all their brethren, whom they in this life had loved so entirely afore, are together in honour and glory, when now the time of frailty hath ceased, and when in the eternal time there can now no cause of heaviness and grief be thought upon, nor found any more at all! Therefore the glory and joy, which the mercy of God shall after the last judgment give unto men that are made whole again of body and soul, shall be without sorrow, and in all points perfect. And like as the ungodly and unbelievers shall be gathered together with the devil and all his companions; so shall also the righteous and elect have the joyful fruition of the company and fellowship of their head Jesus Christ, and of his members, that is, of all faithful believers.

CHAPTER XXXIII.

THE FAITHFUL SHALL KNOW ONE ANOTHER IN HEAVEN.

THEN also shall the blessed know one another again, having joy together, and rejoicing in the obtained health. For if there should be no knowledge, to what end then should the bodies rise again; or what fruit and profit should the resurrection have; or how might the sentence of Daniel [Daniel xii.] the prophet be verified, when he saith, "They that have instructed and taught others unto godliness, shall shine, and be as light as the stars in the firmament?"

When the Lord was risen again from death, and had taken upon him his glorified body, the apostles knew him; yea, so perfectly and thoroughly well knew they him, that, as St. John witnesseth, "none durst say, Who art thou? for [John xxi.] they all knew that it was the Lord." I pass over that the Lord spake in the gospel, saying, "When the Son of man [Luke xxii.]

shall sit upon the seat of his majesty, then shall ye also sit upon twelve seats, and judge the twelve tribes of Israel." For if they that rise again shall not know one another, how shall then the apostles judge and give sentence upon those, to whom they preached here in their lifetime? Note, that the apostles shall not judge in the room and place of their Lord, to whom only is given all power to judge: but this understanding it hath, that the apostles do then judge, when they are there at the judicial court, as witnesses of the righteous judgment of God, with the which he condemneth the unbelievers. For whereas the unbelievers would not give credence to the apostles, that is to say, their preachers, but cried out upon them, as upon ungodly heretics; when they now shall see those present with the Judge of all men, they shall immediately be overcome by the apostles, and have witness in themselves, that they shall be and are justly condemned.

And for this matter read the 4th and 5th chapters of the Book of Wisdom; which serveth very well to this purpose. And seeing it is manifest, that in the life to come even the wicked shall know the good, how much more then shall one good person know another, and one faithful another! In the transfiguration of the Lord upon the mount appeared Moses and Elias, and were known of the three disciples of the Lord; yea, they knew the Lord himself, though he was now transfigured. Hereunto serveth it also that Paul saith: " Ye are come to the city of the living God, to the celestial Jerusalem, and to an innumerable multitude of angels, and to the congregation of the firstborn sons which are written in heaven, and to the spirits of the perfect righteous," &c. Besides this, we have for us the uniform and universal opinion of all faithful, which also witnesseth, that in the life to come the blessed shall know one another. For when we talk of death and of the state and ease of the life to come, we say, though now we must depart asunder, yet shall we see one another again in the eternal country.

Socrates also, the right famous and most excellent among all the wise men of the heathen, marked such a like thing, and saw it as in a dream, when, as Cicero witnesseth of him, he was of death condemned of the judges or council, and now should drink the poison. For he said: " O how much better

Heb. xii.

In Tuscul.
Quæst.[i. 41.]

and more blessed is it to go unto them, that well and uprightly lived here in time, than to remain here in this life
upon earth! O how dear and worthy a thing is it, that I
may talk with Orpheus, Museus, Homerus, Hesiodus, with
those excellent men! Verily, I would not only die once, but
many and sundry times also, if it were possible, to obtain
the same," &c. After this sort, like as in a dream, did the
good philosopher imagine in himself joys vain and of none
effect.

But we promise to ourselves true assured joy, in that we
hope and know, that in the eternal and everduring country,
after the resurrection of the dead, we shall see Adam, our Adam.
first father; Noah, the dearly beloved friend of God; Abra- Noah.
ham, to whom God made special great promises; Moses, the Abraham.
most gentle-hearted man, and one that had greatest expe- Moses.
rience of all the mysteries of God; Samuel, the friendly Samuel.
and loving prophet; David, the king and prophet, who was David.
God's elect, according to his own will and desire; Josiah, Josiah.
the most godly and best among all the kings of Judah; and
also John the Baptist, holier than whom there was none John the
born of woman; and with all these the holy virgin Mary, Baptist.
the mother of God, and highly replenished with grace Mary.
among all women: item, Peter, John, James, chiefest of Peter.
the apostles, with the other disciples of Christ; Paul, the John.
famous teacher of the heathen, and all the holy congrega- Paul.
tion of the patriarchs, prophets, apostles, martyrs, and faithful believers.

As for our glorified and pure understanding and memory,
now endued with immortality, the multitude and infinite
number of the blessed in our said native country shall neither
grieve nor entangle the same.

From the beginning of the creation there was in Adam
a wonderful and excellent efficacy of understanding and
remembrance; forasmuch as unto all things and to every
one in especial, whatsoever was within the whole compass of
the world created, yea, in paradise also, he gave their
names, and knew every one. A much more excellent, more
pure, and more clear understanding shall God give to the
raised up and glorified bodies, so that they shall not lack
nor be destitute of any thing at all. And whereas the
blessed shall rejoice and have joy together one with another;

yet shall their delight be in the only God, who shall be all in all.

Of these everlasting and heavenly things more and further to write I have not at this present.   Howbeit there shall be graciously given us things far greater, much more glorious, more joyful, and more divine, than we can comprehend; namely, salvation, as it is in itself, in that day when we, after the overcoming and treading down of death through our Lord Jesus Christ, shall be carried up and taken to heaven into eternal joy and salvation.   Touching the which I have hitherto written, not according to the majesty and worthiness thereof, but after my small ability in most humble wise.   God the Father of all mercy, through his dear Son our Lord and Redeemer Jesus Christ, vouchsafe graciously to take us poor sinners up to his glory, and after the joyful resurrection of our body, that we long for, to give and shew us the unoutspeakable joy, which he hath prepared for all faithful believers; that we, ever living and having joy in him, may praise him for ever and ever, that is from eternity to eternity!   Amen.

WITH CHRIST EVEN IN DEATH IS LIFE.

THE TABLE.

THE CONTENTS OF THE FIRST PART.

THE CONTENTS OF THE SECOND PART.

[COVERDALE, II.]

THE CONTENTS OF THE THIRD PART.

AN EXHORTATION

TO THE

CARRYING OF CHRIST'S CROSS.

An Exhor

tation to the cari=

enge of Chrystes crosse wyth a

true and brefe confutation

of false and papisticall

doctryne.

☞ 2 Timo. 3.

All, that wyll lyue godly
in Chryste Jesu must
suffer persecucyon.

[AN EXHORTATION TO THE CARRYING OF CHRIST'S CROSS.

This scarce treatise of Bishop Coverdale is here reprinted from a copy in the possession of George Offor, Esq. With respect to the authority on which this work is attributed to Coverdale, it rests on the following evidence. Strype says in his Memorials, (Vol. III. Part I. pp. 239, 40. Ed. 1822,) Anno 1554: "About this time there came forth a little pious work, entitled *An Exhortation to the Cross.* The author's name is not set to it; but it appears that he was a preacher under king Edward, and then an exile: I believe him to be Coverdale. To this was joined another little book, of the same volume, entitled, *The Hope of the Faithful,* and, as it seems, by the same author. And I verily think the work to be Coverdale's." Now the authorship of *The Hope of the Faithful* has been established on conclusive evidence; and it therefore leaves little doubt, but the present treatise also belongs to Coverdale.

To this may be added the internal evidence, derived from the treatise itself, which exhibits a striking similarity of style and sentiments to Coverdale's other writings. There is also evidence from the title-page of this work, that it was not printed separately, but formed part of a volume: and in addition to this, on the blank leaf at the conclusion of *The Hope of the Faithful,* is the set-off or impression of the title to *The Exhortation;* evidently proving, that the two treatises were originally bound together, although they now appear in a separate form. These particulars, which have been obligingly communicated to the Editor by the possessor of this volume, will probably be considered conclusive in support of the former arguments for attributing this treatise to Coverdale.]

AN EXHORTATION

TO THE

CARRYING OF CHRIST'S CROSS.

THE HOLY SPIRIT OF GOD, WHICH IS HIS EARNEST PLEDGE
GIVEN TO HIS PEOPLE FOR THEIR COMFORT AND
CONSOLATION, BE POURED INTO OUR HEARTS
BY THE MIGHTY POWER AND MERITS
OF OUR ALONE SAVIOUR JESUS
CHRIST, NOW AND FOR
EVER. AMEN.

BECAUSE I perceive plainly, that unto the evils fallen upon us which profess Christ's gospel greater are most like to ensue, and after them greater, till the measure of iniquity be upheaped, (except we shrink, and having put our hand to the plough, do look back, and so with Lot's wife fall into God's heavy displeasure incurably, all which God forbid!) and because I am persuaded of you, my dearly beloved brethren and sisters throughout the realm of England, which have professed unfeignedly the gospel of our Lord and Saviour Jesus Christ, (for unto such do I write this Epistle or Book,) how that, as you have begun to take part with God's gospel and truth, so through his grace ye will persevere and go on forwards, notwithstanding the storms risen and to arise; I cannot but write some things unto you, to encourage you to go on lustily in the way of the Lord, and not to become faint-hearted or fearful persons, whose place St John appointed with unbelievers, murderers, and idolaters in eternal perdition; but cheerfully to take the Lord's cup and drink of it, afore it draw towards the dregs and bottom; whereof at length they shall drink with the wicked to eternal destruction, which will not receive it at the first with God's children, with whom God beginneth his judgment; that, as the wicked world rejoiceth when they lament, so they may rejoice when the wicked world shall mourn, and without end feel woe intolerable.

Marginal notes:
Gen. ix.
Luke ix.

Rev. xxi.

Psal. lxxv.

1 Pet. iv.

John xvi.

CHAPTER I.

WHAT WE BE, AND WHERE WE BE.

FIRST, therefore, my dearly beloved in the Lord, I beseech you to consider, that though ye be in the world, yet John xiv. you are not of the world.   You are not of them which look Psal. xvii. for their portion in this life, whose captain is the god of this 2 Cor. iv. world, even Satan, who now ruffleth it apace, as he were wood, because his time on earth is not long.   But you are Rev. xii. of them which look for a city of God's own building.   You Heb. xi. are of them which know themselves to be here but pilgrims 1 Pet. ii. and strangers; for here you have no dwelling-place.   You Heb. xiii. are of them whose portion is the Lord, and which have their Psal. xvi. cxix. hope in heaven; whose captain is Christ Jesus, the Son of God, and governor of heaven and earth.   Unto him is given Matt. xxviii. all power; yea, he is God Almighty with the Father and Rom. ix. the Holy Ghost, praise-worthy for ever.   You are not of 1 John v. them which receive the beast's mark; which here rejoice, Rev. xiii. Luke vi. laugh, and have their heart's ease, joy, paradise, and pleasure: but you are of them which have received the angel's Ezek. ix. mark, yea, God's mark; which here lament, mourn, sigh, Matt. v. sob, and have your wilderness to wander in, your purgatory, and even hell.   You are not of them which cry, Let us eat Isai. xxii. and drink, for to-morrow we shall die.   You are not of that 1 Cor. xv. number which say, they have made a covenant with death and Isai. xxviii. hell for hurting them.   You are not of them, which take it but for a vain thing to serve the Lord.   You are not of Mal. iii. them which are lulled and rocked asleep in Jezebel's bed, [Rev. ii. 22.] a bed of security.   You are not in the number of them that say, Tush, God is in heaven and seeth us not, nor much Ezek. viii. passeth what we do.   You are not of the number of them Psal. lxxiii. which will fall down for the muck of the world, to worship Luke iv. the fiend, or for displeasing of men to worship the golden image.   Finally, you are not of the number of them which Dan. iii. set more by their pigs, than by Christ; which for ease and Matt. viii. rest in this life will say and do as Antiochus biddeth them Luke v. 1 Mac. i. ii. do or say; and will follow the multitude to do evil with Prov. xxiii. Zedekiah and the three hundred false prophets; yea, Achab, 1 Kings xxii. Jezebel, and the whole court and country.

Rom. vi.
Coloss. iii.

But you be of the number of them which are dead already, or at least in dying daily to yourselves and to the world. You are of them which have made a covenant with God to forsake themselves and Satan in this world. You are of them which

Mal. iii.

say, Nay, the Lord hath all things written in his memorial book for such as fear him and remember his name. You

Luke xii.

are of them which have their loins girded about, and their lights burning in their hands, like unto men that wait for their Lord's coming. You are in the number of them that

Psal. xiv.
xxxiii. ci.

say, The Lord looketh down from heaven and beholdeth all the children of men, from the habitation of his dwelling he considereth all them that dwell upon the earth. You are of

Deut. vi.
Matt. ix.
Dan. iii.

them which will worship the only Lord God, and will not worship the works of man's hands, though the oven burn never so hot. You are in the number of them, to whom

1 Pet. ii.

Christ is precious and dear; which cry out rather, because

Psal. cxx.

your habitation is prolonged here, as David did, which Mat-

1 Mac. ii.

tathias followed, and the godly Jews, which knew the way

Matt. vii.

to life to be a strait way, and few to go through it; which

1 Kings xxii.

will not stick to follow poor Micheas, although he be racked and cast into prison, having the sun, moon, and seven stars, and all against him.

Thus, therefore, dearly beloved, remember first that, as I said, you are not of this world; Satan is not your captain, your joy and paradise is not here, your companions are not the multitude of worldlings, and such as seek to please men and to live here at ease in the service of Satan. But you are of another world: Christ is your captain; your joy is

Phil. iii.
Heb. xiii.

in heaven, where your conversation and civility[1] is; your companions are the fathers, patriarchs, prophets, apostles, martyrs, virgins, confessors, and the dear saints of God,

Rev. vii.

which followed the Lamb whithersoever he went, dipping

Job vii. viii.
xiv.
Psal. xc. cii.
James iv.

their garments in his blood; knowing this life and world to be full of evil, a warfare, a smoke, a shadow, a vapour, and as replenished, so environed with all kind of miseries.

[1 Civility: citizenship.]

CHAPTER II.

PERSECUTION IS NOT STRANGE.

THIS is the first thing I would give you often and diligently with yourselves to consider and muse upon, namely,
what you be, and where you be.   Then, secondarily, forget
not to call to mind, that you ought not to think it any strange
thing, if misery, trouble, adversity, persecution, and displea- 1 Pet. iv.
sure come upon you.   For how can it otherwise be, but that
trouble and persecution must come upon you?   Can the John xiv.
world love you, which are none of his?   Worldly men are
the soldiers of your chief enemy, and can they regard you?
Can Satan suffer you to be in rest, which will not do him 1 Pet. v.
homage?   Can this way be easy, which of itself is strait? Matt. vii.
Will you look to travel, and have no foul way, nor rain?
Will shipmen shrink, or sailors of the sea, if storms arise?
Do they not look for such?

And, dearly beloved, did not we enter into God's ship 1 Pet. iii.
and ark of baptism at the first?   Will you then count it
strange, if perils and tempests blow?   Are not you travelling
to your heavenly city of Jerusalem, where is all joy and
felicity?   and will you now tarry by the way for storms or
showers?   The mart and fair will then be past; the night John ix.
will fall; ye cannot travel; the door will be sparred, and Matt. xxv.
the bride will be at supper.   Therefore away with dainty
niceness.   Will you think the Father of heaven will deal
more gently with you in this age, than he hath done with
other his dearest friends in other[2] ages?   What way and
weather, what storms and tempests, what disease, trouble,
and disquietness found Abel, Noe, Abraham, Isaac, Jacob, Gen. iv. vi.
and good Joseph!   Which of these had so fair a life and vii. viii. xi.
restful times as we have had?   Moses, Aaron, Samuel, &c.
David the king, and all the good kings, priests, and prophets
in the old Testament, at one time or another, if not throughout their life, did feel a thousand parts more misery than we
have felt hitherto.   As for the new Testament, Lord God,
how great was the affliction of Mary, Joseph, Zachary, Eli- Matt. ii.
zabeth, John the Baptist, than whom among the children of

[2 Old edition, *our*.]

men none arose greater, of all the apostles and evangelists; yea, of Jesus Christ our Lord, the dear Son and dearling of God! And since the time of the apostles, how many and Eusebius, Eccles. Hist. Tripart. Historia. great are the martyrs, confessors, and such as suffered the shedding of their blood in this life, rather than they would be stained in their journey, or lodge in any of Satan's inns, so that the storms or winds which fell in their travellings might not touch them. Wherefore, dearly beloved, let us think, what we are, and how far meet to be matched with these, whom yet we look to be placed in heaven.

But with what face can we look for this, that are so fearful, unwilling, and backward to leave that which, will we, nill we, we must leave, and that so shortly, as we know not the time when? Where is our abrenouncing and forsaking of the world and the flesh, which we solemnly sware in baptism? Ah, shameless cowards that we be! which will not follow the trace of so many fathers, patriarchs, kings, priests, prophets, apostles, evangelists, and saints of God, yea, even of the very Son of God. How many now go with you lustily, as I and all your brethren in bonds and exile for the gospel? Pray for us; for, God willing, we will not leave 2 Pet. i. you now, we will go before you. You shall see in us, that we preached no lies nor tales of tubs; but even the very true word of God, for which we, by God's grace and help of your prayers, will willingly and joyfully give our blood to be shed for the confirmation of the same, as already we have given liberally our goods, living friends and natural country. For now we are certain, that we be in the high way to heaven's bliss; as Paul saith, "By many tribulations and persecutions we must enter into God's kingdom." And because we would go thither ourselves, and bring you thither also, therefore the devil stirreth up the coals. And forasmuch as we all loitered in the way, he therefore hath received power of God to overcast the weather and to stir up storms, that we, God's children, might go faster, making more speed and haste to go on forwards. As for counterfeits and hypocrites, they will tarry and linger till the storm be past. And so when they come, the market will be done, and the doors sparred, it is to be feared. Read Matthew xxv. This wind will blow God's children forward, and the devil's darlings backward. Therefore, like God's children, let us go on forward apace; the wind is on our back, hoist up the sails, lift up your hearts and hands unto God in prayer, and keep your anchor of faith to cast in time on the rock of God's word, and in his mercy in Christ; and I warrant you. Heb. vi.

And thus much for you, secondly, to consider, that affliction, persecution, and trouble is no strange thing to God's children; and therefore it should not dismay, discourage, or discomfort us, being none other thing than all God's dear friends have tasted in their journey to heavenward. As I would in this troublesome time, that ye should consider what you be by the goodness of God in Christ, even citizens of heaven, though you be presently in the flesh, even in a strange region, on every side full of fierce enemies, and what weather and way the dearest friends of God have found; even so would I have you, thirdly, to consider for your further comfort, that if you shrink not, but go on forward pressing to the mark appointed, all the power of your enemies shall not overcome you, neither in any point hurt you.

CHAPTER III.

TROUBLE CANNOT HURT GOD'S CHILDREN.

BUT this must you not consider according to the judgment of reason and her sense, but after the judgment of God's word and the experience of faith; else you mar all. For to reason and experience or sense of the outward man we poor souls, which stick to God's word to serve him as he requireth only, are counted to be vanquished and overcome, in that we are cast into prison, lose our livings, friends, goods, country, and life also at length concerning this world. But, dearly beloved, God's word teacheth otherwise, and faith falleth accordingly. Is it not written, "Who shall separate us from the love of God? shall tribulation, Rom. viii. or anguish, or persecution, either hunger, either nakedness, either peril, either sword? As it is written, For thy sake are we killed all day long, and be counted as sheep ap- Psal. xliv. pointed to be slain. Nevertheless in all these things we overcome through him that loved us. For I am sure that

neither death, neither life, neither angels, nor rule, neither power, neither things present, neither things to come, neither height, nor loweth, neither any other creature, shall be able to part us from that love, wherewith God loveth us in Christ Jesus our Lord." This spake one, which was in affliction, as I am, for the Lord's gospel's sake; his holy name be praised therefore, and he grant me grace with the same to continue in like suffering unto the end! This, I say, one spake, which was in affliction for the gospel; but yet so far from being overcome, that he rejoiced rather of the victory
2 Tim. ii. which the gospel had. For though he was bound, the gospel was not bound; and therefore rendered he thanks unto God,
2 Cor. ii. who always giveth victory in Christ, and openeth the savour of his knowledge by us and such' as suffer for his truth; although they shut us up never so much, and drive us never so far out of our natural country in every place.

The world for a time may deceive itself, aye thinking it
Gen. iv. hath the victory; but yet the end will try the contrary. Did not Cain think he had the victory, when Abel was slain? But how say ye now? Is it not found otherwise? Thought not the old world that they were wise and well, and Noe a fool,
Gen. vii.
viii. which would creep into an ark, leaving his house, lands, and possessions? For I think he was in an honest state. As for the world, they judged that he was a dastard and a fool: but I pray you, who was wise when the flood came?
Gen. xii. Abraham, I trow, was counted a fool to leave his own country and friends, kith and kin, because of God's word. But, dearly beloved, we know it proved otherwise. I will leave all the patriarchs, and come to Moses and the children of Israel. Tell me, were they not thought to be overcome,
Exod. xiv. and stark mad, when for fear of Pharao, at God's word, they ran into the Red Sea? Did not Pharao and the Egyptians think themselves sure of the victory? But, I
1 Sam. xvi.
&c. trow, it proved clean contrary. Saul was thought to be well, and David in evil case and most miserable, because he had no hole to hide him in; but yet at length Saul's misery was seen, and David's felicity began to appear. The prophet
1 Kings xxii. Michaias, being cast into prison for telling Achab the truth, was thought overcome of Zedechias and other false prophets: but, my good brethren, and sisters, the holy history telleth
Jer. xx. otherwise. Who did not think the prophets unhappy in

their time? for they were slain, imprisoned, laughed to scorn, and jested at of every man. And so were all the 1 Cor. iv. apostles; yea, the dearly beloved friend of God, John the Baptist, who was beheaded, and that in prison, even at a dancing damsel's desire. As all these, to the judgment of reason, were then counted heretics, runagates, unlearned, fools, fishers, publicans, &c., so now unhappy and overcome in deed, if God's word and faith did not shew the contrary.

But what speak I of those? Look upon Jesus Christ; Rom. viii. to whom we must be fashioned here, if we will be like him elsewhere. How say you, was he not taken for almost a fool, a seditious person, a new fellow, an heretic, and one overcome of every body, even forsaken both of God and men? But the end told them and telleth us another tale; for now is he in majesty and glory joyful. When he was led to Pilate or Herod, or when he was in prison in Caiphas' house, did not their reason think that he was overcome? When he was beaten, buffeted, scourged, crowned with thorns, hanged upon the cross, and utterly left of all his disciples, taunted of the high priests and holy fathers, cursed of the commons, railed on of the magistrates, and laughed to scorn of the lewd heathen; would not a man then have thought, that he had been out of the way, and his disciples to follow and believe him? Think you, the whilst he lay in his grave, men did not point with their fingers, when they saw any that had loved and believed in him and his doctrine, saying, Where is their master and teacher now? What! is he gone? Forsooth, if they had not been fools, they might well have known this learning he taught could not long continue. Our doctors and Pharisees are no fools, now they may see. On this sort men either spake or might have spoken against all such as loved Christ or his doctrine: but yet they and all such were proved fools and wicked wretches. For our Saviour arose maugre their beards, and published his gospel plentifully, spite of their heads and the heads of all the wicked world, with the great powers of the same; always overcoming, and then most of all, when he and his doctrine was thought to have the greatest fall.

Now, dearly beloved, the wicked world rejoiceth, the papists are puffed up against poor Christ and his people:

after their old kind now cry they, Where are these new-found preachers? Are they not in the Tower, Marshal-sea, in the Fleet, in Newgate, &c., and beyond the seas? Who would have thought that our old bishops, doctors, and deans were fools, as they would have made us believe, and indeed have persuaded some already, which are not of the wisest, specially if they come not home again to the holy church? These and such like words they have to cast in our teeth, as triumphers and conquerors. But, dearly beloved, short is their joy. They beguile themselves; this is but a lightning before their death. As God, after he had given the wicked Jews a time to repent, visited them *Eusebius, Eccles. Hist. Lib. III. cap. 5, 6, 7, 8, 9.* by Vespasian and Titus most horribly, to their utter sub-version, delivering first of all his people from among them; even so, my dear brethren, will he do with this age. When he hath tried his children from amongst them, as now he beginneth, and by suffering hath made us like to his Christ, and by being overcome to overcome indeed to our eternal *1 Thess. iv.* comfort; then will he, if not otherwise, come himself in the clouds: I mean, our dear Lord, whom we confess, preach, and believe on. He will come, I say, with the blast of a trump and shout of an archangel, and so shall we be caught up in the clouds to meet him in the air; the angels gathering *Matt. iii.* together the wicked wretches, which now welter and wallow, as the world and wind bloweth, to be tied in bundles, and cast into the fire which burneth for ever most painfully. There and then shall they see, who hath the victory, they *Luke xvi.* or we. When they shall see us afar off in Abraham's bosom, then will they say, Alas! we thought these folks fools, and *[Wisd. v.]* had them in derision; we thought their life madness, and their end to be without honour. But lo! how are they counted among the children of God, and their portion is with the saints. Alas! we have gone amiss, and would not hearken. Such words as these shall the wicked say one day in hell, though now they triumph as conquerors.

And thus much for you, thirdly, to look often upon; namely, that whatsover is done unto you, yea, even very death, shall not baffle or hurt you no more than it did Abel, David, Daniel, John the Baptist, Jesus Christ our Lord, with other the dear saints of God, which have suffered for his name's sake. Let not, therefore, reason be judge in this matter, but faith and God's word; in the which if we set before our eyes the shortness of this present time wherein we suffer, and consider the eternity to come, we shall find it most certain that our enemies and persecutors shall be helpless in intolerable pains, and we, if we persevere unto the end, shall be dangerless in such felicity and joy, as the very heart of man in no point is able to conceive. Consider- ing this, I say, we cannot but even contemn and set nothing by the sorrows and griefs of the cross, and lustily go through thick and thin with good courage.

The time of suffering is but a trifle.

1 Cor. ii. Isai. lxiv.

Now have I declared unto you three things necessary to be much mused upon of every one, which will abide in Christ and his gospel in these troublesome times, as I trust you all will: namely, first, to consider, that we are not of this world, nor of the number of the worldlings, nor any retainer to Satan; that we are not at home in our own country, but of another world, of the congregation of the saints and retainers to Christ, although as yet in a region replete and full of untractable enemies. Secondly, that we may not think it a strange thing to be persecuted for God's gospel, from the which the dearest friends of God were in no age free; as indeed it is impossible they should be any long time, their enemies being always about them, to destroy them if they could. And thirdly, that the assaults of our enemies, be they never so many and fierce, shall in no point be able to prevail against our faith, albeit to reason it seemeth otherwise; wherethrough we ought to conceive a good courage and comfort: for who will be afraid, when he knoweth that the enemies cannot prevail?

Heb. xii.

CHAPTER IV.

THE CROSS IS COMMODIOUS AND PROFITABLE.

FURTHERMORE, for the more encouraging of you unto the cross, I will give you a fourth memorandum, namely, of the commodities and profits which come by the trouble and affliction now risen, and hereafter to arise, unto us which be God's children, elect through Jesus Christ. But here ye may not look to have [from] me a rehearsal of all the commodities which come by the cross to such as are well exercised therein; for that were more than I can do. I will only speak of a few; thereby to occasion you to gather, and at the length to feel and perceive more.

The first commodity of the cross.

Amos iii.
Matt. x.
Isai. xlv.
Psalm cxlv.

First, there is no cross which cometh upon any of us without the counsel of our heavenly Father. As for the fancy of fortune, it is wicked, as many places of scripture do teach. We must needs, to the commendation of God's justice, who in all things is righteous, acknowledge in ourselves that we have deserved of the hands of our heavenly Father this his cross and rod, now fallen upon us. We have deserved it, if not by our own unthankfulness, sloth, negligence, intemperance, and our sins done often by us, (whereof our consciences can and will accuse us, if we call them to council, with the examination of our former life;) yet at least by our original and birth sin, as by doubting of the greatness of God's anger and mercy, by self-love, concupiscence, and

Psalm li.
Heb. xii.

such like sins, which as we brought with us into this world, so do the same ever abide in us, and, even as a spring, they alway bring forth something in act with us, notwithstanding

Gal v.

the fight of God's good Spirit in us against it. The first commodity, therefore, that the cross bringeth, is knowledge,

Psalm v.

and that double, of God, and of ourselves: of God, that he

Psalm li.

is just, pure, and hateth sin; of ourselves, that we are born

Gen. viii.
Jer. xvii.
Ephes. ii.
1 Kings viii.

in sin, and from top to toe defiled with concupiscence and corruption, out of the which have sprung all the evil that ever at any time we have spoken and done. The greatest and most special whereof we are by the cross occasioned to

Gen. xlii.

call to mind, as did the brethren of Joseph their evil fact against him, when the cross once came upon them. And so by it we come to the surest step to get health for our souls; that is, we are driven to know our sins, original and actual, by God's justice declared in the cross.

The second commodity of the cross.

Secondly, the end, wherefore God declareth his justice against our sin original and actual, and would have us by his cross to consider the same, and to call to mind our former evil deeds; the end thereof, I say, is this, namely, that we may lament, be sorry, sigh, and pray for pardon; to the intent, that so doing we might obtain and have the same by the means of faith in the merits of Jesus Christ his dear Son; and that we, being humbled because of the evil that dwelleth in us, might also become thankful for God's goodness, living in continual vigilance and wariness, and suppressing the evil which liveth in us, that it bring not forth fruit unto death at James i. any time.   This second commodity of the cross, therefore, must not we count to be only a knowledge, but also a great Note. gain of God's mercy with wonderful rich and precious virtues of faith, repentance, remission of sins, humility, thankfulness, mortification, and diligence in doing good.   Not that properly the cross worketh these things of itself; but because the cross is the mean and way by the which God worketh the know-ledge and feeling of these things in his children: as many both testimonies, and also ensamples in scripture, are easily found of them that diligently weigh what they hear or read therein.

To these two commodities of the cross join this third, of The third commodity God's singular wisdom, that it may be coupled with his justice of the cross. and mercy.   On this sort let us overcome it.   When we see the gospel of God and his church persecuted and troubled, as now it is with us, thus, I say, let us receive the matter; namely, that because the great learned and wise men of the world use not their wisdom to love and serve God, as to natural reason he openeth himself manifestly in his visible Rom. i. creatures, therefore doth God justly infatuate them, and maketh them foolish, giving them up to insensibleness, espe-cially herein.   For concerning the affliction which cometh for the gospel upon the gospellers, they reason on this manner. If this were God's word, say they, if this people were God's Man's reason concerning children, surely God would then bless and prosper them and the affliction of the church. their doctrine.   But now in that there is no doctrine so much hated, no people so much persecuted as they be, therefore it cannot be of God.   This is of God, which our queen and old bishops have professed.   For how hath God prospered and kept them!   What a notable victory hath God given to her; Success. whereas else it was impossible that things so should have come to pass, as they have done!   And did not the great The book of North. captain confess his fault, that he was out of the way, and not of the faith which these gospellers profess[1]?   How many are The relenting of many. come again from that which they professed to be God's word!

[1 Allusion is here made to the duke of Northumberland. An account of the circumstances mentioned may be found in Strype's Life of archbishop Cranmer, Book III. chap. iii. pp. 450—4. Ed. Oxf.]

The most part of this realm, notwithstanding the diligence of preachers to persuade them concerning this new learning which now is persecuted, never consented to it in heart, as *Plagues.* experience teacheth. And what plagues have come upon this realm since this gospel, as they call it, came in amongst us! Afore we had plenty; but now there is nothing like as was. *Parliament.* But, to let this pass, all the houses of the parliament have overthrown the laws made for the stablishing of the gospel, and new laws are erected for the continuance of that which is contrary, and was had before. All these things do teach plainly, that this their doctrine is not God's word.

Thus reason the worldly-wise, which see not God's wisdom. *The cause of our persecution.* For else, if they considered that there was with us unthankfulness, no amendment of life, but all kind of contempt of God, all kind of shameless sinning against the preaching of the gospel, they must needs see that God could not but *Rev. xx.* chastise and correct; and that, as he let Satan loose after he had bound him a certain time, so for men's unthankfulness, and to punish the same, he hath let those champions of Satan run abroad to plague us by them. Great was God's anger *1 Kings xx.* against Ahab because he saved Benadad the king of Syria, when he had given him into his hands; and afterwards it turned to his own destruction. God would that double sorrow should have been repaid unto them, because of the sorrow that they did to the saints of God. Read Rev. xviii. As to *Causes of victory.* the victory given to the queen's highness, if men had any godly wit, they might see many things in it. First, that God hath done it to win her heart with kindness unto his gospel; and as well because that they which went against her, put their trust in horses and power of men, and not in God, as because in their doctrine they sought not the propagation of God's gospel. Which thing is easily now seen by the confession of the captain; his heart loved popery, and hated the gospel. Besides this, men may easily see he was purposed never to have furthered the gospel, but so to have handled the livings of ministers, that there should never have been any minister in manner hereafter. And what one of the councillors, which would have been taken as gospellers in one of our good king's days, declare now that even they loved the gospel? Therefore no marvel why God fought against them. They were hypocrites, and under the cloke of the gospel would have debarred the queen's highness of her right. But God would not so cloke them.

Now for the relenting, returning, and recanting of some from that which they have once professed or preached, alas! who would wonder at it? For they never came to the gospel, but for commodity or gain's sake; and now for gain leave it. The multitude is no good argument to move a wise man. For who knoweth not more to love this world better than heaven; themselves better than their neighbours? "Wide is the gate," saith Christ, "and broad is the way that leadeth to destruction, and many there be which go in thereat. But strait is the gate, and narrow is the way which leadeth unto life, and few there be that find it." All the whole multitude cried out upon Jesus, Crucify him, truss him up; but I trow they were not the better part, although they were the bigger. All Chaldeans followed still their false gods; only Abraham followed the true God. And whereas they say that greater plagues are fallen on the realm in poverty and such gear than afore, it is no argument to move others than such as love their swine better than Christ. For the devil chiefly desireth his seat to be in religion. If it be there, then will he meddle with nothing that we have; all shall be quiet enough: but if he be raised there, then will he beg leave to have at our pigs. As long as with us he had the ruling of religion, which now he hath gotten again, then was he a Robin Goodfellow; he would do no hurt: but when he was tumbled out of his throne by the preaching of the gospel, then steered he about as he hath done. Notwithstanding, to be short, surely effectual he hath not been, but in the children of unbelief: them indeed he hath stirred up to be covetous, oppressors, blasphemers, usurers, whoremongers, thieves, murderers, tyrants.

And yet perchance he suffered them to profess the gospel, the more thereby to hinder it, and cause it to be slandered. How many do now appear to be true gospellers? As for the parliament and statutes thereof, no man of wisdom can think otherwise, but that look what the rulers will, the same must there be enacted. For it goeth not in those houses by the better part, but by the bigger part. It is a common saying, and no less true, *Major pars vincit meliorem;* the greater part overcometh the better. So they did in con-

Why many relent and recant.

The greater sort.

Matt. vii.

Gen. xii.

Plagues.

Matt. viii.

The parliament.

John vii.

16—2

demning Christ; Nicodemus' counsel not being regarded. So did they in many general councils, which purposely I will not recite; for all wise men know that acts of parliament are not for God's law in respect of God's law, but in respect of the people.

Now what we are, God knoweth, and all the world seeth; more meet a great deal to have the devil's decrees, than God's religion; so great is our contempt in it. And there-*Job xxxiv.* fore justly for our sins, as Job saith, God hath set hypocrites to reign over us; which can no more abide God's true religion, than the owl the light, or bleared eyes the bright sun. For it will have them to do their duties, and walk in diligent doing of the works of their vocation. If God's word, I mean, had place, bishops could not play chancellors and idle prelates, as they do; priests should be otherwise known than by their shaven crowns and appetites. But enough of this. I will now return to the third commodity coming by the cross.

Here let us see the wisdom of God, in making the *The igno-* wisdom of the world foolish. For it knoweth little of man's *rance of* corruption, how foul it is in the sight of God, and displeaseth *worldly* him. It knoweth little the portion of God's people to be in *wisdom.* another world. It knoweth little the portion of Christians, Christ Jesus. It knoweth little the judgments of God, the great malice of Satan to God's people, the price and estimation of the gospel. And therefore in the cross it seeth not, as God's wisdom would men should see, namely, that God *Luke xiii.* in punishing them which sin least, would have his anger against sin better considered and feared; and that in punishing his people here, he kindleth their desire towards their *2 Cor. v.* restful and peaceable home. For in punishing his servants in this life, he doth by these means conform and make them *Philipp. i.* like to Christ; that as they be like in suffering, so they may be partakers in reigning. In punishing his church in the world, he doth thereby give even a demonstration of his judgment, which shall come on all men, when the godly *2 Thess. i.* shall there find rest, though now they be afflicted; and the *2 Pet. ii.* wicked now wallowing in wealth shall be wrapped in woe *Job i.* and smart. In punishing the professors of his gospel on *Acts xvi.* earth, he doth by the same set forth the malice of Satan *xvii. xviii.* *&c.* against the gospel and his people, for the more confirming

of their faith, and the gospel to be God's word indeed, and
them to be God's people : for else the devil would let them
alone.   In punishing the lovers of his truth more than
others which care not for it, he thereby putteth them in
mind, how they have not had in price, as they should have Psalm cxix.
had, the rule of his word and gospel.   Before such trial and
experience by trouble, perchance they thought they had
believed and had had faith; which now they see was but
a lip faith, a mock faith, or an opinion.   All which things
we see are occasions for us to take better heed by means
of the cross.

Therefore, thirdly, let us see the cross to be commodious
for us to learn God's wisdom, and what is man's foolishness,
God's displeasure at sin, how the elect desire to be with
God, and their conformity with Christ, the general judgment,
the malice of Satan, hatred of sin, the gospel to be God's
word, and how it is much to be esteemed, &c.   Thus much
for this.

Now will I briefly shew you the cross to be profitable The fourth
for us, to learn and behold better the providence, presence, of the cross.
and power of God; that all these may be coupled together,
as in a chain, to hang about our necks: I mean God's
justice, mercy, wisdom, power, presence, and providence.

When all things be in rest, and men be not in trouble,
then are they forgetful of God commonly, and attribute too
much to their own wisdoms, policies, provisions and diligence;
as though they were the procurers of their own fortune and
the workers of their own wealth.   But when the cross
cometh, and that in such sort as their wits, policies, and
friends cannot help them, then though the wicked despair
and run from God to their anodynes, saints, and unlawful
means, yet do the godly therein behold the presence, providence, and power of God.   For the scripture teacheth, that
all things, weal and woe, should be considered as God's work, Amos iii.
although Satan, the devil, be the instrument by whom God Matth. x.
worketh justly and mercifully; justly to the wicked, and
mercifully to the godly; as by the ensamples of wicked Saul The devil
and godly Job we may easily see God's work by Satan his strument.
instrument in them both.

The children of God, therefore, which before forgat God
in prosperity, are now in adversity awaked to see God and

his work; and no more to hang on their own forecasts, power, friends, wisdom, riches, &c.; but learn to commit themselves unto God's providence and power, whereby they are so preserved and governed, and very often even miraculously delivered, that the very wicked cannot but see God's providence, presence, and power in the cross and affliction of his children; as these (his children, I mean) to their joy do feel it, thereby learning to know God to be the governor of all things. He it is that giveth peace, he it is that sendeth war, he giveth plenty and poverty, he setteth up and casteth down, he bringeth to death, and after giveth life; his presence is everywhere, his providence is within and without, his power is the pillar whereby the godly stand, and to it they lean, as to a thing no less able to set up than to cast down.

Which thing full well the apostle saw in his afflictions, and therefore rejoiced greatly in them, that *eminentia virtutis Dei*, God's power might singularly be seen therein.

Concerning this I might bring forth innumerable ensamples of the affliction of God's children, both in the old and new Testament, wherein we may see how they felt God's presence, providence, and power plentifully. But I will omit ensamples; because every one of us that have been or be in trouble, cannot but by the same the rather remember God's presence, which we feel by his hand upon us presently; his providence, which leaveth us not uncared for, without any of our own provision; his power, which both preserveth us from many other evils, that else would come upon us, and also maketh us able to bear more than we thought we could have done. So very often doth he deliver us by such means as have been thought most foolish, and little to be regarded.

And, therefore, we spake of our sleep of security and forgetting of God, our trust and shift in our own policy, our hanging on men and on our own power. So that the cross, you see, is commodious, fourthly, for us, to see God's presence, providence, and power; and our own negligence, forgetfulness of God, security, love, trust, and confidence in ourselves and in things of this life to be cut off, as the other are to be taken hold upon.

And this shall suffice for the commodities that come by the cross; wherethrough we may be in love for it for the commodities' sake, which at length we shall find, though presently in sense we feel them not.   "No castigation or Heb. xii. punishment is sweet or joyous for the present time, but grievous; nevertheless afterward it bringeth the quiet fruit of righteousness unto them which are exercised therein." As we see in medicines, the more wholesome they be, the more unpleasant oftentimes is the taste, as in purgations, pills, and such like bitter things; yet upon the physician's word we will gladly drink them for the profit which cometh of them.   And, dearly beloved, although to lose life, goods, or friends for God's gospel's sake seem a bitter and sour thing; yet seeing our Physician which cannot lie, Jesus Christ, I mean, telleth me, that it is very wholesome, howsoever it be toothsome[1], let us with good cheer take the cup at his hand, and drink it merrily.   If the cup seem unpleasant, and the drink is bitter, let us put some sugar therein, even a piece of that which Moses cast into the bitter Exod. xv. water, and made it pleasant; I mean an ounce or quantity of Christ's afflictions and cross, which he suffered for us.   1 Pet. iv.

If we call these to mind, and cast of them into our cup, considering what he was, what he suffered, of whom, for whom, to what end, and what came thereof; surely we cannot loathe our medicine, but mix and drink it lustily. Lustily, therefore, drink the cup; Christ giveth it, and will give it unto you, my good brethren and sisters: I mean, prepare yourselves to suffer whatsoever God may lay upon you for the confession of his holy name; if not because of these three things, that you be not of this world, that ye suffer not alone, and your trouble shall not hurt you; yet because of the commodities that come of the cross, I beseech you heartily to embrace it.

[1 Probably a mistake for *untoothsome*.]

CHAPTER V.

HOW THE PAPISTS HOLD THEIR FOUR SPECIAL ARTICLES, THAT THEY CHIEFLY PERSECUTE FOR.

AND here, because the persecution and cross which is come and will come upon us, is specially for these four points of religion, namely, of the sacrament of Christ's body and blood, and for the sacrifice of Christ, for praying for the dead, and for praying to the dead, that is, to saints; I am purposed by God's grace to write hereof a little unto you, thereby to confirm you in the truth, to your comfort in the cross about the same. And first, concerning the first doctrine, what they would have us believe on these points.

Of the Sacrament.

John vi.

This is their doctrine. The catholic church hath taught, as she hath learned and received of Christ, how that he in his last supper, according to his promise, when he promised to give a bread, even his flesh, in instituting the sacrament of the altar (as they call it) performed the same, and that as in all things which he promised he was found true, so in this the catholic church hath believed and doth believe no less. And therefore so soon as the priest in the mass hath fully spoken these words, " This is my body," if he purpose or his intention be as he speaketh, (for that is requisite, teach they,) then that which before was bread, and seemeth to the eye to be bread, is made in very deed Christ's body, flesh, blood, and bone, even the selfsame which was crucified, rose again, and ascended up into heaven. So that he which believeth not this, is a most heinous heretic, and cut off from the catholic church, and is not meet to receive this holy sacrament; because he cannot without this faith of Christ's natural, real, corporal, and carnal body, under the form or accident of bread and wine, otherwise receive this sacrament than unworthily and to eternal damnation. This is a short sum of their doctrine concerning the supper.

Now concerning the sacrifice they teach, that though our Saviour himself did indeed make a full and perfect sacrifice, propitiation, and satisfaction for the sins of all the whole world, never more so, that is to say, bloodily, to be offered again; yet in the supper he offered the same sacrifice to his Father, but unbloodily, that is to say, in will and desire; which is accounted often even for the deed, as this was. Which unbloody sacrifice he commanded his church to offer in remembrance of his bloody sacrifice, as the principal mean whereby his bloody sacrifice is applied both to the quick and dead; as baptism is the mean by the which regeneration is applied by the priest to the infant or child that is baptized. For in that the supper of Christ is to them not only a sacrament, but also a sacrifice, and that not only applicatory, but also propitiatory, because it applieth the propitiatory sacrifice of Christ to whom the priest or minister will, be he dead or alive; and in that, even from the beginning, the fathers were accustomed in the celebration of the supper to have a memorial of the dead[1]; and also in that this sacrifice is a sacrifice of the whole church; the dead being members, of the church, of charity, as they cannot but offer for them, even so they cannot but pray for them after the ensample of the catholic church; because it is a wholesome thing, saith Judas Maccabeus, to pray for the dead, that they may be delivered from their sins. Whereunto all the doctors do consent, say they.

Prayer for the dead.

[2 Mac. xii. 44, 45.]

Now, as for praying to saints, they teach, that albeit there is but one Mediator of redemption, yet of intercession the holy saints of God departed this life may well be counted mediators. And, therefore, it is a point of a lowly heart and humble spirit, which God well liketh, to call upon the saints to pray for us first, lest by our presumption to come into God's presence, we being so unworthy, and God being so excellent and full of majesty, we more anger and displease God; whereas by their help God may be entreated to make us more worthy to come unto him, and the sooner to grant us our petitions. For if the holy saints of God, here being upon the earth, could and would pray for the people, obtaining many things at God's hand; it is much more to be believed now, say they, that they can and will, if we pray to them, obtain for us our 'humble and godly desires. And therefore to the end their sacrifice propitiatory, which in the

Prayer to saints.

[1 On this subject see Bingham's *Origines Ecclesiasticæ*, Lib. xv. chap. iii. sect. 15—17.]

mass they offer, may be the more available, they use about
it much praying to saints. So of these four, as of four pillars, the mass standeth. The which mass, you may see what
it is, and how precious and worthy a piece of work it is, by
their doctrine concerning the supper, the sacrifice, the praying for the dead and to the dead; whereof I have given you
a sum in the most honest, godly, and religious wise, that the
best of them do set it forth in. For else, if I should have
shewed you this their doctrine, as some of them set it forth,
as I know you would abhor it, so the subtle papists would
say that I railed and misrepresented them. Therefore because they shall have no such occasion, nor you by their most
subtle colours be deceived, I have, in the best manner I can,
repeated a sum of their doctrine. The which to the end
you might the better consider and have, I will now tell you,
as God's word teacheth, how these four points are to be
believed and received; and then will I open the filthiness
and abomination, which in this their doctrine is devilishly
contained.

CHAPTER VI.

HOW GOD'S WORD TEACHETH OF THE SUPPER, WITH CON-
FUTATION OF THE PAPISTS' HERESY OF TRANSUBSTAN-
TIATION ABOUT THE SAME.

CONCERNING the supper of our Lord, which Christ Jesus
did institute to be a sacrament of his body and blood, we
believe that his words in the same supper accordingly are
to be understood, that is, sacramentally, as he meant them;
and not simply, contrary to his meaning, as the papists wrest
them. And this is taught us, not only by innumerable such
like places, as where baptism is called regeneration, because

Titus iii.

Gen. xvii.

it is a sacrament of it; circumcision is called God's covenant,
because it is a sacrament of it; but also by the plain circum-

Matth. xxvi.
Mark xiv.
Luke xxii.
1 Cor. x. xi.

stances of the text, as thereof the evangelists with the apostle
St Paul do write plainly, affirming that our Saviour Christ
did give, and his disciples did eat, that which he took and

brake, and bade them divide among themselves, that is, bread and wine. For we may not think that Christ's natural body was broken, nor that his blood can be divided. And plainly, our Saviour saith concerning the cup, that he would not drink Matth. xxvi.
Mark xiv. any more of the fruit of the vine, (which is not his blood, I trow, but wine,) until he should drink it new with them after his resurrection.

But to make this matter more plain, like as many things in Christ's supper were figuratively done and spoken, as the washing of the disciples' feet, the paschal lamb was called the John xiii.
Luke xxii. passah, Judas was said to have lifted up his heel against him; so doth Luke and Paul plainly alter the words concerning the cup, calling that the new Testament, which Matthew and Mark call his blood; yea, expressly five times the apostle calleth the sacrament of Christ's body after the consecration spoken (as they term it) bread. "Is not the bread, 1 Cor. x. xi. which we break," saith he, "the communion of Christ's body?" Whose exposition I will more boldly stick unto, than unto all the papists' dreams, as long as I sleep not with them, by God's grace. They have none other sentence but these four words, "This is my body." But ask them, what this is, and they will not say, as the apostle doth, namely, that it is bread. No; then they will say, that we hang all by reason, the matter being a matter of faith. Whereas they themselves altogether hang on reason, as though Christ cannot be able to do that which he promiseth, (bread still in substance remaining, as the accidents do,) except it be transubstantiate. Is not this, trow you, to make it a matter of reason, and to hedge God's power in within the limits of reason? If Christ's words that follow, "which is given for you," be to be understood for, "which shall be given, or shall be betrayed for you," and not so precisely, as they be spoken, (for that were to make Christ a liar;) why is it so heinous a matter with the papists, because we do not so precisely take the words immediately going before, namely, "This is my body," as to admit, that if there be bread, then Christ is a liar? Might not we reason and say, Then if Christ's body at the time was not betrayed, (as indeed it was not,) nor his blood shed, then is Christ a liar. But here they will say, All men may know that Christ by the present tense meant the future tense; and in the scripture it is a most usual thing so to take tense

for tense.   And, I pray you, why may not we say, that all
men may know it is most common in scripture to give unto
signs the names of the things which they signify ?   And no
man is so foolish, but he knoweth that Christ then instituted
a sacrament, wholly sacramentally to be understood; that is,
that the sign or visible sacrament should have not only the
name of the thing signified, but also some similitude therewith, or else it were no sacrament.   But take bread away,
as the papists do, leaving there but the accidents only, which
do not feed the body; and then what shall resemble and
represent unto us Christ's body broken for the food of the
soul ?   As wine comforteth the heart, so doth Christ's blood
shed on the cross comfort the soul.   But take wine away
by transubstantiation, as the papists do, and tell me, what
similitude remaineth ?   None at all : so no sacrament at all.
So Christ's institution is taken away.   Well do they reject
God's commandment for their tradition's sake.

     Our faith, therefore, is, that the supper of the Lord is
the sacrament of Christ's body and blood.   These words,
" This is my body, which is broken for you; this is my blood
of the new Testament, which is shed for your sins," are
most true words, and plain according to Christ's meaning to
all them which do as he biddeth them, that is, to all such
as take, eat, and drink.   Which words the papists keep in
their purse, or else their private masses could not stand.   To
such, I say, as take and eat this sacrament, in sorrowing for
their sinful life past, and purposing to amend, above all
things remembering and believing that Christ's body was
broken for their sins, and his blood shed for their iniquities;
all such, I say, as verily as they see, take, taste, and eat
bread, and drink wine, which goeth into their body, feedeth
it, and nourisheth it; even so verily the soul and spirit by
faith receiveth, not only Christ's body broken, or his blood
John vi.   shed, (for "the flesh profiteth nothing, it is the spirit that
quickeneth," saith Christ;) but even whole Christ, into whom
Ephes. v.   they are incorporate and made one with him, flesh of his
flesh, and bone of his bones.   That is to say, as Christ's
body is immortal and glorious, even so are theirs now by
faith and hope, and at the [last] day they shall be in very
deed.   Than which thing what can be greater ?   This we
teach and believe concerning this sacrament, detesting and

abhorring the horrible error of transubstantiation, which maketh bread and wine our God and Christ; and causeth men to be gazers, gapers, and worshippers, yea, idolaters, rather than tasters and eaters, as Christ commandeth; and which maketh Christ's sacrifice of none effect, as now shall be shewed by God's grace.

For this shall suffice to the declaration of our faith concerning the Lord's supper; whereunto agreeth the catholic church, and all the fathers; as full well thou mayest see in the bishop of Canterbury's book, which is far from being answered either by the bishop of Winchester his book in English, or Marcus Constantius in Latin[1], which thou needest no more to confirm thy faith in this matter, than to read them with an indifferent mind, not being addict otherwise than to the desire of the truth. As for this doctrine of transubstantiation, it is a new-found thing about six hundred years old; even then brought out, when Satan was let loose after a thousand years that was bound. Even then was it established, when there was more mischief among the prelates, specially the popes, about the see of Rome, who could catch it, than ever there was among the emperors for the empire. In the primitive church popes were martyred for Christ's spouse's sake, that is, the church; but now one poisoned another, and one slew another, for the rose-coloured whore of Babylon's sake, that is, the popish church. In one hundred and sixty years there was near hard fifty popes[2]; whereas in no such time there were above thirty-three emperors. And in the midst of this miserable state and time this doctrine of transubstantiation was the pope's beginning, as they might have leisure from conspiring against princes, and one against another, to establish it as the very principal pillar of all their power. And no marvel: for this being admitted, then have they power over Christ the King of all kings, that he be where they will, when they will, and as long as they will, under their power; wherethrough the

Rev. xx.

Rev. xvii. xviii.

[1 By Marcus Constantius is meant bishop Gardiner, who under this fictitious name published his *Confutatio cavillationum, &c.* See archbishop Cranmer's writings and disputations relative to the Lord's supper. Parker Soc. Ed. p. 419. note.]

[2 The period alluded to is probably contained between the beginning of the tenth and the latter part of the eleventh century.]

other must needs follow, that if they have power over Christ, and that in heaven, to bring him down at their pleasure, much more then over all earth, emperors, kings, princes, and people; yea, even over the devil, purgatory, and hell, have they full power and jurisdiction, being now gods on earth, which sit in the holy place, even as God, yea, above God; to make what article of faith shall please them, as they have done this of transubstantiation; which might as well be denied as granted, saith Duns, one of their own doctors, and master Gabriel also, if it so pleased the holy father, and his spouse, the church of Rome[1]. Before this time all the fathers' diligence, labour, and care was to call men to the receiving of this sacrament for the confirmation of their faith; that as verily as they did eat bread and drink wine here, so should they not doubt but that by faith they did feed on the body of Christ, broken for their sins, and on his blood shed for their iniquities. And therefore sometimes would they call the sacrament bread, a figure or a sign; sometime would they call it the body and blood of our Saviour Jesus Christ, as the nature of sacraments is to be called with the name of the things which they do signify; that thereby men's minds might be withdrawn from the consideration of sensible and visible things to things heavenly, which they do signify and represent. And their care and crying unto the people was to receive it; and therefore they made decrees that such as would not receive and be present, should be spurned out of the church. Oh, how earnest was Chrysostom herein! Read his sixty-first homily unto the people of Antioch[2]. But after that this decree and doctrine of transubstantiation came in, no crying out hath there been to receive it, (no, that is the prerogative of the priest and

Marginal notes:

2 Thess. ii.

Scotus super 4. Senten. dist. 11. Gabriel. super canon. missæ. Lect. 40.

[1 Joann. Duns Scoti Opera, Lugd. 1639, in Lib. IV. Sentent. Dist. XI. Quæst. 3. Tom. VIII. pp. 6, 16, 18, 19; and Gabriel Biel. Canon. Miss. Expos. Basil. 1515. Lect. XL. fol. 94, 2. The passages are referred to by archbishop Cranmer in his second book against Transubstantiation, p. 302, Parker Society's Edition; and they are given at length in his *Defensio veræ et Catholicæ doctrinæ de Sacramento corporis et sanguinis Christi Servatoris nostri*, p. 34. Ib.]

[2 The homily referred to is the 61st ad Pop. Antioch. in the Latin edition of Chrysostom, and will be found Tom. v. p. 336. ed. Paris. 1570.]

shaven shorelings;) but altogether the end of their crying out was as now to believe transubstantiation, Christ to be their flesh, blood, and bone at every altar, between every priest's hands, yea, in every priest's mouth, when it pleaseth them......The crying and teaching of the clergy continually hath been to believe transubstantiation, and then to come to church to see their Maker once a day, to hold up their hands, to knock on their breasts, to streak their faces, to mutter with their Latin prayers, to take holy water and holy bread, to live in obedience to holy father, and holy church his spouse.   This was all they required.   Drink, dice, card, fight, swear, steal, no matter; so that in the morning they see their God, all is well; good catholic people; no man shall hurt them, or persecute them.   But if any man should not allow nor worship this God of their making, although he lived a most godly life, and were a man full of charity, sobriety, and very religious, O, such is an heretic or schismatic.   Nothing would please these wolves but even the blood and life of such a poor sheep; as men have felt before, and now begin to feel.   Let all the pack of them burthen those justly, whom now they imprison and cause to fly the realm, of any other thing than only of this, that we will not serve their God of bread and wine, and then will we suffer shame.   But I have been too long herein. Now to our doctrine and belief, for the second point concerning Christ's sacrifice.

CHAPTER VII.

HOW GOD'S WORD TEACHETH OF CHRIST'S SACRIFICE, AND THE POPE'S BLASPHEMY THEREIN REVEALED.

THE doctrine and faith in this behalf is as in the other, that is, according to God's holy word; namely, that Jesus Christ, the Son of God and second Adam, by whom we receive righteousness unto life, as by the first Adam we received sin unto death,—our faith is, I say, that this Christ in our flesh, which he took of the substance of the virgin Mary, but pure and without sin, for the satisfying of God's just displeasure deservedly and in our flesh, did in the same suffer unjustly all kinds of misery and affliction, and offered up himself unto his eternal Father with a most willing obedient heart and ready mind, when he was crucified upon the cross. And thereby as he satisfied God's justice, so he merited and procured his mercy, peace, and favour for all them which either before that time were dead, either were at that time present, either that should afterwards come and believe, by and in that offering done for them and their sins; so that God the eternal Father, I say, would be, in this their Christ, their God and Father, and not lay their sins committed to their charge to condemnation.

This doctrine the holy scripture teacheth almost every where; but specially in the Epistle to the Hebrews, chaps. i. vii. viii. ix. This is most lively for faith, how that by one oblation once offered by this Christ himself all that be God's people are sanctified. For as in respect of them that died in God's covenant and election before Christ suffered his death, and offered his sacrifice, one, alone, and omnisufficient, never more to be offered, he is called the Lamb slain from the beginning of the world, and the one alone Mediator between God and man, whose forthcoming was from the beginning; even so in respect of the virtue and efficacy of this one sacrifice to all God's people continually unto the world's end, the Holy Ghost doth tell us, that thereby he hath made holy such as be children of salvation: and saith not, shall make holy, or doth make holy; lest any man

Rev. xiii.
1 Tim. ii.
Mic. iii. v.

should with the papists indeed reiterate this satisfaction again: although in words they say otherwise, as anon we shall see, if hereunto I shew you the means whereby to apply this sacrifice; which I will do very briefly.

For in the seventeenth of John our Saviour doth very plainly shew this in these words: "For their sakes," saith he, "I sanctify myself, that they also might be sanctified through the truth. I pray not for them alone, but for those also which shall believe on me through their preaching." Here our Saviour applieth his sacrifice in teaching and praying for them. And as he teacheth them as ministers to do the like, that is, to preach and pray for the application of his sacrifice to the church, so doth he teach them and all the church to apply it unto themselves by believing it and by faith. The which thing the apostle St Paul in many places, but more plainly in the second to the Corinthians, the first chapter in the latter end, doth teach. Read it and see. So that, as ye have now Christ's one only sacrifice, which he himself on the cross offered once, as sufficient for all that do believe, and never more to be reiterated; so have you, that for the applying of it to his church the ministers should preach, and pray that their preaching might be effectual in Christ. And as Paul was ready himself to suffer death for the confirmation of the faith of the elect, so should the church and every member of the same, which is of years of discretion, by believing in Christ through the minister's preaching, apply it to themselves. As for infants, I need not in this place to speak of God's election. It is most certain this kind of applying, as it killeth the papistical priests, which hate not the dead worse than true preaching, so doth it cast down all their soul-massing and foolish foundations for such as be dead and past the ministry of God's word. And also it putteth away the opinion of *opus operatum*, and perseverance in impiety, from such as would enjoy the benefits of Christ's death.

CHAPTER VIII.

OF PRAYING FOR THE DEAD, THE TRUE DOCTRINE.

Now as concerning the third, that is, praying for the dead and sacrificing for them, as in the other we confess, teach, and believe according to God's word, so do we in this; namely, that in holy scripture, throughout the canonical books of the old and new Testament, we find neither precept nor ensample of praying for any, when they be departed this life; but as men die, so shall they arise: if in faith in the Lord towards the south, then need they no prayers; then are they presently happy, and shall arise in glory: if in unbelief without the Lord towards the north, then are they past all help, in the damned state presently, and shall rise to eternal shame. Wherefore according to the scripture we exhort men to repent, and while they have time, to work well. Every man shall bear his own burthen; every man shall give account for himself, and not for John, nor for Thomas, that sing and pray for him. Every man shall receive according to that he himself doeth in this body, while he is here alive, be it good or bad; and not according to that his executors, or this chantry priest and that fraternity doth for him. Whereby we may well see, if we will, that as prayer for the dead is not available or profitable to the dead, so is it of us not allowable, or to be excused. For as they that are departed are past our prayers, being either in joy or in misery, as is above shewed; even so we, having for it no word of God, whereupon faith leaneth, cannot but sin in doing it, in that we do it not of faith, because we have no word of God for it. Therefore with Abraham, Isaac, Jacob, Moses, the prophets, Christ Jesus, and the apostles, we bury the dead in a convenient place, and mourn in measure, as men having hope of the resurrection, not because of them, for that were a great point of ingratitude, they being departed out of miserable condition unto a most blessed state. Therefore we give thanks to God for them, praise his name for his power and might shewed in them, and pray that we may depart in the same faith, and joyfully rise with them in

Marginal references:
Eccles. xi.
John v.
Gal. v.
Coloss. iii.
Rom. xiv.
2 Cor. v.
Rom. x. xiv.
1 Thess. iv.
Rev. xiv.

the resurrection; which we desire and wish the Lord would hasten. We mourn, I say, not because of them, but of ourselves, that have lost the company of such our helpers, and further us in spiritual and temporal benefits, by them being admonished of our immortality and of the vanity of this life, that we might the more contemn it, and desire the everlasting life, where they and we shall never be separated.

This is our faith and doctrine for them that be departed; who though they be members of the same holy mystical body of Christ that we be of, yet should they in this case be discerned from the militant members, they being at rest, and having finished their course and fight, in no point needing any of our help, unless we should too arrogantly set up our own merits and prayers, and pull down Christ, as though we were able to get pardon and higher crown in heaven for others; where all our righteousness and the best thing we do is so far from helping others, that thereby we cannot help ourselves; but had need to cry, *Dimitte nobis debita nostra*, being no better in God's sight than a defiled woman's cloth, although to the sight of men they may seem gorgeous and gay. For if the papists would say, (as, when they are pressed with blasphemy in extolling their own merits and works of supererogation against Christ, they use,) that our prayers do them no good in respect of the worthiness of their prayers, but in respect of God's goodness, in that God's goodness is not to be looked for otherwise than he hath promised; let them either give men his promise, or else in this behalf keep silence, and exercise themselves better in doing their duties to their brethren that be alive; towards whom their charity is very cold, although when they are dead, then they will pretend much, then will they pray for them, but yet not for nought and freely, as true charity worketh; for no penny, no paternoster. Give nothing, and then they will neither sing nor say *requiem*, nor *placebo*, I warrant you. But of this sufficient. Now to the last, of praying to the dead, or to saints departed this life.

2 Tim. iv.

Luke xi.
Isai. lxiv.

CHAPTER IX.

OF PRAYING TO SAINTS.

HERE we confess, teach, and believe, as before is said, according to God's holy word, that as all and every good thing cometh only from God the Father by the means of Jesus Christ, so for the obtaining of the same we must call upon his holy name, as he by himself commandeth very often. But forasmuch as God dwelleth in light inaccessible, and is a consuming fire, and hateth all impiety and uncleanness, and we be blind, stubble, grass, hay, and nothing but filth, unclean, and sinful; and because that therefore, as we may not, so we dare not approach to his presence; it hath pleased this good God and Father of his love to send a spokesman and mediator, an intercessor and advocate between him and us, even Jesus Christ, his dearly beloved Son; by whom we might have free entrance with boldness to come before his presence and throne of mercy, to find and obtain grace and help in time of need. For this our Mediator and Advocate is with his Father of the same substance, power, wisdom, and majesty, and therefore may weigh well with him in all things; and with us he is of the same substance which we are of, even flesh and man, but pure and without sin, in all things being tempted like unto us, and having experience of our infirmities; that he might be merciful and faithful in our behalf, to purge us from our sins, and to bring us into such favour with the Father, that we might be not only dearly beloved through him, the only dearling of the Father, but also obtain whatsoever we shall ask, according to his word and will, in the name of this same our Mediator, Saviour, Intercessor and Advocate. So that easy it is to see, that as it is an obedient service to God the Father, to call always upon him in all our need; so to come to his presence through Christ is to the honour of Christ's mediation, intercession, and advocateship. And therefore, as it cannot be but against the Almighty God and Father, to ask or look for any thing elsewhere, at the hands of any that be departed this life, as though he were not the giver of all good things, or as though he had not commanded us to come unto him; so we

Marginal references:
James i.
Psal. l.
1 Tim. vi.
Heb. xiii.
Psal. v.
Heb. ii. iv.
Heb. iii. iv.
1 Pet. ii.
Matt. iii. xvii.
Matt. vii.
1 John v.
John xiv.
Psal. l.

see it is manifestly against Christ Jesus our Lord, by any other saint, angel, or archangel, to come and move any thing at our Father's hands, as though he were not our Mediator, Advocate, and Intercessor, or else not a sufficient Mediator, Advocate, or Intercessor, or at least not so merciful, meek, gracious, loving, and ready to help, as others: whereas he only so loved us, as the very hearts of all men and angels never were able to conceive any part of the height, depth, *Ephes. iii.* breadth, and length of the same, as it is. If his own heart-blood was not too dear for us, being his very enemies, and never desirous to do his will; how is it possible that he will contemn us for coming unto him with purpose and desire to serve him?

Many other reasons I could give you, wherefore the saints are not to be prayed unto; for that pulleth from faith in Christ: it maketh them gods; it is idolatry, &c. But this may suffice. So that now you see by God's word, what our faith is concerning these four things. Which that you may the more love, embrace, and be content to carry with you through fire and water, I will now go about with God's grace, as briefly as I can, to shew how abominable their doctrine is, even out of the short sum thereof already before by me rehearsed.

CHAPTER X.

THE POPISH DOCTRINE OF THE SACRAMENT CONFUTED MORE LARGELY.

FIRST, where they allege the catholic church to have taught concerning the supper the doctrine of transubstantiation, of Christ's real and carnal presence, dearly beloved, know that this is a manifest lie. For as the catholic church never knew of it for nine hundred years at the least after Christ's *Transubstan-* ascension; so after that time no other church did obstinately *tiation is a new doc-* defend, cruelly maintain, and wilfully wrest the scriptures *trine.* and doctors for the establishing of it, save only the popish church, and their own doctors, Duns and Gabriel, do teach[1].

[1 See above, p. 254.]

Read the bishop of Canterbury's book against Winchester[1], and see. Whereas they say, that Christ in his supper by taking bread and speaking the words of consecration did make it his flesh, according to his promise in John, when he

John vi. saith, "And the bread which I will give is my flesh, &c.;" so that they would thereby seem to have two places of scripture for this their doctrine of transubstantiation and real or carnal presence; although diversly I could improve[2] this, yet because for that I would not be over tedious unto you, even by the same their sentence you shall see how learnedly they lie.

The sentence is this: "And the bread that I will give is my flesh, which I will give for the life of the world." First mark that he saith, "The bread is my flesh." He saith not, "shall be my flesh," but it "is my flesh." This, I trow, maketh against them; for the sacrament a year after at the least was not instituted. Again he saith, that the bread is his flesh, which he will give for the life of the world. Here would I ask them, whether Christ's death was for the life of the world, or in vain. If they say it was for the life of the world, then why do they apply and give it to the sacrament? Was it crucified? Or if it be the same sacrifice, (for so they say,) either it was effectual, or not. If it was effectual, then Christ's death needed not. If it was not effectual, then Christ was not God, and could not do that he would. Thus ye may see their ungodly foolishness, or foolish ungodliness,

Of the priest's intent. I cannot tell which to call it well. Whereas they require the intent of the priest to consecrate Christ's body; forasmuch as we know not any man's intent, (God only knoweth the heart,) yea, the words we know not, they are so spoke in *hucker mucker;* I pray you, in what a doubtfulness are we brought whether it be the sacrament or not! In what peril are we of worshipping a piece of bread for our Christ! Is not this, trow you, sweet and comfortable gear, that a man shall always stand in doubt whether he have received the sacrament or not? Whereas they will have it bread to the eye, and not to the mouth, judge then, whether a dog may not eat Christ's body; judge whether the devil, if he would come in the likeness of a priest, might not swallow up

[1 Archbishop Cranmer's *Answer to a Crafty and Sophistical Cavillation devised by Stephen Gardiner.*]

[2 Improve: disprove.]

Christ, and so bring him into hell, from whence, because there is no redemption there, Christ's body should never come, but be damned. Judge, whether the taste of thy mouth is not as much to be credited, as the sight of the eye; specially in that the scripture so often calleth it bread after the consecration, as before I have shewed. Judge, whether Christ's body be not very petty, that it can be in so little a room. Judge, whether Christ hath more bodies than one, when perchance the priest hath twenty or a hundred before him. Judge, whether the priest brake not Christ's body in breaking of it. Judge, whether it be seemly to chew Christ's body with the teeth. Judge, whether Christ did eat his own body; yea, or no? Christ did eat the sacrament with his disciples. Judge, whether it be seemly that Christ should be kept so in prison, as they keep him. Judge, whether it be seemly that Christ's body should be so dindle-dandled and used, as they use it. Judge, whether the people, knocking and kneeling at the elevation of that they see, (for they see but the forms of bread and wine, and not Christ's body, if it be as the papists feign;) judge, I say, whether the people by the papists' own doctrine be not made idolaters.

Many more absurdities there be, which I purposely omit. This little is enough hereby to give you occasion to know the more. Where they say that the bread is made Christ's body, flesh, blood, &c., that is, that Christ's body is made of the bread; as the bishop of Winchester in his book for this matter of the *Devil's Sophistry* and elsewhere doth affirm; you may see how shamelessly, yea, blasphemously they speak. For Christ's body crucified was born of the virgin Mary, even of her substance; but they say the supper is that body which was crucified. Now, I trow, bread is one thing, and the virgin's flesh another thing: therefore indeed they deny Christ in the flesh, that they may stablish their Christ in the bread; which is the very root of antichrist. Last of all, whereas they say that they receive the sacrament to damnation, which do not believe their transubstantiation; if with Paul their words were conferred, you should see otherwise. For he saith, they receive this bread (for so he calleth it after the words of consecration) unworthily, which do not esteem

Christ's body: as indeed the papists do not, which would bring Christ down out of heaven for thieves and whores to chew and eat, for moths to corrupt, and to be in danger of moulding; as, if they kept their hosts long, indeed they will mould, and then will they burn them. Do these men, trow you, esteem Christ's body? Paul plainly sheweth in the same place, that the wicked man which receiveth the sacrament unworthily, eateth not Christ's body, but his own damnation, which I trow be not Christ's body. And this shall serve for this time to shew you, how shameless, filthy, and abominable this their doctrine of transubstantiation is. If in so short a sum of their doctrine there be so many abominations, I pray you, how much is in the whole sum of the same? Now for the sacrifice.

CHAPTER XI.

THE POPISH DOCTRINE OF THE SACRIFICE CONFUTED.

FIRST, in that they grant Christ's sacrifice on the cross done by himself to be full and perfect enough, we may well see that we need not this which they have found out, indeed to make the other imperfect; for else it needed no reiteration. But seeing they reiterate it by this, and make it needful even as baptism, easily may all men know, that though they speak one thing, they mean another, and so are dissemblers and destroyers of Christ's sacrifice, little considering the great pain that Christ suffered, seeing they weigh it no better.

Whereas they say, that it is the same sacrifice which Christ offered on the cross, but unbloodily, (wherein they seem to deny transubstantiation; for else I trow it must needs be bloody,) I would thus reason with them. Inasmuch as Christ's sacrifice on the cross was the only perfect and all-sufficient propitiatory sacrifice for the sins of the world, as they confess; this could not be the same, because it was done before that upon the cross. Or else the full perfect sacrifice was then in the supper finished, and so Christ's death is in vain, and a foolish thing. If Christ's death be not foolish, but indeed, as it is, the full aud perfect sacrifice for the sins of the world; then this, which they feign he offered in his last supper, is not the same, prate what pleaseth them; or else it is not of value, take whether they will. Whereas they prate of Christ's will, that it was accepted before his Father for the deed; as they shall never be able to shew one word to prove that Christ would in his supper sacrifice himself to his Father for the sins of the world, (for there is not one word thereof throughout the whole bible,) so do they belie God the Father, which would indeed have his Son to drink the cup that he prayed to be taken from him, or else make Christ's death frustrate and more than need; which is the only thing that all their doctrine tendeth unto. For if the Father alloweth his will for the deed, I pray you, who seeth not now the deed to be more than needeth?

Where they say, that Christ commanded his church to offer this sacrifice to his Father in remembrance of his bloody sacrifice; I would pray them to shew me, where he commanded it, and then good enough. But, dearly beloved, they can never shew it. If they will say, *hoc facite*, to take *facere* for *to sacrifice*, as some teach it; then will I say, that a boy of twelve years old can tell they lie. For *hoc facite, do you this*, pertaineth to the whole action of Christ's supper, of taking, eating, and drinking of the sacrament, &c., and as well spoken to the laymen as the priests: but I trow they will not suffer the laymen to say mass another while for them. No, this were too much against their honour and gain also.

But if one would ask them, what they offer to the Father, then a man should see their abominations. For if they should say nothing, then men would take them as they be, liars. If they say, bread and wine, as indeed they do in their mass horribly; then in that they say they offer the same thing which Christ offered on the cross, and he offered his body, bread must needs be Christ's body, and so Christ's body is bread and wine. If they say, that they offer up Christ, in that the offerer must needs be as good at the least, yea, a better than the thing offered, then must they needs shew themselves open antichrists. For they make themselves equal with Christ, yea, better than he: which thing indeed their holy father and grandsire the pope doth. For where Christ would take upon him to teach nothing, but that he had received of his Father, and therefore willed men to search the scriptures, as all his apostles did, whether their doctrine was not according thereunto; the pope and his prelates will be bold to teach what please them more than God biddeth, yea, clean contrary to that which God biddeth; as it is plain by all these four points, transubstantiation, sacrifice, praying for the dead, and to the dead. But see, I pray you, these abominations. The sacrifice of Christ for the redemption of the world was not simply his body and his blood, but his body broken and his blood shed, that is, all his passion and suffering in his body and flesh. In that therefore they offer, as they say, the same sacrifice which Christ offered, dearly beloved, do they not, as much as in them is, kill, slay, whip, and crucify Christ again with wretches and antichrists? Who would not desire to die for his master Christ's cause against this their heinous and stinking abomination?

Whereas they call this sacrifice of the mass the principal mean to apply the benefit of Christ's death to the quick and dead, I would gladly have them to shew, where and of whom they learned it. Sure I am they learned it not of Christ. For when he sent his disciples abroad to apply unto men the benefit of his death, he bade them not mass it, but preach the gospel, as the mean by the which God had appointed believers to be saved. The which thing Peter told Cornelius plainly; as Paul also teacheth almost every where in his epistles. But indeed preaching they may not away with, as well for that it is too painful, as for that it is nothing so gainful, nor of authority and estimation in the world. Nothing so displeaseth the devil as preaching the gospel, as in all ages easily we may well see, if we will mark to our comfort in this age. And therefore by giving his daughter idolatry, with her dowry of worldly wealth, riches, and honour, to the pope and his shaven shorelings, they have by this means in many years been begetting a daughter, which at length was delivered to destroy preaching, even the minion *Missa;* mistress Missa, who danced daintily before the Herods of the world, and is the cause even why John the Baptist and the preachers be put into prison and lose their heads. This dancing damsel, the darling of her mother, the fair garland of her fathers (for she hath many fathers), the gaudy gallant of her grandsire, is trimmed and tricked in the best and most holy manner or wise that can be, even with the word of God,

Matt. xxviii.
Mark xvi.
Luke xxiv.

Acts x.

Col. i. ii.
2 Cor. v.

the epistle and the gospel, with the sacrament of Christ's body and blood, with the pomander[1] and perfumes of prayer, and all goodly things that can be; but blasphemously and horribly abused to be a mermaid to amuse and bewitch men, sailing in the seas of this life to be enamoured on her. And therefore besides her aforesaid goodly apparel, she hath all kinds of sweet tunes, ditties, melodies, singing, playing, ringing, knocking, kneeling, standing, lifting, crossing, blessing, blowing, mouthing, incensing, &c. Moreover she wanteth no gold, silver, precious stones, jewels, and costly silks, velvets, satins, dumasties, &c., and all kind of things which are gorgeous in the sight of men; as, if you call to mind the chalices, copes, vestments, crucifixes, &c., you cannot but see. And hereto is she beautified yet more, to be shewed and set forth in lying words and titles given to her; that she hath all power in heaven, earth, and hell, that she hath all things for soul and body, for quick and dead, for man and beast. And lest men should think her too coy a dame, lo, sir, she offereth herself most gently to all that will come, be they never so poor and stinking and foul, to have their pleasure on her. Come who will, she is "Hail, good fellow;" and that not only to make herself common to them that will, but also to ply them plentifully with most pleasant promises falsely, and giving most licentious liberties to all her lovers, and great fees and wages to her diligent servants and ministers; so that there needeth no preaching of the gospel. She hath all things, she will give all things; the death of Christ she will apply and can to whom she will, and when she will. For this daughter the mothers, the fathers, and the grandfathers watch night and day, as the only mean whereby Herod and Herodias may live as they lust........But, dearly beloved, as from the devil's dearling indeed, fly from her; and know that the true and only way to apply the benefit of Christ's death and sacrifice, is in the minister's behalf by preaching, and in your behalf by believing.

This is a sacrament, and not a sacrifice; for in this, using it as we should, we receive of God obsignation and full certificate of Christ's body broken for our sins, and his blood shed for our iniquities. As in baptism we are confirmed, and settle ourselves in possession of the promise of salvation to

[1 Pomander: a ball made up of several perfumes.]

appertain unto us, God to be our God, Christ to be our
Christ, and we to be God's people; the promise of the word
of God giveth and offereth, faith in us applieth and receiveth
the same, and the sacraments do confirm and (as it were) seal
up : baptism, that we are regenerated with the Spirit of God,
made his children, brethren to Christ, and engrafted into
him; the supper, that we are fed with Christ spiritually, with
his body and blood, yea, that we be incorporated into Christ,
to be flesh of his flesh and bone of his bones, as he by being
born of the virgin Mary was flesh of our flesh and bone of
our bones. Away therefore with their abominable doctrine,
that the sacrifice of the mass is the principal means to apply
Christ's death to the quick and dead; wherein all men may
see that they lie boldly. For as the word of God in the
ministry pertaineth not to the dead, (for who will be so mad
as to go and preach on dead men's graves, that the dead
men may hear?) so likewise do not the sacraments. Little
beholden were men to Christ and to the apostles, if this were
the principal mean to apply salvation, that they would use
it so little, and preach so much. Paul, having respect to the

1 Cor. i.

chiefest end wherefore he was sent, said, that he was not sent

Rom. i.
Gal. i.

to baptize, but to preach. And often saith he, that he was
an apostle segregate of God to preach the gospel. And the

2 Tim. iv.

bishop Timothy did he warn to preach in season and out of
season, speaking never a word of this massing or sacrificing
Christ's body.

Last of all, where they make a similitude, that as by
baptism the minister applieth to the child regeneration, so
in this, &c. O that this similitude were well looked on!
then would it make them to bluster; for they are no more
like than an apple like an oyster. In baptism the child
is alive, but here the man is dead: in baptism the child
is present, but here the man is perchance forty miles off, if
he sacrifice for the quick,' yea, hundred miles from him : in
baptism the child receiveth the sacrament, but here you must
look and gape; but beware you take not; for ye may receive
but once a year, and then also you must receive but the one
half, the cup he will keep from you. In baptism is required
God's election, if he be an infant; or faith, if he be of age;
and therefore he reciteth the promise, that it may be heard :
but here is no faith required; for how can men believe,

when they are dead? No promise is then preached or heard. So that even this their similitude maketh the matter plain enough: for baptism all men know to be no sacrifice. But of this I have spoken a little before, that if applying come by the priest's massing, then were preaching in vain, believing in vain, godly life in vain; the priest were God's fellow, yea, Christ's superior, as is aforesaid. Now for the third, of praying for the dead; wherein I will be brief.

CHAPTER XII.

THE CONFUTATION OF THE PAPISTS' SACRIFICING AND PRAYING FOR THE DEAD.

First, when they say, this applicatory sacrifice may be called a propitiatory sacrifice, because it applieth the propitiatory sacrifice to whom the priest will, be he dead or alive; as I would have you to note, how they grant, that of itself it is not a propitiatory sacrifice, whereby they vary from that which they elsewhere teach, that it is the selfsame sacrifice which Christ offered on the cross unbloodily; so, I pray you, forget not, that the priest is God's fellow, for he may apply it to whom he will. Therefore honour sir John, and make much of sir Thomas: for though God could make thee alone, yet alone, without the priest, he cannot save thee. Again, if sir John be thy friend, care neither for God nor the devil; live as thou wilt, he will bring thee to heaven, although thou slip into hell. So they write, that Gregory by massing did with Trajan the emperor. It maketh no matter how thou live here, so thou have the favour of the pope and his shavelings.

Whereas they say, that the fathers from the beginning were accustomed to make memorials for the dead; this I grant to be true, as we do in our communion. But to gather that therefore they prayed for them, it no more followeth, than to say, that our English service doth allow it, where it doth not. For ye must note, that there is a memorial for the dead, as well in giving thanks to God for them, as in praying for them; for to say, to pray for the dead, is a general word, including in it giving of thanks. And therefore when

we read in the ancient fathers of the primitive church of
memorials for the dead[1], or praying for the dead, it is not
to be understood that they prayed for to deliver them from
purgatory, (for that was not found out then,) or from hell,
(as our papists do in their prayers of the mass,) for there is no
redemption; or for pardon of their sins, as though they had
it not; for if they depart without it, they are damned; or
for to get them a higher place in heaven, for that were in-
jurious to Christ, that we should purchase places and higher
crowns in heaven for others: but either for the desire of the
more speedy coming of Christ, to hasten the resurrection;
either that they might not be thought negligent or careless
over the dead; either that the living might be occasioned to
increase in love to the church here in earth, who still followeth with good will and love even men when they be departed;
either to admonish the church to be diligent over such as
live, and careful to extend her love, if it were possible, even
to the dead.   On this wise should we expound, not only
the former, but also the later fathers, as Austin, Chrysostom,
and others; which though in some places they seem very
manifestly to allow praying for the dead, yet they are not
to be understood otherwise than I have said for them.   For
never knew they of our merits and purgatory; for if they
had but dreamed thereon, surely they would have been
much more circumspect in their speakings and writings of
this, than they were.

Where they say, that because this sacrifice is the sacrifice
of the whole church, whereof the dead be members, therefore
they should be prayed for; as before I have shewed, that
we must put a difference between the members of the church
militant here on earth, and those which be now at rest and
peace with God; so would I have you to note here, that they
should pray for none other dead, than such as be members
of Christ's church.   Now in that all such die in the Lord,
and therefore are happy, I would gladly learn, what good
such prayer doeth to those so departed.   As for purgatory
pike-purse, they pass not upon it.   But that this is a sacrifice
applicatory or propitiatory, the papists can never prove.

Where they say, charity requireth it; I answer, that
inasmuch as charity followeth faith, and will not go a foot

[1 See above, p. 249.]

further than faith sheweth the way; seeing faith is not Rom. x.
but of the word of God, and God's word for this they have
not, easy it is to perceive that this praying thus for the
dead is not of christian charity. But be it that charity
required it, I then marvel why they are so uncharitable,
that will do nothing herein without money. Why will
they not pray without pence? If the pope and his prelætes
were charitable, they would, I trow, make sweep-stake at
once with purgatory.

Where they allege the sentence of the Maccabees; as all
men of learning know, the Fathers allow not that book to be
God's Spirit or catholic, so do I wonder that in all the old
Testament this sacrificing for the dead was never spoken of
before. In all the sacrifices that God appointed, we read of
never one for the dead.

This gear came not up till the religion was wonderfully
corrupt among the Jews: as with us it was never found out
till horrible corruption of religion and ignorances of God's word
came into the church of God, when preaching was put down,
and massing came up. Then faith in Christ was cold, penance
became popish, and trust was taught in creatures, ignorance
abounded, and look, what the clergy said, that was believed.
Then came up visions, miracles, dead spirits walking, and
talking how they might be released by this mass, by that
pilgrimage gate-going. And so came up this pelf of praying
for the dead, which Paul the apostle and all the prophets
never spake one word of; for all men may easily see, that it
is a thing which helpeth much vice, and hindereth godliness.
Who will be so earnest to amend, to make restitution of that
he hath gotten unjustly, and live in a godly life, and true
fear of God, being taught that by prayers, by masses, by
founding of chauntries, &c., when he is gone, he shall find
ease and release, yea, and come to joy eternal? Christ's
doctrine is, that the way of salvation is strait; but this
teaching, heaping of masses one upon another, when we are
dead, maketh it wide. Christ's teaching is, that we should
live in love and charity, the sun should not go down on our
wrath; but this doctrine, to pray for the dead to be delivered
out of purgatory, teacheth rather to live in little love, in
wrath even to our death's day: for sir John can and will
help; sir Thomas, by a mass of *scala cœli* will bring us into

heaven. Christ's doctrine is, that he is the way; but this doctrine maketh the massing priest the way : a way indeed it is, but to hell and to the devil. Dearly beloved, therefore take good heart unto you for this gear, rather than you would consent unto it, to lose life and all that ever you have. You shall be sure with Christ to find it, and that for ever, with infinite increase.

Last of all, when they allege the catholic church and consent of all the doctors on this matter; as I wish you should know that to be the true and catholic church which is grounded upon God's word, which word they have not for them in this matter; so would I ye should know that there is no member of the church, but he may err; for they be men, and "all men be liars," as David saith. Now if all the members may err, then you may easily see, whereto your faith ought to lean, even unto God's weighty word. Hear the church and the doctors of the church ; but none otherwise, than as teachers, and try their teaching by God's word. If they teach according to it, then believe and obey them; if contrary, then know they be but men, and always let your faith lean to God's word.

Howbeit, for this matter of praying for the dead, know of truth that there be no doctors of four hundred or five hundred years after Christ's ascension, but if they in some places seem to allow praying for the dead, yet they would be taken in some of the senses which I have specified. In many places do they by divers sentences declare it themselves. But of this enough.

CHAPTER XIII.

THE REFUTATION OF THE HERESY OF PRAYING TO SAINTS DEPARTED OUT OF THIS WORLD.

Now to the last, of praying to saints. First, where they say, there be more mediators of intercession than Christ, making a distinction not learned out of God's book, in such sense and for such purpose as they allege; I wish they would look on the epistle to the Romans, and 1 John ii. and there shall they learn to take better heed. The one saith, " Christ [Rom. viii.] sitteth on the right hand of his Father, and prayeth for us:"

the other saith, "He is our advocate," that is, a spokesman, comforter, intercessor, and mediator. Now would I ask them, seeing that Christ is a mediator of intercession, (as I am sure they will grant,) whether he be sufficient or no. If they say, no; then all men will know that they lie. But if they say, yes; then may I ask, why they are not content with sufficient? What fault find ye with him? Is there any more merciful than he, any more desirous to do us good than he? any that knoweth our grief and need so much as he? any that knoweth the way to help us so well as he? No, none so well. He crieth: "Ask, and ye shall have; come to me, Matt. vii. and I will help you; ask, that your joy may be full. Hitherto Matt. xi. ye have not asked any thing in my name." Therefore, my John xvi. good brethren and sisters, let us thank God for this mediator; and as he is our alone mediator for redemption, let us take him even so for intercession. For if by his work of redemption of enemies we are made friends; surely we being friends, and having him above on the right hand of his Father, shall Rom. v. by him obtain all things. Heb. i.

Where they call it a point of a lowly and an humble spirit to go to saints, that they may pray for them; you may easily see, it is a point of an arrogant heart and a false untrue spirit. For inasmuch as God plainly biddeth thee, Deut. xii. that thou put nought to his word, nor take aught therefrom; Rev. xxii. in that his word is, "Thou shalt call upon him in thy need;" Psal. l. why art thou so arrogant and proud, that you will go to Peter or Paul to pray for thee? Where hast thou God's word? Dost thou think God is true of his promise? Why then dost thou not go unto him? Dost thou think that God at any time receiveth thee for thy worthiness? Upon whom be his eyes, but upon him that trembleth at his word? Isai. lxv. Blessed are they that be poor in spirit, and think themselves Matt. v. unworthy of God's help. Wherefore hath God sworn that he will not the death of a sinner, but that sinners might be Ezek. xxxiii. most certain of his love and mercy to be much greater than they be able to conceive? His mercies are above all his Psal. cxlv. works. But thou, that runnest to saints, thinkest that it is not so; for else wouldest thou go to him thyself, that thou, seeing his so much goodness, mightest the more love him, which thou canst not, if thou use other means than by Christ only.

[COVERDALE, II.]

18

Where they bring in the ensample of saints praying for the people, and obtaining benefits for them, whilst they were living here on earth, and so gather, that much more they will and can do it now for us, in that they be with God, if we will pray unto them; very easily may we put this away by many reasons. First, that the cases be not like. For when they were alive, they might know the need of the people : but now who can tell whether they know any thing

Isai. lxiii.

of our calamities and need? Isaiah saith, Abraham did not know them that were in his age. Again, if the people had come to them to have desired their prayers, as they would have taken this for an admonishment of their duty to the people, so would they again have warned the people of their duty, that with them they also would pray unto God themselves. Whereas there be no such reciprocal and mutual offices between the dead and the living. Now cannot we admonish them, and tell them of our needs; or if we should go about it, surely we should still stand in a doubt, whether they did perceive us or no. But if they did perceive the miseries of their brethren, surely their rest would not be without great grief; and of this we are sure, that they can tell us nothing also. Besides this, this their reasoning smell-

1 Cor. i.
Rom. x.

eth, as it that went before, of man's reason, which is a fool in God's service, and of a good intent which is not according to knowledge. We may not do after that which is good in

Deut. xi.

our own eyes, but according to that which God biddeth us do. In our eyes it seemeth good, that as to kings and great men we use means by men, which are of their privy chambers, or are about them, either to come to their speech, or to attain our suits, so we should do to God by his saints. But to dream on this sort with God, to use saints so, were and is unto faith very foolish : for God useth no such privy chambers to hide himself in. "He is at hand," saith

Psal. cxlv.
Deut. iv.

David, "to all that call upon him." And Moses said before him : "God is near thee in all thy prayers. No nation hath their gods so nigh unto them as our God is unto us in all our prayers." He needeth none to put him in remembrance

Heb. iv.
Psal. xxxiii.
xcv.

of us; for he hath all things open to his eyes : the height of the hills and the bottom of the depths are in his sight. Nothing can hide itself from his knowledge. He hath ordained Christ Jesus alonely to be the mean by whom we

shall speed and receive our requests, which be according to 1 Tim. ii.
his will, if we open our purse-mouth, that he may pour into
the same ; I mean faith.   For as a thing poured upon a
vessel or other thing, the mouth being closed, is spilt and
lost ; so if we ask any thing according to God's will by
Christ, the same doth us no good, except the purse-mouth
of our hearts be opened by faith to receive it.

But to make an end.   St Paul telleth plainly, that with- Rom. x.
out faith prayer is not made.   Now in that faith is due only
to God, (for cursed is he that hath his faith in man, saint,
or angel,) to God only let us make our prayers, but by
Jesus Christ, and in his name only ; for only in him is the
Father well pleased.   This if we do, and that often, as Christ Matt. iii.
                                                                xvii.
willeth, *oportet semper orare*, we must pray alway ; then Luke xviii.
shall we undoubtedly in all things be directed by God's holy
Spirit, whom Christ hath promised to be our doctor, teacher, John xiv.
                                                              xv. xvi.
and comforter.   And therefore need we not to fear what Psal. xxvii.
man or devil can do unto us, either by false teaching or
cruel persecution : for our pastor is such one, that none can John x.
take his sheep out of his hands.   To him be praise for ever.
Amen.

CHAPTER XIV.

THE KNITTING UP OF THE MATTER, AND CONCLUSION OR
    PERORATION, WITH THE AUTHOR'S DESIRE AND PRAYER
    FOR THE PERSECUTED BRETHREN.

AND thus much, my good brethren and sisters, on our
dear Lord and Saviour Jesus Christ I thought good to write
unto you for your comfort in these troublesome days, and
for the confirmation of the truth that ye have already received : from the which if you for fear of man, loss of goods,
friends, or life, do swerve or depart, you depart and swerve
from Christ, and so snare yourself in Satan's sophistry to
your utter subversion.   Therefore, as Peter saith : " Watch, 1 Pet. v.
and be sober : for as a roaring lion he seeketh to devour
you."   But be ye strong in faith, that is, stagger not, waver

18—2

Acts ii.
Deut. xx.

Psal. xci.

Matt. xxvi.

Luke xxii.

2 Pet. ii.

Heb. vi. x.

Matt. x.
Mark viii.
Luke xi.
Gen. xix.
Matt. xxvii.

Matt. xvi.

not in God's promises, and be assured that they pertain unto you, that God is your God, that he is with you in trouble, and will deliver you and glorify you. But yet see that ye call upon him, specially that you enter not into temptation, as he taught his disciples to pray, even at such time as he saw Satan desire to sift them, as now he hath desired to sift us. O most dear Saviour, prevent him now, as thou didst then, with thy prayer, we beseech thee, and grant that our faith faint not; but strengthen us to confirm the weak, that they deny not thee and thy gospel, that they return not to their vomit and puddle of mire in popery and superstition, as massing, praying to saints, praying for the dead, or worshipping the work of men's hands instead of thee their Saviour. Oh, let us not so run down headlong into perdition, stumbling on those sins, from the which there is no recovery, but a causing of thee to deny us before thy Father, making our latter end worse than the beginning; as chanced to Lot's wife, Judas Iscariot, Franciscus Spira[1] in these our days, and to many others: but rather strengthen us all in thy grace, and in those things which thy word teacheth; that we may here hazard our life for thy sake. And so shall we be sure to save it; as, if we seek to save it, we can but lose it: and it being lost, what profit can we have, if we win the whole world? Oh, set them always before our eyes, not as reason doth this life, or the pleasures of the same, death of the body, prisonment, &c.; but everlasting life, and those unspeakable joys, which undoubtedly they shall have, that take up their cross and follow thee. Set ever before us also the eternal fire, and perpetual destruction of soul and body, that they must needs at length leap into, which are afraid of the hoar-frost of adversity, that man or the devil stirreth up to stop and hinder us from going forward in our journey to heaven's bliss; to the which, O Lord, do thou bring us for thy name's sake. Amen.

Pray for all your brethren which be in prison and exile, and so absent from you in body, but yet present with you

[1 An eminent lawyer of Citadella near Padua, who embraced, and afterwards renounced, the reformed faith, A. D. 1546. Some account of him may be found in Seckendorf, Hist. Lutheranismi, Lib. III. sect. cxxix. Vol. II. p. 601, and Sleidan, History of the Reformation, Book XXI.]

in spirit; and heartily pray God once to prove us, and trust us again with his holy word and gospel; that we may be suffered to speak, and you to hear his voice, as heretofore we and you have done, but unthankfully and negligently, I may say, yea, very unworthily and carnally. And therefore is his most just anger fallen now upon us. He remember his mercy towards us in his time, we beseech him! Amen.

THE CONTENTS OF THIS BOOK

AS THEY FOLLOW IN EVERY CHAPTER.

EXPOSITION

UPON THE

TWENTY-SECOND PSALM.

A very

excellent and swete

exposition upon the two

and twentye Psalme of

David, called,

in latyn,

Dominus regit me, et nihil.

Translated out of

hye Almayne

in to En-

glyshe

by

Myles Coverdale.

1537.

[PARAPHRASE OF THE TWENTY-SECOND PSALM.

THE original of this Treatise, which is entitled a Paraphrase on the twenty-second Psalm, according to the Septuagint Version, or the twenty-third, according to the notation of the Hebrew text, is found in the Latin edition of Luther's Works, Vol. II. pp. 226—254, ed. Jenæ, 1600, among his "Operationes in Psalmos xxii. priores." The present edition of Coverdale's translation is printed from a copy in the Bodleian Library, Oxford.]

UPON THE TWENTY-SECOND PSALM.

The effect of this psalm.

IN this psalm doth David and every christian heart give thanks and praise unto God for his most principal benefit, namely, for the preaching of his dear and holy word, whereby we are called, accepted, and numbered among the multitude, which is the congregation or church of God; where only, and in no place else, the pure doctrine, the true knowledge of God's will, and the right service of God is found and had.

But this same noble treasure doth holy David praise and extol marvellous excellently, with goodly, sweet, fair, and pure words, yea, and that with likenesses borrowed out of the God's service of the old Testament.

A sheep.

First, he likeneth himself to a sheep, whom God himself, as a faithful diligent shepherd, doth wondrous well take heed unto, feedeth him in a pleasant green pasture, which standeth full of good thick grass; where there is abundance also of fresh water, and no scarceness. Item, he likeneth God also

The shepherd.

unto such a shepherd, as with his staff leadeth and bringeth the sheep the plain right way, that it cannot go amiss, and defendeth his flock so with the sheep-hook, that the

A guest.

wolf cannot break in. After this doth he make himself a guest, for whom God prepareth a table, where he findeth both strength and comfort, refreshing and joy, and that plenteously.

The word of God hath many names.

And thus the prophet giveth the word of God divers names, calleth it goodly pleasant green grass, fresh water, the right way, a staff, a sheep-hook, a table, balm, or pleasant oil, and a cup that is alway full. And this he doth not without a cause: for the power of God's word is manifold. For why? Like as a sheep in a fair pleasant meadow, beside the green grass and fresh water, in the presence of his shepherd which leadeth it with the staff or rod, so that it cannot go astray, and defendeth it so with the sheep-hook, that no harm can happen unto it, hath his food and pleasure in all safeguard; or like as a man lacketh nothing that sitteth at a table, where there is plenty of meat and drink, and all manner of comfort and gladness: so much more they that be the sheep of this shepherd, whereof this psalm singeth, lack no good thing, are richly provided for, not only in soul, but also in body; as Christ saith in the sixth of Matthew: "Seek first the kingdom of God and the righteousness thereof; so shall all these things be ministered unto you." For as they that want bodily food live in great straitness and pensiveness, not being able to fulfil the body's request in this behalf; even so also those that want this wholesome and necessary word of God, cannot rejoice nor be pacified inwardly. Yea, even as bread and wine refresh a man's fleshly heart, and make him joyful; even so the word of God quickeneth and refresheth a man's soul inwardly.

For when the word of God is truly and sincerely preached, look how many divers names the prophet giveth it here, so many commodities and fruits doth it bring. Unto them that are diligent and earnest to hear it, whom our Lord God knoweth only for his own sheep, it is a pleasant green grass, a fresh water, wherewith they are satisfied and refreshed. It keepeth them also in the right way, and preserveth them, that no misfortune nor harm happen unto them. Moreover, it is unto them a continual wealth, where there is abundance of meat and drink, and all manner of joy and pleasure: that is, they are not only instruct and guided, refreshed, strengthened, and comforted by the word of God, but ever more and more preserved in the right way, defended in all manner of trouble both of body and soul. And finally they have the victory, and prevail against all temptations and troubles, whereof they must abide right many, as the fourth verse doth specify. Shortly, they live in all manner of safeguard, as they unto whom no misfortune can happen, forasmuch as their shepherd doth feed them and preserve them. *The preaching of God's word bringeth prosperity.*

Therefore should we take instruction out of this psalm, not to despise the word of God, but gladly to hear and learn the same, to love it, and to make much of it, and to resort unto the little flock where we may have it; and again, on the other side, to fly and eschew those that do blaspheme and persecute it: for where this blessed light doth not shine, there is neither prosperity nor health, *The doctrine to be taken of this psalm.*

neither strength nor comfort, either in body or soul; but utter disquietness, terror, and despair, specially when trouble, distress, and painful death is at hand. Howbeit the un-
Isai. lvii.
godly, as the prophet saith, have never rest, whether they be in wealth or woe. For if they be in prosperity, then are they presumptuous, proud, and high-minded, forget our Lord God utterly, boast and crack only of their own power, riches, wisdom, &c.; and take thought beside, how they may maintain and increase the same, and how they may persecute and oppress other men that lie in their ways. But if the leaf turn about with them, as doubtless it must
Deposuit po-tentes de sede, et di-vites dimisit inanes.
needs do at the last; (for that sweet virgin Mary is a very sure prophetess, which yet hath not failed in her song;) then are they of all the most miserable and carefullest people, which immediately fall to despair and mistrust. What aileth them? They know not where nor how they shall seek comfort, seeing they have not the word of God, which only teacheth the right way how to be patient, and to have a good hope even in adversity. Rom. xv.

An ensample for us.
This thing ought to warn us and move us, that we esteem nothing more excellent nor worthy upon earth, than this benefit, namely, to have that dear blessed word, and that we can be in a place where it may be freely preached and professed openly. A christian man therefore, that be-longeth unto a church wherein the word of God is taught, as oft as he goeth in, should think upon this psalm, and out of a joyful heart with the prophet to give God thanks for his unoutspeakable grace, that he hath set him, as his own sheep, in a pleasant green meadow, where there is plenty of good grass and fresh water; that is, that he may be in a place where he may hear and learn the word of God, and conceive rich comfort thereout, both in body and soul.

This blessed David did well understand, how worthy a treasure it is, when it may be so had: therefore can he boast and sing so well of it, and magnify this benefit above all that
What we ought to learn here of David.
is in any estimation or worship upon earth. At him ought we to learn this science, and according to his ensample not only to be thankful unto God our loving and faithful shep-herd, and to magnify his unoutspeakable gift, which he of very loving-kindness hath given us, as David doth here in the first five verses; but also earnestly to desire and pray

him, as he doth in the last verse, that he may abide by his riches, and never to fall away from his holy christian church.

And such a prayer is exceeding necessary : for we are very weak, and, as the apostle St Paul saith, we carry this *2 Cor. v.* treasure about in earthen vessels. The devil also, our adversary, beareth deadly hate unto us for this treasure's sake. Therefore doth he not rest, but goeth about as a roaring lion, and seeketh how he may devour us. Beside all this, he hath a quarrel unto us, because of our old sack which we carry yet upon our necks, wherein there be yet also divers concupiscences and sins. Moreover, the dear flock of Christ is spotted and filled with so many horrible offences, or slanders, that because of the same there do many fall away from them. Therefore, I say, it is necessary that we pray, and put this uncorrupt doctrine still in practice, and defend ourselves therewith against all slanders, that we may continue unto the end, and be saved.

This mad and blind world knoweth utterly nothing of *The blindness of the world.* this treasure and precious stone, but imagineth only, even as a swine or unreasonable beast, how they may here fill the belly; or else, when it cometh to the point, they follow lies and hypocrisy : as for the truth and faith, they let it pass. Therefore do they sing no psalm unto God for his holy word; but rather, when he offereth it unto them, they blaspheme it and condemn it for heresy. And as for those that teach it or will be known of it, the world persecuteth them and putteth them to death, like as if they were deceivers, and the most ungracious wretches that are in the world. It shall be good therefore for this small flock to knowledge such a benefit, and with the prophet to sing a psalm or song of thanksgiving unto God for it.

But what say ye of them that cannot have the preach- *Of them that would and cannot have the word of God.* ing of God's word; as namely, they that dwell here and there among tyrants and enemies of the truth? No doubt, where as the word of God is preached, there can it not pass away without fruit, as Esay saith in the fifty-fifth chapter. The good christian people also of the same place have one vantage, which indeed is dear unto them : for they that be christian men count it a very great thing, that they may be in a place where the word of God is freely and openly taught and knowledged, and the sacraments ministered after Christ's institution.   But as for those, they be sown very thin.   The false Christian are always more than the good.   The great multitude careth nothing for God's word, neither do they knowledge it for a benefit, that they may hear it without all harm and peril.   Yea, they are soon filled and weary of it, and esteem it but a pain to hear it, and to receive the holy sacrament.

Again, they that suffer under tyrants complain day and night, and long greatly for it.   And if a small morsel of our bread, that Christ hath given us so richly, doth come unto them, they receive it with great joy and thankfulness, and do themselves much good withal; whereas our swine in the mean season, having that worthy bread themselves so richly, and many whole baskets full thereof, cannot reach unto it, they are so weary of it.   Yea, they cast it down, wallow themselves therein, tread it under their feet, and run over it.

Men wear weary of the word of God. Therefore goeth it even after the proverb.   When a thing beginneth to be common, it is no more set by, but despised, be it never so precious.   And such proverbs are specially found true in the word of God.   Where men have it, there will they not away withal.   Again, where men have it not, there would they be glad to have it.   Where men have a church at their doors wherein the word of God is taught, there go they up and down in the market in the preaching time, and lurk about the graves.   Where they be ten or twenty miles from it, there would they be glad to go with the multitude, and to pass over with them unto the house of God with joyfulness and thanksgiving, [Psalm xlii.] as it is in the forty-first psalm.

Of them that dwell under tyrants. Therefore shortly this is mine answer unto the question concerning them that dwell under tyrants.   Blessed be they which are now scattered abroad under the Turk or pope, being destitute of God's word, and would yet be glad with all their hearts to have it, and in the mean season receive with thanksgiving such morsels as they can get, till the meal be better.   Now if they be not far from the place where the word of God is preached, and the blessed sacrament ministered according unto Christ's institution, they may well go thither and enjoy the same treasure, like as many do, and are therefore punished of their wicked rulers, both in body and goods. But if they dwell far from such places, yet do they not cease at the least to sigh thereafter. No doubt Christ our Lord will hear their sighing, and in process of time will he turn back their captivity. Again, unhappy, yea, and unhappy again are they that have this treasure plenteously at their doors, and yet care not for it. On them shall the word of Christ be fulfilled, where he saith: "Many Matt. viii. shall come from the east and west, and shall sit with Abraham, Isaac, and Jacob in the kingdom of heaven; but the children of the kingdom shall be cast out," &c.

Let this be said for an introduction. Now will we shortly go over the psalm.

The Lord is my shepherd : I shall lack nothing.

First of all, the prophet and every faithful heart calleth God his shepherd. Now though the scripture giveth God A sweet many loving names, yet this which the prophet giveth here name. unto God is a much more sweet and gracious name, where he calleth him a shepherd, and saith: "The Lord is my shepherd."

It is very comfortable, when the scripture calleth God our hope, our strength, our stony rock, our castle, our shield, our comfort, our deliverer, our king, &c.; for verily he declareth the thing so still indeed unto his own, that he is even so as the scripture describeth him. But exceeding comfortable is it, that he is called here, and many times else in the scripture, a " shepherd." For in this only word, " shepherd," is almost all comprehended together, what good and comfortable thing soever is spoken of God.

Therefore doth the prophet speak this word with a joyful The cause and sorrowless heart, which is full of faith, and for very that moved the prophet great gladness and comfort exceedeth; and saith not, "The to call God Lord is my strength, castle," &c., which were a marvellous his shepherd. comfortable saying; but, "the Lord is my shepherd." As if he would say: If the Lord be my shepherd and I his sheep, then am I wondrous well provided for, both in body and soul: he shall get me a competent living; he shall defend me and keep me from misfortune; he shall care for me; he shall help me out of all trouble; he shall comfort me; he shall strengthen me, &c. Summa, he shall do for me whatsoever a good shepherd ought to do. All these benefits and more doth he comprehend in this only word "shepherd," as he expoundeth it himself immediately, where he saith: "I shall lack nothing."

Besides this, some of the other names which the scripture ascribes unto God, sound partly too glorious and too high, and bring in a manner a fear with them, when men hear them to be named; as when the scripture calleth God our Lord, King, Maker, &c.

Of such a nature is not this word "shepherd," but soundeth very friendly; and unto them that be godly it bringeth in a manner a confidence, comfort, and trust with it, when they read or hear it; like as this word "Father," and other more, when they be appropriated unto God.

A very
comfortable
similitude.

Therefore is this one of the most loving and comfortable similitudes, and yet very common in the scripture, that it likeneth the majesty of God to a virtuous, faithful, or, as Christ saith, a good shepherd; and us poor, weak, and wretched sinners to a sheep.

Now cannot this comfortable and loving similitude be better understand, than to go into the creatures themselves, whereout the prophets take this and such other like similitudes; and to learn diligently thereby, what the condition and property of a natural sheep is, and the office, labour, and diligence of a good shepherd. Whoso taketh good heed thereunto, may not only with ease understand this and other similitudes in the scripture concerning the shepherd and the sheep; but also they shall be unto him exceeding sweet and comfortable.

The con-
dition of a
sheep.

A sheep must live only by the help, defence, and diligence of his shepherd. As soon as it leaveth him, it is compassed about with all manner of peril, and must needs perish; for it cannot help itself. For why? it is a poor, weak, and innocent beast, that can neither feed nor guide itself, nor find the right way, nor keep itself against any unhappiness or misfortune; seeing this, that of nature it is fearful, flieth and goeth astray. And if it go but a little out of the way, and come from his shepherd, it is not possible for itself to find him again, but runneth ever farther and farther from him. And though it come to other shepherds and sheep, yet is it nothing helped therewith: for it knoweth not the voice of strange shepherds; therefore flieth it from them, and runneth so long astray, till the wolf ravish it, or till it perish some other ways.

Nevertheless, as weak a beast as it is, yet has it this condition, that with all diligence it bideth with his own shepherd, and seeketh comfort at his help and defence; and how or whither soever he leadeth it, it followeth. And if it can but be with him, it careth for no more, neither feareth it any man, but is careless and merry; for it lacketh nothing. It hath also this good virtue in it, which is well to be marked, (for Christ doth specially praise the same in his sheep;) this virtue, I say, it hath, that it will be earnest and sure to hear and know the voice of his shepherd, and ordereth itself thereafter, and will for nothing go from it, but followeth straight the same. Again, it regardeth no strange shepherd's voice: and though they call and whistle upon it never so friendly, yet careth not it therefore; much less doth it follow them. *The property of a sheep.*

Again, this is the office of a good shepherd, that he doth not only provide for his sheep pasture, and other more things that belong thereto, but defendeth them also, that no harm chance unto them. Besides this, he taketh diligent heed that he lese none. If any go astray, he runneth after it, seeketh it, and fetcheth it again. As for such as be young, feeble, and sick, he dealeth gently with them, keepeth them, holdeth them up, and carrieth them, till they be old, strong, and whole, &c. *The office of a shepherd.*

Even thus goeth it also in the spiritual sheepfold, that is to say, in the flock of Christ. Look, how little a natural sheep can keep, guide, rule, save, or defend itself against danger and misfortune, (for it is a feeble and weaponless beast;) so little can we poor, weak, and miserable people keep and rule ourselves spiritually, walk and endure in the right way, or of our own strength to defend us against all evil, and to get us help and comfort in trouble and distress. *How it goeth in the sheep-fold of Christ.*

For how should he have skill to guide himself after a godly fashion, that knoweth nothing of God, that is conceived and born in sin (as we all are), and of nature the child of wrath and the enemy of God? How should we find the right way, and continue therein, seeing that (as the prophet Esay saith) we can do nothing but go astray? How is it possible that we should defend ourselves from the devil, *The misery of our nature.*

which is a prince and lord of this world, whose prisoners also we be every one, seeing that with all power and might we cannot do so much as to hinder a small leaf to hurt us, or a poor flea from grieving us? Why will we poor wretched people boast so much of great comfort, help, and counsel against the judgment of God, against God's wrath and everlasting death, seeing that by ourselves and other we have experience daily and hourly, how we can neither counsel nor comfort ourselves in small bodily necessities?

A plain com-
parison.
Therefore conclude thus hardly: as little as a natural sheep can help itself in the things that be least of all, but must look for all benefits at his shepherd's hand; much less can a man rule, comfort, help, or give counsel unto himself in things belonging to salvation, but must look for all such at the only hand of God his shepherd; which to fulfil anything for his sheep that is to be done is a thousand times more willing and diligent, than any other virtuous shepherd in the world.

Christ is our
shepherd.
As for this shepherd, of whom the prophet had spoken so long before, it is even Christ our loving master, which is far another manner of shepherd than Moses, which is hard and extreme unto his sheep, and driveth them back into the wilderness, where they find neither pasture nor water, but plain scarceness, Exod. iii. But Christ is the gracious and loving shepherd, which runneth after the famished and lost sheep in the wilderness, and seeketh it there; "and when he findeth it, he taketh it up gladly upon his shoulders," Luke xv.; yea, "and giveth his life also for his sheep," John x. This must needs be a loving shepherd. Who would not be glad then to be a sheep of his?

The shep-
herd's voice.
This shepherd's voice, wherewith he speaketh and calleth unto his sheep, is the holy gospel, whereby we be taught that we obtain grace, remission of sins, and everlasting salvation, not by Moses' law, (wherethrough he putteth us in the more fear, dread, and despair, which were too fearful, too sore afraid, and despaired too much afore,) but by Christ, which is "the shepherd and bishop of our souls," 1 Pet. ii.; which hath sought us miserable and lost sheep, and fetched us out of the wilderness, that is to say, from the law, from sin, from death, from the power of the devil, from everlasting damnation; and in that he gave his life for us, obtained

he us grace, remission of sins, comfort, help, and strength against the devil and all misfortune, yea, and everlasting life also. This is now unto the sheep of Christ a loving sweet voice, which they are heartily glad to hear, which they know right well, and order themselves thereafter. "As for a strange voice that soundeth otherwise, they neither know it nor hearken unto it, but avoid and fly away from it," &c. John x.

The pasture, wherewith Christ feedeth his sheep, is also *The pasture.* the comfortable gospel, whereby the souls are fed and strengthened, kept from error, comforted in all temptations and troubles, defended against the craft and power of the devil, and finally delivered out of all trouble. Nevertheless, forasmuch as his sheep are not all alike strong, but some yet lost and scattered here and there abroad, wounded, sick, young, and feeble; he doth not therefore cast them away, but hath much more respect unto them, and careth more diligently for them, than for the other that have no such need. For as the prophet Ezekiel saith in the xxxivth chapter: "He seeketh them that be lost, bringeth together them that be scattered abroad, bindeth up such as be wounded, looketh to them that be sick." And the weak lambs that be but young at the first, saith Esay, "he taketh up in his arms, and beareth them, and such as be with young ones doth he drive forth fair and softly." All this doth our loving master Christ by the office of preaching and distributing of the holy sacrament; as it is oft and with many words taught in other places. For to set it forth here word by word as need should require, it were too long. The prophet also himself will declare it afterward in the psalm.

By this then may we easily perceive, how shamefully *We have been deceived.* we have been seduced under the papacy. For Christ was not so lovingly set forth unto us as the dearly beloved prophets, apostles, and Christ himself doth: but so fearfully was he described unto us, that we have been more afraid of him than of Moses; yea, we thought Moses' doctrine much more lighter, and to have much more sweetness in it, than the doctrine of Christ. And so we knew nothing else, but that Christ had been a wrathful judge, whose displeasure we might have reconciled with our good works and with our holiness, and whose pardon we might have obtained through the merits and intercessions of saints. This is not only a shameful lesson, and a miserable deceiving of poor consciences, but also the highest blasphemy of the grace of God, a denying of the death, resurrection, and ascension of Christ, &c., and of all his unoutspeakable benefits, slandering and condemning of his holy gospel, a destroying of faith, and instead thereof a setting up of utter abominations, lies, and errors, &c.

Blindness.

If this be not darkness, then cannot I tell what darkness is. Yet could no man in a manner perceive it, but every man took it for the plain verity; and yet unto this day will our papists needs take it for the right way, and shed much innocent blood for the same. Go to then, if we can preserve ourselves from error, if we can obtain grace and remission of sins, resist the devil and all misfortune, overcome sin and death by our own merits; then must all the scripture be false, which testifieth of us, how that of ourselves we are but lost, scattered abroad, wounded, weak, and feeble sheep. And so should we have no need of Christ to be shepherd, to seek us, to bring us together, to guide us, to bind us up, to look upon us, and to strengthen us against the devil. And so hath he also given his life for us in vain. For if we can bring all this to pass, and obtain it through our own strength and goodness, then have we no need of Christ's help.

Mark this well.

But here thou hearest the contrary, namely, that thou art but a lost sheep, and of thyself canst not come to the shepherd again; but to go astray, only that canst thou well do. And if Christ thy shepherd did not seek and fetch thee again, thou must needs be a prey unto the wolf. But now he cometh, seeketh, findeth, and bringeth thee unto his fold, that is to say, into his christian congregation, through the word and sacrament; giveth his life for thee, and holdeth thee still by the right hand, lest thou shouldest fall into any error. There hearest thou nothing of thine own strength, of thine own good works and merits; except thou wilt call it strength, a good work, and merit, to go astray, to be feeble and lost. Christ worketh, deserveth, and sheweth here his power only. It is he that seeketh, beareth, and guideth thee. He through his death deserveth life for thee. He only is strong, and defendeth thee, lest thou shouldest perish and be taken away out of his hands. John x. Unto all this canst thou do nothing, save apply thine ears to hear, and with thanksgiving to receive such an unoutspeakable treasure, and to learn to know well the voice of the shepherd, to follow him, and to eschew the voice of strangers. Wherefore, if thou wilt be richly provided for, both in body and soul, above all things take good heed then to the voice of this shepherd; hearken well what he saith unto thee; let him feed thee, rule thee, guide thee, defend thee, comfort thee, &c. : that is to say, keep thee unto his word, be glad to hear it and to learn it, and so no doubt thou shalt be well provided for, both in body and soul.

Take heed to thy shepherd's voice.

By this that hath been spoken of hitherto, I think it but easy to understand these words, " The Lord is my shepherd ;" yea, and all the whole psalm beside. They are but few words : " THE LORD IS MY SHEPHERD ;" but a great weight and pith. The world maketh great boasting and cracking of honour, power, riches, favour of men, &c. But the prophet maketh his boast of none of these; for they be all uncertain and transitory. He speaketh but few words and good : " The Lord is my shepherd." Thus speaketh a sure and constant faith; which turneth her back upon everything that is temporal and transitory, how high and precious soever it be; and turneth the face and heart straight unto the Lord, which is only and altogether, and doth it himself alone. Even he, and else none, whether he be king or emperor, saith he, " is my shepherd." Therefore goeth he forward in all quietness, and saith :

I shall lack nothing.

This doth he speak in general of all the benefits bodily and ghostly, that we receive by the office of preaching. As though he would say : That the Lord be my shepherd, then doubtless I shall lack nothing; I shall have abundance of meat, drink, clothing, a living, defence, peace, and all manner of necessaries, whatsoever serveth for the sustentation of this life : for I have a rich shepherd, which shall not suffer me to lack. Nevertheless he doth speak most specially of the spiritual goods and gifts, that the word of God bringeth with it, and saith : ' Forasmuch as the Lord hath taken me among his flock, and provideth for me with his own pasture,

A general sentence.

that is, forasmuch as he hath richly given me his holy word,
he shall not suffer me to have scarceness in any thing. He
shall give his blessing unto the word, that it may have
strength, and bring forth fruit in me. He shall likewise
give me his Spirit, to stand by me and to comfort me in all
temptations and troubles, to make my heart also sure and
certain, and that I doubt not therein, but that I am one
of my shepherd's dear sheep, and he my faithful shepherd,
which will deal gently with me, as with a poor weak sheep,
and will strengthen my faith, endue me also with other
spiritual gifts, comfort me in all troubles, hear me when I
call upon him, defend me from the wolf, that is, from the
devil, so that he shall not be able to do me harm; and
finally deliver me from all misfortune.'

I shall lack nothing.

An objection. Thou wilt say, Yea, and whereby shall I perceive that
the Lord is my shepherd? I cannot perceive that he dealeth
so lovingly with me, as the psalm speaketh; yea, the contrary do I well perceive. David was an holy prophet, and
a man dearly beloved unto God: therefore could he easily
talk of the matter, and believe well as he said. As for
me, I shall not be able to do it after him; for I am a poor
sinner.

An answer. I have declared above, that a sheep hath this good
condition and proper virtue in it, that it knoweth well the
voice of his shepherd, and ordereth itself rather after the
ears, than after the eyes. The same virtue doth Christ
praise also in his sheep, when he saith, (John x.) "My
sheep know my voice." Now his voice soundeth after this
manner: "I am a good shepherd, and give my life for my
sheep. And I give them everlasting life, and they shall
never perish, and no man shall pluck them out of my hand."
Take good heed now unto this voice, and order thyself
thereafter: if thou do so, then be sure that thou art one
of Christ's sheep, and he thy shepherd, which knoweth thee
right well, and can call thee by name. Now if thou hast
him for thy shepherd, then shalt thou verily lack nothing;
yea, thou hast already that thou shouldest have, even everlasting life. Item, thou shalt never perish, neither shall
there be any power so great and mighty, as to be able to

pluck thee out of his hand. Only be thou sure of this: for doubtless this shepherd's voice shall never fail thee. What wilt thou more? But if thou lettest this voice go, and orderest thyself after the sight of the eyes and after the feeling of that old Adam; then leseth thou the faith and confidence, which thou as a sheep shouldest have unto him, as to thy shepherd. And so falleth thee upon the now one imagination, now another, so that thou canst not be in quiet, but disputest by thyself, and sayest: If the Lord be my shepherd, why suffereth he then the world to plague me and persecute me too miserably, contrary to all my deserving? I sit among wolves, and am not sure of my life the twinkling of an eye; but I see no shepherd that will defend me. Item, why giveth he the devil licence to do me so much harm with fear and despair? Besides this, I find myself all unapt, feeble, unpatient, and laden yet with many sins; I find no certainty, but doubtfulness; no consolation, but fearfulness and quaking for the wrath of God. When beginneth he to declare to me, that he is my shepherd?

Leave not the voice of thy shepherd.

Such and many other no wonderful cogitations shalt thou have, if thou let his voice and word pass. But if thou cleave still fast unto it, then sufferest thou neither the deceitfulness of the devil, the displeasure and madness of the world, neither thine own infirmity and unworthiness, to overcome thee by temptation; but goest on boldly, and sayest, Whether the devil, the world, or mine own conscience do take part against me never so fiercely, yet will not I therefore take overmuch thought. It must and shall be thus, that whosoever is a sheep of the Lord, he cannot remain untempted. Let it go with me as it may, yea, whether they seethe me or roast me, yet is this my comfort, that my shepherd hath given his life for me. Besides this, he hath also a sweet and loving voice, wherewith he comforteth, and saith, I shall never perish, neither shall there any man pluck me out of his hand, but I shall have everlasting life. This promise will be faithfully kept with me, whatsoever become of me. And though sometime there chance a sin or other impediment by the reason of mine infirmity, yet will he not therefore cast me away; for he is a loving shepherd, which looketh to the weak sheep, bindeth up their wounds, and healeth them. And to the

What good followeth when one cleaveth fast to God's words.

intent that I should be the surer of this, and not to doubt
thereon, he hath left me here the holy sacrament, for a
token that it is so indeed.

Even thus hath the prophet done. He was not merry
alway, neither could he at all hours sing, "The Lord is
my shepherd, I shall lack nothing." He hath been sometime
at many a great exigent, yea, all too many; so that he
neither felt the righteousness, comfort, nor help of God, but
plain sin, the wrath of God, fearfulness, despair, the pains
of hell, &c.; as he complaineth himself in many psalms.
Nevertheless he turneth him from his own feeling, and
taketh hold of God by his promise concerning Messias that
then was for to come, and casteth this in his mind: 'Howsoever it stand with me, yet is this the comfort of my
heart, that I have a gracious and merciful Lord, which is
my shepherd, whose word and promise doth strengthen and
comfort me; therefore shall I lack nothing.' And even
therefore hath he written this and other psalms, to the
intent that we should be sure, that in very temptations
there is elsewhere no counsel and comfort to be found; and
that this is the only golden science, namely, to cleave unto
the word and promise of God, and to judge after the same,
and not after the feeling of the heart. And so, no doubt,
there shall follow help and comfort, and not fail in anything.

Now followeth the second verse.

*He feedeth me in a green pasture, and leadeth me to
the fresh water.*

In the first verse hath the prophet shortly comprehended
the meaning of the whole psalm, namely, that whosoever
hath the Lord for his shepherd shall lack nothing. More
than this doth not he teach in this psalm; but only setteth
forth the same more at large with goodly ornate words and
similitudes, how it chanceth that they which are the Lord's
sheep lack nothing, and saith: "He feedeth me," &c. But
almost throughout the whole psalm (as his manner is ofttimes
to do) he useth words, which signify somewhat else than they
sound. As when he maketh mention of the shepherd, of the
feeding of the green pasture, of the fresh water, the staff,
the sheep-hook, &c., it is easy to perceive, that he will have
somewhat else understood thereby than we men use to speak

thereof. Such manner of speaking is very common in the scripture; and therefore should man take diligent heed thereunto, that they may be accustomed withal, and learn to understand it.

But see how well-favouredly he can speak. I am, saith he, a sheep of the Lord's, which feedeth me in a green pasture, &c. A natural sheep cannot be better than when the shepherd feedeth it in a pleasant green pasture, and beside fresh water. If it can have this, it thinketh no man upon earth is more rich or happier than it; for there it findeth every thing that it can desire: a goodly thick plentiful grass, whereof it waxeth strong and fat; a fresh water, wherewith it can refresh and quicken itself. There hath it pleasure and joy. Even so will David say here likewise, that God never shewed him a greater grace and benefit upon earth than this, that he might be in the place and among the people, where the word and dwelling of God and the right God's service was. For where that treasure is, there goeth it well both in the spiritual and worldly regiment. As if he would say: 'All the nations and kingdoms upon earth are nothing. They are indeed richer, mightier, and more glorious than we Jews, and make great boasting thereof. They boast also of their wisdom and holiness, for they have gods also whom they serve: yet with all their pomp and glory, they are but even a plain wilderness and desert. For there is neither shepherd nor pasture; therefore must the sheep needs stray, be famished, and perish. As for us, though we have many wildernesses about us, yet sit we here at rest, safe and merry in paradise, and in a pleasant green pasture, where there is plenty of grass and fresh water, and have with us our shepherd, which feedeth us, leadeth us to the drink, defendeth us, &c. Therefore can we lack nothing.'

This man had ghostly eyes, and therefore saw he right well what is the best and noblest good upon earth. He maketh no boast of his kingly worship and power: he knowledgeth well, that such goods are also the gifts of God; neither runneth he from them, and letteth them lie, but useth them unto the honour of God, and giveth him thanks therefore. But of this maketh he specially his boast, namely, that the Lord is his shepherd, and he in his pasture and feeding; that is, that he hath God's word. This benefit

The chiefest good upon earth is to have God's word.

can he never forget; but speaketh thereof marvellous excellently, and with great joy, and praiseth it far above all the goods upon earth. And this he doth in many psalms, as [Psal. cxix.] in the 118th, where he saith: "The law of thy mouth is dearer unto me than thousands of gold and silver." Item: "I love thy commandments above gold and precious stone. O how sweet are thy words unto my throat! Yea, more than honey unto my mouth."

What we
ought here
to learn. This science should we learn also, namely, to let the world boast of their great riches, honour, power, &c. For it is loose, uncertain, and transitory ware, which God casteth into the dungeon. It is a small matter for him to give an ungracious person, that blasphemeth and dishonoureth him again, for his reward, a kingdom, a dukedom, or any other worship and good upon earth. These worldly goods are his draff and swillings, wherewith he filleth the hogs' bellies, that he is disposed to kill. But unto his children, as David speaketh here thereof, he giveth the right treasure. Therefore should we, as the dear children and heirs of God, neither boast ourselves of our wisdom, strength, nor riches, but of this, that we have the precious pearl, even that worthy word, whereby we know God our loving Father, and Jesus The word of Christ whom he hath sent. This is our treasure and inheritance, which is sure and everlasting, and better than all the good of the world. Whoso hath this, let him suffer other men to gather money together, to live voluptuously, to be proud and high-minded: but though he himself be despised and poor in the sight of the world, yet let not that tempt him; but let him thank God for his unoutspeakable gift, and pray that he may abide thereby. It maketh no matter how rich and glorious we be here upon earth; if we keep this treasure, we have plenty of riches and honour. St Paul was a man of light reputation, and poor upon earth, having the devil and the world very fierce against him: but in the sight of God he was a man right dear, and greatly set by. Besides this, he was so poor, that he was fain to get his living with the labour of his hands. And yet for all that great poverty he was richer than the emperor of Rome; having nevertheless none other riches but the knowledge of Christ. "For the which," saith he, Phil. iii. "I count all things nothing upon earth, except very loss and dung."

The God of mercy grant us grace, that we also, after the ensample of David, Paul, and other holy men, may count our treasure, which is even the same that they had, as great, and magnify it above all the goods upon earth, and heartily to give God thanks therefore, that he hath vouchsafed it upon us afore many thousands of other! He might have suffered us to go astray, as well as the Turks, Egyptians, Jews, and other idolaters, which know not of that treasure; or else he might have suffered us still to be hard-hearted, as are the papists, that blaspheme and condemn this treasure of ours: whereas he hath set us now in his own green meadow, and provided us so richly with good pasture and fresh water. It cometh even of his grace; therefore have we the more to thank him for. God hath done more for us than for many other.

As for the people of God, or the holy congregation of Christ, the prophet calleth it a green meadow. For it is a pleasant garden, garnished and beautified with all manner of spiritual gifts. The pasture or grass therein is the word of God, whereby the consciences are strengthened and refreshed. In the same green meadow doth our Lord God gather his sheep together, feedeth them therein with good grass, and refresheth them with fresh water: that is, he committeth unto the holy christian church the shepherd's office, delivereth and giveth her the holy gospel and the sacraments, to take charge and look to his sheep therewith, that they may be richly provided for with doctrine, with comfort, with strength, and with defence against all evil, &c. As for those that preach the law of Moses, or the commandments of men, they feed not the sheep in a green pasture, but in the wilderness, where they famish, and lead them to foul stinking waters, whereof they perish and die. The meadow.
The grass.
What they be that feed sheep in the wilderness.

By this allegory of the green pasture will the prophet declare the great abundance and riches of the holy gospel and of the knowledge of Christ among the faithful. For like as the grass in a green meadow standeth goodly thick and full, and ever groweth more and more; even so have the faithful not only God's word with all plenteousness, but also the more they use and meddle withal, the more it increaseth and groweth among them. Therefore setteth he the words marvellous plainly. The great riches of such as believe.

He saith not, he bringeth me once or oft into a green

pasture; but feedeth me still therein, that I may lie, take my rest, and dwell even in the midst of the grass, and need never to suffer hunger or any scarceness beside. For the word that he here useth may be called lying, or resting, as a beast lieth and resteth upon his four feet. After the same manner [Psal. lxxii.] doth Solomon speak also in the seventy-first psalm, where he prophesieth of the kingdom of Christ and the gospel, that it should mightily go through and come into all places, and saith : " There shall be an heap of corn in the earth high upon the hills, &c., and shall be green in the city, like grass upon the earth." That David also in this psalm speaketh likewise of the gospel, he declareth himself afterward, when he saith : " He quickeneth my soul." Item : " Thy staff and thy sheep-hook do comfort me."

The first fruit of God's word.   This is now the first fruit of the word of God, that the christians are so instructed thereby, that they increase in faith and hope, learn to commit all their doings unto God, and whatsoever they have need of, either in soul or body, to look for it at his hand, &c.

And leadeth me to the fresh water.

The second fruit of God's word.   This is the second fruit of God's word. It is unto the faithful not only pasture and grass, whereby they are filled and strengthened in faith ; but it is also unto them a goodly cold fresh water, whereby they take refreshing and comfort. Therefore leaveth he not there where he said, " He feedeth me in a green pasture ;" but addeth this also unto it, " And leadeth me to the fresh water." As if he would say : In the [Psal. cxxi.] great heat, when the sun doth sore burn (Psal. cxx.), and I can have no shadow, then leadeth he me to the fresh water, giveth me drink and refresheth me : that is, in all manner of troubles, anguishes, and necessities, ghostly and bodily, when I know not elsewhere to find help or comfort, I hold me unto the word of grace. There only, and nowhere else, do I find the right consolation and refreshing, and that plenteously. Now, whereas he speaketh here of this comfort with garnished words, he talketh of it in another place with plain and mani- Psal. cxviii. fest words, and saith : " If thy word were not my comfort [cxix.] and delight, I should perish in my trouble." " I will never forget thy word, for in my trouble it is my consolation ; yea, thy word quickeneth me."

Nevertheless he continueth still in the similitude of the Why the scripture rehearseth so oft this similitude. shepherd and of the sheep; and, no doubt, it is common in all the prophets. For of the sheep and other cattle had the Jews their best living, and were commonly shepherds, as was David and the patriarchs. Therefore is this similitude ofttimes spoken of in the scripture. But David speaketh of this matter after the nature of the country. For the land of promise is an hot, dry, sandy, and stony land, which hath many wildernesses and little water. Therefore in the first book of Moses it was more than once declared, how that the heathen shepherds strove with the shepherds of the patriarchs because of water. For the which cause in the same country they take it for a special treasure, if they might have water for their cattle. In our countries we know not thereof; for there is water enough every where. Of this did David see, and he rehearseth it for a special benefit, to be under the custody of the Lord, which should not only feed him in a green pasture, but also in the heat bringing him to the fresh water, &c.

Shortly, his meaning is to declare, that as little as a man can come to the knowledge of God and the truth, and to the right faith, without the word of God; so little can there any Without God's word can no man's conscience be at rest. comfort and peace of conscience be found without the same. The worldly have also their comfort and joy; howbeit that endureth but the twinkling of an eye: when trouble and anguish cometh, and specially the last hour, it goeth away; as Solomon saith: "After laughter cometh sorrow, and after Prov. xiv. joy cometh heaviness." But as for them that drink of this fresh and living water, they may well suffer trouble and disease in the world; but they shall never lack the true consolation. And specially when it cometh to the point, the leaf turneth over with them: which is as much to say as, 'After short weeping cometh everlasting laughter, and after a little sorrow cometh excellent joy.' 2 Cor. v. For they shall not weep and mourn both here and there; but, as Christ saith: "Blessed are you that weep here, for ye shall laugh." Luke vi.

He quickeneth my soul, and bringeth me forth in the way of righteousness for his name's sake.

Here doth the prophet declare himself, of what manner Spiritual pasture and water. of pasture and fresh water he spake, namely, even of the same that strengtheneth and quickeneth the soul. This can be nothing else but God's word. But forasmuch as our Lord God hath two manner of words, the law and the gospel, the prophet, when he saith, "He quickeneth my soul," giveth sufficiently to understand, that he speaketh not here of the

The law. law, but of the gospel. The law cannot quicken the soul; for it is a word that requireth and commandeth us to love God with all our hearts, &c., and our neighbour as ourselves. Whoso doth not this, him it condemneth, and speaketh this sentence over him: "Cursed be every man which doth not all that is written in the book of the law." Deut. xxvii. Gal. iii. Now is it certain, that no man upon earth doth this; therefore cometh the law with his judgment, fearing and vexing the consciences: and if there be no help, it goeth through; so that they must needs fall into despair, and be condemned for ever. Of this occasion doth St Paul

Rom. iii. say: "By the law cometh but the knowledge of sin." Item,

Rom. iv. "The law causeth but wrath."

The gospel.   As for the gospel, it is a blessed word; it requireth none such of us, but bringeth us tidings of all good, namely, that God hath given us poor sinners his only Son, to be our shepherd, to seek again us famished and dispersed sheep, and to give his life for us, that he might so deliver us from sin, from everlasting death, and from the power of the devil. This is the green grass, and the fresh water, wherewith the Lord quickeneth our souls. And thus are we made loose from evil consciences and heavy thoughts. Of this shall we speak more in the fourth verse.

He bringeth me forth in the way of righteousness.

Here, saith he, doth not the Lord my faithful shepherd leave, that he feedeth me in a green meadow, and leadeth me to the fresh water, and so quickeneth my soul; but he bringeth me forth also in the right way, that I depart not aside, go

To be led in the right way what it is. astray, and so perish: that is, he holdeth me fast to the pure doctrine, that I be not deceived by false spirits, and that I fall not away by any other temptation or offence; item, that I may know how I ought to lead mine outward conversation and life, and that I suffer not myself to be persuaded by the holiness and strait life of hypocrites; item, what is the true doctrine, faith, and service of God, &c.

This is now again a goodly fruit and virtue of the word An excellent virtue of God's word. of God, that they which cleave fast thereunto, do not only receive strength and comfort of soul thereby, but are preserved also from untrue doctrine and false holiness. Many men obtain this treasure, but they cannot keep it. For as soon as a man is too bold and presumptuous, and thinketh himself sure of the matter, it is done with him: or ever he can look about him, he is deceived. For the devil also can pretend holiness, and transform himself into an angel of light, as St Paul saith: and even so likewise can his ministers shew themselves, as though they were the preachers of righteousness, and come in sheep's clothing among the flock of Christ, but inwardly are they ravening wolves. Therefore is it good here to watch and pray, as the prophet doth in the last verse, that our shepherd may keep us by this treasure which he hath given us. They that do not this, certainly they shall lese it. "And the end of that man," as Luke xi. Christ saith, "shall be worse than the beginning." For they shall afterward become the most poisoned enemies of Christ's flock, and do more harm with their false doctrine than the tyrants with the sword. This had St Paul well proved by the false apostles, that made the Corinthians and Galatians to err so soon, and afterward made division in all Asia. We see it ourselves also this day by the anabaptists and other false spirits.

For his name's sake.

The name of God is the preaching of God, whereby he The name of God. is magnified and known to be gracious, merciful, long-suffering, true, faithful, &c.; which, notwithstanding that we be the children of wrath, and guilty of everlasting death, forgiveth us all our sins, and taketh us for his own children and inheritors. This is his name, this doth he cause to be proclaimed by his word. Thus will he be known, magnified, and honoured; and, according unto the first commandment, he will even thus declare himself toward us, as he hath caused it to be preached of him: like as he doth still, strengtheneth and quickeneth our souls spiritually, and keepeth us that we fall not into error, getteth us living for our body, and preserveth us from all misfortune.

This honour, that he so is as we have now said, is given

him only of them that cleave fast unto his word: these believe
and confess plainly, that all the gifts and goods which they
have, ghostly and bodily, they receive them of God, even of
his mere grace and goodness; that is to say, "For his
name's sake," not for their own work and deservings. For
this do they give thanks unto him, and declare the same
unto other. This honour cannot be given unto God of any
presumptuous justiciaries, as heretics and false spirits, or enemies and blasphemers of God's word; for they magnify not
his name, but their own.

*And though I walk in the valley of the shadow of
death, yet fear I no evil; for thou art with me: thy staff,
thy sheep-hook do comfort me.*

Hitherto hath the prophet declared, that they which have
and love the word of God can lack nothing. For the Lord
is their shepherd, which doth not only feed them in a green
pasture and leadeth them to the fresh water, that they may
be fat, strong, and refreshed both bodily and ghostly; but
also taketh such care for them, that they be not weary of
the good pasture and fresh water, leaving the green meadow,
and depart again from the right way into the wilderness.

What the prophet teacheth in this verse.

This is the first part of this psalm. Now teacheth he farther,
how that they which are the sheep of this shepherd be compassed about with many jeopardies and misfortunes. Nevertheless the Lord, saith he, not only defendeth them, but
delivereth them also out of all temptations and troubles:
for he is among them. Now after what manner he is with
them, he declareth likewise well-favouredly.

Here thou seest, that as soon as the word of God goeth
forth, and as soon as there be any that receive it, and abide
by it, immediately the devil and all his angels step forth and
move the world with all the power thereof against it, to
put it down, and utterly to destroy them that have it and

Persecution.

knowledge it. For look, what our Lord God speaketh or
doth, it must be tried and go through the fire. This is very
needful for christian men to know; else might they fail and
think thus in their minds: How standeth this together?
The prophet saith afore, "The Lord is my shepherd, I shall
lack nothing." And here he saith contrary, namely, that he
must walk in the dark valley. And in the next verse follow-

ing he confesseth, that he hath enemies: whereby he giveth sufficiently to understand, that he lacketh many, yea, all things. For he that hath enemies, and lieth in a dark valley, seeth no light; that is to say, he hath neither comfort nor hope, but is forsaken of every man, and every thing is black and dark before his eyes, yea, even the fair clear sun. How is this true then, that he should lack nothing?

Here must thou not order thyself after thine own eyes, and follow natural reason, as doth the world, unto whom it is impossible to see this rich and glorious comfort of christian men, that they should lack nothing. Yea, certainly they hold that the contrary is true, namely, that there are no people upon earth more poor, more miserable, and more unhappy than christian men: yea, with all their diligence and courage help they thereto, that they may be most abominably persecuted, banished, shamed, and put to death: and in so doing they think they do God's service therein. It appeareth therefore outwardly, as though christian men were but sheep driven away and forsaken of God, and given over already into the wolves' mouths, and to be even such as lack nothing but altogether[1]. *We may not order ourselves after the outward sight.*

Again, they that serve that great god Mammon, or the belly, appear in the world to be those good sheep, which, as the psalm saith, lack nothing; being richly provided for of God, comforted, and preserved from all peril and misfortune. For they have their own heart's desire, honour, good, joy, pleasure, every man's favour, &c. Neither need they be afraid to be persecuted or put to death for the faith's sake. For as long as they put not their trust in Christ, the only true Shepherd, nor knowledge him; whether they believe on the devil or his dam, or do whatsoever they will beside with covetousness, &c., they are taken not only for welldoers therein, but also for the living saints, which bide still by the old faith, and will not be deceived through heresy; which is, as David teacheth here, that the Lord only is the shepherd. So abominable and grievous mortal sin is it to believe on this shepherd, and to knowledge him, that there came never such a sin upon earth. For even the pope's holiness, which else can dispense with all sins and forgive them, cannot remit this only crime. *The servants of Mammon.* *The pope will not forgive him that putteth his whole trust in Christ.*

[1 Perhaps for, *lack not one thing, but all together*.]

Therefore, I say, in this thing do not thou follow the world and thine own reason, which, while they judge after the outward appearance, become foolish, and hold the prophet but for a liar in that he saith, "I shall lack nothing." But, as I said afore, hold thou thee fast unto the word and promises of God; hearken unto thy shepherd, how and what he saith unto thee; and order thyself according unto his voice, not according to that which the eye seeth, or the heart feeleth: and so hast thou the victory. Thus doth the prophet: he confesseth that he walketh in the valley of the shadow of death, that is, that he is compassed about with trouble, heaviness, anguish, necessity, &c.; as thou mayest see at more large in his stories and other psalms. Item, that he hath need of comfort; whereby it is sufficiently declared, that he is in heaviness. Item, that he hath enemies; and yet he saith: Though my temptations were more and greater, and though I were in a worse case; yea, though I were in death's mouth already, yet do not I fear any misfortune. Not that I am able to help myself through mine own provision, travail, labour, or succour; neither do I trust to mine own wisdom, virtue, kingly power, and riches: for in this matter the help, counsel, comfort, and power of all men is far too little. But this is it that doth it, even that the Lord is with me. As if he would say: Certainly of mine own behalf I am feeble, in heaviness, vexed, and compassed about with all manner of peril and misfortune. My heart also and conscience is not quiet, because of my sins. I feel an horrible fearfulness of death and hell, so that I might in manner despair. But though all the world, yea, and the gates of hell be set against me, yet will I therefore not be discouraged. Yea, I will not be afraid for all the misfortune and pain that they are able to lay upon me. The Lord is with me: the Lord, I say, which made heaven and earth, and all that therein is, unto whom all creatures, angels, devils, men, sin, death, &c., are subject. Summa, he that hath all things in his own power, is my counsel-giver, my comforter, my defender, and helper. Therefore am I afraid of no misfortune.

How the prophet behaveth himself in temptation and trouble.

Asaph.

[Psal. lxxiii.]

After this manner doth Asaph speak also in the seventy-second Psalm, where he comforteth the Christian against that great stumbling-block, that the ungodly have such prosperity upon earth, and that the beloved saints of God, on the other side, are ever plagued, &c., and saith: "If I have but thee, O Lord, I pass not upon heaven nor earth. Though both body and soul should perish, yet thou, O God, art the comfort of my heart, and my portion."

Now after what manner the Lord is with him, he sheweth farthermore, and saith:

Thy staff and thy sheep-hook do comfort me.

The Lord, saith he, is with me; but not bodily, that I may see or hear him. This presence of the Lord, whereof I speak, is not comprehended with the five wits. Only faith seeth it. The same is sure, that the Lord is nigher unto us than we are to ourselves. Whereby? even by the word. Therefore saith he: "Thy staff and thy sheep-hook comfort me." As if he would say: In all my troubles and necessities I find nothing upon earth, whereby I may be helped to be at rest. Only the word of God is my staff and sheep-hook, whereby I hold me, and stand up again. And sure I am likewise by it, that the Lord is with me, and doth not only strength and comfort me by the same word in all troubles and temptations, but also delivereth me from all mine enemies, spite of the devil and the world. ^{How the Lord is present with many faithful men.}

With these words, "Thy staff and thy sheep-hook do comfort me," cometh he again unto the similitude of the shepherd and the sheep, and will say thus much: Like as a bodily shepherd ruleth his sheep with the staff or sheep-hook, and leadeth them to the pasture and to fresh water, where they find meat and drink, and defendeth them with the sheep-hook against all peril; even so doth the Lord, that true shepherd, guide and rule me with his staff, that is to say, with his word; to the intent that in his sight I should walk with a good belief and a merry conscience, and know to beware of untrue doctrine and false holiness. Besides this, he defendeth me also against all jeopardy and misfortune, bodily and ghostly, and delivereth me from all mine enemies with his staff; that is to say, with the same word doth he strength and comfort me so richly, that there is no misfortune so great, whether it be bodily or ghostly, but I am able to come out of it, and to overcome it. ^{The similitude of the shepherd.}

By this thou seest, that the prophet speaketh here of no help, defence, or comfort of man. Neither draweth he out ^{This goeth spiritually to work.}

20—2

any sword, &c. It goeth here all secretly and privily to
work, even by the word : so that no man can spy this
defence and comfort, but only they that believe. And here
doth David write a general rule for all christian men, which
is well to be noted ; namely, that there is none other mean
way upon earth for any man to be delivered out of all temptations, save only to cast all his burden upon God, and to
hold him fast by his word of grace, to cleave surely unto it,
and in no wise to suffer it to be taken from him. Whoso
doth this can be content, whether he be in prosperity or
adversity, whether he live or die. And, finally, he can endure, and must needs prosper against all devils, the world,
and misfortune. This, methink, is a great praise of that
good word of God ; and a greater power is ascribed here
unto it, than is the power of all angels and men. Thus doth
St Paul praise it also, Rom. i. : "The gospel," saith he, "is
the power of God for the salvation of all them that believe
thereon."

The office of
preaching.
        And with this doth the prophet touch the office of preach-
ing : for by the mouthly preaching of the word, which goeth
in at the ears, and that the heart taketh hold upon by faith,
and by the holy sacraments, doth our Lord God bring all
this to pass in his christian congregation ; namely, to the
intent that the people may have faith, be strengthened in
belief, and preserved in the true doctrine : item, that they
may finally endure against all temptations of the devil and
the world. For since the beginning of the world hath God
dealt thus with all his saints by his word, and beside the
same hath he given them outward tokens of grace. This
I say, because that no man should take upon him without
these means to meddle with God, or to choose himself a
peculiar way unto heaven ; else shall he fall and break his
neck, as the pope and his hath done, and as the anabaptists
and other seditious spirits do yet this day. And with these
words, "Thy staff and thy sheep-hook do comfort me," will
the prophet shew some special thing. As if he would say :
Moses is a shepherd likewise, and hath also a staff and a
sheep-hook: nevertheless he doth nothing else but compel and
punish his sheep, and overladeth them with an untolerable
burthen. Acts xv. Isai. ix. Therefore is he a fearful and
a terrible shepherd, of whom the sheep are afraid, and fly

from him. Nevertheless thou, Lord, with thy staff and sheep-hook compellest not thy sheep, neither makest them afraid, nor overchargest them, but giveth them comfort.

Therefore speaketh he here of the office of preaching the new Testament, whereby tiding is brought unto the world, that Christ came upon earth to save sinners, and thereby hath obtained them such a salvation, that he hath given his life for them. All they that believe this shall not perish, but have everlasting life. John iii. This is the staff and sheep-hook, whereby the souls take refreshing, comfort, and joy. Wherefore in the spiritual sheepfold, that is to say, in the kingdom of Christ, there ought none other law to be preached, but the gospel; which the prophet with ornate words calleth the staff and sheep-hook of comfort, whereby they be strengthened in faith, refreshed in their hearts, and receive consolation in all manner of troubles, and even at the point of death. *The staff and the sheep-hook.*

They that so preach use the spiritual shepherd's office aright, feed the sheep of Christ in a green meadow, lead them to the fresh water, refresh their souls, keep them that they be not deceived, and comfort them with the staff and sheep-hook of Christ, &c. And where thou hearest such one, be sure thou hearest Christ himself. Such men also ought to be taken for true shepherds, that is to say, for the ministers of Christ and the stewards of God. Neither ought it to be regarded, that the world crieth out upon them, and calleth them heretics and deceivers. Again, they that teach any thing else contrary to the gospel, causing men to trust to their own works, merits, and to their own feigned holiness, these no doubt, though they boast never so much to be successors of the apostles, and deck themselves with the name and title of the christian church, yea, though they raised up dead men, yet are they wolves and murderers; which spare not the flock of Christ, scatter them abroad, torment them, and kill them not only spiritually, but bodily also, as men may see now before their eyes. *What they be that lead Christ's sheep in a green meadow.*

Like as the prophet here afore doth call God's word, or the gospel, grass, water, the right way, a staff, and a sheep-hook; even so afterward in the fifth verse he calleth it a table prepared, an ointment, a full cup. And this similitude of the table, ointment, and cup, doth he take out of the old *The names that the word of God hath in this psalm.*

Testament from the God's service of the Jews, and saith even in a manner the same that he had said afore, namely, that they which have the word of God are richly provided for in all points, both concerning the soul and body, save only that he speaketh it here with other figures and allegories. First, bringeth he in the similitude of the table, whereupon the shewbread lay continually. Exod. xxv. xl. And then declareth he what the same did signify, and saith:

Thou preparest a table before me against mine enemies.
Thou anointest mine head with oil, and fillest my cup full.

Here doth he knowledge plainly, that he hath enemies. But he saith, he keepeth him from them, and driveth them back by this means, namely, because the Lord hath prepared a table before him against those his enemies. Is not this a wonderful defender? I would have thought he should have prepared before him a strong wall, a mighty bulwark, deep ditches, armour, and other harness and weapons, whereby he might be sure from his enemies, and discomfit them. And now cometh he and prepareth him a table, to eat and to drink on, and so to smite his enemies.

There could I be content to fight also, if the enemies might be overcome without any jeopardy, care, travail, and labour, and I too do nothing else but to sit at a table, to eat and drink and be merry.

With these words, " Thou preparest a table before me against mine enemies," will the prophet declare the great,

The great power of God's word.

excellent, and wonderful power of the word of God. As if he would say: Thou offerest me such kindness, O Lord, and feedest me so well and richly at thy table which thou hast prepared for me, that is, thou enduest me so plenteously with the exceeding knowledge of thy good word, so that through the same I have not only plenteous consolation inwardly in my heart, against mine own evil conscience, against fear and dread of death, and the wrath and judgment of God; but outwardly also, through the same word, I am become so valiant and so invincible a giant, that all mine enemies can bring nothing to pass against me. The more wroth, mad, and unreasonable they are against me, the less I regard it: yea, I am so much the more quiet in myself, glad, and content; and that of none other occasion, save only that I have thy word. The same giveth me such power and courage against all mine enemies: so that when they rage fiercely and are most mad of all, I am better content in my mind, than if I sat at a table where I might have all that my heart could desire, meat, drink, mirth, pleasure, minstrelsy, &c.

There hearest thou again, how highly this holy David magnifieth and praiseth the good word of God; namely, how that by the same they that believe overcome and win the victory against the devil, the world, the flesh, sin, a man's own conscience, and against death. For if a man have the word, and take more hold of it by faith, then must all these enemies, which else are invincible, be fain to give back and to yield themselves. And it is a marvellous victory and power, yea, and a very stout boasting of such as believe, that they subdue and overcome all these horrible, yea, and in manner almighty, enemies; not with raging, not with biting, not with resisting, not with striking again, not with taking of vengeance, not with seeking of counsel and help here and there; but with eating, drinking, pleasure, sitting, being merry, and taking of rest. Which things, as it is said afore, come all to pass through the word. For to eat and drink is called in the scripture, to believe, to take sure hold on God's word, whereout there followeth peace, joy, comfort, strength, &c.

An high commendation of God's word.

Natural reason can give no judgment in this wonderful victory of the faithful; for here cometh the matter to pass clean contrary to the outward senses of man. The world doth alway persecute and slay the Christian, as the most hurtful people upon earth. Now when natural reason saith this, it cannot think otherwise, but that the Christian lie under; and again, that their enemies prevail and have the victory. Thus did the Jews entreat Christ, the apostles, and the faithful, and put them ever to execution. When they had slain them, or at the least banished them, then cried they, Now have we the victory; these followers that have hurt us shall now trouble us no more. Now shall we handle every thing as we will. But when they thought themselves to have been surest of all, our Lord God sent upon them the Romans, which dealt so horribly with them, that it is a terrible thing to hear. Then after certain hundred years, as for the Romans, (which throughout all the

The natural reason of man.

empire of Rome had slain many thousand martyrs,) God rewarded them afterward, and suffered the city of Rome in a few years to be four times spoiled by the Gothics and Vandals, and finally to be burnt, destroyed, and the empire to decay. Who had now the victory? The Jews and Romans, that shed the blood of saints like water; or the poor Christians, that suffered themselves to be ordered like slaughter-sheep, and had none other harness and weapon, but the good word of God?

How it goeth with the multitude of them that believe in Christ.

Thus doth David declare with these words, how it goeth with the holy christian congregation, (for he speaketh not here of his own person only,) setteth her forth in her colours, and describeth her well-favouredly; namely, how that in the sight of God she is even as a pleasant green meadow, which hath plenty of grass and fresh water: that is to say, that she is the paradise and pleasant garden of God, garnished with all his gifts, and hath his unoutspeakable treasure, the holy sacraments, and that good word, wherewith he instructeth, guideth, refresheth, and comforteth his flock. But in the sight of the world hath this congregation a far other appearance, even as though she were a black dark valley, where a man can see neither pleasure nor joy, but trouble, sorrow, and adversity. For the devil with all his power setteth himself against it, for this treasure sake. Inwardly plagueth he the congregation of God with his venomous fiery darts: outwardly treadeth he her down by sects and offences. Then kindleth he also his brand upon her, even the world, which ministereth unto her all sorrow and heaviness of heart, with persecuting, slandering, blaspheming, condemning, and murdering; insomuch that it were no wonder that dear flock of Christ were utterly destroyed in the twinkling of an eye, by such great subtilty and might both of the devil and of the world. For she cannot keep herself from her enemies; they are far too strong, too deceitful, and too mighty for her. She is even as the prophet doth here describe her, an innocent, simple, and weaponless lamb, which neither will nor can do any man harm, but is alway ready, not only to do good, but also to take evil for good.

How the flock of Christ winneth.

How happeneth it then, that the congregation of Christ in such weakness can escape the craftiness and tyranny of the devil and the world? The Lord is her shepherd; therefore lacketh she nothing. He feedeth and refresheth her ghostly and bodily; he keepeth her in the right way; he giveth her also his staff and sheep-hook instead of a sword, which she beareth not in the hand, but in the mouth; and not only comforteth the sorrowful therewith, but driveth away the devil also and his apostles, be they never so subtle and spiteful. Besides this, the Lord hath prepared for her also a table and Easter lamb. When her enemies are very wrothful, gnash their teeth together over her, are mad, unreasonable, in a rage, and out of their wits, and take all their subtilty, power, and might to help them for to destroy her utterly; then doth the beloved Bride of Christ set her down at her Lord's table, eateth the Easter lamb, drinketh of the fresh water, is merry, and singeth: "The Lord is my shepherd, I shall lack nothing."

These are her weapons and guns, wherewith she hath hitherto smitten and overcome all her enemies; and after the same manner shall she have the victory still unto doomsday. The more also that the devil and the world doth hurt and vex her, the better is it with her. For her edifying and increase standeth in persecution, affliction, and death. Out of this occasion did one of the old fathers say: "The blood of martyrs is a seed; where one is cast, there rise an hundred up again[1]." Of this wonderful victory sing certain psalms, as the ninth, tenth, &c. A notable saying.

After this same manner have I also, through the grace of God, behaved myself these eighteen years: I have ever suffered mine enemies to be wroth, to threaten, to blaspheme and condemn me; to cast their heads still against me, to imagine many evil ways, and to use divers unthirsty points. I have suffered them to take wondrous great thought, how they might destroy me, and mine, yea, God's doctrine. Moreover, I have been glad and merry, (but more at one time than at another,) and not greatly regarded their raging and madness, but have holden me by the staff of comfort, and had recourse unto the Lord's table; that is, I have com- The author of this book.

[1 The sentiment is found in Augustine, Enarrat. in Psalm lv. (lvi.) Pars I. Opera, Tom. VIII. p. 128. C. Ed. 1541. Effusus est multus et magnus martyrum sanguis: quo effuso, tanquam seminata seges ecclesiæ fertilius pullulavit.—Compare also Enarrat. in Psalm. cxl. (cxli.) Ib. p. 354. I. Tertull. Apol. adv. Gentes, c. 50.]

mitted the cause unto God, wherein he hath so led me, that
I have obtained all my will and mind. And in the mean
time have I done little or nothing, but spoken unto him a
Paternoster, or some little psalm.   This is all my harness,
wherewith I have defended me hitherto, not only against
mine enemies; but also through the grace of God brought
so much to pass, that when I look behind me, and call to
remembrance, how it hath stood in the papistry, I do even
wonder that the matter is come so far.   I would never have
thought that the tenth part should have come to pass, as it
is now before our eyes.   He that hath begun it shall bring
it well to an end; yea, though nine hells and worlds were
set on an heap together against it.   Let every christian man,
therefore, learn this science; namely, that he hold him by
this staff and sheep-hook, and resort unto this table, when
heaviness or any other misfortune is at hand.   And so shall
he doubtless receive strength and comfort against every thing
that oppresseth him.

The oint- ment.   The second similitude is of the ointment, whereof there
is mention made oft-times in the holy scripture.   It was some
precious oil, as balm, or else some other sweet-smelling water;
and the use was, to anoint the kings and priests withal.   When
the Jews also held their solemn feasts, and were disposed to
be merry, they did anoint or sprinkle themselves with such
precious ointment, as Christ declared likewise in the sixth of
Matthew, where he saith: "When thou fastest, anoint thine
head, and wash thy face," &c.   The use then of this ointment was had among those people, when they were disposed
to be merry and glad: like as the Magdalene also thought
to make the Lord merry, when she poured upon his head the
precious water of nardus; for she saw that he was heavy.

The full cup.   The third similitude is of the cup, which they brought in
their God's service, when they offered drink-offerings, and
were merry before the Lord.

The rich comfort of christian men.   With these words then, " Thou anointest my head with
oil, and fillest my cup full," will the prophet describe the
great rich comfort, which they that are faithful have by the
word of God; so that their consciences are quiet, glad, and
at rest in the midst of all temptations and troubles, yea,
even of death.   As if he would say: Doubtless the Lord
maketh me a marvellous man of war, and harnesseth me

wondrously against mine enemies. I thought he should have put material harness upon me, set an helmet upon mine head, given me a sword in my hand, and have warned me to be circumspect, and to take diligent heed to my matter, lest mine enemies should overtake me. Now cometh he and setteth me down at a table, and prepareth me a goodly banquet, anointeth mine head with precious balm: or, after the manner of our country, setteth a garland upon mine head, as if I should go to some pastime or dancing, and not fight with mine enemies; and to the intent that there should be no scarceness, he filleth my cup full, that I may drink, make good cheer, and be drunken. The table then prepared is my harness, the precious ointment is my helmet, and the full cup is my sword. With these do I overcome all mine enemies. Is not this a marvellous preparing to war, and yet a more wonderful victory? Thus will he say: Lord, thy guests which sit at thy table, that is to say, the faithful, shall not only be strong and valiant giants against all their enemies, but they shall be merry also and drunken. For why? thou makest them good cheer, *Spiritual drunkenness.* as a rich host useth to do to his guests; thou feedest them well, thou makest them lusty and glad, thou fillest into them so much, that they must needs be drunken. This is all done by the word of grace. For by the same doth the Lord our shepherd feed and strength so the hearts of his faithful, that they dare defy all their enemies, and say with the prophet, "I am not afraid for thousands of the people, that compass me around about." Psalm iii. And here afore in the fourth verse: "I fear no evil; for thou, Lord, art with me." With this, yea, even through the same word, doth he give them also the Holy Ghost, which maketh them not only to take good stomachs unto them, and to be of good courage, but so quiet also in themselves and merry, that for the same great exceeding · joy they are even drunken.

He speaketh here then of a spiritual strength, of a spi- *This must be spiritually understand.* ritual drunkenness, which is a godly strength, Rom. i.; "a joy," as St Paul calleth it, "in the Holy Ghost," Rom. xiv.; and a blessed drunkenness, when people are not full of wine, whereout followeth inconvenience, but full of the Holy Ghost. Ephes. v. This is the harness and the weapons, wherewith our Lord God prepareth his faithful against the devil and the world; namely, in their mouth giveth he them his word, and in their heart he giveth courage, that is to say, the Holy Ghost. With such ordnance put they from them all fear, and with gladness buckle they with all their enemies, smite them and overcome them with all their might, wisdom, and holiness.

Such soldiers were the apostles on Whit-Sunday, when they went up to Jerusalem against the commandment of the emperor and the high priests, and ordered themselves, as if they had been very gods, and all the other but grasshoppers, and went even through with all power and joy, as if they had been drunken; insomuch that some had them in derision therefore, and said, They were "full of sweet wine." Nevertheless St Peter declared out of the prophet Joel, that they were not full of sweet wine, but full of the Holy Ghost. And so he smote about him with his sword, that is, he opened his mouth, and preached the word of God, and felled down three thousand souls at once from the power of the devil. Acts ii.

This strength, joy, and blessed drunkenness doth not only shew itself in the faithful, when they be in prosperity, and have peace; but also when they suffer and die. As when the council at Jerusalem caused the apostles to be beaten, they were glad of it, that they were worthy to suffer rebuke for the name of Christ. Acts v. And in the fifth to the Romans doth St Paul say: "We rejoice also in troubles," &c. Afterward were there many martyrs also, which with merry hearts and laughing mouths went unto their death, as if they had gone to some pastime or dance. Like as we read of St Agnes and St Agatha, which were virgins of thirteen or fourteen years old[1], and of other more, which were of such inward courage and confidence, that they did not only overcome the devil and the world by their death, but also made good cheer even then with their hearts, as though they had been drunken of very joy. And this grieveth the devil exceeding sore, namely, when men are

The stedfast and joyful hearts of them that have suffered death for the word of God.

[1 Some account of these persons, together with the hymns composed to their memory, may be found in Daniel's Hymnologus Christianus, Vol. I. p. 945. Ed. 1841. See also Nichols on the Common Prayer.]

at such quietness in themselves, that they despise his great
might and guile. In our time also have there been many,
which for the knowledge of Christ have been glad to suffer
death. We see moreover, that there be many, which with
perfect understanding and faith die upon their beds, and say
with Simeon, "Lord, now lettest thou thy servant depart
in peace," &c., that is to a joy to behold them; of whom
I have seen many myself. And all this cometh because
that, as the prophet saith, they be anointed with the oil,
which the forty-fourth Psalm calleth the oil of gladness; [Psal. xlv.]
and because they have drunk of the full cup, which the
Lord hath filled.

    Yea, but thou wilt say, I feel not myself yet so apt, Objection.
that I could be content to die, &c. That maketh no matter.
David also, as it is said afore, hath not been sure of that Answer.
science at all hours, but sometime complained, that he was
cast out of God's sight. Other holy men also have not
alway had an hearty confidence toward God, and a perpetual delight and patience in their troubles and temptations. Note this
St Paul sometime is so sure and certain in himself, and well.
maketh such boast of Christ, that he careth not the curse
of the law, for sin, death, nor for the devil. "I live not
now," saith he, Gal. ii., "but Christ liveth in me." Item,
"I desire to be loosed and to be with Christ." Phil. i. Item,
"Who shall separate us from the love of God, which spared
not his own Son, but hath given him for us all? How shall
he not with him give us all things also? Shall trouble,
anguish, persecution, sword, &c., separate us from him?"
Rom. viii. There speaketh he of death, of the devil, and
of all evil with such a courage, as if he were the strongest
and greatest of all saints, unto whom death were but a sport.
But incontinently in another place he speaketh, as though he
were the weakest and greatest sinner upon earth. 1 Cor. ii.
"I was with you," saith he, "in weakness, in fear, and in
much trembling." "I am carnal, sold under sin, which is in
my members. O wretched man that I am! who shall deliver
me from the body of this death?" Rom. vii. And in the
fifth to the Galatians he teacheth, that in the saints of God
there is a continual strife of the flesh against the spirit, &c.
Therefore oughtest thou not immediately to despair, though

thou feelest thyself feeble and faint-hearted: and pray diligently, that thou mayest endure by the word, and increase
in the faith and knowledge of Christ; as the prophet doth
here, and teacheth other men likewise so to do, and saith:
" Oh let thy lovingkindness and mercy follow me all the
days of my life, that I may dwell in the house of the Lord
for ever."

Forasmuch as the devil never ceaseth to plague the
faithful inwardly with deceitfulness of false teachers, and
with the violence of tyrants, he prayeth here therefore at
the end earnestly, that God, which hath given him this
treasure, will keep him fast by it also unto the end, and
saith: " O gracious God, shew me such favour, that thy
lovingkindness and mercy may follow me all the days of
my life." And immediately he declareth, what he calleth
this lovingkindness and mercy, namely, that he may remain
in the house of the Lord for ever. As if he would say:
Thou hast begun the matter; thou hast given me thy holy
word, and accepted me among them that are thy people,
which do knowledge, praise, and give thanks unto thee: grant
me, therefore, such grace from henceforth, that I may continue still by the same word, and never to be separated
more from thy holy christian flock. Thus doth he pray
also in the twenty-sixth Psalm: " One thing," saith he,
" have I desired of the Lord, which I would fain have;
namely, that I may dwell in the house of the Lord all the
days of my life, to behold the fair beauty of the Lord,"
that is to say, the true service of God, " and to visit his
temple."

The prophet then here, by his ensample, teacheth and
exhorteth all such as put their trust in God, that they be
not careless, proud, or presumptuous in themselves; but to
fear and give themselves unto prayer, that they lose not
this treasure. And doubtless this earnest exhortation should
tear us up, and make us fervent unto diligent prayer. For
seeing that holy David, which was a prophet, so highly
endued with all manner of godly wisdom and knowledge,
and with divers great excellent gifts of God, seeing he, I
say, did pray so oft and with such great earnest, that he
might abide by this treasure; much more shall it be meet

Marginal notes:

Why the pro-
phet maketh
this prayer.

[Psal. xxvii.]

A notable
ensample.

for us, which are utterly nothing to be compared unto him, and live also now at the end of the world, when, as Christ and the apostles say, it shall be an horrible and perilous time; it shall be much more convenient, I say, to watch and pray with all earnest and diligence, that we may continue in the house of the Lord all the days of our life; namely, that we may hear the word of God, and receive the manifold commodities and fruits that come of it, as it is rehearsed afore, and continue in the same unto the end. Which grant us Christ, our only Shepherd and Saviour! Amen.

We have most need to watch and pray.

Imprinted in Southwark by James Nycolson, for John Gough.

Cum privilegio.

A confutacion of that

treatise which one John Stan=
dish made agaynst the protestacion of
D. Barnes in the yeare
M.D.XL.

Wherin the holy scriptures (perverted and
wrested in his sayd treatise) are restored to their
owne true vnderstanding agayne
by Myles Couer=
dale.

Iacobi iij.

Nolite gloriari, & mendaces esse adver-
sus ueritatem.

CONFUTATION

OF THE

TREATISE OF JOHN STANDISH.

[CONFUTATION OF STANDISH.

THE history of the life and martyrdom of Dr Robert Barnes, and of the Protestation which he made on that occasion, is given by Foxe, in his Acts and Monuments, Vol. II. p. 435, &c. ed. 1684. This Protestation was assailed by John Standish, a Fellow of Whittington College, London, in a violent book, of which an account is given by Coverdale in the address to the reader, which is prefixed to this work; and also by Strype, Ecclesiastical Memorials, Vol. I. p. 570, ed. Oxf. 1822[1]. It was in answer to this attack that Coverdale wrote this able Treatise in defence of the memory of his instructor and friend. This present edition is printed from a copy formerly belonging to his late royal highness the duke of Sussex, and now in the possession of the Parker Society.—The extracts from Barnes's Protestation, which are introduced into this work, either as the subject of attack on the part of Standish, or of defence on the part of Coverdale, are distinguished by a different type.]

[1] This scarce Tract is in the University Library, Cambridge.

TO THE READER.

TO ALL THEM THAT EITHER READ OR HEAR GOD'S HOLY
WORD, AND GIVE OVER THEMSELVES TO LIVE UN-
FEIGNEDLY ACCORDING TO THE SAME, DO
I HEARTILY WISH THE GRACE, PEACE,
AND MERCY OF GOD THE FATHER,
IN AND THROUGH OUR LORD
AND ONLY SAVIOUR,
JESUS CHRIST.

THE seventh day of December was delivered unto me
a certain treatise, composed by one John Standish, fellow of
Whittington College in London, (so is the title of it), and
printed by Robert Redeman, Anno M.D.XL., iii. nonas Octobris. At the reading whereof I mourned sore within myself
for certain occasions offered unto me in the said treatise:
first, that under the king's privilege any thing should be
set forth, which is either against the word and truth of
Almighty God, or against the king's honour: secondly,
that good, wholesome, and christian words should be calum-
niated and reviled: thirdly, that the said John Standish,
pronouncing doctor Barnes to have taught heresy so long, is
not ashamed all this while to have held his pen, but now
first to write against him, when he is dead, &c.

As touching the first, whether I have cause to mourn or
no, I report me to all true christian hearts: for, as I am
credibly informed, and as I partly have seen, there is now a
wonderful diversity in writing books and ballads in England, Diversity
one envying against another, one reviling and reproving among writers.
another, one rejoicing at another's fall and adversity. And
not only this, but at the end of every ballad or book in
manner, (whether it be the better party, or worse,) is set the
king's privilege. Which as it is against the glory of God,
that one should revile another; is it not even so against
the king's honour, yea, the shame is it of all England, that
under his privilege any erroneous, contentious, or slanderous
book or paper should be printed? Men wonder in other
countries, that there is so great negligence of this matter

21—2

in a realm where so wise and prudent a council is. And they that are moved with godly compassion do lament England; sorry, that there is so great dissension in it; sorry, that blasphemous jesting and railing ballads or books against the manifest word of God should either be suffered or privileged; sorry, that God's truth should thus spitefully be entreated of so great a number. Now the reformation of this and all other defaults lieth only in the hand of God, to whom I refer it, and to the rightful administration of his holy ordinance and authority in the king's highness; who, *Trifles are printed with the king's privilege unknown to him.* when he knoweth the said inconvenience, how trifling and railing books and rhymes are printed under his privilege, will no doubt set a redress herein.

Concerning the second occasion above rehearsed, Is it not cause enough for me and all other Christians to be right sorry, to mourn and lament, that the words which are good, wholesome, and according to the holy scripture and Christ's faith, should be either blasphemed or taken to the worst? If the king's grace should put forth a wholesome proclamation, injunction, or commandment (as he doth many), what true subject, loving God's holy ordinance and authority in his prince, would not be grieved to see any man either spit at those his sovereign's words, or to defy them? If we now, which are Christians, have so just occasion, and are bound to be thus-wise minded in this outward regimen, wherein God hath appointed us to be obedient to the higher powers; how much more cause have we to water our eyes with sorry hearts, when the proclamation, injunction, commandment, *Good words are blasphemed.* and word of him, which is King of all kings, and Lord of all lords, is thus reviled and evil spoken of! That the words of D. Barnes, spoken at the hour of his death, and here underwritten, are good, wholesome, according to God's holy scripture, and not worthy to be evil taken, it shall be evidently seen, when we have laid them to the touchstone, and tried them by God's word. To the open text whereof if ye take good heed, ye shall see the perverse doctrine and wicked opinions of Standish clearly confuted. And, no doubt, God will so have it; because that under the pretence of bearing a zeal toward God's word, he taketh upon him to be judge and giver of sentence against God's word, and to condemn it that God's word alloweth.

And this, as I said, is another cause of the sorriness of my heart, that he which dare avow another man to be an open heretic, is not ashamed thus long neither to have written nor openly preached against him by name, but now to start up, when he is dead. Is it not a great worship for him to wrestle with a shadow, and to kill a dead man? Is he not a worthy soldier, that all the battle-time thrusteth his hand in his bosom; and when men are dead, then draweth out his Standish will kill a dead man. sword, and fighteth with them that are slain already? Judge ye, gentle readers, if Standish playeth not such a part with D. Barnes; to whom also he imputeth treason, and yet proveth never a point thereof against him. Yet were it as charitable a deed to confute all treason, and to give us warning of it by name, as either to establish false doctrine, or to inveigh against good sayings: yea, a christian and charitable act were it, in reproving any traitor, to tell the king's subjects, in what thing he committed the treason, that they may beware of the same. But thus doth not Standish here in this his treatise; which, because it is builded on sand and on a false foundation, I doubt not, but with God's word, Ephes. vi. which is the sword of the Spirit, and a weapon mighty to overthrow every imagination that exalteth itself against the 2 Cor. x. knowledge of God, to give it a fall, and with holy scripture to shew evidently, that Standish hath far overshot himself in condemning the sayings, which God's word doth not disallow. He that would write against any man, should level his ordnance against his evil words, if he hath spoken or written any, and not against his good words: for God is the author of all good, which as his holy scripture alloweth, so will he himself defend the same. He that is therefore an enemy to the thing which is good, or resisteth it, is God's adversary, and withstandeth him. Wherefore let Standish from henceforth, and all others, beware, that they take no Let no man take part against the truth. part against God's word, nor defend any false matter, lest God be the avenger: for if the lion begin to roar, he will make all his enemies afraid.

And if D. Barnes died a true christian man, be ye sure, his death shall be a greater stroke to hypocrisy, than ever his life could have been. If he was falsely accused to the king's highness, and so put to death, woe shall come to those accusers, if they repent not by times. And if D. Barnes in his heart, mouth, and deed, committed no worse thing toward the king's highness, than he committed against God in these his words at his death, he is like at the latter day to be a judge over them that were cause of his death, if they do not amend.

Now, indifferent reader, to the intent that thou mayest the more clearly discern light from darkness, and know God's true word from false doctrine, I shall, when I have said somewhat to Standish's preface, rehearse unto thee D. Barnes' words. Secondly, though I rehearse not unto thee all Standish's words, lest I should make too great a book, I shall point thee to the beginning of his sentence, requiring thee, if thou wilt, to read out the rest thyself in his treatise. Thirdly, though he hath deserved to be roughly handled, yet do I purpose, by God's only grace, to deal more gently with him being alive, than he doth with the dead. This enterprise now as I take in hand against Standish in this behalf; so am I ready to do the same against the great grandsire and captain of false teachers, I mean great Goliath of Rome and his weapon-bearer; that is, against all such as are enemies to king David, our Lord Jesus Christ:
for whose most comfortable Spirit, gentle reader,
I beseech thee to pray with me unto our
most dear Father in heaven, whose
name be praised, whose kingdom come, whose only
will be fulfilled, now
and ever.
Amen.

HERE FOLLOWETH THE PREFACE OF JOHN STANDISH TO THE READER.

STANDISH.

To see the most victorious and noble prince our sovereign lord the king labouring and watching continually with all diligent study to expel and drive out, I may say, to purge and cleanse this his catholic region, &c.

COVERDALE.

Though ye abuse your terms, in reporting that the king goeth about to expel and drive out his catholic region, I will impute those your words to the weakness of your brain, and to the scarceness of honest eloquence therein. But if the king's labour, watching, and diligent study in purging and cleansing his realm from all heresies and schisms be occasion sufficient, as it is in deed, to compel every true subject to help unto the same, why have ye then been so slack therein all this while? Your own words bring you into a shrewd suspicion: for ye know and have seen with your eyes, Suspicion. that the king hath these many years been labouring and busy in abolishing out of his realm the usurped power of the bishop of Rome, his manifold sects of false religions, his worshipping of images, his deceitful pardons, his idolatry and pilgrimages, &c. Were not all these great heresies and schisms? Or can ye excuse yourself of ignorance, that ye have not seen, how the king hath laboured in putting down the same? If ye then be a writer against heresies and schisms, why have ye written against none of these all this while? Thus every man which readeth your words may see, that ye have bewrayed yourself to be a favourer of such things.

STANDISH.

Wherefore marvel not, gentle reader, &c.

COVERDALE.

Contrary now to your request, will every man marvel at you, not only because ye declare yourself to have borne all this while no right love toward God's word, to the salvation of men's souls, nor to the duty that ye owe to your prince;

but also because that now, through the occasion of a poor man's death, ye first start up to write, as though the king had put down no heresies afore D. Barnes died. Is this the zeal, that ye bear toward God's word and toward his people? Such a zeal had they, of whom the apostle speaketh to the Galatians, saying: "They have no good zeal unto you; but would thrust you out, namely from the truth, that ye might be fervent to themward." Whereas ye write the day and year of D. Barnes' death, it increaseth your own confusion, and shall be a clear testimony against yourself, for resisting those good words of his protestation, if ye forsake not your heresy in time. Yea, even by your own pen have ye brought it to pass, that it shall not be forgotten till the world's end, what a christian testament and last will D. Barnes made at his death, and how patiently he forsook this life.

Gal. iv.

STANDISH.

For in his protestation is both contained heresy and treason.

COVERDALE.

"For," say ye, "in his protestation, &c." Is that the cause why ye do enterprise and take in hand to write against it? Then verily declare ye yourself not only to be partial, but also a favourer of heresy and treason, knowing so many to have been attainted thereof within these seven years.

STANDISH.

Albeit, do not think, that I write this through any malice toward him that is burned, &c.

COVERDALE.

He that compareth your words to your deed shall soon perceive, that ye have cast milk in your own face, and that, for all your holy pretence, some spice of Cainish stomach hath made you now do more than all the king's noble acts in abolishing the said abuses could make you do many years before; though the same, if you were a true subject, were, by your own confession, sufficient cause for you so to do. Howbeit it is not I that go about to lay malice to your charge; your own act is not your best friend: I pray God your conscience accuse you not thereof.

But why take ye God to record in a false matter? Do ye not confess yourself, that the king's grace's labour, watching, and diligent study, is the thing that causeth and compelleth you to write against D. Barnes' protestation, and that through the love and fervent zeal ye bear toward God's word and the salvation of men's souls, &c.? And now take ye God to record, that ye do it for fear, lest the people should be infect with the multitude of copies of the said protestation. Against the which fear I know none other comfort for you, (as long as ye will not hearken to God's word), but that Wisdom itself giveth you in Salomon's Proverbs, namely, that "the thing that ye fear shall come upon you, and even it that ye are afraid of shall fall in suddenly among you." This am I certified of, not only by the same place of scripture, but even by this your present act in putting forth your treatise to be printed with and against the said protestation. For if ye fear the great infection of the people through the multitude of copies thereof, why caused ye it to be printed, or any man else for you? Is the printing of the said protestation the next way to keep copies thereof from the people? Ye may well have wit, but sure ye lack policy. Such a like wise way was taken in England within these few years by certain abbots, which, thinking thereby to uphold their false religions, wrought, moved, or else consented to insurrection within divers parts of the realm [1]; and yet was the same their wisdom a cause that hasted their own destruction. And even so now, by your printing of the said protestation, ye have brought it so to pass, that the thing which ye feared is come to light. Thus can God pull down his enemies' houses with their own hands. Certainly, like as I never heard, that there was any copy thereof, till I saw it in your book, so am I credibly informed, that it was never in print afore.

Whereas ye say, that it is an erroneous and traitorous protestation, it is sooner said than proved; neither maketh it greatly for your honesty, to know many secret embracers of heresy and treason, and not to utter them. But ye may twice say it, afore ye be once believed: only they that are

Standish is afraid.

Prov. i.

The enemies of God's word fight against themselves.

[1 This probably alludes to the rebellions, which took place in Lincolnshire and Yorkshire in the year 1536; for an account of which see Burnet, History of the Reformation, Book III.]

of God will, when they have tried and examined all things, keep that which is good, and eschew the contrary.

STANDISH.

But I trust in Almighty God, if it please you to read this little treatise with a loving zeal toward our mother the holy church, &c.

COVERDALE.

Here do ye manifestly declare, what zeal moved you to write against D. Barnes' protestation, namely, not any just zeal or love toward God's word, or his people, but even because ye fear lest your mother should come to shame, if the truth were known : therefore to shew your mother a pleasure, ye thought to do your best in defending her. Neither helpeth it your pretence any thing at all, though ye call her holy : for every such sect as ye be of hath a sundry holiness, which cometh not of the Spirit that sanctifieth. Now like as your own act came of that zeal which ye bear toward the church of the wicked, so would ye have your treatise read with the same zeal; to the intent that the readers might smell heresy and treason, where none is, and be poisoned with such a corrupt judgment, as ye be of yourself.

Again, how are ye, or all men living, able to prove, that this protestation of D. Barnes doth smell and savour nothing but heresy and treason ? Is it heresy and treason to teach no erroneous doctrine, to teach only those things that scripture leadeth unto, to maintain no error, to move no insurrection, to be falsely slandered, to confute the false opinion of the Anabaptists, to detest and abhor all such sects, to set forth the glory of God, obedience to the higher powers, and the true religion of Christ ? Doth it smell and savour nothing but heresy and treason, to believe in the holy and blessed Trinity, to believe the incarnation, passion, death, and resurrection of our Lord and Saviour Jesus Christ ? Is it heresy and treason, for a sinner to desire God to forgive him, to trust only in the death of Christ, to set forth good works, to believe that there is a holy church, to believe a life after this, to speak reverently of saints, to call our lady a virgin immaculate and undefiled, to acknowledge a christian belief concerning the body and blood of our Lord, to ascribe unto saints the honour that scripture willeth them to have,

Marginal notes:

All is not gold that shineth.

Standish smelleth here nothing but heresy and treason.

to pray for the king and his council, &c.? Do such things smell and savour nothing but heresy and treason? "Woe Isai. v. unto them that call good evil, and evil good, darkness light, and light darkness, sweet sour, and sour sweet!"

Though ye do also esteem them to be heretics and traitors, that take part with D. Barnes' protestation, yet doth not your estimation or judgment discourage me in this behalf. Neither is it my mind or will to meddle with his offence (if he committed any against the king), neither to defend this his protestation with any hand or weapon of man; but by the scriptures to bear record unto the truth, and to reprove your perverse and strange doctrine, which ye do teach against the same.

STANDISH.

For surely such as do improve them, &c.

COVERDALE.

This your saying proveth not the contrary but that, seeing ye resist the truth, I may tell you your fault, and inform you better, according to the apostle's doctrine; if 2 Tim. ii. God at any time will grant you repentance for to know the truth, and to turn from the snare of the devil, &c. If I can understand, that through this information ye will give place to the open and manifest truth, God shall have the praise, and I shall think my labour well bestowed. If the truth can have no place in you by fair means, but ye will still resist it obstinately, and belie it, as ye do here in this your treatise; then verily ye may be sure to be afterward so handled, as the limits and bounds of God's holy scripture will suffer. I beseech God, according to his good pleasure, that ye may have eyes to see, ears to hear, and an heart to understand his holy word, to consent unto the same, and in all points to live thereafter. Amen.

HERE FOLLOWETH THE PROTESTATION OF D. ROBERT BARNES.

BARNES.

I am come hither to be burned as an heretic, and you shall hear my belief; whereby ye shall perceive what erroneous opinions I hold.

STANDISH.

I am sorry to see the obstinate blindness and final induration in this his protestation, which would clear, justify, and excuse himself by colour and deceit.

COVERDALE.

Christ our Saviour, making mention of his own death, before he was hanged upon the cross, said these words: "Behold, we go up to Jerusalem; and the Son of man shall be betrayed, condemned, mocked, scourged, crucified," &c. When a true man cometh to be hanged on the gallows, is it obstinate blindness and final induration for him so to say? Peradventure ye will say unto me, Take ye D. Barnes then for a true man? I answer, Verily: these his words prove him no false man; for he said that he came to be burned: and sure I am, that he came not to the fire to be made a bishop.

Moreover, D. Barnes told the people that they should hear his belief, &c. And ye lay to his charge for his so doing, that he would clear, justify, and excuse himself with colour and deceit. As though he justified himself with colour and deceit, which, according to St Peter's doctrine, is ready alway to give answer unto every man that asketh him a reason of the hope which is in him. Was not D. Barnes instantly required to shew his faith, and to open his mind in sundry things? Again, though he or any man else would clear himself from such things as are wrongfully laid to his charge, did he evil therein? If it be so, then did holy St Paul leave us a shrewd example in the Acts.

Matt. xx.

1 Pet. iii.

Acts xxiii. xxiv. xxv.

STANDISH.

Which ought to have accused, condemned, and utterly forsaken all that he had offended in. Si nos ipsos judicaremus, non utique dijudicaremur a Domino.

1 Cor. ii.

COVERDALE.

I answer: By your own words then it followeth not, that he was bound to accuse and condemn himself of the things that he had not offended in. But by your leave, whereas ye bring in this text of St Paul, *Si nos ipsos &c.*, ye pervert it;

not alleging it as it standeth, but thus, *Si nos ipsos judi-* Standish per-
verteth the
text.
caremus, non utique dijudicaremur a Domino; that is to
say, "If we judged ourselves, we should not be judged of the
Lord." But St Paul's words are these, *Quod si nos ipsos
dijudicaremus, non utique judicaremur. Dum judicamur
autem, a Domino corripimur, ne cum hoc mundo damnemur.*
That is to say, "If we would judge, or reprove ourselves, we
should not be judged. But when we are judged, we are
chastened of the Lord, lest we should be damned with this
world." Wherefore the perverting of this text now at the first
brunt causeth me the more to suspect you, and to trust you
the worse; because the devil himself is schoolmaster to such Matt. iv.
Luke iv. out
of the xcth
(xci.) Psalm.
chopping up of the text, as we may see in the gospel of
Matthew and Luke. Now go to: if I find any more such
juggling casts with you, ye are like to hear of it, before I
come to the end of your book. For weakness and ignorance
can I well away withal, so long as it is not wilful; but the
perverting or chopping up of a text of holy scripture is not
to be borne unrebuked.

STANDISH.

Mark here, how he useth ironia, *&c.*

COVERDALE.

Ye confess that D. Barnes in his foresaid words doth use
ironia; and yet, contrary to the signification of the word, ye
are not ashamed to affirm, that he confessed herewithal both
heresy and erroneous opinions. Now is *ironia* as much to say εἰρωνεία.
as a mockage, derision, or meaning of another thing, than is
expressed in the words. Which manner of speaking is much
used, not only throughout the prophets in holy scripture, but
also among the heathen poets. And the same phrase of speech
have we in English; as when a man sayeth to a shrewd boy:
"Come hither, good sir, ye are a virtuous child indeed, &c."
meaning nothing less. Forasmuch then as ye yourself confess, that D. Barnes doth here use *ironia;* it is evident, that
when he said these words, "you shall perceive what erroneous
opinions I hold," his meaning was, how that the people should
know, that he held no erroneous opinions, as it appeareth by
these his words following.

BARNES.

God I take to record, I never to my knowledge taught any erroneous doctrine; but only those things which scripture led me unto.

STANDISH.

Justly ponder by the prophet, Psal. cxl. (cxli.) how grievous offence is Pertinax excusatio in peccatis, &c.

COVERDALE.

Like as ye cannot justly lay any pertinacity to D. Barnes for those his words, so prove ye the grievousness thereof full slenderly out of Psalm cxl, if the true reading of the text be well and justly pondered. Whereas he taketh God to record in the truth of so weighty a matter, the scripture is full of holy ensamples, that bear him therein. What pertinacity is there then in that act?

He durst avow also, that, to his knowledge, he never taught any erroneous doctrine: and yet are ye not ashamed to ascribe pertinacity unto him, and to call him an obstinate heretic; whereas St Jerome in his fourth book, the xxivth chapter upon Matthew, writeth thus: "He is a heretic, that under Christ's name teacheth the things which are against Christ[1]." If D. Barnes, therefore, had wittingly and willingly taught any thing against Christ, ye might have laid great pertinacity to his charge. Truth it is, that he being in ignorance, and deceived sometime by a multitude, as you be, did both err and teach erroneous doctrine for the preferment of the bishop of Rome's usurped authority, and other abuses; according as many learned men more in the realm have done, which have since both repented toward God, and also received the king's gracious pardon many years ago. Again, if ye will lay pertinacity to his charge, because he was sometime in such gross ignorance; by the same argument might ye condemn Christ's disciples, of whose ignorance mention is made in many places of the new Testament. I say not this to excuse ignorance; but to reprehend

[Margin notes:]
Gen. xliv.
Rom. i.
2 Cor. i.
2 Cor. xi.
Gal. i.
Judg. xi.

Who is an heretic.

Mark vi. ix.
Luke ii. ix.
xviii.
John xvi.

[1 Ego reor omnes hæresiarchas Antichristos esse, et sub nomine Christi ea docere, quæ contraria sunt Christo. Hieron. Comment. in Matth. Lib. iv. c. 24; v. 5. Op. Tom. vii. p. 193. ed. Veron. 1737.]

the rashness of your judgment, which presume to condemn them whom God hath called to repentance.

But peradventure the pertinacity that ye lay to his charge is, because he saith he taught only those things which scripture led him unto. For that is no small corsie[2] to your sore. Ye would not have scripture taught only, without other doctrines: nevertheless, they that love God's commandment, will teach nothing but his word only; for so hath he himself given commission. Of his promises is mention made both in Jeremiah, and in the Gospel of Matthew. As for ensamples, we have sufficient both of the prophets and apostles, which, to die for it, would teach nothing but scripture. Read the thirteenth chapter of the second epistle to the Corinthians, the fifteenth to the Romans, and the most godly protestation that St Peter maketh in his second epistle. "Let us give place and consent to the holy scripture," saith St Augustine; "for it can neither deceive, nor be deceived[3]." The bishops also and clergy of England, in the epistle of their book to the king's grace, do affirm, that "Holy scripture alone sheweth men the right path to come to God, to see him, to know him, to love him, to serve him, and so to serve him as he most desireth[4]." Wherefore they are rather obstinate against God, which, instead of his only word, preach and teach other doctrines. But let us hear what D. Barnes saith more.

Deut. xii.
Matt. xxviii.
Gal. i.
2 John i.
Jer. xvi.
Matt. v.

2 Cor. xiii.

Rom. xv.
2 Pet. i.

De peccatorum meritis et remissione, cap. xxiii.
The bishops of England.

BARNES.

And that in my sermons I never maintained any error, neither moved nor gave occasion of any insurrection.

STANDISH.

What blindness would he lead us into? Who hath not heard him preach against all the ordinance of Christ's church? &c.

[2 Corsie : corrosive.]

[3 Cedamus et consentiamus auctoritati sanctæ scripturæ, quæ nescit falli, nec fallere. August. de peccatorum meritis et remissione. Lib. I. cap. 22. Op. Tom. VII. p. 144. B. ed. 1541.]

[4 Preface of the prelates to the king's majesty, prefixed to *The institution of a christian man;* among the Formularies of Faith, put forth by authority, in the reign of Henry VIII. p. 24. Oxford, 1825.]

COVERDALE.

As for blindness, ye need no leader to bring you into it: our Lord, when his will is, bring you out of it! This man took God to record, that he never maintained any error: whereby, like as he denied not but that he might err (as he did err grossly when he lived in the papistry), even so left he us an ensample to forsake all errors, and to maintain none. Call ye this a leading into blindness? Then farewell all good ensamples of humility and repentance.

A good en-
sample in
D. Barnes.

To the other part of your cavillation I answer. It would be too long a register for you to rehearse the names of all those, which never heard D. Barnes preach against the ordinance of Christ's church. I also am one of them, which have heard him as oft as ever did ye; and yet, as I hope to have my part of God's mercy in Christ's blood, I never heard him preach against any such, since he was converted first from the wicked papistry. Against some of the ordinances or ceremonies used in your church have I heard him preach oft and many times. As for you, ye are none of Christ's church, by your own saying. For hereafter in your treatise ye confess yourself, that the congregation of Christ's church in this region of England is the king's majesty with his learned council. And truly like as I am sure that ye are not king of England, so do I perceive by your writing, that ye are none of the king's learned council; and so, by your own confession, none of Christ's church. The ordinance of Christ's church is, that every one, from the prince to the lowest subject, shall be diligent to wait upon his office, and to do the thing that God hath called him unto. To the ordinance of Christ's church pertaineth all that is written concerning the duty of every estate, and also concerning such order, as is meet to be kept in the church, according to the doctrine of the apostle, 1 Cor. xiv; 1 Cor. xi. Did you ever now hear D. Barnes preach against any such holy ordinance of God, or of his church? No, verily, I suppose; for then doubtless, we should have heard of it in this your thundering treatise.

Standish
writeth him-
self to be
none of
Christ's
church.

Whereas D. Barnes now hath been earnest against your wicked church of the papistry, and preached against the horrible abuses thereof, call ye that erroneous railing and traitorous speaking? By that reason were the prophets erroneous railers, which rebuked the abuses of the Jews' church so earnestly. Yea, and against the superstitious observing of fasting days did the prophets preach, as did also the apostle St Paul. All these, and many other more of God's servants did speak against superstitious observing of vain fasts, and against the abusing of that fast, which God had commanded. But against true fasting, whereof mention is made in many places of holy scripture, have not ye yet proved that D. Barnes did ever preach in his sermons, neither against such days as by lawful authority are appointed without superstition for general fastings.

Isai. i. lviii. lxvi. Zech. vii. Amos v. viii. Mal. ii. Gal. iv. Coloss. ii. Matt. vi. 1 Cor. vii.

If ye will blame him for preaching against the abuse of prayer, why do ye not also blame the prophet Esay, our Saviour Christ himself, the apostle St James, St Ambrose, Gregory, Bernard, Chrysostom, Jerome, Cyril, Fulgentius, Origen, &c.? Can ye say now, that ye have justly blamed D. Barnes in this behalf? But, thanks be unto God! against the right use of prayer, whereof mention is made by our Saviour and his apostles throughout the new Testament, have ye not yet proved, that D. Barnes at any time did preach, since he forsook the papistry; neither against such lawful days, as by just authority are appointed for general prayers and thanksgivings to God, and for the accomplishing of other spiritual exercises grounded upon God's word.

Isai. i. Matt. vi. xxiii. James i. iv.

Nevertheless I marvel the less, that ye blame him unworthy in this point: for ye are not ashamed also to belie him, and to report of him, that he denied godly ordinance to bind unto deadly sin, contrary to St Paul, Romans xiii.; which chapter, with the contents thereof, he defended in his sermons and writings very earnestly, and diligently set forth due obedience to the higher powers, to the great hinderance of hypocrites and their wicked church, whose ordinance he denied utterly to bind unto deadly sin, because it is not grounded on God's word. But godly ordinance, that is to say, the ordinance and institution of God, did not he deny, but that the breakers and offenders thereof do commit deadly sin. As for man's ordinance, not institute of God, nor justly grounded upon his word, what christian man, having wit to discern between chalk and cheese, will say or grant, except it be such wavering reeds as fear man more than

Godly ordinance.

God, that it bindeth unto deadly sin; seeing it is sinful,
wicked, and abominable itself, invented by Satan, and repug-

Isai. xxix.
Matt. xv.
xxiii.
Mark vii.
Col. ii.
Gal. iv.
1 Tim. iv.

nant unto God's word? Is not such stuff most vehemently
rebuked by God's own mouth, and also by his holy apostle?
Are ye not ashamed then to affirm, that man of his authority
may restrain the things which are free by the gospel? May
a man bind that God looseth, condemn that God saveth, or
hold him in prison whom God delivereth? Is man stronger
than God, or man's authority above the authority of God?
or be they both alike?

Whereas ye say, that it is the church which hath this
authority to restrain the things that are free by the gospel;
I answer, the church of Christ is his spouse, and the fold
of those sheep that hearken to his voice; unto his voice, I
say, and not unto the voice of strangers. He himself also,
sending out his apostles, biddeth them teach all that he hath
commanded them, and not to bind that he hath made free,
neither to make free that he hath bound. Again, the nature
and condition of an honest wife is to hearken to the wholesome words of her husband, to prefer his commandment, and
to see that his household folk keep it. A strumpet indeed,
and an harlot, careth not to control her husband, to disobey
him, and to maintain evil rule in his house against his mind.
That church therefore, which taketh upon her any such
authority, as is not given her by Christ, is not his lawful
spouse, neither can ye prove, that he hath given your church
any power to restrain the things which he hath made free;
except ye do it with the words of St James, that saith,

James iv.

"There is one lawgiver, which is able to destroy and to
save;" or else with the words of St Paul, that asketh the

Col. ii.

Colossians this question, "If ye be dead with Christ from the
ordinances of the world, why are ye holden then with such
traditions, as though ye lived after the world?" &c.

STANDISH.

*Who hath not heard him preach a carnal liberty, with
a damnable justification of only faith to justify, &c?*

COVERDALE.

Truly, it would make your head ache, to read all the
names ~of them, that never heard D. Barnes preach any such

unlawful liberty as you speak of. But first, I pray you, what carnal or fleshly liberty doth he preach, that exhorteth men "with well doing to put to silence the ignorance of foolish men; 1 Pet. ii. as free, and not as having the liberty for a cloke of wickedness?" How oft hath he taught this doctrine, as they that have heard him can tell, if they be not either malicious, or else forgetful! Who can justly deny, but he oft and many times, upon due occasion, in his writings and sermons did exhort his hearers, that they would not live after the flesh, nor Rom. viii. xiii. accomplish the lusts thereof; but to cast away the works of darkness, to put on the armour of light, to walk honestly in the light that God hath given them; to follow such things as pertain to peace, and things whereby one may edify another; Rom. xiv. to walk every man in his calling; to give no occasion of fall- 1 Cor. vii. x. ing unto any man; to mortify their earthly members, &c. 2 Cor. vi. Col. iii. according to the wholesome doctrine of the apostle? Call ye this a preaching of a fleshly and carnal liberty? Is this a doctrine that maketh men run at riot, and to do what they list? I wonder, verily, that ye shame not thus to belie the truth so oft.

As pertaining to your blasphemy, which say that it is a damnable justification, where faith is preached only to jus- Justification. tify, it is damnably spoken of you; yea, though an angel of heaven should speak it, if holy St Paul be true, which saith, Gal. i. he ought to be holden accursed, that preacheth any other gospel, than that he himself and the other apostles had preached. If ye of a cankered hatred to the truth have not wilfully and maliciously taken part against the Holy Ghost, so that ye are but led ignorantly by a blind multitude to affirm the said inconvenience; I pray God send you a clearer light in the kingdom of Christ. But if ye be minded, as were Matt. xii. the Pharisees, and maliciously ascribe damnation to it, where- Mark iii. Luke xi. by only we receive salvation, as they ascribed unto the devil it, that was the only working of the Holy Ghost; then am I sore afraid for you, and for as many as are of that mind. For if it be damnable to teach or preach wittingly against the express word of God, then verily is this a damnable heresy to affirm, that faith only doth not justify; seeing that holy scripture so teacheth: as Gen. xv. Esai. liii. Abac. The scriptures. ii. Mark xvi. Luke i. viii. xxiv. John v. xvii. Acts xiii. xvi. Rom. iii. iv. v. x. Gal. ii. iii. iv. v. Philip. iii. 1 Pet. i. ii.

Heb. iv. xi. Of this faith, that scripture speaketh of so plentifully, I have made sufficient mention in the prologue of that little book, which I lately put forth in English concerning the true *Old Faith of Christ*[1]. Now like as the scriptures before alleged do testify for us, that we mean no false nor vain faith; even so is the same article of justification defended and maintained by the doctors in many and sundry places, specially by St Augustine in the ccclii. chapter *De vera innocentia*[2]. *De verbis Domini, Sermone* xl.[3] *De verbis Apostoli, Ser.* xxvii.[4] *In the book of the fifty Sermons, the 17th Sermon*[5]. *In the first book of the Retracts, the 23rd chapter*[6]. *In the 105th epistle unto Sixtus the bishop*[7]. *In the 25th treatise upon John, the sixth chapter*[8]. *In his Manual, the 22nd and 23rd chapter*[9]. *In the exposition of the 67th and of the 70th Psalm*[10]. *In the 53rd Sermon, De tempore*[11]. *In the 5th Book of his Homilies, the 17th Homily*[12]. *In the book of the 83 questions, the 66th chapter*[13]; *and in the Prologue of the 31st Psalm*[14]. I might allege Cyril, Ambrose, Origen, Hilary, Bernard, Athanasius, with other more: but what helpeth it? Yet shall all the world know, that your heresy is not only condemned by the open and manifest scripture, but also by many of the

Natural reason. doctors. As for natural reason, it fighteth clearly against you also, if ye ponder well the parable of the marriage in the twenty-second of Matthew, and in the fourteenth of Luke, the parable of the unthrifty son in the fifteenth of Luke, the parable also of the debtor in the eighteenth of Matthew, and in the seventh of Luke.

[1] *Old Faith*, pp. 4-11, Coverdale's works. Parker Society Ed. 1844.]

[2] August. Op. Tom. iii. p. 240, M. ed. 1541.]

[3] Ib. Tom. x. p. 34, F. But it would appear that the reference ought to be to Serm. lx. Ib. p. 50, B.]

[4] The reference, as appears, ought to be to Serm. xv. Ib. pp. 72, 73.]

[5] Homiliarum quinqaginta Liber. Homil. xvii. Ib. p. 99. B.]

[6] Ib. Tom. i. p. 8, B.]   [7] Ib. Tom. ii. p. 95. I.]

[8] Ib. Tom. ix. p. 46, L.]

[9] Ib. Tom. ix. p. 174, E. F. But this is admitted not to be a genuine work of Augustine. See Cave, Hist. Lit. Vol. i. p. 248. ed. 1688.]

[10] Ib. Tom. viii. p. 152, B ; and p. 164, E.]

[11] Ib. Tom. x. p. 153, L.]   [12] Compare above, note 5.]

[13] Ib. Tom. iv. 133, C.]   [14] Ib. Tom. viii. p. 40, K.]

Whereas it was laid to D. Barnes' charge, how that he should teach that God is the author of sin, verily he pro- God is not the author of tested openly at St Mary's spital the Tuesday in Easter week, sin. that he was never of that mind : howbeit he confessed, as the truth is, that whereas in his book he had written of pre-destination and free-will, there was occasion taken of him by his writing, that he should so mean. But verily, if he had in that matter been as circumspect, as the children of this world are wise in their generation, he might the better have avoided the captiousness of men aforehand. Nevertheless it appeareth plainly, that he mistrusted no such thing; and therefore did too much simplicity deceive him in that behalf, as it doth many more, which are not so wise as serpents. Neither find ye in all his book these words, GOD IS THE AUTHOR OF SIN; but you may find these words : " The Governor of D. Barnes' all things is most wise, most righteous, and most merciful ; words. and so wise, that nothing that he doth can be amended ; so righteous, that there can be no suspicion in him of unright-eousness, &c.[15]" Item : " All thing that he doth is well done." Wherefore, if they that laid that heresy to D. Barnes' charge, had remembered their own distinction of *malum pœnœ*, and *malum culpœ*, at the reading of his words, as well as they can note it in other places; they might easily have perceived his meaning, and not have mistaken him.

Ye say also, D. Barnes did preach, that " Works do not Works. profit." If ye mean works invented by men's own brains, not grounded on God's word, then verily might he well say, that such works do not profit to salvation : for whatsoever Rom. xiv. is not of faith is sin. But if ye mean such good works as are comprehended in the commandments of God, and within Hos. xii. the precinct of his word, then truly ye fail so to report of him ; for though salvation be God's work only, yet D. Barnes in his book doth not only condemn the fleshly and damnable reason of them, which say, " If faith only justifieth, what need we do any good works, &c.?" but also he af-firmeth plainly, that we must needs do them, and that they which will not do them, because they be justified alone by faith, are not the children of God, nor children of justification, &c. For if they were the very true children of God, they would be the gladder to do good works, &c. " Therefore,"

[15 " Treatise on Free-will." Barnes' Works.]

D. Barnes'
words. saith he, "should they also be moved freely to work, if it were for none other purpose nor profit, but only to do the will of their merciful God, that hath so freely justified them, and also to profit their neighbour, whom they are bound to serve of very true charity [1]." Are these words now as much to say, as "Works do not profit?" Lord God! what mean ye, thus untruly to report of the dead?

A fond ob-
jection
against the
justification
of faith. Whereas ye make this blind objection, and say, "If works profit not, so that faith only justifieth, and Christ's death be sufficient, then penance is void and superfluous;" I answer, A goodly consequent, gathered neither of witty sophistry, wise logic, nor of good philosophy, (except it be of philosophy unnatural), no, nor of right divinity. "Works profit not to salvation: ergo, they profit nothing at all:" is this a pretty consequent? Your consequent is naught, saith St Peter; [2 Pet. i.] for "by good works must ye make your vocation certain and sure." A like argument might ye make after this manner, and say: "Iron is not profitable to chew or to eat; therefore it is nothing worth." Were not this a wise consequent? The smith will tell you a better tale.

Peradventure ye will excuse yourself, and say: "This consequent is not mine, but Barnes's words." I answer: "Yes, verily, they be your own words;" for ye say plainly afterward, in your treatise: "If Christ had delivered us from all pain satisfactory, &c. we should neither mourn nor be penitent for our offence committed against God, neither need we to mortify our flesh." This your fleshly and damnable reason, this your heresy, this foul stinking opinion, this pestilent error and spiritual poison, did Barnes utterly abhor, and condemn it by St Paul's own words in the forty-ninth leaf of his book. So that the more I look upon your words, the more I wonder at your shameless slandering of the truth. But as touching this, I shall have more occasion to talk with you afterward.

Now to put you to your probation. How are ye able justly to prove, that penance is void and superfluous, where faith is preached only to justify? The true faith of Christ is Gal. v. it that we speak of. Is it not occupied then, and worketh through godly love and charity? They then that duly receive this faith, do not receive it to live worse or as evil

[1 " Treatise on Justification." Barnes' Works.]

afterward, as they did afore God gave it them. For though Ephes. ii.
"we be saved by grace through faith, and that not of ourselves,
though it be the gift of God, I say, not of works;" yet are
we "his workmanship, created in Christ Jesu unto good
works, to the which God ordained us before, that we should
walk in them." Neither hath our Saviour given us any
liberty to receive it in vain; but teacheth us to "forsake all 2 Cor. vi.
ungodliness and worldly lusts, and to live discreetly, justly, Tit. ii.
and godly in this world." Therefore whoso despiseth to live
virtuously, and to do good works, despiseth not man, but 1 Thess. iv.
God. The same faith that only justifieth, setteth forth this
doctrine; therefore doth it not destroy good works and penance. Take you heed then, and beware what ye say
another time. I might point you also to St Ambrose, who, Lib. i. cap. 8.
treating of the calling of the heathen, and declaring the true
original of our salvation, allegeth the place afore rehearsed
of the second to the Ephesians, and sheweth, that faith goeth
as it were with child, being replenished with all good thoughts
and deeds, and in due season bringeth them forth[2]. And
St Augustine saith these words: "If faith be the foundation De vera et
of penance, without the which there is nothing that can be cap. 2.
good, then is penance earnestly to be required, which, as it
is evident, is grounded in faith. For a good tree cannot
bring forth evil fruits. Matth. xii. Penance therefore, which
proceedeth not of faith, is not profitable[3]," &c. These are

[2 The passage to which allusion is here made, is probably the
following, in the treatise *De vocatione gentium*, Lib. i. cap. 8; towards
the latter end of which the author, having quoted Ephes. ii. 10, thus
proceeds: Proprium ergo hoc habet nova creatura per gratiam, ut
qui figmentum Dei sunt, qui nativitate cœlesti conduntur in Christo,
non otio torpeant, nec desidia resolvantur, sed de virtute in virtutem
proficiant, per viam bonorum operum ambulando.—Ambros. Opera,
Tom. iv. p. 528. Paris. 1603. But the Benedictine editor says, that
all critics are agreed that the books *De vocatione Gentium* are not by
St Ambrose; and the same is the opinion of Cave. Hist. Lit. Vol. i.
p. 215.]

[3 Si fides fundamentum est pœnitentiæ, præter quam nihil est quod
bonum sit, appetenda est pœnitentia, quam constat in fide esse fun-
datam. Non enim potest arbor bona malos fructus facere. Pœnitentia itaque, quæ ex fide non procedit, utilis non est.—De vera et
falsa pœnit Angust. Opera, Tom. iv. p. 248, G. Ed. 1541. This
work however is believed to be improperly ascribed to Augustine. See
Cave, Hist. Lit. Vol. i. p. 249.]

St Augustine's words. Faith then destroyeth neither penance, nor good works; but is the womb that beareth them both, and of whom they both proceed.

Touching the article of forgiveness, where ye say, that it is contrary to the order of our Saviour's prayer, that we must be forgiven of God afore we can forgive; are ye not ashamed thus to proceed forth in blasphemies against the manifest word of God, yea, and clearly against your own words? Do ye not confess yourself, that first God of his mercy only giveth us grace, without which we can do nothing that is good? Is it not a good thing, one man to forgive another? Do ye not grant also, that God first loved us, yea, even when he was not loved of us? Why then shame ye not to write, that it is against the order of our Lord's prayer, to be forgiven of God afore we can forgive? Is the love of our Saviour against the order of his prayer? Or did he not forgive us, when he loved us first? Can he love, and not forgive? Think ye God to be of the nature of those, which forgive and love not, or that shew tokens and countenance of love in outward appearance, and forgive not in their hearts?

A shame is it for you, to take upon you the office of a teacher, of a reader, of a preacher, and to handle such a weighty matter as this is so slenderly, so frowardly, so crookedly, so far out of frame, so wide from the order of Christ's sincere and true doctrine. Read ye never the pa-
Matt. xviii. rable of forgiveness, that our Saviour telleth in the eighteenth of Matthew? Which parable, like as it setteth forth our duty, and teacheth us every one to forgive our brethren's trespasses from our heart roots, proveth it not likewise, that the Lord first pitieth us, dischargeth us, and forgiveth us our great debt? Is not love and gentleness, that one christian
Gal. v. man oweth to another, a fruit of the Holy Ghost? Is it not a work of faith then and of the Holy Ghost, yea, a fruit of that penance which proceedeth from them both, one man
John xiii. to forgive another? Doth not our Lord himself say, "A new commandment I give you, to love one another, that even as I have loved you, ye also may love one another?" &c.
Ephes. iv. "Be ye courteous," saith St Paul, "one to another, merciful, and forgive one another, even as God hath forgiven you in
Cor. iii. Christ." Item, "Now therefore, as the elect of God, holy

and beloved, put on tender mercy, kindness, humbleness of mind, meekness, long-suffering, forbearing one another, if any man have a quarrel against another. Even as Christ hath forgiven you, so do ye also."

Be these scriptures now against the order of our Lord's prayer? The words whereof if we rehearse in order as he taught them, then, before we ask any petition, we first confess, that Almighty God is our father, and we his children; Luke xi. Matt. vi. which we cannot be, except he hath granted us forgiveness for Christ's sake. Again, there is no prayer good and acceptable without faith; "for how shall they call upon him," Rom. x. saith St Paul, "in whom they have not believed?" They therefore that truly say their Paternoster, are faithful believers, to whom eternal life is promised by Christ's own John iii. vL xi. Mark xvi. mouth, and have their sins forgiven them of God.

Do ye not consider, that they, to whom our Lord taught this prayer, were his apostles, and true christian men? which like as they themselves first have forgiveness of God, (they John xiii. Matt. xviii. should never else be christian men,) so use they to forgive others, according to the doctrine of scripture. For the apostle saith: "Be ye the followers therefore of God, as dear Ephes. v. children, and walk in love, even as Christ loved us," &c. And what christian man, being in his right wit, did ever deny, but that if we, which have forgiveness of God, will not forgive our trespassers, he shall withdraw his forgiveness from us? But you, not regarding the order that God hath taken in the salvation of his people, turn the root of the tree upward, draw the thread through afore the needle, set the cart before the horse. Yea, your doctrine will have us to be the foregoers of God, and not the followers of him, as scripture biddeth us.

STANDISH.

A revocation of these was read in Octavis Paschæ, &c.

COVERDALE.

What revocations ye make in men's names, they being absent, I cannot tell. But like as ye come to the sermon to take Christ in his words, so are ye not to learn to turn the cat in the pan. This may all the world spy here in you, that as ye are crafty and subtle to bring men to revocations, so are ye malicious in defaming of them.

STANDISH.

Furthermore, read his detestable books, and you shall see what detestable seed he hath sowed.

COVERDALE.

If D. Barnes' books be detestable and to be abhorred, why do ye bid us read them? Will ye have the king's subjects to read abominable books?

As for the seed which he did sow, I cannot greatly marvel at you, that call it a pestilent seed; for in his book he said these words: "When I am dead, the sun and the moon, the stars and the element, water and fire, yea, and also the stones, shall defend this cause against them (meaning the cause of God's word against the spirituality), sooner than the verity should perish." This is one corn of the seed D. Barnes did sow. And verily, so far as I can perceive, this same little pretty seed, verity, will grow and come up. Yea, I may tell you, it will grow in your own gardens, when ye are most against it. For Christ told your predecessors plainly, that if his disciples would not speak, the very stones should cry; according to the prophecy of Abacuc. It is no wonder, therefore, though ye call this a pestilent seed. For pestilent is as much to say, as hurtful or unwholesome: so that, if ye suffer this seed of the verity to grow, it will hurt your false doctrine; and the physicians that have seen your water, say that it is unwholesome for your complexion.

margin: D. Barnes' words in the thirty-fourth leaf of his book.

margin: Luke xix.

margin: Hab. ii.

STANDISH.

And thereby you shall perceive how shamefully now he doth lie, like as he hath done ever heretofore.

COVERDALE.

By D. Barnes' book may every one perceive, that he confesseth the articles of the christian belief. And if he lied ever heretofore, as you report of him; then said he never truth. Now is it manifest also, that in his book to the king's highness he confesseth, that no man in England is except from the subjection of the king's power, neither bishop, nor other. He confesseth also, that the king's prerogative is allowed by God's word. He saith likewise, in the next leaf, that it is not lawful for the spirituality to depose a king. Is not this

margin: In the fourth leaf.

margin: In the fifth leaf.

truth? Will ye say then, that he hath lied ever heretofore? Let not the king nor his council hear these your words, I will advise you. Now like as D. Barnes spake truth in these things, so heard I him say to a sort of malicious enemies of God's word even the saying of Christ to the wilful Jews: "Ye are of the father the devil, and after the lusts of your John viii. father will ye do. He was a murderer from the beginning, and abode not in the truth, for the truth is not in him. When he speaketh a lie, he speaketh of his own; for he is a liar, and father of the same," &c. Ye will grant these words to be true, I think.

STANDISH.

Which would have us here to believe contrary to our hearing and seeing, that he never taught nor preached heresy, nor erroneous opinions.

COVERDALE.

To that doth D. Barnes say himself, in his before re-hearsed words, that to his knowledge he never taught any erroneous doctrine. Somewhat also have I said unto you already concerning this matter.

STANDISH.

I pray you, what was his own revocation, &c.

COVERDALE.

Ye make answer to your own question yourself. Ye say, that he utterly there forsook many of his old damnable heresies. If, as you say, he forsook there his old dam-nable heresies, then did he there, as he did in other his sermons, even shew himself to abhor the heresies of the papistry; for those were the old infections, that he was tangled withal sometime.

BARNES.

Although I have been slandered to preach, that our lady was but a saffron bag, which I utterly protest before God, that I never meant it, nor preached it; but all my study and diligence hath been, utterly to confound and confute all men of that doctrine, as are the Anabaptists, which deny that our Saviour Christ did take any flesh of the blessed virgin Mary; which sects I detest and abhor.

STANDISH.

Here he cleareth himself to be no Anabaptist; as though there were no heresy but that alone.

COVERDALE.

Ye would be loth yourself, that other men should so understand your words, or gather such a consequent of them. If ye were accused to be a privy thief, and came before a multitude to clear yourself from that vice; would ye men should judge you to be therefore of so fond opinion, as to think, that there were no more vices but theft alone? I doubt not, but if ye were straitly examined, ye would say, that there were also the vice of lying, the vice of malice, of slandering, of backbiting, of frowardness, of foolishness, of wilfulness, &c.

STANDISH.

And yet this opinion, to say, Christ did pass through the virgin's womb, as water through a conduit, was none of the Anabaptists' own opinion. It was one of the Manichees' error[1], and also Eutice's[2] error, whom some of the Anabaptists herein did follow.

COVERDALE.

Whose error soever it was, I refer that to you; for your treatise declareth, that ye be well acquainted with heretics.

STANDISH.

Wherefore M. Barnes hereby doth not purge himself from the Anabaptists' heresy concerning the baptism of infants.

[1 This heresy is alluded to by Irenæus, *Adversus Hæreses*, Lib. I. cap. 13. p. 33. 1. ed. Grabe, 1702. εἶναι δὲ τοῦτον τὸν διὰ Μαρίας διοδεύσαντα, καθάπερ ὕδωρ διὰ σωλῆνος ὁδεύει, κ. τ. λ.; also, Lib. I. cap. 12. 3, and in other places. See also Tertullian, *De carne Christi*, cap. 1, and *De resurrectione carnis*, cap. 2. Dr Lardner has collected much information on this subject in his Credibility of the Gospel History, part II. sect. iv. Works, Vol. II. pp. 200-3. ed. 1815; and Dr Grabe, in his note on the first passage quoted, shews that this heresy descended from the Gnostics, from whom, with many other of their opinions, it was adopted by the Manichees.]

[2 Most probably a mistake for *Eutyches's*.]

COVERDALE.

His disputations had oft-times with them, his continual preaching against them, his daily words also and conversation, was record sufficient, that he abhorred their error also in that behalf. Why would ye have him then to purge himself thereof? Your physic is not good, to give a man a purgation, which is not infect with such evil or gross humours as require a purgation.

STANDISH.

Here he saith, he never gave occasion to insurrection. But how say you? Did he not offer himself to cast his glove in defence of his errors at Paul's cross?

COVERDALE.

He said at the cross, the third sunday in Lent: "Here is my glove, not in defence of any error, (as ye untruly repeat,) neither with material sword, buckler, or spear to defend any such thing; but with the sword of God's word to prove, that God first forgiveth us afore we can forgive, and that they be no breakers of order, which set forth God's word and due obedience to their prince; but they that maintain their own traditions, burn God's word, and regard not the king's injunctions, &c."

STANDISH.

Did he not openly say these things (meaning his errors) must be tried by blood?

COVERDALE.

Ye are to blame to be so malapert, as to enter so presumptuously into a man's thought, and so to judge it. For his very death declareth, that he meant not to fight, nor to hurt any man's blood, neither to set men together by the ears for any article of his belief; but that they which are of the truth, must in the cause thereof suffer their blood to be shed, and be content to die for the name of Christ, if they be called thereunto.   Matt. x. xvi.

STANDISH.

What call you this, but giving occasion of insurrection?

COVERDALE.

If this be insurrection, then did the apostles send out two
seditious men, Paul and Barnabas; for in their epistle they
testify of them, that they jeoparded their lives for the name of
our Lord Jesus Christ. And yet their weapons were not
carnal, as St Paul saith. If it be insurrection therefore, when
a man offereth himself to die in the cause of Christ, then did
he himself preach insurrection, when he said, "He that loseth
his life for my sake shall find it." "Whosoever loseth his life
for my sake and the gospel, shall save it." " I say unto you
my friends, be not afraid of them which kill the body, and
afterward have no more that they can do. But I will shew
you whom ye shall fear; fear him, which after he hath killed,
hath power to cast into hell : yea, I say unto you, fear him."
D. Barnes therefore, offering himself to die in the cause of
Christ and his gospel, shameth you and all your affinity, as
ye call it; which will not jeopard to put your little finger,
where he hath suffered his whole body to be burned for the
trial of the truth.

Acts xiii.

2 Cor. x.

Matt. x. xvi.
Mark viii.
Luke xii.

STANDISH.

He saith he never called our lady a saffron bag.
Whether he did or no, I wot not; but I heard him at
Barking, two year and more afore he was burned, in de-
claring the canticle, Magnificat, slanderously speak of her.

COVERDALE.

Our lady hath but a faint friend of you that, hearing
one slander her in his sermon, could not find in your heart,
by the space of two year and more, to see him openly
rebuked for it; but now, like a coward, to stand up, when he
is dead, and to accuse him that cannot answer for himself.
Verily, like as he, whatsoever he be, that slandereth our
lady, is worthy of open punishment to the ensample of other;
even so, seeing that, by your own confession, ye heard him
slander her so long before his death, and complained not of
it, ye make yourself guilty of the crime, by the same text
that ye allege out of the Romans in the latter end of your
preface. Neither can I believe, that any of the king's council, hearing of any such inconvenience, and having sufficient
proof thereof, would defer the punishment so long.

Rom. i.

STANDISH.

Making her no better than another woman, &c.

COVERDALE.

Indeed it was not D. Barnes, nor any other creature, that made her better than other women; but even the holy and blessed Trinity, whose good pleasure it was to choose her before all other to be the worthy mother of our Saviour Jesus Christ, in whom all faithful should be blessed. But if ye say, that he in his sermons reputed her no better than another woman, then declare ye yourself to be a very malicious slanderer of the dead: against whom like as ye prove nothing, so were not only his sermons gathered at his mouth in writing, but also the learned men that heard him preach, and were then present at Barking, do testify and report, that in their life they never heard man speak more reverently of the blessed virgin Mary, than he did in that place.

BARNES.

And indeed in this place there hath been burned some of them, whom I never favoured nor maintained.

STANDISH.

Here he saith, that he doth detest and abhor some that hath been burned in Smithfield: whereby we may see, that in all things heretics do not agree among themselves, &c.

COVERDALE.

By the same collection should ye have inferred also, that an heretic agreeth not with himself, and have proved it, when ye have done; as ye do well-favouredly in that your treatise, where, when ye have said one thing in one place, ye affirm the contrary in another, as I shall shew more plainly afterward.

An heretic agreeth not with himself.

BARNES.

But with all diligence evermore did I study to set forth the glory of God, the obedience to our sovereign lord the king, and the true and sincere religion of Christ.

COVERDALE.

Here, gentle readers, note well and forget not, that to these words of D. Barnes John Standish saith nothing: whereby it appeareth, that he cannot deny, but that D. Barnes was a diligent setter forth of God's glory, of due obedience, and Christ's religion; which three things whoso doth, is, in my mind, no heinous heretic.

BARNES.

And now hearken to my faith: I believe in the holy and blessed Trinity, that created and made all the world; and that this blessed Trinity sent down the second person Jesus Christ into the womb of the blessed and most purest virgin Mary. And here bear me record, that I do utterly condemn that abominable and detestable opinion of the Anabaptists, which say, that Christ took no flesh of the blessed virgin. For I believe that, without the consent of man's will or power, he was conceived by the Holy Ghost, and took flesh of her, and that he suffered hunger, thirst, cold, and other passions of our body, sin except; according to the saying of St Peter, he was made in all things like to his brethren, except sin. And I believe, that he lived here among us; and after he had preached and taught his Father's will, he suffered the most cruel and bitter death for me and all mankind: and I do believe, that this his death and passion was the sufficient price and ransom for the sin of all the world: and I believe, that through his death he overcame the devil, sin, death, and hell.

STANDISH.

This is well said: but mark the devil and Peter, the one Matt. xvi, the other Mark v. &c.

COVERDALE.

What, are ye so forgetful of yourself? said ye not in your preface, that the protestation of D. Barnes doth smell and savour nothing but heresy and treason? And now ye confess, that in these fore-rehearsed words he said well; which could not be, if they smelled either of heresy or treason. Thus are ye become not only contrary to yourself, but also a defender of D. Barnes' protestation, and approve the same. And in this do ye prove the sentence true, that I spake of before ; namely, that he which is given to false doctrine agreeth not with himself, after the example of you, which teach one thing in one place, and deny the same in another.

Standish contrary to himself.

Whereas ye compare the confession of D. Barnes to the confession of the devil, we will try your doctrine by the text of St Mark; and thereby shall we see, how well these two confessions do agree, and how clerkly ye have joined them together. St Mark reporteth, that the legion of devils which had possessed a certain man, and taken his right mind from him, &c., cried out, and said unto our Saviour, " What have I to do with thee, thou Son of the most High God?" Here is it manifest, that the devil crieth out of our Saviour Christ, and would have nothing to do with him. When did D. Barnes cry out of him? A great part of the world can testify, that he hath cried out of antichrist and his chaplains, yea, and that so loud, that he hath awaked a great number with his crying.

Mark vi.

Yea, but to my purpose, will ye say, the devil also confesseth Christ to be the Son of God. I answer, their confessions be not alike. For D. Barnes doth not only confess that Christ is the Son of God; but saith also, I believe that he suffered the most cruel and bitter death for me, &c. When did the devil believe that Christ died for him? Again, this confession of D. Barnes condemneth the heresy of the Anabaptists concerning the incarnation of the Lord Jesus. When did the devil condemn any such false opinion? Will ye make it not devilish doctrine to be of that sect? Beware what ye say. Are ye not ashamed then to compare these blessed words to the confession of the devil, and yet to write that they be well said ?

The confession of D. Barnes.

STANDISH.

This your confession doth not prove you to be a good christian man.

COVERDALE.

By your judgment, to confess the true belief in the blessed Trinity, to confess the incarnation of Christ, to abhor the false opinion of the Anabaptists, to believe in Christ's death, resur-

Matt v.
Luke xii.
Rom. x.
rection, &c. is no proof of a christian man; no, though Christ himself say, "Whosoever doth acknowledge me before men, him will I acknowledge also before my Father which is in heaven;" and St Paul, "To believe with the heart justifieth, Isai. xxviii. and to acknowledge with the mouth saveth; for the scripture saith, Whosoever believeth on him shall not be confounded."

Wherefore, if men consider your words, ye bring yourself verily into a shrewd suspicion; for ye seem to favour the miscreants and infidels, even them that believe not the articles of the christian faith. It seemeth, that ye believe in some other thing than God; else would ye make more of the christian belief than ye do.

STANDISH.

For the most part of the heretics condemned by scripture and our mother the church, &c.

COVERDALE.

Where find ye in the scripture, that he is condemned, which believeth in the Son of God, although ye call him and write him heretic ten thousand times? But I see well ye lack help. I will tell you, where ye shall find a text of scripture for your purpose. St John the Baptist saith: "He that believeth on the Son of God hath everlasting life." And Christ our Saviour saith a little before, in the same chapter: John iii. "God so loved the world, that he gave his only-begotten Son, that whoso believeth in him, should not perish, but have eternal life, &c." "He that believeth on him is not condemned."

And whereas ye say, that they were condemned by the church, I answer: If ye mean the church of Christ, (which I doubt not to be in England, as well as in other realms;) then blaspheme ye it, for saying, that it condemneth them, whom Christ with his own mouth pronounceth not to be condemned: for Christ's church never condemneth them whom he saveth. Yea, and in your so reporting ye blaspheme the king's highness, chief and supreme head next under God of this said church of England, without whose authority no execution may lawfully be done within his dominion. Howbeit, among the bushes and in a corner, without the king's knowledge, a true man sometime may chance peradventure to be hanged, as soon as a thief.

If ye mean your own mother, the church of the froward

and multitude of wicked doers, then verily, like a good child,
ye have disclosed and uttered your mother's secrets, and told
us her very nature; which, as she is a very spiritual strumpet
and common harlot, so is she a mother of murder, a shedder
of innocent blood, and, by your own confession, a condemner
of them whom Christ dare avow to be saved.

What ye mean by the censure of the powers, a man cannot well perceive by your words, ye speak so confusedly.
But if ye mean the sentence, judgment, or determination of
the higher powers, then slander ye them, (as I said before,)
in that ye report, how they should be the condemners of those
whom Christ hath not condemned.

If by the censure of the powers ye mean your own
usurped authority, or the stolen and untruly gotten authority
of your mother the wicked church, then we believe you:
for in her, as the angel saith, is found the blood of the pro- Apoc. xviii.
phets and saints.

If ye mean the firepan that ye cast incense in, then may
we see, that your censer is hotter than others men's fire; and
therefore the more perilous for any man to meddle withal.

If by the censure of the powers ye mean the censure
of your excommunication, then declare ye yourselves to be
the cursers of them whom God hath blessed; and so are ye
cursed of God, which saith unto Abraham, and in him to
every faithful believer: "I will curse them that curse thee." Gen. xii.
And, "He that toucheth you," saith the prophet, "toucheth Zech. ii.
the apple of God's own eye."

BARNES.

And that there is none other satisfaction unto the
Father, but this his death and passion only.

STANDISH.

*Among other this was one of his errors, that he revoked
the last Easter at the Spital.*

COVERDALE.

Here ye take your pastime upon the dead, and stray
abroad almost as far as six leaves of your treatise will extend. And now and then, because the common people that
be unlearned should the better understand your words, ye
give them a sentence of Latin, and now and then half a
sentence. I could tell wherefore, if I would.

Among other, ye say, this was one of his errors. Ye judge it an error to affirm, that there is none other satisfaction unto the Father, but the death and passion of Christ only; and yet (like a learned man, full sure of yourself) ye confess plainly on the other side of the leaf in your book, that no man can satisfy for the offence. Upon this ye must give me leave to demand this question of you. If it be erroneous to say, that Christ is the satisfaction unto the Father, and ye yourself confess, that no man else doth satisfy for the offence; to whom then shall we ascribe this honour of satisfying for our sins? Alas, what a gross error be ye in! O blind guides, what way will ye lead the people of God! Unhappy is the flock that is under your keeping; and "happy is the man whom thou, Lord God, instructest, and teachest him out of thy law." "It is time Lord, to lay to thine hand; for they have wasted away thy law."

Standish is full of his Latin.

Standish is contrary to himself.

Psal. xciv.

Psal. [cxix.]

This article, that Christ's death only is the satisfaction to the Father for all the sins of the world, is plain, manifest, and approved throughout all the holy scripture. The whole sentences whereof are here too long to rehearse: but the text is open and evident, though sometime it use one vocable, and sometime another. For to this article pertain all those scriptures, that report him to be the pacifier and reconciler of his Father's wrath, the cleanser, the purger, the maker of atonement, or agreement, the obtainer of grace, the sacrifice and oblation for our sins, &c. The Father of heaven himself doth testify, that it is his Son Jesus Christ, in whom or by whom he is pleased and content. Who taketh away the sin of the world, but he? In whom are we complete, and have all heavenly and necessary things pertaining to salvation, but in him? I pass over the rehearsal of the scriptures written: Isai. liii.; Hos. xiii.; 1 Pet. i. ii.; 1 John i. ii. iii.; Apoc. i.; Heb. i. v. vii. ix. x.; Tit. ii.; Coloss. i. ii.; 1 Tim. ii.; 1 Cor. i.; 2 Cor. v.; Rom. iii. v.

Matth. iii. xvii.
2 Pet. i.
John i.

Whatsoever D. Barnes revoked, (as ye report of him,) I refer that to you, which seem to know more thereof than I. If ye were compelled by force to write, read, or say anything against right and conscience; then like as they be to blame, that will fear man more than God in that behalf, so will God certainly be the visitor of such extreme handling. I would

wish with all my heart (if I might lawfully so do), that the
king's most royal person might see as far as his high autho- The king's grace knoweth not of all the evil that is done in his realm.
rity extendeth : for I fear the common proverb be too true,
that there runneth by the mill much water, which the miller
knoweth not of; neither be all they gentle and loving en-
treaters of the king's subjects, that speak to his majesty
fair words in his face ; yea, the king's grace may have
Judas in his realm, as well as Christ had him in his small
court. I am sorry at my heart root, when I remember
how oft the king's highness hath proved this conclusion true
in his time. I can say no more : but refer all secrets to God;
who, I am sure, will do as he was wont, and bring all falsehood to light at the last.

As for D. Barnes' preaching at the Spital, so far as I
can learn, there is nothing maketh more against you than
that same his day's work. For like as he there openly gave
a godly example of charity and fraternal reconciliation, so An example of charity.
is the same a confusion to you and all your wanton sect ;
which, belying the truth, blaspheming the Holy Ghost, and
slandering them that are the price of Christ's blood as well
as you, (which points smell of greater heresy than ye can
prove against D. Barnes in this his Protestation,) will not
repent, nor ask open forgiveness. Which of your cankered
sort hath yet of his own free mind, uncompelled, come into
an open audience, and played such a part, or desired reconciliation ? Not one of you all, that I know of; no, though
the king hath commanded you in his injunctions, and though
some of you hath not been ashamed to burn God's word.

Standish.

As it was declared at Paul's cross, &c.

Coverdale.

D. Barnes' last will and testament, whereupon he taketh A man's last will must stand.
his death, is this; that there is no other satisfaction unto
the Father, but the death and passion of Christ only. Therefore, though it had been ten thousand times revoked before,
yea, and declared never so oft at Paul's cross, either in the
rehearsal sermon or otherwise; yet shall no man's revoking,
no, nor your blasting and blowing, your stamping and staring,
your stormy tempests nor winds, be able to overthrow this

truth and testimony of the Holy Ghost throughout the scriptures, that the death of Jesus Christ only doth satisfy and
John i. ii. content the Father of heaven, and maketh the atonement for
our sins.   Neither do ye ought but bark against the moon,
so long as ye labour to diminish the glory of Christ, as
though he obtained not grace for all the sin of the world.

Your opinion and doctrine will not suffer Christ to be a
full satisfier unto his Father for all sins. Ye say, he delivered
us from original sin and actual : and yet yourselves confess
that there be also venial sins, which if ye taught not to be
washed away with some other things of your own choosing,
no doubt ye would confess, that Christ delivered us from
them also, as well as from the other.

Diversity. In this your doctrine ye confess, that through Christ we
may avoid and escape the eternal and second death; and
yet afterward say ye, that our satisfaction doth please and
content Almighty God, as satisfactory for our trespass.

But how faintly bring ye out these words, " We may!"
O how loth are ye, that Christ should have his due honour!
Again, how stand your words now together? If we escape
the eternal and second death by Christ, how can we ascribe
the pacifying and contenting of Almighty God to our own
satisfaction? Moreover, how doth God accept our satisfaction
as satisfactory for our trespass, when no man, by your own
confession, can satisfy for the offence? Is not trespass and
offence all one thing?

Heresy. Ye affirm in your Latin words, that a man suffereth not
the eternal and second death through the sin of Adam :
which saying includeth a very heinous heresy, and is openly
Rom. v. confuted by the apostle to the Romans, where like as he
proveth, that the salvation of all men came only by Christ,
so affirmeth he also, that condemnation came on all men
through Adam.

STANDISH.

No man can, I grant, satisfy pro culpa, *&c.*

COVERDALE.

Diversity. Ye grant now, that no man can satisfy for the offence;
and yet ye said before, that our satisfaction is accepted of God,
as satisfactory for our trespass.   Item, ye say here, that
Diversity. every man must satisfy for the punishment belonging to sin;

and ye granted afore, that through Christ we avoid and escape the eternal and second death. Look better on your book, man, for shame. Is not the eternal and second death everlasting damnation and punishment due for sin? How can we then satisfy for the punishment belonging unto sin, when, by your own confession, we escape it by Christ? Alas, that ye are so blind, or that ye should build upon so weak a foundation!

STANDISH.

According to that of St Paul, 1 *Cor. xi.,* Et nos ipsos judicaremus, *&c.*

COVERDALE.

Remember yourself well, and forget not, that ye have brought in this text, to prove that every man must satisfy for the punishment belonging unto sin. Nevertheless let us see whereupon the apostle speaketh, and ponder the circumstance of his words; so shall we try whether Paul and you agree, and whether ye have judged with the text, or no. For I fear me, we shall find, that ye have played another false cast, even with this same poor text. The words of the 1 Cor. xi. apostle are these: "If we would judge, or reprove ourselves, we should not be judged. But while we are judged, we are chastened of the Lord, lest we should be damned with this world." These are St Paul's words.

Afore, in another place of your treatise, ye bring in this text for another purpose, namely, to prove, that D. Barnes ought to have accused and condemned himself. And now, forgetful what ye said before, or else wilful blind (as it seemeth), ye allege the same text, to prove that every man must satisfy for the punishment belonging unto sin. Thus make ye of God's holy scripture a shipman's hose, wresting and wringing it to what purpose ye will. Verily, such perverting of the scripture can ye not use without your own damnation, except ye amend, if St Peter be true. 2 Pet. iii.

The apostle, shewing the Corinthians the true institution of our Lord's holy supper, and the right use thereof, concludeth with these words, saying: "Let a man examine himself, and so let him eat of this bread, and drink of this cup. For he that eateth and drinketh unworthily, eateth and The text drinketh his own damnation, because he discerneth not the 1 Cor. xi.

Lord's body from other meats. Therefore are many weak
and sick among you, and many sleep. For if we judged
ourselves, we should not be judged. But while we be judged,
we are chastened of the Lord, lest we should be damned with
this world. Wherefore, my brethren, when ye come together
to eat, tarry one for another," &c.

By the circumstance then of this chapter it is evident,
that these words of the apostle extend to the right use of
the holy sacrament, teaching us that, before we come to the
Lord's board, we ought first to judge, to try, to prove, and
to examine ourselves, in what case we stand toward God and
our neighbour; considering that it is no childish play, nor
a thing lightly to be regarded, but a most weighty and
earnest matter concerning our salvation, the glory of God,
and edifying of the world: and when we have duly and
unfeignedly tried ourselves, by comparing our whole conversation, both inward and outward, to the just commandments of God, and by occasion thereof have heartily acknowledged and confessed our sins, being sorry and penitent for
them, believing stedfastly in the promises of God, received
the absolution of his word, entered into true repentance and
earnest amendment of our living, being reconciled and at one
with all men, purposing without fail so to continue till our
life's end, then to come and sup with the Lord. This is now
the thing that St Paul teacheth in this chapter; and proveth
here no such article as ye go about. Therefore do ye wrong
to the text, in wresting it to this sense, that every man must
satisfy for the punishment belonging to sin. By the which
your doctrine, like as ye rob Christ of his worship, deface
the merits and fruit of his death, and set every man in
Christ's room, even so doth your said article condemn every
man. For like as Christ only satisfied his heavenly Father
for our sins, and for the punishment due to the same; even
so, if we should not avoid the eternal pain of hell, which is
the second death and reward of sin, till we made satisfaction
for it ourselves, we should continue still in the wrath of God,
and so be damned for ever.

*The holy
scripture of
our Lord.*

*O wicked
opinion!*

STANDISH.

*And to prove this satisfaction, the words of John Bap-
tist, Matth. iii., be very strong, &c.*

COVERDALE.

Be these words, "Bring forth the worthy fruits of penance," as much to say as, Ye must satisfy for the punishment due unto sin? Prettily well expounded of you! O shameless controllers of the Holy Ghost! Will ye make John the Baptist contrary to himself? Doth he not say manifestly in another place, "Whoso believeth on the Son John iii. of God hath everlasting life"? And what is it else to have everlasting life, but to escape the eternal and second death, even everlasting damnation and punishment due unto sin? Which, as ye confess yourself, we do avoid through Christ. Why do ye then wrest the scripture to your own purpose? But one question will I ask you: Who speaketh the words, which are written in the prophet Oseas, saying, "From the Hos. xiii. hand of death will I deliver them, from death will I redeem them: O death, I will be thy death; O hell, I will be thy sting"? Find me now any creature in heaven or in earth, that may of himself verify and pronounce these words of Christ's person; and I shall grant that he may make satisfaction for the punishment due unto sin, which, as this text declareth, is eternal death and hell. Else if there be but one Jesus, one Saviour, one destroyer of damnation and hell; then shall he verily have my poor voice to be called also, as he is indeed, the only satisfier for the punishment due unto sin, as well as he is the satisfier for sin itself.

As for the words of John the Baptist, they prove evidently, The words of John Baptist. that when men convert unto God, (as those Pharisees pretended to do at the baptism of John,) they shall do it unfeignedly; and not to be hypocrites still, nor to lean to their old leaven, but to bring forth the worthy fruits of penance; whereof he nameth part in the third of Luke to the people, and speaketh of no such satisfaction as you feign.

But remember, that ye have named fasting, prayer, and alms-deeds to be the fruits of penance: for I fear me, ye will deny it again anon, when we come to Cornelius the captain.

STANDISH.

Fructus n. dignus pœnitentiæ est opus restaurans ea, &c.

COVERDALE.

There are some of you, that call us English doctors for

writing so much in English, as though in the understanding of other tongues we were inferiors to you; but now ye make us your English interpreters, for putting us to the pain to English the words, which ye wrap up in Latin from the understanding of the people. For the worthy fruit of

Standish. penance, say ye, is a work amending those things, whereof the penance is; that is, repairing such things, as it repenteth us to have left undone, or to have committed; and this is it that we call satisfaction for sins.

Coverdale. That to bring forth the worthy fruits of penance is as much as to amend, whereinsoever we have thought or done amiss, I grant; for the scripture alloweth the same. But whereas ye call that the satisfaction to God for sins, ye speak it not out of the mouth of the Lord.

Diversity. Again, ye said afore, that no man can satisfy for the offence; and now ye call the fruit of penance the satisfaction for sins. Is not every offence sin? Lord God! what hold is there in your words? Fie on such doctrine!

STANDISH.

And here let us note, that it is not all one to bring forth good fruits, and to bring forth worthy fruits of penance.

COVERDALE.

No? Where have ye authority of God's word for you? Be not the good fruits of penance worthy fruits? Or be not they good fruits that are worthy? O unworthy teachers! What an unworthy doctrine is this?

STANDISH.

For he that doth commit no deadly sin, &c.

COVERDALE.

If I should teach any man, when he hath unlawfully behaved himself, to use unlawful things still; I am sure, that like as God's word would condemn me, so would the prudent rulers of the world, according to their duty, look sharply upon me, and judge me little better than a seditious teacher. If the rulers, therefore, of the world will wink at such a pestilent doctrine, and suffer it to be sown among their people, I beseech God to send them his discipline, to their

better information; and so to lighten the eyes of their understanding, that they may as well remember, what hurt cometh
of seditious doctrine, as many. of their subjects, yea, they
themselves also, have proved it by experience. Well, yet
remember the end.

Whereas ye separate the fruits of innocency, of goodness,
&c., from the fruits of penance, where find ye that in holy
scripture? For albeit that some man offendeth more than
another, who yet, I pray you, is not bound to confess himself
a sinner, to declare himself sorry for the imperfectness of his
own nature, to mortify his flesh, and to live in repentance
all the days of his life; yea, be he never so innocent, just, or
righteous in the estimation of man? Thus, by your slender
division, ye prove but slenderly, that the works of Mary
Magdalene and David were not fruits of goodness, but only
fruits of penance; as though penance were not good, or as
though the fruits of penance were not good fruits.

As for the carnal liberty of man, it must be alway
restrained: abuse of all things is utterly forbidden. Yet
must the body of man have his worship at his need; at his
need, I say, not at his lust. If you now, through any shine
of wisdom or chosen spirituality, will teach the contrary; then
is your doctrine condemned by St Paul to the Colossians. Coloss. ii.

STANDISH.

*Yea, and according to the quality of the offence must
be the satisfaction.* Pro mensura peccati erit plagarum
modus. *Deut. xxv.*

COVERDALE.

This text verily, as it is slenderly alleged, so proveth it
your purpose but faintly. Moses' words, which you bring in,
are these: "According to the measure of the offence shall
be also the measure of stripes." But let us see the circumstance of the text, and so shall we try whether ye have
played a juggler's cast or no. And forget not, I pray you,
that ye have alleged this text, to prove that the satisfaction
must be according to the quality of the offence.

Moses writeth thus: "If there be a matter of plea Deut. xxv.
between any men, and they come to the law, then look, whom
the judges consider to be just, him shall they declare to be
in the right cause; and him whom they perceive to be un-

godly, shall they condemn for his ungodliness. But if they
see him which hath offended to be worthy of stripes, they
shall take him down, and cause him to be beaten in their
presence. According to the measure of the offence shall be
also the measure of the stripes; but so that they pass not the
number of forty," &c.

This law, as it is evident, was a civil ordinance, made for
the commodity of the people, and not without mercy. The
text also speaketh of no such satisfaction as ye mean. But
here, forgetting the rules of your logic, ye would make a
quality of a quantity. For in your article ye speak of a
quality, and the text maketh mention of a quantity, number,
or measure. Again, this law will, that the party which is to
be beaten shall not have above forty stripes. And then, by
your doctrine, it must follow, that though we be compelled
to be punished, and so to make satisfaction for the pain due
unto our sins, yet should each one of us have but forty
stripes; for the text speaketh of no more. May ye not be
ashamed then thus to mock with the scripture?

*Note well
now, how
the text and
Standish
agreeth.*

STANDISH.

Not like nor equal in the great offender and the less.
Unde *Apoc. xviii.,* Quantum quis se glorificavit, et in deliciis
fuit, tantum illi inferendum est tormentum.

COVERDALE.

Whereas the voice from heaven speaketh of the whore
of Babylon, and saith, "Come away from her, my people,
that ye be not partakers of her sins; lest ye receive of her
plagues, &c.: as much as she glorified herself, and followed
her own lusts, so much give ye her of punishment and sorrow," &c; by the last part of this text would ye prove,
that satisfaction may not be equal in the great offender and
the less. Now saith the text: "As much as she glorified
herself, &c., so much give ye her of punishment." Here is
rather equality.

Rev. xviii.

Equality.

And whereas the text speaketh of the whore of Babylon,
ye say, *Quantum quis, &c.;* turning not only the feminine
gender to the masculine, (which a boy that goeth to the
grammar school would not do;) but also proving an universal
by a particular.

*The feminine
gender turned
to the mascu-
line.*

Again, this text speaketh of her that is damned to hell; and the article that ye go about to prove, speaketh of those whom ye have affirmed already to make satisfaction unto God for their sins by the fruit of penance; which, by your own judgment, are not damned unto hell. Lord God! when will this blindness have an end? Note this well.

STANDISH.

It is not enough, saith Chrysostom, &c.

COVERDALE.

The doctrine of God is, that when Christ hath made us whole, (for without him is no remission,) we shall sin no more: he that hath stolen, must steal no more; he that hath not the gift of chastity, must for the avoiding of fornication take a lawful wife; for better it is to marry than to burn. On the backside of the book, therefore, is that doctrine written, which teacheth, that when a man hath long continued in whoredom, he shall then abstain from the lawful use of wedlock; for wedlock is the remedy appointed of God against all bodily fornication and whoredom. Job v. viii.
Ephes. iv.
1 Cor. vii.

STANDISH.

Whereby we may perceive, &c.

COVERDALE.

Yes, there be worthy fruits of repentance to bring forth; there is a new man to put on; the tree hath good fruits to bear; the spouse of Christ, which is every true faithful soul, hath lawful children, that is, lawful thoughts, lawful words, lawful deeds, to bring up and to nourish. Good works must needs follow faith; but not that we may set any of them in the room of Christ, nor make them the satisfaction to God for our sins. "God hath called us," saith the scripture, "unto good works, TO WALK IN THEM;" but not to make our Saviour or satisfaction to God of them. Ephes. ii.

STANDISH.

Christ, Luke xi., when he had rebuked the Pharisees for their vice, said, Date eleemosynam, et omnia munda sunt vobis.

COVERDALE.

That text, if it be not *ironia*, proveth, that we are bound to do good works; to the which though God join his loving promise, (as he doth commonly throughout the scripture,) yet calleth he not them the satisfaction to him for sins. But like as in the [fifty-]eighth of Esa. the Holy Ghost rebuketh the superstition and hypocrisy of the Jews, that had fallen to works of their own inventing; and then telleth them the true fast and good works, which God requireth, adding a loving promise to the fulfillers thereof; even so doth our Saviour here in this chapter. For when the Pharisee was so superstitious, that he marvelled why he washed not his hands before dinner, then said he unto him : "Now do ye Pharisees make clean the outside of the cup and platter; but your inward parts are full of robbery and wickedness, &c. Nevertheless, give alms of that ye have, and behold, all things are clean unto you." Lo now, first he rebuketh their superstition; secondly, sheweth them, what good works he alloweth, commanding them to do the same; and thirdly, addeth a promise thereto.

The text Luke xi.

STANDISH.

And the preacher, Eccl. xxi. Fili, peccasti? &c.

COVERDALE.

Those are not the words of the preacher, whom the scripture calleth Ecclesiastes, but they are the words of Jesus Sirack, saying : "My son, hast thou fallen into sin? Do no more so; but pray instantly for thy former sins, that they may be forgiven thee. Flee from sins, even as thou wouldest flee from a noisome serpent," &c. This text then proveth no more your feigned satisfaction, than it proveth the Jews' circumcision. And like as your fond alleging of it declareth, that ye are an hider of the scripture from the unlearned; so proveth the Holy Ghost in the text, that if we have broken the profession of our baptism, and be fallen unto sin, we shall do no more so, but convert and turn unto God, continuing in the fear of him and in fervent prayer, to be at the stave's end with sin, and to abhor it all the days of our life.

The text Eccles. xxi.

STANDISH.

He that thinketh this insufficient, &c.

COVERDALE.

Suspecting, as it appeareth, that your wresting of the former scriptures will not be taken for a sufficient proof of your feigned satisfaction, ye bring in ensamples of David, Moses, Aaron, and the children of Israel; as though their punishment had been their satisfaction. But where find ye that in any of those places of scripture? If ye say, Why doth God then punish, after that he hath remitted the fault? I answer, Like Objections. as he is the Father of mercy and God of all comfort, so doth 2 Cor. i.
Wisd. iii. he correct and chasten his own, yea, exerciseth and trieth them, Prov. iii.
Heb. xii. as the gold in the fire; partly, because he loveth them, and partly for the example of other, that they may beware of such falls. The same examples therefore, that ye bring in, make clearly against you, and prove manifestly, that ye are but blind and ignorant of the scriptures. For the apostle, speaking of the same children of Israel, and of their punishment, saith plainly, that all such happened unto them for ensamples; 1 Cor. x. but are written to warn us, that we should not lust after evil things as they lusted; that we should not be worshippers of images, that we should not commit whoredom, that we should not tempt Christ, nor murmur against him, as they did. Shame ye not then, so irreverently to handle the holy word of the living God?

STANDISH.

Furthermore Daniel, cap. iv. exhorteth Nabuchodonosor, &c.

COVERDALE.

If that text should prove any satisfaction to be done by man to God, as it proveth our duty to our poor neighbours, it should rather maintain a satisfaction for sin than for the By sin doth
Standish
understand
satisfaction
for sin. pain belonging to sin; for the text speaketh of sins and iniquities, and maketh mention of no punishment. Have ye no better judgment nor clearer sight in discerning of a text? Ye may be ashamed, verily.

The words of Daniel, as they include in them a commandment to do alms-deeds, and shew mercy to the poor, which thing every man is bound to do; so include they in them a loving promise to all such as are merciful in distributing to them that lack help. And as it is an eternal worship for

them that follow this most wholesome counsel of the prophet; so is it a shame and perpetual confusion to all churlish hearts and unkind people, (specially to covetous princes, rulers, and rich men,) that will not do their best in providing for the
What a charitable heart Daniel bare toward the poor.
poor, after the example of Daniel; who, no doubt, seeing so many poor prisoners and helpless people driven from Jewry to Babylon, had a singular respect to their necessity, and therefore spake to the king in their cause. Which thing would God they that are great with princes, or of their council, were as diligent to do, as they are to make suit in their own private causes! And doubtless they would be the more inclined so to do, if it were not for you and such other, which allege not the scripture to such purpose as the Holy Ghost hath caused it to be written for, but frowardly wrest it for the maintenance of your own fond opinions.

STANDISH.

Look also, Jonas iii., what satisfaction the Ninivites made, &c.

COVERDALE.

The text declareth, that God first sendeth his word;
The story of Jonas.
which when it is preached, (as it was by Jonas the prophet,) then the children of salvation believe, after the example of the Ninivites, and earnestly turn unto God from their old evil way, and from that time forth give over themselves wholly to all manner of good works. Then God approveth and alloweth their works, accepteth them, hath mercy of them, and poureth not upon them the wrath, that he hath threatened to such as will not repent. This is the sum of that whole third chapter of the prophet Jonas. But in all the text is there no mention made of any such satisfaction as you feign.

Is it not an ungodly thing then, so to wrest and wring the scripture violently? The ever living and merciful God
A thing to be wished.
amend it! It were greatly to be wished, that like as the king of the Ninivites, receiving God's word, made a proclamation for all his subjects to fast and pray, there were even such restraints made likewise in every country, that no man should wrest the scripture of God, nor allege any thing thereof, which may not justly be gathered by the words of the Holy Ghost, that is, that no man should belie the text.

STANDISH.

This satisfaction Paul speaketh of, Rom. xii. Obsecro
vos, *&c.*

COVERDALE.

"I beseech you, brethren," saith the apostle, "for the mercy of God, that ye will give over your bodies, to be a living, holy, and acceptable sacrifice to God, which is your reasonable serving of God. And fashion not yourselves like unto this world: but be changed through the renewing of your mind." These are St Paul's words; which as ye partly hide from the unlearned, so cut ye them very short; lest, I fear, if we heard out St Paul's mind, we should understand him the better. *(The text Rom. xii.)*

St Paul's doctrine is, that we must mortify our bodies: but to what intent? To make any such satisfaction, as ye would prove? Nay, so saith not the text; but to the intent that we may serve God, as we should serve him; to forsake vanity, and to be altered from an evil mind to a good. Even so likewise saith the other text, which I must English for you, in the sixth to the Romans: "Like as ye have in times past given over your members to serve sin from one wickedness to another; so must ye now give over your members to serve righteousness, that ye may be holy." "That ye may be holy," saith he; and speaketh of no such satisfaction as ye invent. *(The text Rom. vi.)*

STANDISH.

If I do not thus satisfy, then I shall have the reward and pain belonging to sin, &c.

COVERDALE.

To the intent that ye may spy the better, in what case ye stand by your own words, (I pray God ye may look to yourself by times, as a christian man should,) I will make you an argument or two out of the scripture.

To deliver from eternal death is to satisfy for the pain due unto sin. *(Major.)*

But Christ only delivereth from eternal death. *(Minor.)*

Ergo, Christ only satisfieth for the pain due unto sin. *(Conclusio.)*

The major is manifest by St Paul, whom ye yourself allege, saying: "The reward of sin is death," even eternal *(Rom. vi.)*

[COVERDALE, II.] 24

death, by your own confession. The minor is proved by the prophet, and by the apostle. Of these two premises gather you the conclusion.

Another argument.

By what one soever we are delivered from the wrath of God, both past and for to come; by the same is made sufficient satisfaction for the pain due unto our sin.

But Christ only delivereth us from the wrath of God, both past and for to come.

Ergo, He only satisfieth for the pain due unto our sin.

The major is manifest; for the pain due unto sin is the wrath and indignation of God.

The minor is evident by the apostle: First, That we are delivered only by Christ from the wrath of God past; for he hath made the peace between his heavenly Father and us, and by him is the Father reconciled. Secondly, That we are delivered by him from the wrath to come, it is clear, Rom. v. and 1 Thessa. i. By these two premises may you gather the conclusion.

Now to your words.

To satisfy for the pain due unto sin is the only office of Christ.

But ye take upon you to satisfy for the pain due unto sin.

Ergo, ye take upon you the office of Christ.

The major is proved by the scriptures alleged before in the two first arguments.

The minor is gathered from your own plain words. Of these two followeth the conclusion.

Then thus.

Ye say, that if ye do not thus satisfy, ye shall have eternal death.

But so ye cannot do; for it is the only office of Christ.

Ergo, ye shall have eternal death.

Behold now, what a dangerous case ye be in by your own words! Alas, man, that ever ye should be so blind, as to sit thus in judgment, and to give sentence against your own soul, that Christ hath shed his blood for, if ye conform yourself to be partaker thereof! Who would not note me to be five mile from my right wit, if I should make such an argument, and say thus:

If I be not Christ the Son of God, I shall have eternal death and damnation.

But so it is, that I am not Christ. Ergo, &c.

If I should thus believe, and affirm this matter, would not ye abhor me? Turn therefore, turn, for God's sake, into your own conscience, and rebuke it earnestly between God and you, for suffering either your hand to write, or your mouth to speak, any such inconvenience.

STANDISH.

And now of this satisfaction finally to conclude, if there were need of no satisfaction, after by repentance we be come into the favour again with God, why then did Christ say, Luke vii. To them that love much many sins are forgiven, and to them that love little fewer sins are forgiven?

COVERDALE.

Your opinion upon that place of the gospel doth utterly destroy the parable of the lender and two debtors; yea, and Simon's answer, which our Saviour Christ alloweth. For Simon saith, that "To whom most is forgiven, the same loveth most;" and again, our Saviour saith, "Unto whom less is forgiven, the same loveth less:" by the which two sentences every man may easily perceive, that the text speaketh of no such satisfaction as ye imagine. *The place, Luke vii.*

But I have spied you now at the last. O very cruel enemies to God's holy word, how falsely have ye perverted and turned our Saviour's words, to maintain your heresy withal! Cannot Christ's words stand in the gospel for you, as he spake them, and as the evangelist wrote them, but ye must teach him how he should say? Doth he say in that place, To them that love much, many sins are forgiven, and to them that love little, fewer sins are forgiven? Nay, verily, these are his words: "Many sins are forgiven her, for she hath loved much: but unto whom less is forgiven, the same loveth less." Will ye still then take upon you to control the Holy Ghost? Well, beware, that this your juggling come not to light. Beware, I say, that the breath of God blow not down your house; for a rotten foundation cannot stand long. Take heed by times, and say, ye be warned. *Standish maketh a new text.*

STANDISH.

This saying cannot be concerning culpam, *&c.*

COVERDALE.

Our Saviour speaketh of sins, and of forgiving the sins;
and yet are ye not ashamed to affirm, that his saying cannot
be concerning the fault, but concerning the punishment. Can

Standish
would make
Christ a
liar.
not Christ speak a thing, and mean the same? Can he not be
true in his words? O blasphemers of the Son of God, yea, and
of that blessed woman, Mary Magdalene, which must needs
be yet in her old faults and a sinner still, if he meant not as
he said; if his saying were not concerning the fault, when he
spake these words : " Many sins are forgiven her, &c."

STANDISH.

Whereby we see, that post remissam culpam, *&c.*

COVERDALE.

Ye have heretofore called this satisfaction the works of
penance; and now say ye, but in Latin, that there remaineth sometime a duty of punishment to be purged, or reconciled, with a worthy satisfaction : which if it be a work of
penance, what time can you assign me, in the which I am
not bound to be exercised in some fruit thereof? And now
come ye in with "sometime." Again, ye said afore, that the
satisfaction must be according to the quality of the offence ;
and now ye say, that the punishment due unto sin must be
purged with a worthy satisfaction. Now is it manifest, that
unworthiness is a quality of every offence, for all faults are
unworthy things ; wherefore by your own confession it followeth, that the pain due unto the same must be satisfied
with an unworthy satisfaction. And verily so I take it; for
unworthy is it, whatsoever a man of his own brain inventeth,
without some sure ground of God's word.

STANDISH.

And this is signified by that of the prophet Joel, &c.

COVERDALE.

The words of the prophet, though ye chop them very

The text
Joel ii.
short, are these : " Now therefore," saith the Lord, " be ye
turned unto me in your whole heart, in fasting, weeping, and

mourning. And rend your hearts, and not your clothes, and
be ye turned to the Lord your God; for he is gracious and
pitiful, long-suffering and of great mercy, and will be entreated as touching sin," &c. Doth this text now signify, that
after the fault is forgiven, there remaineth sometime a duty
of punishment to be purged with a worthy satisfaction? Is
this your judgment in scripture? O shameless beliers of the
open and manifest text!

Standish.

*Now if you say, Esay, cap. liii. saith, Our Saviour bare
our sins on him, &c.*

Coverdale.

"Of a truth," saith the prophet, "he hath taken away ^{The text}
our sorrows, and he himself hath borne our pains, &c. The ^{Isai. liii.}
correction of our atonement was laid upon him," &c. These
are the words of Esay: which, as they are manifest and
plain, so do not you truly rehearse them as they stand; and
yet can ye not deny, but that if we conform ourselves unto
Christ, then hath he satisfied for us most abundantly. To
what point now have ye brought your former doctrine of
satisfaction? Verily, even to this point, that Christ hath
taken away their sorrows and pains, yea, and borne the
correction of their atonement, which conform themselves
unto him.

For all this your confession, yet deny ye the truth
again, and say, that he delivered us not from all pain satisfactory. Now saith the prophet, that he took away our
sorrows and pains. What pain satisfactory then is there,
that he hath not delivered us from? If it be our pain, then,
saith Esay, Christ hath borne it. But peradventure ye do
mean some pain of your own. Ye seem to be yet dreaming
of your painful purgatory; for if ye conformed yourself to
Christ and to his doctrine, ye should be persuaded and certified in your conscience, even by the same chapter of Esay,
that Christ hath as well satisfied his heavenly Father for the
pain due unto your sin, as for your sin itself.

Standish.

For if he had so done, we should neither mourn, &c.

COVERDALE.

Ye say, that if Christ had delivered us from all pain satisfactory, we should neither mourn nor be penitent for our offence committed against God, nor we need not to mor-
An heinous heresy. tify our flesh. O damnable heresy! And are ye one of the authors thereof? Are ye one of the destroyers of penance, of converting to God, and of mortifying the flesh? But as touching such another like ungodly consequent, I have talked somewhat with you afore. All the world therefore shall know, that ye are the teachers of such pestilent doctrine, and not we.

Behold now, how unsure ye are of yourself. Ye say, that if Christ had delivered us from all pain satisfactory, we should neither mourn nor be penitent for our sin, nor mortify our flesh. And yet ye confessed before, that through Christ we avoid and escape eternal death; which likewise, by your own confession, is the pain due unto sin. How stand your words now together?

Whereas ye condemn your own perverse doctrine by the sixth chapter to the Romans; it were sufficient to deliver you from suspicion, if ye did abide thereby. But that do ye recant, and fall to your vomit again, saying,

STANDISH.

But we should with their fleshly liberty have a joyful penance full of mirth.

COVERDALE.

Your doctrine is, that if Christ had taken away the pain due unto your sin, ye should not repent for your sins, but follow your own fleshly liberty, &c. Whereby ye declare yourself to be still of that rotten opinion, which ye defended afore.

Now whereas ye report of us, that our penance is with a fleshly liberty, I answer: Even as by your former words ye prove yourself to be one of their number, which say, "Let us
Rom. iii. do evil, that good may come thereof; Let us continue in
Rom. vi. sin, that there may be abundance of grace; Let us sin, because we are not under the law, but under grace;" even so, I say, do ye declare yourself to be one of them that speak evil of us, and report us to be the affirmers of your wicked words: as though we were they that exhorted men to a fleshly liberty, or not to live in virtue and good works.

Now God is the true judge, who, as he abhorreth all liars, Psal. v.
Deut. xxxii. even so refer I all vengeance to him; for it is his office by Rom. xii. right. But in the mean season, till all falsehood be disclosed, our earnest watching and labouring for your salvation, the poor life which we lead in this world, and the fruits of our good-will that grow in your own gardens, for all your weeds, shall testify somewhat with us also against your evil tongues. And God, which is able to restore the blind to their sight, shall lend men eyes to see, and understanding to discern, whether the doctrine and open word of God, which we teach, would have men to live after their own lusts; or whether your doctrine, which is of men's inventing, be not rather cause of all wickedness, robbing men of their wits, and making them to run at riot from God's word, from his ordinance, from his commandments, from his promises, and from the most virtuous ensamples of God's children.

Now as touching our penance, ye would make the world believe, that when we speak thereof, we mean some morris-dance, some such delicate banquetting as is among the ungodly, some unlawful chambering, some such excess of eating and drinking as (God amend it!) is commonly used in the world. Again, your doctrine is, that repentance should be without joy. And our belief is, that if the Holy Ghost and the true faith of Christ go together, then like as repentance proceedeth of faith, so is the joy of christian men a fruit of Gal. v. the Holy Ghost, as the apostle saith. Thus also to be merry and joyful are we taught by the scripture, Hiere. ix; 1 Cor. i; 2 Cor. xi; Rom. v. viii; Matt. v; Luke x. Shall we then be sorry, because God hath done so much for us? For our sins and trespasses we will be sorry and mourn; though when we fast, we rend not our garments, nor put on sack- Joel ii.
Isai. lviii. cloth, neither disfigure our faces to be seen of men; though Matt. vi. iii.
Rev. xviii. when we pray unto God, we prick not ourselves with bod- Matt. vi.
Isai. i. kins, nor make too much babbling of words. Such flings, Eccles. v. such morris-dances, such wanton gestures, such light mirth we make not; for our joy and gladness is inward, conceived in our breasts, when we feel the inestimable mercy and love of God therein, yea, even when we are put to trouble and adversity.

Another love have we also, and the same is likewise a fruit of our repentance, appointed in scripture; as when we joy with them that joy, when we are glad of our neighbour's Rom. xii.

welfare, glad and cheerful to do him good, glad to give him lodging, &c. Wherefore to call such fruits of repentance any light or wanton mirth, ye are to blame, and of a wanton judgment.

STANDISH.

All these new fellows would have penance to be, &c.

COVERDALE.

To be called "new fellows" of your mouth, we do not greatly force. But first, whereas ye jest upon us for casting our sins and care on Christ, and for rejoicing that he hath taken them on him, ye shew yourself not only ignorant in this spiritual cause of Christ's faith, but also blasphemous both against him and his. I pray you, who hath so broad a back, or so meet to bear the sins of penitents, as Christ

Isai. liii. hath? Hath not his heavenly Father laid our sins upon him, as ye yourself have confessed out of Esay? And doth he

Matt. xi. not say unto us himself, " Come to me all ye that labour and are laden, and I shall refresh you?" Is not he " the

John i. Lamb of God, that taketh away the sins of the world?" And

1 John i. doth not his " blood cleanse us from all sin ? "

Secondly, whereas ye blame us for casting our care upon Christ, we do not greatly pass upon it, though we lament your blindness; for we have God's word on our side, yea, not only his commandment and precept, but also

Psal. liv.
Matt. vi.
Luke xii. his promise, that so doing he will nourish us and not suffer us to lack. Nevertheless, in casting our care upon God, we rob not our body of his duty; but set the hands to labour, the feet to go, the mouth to speak, and every member to work in

Deut. vi. his calling, lest we tempt God, contrary to his commandment.

STANDISH.

This penance Peter did not take.

COVERDALE.

What, will ye belie St Peter? Did not he cast his sins

1 Pet. ii. upon Christ? Saith he not plainly, that " Christ himself bare our sins on his body upon the tree, to the intent that we might be delivered from sin, and live unto righteousness ?"

Or did not holy St Peter cast his care upon Christ?

1 Pet. v. Why biddeth he us then to " cast all our care upon him," adding also, that " he careth for us"?

Again, doth not St Peter also bid us "rejoice, inasmuch 1 Pet. iv. as we are partakers of Christ's passions?" &c.   Or think ye, that he did not as he taught?   Was he not one of those disciples, which "were glad when they saw that their Lord" John xx. was alive?   Why are ye not ashamed then to belie him? Fie, fie! take better heed to your words another time.

STANDISH.

But his penance was mournful.

COVERDALE.

Though he mourned and wept bitterly, when he had denied our Saviour, as every true penitent doth; yet proveth not this the contrary but that, in consideration of the goodness of Christ, he also rejoiced, as appeareth by his own words afore.

STANDISH.

Theirs glad and jocund, &c.

COVERDALE.

So glad are not we in our penance, but we may find cause enough of sorriness, though we considered nothing else save the blind understanding that is in you.   Ye say, that we think justification to be without works of penance. But like as ye are too malapert to enter into men's thoughts, so am I glad that ye cannot report, that we should preach, teach, talk or write, that we would have justification to be without works of penance following.   For our books, our We have sufficient papers, our pens, our hands, our whole conversation, (though testimony of this. we have our faults as well as other men,) yea, and the mouths of them that know us, can testify that we are of a contrary opinion.

STANDISH.

If you say, remission of sin is freely forgiven in baptism, therefore we need no more penance, &c.

COVERDALE.

I wonder in whose name ye make that objection.   If ye know any man to affirm, teach, or write, that we need no more penance, because sin is freely forgiven in baptism, he ought to have an open rebuke.   Howbeit the same is like unto your own doctrine, where ye say, that if Christ had taken away the pain due unto your sin, ye should not repent, but follow your carnal liberty.

Now to your satisfaction, ye say here, that it springeth out of the third kind of penance; and before, in the eighth leaf of your treatise, to prove it strongly, ye bring in St John Baptist's words, which ye join now to the first kind of penance. Is it not now strongly proved? Are ye not very sure now of the doctrine that ye teach?

Note this well.

Again, to prove, that by the second kind of penance godly men are purged from such sins, without which a man cannot here live; ye allege the first chapter of the first epistle of John, who in the same place saith these words: "If we say that we have fellowship with God, and yet walk in darkness, we lie, and do not the truth. But if we walk in light, even as he is in light, then have we fellowship together, and the blood of Jesus Christ his Son cleanseth us from all sin." This scripture now maketh clearly against you, and proveth your opinion to be false; for Christ's blood cleanseth us from "all sin," none except, so long as we walk in his light, and not in darkness. Why ascribe ye then the purgation of men's sins to any kind of penance, seeing Christ's blood hath and must have the honour thereof?

The place, 1 John i.

Ye allege here sundry places of scripture, the circumstances whereof doth utterly disapprove your doctrine; as plainly appeareth to him that conferreth the same to the open words of the text, which I heartily require all indifferent readers to do.

Ezek. xviii.

The place of Ezechiel is manifest, that God will no more think upon their sins that truly repent and turn from them.

Isai. lv.

The place of Esay sheweth, that God will have mercy on

Jer. xviii.

such penitents. The place of Hieremy is plain, that if people convert from their wickedness, God will no more plague them

Wisd. xi.

therefore. The eleventh chapter of Wisdom declareth evidently, that the punishments which happened to the Egyptians were sent through the indignation of God, and that the trouble, nurture, and correction, which the Israelites had, came of his fatherly mercy. The hundred and forty-fourth Psalm wit-

Psal. cxlv.

nesseth, that "the Lord is gracious and merciful, long-suffering, of great goodness, loving to every man, &c.; lifteth up all them that are cast down, and is nigh to all such as

Matt. xviii.

faithfully call upon him." The eighteenth of Matthew is evident, that whosoever converteth from his sin, Almighty God will not that he shall perish. Item, that like as all true penitent sinners have their debt freely forgiven them, so shall they be partakers of the same forgiveness still, if they will heartily do unto others as they are dealt withal themselves. These places of scripture, though ye tell not forth the words, are of your own alleging; and yet are ye not ashamed to write, yea, even of penitents, that none of their sins shall be unpunished. Now is it manifest in the said chapter of Ezechiel, *Ezek. xviii.* that like as God will not reward their good deeds, that forsake him, and turn away again to their vomit of wickedness; so will he not think upon their sins, that truly convert *Ezek. xviii.* therefrom unto him. Yet call ye them happy, that punish themselves, and take upon them to be satisfactors in that behalf; as though it were a blessed thing for men to lay crosses upon their own backs. Thus by your judgment were Baal's priests happy, and the hypocrites that the prophet *1 Kings xviii.* Esay speaketh of. O deceitful teachers! full well might the *Isai. lviii.* prophet say unto God's people of England, and in this behalf: " O my people, they that do call thee happy, do but deceive *Isai. iii.* thee, and mar the way that thou shouldest go in." *Popule meus, Qui te beatum dicunt, &c.*

Now let us hear more of D. Barnes' words.

BARNES.

And that no work of man did deserve any thing of God, but only his passion, as touching our justification.

STANDISH.

This manner of justification plainly appeareth to be false, even by that one place, if we had no more, of Cornelius, Acts x., &c.

COVERDALE.

The words of the text are these: "There was at Cesarea *The text* a man named Cornelius, a captain of the Italianish company, *Acts x.* a devout man, and one that feared God with all his house, and gave much alms to the people, and prayed God alway."

The text saith in order, first, that Cornelius was a devout man, and feared God with all his house; and then speaketh it of his good works, as alms, prayer, &c. Whereby it is manifest, that he himself was first accepted of God and justified: for, as St Peter saith afterward in the same chapter, "God hath no respect of persons, but in all people he that feareth him, and worketh righteousness, is accepted

Isai. lvi. unto him." And, as the prophet saith: "The strangers, gentiles, or heathen, which cleave unto the Lord in worshipping him and loving his name, are accepted unto him, as his

Ecclus. ii. own servants." Again, the scripture saith: "They that fear
Heb. xi. the Lord give credence to his word." "And without faith
Rom. xiv. it is not possible to please God." Item, "Whatsoever is not of faith is sin." By this it is manifest, that those good works of Cornelius were fruits of his faith and of the fear of God, and he justified afore he did them. Ye confessed also before, that fasting, prayer, and alms-deeds, are the

Diversity. fruits of penance: then must ye needs grant, that the tree was afore them.

This text then proveth not, that our justification, deserved only by the death of Christ, is a false justification, nor that Cornelius' works deserved much of Almighty God afore he was justified. For, as I shall rehearse afterward, ye confess yourself, not only that we are justified freely, but also that

Diversity. God first giveth us grace, without which we can do nothing that is good.

STANDISH.

As did the work of king Ezechias, 2 Reg. xx, &c.

COVERDALE.

Your purpose is by the ensample of Ezechias to prove, that our works deserve much of Almighty God, afore we be justified: and that work of Ezechias, which ye allege, was done long after his justification. For the text saith, that

2 Kings xx. when he lay sore sick, the prophet Esay came to him, and told him the message of God; and that he then made his fervent prayer, and wept. After the which God sent him word, that "he had heard his prayer, and seen his tears," &c. And afore, in the same book, it is evident, that the same

2 Kings xviii. king Ezechias "did the thing that was good in the sight of the Lord, according as his father David had done, put his trust in the Lord God of Israel, &c., cleaved unto the Lord, went not out of his paths, but did according to all the precepts that God had commanded Moses;" and "therefore," saith the text, "was the Lord with him in all that he took in hand."

Wherefore by the circumstance of the text it is manifest, that Ezechias was justified afore he lay sick, and that his prayer was a worthy fruit of his repentance long after he was justified, and no work that deserved any thing afore his justification. Neither did his prayer, nor the work of the Ninivites, change the sentence of God; for God is neither Heb. vi. James i. changeable nor double in his words. But like as, afore the Ninivites believed in him, he first sent his word, and Jonah iii. threatened them, that if they would not convert, their city should be destroyed after forty days; even so, when Eze- 2 Chron. xxxii. chias was fallen into sin, God threatened him, that if he would not repent, he should die. And like as God, when we receive his word earnestly, believe stedfastly in him, and bring forth good works, doth accept us, as he did the Nini- Jonah iii. vites; even so, though we have fallen from the profession of our faith, yet if we now do earnestly repent and convert, he is merciful and true to forgive us our sins, and to grant us 2 Kings xx. our petition, after the example of Ezechias: at whom like as all kings and princes may take instruction of good governance, even so in him have all other sinners, that have broken their covenant with God, a very notable ensample of true repentance.

But how rhymeth the example either of Ezechias, or of the Ninivites, for the probation of your purpose? Did either Ezechias, after he was fallen into sin, or the Ninivites, afore they believed, deserve any thing of God? Or doth any of both these examples prove that our justification, deserved only by the death of Christ, is a false justification?

Afore, in the tenth leaf of your treatise, ye allege the example of the Ninivites, to prove, that after the sin is forgiven, we must make satisfaction unto God for the pain due thereunto. And now bring ye the same in, to prove that Diversity. our works may deserve much of Almighty God, afore we be justified. If this be not a mocking with God's word, let them judge that are learned therein.

STANDISH.

Scripture is full of such ensamples, &c.

COVERDALE.

Scripture is full of ensamples; but to bring us unto the faith of Christ, and also to make us rise up by true repentance, when we are fallen from the same. But in all the scripture find ye no ensample, that teacheth you to call our justification, deserved only by the death of Christ, a false justification, or to affirm that we may deserve much of Almighty God afore we be justified. And yet would ye fain prove the same, yea, even by the ensamples of those that were justified afore.

STANDISH.

Notwithstanding I am not ignorant of the order of our justification, &c.

COVERDALE.

Are ye not ignorant, what order God taketh in justifying his people, and will yet teach the contrary? The more shame for you! Now may every man, that noteth your former doctrine, perceive evidently, that ye are a wilful teacher against the order of our justification. For if God first of his mercy only giveth us grace, without which we can do no good thing; then teach ye contrary to this order, when ye say, that men's works deserve much of Almighty God, afore they be justified. Thus doth your own doctrine prove you not only to be contrary to yourself, but also a wilful breaker of godly order.

STANDISH.

Ille prior dilexit nos, 1 *John iv.* Non dilectus dilexit, &c.

COVERDALE.

Here in this place of your treatise ye make a long process in Latin; which as it is fondly printed, and patched of you with little morsels of scripture, so do the same make clearly against your purpose.

1 John iv.
Rom. v.

Ye grant, that God first loved us, afore we loved him; and that Christ died for us, when we were yet sinners: which if it be true, then is it manifest that God first forgave us for Christ's sake. If he first forgave us, then is your doctrine false, when ye call it against the order of our Saviour's prayer, that we must be forgiven of God, afore we can forgive; and that our justification, deserved only by the death of Christ, is a false justification ; seeing ye confess also, that the mercy of God goeth both before and behind us, and that we are freely justified.

Whereas ye grant also, that through faith we obtain the grace of God, how agreeth that with your former doctrine against the justification of faith? Yea, even the same third chapter to the Romans, that ye here allege, is against you : Rom. iii. for St Paul's words are these : " The righteousness of God cometh by the faith of Jesus Christ unto all and upon all them that believe," &c. Item, " Freely are they justified, even by his grace, through the redemption that is in Christ Jesu, whom God hath set forth to be the mercy-seat through faith in his blood," &c.

BARNES.

For I knowledge, the best work that ever I did is unpure and unperfect.

STANDISH.

Taking this saying as it is, Job xxv. &c.

COVERDALE.

Take D. Barnes' words none otherwise than he spake them ; and let them be tried by the same place of scripture that ye allege, where Baldad the Suhite saith thus : "May a man compared to God be justified? Or can he that is Job xxv. born of a woman appear clean? Behold, the moon is not clear, and the stars are not clean in his sight. How much more man, which is corruption, and the son of man, a worm !" And in the ninth chapter saith Job himself plainly : " God is he, whose wrath no man may resist, and under Job ix. whom are subdued the proud of the world. Who am I then to answer him, or to talk with him in my words? Yea, and though I have any righteous thing, I will not answer, but make my humble supplication to my judge, &c. If equity of judgment be required, no man dare bear record on my side. If I will justify myself, mine own mouth shall condemn me. If I will shew myself innocent, he shall declare me to be naught."

Do not these scriptures prove now, that, in consideration of God's judgment, all men's works are unpure and unperfect?

STANDISH.

Unde *Isai. lxiv.* Omnes nos immundi et quasi pannus menstruatus : *but thus to his purpose it cannot be taken, &c.*

COVERDALE.

What mean ye, man, so perversely to handle with the dead ? D. Barnes confessed, as appeareth by his words, that the best works, that were done by him upon earth in this corrupt body, were not so purely and perfectly done as the equity of God's law requireth ; and therefore, as appeareth afterward, in consideration thereof he made his prayer with the prophet, saying : "Lord, enter not with me into judgment." "If thou, Lord, wilt straitly mark our iniquities, Lord, who will abide it ?" Notwithstanding, though his words be manifest, yet ye say, not only that it cannot be taken to his purpose, as Esay wrote in that chapter ; but also upon the same ye gather an intent, (for ye are good at that, ye are well skilled in judging men's intents and thoughts,) that he should mean, " All good works are naught, and that it is sin to obey the voice of God :" which your collection is clean contrary to D. Barnes' words.

And if we confer them to that place of Esay whom you allege, this matter shall be the more manifest. The words of the prophet are these : " All we are become as an unclean man, and all our righteousnesses are as filthy rags." This text, as it maketh clearly for D. Barnes' purpose against yourself, even so in alleging of it have ye diminished it, and left out of it those words that make most against you. But the abbot of lies and father of falsehood, even the devil, taught you that lesson, as I told you before, out of the fourth of Matthew ; because ye play such another part with a text of St Paul, 1 Cor. xi.

In your Latin ye read the text thus : " All we are unclean, and as filthy rags." So that ye leave out, *All our righteousnesses.* Now if the text may stand still for you, as the Holy Ghost left it, that all our righteousnesses and best works are unclean, and not without some blemish ; then happily will you have little thank, not only for holding against it, but also for minishing the text.

As touching the Germans, (to whom ye impute error in this behalf,) their doctrine is, that when the servants of God

Marginal notes:
Psal. cxliii.
Psal. cxxx.

Isai. lxiv.

Standish doth diminish the text.

have done all that is commanded them, they must acknow- Luke xvii.
ledge themselves to be unprofitable; to have occasion continually to cry unto God, and to say, "O forgive us our Matth. vi.
Luke xi.
trespasses;" to acknowledge, that "in their flesh dwelleth no
good thing;" yea, and to confess, that though they "delight Rom. vii.
in the law of God after the inward man, yet there is another
law in their members, which striveth against the law of their
mind, and taketh them prisoners in the law of sin, which is
in their members;" that "there is no man but he sinneth;" 1 Kings viii.
2 Chron. vi.
that "the whole life upon earth is a very battle," where "the Job vii.
Gal. v.
flesh lusteth against the spirit, and the spirit against the
flesh;" so that christian men cannot bring every thing to
such a perfection as they fain would.

This is now the doctrine of the Germans; and thus taught
also St Augustine, writing *De verbis Domini secundum Jo-* The scrip-
ture and St
hannem, Sermo XLIII., where he saith these words: "We Austin
maintain the
cannot do that we would. Why so? For we would that Germans'
doctrine.
there were no concupiscences; but we cannot have our will.
For whether we will or no, we have them; whether we will
or no, they tickle, they flatter, they prick, they vex, they
will up; they are kept down, but not yet utterly extinct,
as long as the flesh lusteth against the spirit, and the spirit
against the flesh [1]." The same affirmeth he in the sixteenth
sermon *De verbis Apostoli* [2]. And in the forty-ninth chapter,
De definitionibus orthodoxæ fidei, he saith after this manner:
"And therefore all holy men do truly in pronouncing themselves sinners; for of a truth they have whereof to complain;
and though not through any reproof of conscience, yet

[1 Non quod volumus facimus. Quare? Quia volumus ut nullæ
sint concupiscentiæ, sed non possumus. Velimus nolimus, habemus
illas; velimus nolimus, titillant, blandiuntur, stimulant, infestant, sur-
gere volunt; premuntur, nondum extinguuntur, quamdiu caro con-
cupiscit adversus spiritum, et spiritus adversus carnem.—August. De
verbis Domini in Evang. sec. Johan. Serm. XLIII. Opera, Tom. x. p.
36, M. Ed. 1541.]

[2 The following appears to be the passage alluded to: Ecce
enim baptizati sunt homines, omnia illis peccata dimissa sunt, justifi-
cati sunt a peccatis, negare non possumus: restat tamen lucta cum
carne, restat lucta cum mundo, restat lucta cum diabolo. Qui autem
luctatur aliquando ferit, aliquando percutitur, aliquando vincit, aliquando perimitur: quando de stadio exeat, attendatur.—De verbis
Apost. Serm. XVI. Tom. x. p. 75, B.]

through the frailty [1]," &c.   Such doctrine now, though it be approved both by the holy scripture and by St Augustine, yet because the Germans teach it, it must needs be condemned of you for an error.   I wonder ye condemn them not also for holding so little of the pope's church, of his pardons, of his purgatory; for putting down his religions,

The Germans cleanse their church from the papistry. his chauntries, his soul-masses and diriges, his trentals, pilgrimages, stations, &c.; for ministering the sacraments in their mother tongue, for setting their priests daily to preach the only word of God, for bringing in no new customs into the church; for avoiding whoredom and secret abomination from among their clergy, as well as from other; for bringing up their youth so well in the doctrine of God, in the knowledge of tongues, in other good letters and honest occupations, for providing so richly for their poor, needy, fatherless, and aged people, &c.

Now to your ensample of Abraham, which obeyed the voice of God: doth it prove that his obedience was so perfect as the equity of God's justice required? or that his own words

Gen. xviii. were false, when he said unto God, " I am but dust and ashes "?

STANDISH.

Also it is said, Job primo, *In omnibus his non peccavit Job.*

COVERDALE.

The latter part of the text, which declareth the whole meaning thereof, leave ye quite out.   The words of the scrip-

The place Job i. ture are these: " In all these did not Job sin, nor spake any foolish thing against God."   Now is it manifest by the same chapter, that when the scripture hath told of the great ad-

The place Job i. versity that Job had in the loss of his goods and children, it maketh mention also of his notable patience, and then concludeth the chapter with those words.   The one part whereof like as ye leave out, and tell the other in Latin from the unlearned; so make ye of a particular an universal, as though Job might not offend in other things, though he grudged not

[1 The reference ought to be to cap. LXXVI. Et ideo veraciter se omnes sancti pronunciant peccatores, quia in veritate habent quod plangant, etsi non reprehensione conscientiæ, certe mobilitate et mutabilitate prævaricatricis naturæ.—August. De Ecclesiasticis Dogmatibus sive de Definitionibus orthodoxæ fidei. See above, p. 185. n. 12. Op. Tom. III. p. 47, M.]

here against God. For manifest is it, that he did afterward curse the day of his birth, as the third chapter declareth. Job iii. Now because Job was patient in his first adversity, and blasphemed not God, doth that prove it an error to hold with him, when he saith, "If equity of judgment be required, Job ix. no man dare bear record on my side? If I will justify myself, or shew myself innocent, mine own mouth shall condemn me"?

STANDISH.

And St Peter, 2 Pet. i. after he hath recited certain virtues, &c.

COVERDALE.

St Peter, before those words, speaking of the same virtues, saith thus: "If these things be present and plentiful in you, they shall not let you be idle nor unfruitful in the knowledge of our Lord Jesus Christ." Let one place of scripture now open and expound another.

STANDISH.

Furthermore, a strong argument to prove it may be this: Omnis qui in Deo manet non peccat. 1 *John iii.* Sed qui manet in caritate in Deo manet. 1 *John iv.* Ergo qui manet in caritate non peccat &c.

COVERDALE.

To your argument I answer: Like as it is true, when the scripture saith, "They that are born of God sin not," (partly 1 John iii. because God hath covered their sin, and imputeth it not unto Rom. iv. them, and partly because they are at the stave's end with sin, and delight not in it, but keep themselves from sin, as Rom. vii. St John saith in the same fifth chapter;) so is it true also, Gal. v. that "if we say we have no sin, we deceive ourselves, and 1 John i. the truth is not in us," as holy St John saith. In the declaration of the which words St Augustine noteth heresy in the Pelagians and Celestines, for affirming, that the righteous have utterly no sin in this life[2]. Take you heed therefore, that ye smell not of the Pelagians' pan; for it stinketh afar off.

STANDISH.

As David, speaking in the person of every good man, said he did, Servavi mandata tua, Domine, *Psal. cxviii.* [Psal. cxix.

[2 August. de verbis Apost. Serm. xxxi. Op. Tom. x. p. 86. M. &c.]

COVERDALE.

The place
of the
Psal. cxix.

He saith also a little after in the same psalm unto God: "I have gone astray, like a sheep that is lost; O seek thou thy servant." The circumstance also declareth, that it is not only a psalm of consolation, of doctrine, and of thanksgiving; but also an earnest prayer of one that is very fervent in God's cause, and in the defence of his word: so that like as sometime he mourneth and weepeth to see the acts and statutes of God despised, even so complaineth he sore unto God of them that maintain any doctrine contrary to his word. Thus in respect of them he dare boldly say, that he keepeth God's commandments, and no men's doctrines; for he abhorreth all the false learning of hypocrites. But, in consideration of his own infirmity, he saith to God oft-times in this psalm: "O teach me thy statutes; give me understanding, that I may learn thy statutes; save me, help me, deliver me," &c. Like as in another psalm, where he confesseth to have kept the ways of the Lord, he saith a little after in the same psalm: "O my God, give thou light unto my darkness."

Psal. xviii.

STANDISH.

According to God's saying to Jeroboam, 1 Kings xiv.

COVERDALE.

Psal. cxxx.
Psal. cxliii.

Though God covered David's sins, and imputed them not unto him; yet made he his confession unto God, while he was in this body, and said: "If you, Lord, wilt straitly mark iniquities, Lord, who shall abide it?" "Lord, enter not into judgment with thy servant," &c.

STANDISH.

And also as it may be proved by this, that God commandeth us nothing impossible for us to do.

COVERDALE.

One false opinion would ye prove by another; and by this present article, like as by the other afore, ye declare yourself to be a very Pelagian, and partaker of their heresy confuted by St Augustine in the sixteenth chapter of his book *De Libero Arbitrio*[1], and in more other places.

[1 The proper reference is to the treatise De Gratia et Libero Arbitrio. Opera, Tom. VII. p. 28. Ed. 1541.]

STANDISH.

But he saith not only Matt. xix. Si vis ad vitam, &c.

COVERDALE.

Your argument is this : God hath commanded us to keep his law ; ergo, it is not impossible for us so to do. But whether your consequent will be allowed in the chequer or no, we shall see by our Saviour's own words; who, when he had said to the young man, " If thou wilt enter into life, keep the commandments," and told his disciples, "how hard it is for the covetous to enter into heaven;" they asked him, and said, " Who can then be saved? Then answered he them, saying, With men it is impossible : but with God are all things possible." Down then goeth the Pelagians' heresy, and little thank are ye like to have for holding with it. *The place Matt. xix.*

If ye ask, Why then doth God command us to decline from evil, and to do good, if it be not in our power ?—to the same objection doth St Augustine make a sufficient answer in the second chapter *De Correptione et Gratia :* and not only repelleth it by St Paul's words, saying, " It is God which worketh in you both the will and the deed ;" but also putteth us in mind, that if we be the children of God, we are led by God's Spirit to do good; that when we have done any good thing, we may give thanks to him, of whom we are led[2], &c." And in another place : " Therefore doth he command certain things that we cannot do ; because we might know what thing we ought to ask of him[3]." The same doctrine teacheth he also in the sixty-third sermon *De Tempore*[4]. This is confirmed *Objection.* *Answer.* *Phil. ii.* *Rom. viii.* *De lib. arb. cap. xvi.*

[2 Non itaque se fallant, qui dicunt, Ut quid nobis prædicatur, ac præcipitur ut declinemus a malo et faciamus bonum, si hoc nos non agimus, sed id velle et operari Deus operatur in nobis? sed potius intelligant, si filii Dei sint, Spiritu Dei se agi, ut quod agendum est agant, et cum egerint, illi a quo aguntur gratias agant.—August. De Correptione et Gratia, cap. ii. Opera, Tom. vii. p. 286. K. L.]

[3 Compare note 1. Magnum aliquid Pelagiani se scire putant, quando dicunt, Non juberet Deus, quod sciret non posse ab homine fieri. Quis hoc nesciat? Sed ideo jubet aliqua, quæ non possumus, ut noverimus, quid ab illo petere debeamus.—De Gratia et Libero Arbitrio, cap. xvi. Op. Tom. vii. p. 284. C.]

[4 Gratiæ Dei igitur obedientia se humana non subtrahat, nec ab illo bono, sine quo non potest bona esse, deficiat; aut si quid sibi impossibile aut arduum in mandatorum effectibus experitur, non in se remaneat, sed ad adjuvantem recurrat, qui ideo præceptum dat, ut

Rom. vii.   by holy scripture: "For by the law cometh the knowledge of sin. So that even they which are renewed in Christ, find by the law, that when they would fain do good, (for therein is their delight,) evil is present with them."

The words of our Saviour, "If ye love me, keep my commandments," prove no more your purpose, than your wresting of them proveth you to be a true scholar of his. For

John xiv.   after those words he himself saith thus: "I am the way, the truth, and life. No man cometh to the Father, but by me." Nay, saith your doctrine, we may come to God by ourselves; he commandeth us nothing impossible for us to do. Now let me ask you this question: If Christ, when he said these words, "If ye love me, keep my commandments," did mean, that it is not impossible for us so to do; why then, immediately after the same words, doth he promise us the Spirit of comfort? What need have we of him, if we be not comfortless of ourselves, or if nothing that he commanded us be impossible for us to do? What need have the whole of a physician? And St Augustine, writing against them that extol

St Augustine, De verbis apostoli.   their own possibility, in the second sermon *De verbis Apostoli*[1], saith: "Let us be glad to be healed, while we are here in this church. Let us not make our boast of health, being yet sick; lest by our pride we do nothing else but make ourselves incurable."

STANDISH.

Which to the lovers of them be but light. Matt. xi. 1 John v., and Deut. xxx.

COVERDALE.

Ergo, God commanded us nothing impossible for us to do? Is that your consequent? Full faintly are ye able to prove it by those three chapters that ye do allege. First, in

Matt. xi.   the eleventh of Matthew, doth our Saviour bid "all them that are laden, &c. to come to him." And yet saith he in another

John vi.   place, that "no man can come unto him, except his Father draw him." Where is now our possibility?

1 John v.   That fifth chapter of St John's first Epistle sheweth, that

excitet desiderium, et præstet auxilium, dicente propheta, (Psal. lv.) *Jacta cogitatum tuum in Domino, et ipse te enutriet.*—August. Serm. de Temp. LXIII. Op. Tom. x. p. 158. D. ed. 1541.]

[1 August. Op. Tom. x. pp. 55, 6. But the reference is erroneous.]

they which are born of God, do overcome the world by the
victory of faith. Now like as we begat not ourselves in the
kingdom of God, but he himself of his own good will begat James i.
us with the word of life; so is it manifest also, that true faith Ephes. ii.
is the only working of God, and not ours. Where is then, I
say, our possibility? Forsooth, even fled into the isle of
weakness.

If by the thirtieth chapter of Deuteronomy ye will
prove, that God hath commanded us nothing impossible for us
to do, because Moses saith, "This precept that I command thee
this day, is not above thee nor far from thee;" &c. then
must I require you to take the answer of St Paul, who saith,
that it is the righteousness of faith which speaketh those Rom. x.
words; and that the word which Moses there spake of, is the
word of faith, that Paul himself preached.

If ye think there to prove your purpose, because Moses
layeth before the people life and death, good and evil, blessing and cursing, and biddeth them choose life, &c.; then
must I desire you, not only to remember the office of the law,
wherefore it was given, and whereto it serveth; but also to
consider, that in the beginning of the same thirtieth chapter,
Moses himself saith these words: "The Lord thy God shall
circumcise thine heart, and the heart of thy posterity, that
thou mayest love the Lord thy God with all thy heart, and
in all thy soul, &c." Whereby it is evident, that except God
circumcise our hearts, we are not able to love him, nor to
keep his commandments. So that these words of Moses do
prove rather impossibility in us. For "the circumcision of Rom. ii.
the heart," saith the apostle, is the true circumcision, which is
done "in the spirit, and not in the letter; whose praise is not
of men, but of God."

All these three chapters now prove, that like as to be
saved, to keep God's commandments, to have circumcised
hearts, and to overcome the world with the lusts thereof, is
the only working of God in us; even so to them that love
God, are his commandments not grievous; not through any 1 John v.
possibility of man, but partly because Christ hath taken away Gal. iii.
the curse of the law, and delivered them from the heavy Matt. xi.
burdens of their souls, and partly because they delight in
God's commandments, and esteem his word sweeter than
honey, as David did: for love maketh all things light. Psal. cxix.

STANDISH.

Therefore I conclude, in all our working we do not commit sin.

COVERDALE.

Of an evil major and minor followeth a weak conclusion. Ye have wrung and wrested the scriptures violently, to make them serve for your purpose; and now, without any scripture, make ye your conclusion, that in all your working ye do not commit sin. To the probation whereof because ye bring no scripture yourself, I will help you with a text, where the scripture saith thus: "There is no righteous man upon earth, that doeth good and sinneth not." If ye be a man, (I will not reason much with you of righteousness, for I am a sinful man myself,) then must ye needs grant this scripture to be true. If ye be no man, then am I sorry that I have disputed with you so long: for angels have no need of my words; and as for devils, they will not be counselled.

Eccles. vii.

STANDISH.

No, nor our deeds and acts which be good, cannot be called so, &c.

COVERDALE.

Of D. Barnes' secret intent and meaning will not I presume to be judge; but what may be gathered by the circumstance of his words, I have reasoned with you already.

Now because ye cannot prove this last part of your conclusion by scripture, namely, that your good deeds and acts are not unpure nor unperfect in this life; therefore the prophet Esay, to recompense you the wrong that ye did him in minishing his words afore, will yet take the pains for you to prove your purpose, though it be little to your mind, when he saith: "All we are become as an unclean man, and all our righteousnesses are as filthy rags[1]." And the wise man saith also: "Who may say, My heart is clean, I am pure from sin?"

Isai. lxiv.

Prov. xx.

BARNES.

And with this he cast abroad his hands, and desired God to forgive him his trespass.

STANDISH.

Extra ecclesiam nulla salus, &c.

[1 A different translation is cited by the author.]

COVERDALE.

Without the church, ye say, is no salvation. Now is it manifest that, beside the church made of lime and stone, there is also a congregation, church, and multitude of froward and wicked doers, which not only gather themselves together, like roaring lions, fat bulls, wanton calves, and cur dogs, against Christ, as the twenty-first psalm complaineth; but also make [Psal. xxii.] laws, constitutions, statutes, ordinances, and traditions against God's word; whereby it cometh to pass, that though they boast never so much of God's service, yet all is to them in Isai. xxix. vain, as the prophet and Christ himself doth testify. Matt. xv.

Another church is there, which is the holy spouse, congregation, and company of them that are of the fellowship and communion of Christ, and walk not in darkness, but in 1 John i. the truth, having all their sins cleansed by his blood. This church continueth in the apostles' doctrine, runneth not out from Acts ii. the heavenly fellowship of Christ and his members, distributeth the sacraments duly and truly, ceaseth not from praying and well doing, &c., are of one mind and soul, are glad to help one Acts iv. another, as it is manifest in the Acts and Epistles of the apostles. The men of this church "pray in all places, lifting up 1 Tim. ii. pure hands, &c." In this church whosoever asketh hath, he Matt. vii. that seeketh findeth, and to him that knocketh doth God Luke xi. open. In this church is free pardon and remission of sins for Matt. xviii. all true penitents. For God will not the death of sinners, but Luke xxiv. John xx. if they convert unto him, they shall live; and whoso is laden Ezek. xviii. with sin and cometh unto Christ, findeth rest and ease in his Matt. xi, John vi. soul, and shall not be cast out.

Forasmuch then as ye condemn D. Barnes thus doing, and judge him to be none of the church, that desireth God to forgive him his trespass; it is evident, that in your church there is no forgiveness for poor sinners, and so is it not the church of Christ. Wherefore, seeing ye dissent from Christ's church, where the door is ever opened to them that knock, your own sentence condemneth you, that ye can trust to have no salvation by God's promise.

But, alas! what blindness is in you! Though a sinner doth err, or hath erred from the right faith, and from the true use of the holy sacraments that be in the church of Christ, and now cometh to repentance, desiring God to forgive him his trespass; is not this a damnable doctrine to

Luke xxiii. teach, that he cannot trust to have salvation by God's promise? No? Hath God promised, that sinners which repent shall not be saved? The thief that hanged on the right hand of Christ, hath proved the contrary.

Again, If a sinner may not trust to have salvation by God's promise, whereby then may he trust to have it? By himself? by his own works? or by your merits? Even by your merits, as it appeareth, would ye have him trust to have salvation; for ye must needs be full of merits, that in all your working commit no sin, as ye say yourself.

Moreover, the tenor of your words separateth the mercy of God from his promise, as though they concurred not together. But I pray you, who can trust to have salvation by God's promise, and trusteth not in his mercy? When the Gal. iii. apostle saith, "God gave the inheritance unto Abraham freely by promise," was it not done by his mercy? And when he saith in the same chapter, "Ye are the heirs of Christ according to the promise," what meaneth he else but as he saith Tit. iii. to Titus, that "the kindness and love of our Saviour hath appeared, not for the deeds of righteousness which we have done, but according to his mercy hath he saved us?" &c.

St James' words, which ye bring in in Latin, denieth no James ii. forgiveness to them that repent: but like as he rebuketh them that are but christian men in word, and not in good works and deeds; so, if partiality be sin, then doth the circumstance of the same text condemn your former conclusion, that say ye sin not in all your works.

STANDISH.

Look the reward of finalis impenitentia, *&c.*

COVERDALE.

D. Barnes' words testify, what faith and repentance he had toward God, and what heart he bare toward the commonwealth of all christendom; and yet shame ye not to write, that he died without repentance and in errors, because he would not deny Christ, and revoke his word with you.

STANDISH.

Which died by his words, without sign or token of salvation.

COVERDALE.

Is it no token or sign of salvation, to believe in the holy and blessed Trinity, the incarnation, passion, death, and resurrection of our Saviour, and to knowledge the same before men? Is all this utterly no token of salvation? Christ and the ^{Matt. x.}
apostle Paul are of another judgment. Rom. x.

STANDISH.

And so his prayer must needs be void.

COVERDALE.

D. Barnes cast abroad his hands, and desired God forgiveness; and yet dare ye affirm, that his prayer must needs be void. By the which words, like as ye deny the article of forgiveness mentioned in our creed, and promised in the Matt. xviii. scripture to every one that truly repenteth; so declare ye Luke xxiv. evidently, that there is little mercy in your mother, the church of the wicked: for in Christ's church, if the son ask the father a piece of bread, he will not give him a stone, but good Matt. vii. things.

STANDISH.

Mark how he trusteth within an hour, &c.

COVERDALE.

Is it blind arrogancy, when a man, refusing all confidence in his own works, trusteth to have eternal life through the mercy of God? What blind arrogancy was in the apostle, when he said: "We know certainly, that if our earthy house 2 Cor. v. of this dwelling were destroyed, we have a building ordained of God, an house not made with hands, but everlasting in heaven?" Our Saviour also giveth this comfort to such as believe in him, that "they shall not come to damnation, but John v. pass from death unto life." Are ye not a comfortable physician then to men's consciences, that shame not to teach otherwise than Christ doth? But surely these two places of scripture are not for the establishing of your soul-masses and diriges; and therefore no marvel that ye teach a contrary doctrine. For though the name of your purgatory be out of some of your books, yet are not all purse-pickers come to the pillory.

BARNES.

For although perchance you know nothing by me;

yet do I confess, that my thoughts and cogitations be
innumerable. Wherefore, I beseech thee, enter not into
judgment with me, according to the saying of the pro-
Psal. cxliii. phet David, *Non intres in judicium cum servo tuo, Domine;*
Psal. cxxx. and in another place, *Si iniquitates observaveris, Domine,
quis sustinebit ?* "Lord, if thou straitly mark our iniquity,
who is able to abide thy judgment?"

STANDISH.

*See, I pray you, the devil seduced him so far, that he
would not knowledge any sin, but only cogitations, &c.*

COVERDALE.

D. Barnes said not, that he had no sin; but although,
said he, "perchance you know nothing by me, yet I confess,
that my thoughts and cogitations are innumerable." Is this
as much to say as, "I have no sin, but only cogitations and
thoughts?" Or be not thoughts and cogitations sins great
enough? Did he not confess also with the prophet, that if
God would straitly mark his iniquities, he were not able to
abide it? Is iniquity no sin? Not in your judgment, as it
appeareth: for ye dare boldly affirm, that in all your working
ye commit no sin.

STANDISH.

*See how he judged other men perchance to know no sin
in him, &c.*

COVERDALE.

If it be an abominable vice (as it is no doubt) to slander
the scripture or to belie it; then verily are ye infect with
abominable vice, that have misreported it and belied it in so
many places of this your treatise. Now if ye be of counsel
with so many good men that knew such vices in D. Barnes,
I marvel ye tell us not what those vices are. As for your
mother, the unholy church, he called her an harlot many
times. And sure I am, that whoso knoweth her thoroughly,
Ezek. xxiii. and compareth her with her fruits to Aola and Aoliba, will
judge her to be little better.

STANDISH.

*Judge therefore yourselves, what availeth him these his
feigned prayers, &c.*

COVERDALE.

The prayers that D. Barnes useth here are the holy words of God's scripture, and yet ye call them feigned prayers.   Now if the Holy Ghost, which is the author of the scripture, "doth abhor feignedness," as the wise man saith; Wisd. i. then verily is it blasphemous to call those feigned prayers, that he only hath taught.

Again, if they be feigned prayers, why say ye, that ye doubt not but to another man, passing in the faith of Christ, they should have been acceptable, yea, and meritorious before God? Can feigned prayers be acceptable to God? Can feigned prayers merit or deserve any thing of God? Or can he that dieth in the faith of Christ use feigned prayers at his death? How agreeth feignedness with the faith of Christ? Full feigned and false is your doctrine. Our Lord root it once out from among his people.

BARNES.

Wherefore I trust in no good work that ever I did, but only in the death of Jesus Christ.

STANDISH.

To trust in our works, ut in deum credimus, *that they of themselves, &c.*

COVERDALE.

What an unstable doctrine is this that ye bring in among God's people, and would bear them in hand, that Christ allowed your saying in the twentieth of Matthew! Whereas the parable in the same chapter, and the process of the last part of the nineteenth chapter hard afore it, do utterly condemn your doctrine.   Lord God, what a derogation unto God's high glory is this, to teach, that we may trust in our works, that we may challenge our inheritance by our working, that our working may deserve to receive immortality! In the latter end of the nineteenth chapter of Matthew doth our Lord affirm, Matt. xix. that to be saved is a thing impossible through the power of men.   And in this twentieth chapter doth his parable testify, that like as we are first called by him, receive his promise, and are set a-work by his commandment; so is not the reward given for any deserving or pains taking, but according to his own promise.

First, where find ye in any article of the christian faith, contained within the holy Bible, either commandment or promise of God, or example of any good man, that we may put any manner of trust in our works? Again, if our inheritance come by the death of Christ and his promise, how cometh it by our working? Is our working the death of
Christ, or his promise? Now if our working may deserve the inheritance of immortality, then may we make satisfaction unto God for our offence; and that ye have denied afore. Oh, how well agree ye with yourself!

Diversity.

STANDISH.

And this caused Paul boldly to say, 2 Timo. iv. Bonum certamen certavi, &c.

COVERDALE.

When that holy vessel of God, St Paul, had exhorted Timothy to the fervent executing of his duty in preaching God's word, and had told him before of this present perilous time, that men will not suffer wholesome doctrine, &c; he
shewed him of his own death, saying: "For I am now ready to be offered, and the time of my departing is at hand. I have fought a good fight, I have fulfilled the course, I have kept the faith. From henceforth there is laid up for me a crown of righteousness, which the Lord, the righteous judge, shall give me in that day; not only unto me, but to all them that love his coming."

The place 2 Tim. iv.

What caused Paul now to say these words? Any trust or confidence in his own deserving or works? Nay, verily. He confesseth, not only that the crown of righteousness is laid up for him, but also that God shall give it him: neither saith he here, that it shall be given him for his working sake; for then were he contrary to his own doctrine, which utterly
condemneth yours, Roma. iii.; Ephe. ii.; Philip. iii.; 2 Tim. i.; Tit. iii. Note well the places yourself.

St Paul condemneth Standish's doctrine.

STANDISH.

Albeit I fear me these his words, &c.

COVERDALE.

If when he did any good work, he caused no trumpets to

be blown before him, nor mumbled up long prayers in the corners of streets, nor disfigured his face to be seen of men, when he fasted; then was there the less hypocrisy in him. It is a proverb as true as old: 'A still Paternoster is as good as a loud.'

BARNES.

I do not doubt but thorough him to inherit the kingdom of heaven.

STANDISH.

I beseech God, this false and erroneous belief, contrary almost in every sentence to our mother, the holy church, &c.

COVERDALE.

Full unholy and ungracious is your mother, and ye as unwise to take her part, that calleth it a false and erroneous belief, when a man doubteth not but to inherit the kingdom of heaven through Christ. If that belief be contrary to your mother, then is she contrary to it; and so is she the synagogue of Antichrist. Ye are afraid, that the innocent lambs of Christ should hearken to his voice, and not to yours: but set your heart at rest, for they will not hearken to the voice of strangers. _{John x.}

STANDISH.

Who doth believe by any other means contrary to Christ, &c.

COVERDALE.

Yes, forsooth, even you, if ye believe as ye write. For the same pre-eminence, that is due to the death of Christ and his promise, give ye to your working in the vineyard; yea, ye put confidence, that your working shall deserve immortality: remember your own words well. _{Standish's words rebuke himself.}

STANDISH.

But what Christian doth cast off and forsake all duties to our part belonging, and so temerously, &c.

COVERDALE.

One duty, that belongeth to your part, is the sincere and true teaching of God's holy word: which duty though ye cast off and forsake, I will not say all that I might, by your own words; but God amend it that is amiss! Again, this Protestation of D. Barnes testifieth, that he doth not cast off and forsake all duties to a christian man belonging. For he _{This is no casting away of all honest duties.}

believeth in the holy Trinity, he extolleth the merits of Christ, he praiseth our lady, he abhorreth the Anabaptists' heresy, he prayeth for the king's highness, he exhorteth men to good works, he beseecheth God to forgive him his trespass. Be these no duties of christian men? What hath moved you then thus untruly to report of him?

Whereas ye lay presumption to his charge, for trusting to inherit the kingdom of heaven through Christ; I have answered you afore, where ye imputed like arrogancy unto him for so doing.

STANDISH.

Which go about, being blind themselves, &c.

COVERDALE.

Matt. vii.   Those heretics, of whom Christ biddeth us beware, are false prophets, which come in sheep's clothing, but inward are ravening wolves. "Ye shall know them," saith he, "by their fruits." Now in describing unto us their fruits, he sheweth us, that they are such as boast of their works, and say, Have not we done this? Have not we done that? Other blindness speaketh he not of in that chapter. In the fifteenth chapter calleth he those blind leaders of the blind, which, through their own traditions, make the commandment of God to take none effect.

STANDISH.

And Paul speaketh of them, prima *Timo. iv. &c.*

COVERDALE.

1 Tim. iv.   The heretics whom St Paul prophesieth of, 1 Timo. iv., are such as, through their devilish doctrines, forbid men to live in holy wedlock, and command them to abstain from the meats, which God hath created to be received of christian men with thanksgiving.

2 Tim. iii.   The heretics of whom he speaketh, 2 Tim. iii., are such as, among all other vices, are "covetous, boasters, proud, cursed speakers, &c., false accusers, riotous, fierce, despisers of them that are good, traitors, &c. having a shine of godly living, but denying the power thereof, resist the truth, being men of corrupt minds, and lewd in things pertaining to the faith," &c.

Acts xx.   The heretics that he speaketh of in the twentieth of the Acts, are such grievous wolves, as spare not Christ's flock, and speak perverse doctrine to draw disciples after them.

The heretics, whom St Peter speaketh of, are such mockers 2 Pet. iii.
as regard not God's promise, and are not only unlearned, but
also unstable, and pervert Paul's epistles, as they do the
other scriptures also, to their own damnation.

The heretics, whom St Jude speaketh of, are such as, Jude.
among other errors, are " craftily crept into the church, and
turn the grace of our God into wantonness, and deny God the
only Lord, and our Lord Jesus Christ ; even such dreamers
as defile the flesh, despise rulers, &c., speak evil of the things
that they know not, and in such things as they know to be
natural do corrupt themselves as beasts, following the way
of Cain, the error of Balaam for lucre's sake, and the treason
of Core, feeding themselves, making feasts of other men's
kindness, and having men in great reverence because of
advantage," &c.

Have ye not now well described the papistry and the
unholy pillars of your unholy mother, the church of the
wicked?   If ye had joined the second chapter of St Peter's
second epistle and the twenty-third of Matthew to these
places that ye have here alleged, ye had done us the more
pleasure.   But we thank you for pointing us to those scriptures ; we know you now better than we did afore.

Now to Hieremy the prophet. Like as in the nineteenth Jer. xix.
chapter God threateneth destruction to Hierusalem and Tophet,
for shedding of innocent blood, and for their idolatry ; so in
the twenty-third chapter threateneth he sore punishment to Jer. xxiii.
those prophets or preachers, that speak of their own heads,
and not out of God's word.   And in the twenty-seventh Jer. xxvii.
chapter he counselleth king Sedechias and his people, to give
no credence unto those prophets that speak fair words unto
them, and would make them believe that there should come
no such plague as God had threatened.

As for the thirteenth chapter of Ezechiel, which ye allege, Ezek. xiii.
I will heartily desire all christian readers, not only to compare it to the twenty-third of Hieremy ; but also with due
reverence (for so must God's word be entreated) to weigh and
ponder well every sentence thereof. And so doing, I doubt not
but the Holy Ghost shall minister such bright spectacles to
their sight, that they shall clearly discern and see, who be
schismatics, who be false prophets, and who be true.   For I
can wish no man so good a glass to look in, as the scripture.

BARNES.

Take me not here, that I speak against good works.
For they are to be done: and surely they that do them
not, shall never come to the kingdom of God. We must
do them, because they are commanded us of God, to
shew and set forth our profession, not to deserve or
merit; for that is only the death of Christ.

STANDISH.

It is commonly said, No venom or poison is worse, &c.

COVERDALE.

D. Barnes
set forth
good works.

Doth not he set forth good works, that praiseth them,
teacheth men to do them, and threateneth damnation to them
that do them not? Here ye cannot deny, by your own confession, but that he praiseth good works; and yet ye have
reported of him, that he cast off and forsook all duties to our
part belonging. Is it not our duty to praise good works?

STANDISH.

But mark, it is naught that he speaketh afterward, &c.

COVERDALE.

Is it naught and erroneous to say, that we must do good
works, because God hath commanded them? The wise man

Eccles. xxix.

saith: "Take the poor unto thee for the commandment's
sake," &c. Is it not God's commandment to do good unto
the poor?

Moreover, where find you in all holy scripture, that God
hath commanded us to do good works, to the intent that we
should merit or deserve, and not to shew and set forth our

Matt. v.

profession? Must we not "let our light so shine before men,
that they may see our good works, and glorify our Father

Joh. xv.
Rom. vi.

which is in heaven?" Hath not our Saviour "chosen and
ordained us to go and bring forth fruit?" &c. Were we not
made heirs of salvation and baptized, to the intent that we
should now walk in a new life? Are we not dead from the
curse of the law, and married unto Christ, to the intent that
we should now bring forth fruit unto God? Hath not God

Eph. ii.

ordained us to walk in good works? Are we not "chosen of
God to shew now his wonderful works, which hath called us
out of darkness into his marvellous light?" Must we not

"lead an honest conversation in the world, that they which 1 Pet. ii.
backbite us as evil doers, may see our good works, and
praise God?"

Now to do good deeds, to bring forth good fruits, to
walk in a new life, to shew God's wonderful works, to lead
an honest conversation in the world, what is it else, but to
shew and set forth our profession, the life that we have promised and taken us to at the font-stone, even the holy covenant and appointment, that we have made with the eternal
God? Do ye not consider also, that the scripture, appointing 1 Pet. iii.
married women their estate and duty, willeth them to be of
so honest conversation, that even they which as yet will not
believe God's word, may, without the word, be won by their
godly living? And not only this, but so to array themselves
in comely apparel with shamefacedness and discreet behaviour,
without excess, as it becometh women that profess godliness
thorough good works? What can be more plainly spoken
than this? How earnest is the scripture likewise in moving
and commanding us especially, that take in hand to instruct 1 Pet. v.
and teach other, above all things to "shew example of good Tit. ii.
works in the doctrine of God, &c.; that such as resist his
truth may be ashamed of their part, having nothing in us to
report amiss!" And immediately after in the same chapter,
how diligent is the apostle in requiring Titus to exhort
servants to the doing of their duty to their masters, and to
shew all faithfulness? But for what intent? To merit or
deserve immortality? Nay, to the intent that in all things
they may "do worship to the doctrine of God our Saviour,
that the name of God and his doctrine be not evil spoken of."
Thus would he have Timothy also to teach and exhort; and
then saith he these words: "If any man teach otherwise, 1 Tim. vi.
and agreeth not unto the wholesome words of our Lord
Jesus Christ, and the doctrine of godliness, he is puffed up,
and knoweth nothing," &c.

Read ye the text forth, and remember yourself well; consider in what case ye are, and how wide your doctrine dis-
agreeth from the wholesome word of God. If I should say,
ye were puffed up, ignorant, a waste brain, &c. of a corrupt
mind, or robbed of the truth, ye would haply be angry.
Yet be content to let Paul speak to you; for though he rail
not, yet shall ye not find him a flatterer.

STANDISH.

Which thing being true, as the church confesseth, &c.

COVERDALE.

The church of the wicked granteth many more things, than it shall ever be able to prove, except it be with violence and shedding of innocent blood; which is in very deed a fierce, sore, and strong way of probation. Neither be they heretics, that deny this your doctrine; for I have proved unto you by open scriptures, that your doctrine is false.

STANDISH.

Be not our own good works meritorious to ourselves?

COVERDALE.

Isai. lxiv.

Yes, pardie[1]; for the prophet saith, "All our righteousnesses are as filthy rags[2]."

STANDISH.

Whether shall we rather believe St Hierome, &c.

COVERDALE.

1 John v.

"If we receive the witness of men, the witness of God is greater: for this is the witness of God, which he hath testified of his Son, &c.; even that God hath given us everlasting life, and this life is in his Son." St Augustine saith also: "All my hope is in the death of my Lord; his death is my merit, my refuge, my salvation, my life, and my resurrection[3]."

STANDISH.

Which for their detestable opinions deserved justly to be burnt as heretics.

COVERDALE.

If they were not burnt heretics in deed, no force. And if they were just deservers, it is a token that they

[1 pardie: verily.]

[2 The author here follows a different translation of the original.]

[3 This passage is found in August. Manual. c. XXII. Tota spes mea est in morte Domini mei. Mors ejus meritum meum, refugium meum, salus, vita, et resurrectio mea.—Opera, Tom. IX. p. 174. E. Edit. 1541. But the Benedictine editors do not allow this to be a genuine work of Augustine, and with them Cave agrees. See Hist. Lit. Vol. I. p. 249. Edit. 1688.]

meddled the more with righteousness; for no man can justly err, nor justly commit treason.

STANDISH.

What a detestable heresy is it to say, the cause that we be commanded to do good works, is to set forth our profession!

COVERDALE.

Is not our profession the promise and covenant that we have made with God, to seek his glory and our neighbour's profit, even to love him with all our heart, with all our souls, and with all our strength, and our neighbour as ourselves; in the which two points hangeth all the law and the prophets? Are not we bound then, by God's commandment, to set forth the glory of God, our neighbour's profit, and love to them both? Remember, what places of scripture I have pointed you to afore concerning this matter.

STANDISH.

Before whom should we set it forth? before God? He knoweth our profession before.

COVERDALE.

What then? Study alway to have a clear conscience Acts xxiv. toward God and men, after the apostle's ensample.

STANDISH.

Before man? So we may have good works, as the Pharisees had, &c.

COVERDALE.

Though Pharisees do their works to be seen of men, will Matt. vi. you therefore, being a preacher, not give good ensample to other, nor let your light so shine before men, that they 1 Pet. v. seeing your good works, may give the glory unto God? What? are ye so far from the knowledge of this gear, and Matt. v. yet a preacher, a reader, and a post of the church? Who would think, that you (which are so well acquainted with him that can compare the dear blood of Christ to the stinking blood of a swine) should be so far from the understanding of such things? O wicked hogs, whom Satan hath possessed of that sort! Is the worthy price of our redemption come to that worship among you? No marvel

that ye are so blinded in your understanding; for there was
never enemy of Christ's blood, that had yet any clear judgment in his word, till he earnestly repented, and gave himself wholly to the study and life that it teacheth.

BARNES.

I believe that there is a holy church, and a company
of all them that do profess Christ.

STANDISH.

Albeit that every true Christian ought thus to believe, &c.

COVERDALE.

Ye say that every true Christian ought thus to believe;
and yet ye call the same belief erroneous and damnable.   Is
the christian belief erroneous and damnable?   Or is it erroneous and damnable to believe as every christian man ought
to believe?   Thus are ye not only contrary to yourself, but
judge christian men also to be heretics.

Diversity.

STANDISH.

For you judge, as appeareth by your preaching, &c.

COVERDALE.

D. Barnes' words are plain enough. He goeth no further
than the article of your creed, if ye be a christian man.
What will ye more?   Do these his words judge any good
man to be none of Christ's church?   Or be they good men,
that profess not Christ?

STANDISH.

For it cannot be, but either your sect or the other be the
malignant church.

COVERDALE.

To make up
the argu-
ment.

But so it is, that ye, which are of another sect, blaspheme
Christ's blood.   Ergo, ye are of the malignant church.

STANDISH.

Two contraries cannot stand both in one.

COVERDALE.

It is not reason that they should, and yet can ye bring
it so to pass; for ye can prettily[1] well grant to a thing in

[1 prately, old edition.]

one place, and deny the same in another, as I told you oft afore.

STANDISH.

Hinc *Jacobi iii.* Nunquid fons de eodem foramine, &c.

COVERDALE.

It followeth a little after, even in the same place : " If James iii. any man be wise and endowed with learning among you, let him shew the works of his good conversation, in the meekness that is coupled with fear." Which text doth utterly confute your former doctrine, that will not have us do good works, to set forth our profession.

STANDISH.

Unde 2 *Cor. vi.* Quæ societas luci ad tenebras, &c.

COVERDALE.

It followeth immediately in the text: " What part hath 2 Cor. vi. the believer with the infidel ? How accordeth the temple of God with images ?" Now might I ask this question also of you : How do these places of scripture, that ye have now alleged, agree to the confutation of D. Barnes' words, which saith, " I do believe that there is a holy church, and a company of all them that do profess Christ ?"

STANDISH.

Whereby ye prove yourself both an heretic and a traitor.

COVERDALE.

Do ye lay heresy and treason to him, for believing that there is a holy church, and a company of all them that do profess Christ? Sayeth he here any thing else ? And do ye not confess yourself, that every christian man must thus believe, if he will be saved ?

STANDISH.

Making by your devilish doctrine not only us to be the malignant church.

COVERDALE.

To believe that article of the Creed, which D. Barnes here affirmeth, is no doctrine to make you of the malignant church; but your blaspheming of Christ's dear blood, your defacing of his glory, your wresting, perverting, and belying of his holy word, and disagreeing from the wholesome doctrine thereof, maketh you ye may know what, by St Paul's words, 1 Tim. vi.

Ye play here with D. Barnes, though he be dead from this body, as the false prophet Sedechias did with Michee; who, when he had exhorted the king not to break God's commandment, this Sedechias stept forth, among four hundred of his sect, and smote Michee upon the cheek, and said: "What, hath the Spirit of the Lord forsaken me, and spoken unto thee?" Even thus do ye with the dead; whom though ye may not hurt with your fist, yet do ye your worst with your tongue against him. Notwithstanding ye shall be of the malignant church still, for all your facing and bragging, (yea, though ye had ten thousand times four hundred false prophets of your side,) so long as ye resist the manifest truth of God.

2 Chron.
xviii.

STANDISH.

But also our head, the king's grace's majesty, and his honourable council.

COVERDALE.

I dare say, that the king's highness and his honourable council doth judge no malignity to be imputed unto them, when any subject believeth that there is a holy church; for they know, that it is an article necessary to be believed of all christian men. Wherefore this cavillation declareth you plainly to be but a pick-thank in this behalf. Well, yet remember the end of Sedechias: the story is written for your warning. And verily, like as mine humble expectation in the king's highness doth persuade me, so heard I a very famous and prudent councillor of his, who yet is alive, say within these few years, that of all princes living his grace is the greatest enemy to flatterers, when he once hath thoroughly spied them.

A pick-
thank.

The king also hath received his high and supreme office of God, to defend the word, the faith, the congregation and church of God within his dominion, and is no maintainer of any such malignant church. If your doctrine come to light, it will doubtless declare the same.

STANDISH.

By whose laws you be now justly condemned to be burnt.

COVERDALE.

By what law he was condemned, I wot not, no more than I can tell what point of treason was laid unto him. But sure I am, that like as the civil laws of every realm (except the prince grant his pardon) condemn such as are accused by the mouths of many witnesses; so do false witnesses oft-times bring to death even innocent persons, as ye see by the story of Naboth, of Susanna, of holy St Steven in the Acts, and of our Saviour Christ; yea, clean contrary to the judge's mind. Nevertheless, though Cain slay Abel in the bushes, yet will murder come out at the last.

1 Kings xxi.
Dan. xiii.
[Apocr.]
Acts vi.
Matt. xxvi.

STANDISH.

But now to speak of this part of your belief, &c.

COVERDALE.

What is the holy church and company of them that profess Christ, but that true and faithful church, which is ruled by the Holy Ghost according to God's promise; even the congregation of the elect and chosen children of God? What else can ye justly gather of D. Barnes' words, but he confesseth the same, when he sayeth, " I believe that there is a holy church," &c. ?

STANDISH.

For this is the company, that profess Christ with their mouth, &c.

COVERDALE.

So they do also with other good fruits, as well as with their mouth. Now, if this company of Christ's church do profess Christ with their mouth, then have they some injunction of God so to do; for without his commandment will they do nothing, nor consent to that which they know not to be his will. And thus have ye proved yourself at the last, that it is not erroneous to say, how that God hath commanded us to do good works for the setting forth of our profession. Had it not been more worship to you, for to have granted the same at the first, than now with shame to affirm it that ye denied afore ?

Profession
set forth
with the
mouth.

BARNES.

And that all that have suffered and confessed his name be saints, and that all they do praise and laud God in heaven, more than I or any man's tongue can express.

STANDISH.

As you do take it, this is also erroneous, &c.

COVERDALE.

Whatsoever the cause were that he was put to death for, (whereof I am ignorant,) it is no evil token of a christian man at the very point of his death, among other articles of the Creed, to confess, that such a holy church there is, which professeth the name of Christ, and is content to laud and praise it, and to live and die in his cause; neither is it erroneous thus to say. Of arrogancy that ye lay to D. Barnes' charge, I have talked with you afore.

Touching martyrs, like as we have cause sufficient to praise God daily for his word ministered unto us by those martyrs that ye here have named, and for all such as be true followers of them; so have we no little occasion to lament and be sorry, that any man betaking himself to godliness, and making a covenant with God to live unfeignedly after his word, should not profess the same in true fidelity and good works. Our Lord be praised yet, which through the fall of other men hath warned us to beware of unthankfulness! For when they who pretend to be setters up of godliness, are either hypocrites to God, untrue in the affairs of their prince, maintainers of pride, of idleness, of swearing, of excess, and of advoutry in themselves or in their household servants, God's good word must wear the paper, and be jack-out-of-service from other men. Now God shew the right.

God warneth by other men's fall.

BARNES.

And that always I have spoken reverently of saints, and praised them, as much as scripture willed me to do.

STANDISH.

Here he plainly sheweth himself to be an heretic, &c.

COVERDALE.

I am sure that Christ's church hath made no such ordinance, neither given any sentence or judgment, that men should not speak reverently of saints, neither that men shall praise them otherwise than scripture teacheth. How sheweth he himself then to be an heretic in this behalf, that followeth the example of Christ's church, and not of your unholy synagogue? What maketh your definition of heresy to prove, *The definition of heresy.* that he is an heretic, which not only speaketh reverently of saints, but also praiseth them according to the rule of scripture? Verily your definition cometh out of an importunity. Ye might also have defined it thus, and have said, " Αἵρεσις *deducitur ἀπὸ τοῦ αἱροῦμαι, volo, decerno;*" that is to say, *I will so have it, I am at a full point.* For truly I see little in your writing, but wilfulness and obstinate resisting of the manifest truth. Well, God is able to bridle you.

STANDISH.

Also in this his saying, that he will do nothing but that scripture biddeth him, he plainly goeth against scripture, &c.

COVERDALE.

Is he not a worthy apostle, legate, or messenger, that, having commission of his prince, what to say in his message, will speak things of his own head, or more than his master commandeth him? Forsooth ye declare manifestly, whose apostle ye be. But now let us see, how the scripture will maintain this spiritual treason (even treason verily, and no better) against the King of all kings and Lord of all lords.

Christ our Saviour sayeth unto his apostles these words: " As my living Father sent me, so send I you." How did *John xx.* his Father send him? " My doctrine," sayeth he, " is not *John vii.* mine own, but my Father's that hath sent me." " There-*Matt. xxviii.* fore," sayeth he, "go ye your way, and teach all nations, and baptize them, &c.; and teach them to keep all things whatsoever I have commanded you." Ought not stewards to be *1 Cor. iv.* faithful ministers of their masters' goods, to pay every man good money, as they be commanded, and not to give false coin instead of silver and gold? Must we not continue in *2 John* the doctrine of Christ, and speak that thing which is agreeable to God's word? Your doctrine would have us to run *1 Pet. iv.*

at riot, and not to keep us within the bounds that God hath appointed us.

STANDISH.

So that here he proveth himself to have another property of an heretic, which is, to go about with the word of God to destroy the word of God, &c.

COVERDALE.

Like as ye prove not here, with what text of scripture D. Barnes should go about to destroy the scripture; so declare ye manifestly by this your opinion and wresting of the text, to be one yourself, that with the word of God goeth about to destroy the word of God. Now to your three places, that ye bring out of God's word.

Acts xv. Where find ye in the fifteenth chapter of the Acts, that we must obey more than holy scripture biddeth us? First, St Peter confesseth there in that council, that it is a tempting of God to lay any yoke of the ceremonies of Moses' law upon the necks of Christ's disciples, or to trouble the weak consciences of those which lately were turned and converted to the faith: and afore in the same place he confesseth, that God appointed and ordained him to preach the word of the gospel, and maketh mention of none other doctrine. Again, *Acts xv. Galat. ii.* like as by the common consent of the apostles in the same council ye see, that they would not be brought into subjection, nor give place to those false brethren, that would have brought in ceremonies of the law, to bind men's consciences withal; so would they not that the brethren which were turned to Christ should abuse their liberty in him, but *Rom. xiv. 1 Cor. viii.* abstain from certain meats for offending of the weak: which thing also St Paul requireth earnestly in his epistles.

In the sixteenth chapter of the Acts, Paul and Silas preach the word of the Lord; and when Paul saw that to circumcise Timothy was a thing that might be done for the time, and was not required of the Jews as a thing necessary, he was content. Whereby it is manifest, that like as in things indifferent they had alway respect to the time in forbearing weak consciences for a while, so preached they none other doctrine but God's only word.

In the second chapter of the second epistle to the Thessalonians, St Paul, when he hath told them of the great

departing from the faith, doth give thanks to God for calling them to his truth of the gospel; in the which he requireth
them to stand stedfast, and to keep such ordinances, as he
and the other apostles had taught them either by mouth or
by epistle.

Now let me demand of you this question. In the fifteenth Acts xv.
of the Acts, when Peter preacheth the word of the gospel,
and forbiddeth the binding of weak consciences with superstitious things, and consenteth, with the other apostles, to
have such a charitable respect to the time, is that as much
as to will, that men shall obey more than is grounded in
scripture?

In the sixteenth of the Acts, when Paul and Silas preach Acts xvi.
the word of the Lord, and deal gently with the consciences
of the weak according to the time, will they that men shall
obey more than holy scripture teacheth them?

2 Thessa. ii. When St Paul requireth them to stand 2 Thess. ii.
stedfast in the truth of the gospel, and to keep such ordinances as he and the other apostles had taught them, either
by mouth or in their epistles, willeth he them to obey more
than is contained in holy scripture?

Thus is it evident whereabout ye go, namely, even by
your false alleging of such places of God's word to destroy
the word of God. This is verily, as ye say yourself, the
property of an heretic, and this property learn ye of the
father of all heresy, even father Satan; who by *Angelis suis* Matt. iv.
mandavit, &c., would prove, that a man may tempt his
Lord God.

But like as Satan, wresting that place of scripture, which
made most against him, was commanded by our Saviour to
avoid; so be ye sure, that your false doctrine cannot stand.
Daub your wall and spare not; for Ezechiel telleth you plainly, Ezek. xiii.
that God will send such a shower of rain among all lying
prophets, as shall overthrow it. Your labour is but lost, so
long as ye daub your wall with untempered mortar.

STANDISH.

*Also, where he saith that he hath ever spoken reverently
of saints, &c.*

COVERDALE.

Ye granted afore his words to be true, when he said,

that all such as for confessing Christ's name and for his sake do suffer death, are saints in heaven.   This reverent talking and praising of saints did ye allow afore; and now contrary

Diversity. to your own words ye say, that ye wot not whether he ever spake reverently of them or no.   Yet confess ye, that ye have heard him forty times.   Who will now trust you, that are so double in your words?

BARNES.

And that our lady, I say, she was a virgin immaculate and undefiled, and that she is the most purest virgin that ever God created, and a vessel elect of God, of whom Jesus Christ should be born.

STANDISH.

Here yet ignorantly, &c., he goeth further than the scripture speaketh, &c.

COVERDALE.

Be these his words out of the bounds of scripture, or not according to the scripture?   Read them over again.

STANDISH.

He would never willingly grant any thing but that is in scripture, &c.

COVERDALE.

What a report Standish giveth of D. Barnes. Then like as ye prove him to have been a true messenger of God in granting to the holy scripture, (which by your own confession is God's very word;) so declare ye, that if he revoked any thing that is in it, or granted ought contrary unto it, it was done against his will.   Have ye not now a great cause to make such triumphing of revocations in your sermons?

STANDISH.

Albeit here with the church he doth profess, that our lady did continue a virgin still, &c.

COVERDALE.

Doth not the scripture affirm this doctrine, that the mother of our Saviour is the purest virgin that ever God created?   Will not the prophecies of Christ's birth, the performance of the same, and the practices of the Holy Ghost in Christ's blessed mother, allow this doctrine? Have ye noted the work of God in her no better? If she had any need of you, ye shew her but a faint friendship, in reporting that her most pure virginity hath none other ground but the authority of your church. Verily, such your doting doctrine will make both you and your church be less set by.

Isai. vii.
Matt. 1.
Luke ii.

STANDISH.

Deus enim tantam eam fecit, inquit quidam, &c.

COVERDALE.

Is not your doctrine now well sealed with butter? When ye have presumed to controul God's word, and to call the blessed mother of Christ with other names than the Holy Ghost giveth her; now to ratify and confirm your false matter, ye bring in an heretic to help you. Cannot Christ's worthy mother keep still the gracious names the holy Trinity hath given her, but she must now have a sort of heretical ruffians to become new godfathers unto her? Call her, as God's word teacheth you, full of grace, blessed, immaculate virgin, &c. Pray to God, that ye may follow the footsteps of her constant faith, her fervent charity, and godly love, her most meek and humble behaviour, her unfeigned truth, &c.: and when ye talk in matters of Christ's religion, bring forth plain and manifest words of his scripture, and no Romish heretic, nor a text out of frame, to prove your purpose withal.

BARNES.

Then said Mr Sheriff: "You have said well of her before." And he, being afraid that Mr Sheriff had been, or should be aggrieved with any thing that he should say, said: "Mr Sheriff, if I speak any thing that you will me not, do no more but beck me with your hand, and I will straightway hold my peace. For I will not be disobedient in any thing, but will obey."

STANDISH.

Now, as he feigneth, he would give no slander or offence. Sed sero sapiunt Phryges.

COVERDALE.

At this point ye are with D. Barnes, that, though he be out of this life, yet whatsoever he said in this Protestation, or did at the time thereof, ye judge him to the worst, and slander him.   But your own proverb that ye bring in, doth

Sero venisti. admonish you, that it is too late; for though ye belie him and slander him never so much, it cannot hurt him.

STANDISH.

[Psal. xiv.] *Now he saith, he is afraid to displease.* Trepidaverunt timore, ubi non erat timor, &c.

COVERDALE.

Like as ye refer to him the words which are not his own, so report ye of him, that he was afraid where no fear was.   But was there no fear at the fire-side?   The manhood of our Saviour Christ feared death, and so did that

Standish is a manly man. holy king Ezechias.   As for you, ye must needs be of some bold and stout kind, that can kill a dead man.

But how serveth those words of the psalm to this your purpose?   The Holy Ghost speaketh of such wicked workers, as eat up God's people like bread, call not upon God, are afraid to see God standing on righteous men's side, and mock

Standish per-verteth the words of the thirteenth Psalm[1]. poor men for putting their trust in God.   How maketh this scripture now to prove, that there is no fear, where a man seeth death present before his eyes?   O wicked mockers with God's holy word!

STANDISH.

Now see, I pray you, how obedient he saith he will be, which before time was ever disobedient, &c.

COVERDALE.

Ye say much, and prove little, touching this man, whose present Protestation, and his book written afore, declareth

An ensample of obedience in D. Barnes. plainly his obedience toward his prince; whose wholesome commandment if he have at any time disobeyed, contrary to this his doctrine and example, I am the more sorry: but yet have ye not proved it to be so.

Touching bishops, (which are to be esteemed according to their estate,) I wot not what disobedience ye have to prove

[1 Bishop Coverdale quotes according to the notation of the Septuagint Version and the Vulgate.]

against him. Such bishops as labour in the word of God and in the doctrine thereof, are to be counted worthy of double honour: therefore in hearkening unto such, he did well; and if he despised such, he despised Christ. But if he followed St John's bidding, and did not receive such false apostles as bring not the doctrine of Christ, then can ye not justly blame him.

1 Tim. v.
Matt. x.
2 John.

BARNES.

After this there was one that asked him, what he said of the sacrament of the altar. Then said he to Mr. Pope, which was there present: "Mr. Pope, ye know, and Mr. Riche, if ye be alive, that there was one accused before my lord chancellor for denying of the sacrament; and for fault of a better, I was assigned to the examination of him in the gallery. And after long reasoning and disputation I declared and said, that the sacrament being rightly used and according to scripture doth, after the word spoken by the priest, change the substance of the bread and wine into the body and blood of Christ. Were not these my words?" said he. "Yea," said Mr. Pope. "Then bear me witness," said he, "that I err not in the sacrament."

STANDISH.

Although you did not deny that sacrament, yet have you, &c.

COVERDALE.

Ye call it slanderous railing, when a man with God's word doth earnestly rebuke such horrible abuses, as antichrist and his malignant church hath brought in among christian people: so loth are ye to consent unto God's word, or to use any thing according to his holy institution. What could it then have helped you, if he had opened his mind farther, seeing that in his so godly and honest request ye ascribe naughtiness unto him? He did but shew, that he would have the sacrament rightly used and according to holy scripture, and ye are not content with him. Yet well worth the Corinthians! for though they were fallen into abuse about this holy mystery, and about other things, we read not that they

Standish would not have the sacrament used according to the holy scripture.

[COVERDALE, II.]   27

spurned against the Holy Ghost, as you do, when they were called to reformation.

STANDISH.

See also, I pray you, how he saith, &c.

COVERDALE.

If you should say that, for lack of a better, ye did write against this Protestation of D. Barnes, would ye therefore be judged to think, that there were not many better learned men in England to take such a matter in hand than you?

BARNES.

Then said he, " Have ye any thing else to say?" There was one then asked him his opinion of praying to saints. Then said he: " Now of saints you shall hear mine opinion. I have said before somewhat, I think, of them, how that I believe they are in heaven and with God, and that they are worthy of all the honour that scripture willeth them to have. But I say, throughout all scripture we are not commanded to pray to any saints : therefore I cannot nor will not preach to you, that saints ought to be prayed unto. For then should I preach you a doctrine of mine own head."

STANDISH.

There is an old heresy that saith, Saints be not yet in heaven, &c.

COVERDALE.

Is this your next way to confute him that saith, We are not commanded in scripture to pray to any saints? Ye brawl with the dead man, that saith nothing against you in this article of saints being in heaven.

STANDISH.

How can it be in scripture, thou impudent heretic, the prayer unto saints ?

COVERDALE.

Be good to the poor man, and take not the matter so

hot. He goeth not about to prove, that your praying to saints is grounded in scripture.

STANDISH.

As for in the time of the old law, &c.

COVERDALE.

The doctrine of God is, that Christ is the Lamb which Rev. xiii. hath been slain since the beginning of the world, that is, even he, whose power and deliverance hath cleansed and saved all them that ever put their trust in him. Christ Jesus yester- Heb. xiii. day, and to-day, and the same continueth for ever.

STANDISH.

Therefore concerning praying to saints, &c.

COVERDALE.

Must we believe the testimony of men, without it be grounded on God's word? Are ye become such an apostle? Because the church and congregation of Christ must discern, 1 Cor. xiv. judge, try, and examine all manner of doctrine, and so to 1 John iv. eschew the evil and keep the good, hath it therefore autho- 1 Thess. v. rity to make any new article, or to receive a doctrine contrary to God's word? Because Christ hath promised his John xiv. holy Spirit of truth to be alway in his faithful congregation, & xvi. shall they therefore make, ordain, set up, or believe ought that is contrary to his own teaching?

STANDISH.

Dost thou set no more by the authority of it, than so; inasmuch as St Augustine said, Non crederem evangelio, nisi crederem ecclesiæ? &c.

COVERDALE.

Even as ye pervert the words of holy scripture, so do ye with St Augustine; as ye chop and change with it, so do ye with him. And as ye allege the scripture for another Standish per- purpose than the plain circumstance of the text meaneth, so verteth St Augustine's do ye here with this holy doctor. For your purpose is with words. St Augustine's words to prove, that your church by her authority may make new articles, and that we are bound to believe as she believeth, though the same be not grounded in scripture. But if men diligently mark St Augustine's saying, the occasion of his writing, and the circumstance thereof, it shall be evident, that ye are as like him in understanding, as the moon is like a green cheese.

St Augustine, perceiving the great hurt that was growing through the doctrine of wicked Manicheus, took in hand to confute him and his sect; his errors were so noisome and devilish. For he had not only feigned a new doctrine of his own, and named himself Christ's apostle; but also maintained the heresy, which the anabaptists lately held, that the Son of God took not the nature of man of the blessed virgin, and denied rulers to bear office, denied marriage, denied certain kinds of meats to be of God, or to be granted unto christian men; taught also that some men's souls die with their bodies, despised the exterior word of God and ministration thereof, and sought other visions without it: and many other fond and wicked opinions had he, unknown to the holy church and flock of Christ.

The sect of the Manichees.

Now for the repelling of such pestilent doctrine, St Augustine, among other things, wrote one special book against a certain epistle of the Manichees, which was called *Epistola Fundamenti;* and when he had shewed the occasions, which moved him to abide still within the unity of Christ's catholic church, then in the fifth chapter he shewed the cause, that moved him rather to give credence unto Christ's gospel, than to Manicheus; where among other he saith these words: *Nostis enim me statuisse nihil a vobis prolatum temere credere,* &c. "For ye know," saith he, "that I am determined to give no hasty credence to any thing that ye speak of your own heads. I demand therefore, Who is that Manicheus? Ye answer, An apostle of Christ. I believe it not. Now what canst thou say, or do, thou shalt not obtain; for thou didst promise knowledge of the truth, and now thou wilt compel me to believe the thing that I know not. Peradventure thou wilt read me the gospel, and thereby wilt thou essay to affirm the person of Manicheus. If I should find any man then, which as yet believeth not the gospel, what shouldest thou do to him that saith unto thee, I believe not? As for me, I should not believe the gospel, unless the authority of the catholic church did move, teach, or warn me. Seeing that I was obedient unto them, when they said, Be-

Contra Epistolam Manichei, quam vocant Fundamenti.

St Augustine's words.

Ego vero evangelio non crederem, nisi me catholicæ ecclesiæ commoveret auctoritas.

lieve the gospel; why may I not obey them, when they say
unto me, Believe not Manicheus?" &c.[1]

By the circumstance now of St Augustine's words, it is The doctrine of St Augustine.
evident, first, that he would believe no such doctrine as men
brought up of their own heads. Secondly, that he would
believe no uncertain doctrine, nor that he knew not to be
true. Thirdly, that the occasion which moved him to believe the gospel, was the whole consent and authority of the
catholic or universal church. Now like as he reporteth not
of them, that they preached any other doctrine unto him,
save the gospel, so saith he not, that he believed any other
learning, save only it. And in confuting of Manicheus'
error, he bringeth none other doctrine but the scripture, as
it is manifest in the same fifth chapter of his book.

What help have ye now in St Augustine's words, either
to prove praying to saints, or that a particular church may
by her authority make any article necessary to be believed,
except it be grounded in scripture? Ye meant somewhat, Standish choppeth up St Augustine's words.
when ye chopped up St Augustine's words of that fashion.
It is not for nought that ye so have perverted his saying,
and read it otherwise than it standeth in his book. For
these are his words: "I should not believe the gospel, unless
the authority of the catholic church did move me." Now is
καθολικὸς as much to say as *universalis*. Which word like καθολικός.
as ye leave out in your lection, so follow ye the mind of
Franciscus Maronis[2], such another holy father as was your Franciscus Maronis.
inquit quidam; who, coming long after St Augustine, did
gather of these his foresaid words, that the authority of the
church is greater than the authority of holy scripture: where-

[1 Nostis enim me statuisse nihil a vobis prolatum temere credere.
Quæro ergo, quis sit ille Manichæus? Respondebitis, Apostolus Christi.
Non credo. Jam quid dicas aut facias, non habebis: promittebas enim
scientiam veritatis; et nunc quod nescio cogis ut credam. Evangelium
forte mihi lecturus es, et inde Manichæi personam tentabis asserere.
Si ergo invenires aliquem, qui evangelio nondum credit, quid faceres
dicenti tibi, Non credo? Ego vero evangelio non crederem, nisi me
catholicæ ecclesiæ commoveret auctoritas. Quibus ergo obtemperavi
dicentibus, Credite evangelio; cur iis non obtemperem dicentibus mihi,
Noli credere Manichæo?—August. con. Epist. Manichæi, quam vocant
Fundamenti. Cap. v. Op. Tom. VI. p. 26. A. B. ed. 1541.]

[2 A native of France and a pupil of Duns Scotus. For an account
of this person see Cave, Hist. Lit. Vol. I. p. 15. A. He flourished
A.D. 1315.]

as St Augustine meant nothing less; but teacheth us, that whosoever bringeth up any opinion, or setteth up any doctrine, we shall receive none, but that which agreeth with the manifest doctrine of the universal church of Christ: that is, we shall hold us to that doctrine, which was taught by the prophets, by the apostles, and by such other as were true followers of them in Christ's holy congregation and church.

STANDISH.

Is it not still fundamentum et columna veritatis? &c.

COVERDALE.

Tim. iii. The universal congregation and multitude of them that believe in Christ is still the house of God, the church of the living God, the pillar and establishment of the truth. For there dwelleth God, with his mercy, grace, truth, forgiveness, &c. Neither did the apostles contrary to Christ's former institution, when they, to set up his name, which then was so sore spurned at, did baptize in the same, if ye remember well the prerogative of holy baptism, and the presence of the blessed Trinity therein.

STANDISH.

Paul, the vessel of election, fifteen hundred years and more past, desired the Romans, cap. xv., the Collo. [Coloss.] *cap iv., the Tessa.* 1 *Tessa. v.* [Thessa.], *to pray for him, &c.*

COVERDALE.

I turned not over two leaves of your treatise since I read these your words, where ye say thus, "How can it be in scripture, thou impudent heretic, the prayer unto saints?"

Standish will prove by scripture the thing that cannot be therein. Lord Jesu! what mean ye, man? Will ye by scripture prove that thing, which, as ye yourself confess, cannot be in scripture? Do ye not grant yourself, that the holy scripture is the very word of God? Will ye then by God's holy word prove that thing, which cannot be therein? Will ye belie the word of God? Say ye not yourself in another place afore, that it is an abominable vice to slander it? To what point now have ye brought that worshipful doctrine of your unholy mother, the malignant church, which teacheth, that we must now pray unto St Paul and other saints? Now is his request such, that if we should fulfil it

yet for him, as well as when he was living upon earth, then
should we desire God to be good to his holy saints that are
out of this life. And then, God save our Lady, help St Paul,
and comfort sweet St Anthony!

A mocker are ye with God's holy word, and a shameful
slanderer thereof; therefore as unworthy to be answered
unto every vain sentence of your unstable doctrine. So leave
I your long disputation therein, desiring all christian readers
to note well what scriptures ye bring forth, and to compare
the same unto the open text, and then try, which of our
two doctrines is most agreeable to God's holy word.

The doctrine of the prophets of Christ our Saviour, of
his holy apostles, and of such as have and do follow them in
the catholic or universal church and congregation of God, is
his holy word and scripture; which, as holy St Paul dare
avow, is able to instruct us unto salvation, which is through
the faith in Christ Jesu, &c. If your article, therefore, of
praying to saints that be out of this life, were a thing belonging to salvation, no doubt the same holy scripture of God
would have taught it.

The ancient, firm, stable, and true doctrine of Christ's
catholic or universal church, is this, that like as Christ Jesus
took upon him our flesh and blood without sin, and delivered
us from eternal death and hell, so is he still our merciful and
faithful high priest in things concerning God, to make agreement for our sins, and able to succour such as are tempted.
He is the seat of grace, to whom if we resort, we may
receive mercy and find grace to help in time of need: he is
able also ever to save them that come unto God by him, and
liveth ever to make intercession for us, yea, and appeareth
now for us before the face of God.

This doctrine is confirmed by those same texts of scripture that ye bring in, 1 John ii., John xiv., 1 Tim. ii.; and
yet without open scriptures are ye not ashamed to resist it.

We are commanded throughout all holy scripture, both
of the old and new Testament, to pray unto Almighty God,
to call upon him, to make our petitions unto him, and to ask
of him whatsoever we lack.

We have his true and faithful promise, that if we so do,
we shall be heard, we shall have our request, we shall find
that we seek, we shall be delivered, &c.

Margin notes:

Vain words require no answer but reproof.

2 Tim iii. Holy scrip- ture is suffi- cient.

Christ is our high priest. Heb. ii.

Heb. v. The seat of grace.

Heb. vii.

Heb. ix.

Matt. vii. Luke xi. Psal. xlix. Jer. xxix.

Psal. xc. & cxlv. Matt. vii. John xvi. Isai. xxx.

We have ensamples innumerable, that all those faithful people whom the scripture maketh mention of, did make their petitions and prayer to none other but unto God, while *Acts x. &*
xii.   they were in this life.   Let Cornelius, whom we spake of afore, and the practice of the primitive church, bear record.

Shall we now refuse God's holy commandment, think scorn of his loving promise, despise the ensamples of his catholic and universal church, and defy God's holy ordinance, as ye do, and run at riot with your doctrine? Away from *Psal. cxix.*   us, ye wicked! the commandments of our God will we keep, and not yours.

STANDISH.

Which took our sins on him, Pœnam pro peccatis, 1 Pet. ii. &c.

COVERDALE.

Ye taught afore, wresting many scriptures for your *Diversity in*
Standish
doctrine.   purpose, that every man must satisfy for the punishment belonging unto sin; and now ye grant, that Christ took the pain upon him therefore.   As much hold is there at your doctrine, as at an eel's tail.

STANDISH.

But we have more means concerning intercession, &c.

COVERDALE.

The scripture is manifest, that every one of us in this life is bound to pray for another; and daily occasions have we of such petitions and exhortations, as appertain to our estate.   As for praying to saints that be out of this life, ye have mine answer already.

BARNES.

Notwithstanding whether they pray for us or no, that I refer to God.

STANDISH.

A good christian man would have gone no further than the congregation of Christ's church, that is to say, in this region the king's majesty with his learned council.

COVERDALE.

Like as your unreverent handling of the holy scriptures afore rehearsed, and your wicked doctrine against the same, declareth you to be none of Christ's church, unless ye repent and turn; so do ye here exempt yourself from that holy congregation. Marvel not therefore though, when I see you follow your unholy mother, and not Christ's dear spouse, I call you now and then her own white son. ^{Standish excludeth himself.}

In this region of England, ye say, the congregation of Christ's church is the king's majesty with his learned council. But is this a sufficient definition? What a comfort is this now for so many of the king's subjects, both learned and unlearned, to hear that they are not of Christ's congregation! Is it a great consolation for the foot to be none of the body?

Ye repute D. Barnes no good christian man, because he would not define, whether saints pray for us or no, but referred that unto God, and not to the king's majesty and his learned council. What will ye make of the king's grace? A prince that had rather have secret things referred unto him, than unto God, the only knower of all secrets? Or do ye esteem the king's learned council to be such men, as will give judgment in things that be not evident? Or think ye them to be ignorant of the scripture, which forbiddeth men to search out or to meddle with secret things, that God hath not commanded? ^{Prov. xxv. Eccl. iii.}

Barnes.

And if saints do pray for you, then I trust within this half hour to pray for you, Mr Sheriff, and for every christian man living in the faith of Christ, and dying in the same as a saint. Wherefore if the dead may pray for the quick, then I will surely pray for you.

Standish.

O damnable presumption, &c.

Coverdale.

Because this man trusted, thorough the only mercy of God in Christ, to pass from this death unto life, ye note damnable presumption, arrogant presumption, and presumptuous arrogancy in him. And because ye may seem to have scripture to prove, that D. Barnes would temerously appoint and determine the time himself; for his so saying ye bring in,

Quod pater posuit in sua potestate, as right as a ram's horn, and as nigh to the purpose, as Paul's steeple and Mount Falcon. At the time of the ascension of our Saviour, when the apostles were come together, they asked him and said: "Lord, shalt thou at this time set up the kingdom of Israel again?" He said unto them: "It belongeth not unto you to know the times and seasons, which the Father hath kept in his own power," &c. A like answer to such another question giveth he in another place, and saith: "Of that day and hour knoweth no man, no, not the angels of heaven, but the Father only."

What maketh this now to prove, that he which, according to Christ's promise, trusteth to pass from this death to life, doth temerously appoint and determine the same time, day, or season, which our Saviour there speaketh of? or that he is either presumptuous or arrogant, which, according to the example of holy scripture, is certain and sure, that after the destruction of his body he hath an everlasting dwelling in heaven? Have ye not now alleged the scripture well to the purpose? Ye would have men believe, as it appeareth by your doctrine, that when they depart hence, they shall go from the hall into the kitchen, or else into the hot kiln of your purgatory.

STANDISH.

Look what case he is in, that thus ended his life, &c.

COVERDALE.

To prove here that saints pray for us in heaven, ye make a long disputation, and with the scriptures ye do as ye were wont. They have love yet, ye say, and therefore they pray for us, and are our advocates. I answer, The same places of scripture ye bring in yourself, are most against you; for they declare manifestly, that it is the office of Christ to make intercession for us, and that he is with the Father our advocate, which obtaineth grace for our sins. The saints then that be in heaven, knowing this eternal will of God, love us not so, that they desire to be, neither can they be, against it.

It is a token, that your doctrine hath but a weak foundation, when ye go about to prove it by a dream, yea, and that out of such a book, as serveth not for the confirmation of the doctrine of Christ's church: for though it be read among

Acts i.

Mark xiii.
Matt. xxiv.

Joh. v.

2 Cor. v.

Heb. vii.
1 John ii.

2 Mac. xv.
The dream of
Judas Mac-
cabeus.

the stories of other books, yet did not the church receive it Prolog. in
libros Salo-
monis. among the canonical scriptures in St Hierome's time[1].

Neither can ye prove that book lawful by any saying of Luke xxiv. Christ; for throughout all the new Testament he maketh mention of none, but of the Law, the Prophets, and the Psalms, and biddeth not search any other scriptures, but such as bear John v. record and testimony of him.

The fifteenth of Jeremy proveth, (as doth also the seventh, the eleventh, the fourteenth of his book,) that God will not be entreated, where his word is trodden under foot, and where men will needs spurn against it. And verily in all the scripture could ye not have brought in a more manifest place to confute your own doctrine, if it be compared to the fourteenth of Ezechiel.

The sixteenth of Luke proveth nothing for your purpose; in that Abraham prayed not to God, when he was desired. But like as it proveth that there is no redemption in hell, nor time of acceptable repentance and forgiveness after this life; so proveth it evidently, that we ought to hold us to the only word and scripture of God, and not to look for other doctrines, visions, dreams, or revelations.

The place Apoca. vi. proveth, that the voice of Abel's Gen. iv. blood and of such as are slain for the word of God, crieth vengeance from the earth, and under the altar, as St John saith in his vision; and that all such as are malicious per- Matt. xxiii. secutors thereof, are guilty of the righteous blood that is shed upon earth.

St Peter's shadow proveth your doctrine but weakly, Acts v. except ye can make us believe that there be shadows in heaven. No more doth St Paul's napkin, unless ye can Acts xix. prove, that he hath not yet left wiping of his nose.

But where learn ye to belie the word of God? Where find ye in scripture, that Peter's shadow or Paul's napkin could heal the sick? Doth the text say so? Because the people brought their sick into Peter's shadow, did it therefore Acts v. heal them? Peter confesseth himself, that it was not his Acts iii. own power, which made the lame man whole. St Luke also Acts xix.

[1 Sicut ergo Judith, et Tobiæ, et Machabæorum libros legit quidem ecclesia, sed eos inter canonicas scripturas non recipit; sic et hoc, &c. —Hieron. in Prov. Eccles. et Cant. Cantic. Præfat. Tom. III. p. 346. Antverp. 1579.]

reporteth, that "God wrought no small miracles by the hands
Matt. ix. of Paul." And as Christ our Saviour himself witnesseth, that
it was not his vesture, but the woman's faith, which made
Mark xvi. her whole, (though she touched it;) so saith St Mark, that
"the Lord wrought with the apostles, and confirmed the word
with tokens following."

Moreover, whereas St Paul desired to be loosed, and to be
present with Christ, what proveth that the praying to saints?
Phil. i. He said in the same place, that it were more needful for them
to have him yet living among them. Which thing were not
so, if this poor article were so necessary as ye make it. But
Paul's words shall be true still: for great need have we of
many such as he was, if it were for nothing else, but to
preach with his mouth (as he hath done in his epistles)
against your and all other such false doctrines.

STANDISH.

*Nonne confortatus est principatus eorum? Psalm
cxxxviii.*

COVERDALE.

Like as that scripture maketh no mention of any such
The Psalm cxxxix. article as ye imagine; so doth the content of the psalm set
forth the wonderful care and provision, that God maketh for
us; and teacheth us, that God's secret counsels and thoughts
are too high for our capacity.

STANDISH.

Hinc Jero. adversus Vigilantium, &c.

COVERDALE.

C. de Isaac. St Ambrose saith: "Christ is our mouth by the which
we speak unto the Father, our eye by the which we see the
Father, our right hand by the which we offer unto the
Father[1]." Without whose intercession neither we, nor all
saints, have anything with God.

STANDISH.

If you say, Saints do not hear us, &c.

[1 Ipse, Christus scil, sit oculus noster, ut per illum videamus
Patrem; ipse vox nostra, per quem loquamur ad Patrem; ipse dextera,
per quem Deo Patri sacrificium nostrum deferamus.—S. Ambros. De
Isaac et Anima Liber. cap. 8. Opera, Tom. I. p. 380. Ed. Paris. 1696.]

COVERDALE.

What knowledge the saints have, it is truly above my capacity; but well I wot, that the scripture of the old Testament ascribeth only unto God the knowledge of men's hearts. Whereof the gospels also bear record sufficient, and so doth the first of the Acts. Now is it manifest likewise, that as the prayer which cometh from the heart is most acceptable, so doth our Saviour bid us pray unto our Father in secret.

1 Kings viii. 1 Chron. vi. Luke v. vi. xi. xvi.

Matt. ix. xii. Mark ii.

Matt. vi.

Whereas ye bring in the example of Abraham, and the work of God shewed unto him in this life, for to serve your present purpose, it proveth that ye are an unreverent handler of God's word: for the text is plain, that God did there shew unto Abraham, being yet in this life, the destruction of the Sodomites, of his only accustomed goodness and mercy; because Abraham was under his covenant, and did faithfully cleave to his promise, and because he knew that Abraham would command his children and household to keep the way of the Lord, &c. To affirm your purpose then by this place, is even as much as to go about to prove, that saints in heaven have children yet and households to teach in the way of the Lord.

Gen. xviii.

STANDISH.

Whereas the least of them, Qui minor est, &c.

COVERDALE.

Like as of a comparative degree ye make a superlative, and wrest the words to Abraham, that our Saviour spake of John the Baptist; even so to the estate that saints be now in apply ye those words, which St John speaketh of the estate, that God's elect shall have at the second appearing of Christ; even when they shall be like him, when their bodies shall rise uncorruptible, as his is risen, and when he shall change their vile body, that it may be like fashioned unto his glorious body.

Luke vii.

1 John iii.

1 Cor. xv.

Phil. iii.

Again, ye said before, that there were no saints in heaven afore Christ's ascension. And now to prove, that the least of the saints in heaven is more entirely beloved of God than Abraham was in this life, ye allege the words that were spoken long before the death of Christ, *Qui minor est in regno, &c.* Remember yourself well, what a clerkly part ye play with that text.

As for *Sanctorum Communionem*, it is the declaration of the holy catholic or universal church of Christ, that they are a company or fellowship of all such as be sanctified in Christ's blood, and are partakers of his merits, and members one of another. But no probation is it, that saints in heaven do pray for us, if ye note well the description thereof, by St Paul's doctrine.

1 Cor. xii.

Now if ye will prove your purpose by the angels' offices, then must ye prove, that saints are ministering spirits, sent for their sakes which shall be heirs of salvation. But that will be hard for you to do. Neither doth the twentieth chapter of Luke help your matter any thing at all; for, though ye chop up the text at your pleasure with the shortest, these are our Saviour's words: "The children of this world do marry and be married; but they that shall be counted worthy of yonder world and the resurrection from the dead, shall neither marry nor be married, for they can die no more; for they are like unto the angels," &c. This answer now of our Saviour to the Sadducees, as it confuteth their heresy, so doth it prove, that the children of God in heaven be like the angels, in life, in immortality, and in that they are as free from the necessity of marriage, as the angels be; but it proveth not that they are like angels in all things: for then should they have no bodies to be raised up at the general resurrection.

Heb. i.

Luke xx.

STANDISH.

But also that their merits do profit us, as by example we do read, Gen. xxvi., &c.

COVERDALE.

Gen. xxvi.

Whereas Almighty God saith unto Isaac, "Unto thy seed will I give all this land, &c. because Abraham was obedient unto my voice," &c.; upon this are ye not ashamed to say, that the cause is only thorough the merits of his father Abraham? Now saith not the text so, but thus: "Unto thee and thy seed will I give all this land, and will perform mine oath that I sware unto thy father Abraham," &c. This scripture then like as it proveth, according to St Paul's words, that "they which are of faith are blessed with faithful

Gal. iii.

Abraham;" so declareth it manifestly, that this same blessing cometh of God's promise in and thorough the Seed of Abraham and Isaac, that is, even thorough Christ.

But why bring ye in this or any other place of the old Testament to prove, that the merits of saints in heaven do profit us; seeing ye say yourself, that afore Christ's ascension there were none in heaven, and seeing also that those virtues of Abraham and David were things practised here, and not in heaven? God is my record, I wonder greatly, what ye mean, thus to dally with his word.

Touching merits, I have answered you already; but St Paul answereth you better, and saith, that God, giving us his dear Son, hath given us all things with him, and that in him dwelleth all fulness, so that we are complete in him. Sure I am also, that no true servant of God will be otherwise minded, than was holy John Baptist, which said, that "out of Christ's fulness all we receive grace," &c. and that "grace and truth cometh by Jesus Christ." If the merits then that ye speak of be any part of grace and truth, then must ye needs grant, that we receive them only of him. But surely ye have some ungracious and false matter in hand. *Rom. viii. Col. i. ii. John i.*

STANDISH.

He speaketh nothing of our works after our justification, but only of works before faith; which indeed are not meritorious, &c.

COVERDALE.

Afore, to prove by Cornelius' works, that our justification, deserved only by the death of Christ, is a false justification[1], ye say, that his good works before he was justified, something deserved that he should be called into the congregation of our Saviour, and so thorough God's mercy his works did deserve much of Almighty God. These are your own words. And now, clean contrary to the same, ye grant, that works before faith are not meritorious. Thus by your own words condemn ye your own doctrine. *Diversity in Standish's doctrine.*

But though every good work done in true faith after God's commandment shall be rewarded, and hath his promise annexed unto it, as, if I be merciful unto my neighbour, God hath promised to have mercy on me again; shall that reward *Matt. v. xviii. Gal. iii*

[1 See before, p. 379.]

be given for my works' sake, and not rather of his own pro-
2 Cor. iii. mise and blessing in Jesu Christ? Is not all our sufficiency
Phil. ii. of God? Can we think a good thought of ourselves? Is it
not God, which worketh in us both the will and the deed?
" When God rewardeth any good work, doth he not crown his
August. own gifts in us[1]?" Stop ye your mouth then, and know-
Rom. iii. ledge yourself to be in God's danger, and in his debt. Why
Ephes. ii. boast ye of your merits, against the doctrine of God's word?
Luke xvii. Why grant ye not with St Luke, whom ye allege yourself,
that " when ye have done all such things as are commanded
Rom. viii. you, ye are an unprofitable servant?" and with St Paul, that
" the pains taken in this life are not worthy of the glory for
to come?" Do ye not say yourself also these words : " We must
think and surely believe, that all cometh of Christ's liberality,
which freely did call us and love us, before we loved him?"
What practice then of any worldly prince can prove this truth
to be false? Your own words and sentences destroy your
doctrine of merits. Follow St Augustine's counsel then, and
" boast not of men's merits ; but let the grace of God, which
De prædest.
sanc. reigneth through Jesus Christ, have all the pre-eminence[2]."
And if ye have any works following the free and liberal vo-
cation of God, then grant with Chrysostom, that " they are
his reward and your duty, and that the gifts of God are his
own benignity, grace, and greatness of his own liberality[3]."

BARNES.

Well, have ye got any thing more to say? Then
called he Mr Sheriff, and said, " Have you any articles
against me, for the which I am condemned?" And the
sheriff answered, "No." Then said he, "Is there here any
man else, that knoweth wherefore I die, or that by my
preaching hath taken any error? Let them now speak,

[1 Cum Deus coronat merita nostra, nihil aliud coronat quam mu-
nera sua.—August. Sixto Presbytero con. Pelag. Epist. cv. Op. Tom.
II. p. 96, M. Ed. 1541. Compare also, De Grat. et Lib. Arbitr. ad Va-
lentinum. Tom. VII. p. 282, E. F.; Enarrat. in Psalm. xcviii. (xcix).
Tom. VIII. p. 241, D.; and Enarrat. in Psalm. cii. (ciii). p. 252, I. K.]

[2 Humana merita conticescant, et regnet, quæ regnat, Dei gratia
per Jesum Christum, unicum Dei Filium, Dominum nostrum.—August.
de Prædestinatione Sanctorum. Cap. 15. Opera. Tom. VII. p. 270, H.]

[3 The Editor has not been able to discover this passage.]

and I will make them answer." And no man answered. Then said he, "Well, I am condemned by the law to die, and, as I understand, by an act of parliament; but wherefore, I cannot tell, but belike for heresy: for we are like to be burnt."

STANDISH.

Articles against thee? What articles didst thou revoke at the Spittle, &c.?

COVERDALE.

A very spittle fashion is it, no doubt, to ask questions of the dead. And I suppose verily, that except it be a conjurer, a juggler, or a worker with spirits, there is none that useth it.

Touching articles at the Spittle, I am certain D. Barnes did not affirm there, that faith doth not justify, or that Christ's death was not the sufficient satisfaction for our sins. Now whereas he was enjoined to affirm, that though Christ be our only mediator, saviour, justifier, and only satisfaction unto God for the sins of them that believe in him, yet if we lose this grace through sin, then must we rise again by true penance, &c.; if for this article, I say, ye will gather that he should revoke, then do ye interpret his words contrary to his own declaration, that he made of them in the same sermon: insomuch that the Sunday after at Paul's Cross, as I understand, D. Wilson could lay no greater thing to his charge, than that he had expounded penance after his wont manner, by the office of the law and the gospel.

Now like as afore in your words ye compare this his confession to the confession of the devil; so by this and such other your taunts ye would make the world believe that he revoked all truth at the Spittle-field, and that he had all his lifetime taught an ungodly and carnal liberty: the contrary whereof is evident, not only by this present Protestation, but also by his writing and preaching before; namely, that to the true belief and consent of the heart are necessarily required good christian fruits in every man and woman's conversation according to the same. Wherefore this his confession, so long as he maintained no damnable error contrary unto it, (which in all your babbling book ye have not proved, neither shall be able to do,) was a sufficient evidence at his latter end, that he died a true christian man. Neither can ye justly condemn him, that maketh no worse confession on his death-bed. Again, St John saith: "Every spirit which confesseth that Jesus Christ is come in the flesh, is of God." Wherefore ye are too rash in judgment, to affirm that he was justly condemned for heresy, seeing that he neither held any doctrine, nor maintained by evil conversation any thing, out of which ye can truly deduce, that ever he denied the true faith of God, or any one of the benefits or offices of Jesus Christ.

1 John iv.

As for the articles that were laid against him in Cambridge above twelve years ago, verily like as in repeating of them ye accuse your church to pretend an outward forgiveness, and yet to keep hatred still many years; so appear ye to favour them that accused him of the said articles, in some whereof he maintained the prerogative of princes against the tyranny and usurped power ye wot of whom. I say no more; but if ye be at that point, and may so freely write what ye will, I commit my part of the play to God: who, as I doubt not, will defend the king in his right, so am I sure, that although ye be now in your ruff, he is not yet hard asleep. Whereas ye say, that at D. Barnes' death there were three sorts of men, and that the first sort, which by your report were most contrary to him, would give him no answer at his honest request; ye declare plainly, that either they had nothing to say against him, or else little charity; seeing that, according to St Paul's words which ye allege, they found not themselves grieved to see the weak offended, if it were as you say. Neither proveth it them to lean stedfastly unto the pillar of truth, to love God's law, to have true quietness in their conscience, or to be endowed with fervent charity, that follow not the same law of love in the time of need. How do those places of scripture then that ye bring in, allow their act? Let all indifferent readers judge how the cxviii. [cxix.] psalm, the third of the first to Timothy, or the eighth to the Romans, agreeth with their purpose.

2 Cor. xi.

In describing the second sort of people that were at D. Barnes' death, ye fail also: first, in reporting of them, that they ever be and shall be as apt to receive the evil preaching, as the good; secondly, that they are content in these matters

to go whither they be led; thirdly, that they are content
to believe what they be taught; fourthly, that they know
not when they be in the right way, nor when they be forth
of it. Now saith our Saviour, in the same text which ye Matt. xviii.
yourself do allege, that they believe in him. Then like as
they hearken to his voice, and not to the voice of strangers, John x.
so follow they him, and are led of his Holy Spirit; and not Rom. viii.
only prove all doctrines, whether they be of God, but also 1 John iv.
keep that which is good; for they know Christ's voice, and 1 Thess. v.
not the voice of strangers. John x.

Moreover, if that third sort of people did favour no worse
opinions, and were no fuller of fleshly and carnal sensuality,
than this present Protestation of D. Barnes teacheth them;
that text, *Dilexerunt magis tenebras, &c.* may rather be John iii.
verified of you and your sort, than of them.

BARNES.

But they that have been the occasion of it, I pray
God forgive them, as I would be forgiven myself. And
D. Stephen, bishop of Winchester that now is, if he have
sought or wrought this my death, either by word or
deed, I pray God forgive him, as heartily, as freely, as
charitably, and without feigning, as ever Christ forgave
them that put him to death.

STANDISH.

See now whether this be feigned charity or no, &c.

COVERDALE.

It is no point of feigned charity, a man to forgive them
that offend against him, and to pray for them that persecute
him; as it is manifest by our Saviour's doctrine, and example Matt. v.
also at his death. Luke xxiii.

Ye take upon you here the office of a judge, afore ye
be called thereto; yea, even God's only office, in judging men's
hearts, take ye upon you: as who say, he goeth about to
overthrow and cast down a man, that agreeth not with him
in his doctrine. As touching any contentious matter between
my lord of Winchester and D. Barnes, though you and I
both (as I suppose) be ignorant what direction the king's
highness did take therein; yet seeing the one was reconciled

to the other openly at the Spittle, ye should now not take
the matter so hot.

But a pick-thank will ye be still. What mind hath he to
be revenged, that first asketh a man forgiveness, and then
prayeth God to forgive him, as Christ forgave his death, if
he be guilty? Again, will the bishop of Winchester judge
himself to be either seditiously or disdainfully named, or
without reverence, when he is called a bishop? I dare say
he will not. Why play ye Philip Flatterer's part then, as
though the name of a bishop were not a reverent name?

BARNES.

And if any of the council, or any other, have sought
or wrought it through malice or ignorance, I pray God
forgive them their ignorance, and illuminate their eyes;
that they may see, and ask mercy for it.

STANDISH.

Oh, what ignorance, &c.

COVERDALE.

This prayer is neither malicious against God's word, nor
prejudicial to any man; and if they that suffered D. Barnes
to live so long, were to blame for their so doing, then make
ye yourself guilty of the same fault, that have played the
coward all that while, and not helped him to his death.

BARNES.

I beseech you all to pray for the king's grace, as I
have done ever since I was in prison, and do now; that
God may give him prosperity, and that he may long
reign among you, and after him that goodly prince
Edward may so reign, that he may finish those things
that his father hath begun. I have been reported a
preacher of sedition and disobedience to the king's
majesty: but here I say to you, that you all are bound
by the commandment of God to obey your prince with
all humility and with all your heart, yea, not so much as
in a look to shew yourselves disobedient unto him; and

that not only for fear of the sword, but also for conscience sake before God.

STANDISH.

Thou hast been truly reported a seditious preacher, &c.

COVERDALE.

Will ye then wink at sedition so long, and not be an accuser thereof, whereas, by your own confession, ye have heard him preach so oft? yea, and knowing his book to have been so long printed? But how untruly you belie him, it shall be evident to all the world, that will read his book. Ye report of him, that he should say in his book, printed ten years ago, that if the king would by tyranny take the New Testament from his subjects, they should not suffer him. Now is it manifest, that like as he saith here in this part of his Protestation, so saith he also in his book, and bringeth in the same thirteenth chapter to the Romans that ye allege; and addeth moreover these words: "In no wise, be it right or wrong, mayest thou make any resistance with sword or with hand, &c." Item, "If the king forbid the New Testament, &c. men shall first make faithful prayers to God, and humble supplication to the king, that his grace would release that commandment. If he will not do it, they shall keep their Testament with all other ordinance of Christ, and let the king exercise his tyranny, if they cannot fly; and in no wise, under pain of damnation, shall they resist him by violence; but suffer patiently, &c. Nor they shall not go about to depose their prince, as my lords the bishops were wont, &c. But if the king will do it by violence, they must suffer it; but not obey to it by agreement." Item, "Now is it clear, that we may not resist this temporal power, in no wise, by violence, &c.; but if any thing be commanded us that is against the word of God, whereby our faith is hurt, that should we not do in anywise, but rather suffer persecution, and also death."

Be these words now as much to say as, if the king command any thing by tyranny, men shall not suffer him? What mean ye so untruly to report of the dead? But no marvel, when ye shame not to belie so many texts of God's holy word.

[margin note:] In the cxiii. leaf.

[margin note:] D. Barnes' words in the cxv. leaf of his book.

[margin note:] In the cxvi. leaf.

[margin note:] In the cxviii. leaf.

Touching men's laws, it is manifest, that such as are not grounded in God's word, do not bind the conscience of man to deadly sin. For if they be not grounded in God's word, and agreeable to the faith thereof, then are they sinful and naught. Who is bound now to obey sin? But a man may smell you afar off, whose successors ye be. You will not stick to call it a lawful act, for a prince to condemn God's word, and to forbid that thing which is institute and ordained of God : yea, if our prince would take such a thing in hand, (which God forbid!) he should lack no instigation of your malignant church. Neither can I yet conjecture the contrary, but that ye are about such a tragedy. Now go to; set your watchmen to keep the sepulchre, suffer not Christ to rise up in any wise, let not the soldiers lack money, (the church is rich enough,) cast your great heads together, and let Caiphas give you his most subtle counsel. For when ye have done your best, and lied all that ever ye can, yet shall God make your policy to serve for the glory of his truth. Amen.

BARNES.

Yea, and I say further, if the king should command you any thing against God's law, if it be in your power to resist him, yet may you not do it.

STANDISH.

See here the steadfastness, &c.

COVERDALE.

This man neither wrote nor said, that we must obey an earthly prince more than Almighty God; and yet are ye not ashamed so to report of him. He saith, that though the king command us any thing against God's law, yet may we not resist him : which saying ye call an abominable heresy. Thus declare ye yourself manifestly to be of the number of them that teach, how that it is lawful for a man to resist his prince: which thing whether it be not both heresy and treason, let them judge that have authority.

Amos vii.   Because Amos the prophet preached against idolatry at Bethel, that false priest Amasias, whom ye speak of, told the king that he was a seditious fellow, and so found the means to get him out of the court.   Yet played Amasias a more honest part with Amos, than you do ; for he laid rebellion to his charge that was alive, and your accusation is against the dead.   Again, Amasias, being yet a false priest, saith not, that it is lawful for a man to resist his prince ; and you call it abominable heresy to teach the contrary.

Though Peter and John do teach, that we must obey and hearken unto God more than unto men, do they therefore teach, that we must resist our prince? Where find ye that example in them? Peter smote off Malcus' ear indeed ; but little thank had he for his labour.   Doth he not teach us to endure grief, to suffer wrong, and to take it patiently ? 1 Pet. ii. Saith he not, that we are called thereunto? Setteth he not Christ unto us for an example of suffering?

Because our Saviour willeth us not to fear them that kill Matt. x. the body, must we therefore resist them? When a prince doth persecute us for God's word's sake in one city, must we resist him, and not rather fly into another? Doth he call Matt. v. them blessed that resist, and not them rather that suffer for persecution sake?   Did Christ enter into his kingdom by Luke xxiv. resisting, or by suffering?

As for that saying, *Qui timet hominem, &c.* I cannot find it in the xix. of the Proverbs : but I find there written, that Prov. xix. "a false witness shall not remain unpunished, and that he which speaketh lies shall not escape."

Ye call it an abominable heresy to teach, that we ought not to resist our prince, though he command us any unlawful thing ; and to prove your purpose, ye point us to the fifth of Esay, where there is no such words as ye speak of.   But these words find I there : "Woe unto them that call good Isai. v. evil, &c."

As for the example of the seven brethren and their They say not, mother, it utterly condemneth you; for they say these words : to resist. "We are ready rather to suffer, than to offend the laws of 2.] God," &c. ; and as they said, so they did, without making resistance, though the king's commandment was unlawful. What other thing now did D. Barnes teach in his fore-rehearsed words, but (as he had said in his book before) that if the king would command us any unlawful thing, we must suffer him, though we obey not to it by agreement? What danger you be in then for teaching the contrary, I will not define.   I

pray God, according to his good pleasure, have mercy upon
you.

BARNES.

Then spake he to the sheriff and said, " Mr. Sheriff,
I require you of God's behalf, to have me commended
unto the king's grace, and to shew him, that I require of
his grace these requests. First, that where his grace hath
now received into his hands all the goods and substance of
the abbeys "—Then the sheriff desired him to stop there.
He answered, "Mr. Sheriff, I warrant you, that I will speak
no harm ; for I know it is well done, that all such superstition be taken clean away, and the king's grace hath
well done in taking it away. But seeing his grace is
made a whole king, and obeyed in his realm as a king,
(which neither his father, nor grandfather, nor his ances-
tors that reigned before him, ever had,) and that thorough
the preaching of us and such other wretches as we are,
which always have applied our whole studies, and gave
ourselves for the setting forth of the same, and this is
now our reward ;—well, it maketh no matter : now he
reigneth, (I pray God long may he reign among you !)
would God it might please his grace to bestow the said
goods, or some of them, to the comfort of his poor subjects, which surely have great need of them.

" The second that I desire his grace, is, that he will
see that matrimony be had in more reverence than it is,
and that men, for every light cause invented, cast not off
their wives, and live in advoutry and fornication ; and
that these that be not married, should not abominably
live in whoredom, following the filthy lusts of the flesh.

" The third, that the abominable swearers may be
punished, and straitly looked upon. For surely the vengeance of God will come on them for their mischievous
oaths." Then desired he Mr. Pope, which was present, to
have him commended to Mr. Edgar, and to desire him,

for the dear blood of Jesu Christ, that he would leave that abominable swearing that he useth. "For surely, except he forsake it, he will come to some mischievous end. The fourth, that his grace will set forth Christ's true religion: and that, seeing he hath begun, he go forward, and make an end; for many things have been done, but yet much more is to do. And that it would please his grace to look on God's word himself: for it hath been obscured with many traditions of our own brains. Now," said he, "how many petitions have I spoken of?" And the people said, "Four." "Well," said he, "even these four be sufficient, which I desire you, that the king's grace may be certified of them. And say, that I most humbly desire him to look earnestly upon them."

STANDISH.

It was high time to look, &c.

COVERDALE.

The prophet Daniel, I trust, was no arrogant wretch, Dan. iv. though he desired his prince to make some provision for the poor, no more than was holy St Paul, which taught Timothy 1 Tim. vi. to charge the rich men of this world with the same lesson. All they also that were true messengers of God, laboured to have advoutry, fornication, whoredom, and abominable swearing, expelled from among christian men, as all the whole scripture testifieth. Neither did D. Barnes in these his words require any other thing. His words are plain enough: and yet, as your manner is in your treatise, ye imagine an intent and mind clean contrary to the same. Ye grant, that he spake earnestly for the poor and for the commons; and yet call ye him an arrogant wretch, and for his good will report of him, that he desired to have a great stroke in every matter of weight, &c.

D. Barnes said not, that he and his fellows did reform those things that were amiss, (for he knew that to be God's office and the king's;) and yet surmise ye the same untruly upon him. But he saith, that thorough the preaching of

God's word in the ministration of him and such other the king's grace is now more obeyed, than ever he was before. And I pray you, is it not so? Or was it not God's holy word, that gat the king his own again? May he thank any papistical doctrine therefore? No, verily.

Concerning Mr Edgar, if D. Barnes had not had a right good opinion in him, no doubt he would not have sent him that commendation with such an honest request. But because he took him (as he might right well, I trust,) for a gentleman that would suffer a christian exhortation, as they will that pertain unto Christ, therefore was he the bolder of him. As for that swearing, I think verily it cometh rather of a custom (which yet might well be left) than of any set purpose. Neither was D. Barnes' act here against the process required in the eighteenth of Matthew, though he had not spoken with him afore, seeing he might not now come at him.

BARNES.

And that his grace take good heed, that he be not deceived with false preachers and teachers, and evil counsel. For Christ saith, that such false prophets shall come in lambs' skins.

STANDISH.

Oh, how great thank be you worthy, &c.

COVERDALE.

Ye should have proved these words to smell nothing but heresy and treason, as ye say in your preface, because they have the sweet odour of the gospel, where our Saviour biddeth us beware of false prophets, and of the leaven of Pharisees, and telleth us, that many such shall arise and deceive many; yea, even through sweet preachings and flattering words, saith the apostle; and because the scripture biddeth us beware of such merchants as, going in long garments, &c., devour widows' houses under the pretence of long prayers.

This man called not the king's most honourable council evil, and yet (even like a pick-thank still) ye surmise it upon him. If a friend of the king's should say unto him, I beseech your grace, take good heed whom ye receive into your privy chamber, doth he therefore call his chamberlains

Matt. vii. xvi. xxiv.

Rom. xvi.

Mark xii. Luke xx.

evil? Or doth he therefore prefer his own wit above the discreet wisdom of the king's noble council?

Holy St Peter, as long as he was in this body, thought 2 Pet. i. it meet to put christian men in remembrance of their duty; yea, though they were of ripe knowledge themselves, and stablished in the truth. And yet you call it obstinate pride, treason, blindness, and rash foolishness, so to do. Such is your judgment; yea, even when the party doth most humbly desire his prince, to whom he speaketh.

BARNES.

Then desired he all men to forgive him; and that if he had said any evil at any time unadvised, whereby he had offended any man, or given any occasion of evil, that they would forgive it him, and amend that evil they took of him.

STANDISH.

Mark how he doth continue one manner of man, &c.

COVERDALE.

Steadfastness in the way of God's truth is to be commended. And an evident token is it, that he is of the same doctrine, which wittingly teacheth no evil, reconcileth himself unto all men, is sorry if he have offended any man, or given any evil occasion, and giveth other men at their death an ensample of true repentance.

BARNES.

And that they would bear him witness, that he detested and abhorred all evil opinions and doctrines against the word of God; and that he died in the faith of Jesus Christ and the sacraments of the church, by whom he doubted not to [be] saved.

STANDISH.

I know that no good man, &c.

COVERDALE.

Then it appeareth, that if he had not detested and

abhorred all evil and erroneous opinions, but had loved your strange doctrines, which are against God's word, and so died out of Christ's faith, ye would have been a record and witness to him, rather than fail.

BARNES.

And with this he desired them all to pray for him: and then he turned him about, and put off his clothes, making him ready to the fire, and most patiently took his death, yielding his soul into the hands of Almighty God.

STANDISH.

By this it doth appear, that the first writer of these his words was very charitable, &c.

COVERDALE.

Whatsoever he was that first wrote these his words, verily I cannot tell; neither did I ever read them or hear them, till I saw them in your treatise. And though it may be suspected, that this is not the truest copy, because it cometh out of your hands; yet truly a right charitable deed was it to write his words, and to certify us of them: for else, by your present practice we may conjecture that ye would have descanted of his death, as of one whom ye had overcome with your doctrine. Now also that ye can stop the truth no farther, ye would bear us in hand, that it is the writer's judgment only, which ascribeth unto him, that he patiently took his death; as though there were none else that heard him and saw him die, but the writer alone.

COVERDALE.   [STANDISH.]

Albeit I will judge only of the outward behaviour.

COVERDALE.

John vii.   "Judge not after the outward appearance," saith our Saviour, " but give a righteous judgment."

Yet do ye not as ye say; for in many places of your treatise ye judge the man's mind and intent, yea, contrary to his words.

STANDISH.

Taking occasion by his erroneous words, to judge he died an obstinate heretic.

COVERDALE.

Ye cannot deny, but that after the open confession of his faith, and his humble requests unto the king's grace, he then reconciled himself to all men ; and at the last, when he had desired them to pray for him, took his death patiently, and yielded up his soul into the hands of Almighty God. For all this ye do not only call his words erroneous, but also give sentence, that he died an obstinate heretic.

STANDISH.

And as for the inward secrets, whether he be condemned or saved, whether he yielded up his soul into the hands of Almighty God, or no, &c., I remit that to the secret counsel of the blessed Trinity.

COVERDALE.

A wonderful thing is it, that ye are so unstable in your words! Do ye not take upon you afore to judge, that he died an obstinate heretic? And now ye cannot tell whether he be saved or condemned, whether he yielded up his soul into the hands of Almighty God, or no. But can an obstinate heretic yield up his soul, when he is dead already? Can an obstinate heretic be saved? Behold now, to what worship ye bring your doctrine at the last.

STANDISH.

Unto whom be laud, honour, and glory now and for evermore. Amen.

COVERDALE.

Amen. Even to that same blessed Trinity, Father, Son, and Holy Ghost, be honour and glory now and evermore. Amen.

The apostle, describing the office and duty of a minister 2 Tim. ii. or preacher of God's word, willeth him, among all other qualities, to shew himself such a laudable workman, as need not be ashamed, handling the word of truth justly. Where-

fore, seeing ye have so irreverently handled God's holy word,
perverted it, wrested it, and belied it so oft and many times
in your treatise, marvel not at this mine invective against
your false doctrine.   As for simple ignorance, and such frail
weakness as accompanieth the nature of man, whether he
will or no, it may be suffered and borne.   But wilful spurn-
ing at God's holy word, froward and false belying thereof,
must needs be rebuked and improved.   Your zeal, for all
your holy pretence, is to suppress God's truth, to maintain
that doctrine which the catholic universal church of Christ
never received, and to defend the church malignant in her
wickedness.   This is manifest by your present practice.   But
God Almighty, which soweth the seed of his holy word, and
daily increaseth it in the hearts of his faithful, shall, though
no man else will, maintain and defend it himself.   We also,
whom God will not to be idle, shall do our best, and be
carrying stones to the making up of the wall which ye have
broken down; to the intent that Christ our Saviour may
have his own glory, which ye have robbed him of, our prince
his honour, and our neighbour his duty.

TO ALL TRUE CHRISTIAN READERS.

Faint not thou in faith, dear reader, neither wax cold
in love and charity, though the enemies of God's word be
gathered together, and grown into such swarms.   Be thou
strong in the Lord, and in the power of his might; and let
it not discourage thee, that the said word is so little in the
estimation of the world, so greatly despised, so sore persecuted, so wickedly perverted, wrested, and belied, so unthankfully received, so shamefully denied, and so slothfully
followed.

Arm thyself, therefore, with the comfortable ensamples of
the scripture ; and, as touching those jolly Nimrods that
persecute God's word, hunting it out of every corner, whet-
ting their swords and bending their bows against it, be thou

sure, that the God of our fathers, Abraham, Isaac, and Jacob, shall do with them as he ever was wont to do with tyrants in times past. Thou seest thoroughout the stories of the holy bible, how that like as he turneth some of their hearts from cruelty to meekness, even so with death, with fire, with water, and with such other his plagues, destroyeth he them that will needs despise his warning; yea, breaketh their bows in pieces, and killeth them with their own swords. As for Jamnes and Jambres, those wicked sorcerers and covetous chaplains, that teach contrary to God's word, and dissuade the great men of the world from it, their own wresting and belying of it must needs confound them; for though there be many that resist the truth, yet when it is uttered and cometh to light, their madness, as St Paul saith, [2 Tim. iii.] shall be manifest unto all men. And as Moses' rod devoured their rods in the king's presence; so likewise the same places of scripture that they allege for their wicked purpose, shall destroy their false doctrine in the face of the world. Yea, even as little honesty as the papistry hath gotten by wresting of, *Tu es Petrus, &c.*; so small profit are they like to have for belying of other texts. Neither is it to be feared, but God will do for one part of his word as much as for another, when he seeth his time.

Concerning those belly-beasts, that, for no commandment nor promise of God, for no example, warning, nor exhortation, will be counselled, but still blaspheme his holy word thorough their ungodly conversation; let not that withdraw thee from the way of righteousness. Love not thou Christ the worse, though Judas be a traitor. Set not thou the less by his wholesome doctrine, though dogs turn to their vomit, and though swine wallow in their stinking mire again.

I know, gentle reader, that to all true christian hearts it is a great tentation, to see God's holy word either persecuted, belied, or unthankfully received. But first remember thyself well by the practice of all stories, when was it without persecution? When was there not one tyrant or other, that exercised all his power, strength, wit, and counsel against it? When were the children of Israel without some bloody Edomites, Egyptians, Assyrians, Babylonians, Philistines, or other?

Secondly, when was not God's word belied, perverted, or evil spoken of by one false prophet or other? Were there not heretics and flattering chaplains in all ages, that withdrew men from the truth, and misreported the straight ways of the Lord?

Thirdly, when were there not some multitudes, that, pretending a love toward Christ's word, did but follow him for their own bellies' sake? When was the seed of Christ's word sown, but some part of it fell upon the stony ground, where it withered, and among the thorns, that choked it up?

Heb xii. Wherefore, seeing thou art compassed about with so great a number of witnesses, that is to say, with the ensamples of so many godly and holy men, which not only did choose rather to suffer adversity with the people of God than to enjoy the pleasures of sin for a season, but also eschewed false doctrine, and brought forth alway good works in their living; follow thou the same trade, follow thou them, I say, as thou seest they followed Christ, and no farther. And as touching any manner of doctrine, believe no man without God's word, according as St Hierome counselleth thee, *In Epistolam ad Gal.* cap. 5[1]. For certain it is, that like as many times thou shalt spy even great faults in the conversation of God's elect, so readest thou of very few teachers since the apostles' time, which have not erred, and that grossly, in sundry things.

Wherefore, whomsoever thou hearest teach, preach, or write, or whose books soever thou readest, try them by God's word, whether they be agreeable thereto, or no. When thou knowest them, I say, and art certain and sure by Christ's doctrine, that they are false, seditious, or abominable, then hold them accursed, avoid them utterly, eschew them in any wise, and give over thyself to the wholesome hearing and reading of the scripture; but so that thou be sober and discreet in the knowledge and use thereof, and that in professing the true faith and belief of Christ thy heart, mouth, and deed go together, and that thou consent to none opinion contrary to the same; that God may have the praise, and thy neighbour be edified in all thy conver-

[1 Nec illis nec mihi sine verbis Dei consentire debetis.—Hieron. Opera, Tom. VII. p. 487. Ed. 1737.]

sation. So doing, thou shalt not only stop the mouth of
evil speakers; but also allure and provoke other men to
be fruitfully given to faith and good works, and to
help with such their unfeigned faith and godly
living, that the tabernacle of God may
be set up again. The grace of
our Lord Jesus Christ
be with us all.
Amen.

Iacobi. iij.

Yf ye haue a bytter zele, and there be conten-
cions in youre hartes, make no boast,
nether be lyars agaynst the
trueth.

THE DEFENCE

OF

A CERTAIN POOR CHRISTIAN MAN,

&c.

The Defence

of a certayne poore Christen
Man who else shuld habe
bene condemned by
the Popes
Lawe.

Written
in the hye Allmaynes
by a right excellent and
noble Prynce and trans=
lated into Englishe
by Myles Coberdale.

THE DEFENCE

OF

A CERTAIN POOR CHRISTIAN MAN.

LOVE constraineth me, right virtuous judges, to take
upon me the defence of this christian man, whom I see here
accused to have deserved death. Neither do I suppose it
can displease you which be christian, that one christian man
shew a christian work unto another. For although it might
be esteemed a strange and unwont thing, that I take upon
me to defend a man, who neither in name nor visure hath
been known unto me till this present day, neither I also
being of his kin; yet must the hand of christian love be
considered, which knitteth and coupleth unto us not only our
friends and such as do us good, but even our enemies also,
and them that do us evil: insomuch that by the commandment of our Saviour we are bound with body, goods, and
counsel, to help all men without exception, what need soever
they be in. How much less do ye suppose that a christian
brother is to be forsaken, which standeth in danger of his
life, and that for Christ's doctrine sake; for the which no
man (except he were far out of the right way) did ever refuse
to jeopard his neck.

Nevertheless, right dear judges, in this company that
standeth hereby round about us might doubtless many be
found, which could handle this matter with more apt words,
with more gravity, cunning, and eloquence than I. To whom
I was also purposed right gladly with all my heart to give
place. Notwithstanding, as ye do see, among this great
multitude of people there is yet none found, that in such a
virtuous, free, honest, profitable, and needful matter, would
lay to his hands: whereas we see yet daily not a small
number, that willingly and earnestly and with great diligence both maintain open felony, wicked perjury, shameful
adultery, slanderous and venomous matters, horrible robbing,

manslaughter, murder, and other beastly vices; and that
either for vain favour sake, or else, which is yet more
shameful, for a filthy reward or lucre. Only this innocent
christian man, which for the pure doctrine of Christ's sake
standeth in peril of his life, hath not one, I will not say to
maintain him, but so much as one to comfort him. Is not
this a pity, pitiful case? O what a wicked time is this!
But alas! even as the ungodly and wicked are full of malicious
envy, so are the simple both fearful and soon persuaded.

As for me, my lords, I have not feared to take this matter in hand, upon confidence in your wisdom and worship:
specially forasmuch as I consider it is not needful for me to
use many painted words of glorious eloquence or vain appearance, which nothing to this matter appertaineth; forasmuch as it consisteth not in persuasion, but in the truth itself.
It is a free, open matter, and ought also freely and openly
to be handled. Here must be no deceit, no colour, no cavillation, but only the truth; which unto us in this matter shall
be abundant and sufficient. Only I beseech you, right worshipful judges, that ye will lovingly, diligently, and patiently
give audience. Not that I have any suspicion, as though ye
were unrighteously minded against this innocent man. For
by certain manifest tokens and evident signs I have perceived
already, that there is not one of you all which is not minded
to discharge him. Notwithstanding I suppose it ought by
all means to be avoided, that men do not think ye have quit
him more through favour, than by virtue of the law.

For our adversary in his complaint hath used such cavillation, yea, even for the nonce and of set purpose, and hath
mixed therein so many and diverse vain and feigned matters,
which among simple people might easily have an appearance
of the verity, that equity requireth, and necessity constraineth
me, to confute all such with the truth and substantial reasons,
to the intent that no doubt should remain by any man.
Nevertheless I am not therefore so careful to deliver this
man's life, whom I here defend; yea, he himself for the
honour of Christ, if need require, doth not refuse to lose it:
the only doctrine of Christ is it, which I would fain declare
to be without blemish and undefiled. The same only, the
same, I say, have I taken upon me to maintain. For it am
I minded to do my best.

But now, dear judges, afore I come to the head articles, I am advised to talk a little with our adversary. And now I speak unto thee in the long gown, I mean even thee, thou accuser, which (as I hear say) art called an inquisitor of heresy. And first of all, I demand of thee, what moved thee to take that unhappy office upon thee? What worship or profit thoughtest thou to obtain thereby? Methinketh, to say plainly, thou hast sought nothing in this matter, save only either filthy lucre, vain pride, or wicked tyranny: or haply thou art so idle from thine own business, that thou canst handle strange matters, and such as are no point of thy charge: or else thou art so pure and clear from thine own vices, that thou inquirest after other men's offences with such curiosity, as well beseemeth such an holy scribe and earnest defender of the church of Rome. A wonderful holiness, verily, if it be so! And the same only thing, I suppose, is yet lacking unto thy perfect holiness, which hast destroyed certain innocent christian men already. O how sweet a doctrine of divinity is this! Is not this a virtuous defender of the church?

But let us put the case, (nevertheless without prejudice of truth,) that this man whom thou accusest be an heretic and utterly no Christian. Is it thy mind, that he shall therefore in all the haste be hurled unto the hangman, and put to death? Didst thou ever read, that Christ and his disciples command to slay such as received the faith; or that after they had received it, fell away from it again? I suppose not. Nevertheless thou mightest well have read, that the unbelievers ought gently to be instructed and taught, like as they that are fallen ought, after a brotherly fashion, to be helped up again and exhorted; and that they which of an obstinate mind will hear no exhortation, ought to be eschewed and avoided, but not in all the haste put to death. Thou with thy bitter accusation thinkest to bring this christian man into danger of his life. But how far the same thy complaint is from the wholesome doctrine of Christ and his disciples, mayest thou consider thyself.

If thou hadst been minded to make inquisition for heresy, whereby thou mightest help thy brother which is fallen, and bring him from his error unto the right way, then were thy diligonce to be commended. But now, forasmuch as thy desire is to murder him like a beast, thy cruelty must be reproved. Neither can I discern for what intent thou shouldest by right condemn him unto death, except for it be some other offence than lack of faith. For either he hath never been a christian man, (which were temerarious to affirm, forasmuch as he was baptized in Christ, and hath openly confessed Christ, whereof no man doubteth;) or else is he fallen away from Christ, which thou shalt never be able to prove. Now though thou couldest verify one of these two according to thy mind, yet shall it be found, that thou hast wrongfully accused him to have deserved death.

If one should accuse a Jew at the law, that he were worthy to die, because he holdeth nothing of Christ, would not every one say, that he were a mad man? Not that I will excuse the wicked infidelity of a Jew; but because that in this case the judgment appertaineth not unto man, but must be referred unto God. There dwell Jews now also in many parts of Christendom, not only in safeguard, but occupy[1] also, and that openly.

As for the Turks, which of a very unsatiable greediness toward tyranny vex us horribly, and all that we have, yea, spare no manner of age nor kind; no man judgeth it wrong to destroy them in battle. But to murder their wives and children, because they believe not in Christ, do I take for a very beastly thing; and specially out of war, in the time of peace, when the Turks themselves, in matters concerning the faith, are nothing cruel against us.

It is not meet to make a divorce of marriage for only unbelief's sake; so long as the unbelieving husband refuseth not to dwell with the believing wife, neither as long as the unbelieving wife refuseth not to dwell with the believing husband. A christian servant is bound to render to his unbelieving master his due obedience, and that not to the eyesight, but from the heart, even as if he served Christ himself: much less then shall he take upon him to have power to hurt him. And thou thinkest that a man ought to be slain, to whose charge thou canst lay nothing, save only infidelity. Mad and indiscreet art thou, if thou so

[1 Occupy: follow business; as in Luke xix. 13.]

believest; yea, desperate and ungodly, if thou believest no such thing, and yet wilt thou persuade other men to bring this innocent in jeopardy of his life.

Notwithstanding I know already, what thou wilt say thereto. "I accuse no Jew," wilt thou say, "no Turk, no heathen; what have we to do with them that are without, as St Paul saith? I do accuse a runagate and apostate; who though he be baptized in Christ, and lovingly received into the womb of our mother the holy church, yet through the counsel of the devil hath he not been ashamed to fall from the right faith and to cleave unto certain men's heresies, against the commandment of the church: neither was he therewith satisfied, but through his false persuasion hath he gone about to bring many more even into such like errors. Such one, as I suppose, ought to be hewen off from the body, as a corrupt member, to the intent that the sore fret no farther."

Have I understand thy mind? Thou hast nodded with thy head. I perceive that I have not guessed amiss. Now well then, thou grantest that he is baptized in Christ, and lovingly received into the womb of our mother the holy church: I desire no more. Thou art gone from the first step that thou stoodest upon. Whereby I hope, that upon the other step, whereon thou now standest, thou wilt not long continue.

With few, but with true reasons, now have I declared unto thee already, that one which was never no Christian, ought not to be slain for only unbelief's sake, without other offences.

But now will I briefly shew thee what I suppose ought to be done with such as are christened, and yet through heresy and errors concerning faith, or through other sin and vice, are fallen from Christ. For Christ is two manner of ways denied, not only with word, but also with deed; while there be many, that are ever ready to praise Christ with their words, and yet in their deeds are so openly against him, that thereby it may be easily perceived, that, except the vain bare words, they have no christian point in them. If thou now hast taken upon thee, at the judgment-seat of the law, to accuse all such as unchristian, as verily they be indeed; when shall thy accusation then and complaint have an end? If thou meanest, that they ought immediately to

be slain, as soon as they fall, what place then shall repentance have? Who shall have leisure then to do penance,
or to amend?

Wilt thou also be so shameless, as to deny forgiveness
of sins unto them that truly amend? Or canst thou be so
cruel, that thou wilt look for no conversion, but immediately
destroy the man, both body and soul? How canst thou know,
thou unreasonable man, when, how, or by what mean, God
as a merciful Father will call sinners again unto true faith
and repentance, who, upon Peter's question, command him
to forgive his neighbour seven and seventy times? Believest
thou him to be so unmerciful, that what he commandeth a
man to do, he will deny the same to such as pray unto him?
Away, away, I say, with this thy unconvenient and blasphemous opinion. God saith: "I will not the death of a
sinner, but rather that he convert and live." Thou criest:
An heretic ought to be burnt. And why so, I pray thee?
Lest he should convert, and so live. With this voice dis-
coverest thou thyself already, that thou art a child of the
devil, which is a murderer from the beginning. I perceive
thou hast changed thy colour for very anger. I have touched
thy holiness too sore. Pardon me, if I have done amiss. I
would have dealt more friendly with thee, if thou with this
thy undiscreet and unreasonable accusation hadst not bewrayed
thyself.

But lest thou shouldest think, that I favour such as deny
Christ in word or deed, or such as blaspheme God, being oft
exhorted, well and truly taught, yea, convict with substantial reasons out of the scripture, and yet will never leave
their inconvenient and false opinion; lest thou shouldest
think, I say, that I favoured any such, I will declare mine
opinion, and that not out of mine own brain, but such an
opinion as is past all doubt, certain and sure, yea, even
spoken by the holy mouth of Christ himself.

"If he will not hear the church," saith Christ, "then count
him as an heathen and open sinner." Hath not Christ with
these words declared, that such as are disobedient unto his
church and congregation, ought to be excluded from the fellowship of the good? Why lackest thou so heartily, as
though it were but a trifle, a man to be excluded from the
fellowship of saints? Methinketh, thou wottest not well what

matter it maketh, when by the authority of the keys one is separated out of the church. "Verily, I say unto you," saith the Lord, "whatsoever ye bind upon earth, shall also be bound in heaven." Lo, there hast thou no vain opinion, but an assured judgment out of the mouth of our Saviour himself.

The apostle Paul commandeth to eschew an heretic, [Tit. iii.] after that he is sufficiently warned. And the man which kept his stepmother, delivereth he unto the devil, that the [1 Cor. v.] spirit may be saved at the latter day. Did he therefore condemn him unto death, because he writeth to deliver him unto Satan, to the destruction of the flesh? That be far from the excellent love of Paul, that he would not rather help up a brother that were fallen, than utterly to cast him away! The conclusion also of the matter, which followed thereof, declareth itself, that he meant not to have him slain, but to have him purged out, as an old leaven; to the intent that he should not sour the whole lump of dough, and that at the last he might amend, as he did indeed. For in the second epistle to the Corinthians he commandeth, that forasmuch as the same man came to knowledge and repentance, they should with all loving kindness take him up again, forgive him his offence, and comfort him in his heaviness, lest he should be swallowed up, or fall in despair, through overmuch sorrow. All which things could not have come to pass, if the man in all the haste had afore been prevented with death. O! the right godly patience and longsuffering of our Saviour, who, as a good shepherd, leaving the nine and ninety sheep in the wilderness, seeketh it that is lost; not to cast it unto the wolf to be devoured, but lovingly to bring it again into his sheepfold!

Now understandest thou, that mine opinion, yea, the opinion of Christ, is confirmed with scriptures, with examples, and by Paul himself. Neither can it help thee, though thou objectest unto me the parable of the gospel, wherein the householder commandeth his steward to hew down the unfruitful tree, if it bring no more fruit. For such knowledge of time must only be referred unto God, as unto him that only knoweth the hearts of all men. Else had not Christ forbidden to pluck up the weeds afore the harvest.

Yet must I declare unto thee, what bodily hinderance

must grow and follow out of this sentence of excommunication to him that is condemned therein; lest thou shouldest think my mind were to judge no farther, but with bare words only to have him excluded from the communion of the Christian.

[Matt. xviii.]   Thou hast heard the fearful thunderbolt of our Saviour: "Whatsoever ye bind upon earth, shall also be bound in heaven." Thus is he then already put out of the book of life, and living dead. Believe me, it is an heavy punishment. I wot not where to find a sorer. But they that in their hearts are more moved with worldly matters, let them hear this that followeth.

All honest virtuous persons shall eschew him. Howbeit such a one as hath so denied Christ, that he hath also cast from him all shamefacedness and honesty, might peradventure not greatly care therefore. From all worship, if he were in any, and worshipful offices shall he be deposed. All Christians shall abhor him, and earnestly hate his infidelity, and yet love his person, as it becometh the disciples of Christ; to the intent it may appear, that such punishment is laid upon him, not of malice or evil will, but done all to the intent, that he through such temporal correction might convert, and be reserved unto Christ the Lord for ever. Have I said enough now to thy cruelty with this my declaration? Or is not this sufficient? Take heed, I advise thee, that in judging other men too sore, thou condemn not thyself. For I trust I will shortly bring to pass, that it shall be manifest and open unto every man, how that thou thyself art even the same heretic, to whom the foresaid punishment by right and reason belongeth.

Now turn I me again unto you, right prudent judges, having no small confidence in your singular worship and gravity, forasmuch as I know that ye will give no sentence, but such as accordeth with equity, and serveth to the honour of Christ; yea, right glad I am to see, that the same lieth now in your authority.

And because I purpose not to hold you up long with vain words, I will now come to the matter, which I suppose concerneth not only him that here standeth upon life and death, but every one of us also that seek the honour of Christ. I will bring in no new thing, or that hitherto hath not been heard. For in this matter, where we have now continually gone about more than twenty years, what can be spoken, that hath not been oft spoken afore? What can be mentioned, that hath not afore been preached openly, and, as they say, upon the housetops? I suppose it not needful to teach you in this matter, but only to put you in remembrance, and to exhort you. Wherefore I beseech you ye will but even patiently hear me, according as ye have hitherto done already.

I perceive, right dear judges, that our adversary hath grounded his whole accusation hereupon; that he will say how that this christian man is fallen from the holy christian church. Wherefore I see well, I must first endeavour myself to declare unto you the true description of the church; which if it be well known and understood, I perceive that all the rest may lightly be discussed, and peradventure the sooner brought to an end.

As touching this, We believe an holy catholic or general church, which is the fellowship of saints. Here ye see, right dear judges, with how few words the true description of the church is set forth before our eyes.

Whereby we may evidently perceive, that the holy catholic church is nothing else but a fellowship of saints. And the same is also the bride of Christ, without spot or wrinkle, purified through the blood of the Bridegroom himself; even the heavenly Hierusalem, into the which no unclean person cometh; the most holy temple, whereinto is entered our bishop Jesus Christ, who is a priest for ever after the order of Melchisedech. This, I say, is the church builded upon the rock, against the which neither the winds, nor the waves of waters, no, nor the gates of hell can prevail; the head and foundation whereof is Christ himself.

To this church pertain all they, that since the beginning of the world have been saved, and that shall be saved unto the end thereof. For they are the living stones of this heavenly Hierusalem, and of this most holy temple. " Know ye [1 Cor. iii.] not," saith St Paul, " that ye are the temple of God, and that the Spirit of God dwelleth in you? If any man defile this temple, him shall God destroy : for the temple of God is holy, the same temple are ye."

Even this church doth this christian brother of ours

believe stedfastly. Yea, and in this church also believeth
he forgiveness of sins, and after the resurrection of the flesh
an everlasting life. Why sayest thou then, that he is fallen
away from the church? To thee speak I now, thou unreasonable accuser. What hast thou yet more to lay to his
charge? He believeth in God the Father Almighty, maker
of heaven and earth; and in Jesus Christ his only-begotten
Son, our Lord, which was conceived of the Holy Ghost, born
of Mary the Virgin, suffered under Pontius Pilate, was crucified, dead, and buried, descended unto hell, on the third day
rose again from death, ascended unto heaven, sitteth at the
right hand of God the Father Almighty, from thence shall
he come to judge the quick and dead. He believeth also in
the Holy Ghost; and all the rest that we mentioned afore of
the church. He believeth likewise all that is written by the
prophets and other old fathers of the old Testament. In
like manner believeth he all that in the gospels is written of
the acts and doctrine of Christ. He confesseth also, that the
doctrine of the apostles and disciples of Christ is not to be
doubted upon. Moreover he believeth, that whatsoever the
holy fathers of the new Testament have written, is true, so
far as it is not contrary to the doctrine of Christ and of his
apostles.

With this true and free confession of faith I suppose
thou art so satisfied, that now thou wilt not stick with all
expedition to quit this christian man, and faithfully to commit him unto the judges, as a right member of the church:
and forasmuch as thou hast unadvisedly accused him as an
heretic, and as a runagate from the church, and hast done
him wrong, I hope thou wilt therefore ask him forgiveness.
But I see well, thou shakest thy head, bitest thy teeth one
upon another, and art become, as methinketh, nothing the
milder. Wherefore behold, I beseech you, how shameless
this man is, if I may call such one a man, which so unmanly
dealeth, that I suppose he hath forgotten that he himself is
a man. I doubt not, right dear judges, but the same free
confession of this christian man is sufficient enough to quiet
him, and that in your judgment he needeth no further clear-
ing of himself. Notwithstanding, lest our adversary should
report, that I have said nothing to the orderly rehearsal of
his accusation, but wittingly passed over it; or how that I

am so short of memory, that I have forgotten what he hath laid for himself; therefore will I rehearse it all again, to the intent that when I have repeated his unhonest complaint, and confuted it, every man may understand, that he is smitten with his own sword. Ye have perceived, I suppose, that his whole accusation consisted in eight principal articles, which I will now repeat in order; that, if anything therein have been forgotten, it may be called unto remembrance again.

This heretic, saith our adversary, doth affirm,

First. That the bishop of Rome is not the head of the church, nor the true vicar of Christ.

Secondly. That the mass is no sacrifice, nor ought to be used for other.

Thirdly. That the Supper of the Lord ought to be ministered in forms both of bread and wine, and that also unto the lay people.

Fourthly. That there is no purgatory, and that suffrages for the dead are in vain, and superstitious.

Fifthly. That it is not necessary to call upon saints.

Sixthly. That auricular confession was neither commanded nor instituted of Christ and his disciples.

Seventhly. That on the days prohibited and forbidden by the church of Rome, it is no sin to eat flesh.

Eighthly and finally. He saith plainly, that priests may marry.

These, ye dear judges, are the foul misdeeds; these are the horrible vices; these are the detestable blasphemies: hereof cometh the great uproar and horrible noise of heaven and earth, wherethrough it is to be feared that the four elements will come together, and that the world will return into his old darkness and confusion again.

And why do not we all rend our clothes, and stop our ears after the manner of the Jews, and cry with loud voice, "He hath blasphemed; Crucify, crucify"? Such a matter might haply be laughed at, if it were shewed in the way of jesting, and to make the people a pastime withal. But forasmuch as the matter is now handled in judgment, and brought so far forth, that this christian man is like to suffer death; therefore, methinketh, every faithful christian man ought from the ground of his heart to bewail it.

But now let us examine the first article, and ponder well, what is to be holden of the bishop of Rome's power. All christian men do confess, that the holy catholick or universal church is the fellowship of saints. And this is the one only church, wherein is but one Lord, one faith, one baptism, one God and Father of all things. But forasmuch as we say, I believe an holy universal church, we do confess, that the same is not visible nor corporal. Notwithstanding in the scripture there is named yet another church, which is both visible and corporal, whereunto the keys of the kingdom of heaven are committed; which the Lord also meaneth, when he saith, "Tell it unto the church." In the which church all they are comprehended, that are named christian, good and evil; wherein also the tares groweth with the wheat until the time of the harvest.

Nevertheless this is not an one only church, but distributed into many parts: for it were impossible to have in one place an one only congregation of all Christians together, seeing they dwell so far one from another, and be of so sundry languages and manners. Therefore the apostles, as we do read, have in all parts ordained as many churches, as they thought necessary, according to the nature of the countries; and gave unto every church their peculiar bishop, to keep the Lord's flock, whom they also called priest or elder; giving them a title of reputation, either because of their age, or by reason of their excellent gravity and virtuous conversation. To such men was committed the care of Christ's flock and the ministration of God's word, to rule the people, and to feed the flock of Christ withal.

As for high bishop, under Christ they knew none. They had all like authority. Every one had the oversight of the flock that was committed unto him. But when any doubt arose, they used not to shew it unto one alone, as to the head, or to them all (which was impossible), but unto certain; who when they had called upon the name of the Lord, knew in the Holy Ghost what was to be done, as we may openly see in the Acts of the Apostles. Wherefore methinketh it a great wonder, that ever the church of Rome came in such reputation, that it hath hitherto been taken of many for the head of all churches, yea, for the one only catholic or universal church; considering that in holy scripture it hath no testimony that may truly be alleged to any such purpose. For we have declared now already, that there is not one only visible church; which thing appeareth evidently out of the words of Christ, when he saith: "Tell it unto the church." Should he now run from Jerusalem unto Rome, to tell his brother's fault? Therefore be there many churches or congregations, wherein the children of God in this vale of misery are mixed among children of the devil; which inconvenience also they daily complain of.

But let us see, with what reasons, or rather cavillations, our adversary goeth about to maintain this his Romish church, and his grandsire pope, or bishop of Rome. We read in the gospel, that Christ asked his disciples: "Who [Matt. xvi.] say ye that I am? Peter answered and said, Thou art the Son of the living God. Whereupon Jesus said unto him: Blessed art thou, Simon, Jonas' son; for flesh and blood hath not opened that unto thee, but my Father which is in heaven. And I say unto thee, Thou art Petrus, (that is, appertaining to the stony rock;) and upon this rock will I build my church, and the gates of hell shall not prevail against it. And I will give thee the keys of the kingdom of heaven: and whatsoever thou bindest upon earth, shall also be bound in heaven; and whatsoever thou loosest upon earth, shall be loosed also in heaven."

This promise of Christ, which we also believe stedfastly to be fulfilled, taketh our adversary upon him to wrest unto his opinion. "How now?" saith he, "did not Christ plainly say, 'Thou art Petrus, and upon this rock will I build my church; and I will give thee the keys of the kingdom of heaven?'"

Who, I pray thee, denieth, that the church is builded upon a strong rock? Who will not grant, that the keys were committed unto Peter? Nevertheless we will seek the true understanding of this promise. When Peter had confessed Christ to be the Son of the living God, the Lord said unto him: "Blessed art thou, Simon the son of Jonas; for flesh and blood hath not opened that unto thee, but my Father which is in heaven." Whereby Christ is the gift of God, and cometh of the Father of heaven. Now followeth the promise for the Father's sake: "And I say unto thee, that thou art Petrus." Here giveth he him another name, not

Simon, Jonas' son, but Petrus, as one that cleaveth or belongeth unto the rock: "and upon this rock," saith he, "will I
build my church:" as though he should say: "Blessed art
thou; forasmuch as through God's revelation thou confessest,
that I am the Son of the living God. And therefore art thou
Petrus, that is, thou belongest unto the rock. And upon this
rock, whereunto thou cleavest now by thy confession, will I
build my church. For whereas the church of God was
nourished first in hope of the redemption for to come, and,
after that the law came as a schoolmaster, stood much in
outward ceremonies and commandments of the law; now that
the perfect time is come, I will build my church upon myself,
as on the strong rock, that whosoever believeth in me shall
not perish, but have everlasting life." If he had said, *Super
Petrum*, it might haply have been understood of Peter: but
seeing he saith, *Super hanc Petram*, we will search the scripture, whether this rock may signify anything else save only
Christ himself.

[Isai. xxviii.] It is written: "Behold, I lay in Zion a stumbling-stone,
and a rock that men shall be offended at. And whosoever
believeth on him, shall not be confounded:" which scripture
Paul and Peter also declare in manner with the same words.
[1 Cor. x.] And in another place saith Paul: "They drank all of the
spiritual rock that followed them, which rock was Christ."
[Acts iv.] And in the Acts of the Apostles: "This is the stone that was
refused of you builders, and is become the head corner-stone;
neither is there salvation in any other." Lo, here is a true
and sufficient interpretation of this rock. For, as the apostle
[1 Cor. iii.] Paul saith: "No man can lay another foundation, than that
is laid already, namely, Christ Jesus." This much have I
said touching the foundation of the church.

Now will we come to the keys. "And I," saith the
Lord, "will give thee the keys of the kingdom of heaven."
The story now of the gospel declareth, that this authority
of the keys was not given only unto Peter, but unto all the
[John xx.] apostles alike. "And when he had so spoken," saith the
evangelist, "breathed he upon them, and said, Receive ye
the Holy Ghost. Whose sins ye forgive, to them are they
forgiven; and whose sins ye retain, to them are they re-
tained." These are other words than the Lord spake afore
unto Peter alone, and yet is it all one meaning. For what is

this binding else, save only retaining of sins? And what else is loosing, save only remitting of sins? Wherefore not only Peter, but all disciples also, yea, all such as have the Holy Ghost, have free authority to use the keys.

Yet hath our adversary one reason, whereby he thinketh to prove, that Christ gave the superiority unto Peter, vainly; because that in the end of St John's gospel the Lord Jesus said unto him: "Simon Joannes, lovest thou me more than these? Peter answered him, Yea, Lord, thou knowest that I love thee. Jesus said unto him, Feed my sheep;" and that same spake he three times. Out of this will our adversary conclude, that the whole flock of Christ was committed unto Peter to be fed: and because the Lord said, "I have prayed for thee that thy faith fail not," he will that we shall thereby understand the church of Rome.

If he now will have that understand of the church of Rome, as of Peter's habitation to come, then out of Christ's commandment, which followeth immediately after, let him learn, that unto the church of Rome there was given no pre-eminence more than to other churches, but that there is equality. "And thou," saith Christ, "when thou art converted, strength thy brethren." He saith not, "Strength thy sheep, as the chief shepherd; neither, thy children, as the most holy Father;" but, "Strength thy brethren." And as oft as there arose any contention among the disciples for the superiority, Christ alway rebuked them, and said, that they were brethren.

Therefore saith St Paul also: "Unto every one of us is [Ephes. iv.] given grace according unto the measure of the gift of Christ." And immediately after it followeth: "And he himself made some apostles, some prophets, some evangelists, some shepherds and teachers, to the edifying of the saints, to the work and ministration." In this rehearsal of ministrations, where nameth he one of them to be head among the apostles? What is become of the chief shepherd? It followeth also: "Let us follow the truth in love, and in all things grow in him, which is the head, even Christ." Here see we, that all saints are members of one body, whose head is Christ himself: neither is here mention made of any other head. And in another place saith Paul: "They which seemed to be some- [Gal. ii.] what and great, added nothing unto me. But contrariwise, when they saw that the gospel over the uncircumcision was

30—2

committed unto me, as the gospel over the circumcision was unto Peter; (for he that was mighty in Peter in the apostle-ship on the circumcision, the same was mighty in me among the heathen;) when they saw the grace that was given unto me; then James, Cephas, and John, which seemed to be pillars, gave unto me and Barnabas the right hands of that fellowship, that we should be apostles among the heathen, and they in the circumcision." What can be found more plain? St Paul saith, that he had commission of the apostleship among the heathen, as Peter had among the circumcision. Thus, after our adversaries' doctrine, we must have two heads, and two chief shepherds; the one among the Jews, the other among the heathen. And why do not the Romans boast themselves of St Paul, whom every man reputeth an apostle of the heathen, of whom they come? But let them hear the rest of the text, where it saith, that "James, Cephas, and John, seemed to be pillars." Why called he Cephas or Peter a pillar, like the other? Wherefore doth he not call him the foundation of the church? Why nameth he him not the chief among the apostles? "They gave me," saith he, "and Barnabas the right hand of that fellowship." Here he affirmeth, that they were received of them as companions. All which things declare no superiority, but a brotherly equality among the apostles.

But let us grant, that Peter was the chief among the apostles, the chief shepherd of the Lord's flock, and the true vicar of Christ upon earth, (though we need none such; forasmuch Christ hath promised us to be with us unto the end of the world, neither is his kingdom of this world;) but put the case, that it so is: why will the bishops of Rome yet use any such title? What excellent thing soever was in Peter, that same received he at the grace of God through his faith and love. The same grace lacked not Paul and the other apostles. For though Peter's shadow did heal many, yet helped Paul's napkin not a few through like working of the Lord, which confirmed his word with such tokens. But what is that to the bishops of Rome? Doth the same prove, that Peter and Paul preached at Rome? As for Peter, it is not very certain that ever he came there. But let us grant that he was at Rome, and bishop there also. Shall therefore all the bishops of Rome coming after inherit likewise the grace that Peter had? Oh, how blessed an estate hath the bishop of Rome, if even the same grace of God, that was in Peter, be adjoined to his office! if he might inherit the faith and love of Peter, doubtless he should also obtain like grace. But every man knoweth, that these things were gifts of grace in Peter and in the other apostles, considering that virtues or vices come not to inheritance; but every soul that sinneth, the same shall die. Virtue also doth seldom take place in the successors.

Why do the Romish then boast themselves so sore? Do they it only because that Peter was at Rome? That were even as if a shoemaker dwelling in a house, wherein a great learned man dwelt sometime, would boast himself to have obtained some sciences of his predecessor by reason of that dwelling-place. Yea, it were even as if a poor fellow entering into an office, wherein had been a rich man afore, (to whom great debts were owing, not concerning the office,) will require of duty the same his predecessor's debts, because he succeedeth him in the office. Even like arguments in a manner doth our adversary use, whereby he goeth about to make the bishop of Rome like unto Peter in authority. "Peter," saith he, "was ordained chief shepherd of Christ's flock; to him were committed the keys of the kingdom of heaven; and the same Peter was sometime bishop of Rome. Therefore all bishops of Rome are the chief shepherds, and have the keys of the kingdom of heaven." Though this be but a small argument; yet hath God permitted, that through the craft of the devil it is so sunk into many men's minds, that whosoever undertaketh, but with a word, to do ought there-against, must stand in danger of his life. Now is it manifest, that for the maintenance of his opinion he, namely our adversary, hath nothing, except we grant him that Peter was bishop of Rome. If that now alone be sufficient for the establishing of such exceeding great authority, I refer it to the discretion of you that be judges. Now will we speak of the Mass.

This name, Mass, was doubtless in the apostles' time neither used nor heard of; neither can there any certain occasion be shewed, whence this name should come. But certain it is, that all the preparation about it was instituted and ordained, to the intent that the supper and death of the Lord might be had in remembrance; which may easily be perceived by the vestments and other things pertaining to the mass. Now in the primitive church was not the supper of the Lord kept afore noon, as now the use is, but in the evening after supper, as Christ himself kept it. Nevertheless, through the misbehaviour of certain filthy persons, which with their drunkenness dishonoured this holy supper, arose great slander and offence, which St Paul to the Corinthians doth earnestly rebuke. And therefore thought the holy fathers it should not be against the ordinance of the Lord, if men kept this holy supper afore noon, fasting; whereby such inordinate people might somewhat be withdrawn from their inconvenience: which they considered they might well do, forasmuch as they altered nothing of the principal matter.

And at the first was no more added thereunto, save only the Paternoster, the prayer of the Lord. But afterward in process of time, by adding more and more, it grew to the point that it is now at. And besides that with such additions they thought to garnish the supper of the Lord, peradventure of a good intent, they have almost utterly lost the principal points of the remembrance of the supper: so that now the right name of it is altered, and no more called the Lord's supper, but is called mass, which name is both strange and unknown in the scripture: yea, and that worse is, it is named a sacrifice, that may be done for other folks; whereof then sprung the slanderous market of buying and selling of masses in churches. Hereof was renewed the dangerous idolatry, that we ran unto the mass, as to a special work, thinking there to fetch all salvation, which we should have looked for only at Christ's hand.

But let us look, wherefore they call it a sacrifice. Even because, say they, that in the mass Christ the Son is offered up unto God his Father. Oh, what a great blasphemy is this; yea, to be abhorred of all virtuous men! Who would think it possible, that men mortal and sinful could ever have been so malapert, or rather mad, as to presume with their unclean hands to offer Christ the Lord unto his Father yet once again? "Christ," saith St Paul, "is entered into the very heaven, for to appear now in the sight of God for us: not to offer himself often, as the high priest entereth into the holy place every year with strange blood: for then must he have oft suffered since the world began." And afterwards it followeth:

"Thus was Christ offered up once for all, to take away the sins of many." But they will say, "Christ is not so sacrificed in the mass, that he dieth again upon the cross; but it is for the remembrance of the same sacrifice, that once was made." Why do they then call it a sacrifice, seeing it is but a remembrance of a sacrifice? And why say they, that it may be done for other, seeing that of itself it is no such work, but only a remembrance of the supper and passion of our Lord Jesus Christ, which saith, "Take and eat, this is my body?" And of the cup he saith: "Drink ye all thereout; and as oft as ye do this, then do it to the remembrance of me." He saith not, "Offer my body and my blood." Wherefore let the right and true remembrance of the Lord's supper remain in the congregations, and let us shew the Lord's death until he come.

Now if we be disposed to offer, let us "offer our own bodies a quick, holy, and acceptable sacrifice unto God; which is even the reasonable way to serve him." We read in the scripture, that no vice was punished so sore as the abuse of God's service. Wherefore, methinketh, all virtuous men should heartily pray, that the abuse of the mass were put down in the churches. "For if we wilfully sin after the knowledge of the truth, there remaineth no more sacrifice for sins." But I will let the mass go, and treat of both the kinds in the Lord's holy supper, which should also be given unto the lay people.

It is past all doubt by every man, that Christ in the holy supper gave his disciples both the kinds. Therefore it is manifest, that their opinion is not evil, which would have the chalice distributed unto every man. And methinketh the other do err sore, that hold the contrary; and specially because they put such difference between priests and lay people, not considering the priestly office that is committed unto all faithful believers. For in the law of Moses the office of priests was to offer and pray for the people. But now, forasmuch as Christ, being once offered up for us, hath abrogate all other sacrifices, and not only permitted, but also commanded all men to pray; I cannot see what difference can be between priests and lay people, except the governance of the church and ministration of God's word. For St Peter in his epistle saith: "And ye also as living stones are made a spiritual house, an holy priesthood, to offer up spiritual sacrifices, acceptable to God through Jesus Christ." And even there also saith St Peter : "But ye are the chosen generation, the royal priesthood, the holy nation," &c. Here writeth St Peter not only unto bishops and priests, but to the strangers that were dispersed and scattered abroad in Ponto, Galatia, &c.; and calleth them all together an holy and royal priesthood.

St Paul also, writing of this holy supper of the Lord to the common congregations at Corinthum, maketh mention, not only of the bread, but also of the cup. If the cup then at that time was common unto all christian men, why is it now withdrawn from the lay people ?

"The holy fathers," saith our adversary, "have with good conscience brought the supper to this ordaining, that it now is in : and that might they well do, as we read that in the apostles' time certain things were ordained, whereof no mention [Acts xv.] is in the gospel. Among which this is one in the Acts of the Apostles, where they commanded to abstain from things offered unto idols, and from blood, and from strangled; which commandment the apostles esteemed necessary." Whereunto I answer briefly, that the apostles gave no such commandment, for that intent that it should alway so continue; seeing they themselves afterward kept it not. Nevertheless they, having respect unto the time, thought to avoid the offending of the weak. But when the gospel was more clearly come to light, they ceased from such commandments, as things not necessary, the verity being known. Even out of this occasion did Paul circumcise Timothy; whereas nevertheless afterward, when [Gal. ii.] the Jews would needs have had him to circumcise Titus also, he would not give place unto them one hour. Even so, methinketh, should it be now likewise : for though the cup of the Lord be withholden from the lay people for certain causes, which be but trifles; yet now, forasmuch as it is evident to all such as will know it, that the memorial of Christ's holy supper was institute by himself under both the forms of bread and wine, let us forsake our own foolish intents, and turn again to the infallible ordinance of Christ; yea, let us acknowledge, that Christ, who is wiser than all angels or men, did not for nought, or without a cause, ordain this remembrance under both forms of bread and wine; and that if there were any danger for the lay people to have the use of the chalice, (as our adversaries make a babbling thereof,) he could have known it afore well enough: howbeit in the outward use of the sacrament without faith, consisteth but small salvation, as it well hath appeared in the traitor Judas. For as soon as he had received this sacrament with the other disciples at the hand of Christ, immediately went he forth, executed his treason, despaired, and hanged himself. For if the outward use of the bread and wine were necessary to salvation, it should not go well with them that may not away with wine. Therefore the right and wholesome remembrance of the supper of the Lord, is it that is done in faith; namely, when we believe that the body of Christ was given for us, and that his blood was shed for us. But forasmuch as Christ would have the same remembrance kept with outward using of bread and wine; therefore must so great a sacrament in no wise be left unministered, but still observed, according as Christ himself hath ordained it, without all men's inventions. But now will we speak of Purgatory.

The opinion of purgatory, I suppose, is taken out of the books and writings of the heathen; forasmuch as in the holy scripture of the old and new Testament we have no manner of record for the confirmation of any such thing. Christ and his apostles have taught much and evidently of the eternal salvation of the faithful, and damnation of the unfaithful; but nothing of purgatory. Wherefore I think it not needful to inveigh sore against it; considering it is a thing that hath no ground, and must needs fail of itself. Our adversary nevertheless had certain arguments, but so feeble and so wide from the purpose, that I am almost ashamed to repeat them.

We read in the book of the Machabees, Judas sent [2 Macc. xii.] to Jerusalem twelve thousand pieces of silver, to offer for the sins of the dead; because he had a good and devout mind concerning the resurrection. Now, I pray thee, what doth that to purgatory? Who saith, that it is not a good and devout thing to remember the resurrection? And whereas the author of the book addeth these words, "Therefore is it an holy and wholesome cogitation to pray for the dead, that they might be delivered from sins;" the same words do not I so esteem, that they ought to be taken for a certain; forasmuch as the author of the same book is unknown, and the book itself not approved with any testimony of holy scripture.

Furthermore, in the gospel, whereas Christ counselleth us to "agree with our adversary, while we are in the way with him, afore we come to the judge, lest the judge deliver us to the officer, and the officer cast us in prison; whence thou shalt not come forth," saith Christ, "till thou hast paid the uttermost farthing;" with these words will Christ declare, that a gentle agreement is profitable, though it be done with some loss. For if we will not agree with our adversary by the way, but fear a little loss; it is to be feared, that the judge will cast us in prison, and put us to sharper payment, yea, and more intolerable, than peradventure the other was, wherewith our adversary would have been satisfied. But the prison doth our adversary call here purgatory; and that which is spoken concerning the businesses of this world, doth he take upon him to wrest unto the world to come, as though a man might feign out of the words of Christ what he list.

In like manner allegeth he the testimony of St Paul, 1 Cor. iii.; where he saith, that "the fire shall prove every man's work what it is: and if any man's work burn, he shall suffer loss; but he himself shall be saved, nevertheless as through the fire." Here expoundeth he fire to be purgatory; whereas St Paul by a similitude doth say, that our works shall be tried, like as gold, silver, and other metal, is tried in the fire. But who can suffer such juggling? Let him shew us the least letter in the scripture, that plainly proveth purgatory. If we must purge our sins through purgatory, I pray thee then, for what intent died Christ? Wherefore shed he his blood? "If God be with us, who will be against us?" "Who spared not his own only Son, but gave him for us all; and how should he not give us all things with him? Who will accuse the elect of God? It is God that maketh them righteous. Who will condemn them?" Now see we, that the faithful are made righteous, and shall not be condemned. And who is so ungodly, as to think that the righteous God doth after this world punish one uncondemned.

Let this little, but true, be sufficient to overthrow the vain invention of purgatory. And what need was it, with this weak fear of pain to withdraw simple people from the whole love of Christ? who nevertheless in this world hath promised trouble even unto his faithful, to make them feel somewhat of the punishment of much sin, but after death an whole, free, perfect joy and salvation, which we undoubtedly look for in the blessed hope, [from which they] have thrust us down, and therefore feigned they this horrible bog of purgatory; to the intent that we, despairing in the assured and infinite mercy of God which cometh through Jesus Christ, might run to their churches, yea, to their chests, to be free from our sins with unreasonable money; whose judgment tarrieth not behind. Let no man, therefore, be moved by those deceitful spirits, which, as they say, do appear unto men, and desire their help, praying that masses, pilgrimages, and other like superstitious ceremonies, may be done for them; for even the same night-bogs, like as they in old time were among the heathen, so are they now also among the Turks. Neither is it wonder, if the devil can disguise him in the form of a dead man, seeing he can transfigure himself into an angel of light. But to the intent that the unprofitable purgatory do us no harm in our heads, we will go forth farther.

The invocation of saints hath even such a foundation as purgatory hath, namely, none at all. But a wonderful thing is it to express, how the imaginations of men have ever been inclined to idolatry: and therefore is it not for nought, that the first precept among ten was so well beaten into the Jews, that they should honour but one God, and have no strange gods.

Now to have a strange god, what is it else, save to put hope and trust in a creature, and not in God the maker only? Christ saith: "Come to me, all ye that labour and are overcharged, and I will refresh you." And, "Whatsoever ye ask the Father in my name, he will give it you." Is that true? I suppose no man will deny it. If it be true then, why do not we believe it? Wherefore call we not upon God the Father, through his only-begotten Son Jesus Christ, seeing we are sure that he denieth us no petition? But we will see the arguments of our adversary, whereby he goeth about to prove the invocation of saints. "We believe," saith he, "the promise of Christ; but because we trust not to our own strength, therefore seek we advocates to pray unto God for us; like as it is in great princes' courts, where matters are

despatched by the counsellors, whom the prince loveth." O
what a gross likeness is that! Hath a prince mortal anything in this point, that may be resembled unto God? Two
special causes there be, wherefore one must have to do with
lords upon earth through mediators and advocates, namely,
ignorance of the lords, and mutability of their minds. For
they cannot know what one desireth, except somebody tell
them. It is also uncertain, whether they will grant that one
desireth of them, or no. But so is it not with God. Christ
saith: "Your Father knoweth whereof ye have need, afore ye
pray unto him;" and "whatsoever ye pray unto the Father
in my name, he will give it you." Here is it evident, that
neither ignorance nor changeableness of mind hath place with
God. This similitude also concerning the great princes of
the world is false, like as it is false, that they say they believe
the promise of Christ. For if they constantly believed
that they should be heard through Christ, they would seek
no help of other. But seeing they confess, that they trust
not their own error, in that they understood not, that this
promise was made, not through our deserving, but through
the deserving of Christ; and where they will keep themselves from being to hold of God, they fall to their own hurt,
into the head sin of desperation or infidelity. And if they
continue therein, they need not look to obtain anything of
God, as St James testifieth, who exhorted us "to pray in
faith, and not to doubt." "For whoso doubteth," saith he, "is
like unto the waves of the sea, that are tossed and blown of
the wind. Let not such a man think, that he shall receive
anything of the Lord."

In matters of the world is it not accounted no good wit,
for a man to leave a thing certain for a thing uncertain, and,
as the dog did in Esop's fables, to let the flesh fall, and to
follow the shadow thereof? And how much more indiscreet
a thing may it be esteemed, when in such a great matter
concerning everlasting salvation one forsaketh it, that without
contradiction is true, and followeth another thing, where it
may be doubted, whether it be true or no! That we are
heard through Christ, we be certain, while we are so taught
of the verity itself. But how can we be sure, that our prayer
is heard for any saint's sake, seeing that of the invocation of
saints there is no mention made in the scripture; but the

contrary is evidently declared in many places. Christ answereth the devil after this manner: "Thou shalt worship the Lord thy God, and him only shalt thou honour." And what need we many probations? Let him shew us one place in the scripture, where one saint called upon another. If the invocation of saints were profitable, why did not Moses call upon Abraham, Isaac, and Jacob, seeing he heard God himself say, "I am the God of Abraham, Isaac, and of Jacob?" Why did not David and the other prophets call upon Moses, as the chief prophet of God? And wherefore did not the Jews that came after call upon David, who had such good record of God himself, that he said, "I have found a man after mine own heart, which shall accomplish all my will?" And after the coming of Christ, why did not the apostles call upon John the Baptist, concerning whom they had heard these words of our Saviour: "Among such as are born of women, there hath not risen a greater than John the Baptist?"

It is not likely, ye dear judges, that these holy men, of whom I now have made mention, were so negligent or so unkind of stomach toward us, that if they had known and been persuaded, that the invocation of saints were for our salvation, or acceptable to God, they would not let us know thereof. Therefore do I esteem it a dangerous thing, without scripture, yea, against the open scripture, to set up the invocation of saints, as a service acceptable to God. Neither can I allow the objection of those, that go about to maintain such opinions by old and long custom, or by miracles.

For as touching custom, if all were to be commended, that hath been long and of old time used; then the blasphemous use of the heathen with their idols must be set up again, which with one consent of so many nations endured many years afore the coming of Christ. Thus might advoutry also, and other vices also be maintained, seeing they be committed so oft and in so many places. But what is less commendable, than to go about through an evil custom to set up a thing that is openly against the law of God, (yea, men in their laws will suffer no such evil customs,) we to take upon us to be judges over God's word.

Concerning miracles, which God so greatly worketh in his saints, who would not highly wonder at such, as at a singular gift of God? Notwithstanding it is manifest also,

that to do miracles and wonders is not always a sure probation of holiness; seeing we read not ever, that Abraham,
Isaac, Jacob, David, and John the Baptist, did miracles.
Must they therefore not be holy, and should we therefore
despise them? Or why call we not Judas the traitor as a
saint, that did miracles with the apostles, and healed many
people, as we may perceive out of the history of the gospel?
But let us hear the sentence of Christ: "Many," saith he,
"shall say unto me in that day, Lord, Lord, have not we prophesied in thy name? Have not we cast out devils in thy
name? Have we not done great virtues in thy name? Then
will I confess unto them, I never knew you. Depart from
me, all ye evil-doers." What can our adversaries boast now
of saints' miracles, seeing we read, that ungodly and damned
persons have done many great acts in the name of Christ?
And St Paul also prophesieth to the Thessalonians, saying, that
[2 Thess. ii.] "the wicked shall come, namely, the child of perdition, whose
coming is after the working of the devil, with all manner lying
powers, tokens, and wonders." Wherefore let us not believe
every spirit, but prove them whether they be of God, or no.
And let us not be so unadvised, as to ascribe unto saints and
to their merits the honour that only appertaineth unto God.

When Peter and John at the gate of the temple had
made the lame man whole, and the people ran to them won-
dering, Peter said unto them: "Ye men of Israel, why
wonder ye at this thing? or why look ye so upon us, as
though we through our power or virtue had made this man
go?" And afterward it followeth: "Through the faith in his
name," namely Christ's, "hath he upon this man, whom ye see
and know, confirmed his name: and faith through him hath
given this man health before your eyes." Where are now
the miracles, which they say are done through the merits of
saints? Peter and John, pillars of the church, confess plainly,
that this lame man was not made whole through their power
or virtue, but in the faith through Christ. O eternal God,
in what an horrible deep pit of idolatry are we fallen! How
far have we erred from the true faith of Christ! We shall
not lightly find any time, wherein the heathen have honoured
their gods with so great superstitiousness, as some Christians
honour their saints. Every occupation hath his advowry[1],

[1 advowry *or* avowry: justification, *or* justifier.]

every land their own defender, and every sickness a peculiar physician. There be some saints also, whom they do not honour to have profit by them, but because they should do them no harm. To certain peculiar saints commit they their matters of war, their merchandise, and their causes of marriage. The husbandmen also have their own helpers : one increaseth the seed, another keepeth the vineyards, the sheep, the kine, the geese; yea, the filthy swine have likewise their own proper herd. To him offer the foolish people all manner of things, but for the most part ware : so that herein they are almost become like unto the Egyptians, who worshipped such beasts themselves for their gods.

These saints now are all honoured, they are all called upon; only merciful Christ is not regarded. And though they sometime name him with bare words, yet is all their trust in the saints. Neither are they satisfied in such strange honouring of saints, but make also a wonderful difference of holy places. Hereof cometh it, that they think Mary the mother of Christ to be more gracious in one place than in another. New pilgrimages also minish somewhat the reputation of the old. They run to Compostel in Spain, to visit St James; to Akon in Dutchland to salute our lady; and in many other places to saints' graves, as the kites fly to the carrion; and honour many dead bodies upon earth, whose souls are in hell. I pass over the foolish superstition that they use with dead saints' raiment, as coats, hosen, shoes, and regard little the poor saints, that live with us as brethren in Christ upon earth, and have great need of such apparel. Yet would I esteem it a less error, if they worshipped not also the images that have no understanding, and are made with men's hands, of gold, silver, stone, and wood; yea, very little it faileth, that they worship not withal even the worms, the worms that gnaw the bodies of such blessed saints of wood. To such images ascribe they wonders and miracles. Of some one they say that it had spoken. Of another they say, that by his own virtue he is gone from one place to another. The day should be too long for me, if I would say all that might be spoken of this unreasonable matter. Somehow they leave nothing behind, that belongeth to full idolatry.

We may well say, that the Indians had much more right

to worship the Sun, such a dear, profitable, wonderful, and excellent creature, than these mad folks have to worship such a rotten worm-eaten idol. Now though we disallow such idolatry, such perverse honouring and wrong invocation of saints, let no man think that we therefore will withdraw from them anything of their true worship and reputation. Saints have nothing that they have not received.   Paul saith : [1 Cor. iii.] "What is Paul? What is Apollo? Even ministers they are, by whom ye are to believe, and that according as the Lord hath given unto every man."   And afterward it followeth : "Therefore let no man rejoice in men ; for all is yours, whether it be Paul, or Apollo, or Cephas, or the world; whether it be life or death, whether it be things present or for to come, all is yours; but ye are Christ's, and Christ is God's." Wherefore all grace, which cometh through Christ in the Holy Ghost, ascribe we unto God, as unto him that only giveth it.   And heartily we beseech him, that unto us poor sinners also he will grant this infinite mercy, to the intent that we may forsake our sins, and be holy before him, through Jesus Christ, his only-begotten Son, who upon the cross hath delivered us not with a small price, but with his own blood.   Reason it is, that saints have their due honour ; [Heb. iv.] but faith and invocation belongeth only unto God.   "Let us go, therefore, with confidence unto the seat of grace, to help in the time of need. For we have not an high priest, which cannot have compassion on our infirmities; but was in all [Heb. vii.] points tempted as we are, but without sin ;" being "ever able also to save them that come unto God through him, and [Acts iv.] liveth ever to make intercession for us." "Neither is there under heaven given unto men any other name, wherein we [I Tim. ii.] must be saved."   "For there is but one God, and one mediator between God and man, namely, the man Jesus Christ, which gave himself a redemption for all."   To him be honour and praise for ever.

My purpose was, right dear judges, to have defended this christian man's cause with few words.   Nevertheless the subtle complaint of our adversary hath hindered me, as ye see, from making of mine answer. Wherefore the fault of so long communication ought reasonably to be imputed not unto us, but to the unrighteous accuser.

And now will I take in hand the sixth article, namely,

Auricular Confession: which I suppose was first ordained for this purpose, that the simple unlearned people should go to the priests to seek counsel, if they had any grievous thing in their mind, either concerning any doubt in the believe, or concerning sin which vexeth a man's conscience; to the intent that the priests, as they that be learned and have experience in the scripture, might strength such as be weak in faith, warn the unruly and misnurtured, comfort such as be sorry and penitent for their sins; summa, as true physicians, to give due medicines for every sickness. Which ordinance, if it were right kept, and as I now have said, I suppose no man could reprove it. But now, forasmuch as they command that every person shall once in the year confess all his sins to his own priest, not only such as he hath committed in deed, but also whatsoever is come into his thought, yea, and to declare the state, place, time, and circumstance of the persons; considering likewise that they proclaim the same out as a commandment of God, under pain of eternal damnation; I may say, that it is no wholesome confession of sins, but rather a shameful tormenting of men's consciences. Neither can I believe either, but that it was brought in by the special craft and subtilty of the devil, to tangle poor men with a new snare, and utterly to bring them from the wholesome and necessary confession of sins. It is written in the Psalm: "I will even against myself [Psalm xxxii.] confess mine offence unto the Lord, and thou forgavest me the ungodliness of my sin. For the same shall all saints pray unto thee in due season." Without such confession of sin shall no man be saved. For they that desire to be partakers of the grace of Christ, must afore all things know and confess, that they are sinners and worthy of eternal punishment. Such a confession, if it come from the heart, is wholesome and fruitful. Afterward verily followeth a broken heart, which God will not despise.

Our adversary would prove out of the gospel, that this confession to the priest is commanded of Christ, because that when he cleansed the lepers, he bade them go shew themselves to the priests. Here doth our adversary make a cold interpretation: "Shew yourselves," saith he, is as much to say as, "Confess your sins." But the words that follow after in the gospel will not suffer such a slender exposition:

31

"And offer the gift," saith Christ, "that Moses commanded, for a witness unto them." This was the very cause, why they were commanded to go unto the priests; namely, that of them, as of those to whom the knowledge of leprosy was committed, they might be judged clean; to the intent it might be known, that Christ had truly cleansed them. Therefore for a witness against such as resisted him, bade he the lepers offer the gift that Moses had commanded in the law.

[James v.] Out of St James's epistle taketh our adversary these words: "Knowledge your sins one to another, and pray one for another, that ye may be saved." Here doth he, as he did afore, and will have this word "one to another," to be as much to say as, to a priest. Nevertheless the words be so plain, that they need no long interpretation. For St James willeth, that every one shall knowledge himself as a sinner toward his neighbour, and so one to pray for another, that they may fulfil brotherly love, and be saved. I abhor, most prudent judges, to express, what great harm the strait confession hath brought to pass among the simple people. For seeing they think, that they cannot be saved, except they confess everything as narrowly as the same shrift[1] tradition bindeth, and yet leave it undone, sometime for shame, and sometime through forgetfulness; no doubt they fall into despair, and are ever, yea, as long as they live, far from holy hope. It is manifest also, how unreasonably certain priests behave themselves in hearing of confessions, to the great destruction of souls. Some, for all right occasion, will not absolve a penitent, no, though he be very sorry for his sins. Some ask questions of young people concerning wanton and filthy matters, nothing regarding their innocent minds. And whereas they should earnestly desire to help with some wholesome medicine, they make deadly wounds in weak consciences.

But what shall I say? Have they not oft and wilfully, through their constrained confession, abused the chaste simplicity of honest women and virgins to their own unchastity and wantonness? Some of them openly told abroad the thing, that hath been committed to their fidelity in confession; and thereby have they brought much malice to

[1 shrift: from shrive, to hear at confession.]

pass, yea, and sometime murder also. Such are the sweet fruits of this feigned confession; yea, and that as evil is, they preach the same to be a work, for whose sake God forgiveth sins; and therefore have they robbed Christ of his honour, like blasphemous men, as they be. Wherefore considering this tree was not planted by the Father of heaven, but by the children of the devil, to search out craftily the privities of men's hearts, methinketh it should be plucked up by the roots, and men brought again to the right and wholesome confession of their sins.

The rest is, that I make answer touching the difference of meats, and concerning the marriage of priests: which two points I purpose not to sunder, forasmuch as Paul joineth them together in his first epistle to Timothy, where these be his words: "The spirit speaketh evidently, that in the latter [1 Tim. iv.] times some shall depart from the faith, and shall give heed unto spirits of error, and devilish doctrines of them which speak false through hypocrisy, and have their conscience marked with an hot iron, forbidding to marry, and commanding to abstain from the meats, which God hath created to be received with thanksgiving of them which believe and know the truth. For every creature of God is good, and nothing to be refused, that is received with giving of thanks: for it is sanctified by the word of God and prayer." I suppose, dear judges, that as touching these matters, Paul hath with these words sufficiently answered for us, seeing he saith evidently, that they which forbid to marry, and command to abstain from meats, are departed from the faith, and follow the devil's doctrine. Paul also himself writeth thus to the Corinthians: "Whatsoever is [1 Cor. viii.] sold in the flesh-market, that eat, and ask no question for conscience sake. For the earth is the Lord's, and all that is therein." And to the Colossians he writeth: "Let no [Col. ii.] man therefore trouble your consciences about meat or drink, or for a piece of an holy day, or new moon, or of the sabbath-days, which are the shadow of things that were for to come; but the body itself is in Christ." And afterward it followeth: "If ye be dead then with Christ from the ordinances of the world, why are ye holden with such traditions, as though ye lived after the world? As when they say, Touch not this, taste not that, handle not that: all which things do hurt

31—2

unto men, because of their abuse, which cometh only of the commandments and doctrines of men, &c." All this doth Christ confirm, when he saith: "Whatsoever entereth in at the mouth defileth not the man." And what can be more clearly spoken? But so false and unrighteous is the judgment of such unreasonable men, that if a christian man do taste but a little flesh upon a day prohibited by them, immediately, without any farther advisement, they proclaim him to be an heretic, and cast in his teeth such a tradition of fasting, as though a man's salvation depended upon the difference of meats: and yet the hypocrites themselves, though they eat no flesh, are nevertheless so full of fleshly desires, that they can understand nothing but fleshly, and sometime are not ashamed to utter their fleshly lusts with excess.

Even as great wrong do they through their damning of priests' marriage. But to the intent that men should judge them to be excellent maintainers of chastity, they praise virginity out of measure, which in very deed is a singular gift of God, but given unto few. Nevertheless, that they go about to maintain not virginity, but a state to live unmarried, it appeareth plainly by this, that when a priest taketh a wife, they will not only have him deposed from his ministration, but judge him worthy to be put to death also: but if he against all honesty take an harlot, or keep another man's wife, he is suffered as a profitable member of the church, (of Rome, I mean.) Oh what an horrible wickedness is this! Yet was there never a people so wild or unnatural, but they had an ordinance concerning marriage, and keeping concubines. Only Romish priests may in this matter do as they lust themselves. They take harlots of their pleasure, when they will, and where, and ask no question for conscience sake, so that they pay the bishop the whore-toll. And even with like audacity put they them away from them again, and shame never a whit. Yet are they not satisfied with such unmeasurable liberty[1]. Nothing can be safe from them; with their filthy wantonness defile they every thing, the angelical defenders of chastity: all which is so manifest, that it cannot be hid.

But lest I be reputed more to be an accuser of Romish

[1 Eight words omitted.]

priests, than a defender of this christian man, I will pass
over many things, that might be spoken concerning this
matter, and content me with the judgment of Paul, who saith:
" If they cannot abstain, let them marry ; for it is better to [1 Cor. vii.]
marry, than to burn." Wherefore let this judgment remain ;
let troubled consciences be helped, and the ministers of the
church restored again to an honest conversation ; lest if we
continue in this sin, we fall into that horrible judgment,
wherewith God will judge fornicators and advoutres.

Now, thou unreasonable accuser, hast thou a sufficient
answer to all the points of thy complaint. And I would
hope that thy madness should thereby be mitigated, if I
feared not, that the light of thy body were darkened for very
malice. Now "if the light that is in thee be darkness, how
great will the darkness itself be !" Even thou thyself, I say,
knowest well, that all that I have said is true. And why resisted thou then the open truth ? Thou unhappy man, art thou
so far unadvised, that thou canst not ponder, how weak a ground
thou hast in this ungodly matter; and again, how mighty and
invincible an adversary thou hast, namely, Christ Jesus, the
only-begotten dear Son of God ? Thy fury hath now raged
enough against this innocent christian man. Cease now at
the last from perverting the right way of the Lord. Alas,
man, how oft hast thou in this thy envious complaint denied
the faith openly, in that thou hast divers times said, that
only faith maketh not righteous before God ! I pray thee,
art thou not ashamed of so detestable a lie ? Doth not the
scripture teach evidently, that faith only justifieth in the sight
of God ? Who ever denied this, if he were not mad, and
such one as thou art? Thou boastest of great works, whereof
thou thyself hast not touched one with thy little finger. And
who knoweth not, that faith and charity cannot be separated?
If charity then hang upon faith, and cannot be idle, but
alway occupied, how should not the works of charity and
love follow afterward of themselves ? Yea, the same works
are now not ours (lest any man boast himself), but Christ's;
who worketh in us through faith, as in his own members.

Thou takest to record the epistle of St James, whose
words are these : " Faith without works is dead." Here [James ii.]
thou rejoicest, as though thou hadst gotten the victory, and
triumphest, as though thou wast over the hedge already.

St James saith, that "faith without works is no faith; for faith, love, or charity, cannot be sundered." Thinkest thou, that one can love another, to whom he giveth no credence? Or that one can put all his hope and trust in him, whom he loveth not? St Paul saith: "If I had all faith, so that I could remove hills, and had not love, I were nothing." The same putteth he for a thing impossible, and declareth thereby, that faith cannot be without love or charity. Therefore will we discern these three things, faith, hope, and charity, one from another; but so that they remain unseparated. Faith only justifieth before God; love or charity worketh toward his neighbour; hope doth patiently wait for the promise of God, and shall not be confounded. Thou sayest we lack good works,—not such as come of love, or that Christ shall require of us at the day of judgment, but to go a pilgrimage, to set up candles before images, to number up what we pray, to tell over a prayer of beads, to put difference in clothing, in meats, in prayers, in titles or names, where one had rather be called a Charter-House monk, or a barefoot friar, than a christian man. These and such like slender and childish works requirest thou of us; which though one had done them altogether, it were even as much as though he in the mean season had ridden upon a stick with boys in the street.

But declare thou us thy faith out of such works as belong to a christian man, and we will shew thee our works out of faith. Seest thou, how this christian man, whom thou accusest, standeth here so weak and feeble through the stink and tediousness of the prison, that he can scarce stand upon his legs? And why, I pray thee? Hath he committed any evil deed? No. For if he have done ought that deserveth death, or so the judges have the law, they have the sword, let them execute it, I will make no request against it. Wherefore is it then? I will tell thee. Even because he hath freely preached the gospel of Christ, and the grace that is given us through him, (for he "believed, therefore hath he spoken,") and hath taught, that whatsoever is against the gospel ought to be put down, to the intent that the kingdom of God might come unto us, and that "his name might be sanctified." Thus of a fervent love hath he endeavoured himself to instruct all men, and to bring them to the true knowledge of God and of his Son Jesus Christ. Summa, his mind was so set to learn his neighbour, that he hath not abhorred the dark dungeon and prison, to be desolate and alone, in hunger and thirst, yea, and in danger of death. Such are the works for a christian man; which must not be ascribed unto us, but unto the Lord that worketh them in us. Such true fasting is accepted of the Lord, such true obedience belongeth to his saints.

Now forasmuch as I have sufficiently declared, that our adversary's complaint is clean against equity, there is no more to be required, save only that ye, right dear judges, whose mind is to do every man right, quit this christian man according to your benevolence.

A SHORT RECAPITULATION

UNTO THE READER.

HERE hast thou heard, most gentle reader, how benign, how loving, how mindful our most merciful Father is, and ever hath been, over his elect and chosen children, namely even now. And for an ensample have we this poor and simple creature set before our eyes, to call us to remembrance, that he is nigh unto all them that in time of tribulation or persecution will call upon him in truth and verity. See we not here, how mercifully he stretcheth out his hand, he spreadeth abroad his wings, to hide and cover this his tender bride from the glede[1] or buzzard? And in conclusion, he mollifieth and moveth the heart of this virtuous prince; and by him, as by an instrument of his own, doth he not only defend this poor man's cause, or rather the truth itself, but also delivereth him from the cruel hands of all his enemies, no otherwise than even as it were from death to life. Such is his godly nature, such is his property and accustomed mannor, that in the midst of adversities, tribulation, and per-

[1 A glede: a kite.]

secution, where men think him most furthest off, there is he
most nighest and present with such consolation and comfort
as cannot be expressed with tongue.   What more joy can
there come to them which be afflicted, persecuted, and under
the sweet cross of Jesus Christ, than to call to their remembrance the comfortable stories of the scripture, according to
[Rom. xv.]   the saying of St Paul, "Whatsoever thing is written, it is
written for our doctrine and learning, that through patience
and the consolation of God's word we may have sure hope
and trust?"

How like a loving Lord saved he Isaac from the mortal
and deadly stroke of the sword! With how pitiful an eye
looked he on Noe the preacher of righteousness, restoring
him from the rough raging waves of the unmerciful sea! He
delivered Lot at an instant from the conversation and company of the ungodly Sodomites and Gomorrians.   Kept he
not Jonas safe and sound, after he was devoured and swallowed up of that huge and monstrous fish?   Sidrach, Misach,
and Abenago preserved he from the flaming furnace of
burning fire; and Daniel he delivered from the devouring
mouths of the hungry lions.   Moyses, among the reeds
and flags hid and hanged by the water-side in a basket, was
restored again to his natural mother to be nursed of her.
Paul was let down in a basket, and so escaped the hands of
his persecutors.   Susannah was preserved and defended pure
and undefiled from[1] the false priests and judges.   Judith,
with much joy and victory, was delivered from the fiery
violence and mighty power of all the enemies of God.   These
and many more godly ensamples be left in the holy scriptures, to the great comfort and consolation of them that suffer
persecution for Christ's sake, according to the saying of Christ
himself: "Blessed are all they which suffer persecution for
righteousness' sake; for theirs is the kingdom of heaven."
Again, "as many as will live godly in Christ Jesus must suffer
persecution."   It is the blessing of God and the sweet rod of
correction, wherewith all the faith of the faithful must therewith be tried.   For even as our Lord and God doth always
and at all times preserve, keep, and defend his poor persecuted and afflicted in all extremities; so doth he cast down,
and never raise up again, all such that so obstinately and

[1 Four words omitted.]

wilfully resisteth his eternal testament and word, oppressing his preachers, and persecuting Christ the only Son of God in his members.   Seeing now, that such trouble and persecution chanceth always upon the simple and poor afflict, specially now in this dangerous and perilous season, let not therefore the words of Paul be out of the remembrance of them that be at liberty, where he saith: "Remember them [Heb. xiii.] that are in bonds, even as though ye were in bonds with them; and be mindful of them which are in adversity."

Let this short and brief lesson be sufficient at this time to put the most christian reader in remembrance of some part of thy duty, and to render thanks unto the Lord for the great strength and power he gave unto this christian prince to confess his Lord and God : before all men him shall the Lord confess again before the Father of heaven.   The Lord send us many such princes, that will with so ready a mind defend the lively word of God, deliver the innocent, confute the false accuser, and, to conclude, to be first and ready to give his life for his poor brother; to the great discomfort of that hungry horse-leech and blood-thirsty Romanist, the generation of whom is never satisfied till it hath blood! God defend all them that believe in his word from their cruelty, and illuminate the hearts of all princes, that they may once spy and perceive, what kind of people they be, that cause this great dissension, discord, and wars, now in this troublesome time; and though I put no doubt but that kingdom of antichrist, which now hangeth by a twine-thread, shall shortly take a fall, and the kingdom of Christ magnified among all nations, to the great honour and laud of God, to the consolation and comfort of the whole christian congregation of Jesu Christ, to whom be praise both now and ever! Amen.

Printed at Nurenbergh, and translated owt of Douche
into Englishe by Myles Coverdale, in the yeare
of our Lorde M.D.XLV. *in the laste of*
Octobre.

LETTERS.

LETTER I.

MYLES COVERDALE TO Mr CRUMWELL.

Dated from the St Augustin's, *May* 1, [1527.]

[State Papers, Crumwell Correspondence, Vol. vii. No. 62.]

Most singular good master, with due humility I beseech unto your mastership all godly comfort, grace, and prosperous health. Forsomuch as your goodness is so great towards me, your poor child, only through the plenteousness of your favour and benevolence, I am the bolder of your goodness in this my rude style. If it like your favour to revocate to your memory the godly communication, which your mastership had with me your orator in master Moore's house upon Easter Eve, amongst many and divers fruitful exhortations, specially of your singular favour and by your most comfortable words, I perceive your gracious mind toward me. Wherefore, most honourable master, for the tender love of God, and for the fervent zeal that you have to virtue and godly study, *cordis genibus provolutus,* I humbly desire and beseech your goodness of your gracious help. Now I begin to taste of holy scriptures: now, honour be to God! I am set to the most sweet smell of holy letters, with the godly savour of holy and ancient doctors, unto whose knowledge I cannot attain without diversity of books, as is not unknown to your most excellent wisdom. Nothing in the world I desire but books, as concerning my learning: they once had, I do not doubt but Almighty God shall perform that in me, which he of his most plentiful favour and grace hath begun. Moreover as touching my behaviour, (your mastership's mind once known,) with all lowliness I offer myself not only to be ordered in all things as shall please your wisdom, but also as concerning the education and instruction of other alonely to ensue your prudent counsel. *Nam quicquid est in te consilii, nihil non politicum, nihil non divinum est : quicquid enim agis, nihil inconsulte agis, nusquam te primum philosophum præbes ; de rore autem cœli summam, more Jacob, surripuisti benedictionem. De tuo ipso torrente maxime potari exopto, teque coram alloqui non mediocriter cupio. Vale, decus literarum, consiliorum, omnium denique probitatum.* From the Augustin's, this May-day.

Your child and beadman in Jesus Christ,

FRERE MYLES COVERDALE.

Unto the right worshipful and his most singular good master, master Crumwell, this be delivered with due manner.

LETTER II.

MYLES COVERDALE TO MR CRUMWELL.

Dated from CAMBRIDGE, *Aug.* 27, 1527.

[State Papers, Crumwell Correspondence, Vol. VII. No. 67.]

RIGHT honourable master, in my most lowly manner I commend me unto you evermore, desiring to hear of the preservation of your prosperity. So it is, I was required by Mr George Lawson to deliver this writing to your mastership mine own self : notwithstanding such an impediment hath chanced, that I must desire favour on your behalf for my excusation ; for master Moore's kinsman is not all well at ease ; *nam e febribus laborat. Opinandum est sane febris esse speciem ; nam in alimentis lunatico more solet deflectere, sed jam compertum est pene exolevisse.* Wherefore I beseech you to have me excused ; and if I knew that my coming to London might stand with your favour, truly the bird was never gladder of day than I would be to come : but briefly, I am ready at your commandment ; *nam restat tibi facultas apud tuum Milonem mandandi quæ voles. Ceterum nihil apud nos promulgatum est novi, nisi quod rumor est apud nostrates, (cum unus nostratium magis-*

trorum homicidii sit accusatus, alius criminis hæreseos sit dilatus,) quod tertius jam magister sit furtivi criminis deferendus, nempe magister ille Stookes junior; cujus rei subinde manifestius te certiorem faciemus. Denique præter istuc nullum mihi scribendi argumentum relictum est, nisi quod tu tuique rectissime valeatis; quod faxit Christus Optimus Maximus, cui sit honor et imperium in æternum. Amen. Ex Cantabrigia 27 die mensis Augusti, anno Domini 27 supra sesque-millesimum.

Tuus quantus quantus,

MILO COVERDALUS.

Unto the right worshipful master
Crumwell, this be delivered
with speed.

LETTER III.

COVERDALE AND GRAFTON TO LORD CRUMWELL.

Dated from PARIS, *June* 23, 1538.

[State Papers, Crumwell Correspondence, Vol. I. No. 107.]

AFTER most humble and hearty commendations to your good lordship. Pleaseth the same to understand, that we be entered into your work of the Bible, whereof (according to our most bounden duty) we have here sent unto your lordship two ensamples; one in parchment, wherein we intend to print one for the king's grace, and another for your lordship; and the second in paper, whereof all the rest shall be made: trusting that it shall be not only to the glory of God, but a singular pleasure also to your good lordship, the causer thereof, and a general edifying of the king's subjects, according to your lordship's most godly request. For we follow not only a standing text of the Hebrew, with the interpretation of the Chaldee and the Greek; but we set also in a private table the diversity of readings of all texts, with such annotations in another table, as shall doubtless elucidate and clear the same, as well without any singularity of opinions, as all checkings and reproofs. The print, no doubt,

shall please your good lordship.   The paper is of the best
sort in France.   The charge certainly is great; wherein as
we most humbly require your favourable help at this present, with whatsoever it shall please your good lordship to
let us have, so trust we (if need require) in our just business
to be defended from the papists by your lordship's favourable
letters, which we most humbly desire to have (by this
bearer, William Grey) either to the bishop of Winchester[1],
or to some other whom your lordship shall think most expedient.   We be daily threatened, and look ever to be spoken
withal, as this bearer can further inform your lordship; but
how they will use us, as yet we know not.   Nevertheless,
for our further assurance, wherethrough we may be the
abler to perform this your lordship's work, we are so much
the bolder of your good lordship; for other refuge have
[we] none, under God and our king, whom with noble prince
Edward, and all you their most honourable council, God
Almighty preserve now and ever!   Amen.   Written at Paris,
the twenty-third day of June, by your lordship's assured
and daily orators,

MYLES COVERDALE,
RICHARD GRAFTON, *Grocc'.*

To the right honourable and their
singular good lord, the lord
Crumwell, and lord privy seal.

LETTER IV.

COVERDALE AND OTHERS TO LORD CRUMWELL.

Dated from PARIS, *Aug.* 9, 1538.

[State Papers, Crumwell Correspondence, Vol. I. No. 108.]

AFTER most humble and due salutation to your good
lordship.   Pleaseth the same to understand that, your work
going forward, we thought it our most bounden duty to send

[1 Gardiner, who was at this time ambassador at Paris, but was
shortly afterwards succeeded by Boner, bishop elect of Hereford.]

unto your lordship certain leaves thereof, specially seeing we had so good occasion, by the returning of your beloved servant Sebastian. And as they are done, so will we send your lordship the residue from time to time. As touching the manner and order that we keep in the same work, pleaseth your good lordship to be advertised, that the mark ☞ in the text signifieth, that upon the same, in the latter end of the book, there is some notable annotation, which we have written without any private opinion, only after the best interpreters of the Hebrews, for the more clearness of the text. This mark ♀ betokeneth, that upon the same text there is diversity of reading among the Hebrews, Chaldees, and Greeks, and Latinists; as in a table at the end of the book shall be declared. This mark ✳ sheweth that the sentence written in small letters is not in the Hebrew or Chaldee, but in the Latin, and seldom in the Greek; and that we nevertheless would not have it extinct, but highly accept it, for the more explanation of the text. This token † in the old Testament, giveth to understand, that the same text which followeth it, is also alleged of Christ or of some apostle in the new Testament. This, among other our necessary labours, is the way that we take in this work; trusting verily, that as God Almighty moved your lordship to set us unto it, so shall it be to his glory, and right welcome to all them that love to serve him and their prince in true faithful obedience: as is only known to the Lord of heaven, to whom we most heartily pray for your lordship's preservation. At Paris, the 9th day of August, 1538, by your faithful orators,

> MYLES COVERDALE.
> RICHARD GRAFTON.
> WILLIAM GREY.

To the right honourable and their
singular good lord, lord privy
seal, be this delivered.

LETTER V.

COVERDALE AND GRAFTON TO LORD CRUMWELL.

Dated from PARIS, *Sept.* 12, [1538.]

[State Papers, Crumwell Correspondence, Vol. I. No. 115.]

AFTER most humble and due salutations to your most honourable lordship. Pleaseth the same to understand, that we are instantly desired of our host, whose name is Francis Regnault, a Frenchman, to make supplication for him unto your lordship. Whereas of long time he hath been an occupier into England more than forty year, he hath always provided such books for England as they most occupied; so that he hath a great number at this present in his hands, as primers in English, missals, with other such like, whereof now by the company of the booksellers in London he is utterly forbidden to make sale, to the utter undoing of the man. Wherefore most humbly we beseech your lordship to be gracious and favourable unto him, that he may have licence to sell those which he hath done already; so that hereafter he print no more in the English tongue, unless he have an Englishman that is learned to be his corrector; and that is the man well contented withal. He is also contented, and hath promised, before my lord elect of Hereford[1], that if there be found any notable fault in his books, he will put the same out, and print the leaf again. Thus are we bold to write unto your lordship in his cause, (as doth also my lord elect of Hereford,) beseeching your lordship to pardon our boldness, and to be good lord unto this honest man, whose servant shall give attendance upon your lordship's most favourable answer. If your lordship shew him this benefit, we shall not fare the worse in the readiness and due expedition of this your lordship's work of the bible, which goeth well forward, and within few months will draw to an end, by the

[1 Boner, who was at this time ambassador in France, was elected to the bishoprick of Hereford, and was translated to London, without having been ever confirmed in the former see.]

grace of Almighty God, who preserve your good lordship
now and evermore. From Paris, the 12th day of September.

MYLES COVERDALE.
RICHARD GRAFTON.

To the right honourable and their
singular good lord, the lord
privy seal.

LETTER VI.

MYLES COVERDALE TO LORD CRUMWELL.

Dated from PARIS, *Oct.* 30, [1538.]

[State Papers, Crumwell Correspondence, Vol. VII. No. 68.]

IN most humble wise, after like salutation, I beseech your
most honourable lordship to understand, that the 29th day of
this month came to me master Beckynsall, student here at
Paris, in a right lamentable sort, complaining of the injury of
light tongues, which have sinistrally reported, that he should
not be in all things agreeable and conformable to the king's
most lawful acts in England, but rather contrary to the same.
Which, my most singular good lord, if it were so, certainly
as no man is more bound than I to certify your lordship of
the truth in all things, so would I, according to my duty,
pen the same, if I knew it so to be. Again, sure I am that,
forasmuch as Mr Archdeacon Karow and Mr Quene are both
in one lodging with the said Mr Beckynsall, there is neither
of them both, but if they did either hear, see, or perceive
any such thing by him, they would not only certify your
good lordship thereof, but also avoid his company. Which
thing is to me very evident by the peaceable study and right
virtuous conversation of them both. Neither do I understand
otherwise but at this present hour all we, that be here of the
king's nation, are even of one heart and humble mind toward
God and our sovereign, and glad to our power to do one for
another, thanks and praise be [to God, who ever] preserve
the king's highness, noble prince Edward, your lordship, all

other of the king's most honourable council, and the whole realm. Amen. Written at Paris, the 30th day of October,

By your lordship's humble and faithful servitor,

MYLES COVERDALE.

*To the right honourable his singular good
lord, the lord Crumwell, lord privy seal.*

LETTER VII.

COVERDALE TO LORD CRUMWELL.
Dated from PARIS, December 13, [1538.]

[Harleian MSS. 604. fol. 98.]

RIGHT honourable and my singular good lord. After all due salutations, I humbly beseech your lordship, that by my lord elect of Hereford I may know your pleasure concerning the annotations of this bible, whether I shall proceed therein, or no. Pity it were, that the dark places of the text (upon the which I have alway set a hand 𝕀☞) should so pass undeclared. As for any private opinion or contentious words, as I will utterly avoid all such, so will I offer the annotations first to my said lord of Hereford, to the intent that he shall so examine the same, afore they be put in print, if it be your lordship's good pleasure that I shall so do. As concerning the new Testaments in English and Latin, whereof your good lordship received lately a book by your servant Sebastian, the cook, I beseech your lordship to consider the greenness thereof, which, for lack of time, cannot as yet be so apt to be bound as it should be. And whereas my said lord of Hereford is so good unto us to convey thus much of the bible to your good lordship, I humbly beseech the same to be defender and keeper thereof, to the intent that if these men proceed in their cruelness against us, and confiscate the rest, yet this at the least may be safe by the means of your lordship, whom God the Almighty evermore preserve to his good pleasure! Amen. Written somewhat lately, at Paris, the 13th day of December.

Your lordship's humble and faithful servitor,

MYLES COVERDALE.

*To my most singular good lord and master, the lord
Crumwell, lord privy seal, this be delivered.*

LETTER VIII.

MYLES COVERDALE TO LORD CRUMWELL.

No date[1].

[State Papers, Crumwell Correspondence, Vol. VII. No. 64.]

AFTER due commendation to your good lordship. I heartily and in most humble wise beseech the same, that inasmuch as the king's most excellent majesty, of his singular grace, (by the means of your good lordship, as God's instrument in that behalf,) hath granted unto this bearer, James Nycolson, his gracious licence and privilege for the sale of his bibles and new Testaments already printed; and forasmuch as his grace is also informed and hath seen a part of our postils, or ordinary sermons, which the lord archbishop of Canterbury hath corrected; your lordship (according to your most loving and favourable manner of old) will help and further the said James Nycolson to the king's most gracious privilege for certain years to print the same; considering the cost and charge that he hath had, not only for drawing of the said sermons out of scripture, but also in preparing now of his letters and print for the setting forth of the same. This I most humbly require of your lordship, whom God preserve now and ever! Amen.

Your lordship's humble and daily orator,

MYLES COVERDALE.

LETTER IX.

MYLES COVERDALE TO LORD CRUMWELL.

Dated from NEWBURY, February 7, [1539.]

[State Papers, Crumwell Correspondence, Vol. VII. No. 70.]

AFTER my most humble and due salutation to your right honourable lordship. This is to advertise the same, that for lack of diligent inquisition, and through overmuch sufferance,

[1 This letter was probably written early in 1539, shortly after Coverdale's return from Paris.]

there are in these countries (and so I fear me in many more) an innumerable sort of such popish books, as not only be incorrect, but are also great occasion to keep the king's subjects still in error, and to make them fall into such like inconvenience as did lately one John Cowper, whose accusation I trust your lordship hath received, or shall do this week by the justice. In consideration of the premises, I have, under your lordship's favourable correction, required the curate of Newbury to call for all such books, as were either incorrect, or against the king's most lawful act concerning Thomas a Becket, or the bishop of Rome[2]; by the means of the which request there are brought unto me in these two or three days a great number of such books. Wherefore inasmuch as I perceive that this doth turn to the glory of God and to the honour of our most noble king, I humbly require your lordship to grant me authority, and to give me a charge and commandment by your letters, that wheresoever I understand any such unlawful books to be, I may correct them, or cause them to be corrected. In the executing whereof I do not doubt but to win the parties, and to make them not only more fervent toward God and his word, but also to increase in due obedience toward the king's highness; whom with noble Prince Edward, and you all of their most honourable council, the mighty arm of God evermore preserve! Amen. From Newbury, the seventh day of February. Your lordship's favourable answer I most humbly require by this bearer my poor servant.

Your lordship's humble and faithful servant,

MYLES COVERDALE.

To the right honourable my
singular good lord, the lord
privy seal.

[2 With respect to the transactions here alluded to, see Strype's Cranmer, Vol. I. p. 100; and Memorials, Vol. I. i. p. 530—2. Ed. Oxf.]

LETTER X.

MYLES COVERDALE TO LORD CRUMWELL.

Dated from NEWBURY, *February* 8, 1539.

[State Papers, Crumwell Correspondence, Vol. VII. No. 71.]

MY right humble salutation. Considering my most bounden duty in seeking the honour of the king, our sovereign lord, I am constrained to write again unto your good lordship, for none other cause so much as to signify unto the same, that, as methinketh, (I speak under correction,) a great number of the priests of this realm are run in *præmunire* unto the king, inasmuch as they have not utterly extinct all such ecclesiastical service, as is against his grace's most lawful supremity and prerogative. For in the feast called *Cathedra S. Petri* a great part of their matins is plainly a maintenance of the B. of Rome's usurped power. This is evident in all the great matin-books of the church of Newbury, and I doubt not but it is so likewise in many churches more. I found it the seventh day of this month, and I wonder at it, considering that it is so long since the act was made for the abolishing of all such usurped authority. This, my very dear and singular good lord, do I open and shew only unto your lordship, neither doth any man else in the world know that I have uttered this thing; no, not this bearer, good Mr Wynchcombe, unto whom, for his true heart toward the king's highness and love toward your lordship, I might utter right secret things. The everliving God, that never failed your good lordship, guide the same in doing the thing that is to his glory, and to the honour of our most gracious king! Amen. If it be your lordship's good pleasure, that I shall do ought farther herein, I humbly beseech you to know the same by writing, or otherwise by the mouth of Mr Wynchcombe. From Newbury, the 8th day of February.

Your lordship's humble and faithful servant,

MYLES COVERDALE.

To the right honourable and my
singular good lord, the lord
privy seal, this be delivered.
Ad manus.

LETTER XI.

MYLES COVERDALE TO LORD CRUMWELL.

Dated from NEWBURY, *March* 5, [1539.]

[State Papers, Crumwell Correspondence, Vol. VII. No. 69.]

IN my most humble wise, with like salutation to your right honourable lordship.   This is to signify unto the same, that this fourth day of March one Nicolas Hyde and one John Gryese, of Henley upon Thames, came to me unto Newbury, reporting that in a glass window of our lady chapel in the church of the said Henley the image of Thomas a Becket, with the whole feigned story of his death, is suffered to stand still.   Not only this, but that all the beams, irons, and candlesticks, whereupon tapers and lights were wont to be set up unto images, remain still untaken down; whereby the poor simple unlearned people believe that they shall have liberty to set up their candles again unto images, and that the old fashion shall shortly return.   Item, that one Thomas Wolley, of Henley, did forbid five of his neighbours his house for holding with the gospel, and said that he had evil will for receiving such men of the new learning: so that in the said town of Henley poor men are not only discouraged from the truth of God, but it appeareth also, that the king's most gracious commandment is not put in execution.   Now though sir Walter Stonor, knight, be the king's justice of peace at Henley, yet, under your lordship's correction, I reckon great and notable negligence in the bishop of Lincoln[1], which, being so nigh thereby, doth not weed out such faults; yea, I fear it be as evil, or worse, in many more places of his diocese.

It is my duty also to signify unto your good lordship the great oversight of the stationers of London, which for their lucre and gains are not ashamed to sell still such primers as corrupt the king's subjects.   A great number of them have mine neighbours brought unto me, and a great sort of other most ungracious popish books (both contrary to God and the king's highness) have I taken up within the precincts of Newbury, and will do more, if your good lordship do give me

[1 John Longlands.]

authority, or bid me do it : whereof I humbly beseech you, my most dear and singular good lord, to have your loving answer by the mouth of this bearer, young Mr Wynchcombe, and to know your good pleasure, what I shall do with these popish books that I have already, whether I shall burn them at the market-cross, or no. Thus the everlasting God preserve your good lordship long to endure! Amen. From Newbury, the fifth day of March.

Your lordship's humble and faithful servant,

MYLES COVERDALE.

To the right honourable and my very
singular especial good lord, the lord
privy seal, this be presented.

Ad manus.

LETTER XII.

MYLES COVERDALE TO HENRY BULLINGER.

Dated at STRASBURGH, July 27[1].

[From the Archives at Zurich, VI. 108.]

MUCH health in the Lord! I have been prevented by my engagements and by a degree of bodily weakness (not to mention the narrowness of my circumstances), from making my journey to you in company with those very eminent persons, Henry Butler[2] and Richard[3]. But what pain my absence from you causes me, I will not now attempt to describe, so briefly as I am obliged to write to you; for I am very anxious to enjoy your society, and to behold your church.

[1] It does not appear in what year this letter was written, but it was probably during the period of his first residence at Bergzabern, on the occasion of one of his visits to Strasburgh, between 1543 and 1548.]

[2] Henry Butler, a native of Zurich, but of English origin. See Zurich Letters, second series, Letter LXXVII. p. 191; also first series, Letter XCVI. p. 241.]

[3] Richard Hilles, a merchant at London, and contributor to the exiles in queen Mary's reign. He was resident at Strasburgh in 1548. See Strype, Cranmer, Vol. I. p. 280. Memorials, III. i. p. 224. Zurich Letters, first series, p. 224, &c. It was probably during the period of his residence at Strasburgh that this letter was written.]

Since, however, this is not permitted to me, I will patiently wait the good will of my heavenly Father, content in the mean time to have tasted his good spirit through your ministry in his word, and to have experienced your friendship in Christ.   I should in truth have been at a loss what to write to you at the present time, most excellent preceptor, if I had not remembered, how kindly you received my letters, homely as they were, which I sent to you about the middle of last September, and how favourable an interpretation you put upon them.   From whence you see, what confusion of style is caused by an education entirely destitute of all ornament, either of languages or composition.   I am however thankful, that, although otherwise occupied in most important studies, you have condescended again to offer me your remembrances in your letters to Richard.   Finally, I commend to you these eminent men, earnest as they both are themselves in true piety, and the encouragers of it in others, with all the sincerity that I am able, assured that the especial consolation of the Holy Spirit will not be wanting to you both, when you shall have met together in the Lord.   Which that it may be happily accomplished, may he grant, who has already provided that your hearts should be so closely united in the sincere love of himself.   Farewell.   Strasburgh, July 27. My wife offers you her kindest remembrances in the Lord.

Yours,

MYLES COVERDALE.

LETTER XIII.

MYLES COVERDALE TO CONRAD HUBERT[4].

Dated at BERGZABERN, *Dec.* 24, 1543.

[Ex autogr. in MSS. Tom. I. p. 34. Scrin. Eccles. Argent.]

PEACE and joy in the Holy Ghost! Since, on account of the shortness of the time, it is out of my power to indulge in

[4 This learned person was minister of St Thomas's Church at Strasburgh. He was one of the guardians of Bucer's children, and editor of Bucer's *Scripta Anglicana*.   Strype's Parker, Vol. I. p. 56, and Grindal, p. 298.]

a longer epistle, my most dearly beloved brother in the Lord,
cherishing as I do the most pleasing recollection of you, I
know that you will the more readily pardon your affectionate,
humble friend. For yesterday after dinner, at a time when
I was obliged to write more letters on other matters, I understood that the bearer of this was about to set out very early
in the morning on his journey to you. You indeed are sur-
prised, and indeed deservedly so, what can be the reason, that
I, who am now living amongst your friends[1], should altogether
drop my correspondence with you. But in September, when
I came hither by invitation, fortified by your letters of recom-
mendation, I took effectual means, although in a sufficiently
short letter, that you should not be altogether ignorant of the
state of affairs here. Your dear brother John also, during
my intervening absence, without doubt informed you of what
happened subsequently in the business of my own affairs, as
well as those also of the church. For although immediately
before the completion of my business I went down into Lower
Germany, for the purpose of bringing home my wife; yet at
length upon my return, and having learned many things by
experience, which during my former residence I had not sufficiently considered, I see, alas! that the present state of the
churches in these parts is exceedingly calamitous, nay more,
that it is absolutely deplorable. To such an extent do the
princes appear to connive at the abuses which exist, the most
dreadful factions to grow rife, and, what is more, the very
pastors of the Lord's flock to revel in them. Moreover, I
myself wish, as also your very dear father, who by the
mercy of God is still alive, is intensely anxious, that you
could be present with us, even for a couple of days. For
there are many things besides, which I also have to mention
to you in confidence.

But if you will kindly assist our dear brother Abel[2] in
the business of searching for my chest, which, by the mistake
and carelessness of a person at Metz, was carried, as I hear,
to Strasburgh, when it ought to have been conveyed to
Spires, you will do a most acceptable kindness to me, who

[1 Hubert was a native of Bergzabern.—Simler.]
[2 An English merchant resident at Strasburgh, and a contributor
to the exiles in Mary's time. For some account of him, see Strype,
and the Zurich Letters, passim.]

am now a sojourner in a strange land.   Farewell, and be the
messenger of many good wishes from myself and my wife to
your wife, and your beloved Samuel, and to our excellent
preceptor, Peter Martyr.   Again farewell.   Bergzabern,
December 24.

MICHAEL ANGLUS[3],

Minister of the church at Bergzabern.

LETTER XIV.

MYLES COVERDALE TO CONRAD HUBERT.

Dated BERGZABERN, *March* 31, 1544.

[Ex autogr. in MSS. Tom. II. p. 123. Scrin. Eccles. Argent.]

PEACE and joy in the Holy Ghost!   In my former letter
I wrote word, that your beloved father would be with you
within eight days.   He will however inform you in person,
what prevented him from fulfilling his intentions.   I have also
given him seven florins and twelve batzen for this purpose,
that, in your accustomed kindness to me, you may take care
that that money be paid to my creditors; by doing which you
will greatly oblige me.   You are acquainted with what I have
received through your means from master Vindelinus, Riche-
lius, Cephalæus, and James Jucundus.   Besides them I have
these other creditors, Christopher, (the same bookseller who
has a shop under the town-hall, next to Vindelinus,) and that
old man John Grymmus, who has two shops fronting the
western entrance of the great church.   With regard to the
whole amount, this little document written in German will
more clearly shew you what it is.   I pray you not to take

[3 Michael Anglus, or rather Milo Coverdalus, as Hubert himself
observes in the inscription of the letter, lately bishop of Exeter, who
why he assumed the name of Michael Anglus, I am entirely at loss to
know, except perhaps that Milo and Michael have the same meaning
in English.   He was master of the school at Bergzabern, as John
Dodman*, an Englishman, was also at Bissweiler; for he was invited
also to preach to the church at Bergzabern in German, and Edmund
also was invited to be assistant in the school at Landau.—Simler.]

[* Possibly he is the person mentioned by Strype, Annals, I. i. p. 63. Ed. 1822.]

it ill, that I do not cease to avail myself of the kind offices which you have tendered to me; for you appear to have offered your services to me, that I may have the enjoyment of you in the Lord.

I beg you to take care that Cephalæus sends to you the paper, which I mentioned in my letter to him; likewise also that James Jucundus delivers to you the books, of which the names are written in this document. Moreover, I wish that you would take care, that the table which our friend Edmund is about to send, may be conveyed to me as soon as possible. Farewell. I and my wife offer to you and your beloved wife many good wishes in the Lord. Again farewell. From Bergzabern, March 31.

MYLES COVERDALE.

April 1st. This morning, just when I was going to seal this letter, your beloved father came to me; who from bodily weakness cannot at present attempt the journey which he had proposed. However he does not despair of being able to set out in a short time; nor does he appear to be much amiss hitherto. God be thanked! Wherefore there is no necessity for your being any more anxious on this account; for he would have come to you at the present time, if the coachman had not refused to carry him.

LETTER XV.

MYLES COVERDALE TO CONRAD HUBERT.

Dated BERGZABERN, *April* 10, 1544.

[Ex autogr. in MSS. Tom. I. p. 29. Scrin. Eccles. Argent.]

PEACE and joy in the Holy Ghost! Our friend Edmund delivered to me your letter dated March 11: in whose business, that he might obtain admission into some situation connected with education resembling that in which we are engaged, I have exerted myself to the utmost for the last three months; and the Lord Jesus, whose interest is at stake, has not been wanting in assisting our endeavours: nor can I doubt of a most prosperous issue, even though he should

meet with boys educated in the worst manner; and therefore
his undertaking of the school at Landau will on this account
be especially rendered a very difficult task.   With regard to
the matter relating to the English boys of our country, who
are there, I settled this business, as far as I was able, fifteen
days ago, during the absence of master Nicolas, and when
our illustrious prince was present, on his road down to Spires;
not indeed after an introduction to the prince himself, but in
the presence and hearing of the prince, in the company of
our prefect; who in the name of the most illustrious prince
gave me this answer, namely, that it had been already
determined by his highness, that in the next visitation, which
we have thought will take place in May, the best attention
should be given to this business.   Besides, we, together with
your very dear parents, are continually mindful of the welfare of yourself and the church which is in the Lord with
you, which we do not doubt that you do in return unceasingly for us.   Farewell.   From Bergzabern, April 10, 1544.

Yours in the Lord,

MICHAEL ANGLUS.

To Conrad Hubert, my worthy
friend in the Lord, at
Strasburgh.

LETTER XVI.

MYLES COVERDALE TO CONRAD HUBERT.

Dated WEISSEMBERG, *April* 13, 1544.

[Ex autogr. in MSS. Tom. I. p. 38. Scrin. Eccles. Argent.]

HEALTH! That happy and illustrious youth has shewn
towards me the greatest friendship, inasmuch as he not only
brought the letter from you to me hither, namely, to Bergzabern, but also took upon himself the charge of conveying
this money to you by a faithful messenger.   It is almost
impossible for me to describe in a few words, how unwillingly
I have detained it so long.   For your father, as you know,

was to have been the bearer of it. What amount is due to
each person, you understand from the account, which I sent
to you in my letter of the first of April; so that I need not
trouble you with any further account at the present time.
I beg you to salute your dear wife for me and my wife.
We hear with satisfaction that your little boy is restored to
health.   Farewell.

Yours from the heart,

MICHAEL ANGLUS.

In the mean time, in conformity with the mutual friendship which exists between us, I request that I may receive
from Vindelinus, Cephalæus, and James Jucundus, the books
which I mentioned in my former letter. Again farewell.
In haste.   From Weissemberg, April 13.

LETTER XVII.

MYLES COVERDALE TO CONRAD HUBERT.

Dated BERGZABERN, *April* 21, 1544.

[Ex autogr. in MSS. Tom. II. p. 126. Scrin. Eccles. Argent.]

GRACE and peace from the Lord! This beloved messenger having signified to me by letter his intention of setting
out to Strasburg within so few days, I called on your dear
father; with respect to whose journey to you nothing further
is settled, except that he has determined to visit you about
Ascension-day. For he has now partially recovered from the
attack in his feet; and your mother also, although she is
visited with a troublesome scorbutic eruption, appears to
be in good spirits. But the Lord, who is always righteous
in all his works, in his good pleasure deprived your brother
John eight days since of that sweet child, which his wife had
brought forth to him about Christmas. To-morrow, if the
Lord will, we shall celebrate his holy supper. The business
of catechizing, which we attempted two previous weeks in
church, we now, God be thanked, find succeed prosperously,

and to be not without fruit. May God grant, that what we have begun to plant and water, may increase more and more to his glory.

With regard to the money which D. Valentius Brentius will give you, I sent at the same time with my letter of March 31, a document mentioning the sum which was due to each individual. Wherefore I beg you to attend to this business of mine, and carefully remind Vindelinus, Cephalæus, and Jucundus, to send to me the paper and the books; for I am now in need of them. I have now sent a letter privately to Vindelinus and Cephalæus, but not to James Jucundus. Wherefore, in consideration of the friendship which exists between us, I wish that you would take care that I have also from his shop twelve copies of the smaller edition of Donatus, the same number of the colloquial formularies of Seobald Heiden, and six or eight copies of the Bucolics of Virgil, and that they be transmitted to me with the paper of Cephalæus and the books of Vindelinus: and I wish this to be done as soon as possible; for you cannot believe, how greatly we are distressed from the want of books and the scarcity of paper. I should wish these things to be conveyed at least to Weissemberg, if possible. And I would not trouble you, engaged as you are in your sacred office, if there were any other person whom I could safely entrust with this business. Farewell, with many good wishes from myself and my wife, who desires her best wishes to your dear wife. Again farewell. From Bergzabern, April 21, 1544.

Yours,

MYLES COVERDALE.

To my most courteous friend,
Conrad Hubert, preacher of
the gospel at St Thomas's
church, Strasburgh.

LETTER XVIII.

MYLES COVERDALE TO CONRAD HUBERT.

Dated BERGZABERN, *May* 22, 1544.

[Ex autogr. in MSS. Tom. I. p. 36. Scrin. Eccles. Argent.

PEACE and joy in the Holy Ghost! How kind the Lord hath been to us in sending to us our dearly-beloved preceptor in Christ, Bucer[1], I can scarcely either declare or write, from the lively emotions of my heart. For the space of three days he displayed towards us, not without the greatest exertions, many offices both of charity and piety; by which I am assured that our churches will be not a little established in the Lord. These things, however, our friend Christopher will better explain by word of mouth, than I can by writing. I took Bucer twice to the house of your dear parents; and how great comfort it afforded to them, the feelings of both your parents, and also of your brother, sufficiently shewed. But our little town has, alas! received very great damage from the late hail-storm, which took place eight days ago. But if we would seek for the true reason of this scourge, we must attribute it to the goodness of God, who is accustomed to chasten his adopted child, and thus invites us to repentance. With respect to the son of Matthew, the prefect of Barbelrode[2], since you have given clear evidence in your letter to me, how kindly you are disposed to him in the Lord, I also have given consideration to his case; nor does it appear advantageous, either for himself or for the church of God, that he should be admitted before his twenty-second year into the sacred ministry. My reasons for this declaration are too numerous for me to detail them in a few words. Finally, your beloved father has determined to visit you before Whitsuntide; by whom I will gladly write to you, if the Lord permit, at greater length concerning the condition of our church, to which you are so kindly disposed.

[1 Bucer was probably at this time living at Strasburgh. With reference to the circumstances which led him thither, see Strype, Cranmer, Vol. I. p. 362. Ed. 1812.]

[2 See Letter XXIX.]

That most excellent widow, the sister of your dearest mother, has sent the two gold pieces, which I have given to Christopher: she has given another a present to his sweet little boy Samuel; another she has sent for this purpose, that a bed may be bought with it and sent to us, as soon as an opportunity offers. Farewell, with many good wishes from your parents and my wife, in the Lord. Many good wishes from us to your wife. From Bergzabern, May 22.

Yours,

MICHAEL ANGLUS.

To his courteous friend and faithful minister of the gospel, Conrad Hubert, his dearly-beloved brother in Christ, at St Thomas's, Strasburgh.

LETTER XIX.

MYLES COVERDALE TO CONRAD HUBERT.

Dated BERGZABERN, *Aug.* 13, 1544.

[Ex autogr. in MSS. Vol. II. p. 125. Scrin. Eccles. Argent.]

PEACE and joy in the Holy Ghost! Even though I had not more reasons for writing to you, I was nevertheless desirous even on this ground to offer you my good wishes, my dearly beloved in the Lord, lest from my long intermission of correspondence you should think me unmindful of you. Your dear parents are in very tolerable health, and offer their best wishes to yourself and your wife. I do not doubt that the interests of religion here will daily prosper more and more; for having already experienced some proof of this, I write this, that you, who are so earnestly zealous for the church of God, may render thanks to him for it, and unceasingly offer up your prayers for still greater success. But I earnestly request this of you, that having ascertained the extent of Bucer's influence in this most troublesome time, you would enable us also to know it. The rumours which we hear at this place hold out a poor prospect of peace. For as they say the emperor is willing to admit of no peace, not even on the earnest exhortation of the princes; so it is reported, that he has just made a fresh invasion[1] into the art of Brabant belonging to the duchy of Cleves, and the Dutch territories, with great violence. A dreadful beginning in truth! May God grant that, roused by such great evils, and truly acknowledging our great ingratitude, we may sincerely repent! I should be glad to be remembered to such of our countrymen as are there, especially to Richard[2] and the rest. You will very much oblige me also by conveying my remembrance on my behalf to Vindelinus, Conradus the clergyman, and to Sturmius and Severus. Farewell. From Bergzabern, August 13, 1544.

M. COVERDALE.

To the most excellent Conrad Hubert,
preacher at St Thomas's, Stras-
burgh, my very dear friend.

LETTER XX.

MYLES COVERDALE TO CONRAD HUBERT.

Dated from BERGZABERN, *Aug.* 31, 1545[3].

[Ex autogr. in MSS. Tom. I. p. 31. Scrin. Eccles. Argent.]

PEACE and joy in the Holy Ghost! If our common preceptor, master Bucer, has at the present time composed anything against the enemies of the gospel, especially against the bishop

[1 The transactions here referred to relate to the war which was waged by Charles V. against William duke of Cleves, in 1543-4; when he made an irruption into his territory, and was guilty of great oppression towards him. For some account of the transactions referred to, see Robertson, History of Charles V. Book VII. Seckendorf. Hist. Luth. Vol. II. p. 427.]

[2 Probably Richard Hilles. See page 502, *n.* 3.]

[3 Compare Letter XXVII. and note 1, p. 520. Whatever may be the true date of that letter, this is evidently to be assigned to an earlier period.]

of Winchester[4], I particularly request you to procure for
me a copy of any work of this description. Through the
mercy of God we are all well. Your parents are looking
for you towards the approaching vintage, and desire their
best remembrances. Farewell. From Bergzabern, August 31,
1545.

MICHAEL ANGLUS.

*To Conrad Hubert, preacher of the gospel
at St Thomas's, my friend and most
reverend brother, at Strasburgh.*

LETTER XXI.

MYLES COVERDALE TO CONRAD HUBERT.

Dated BERGZABERN, *Sept.* 13, 1544.

[Ex autogr. in MSS. Tom. ii. p. 124. Scrin. Eccles. Argent.]

PEACE and joy in the Holy Ghost! You give a great
proof of your kindness, most learned sir, in not ceasing to
spur on with your most agreeable letters your friend Michael,
or, if you wish it, Myles, who would otherwise advance but
slowly to more favourable progress. Your letter written on
the 30th of August was faithfully delivered to me on the
3rd of November; from which I understood that Bucer,
contrary indeed to the opinion of us all, had not yet returned: at which circumstance you need not doubt that we
are much grieved. But I know that the church is pleading
continually with many prayers; and there is no reason for our
despairing, that God, in his accustomed mercy, will set him at
liberty[5]. Dr Nicholas has returned home in good health and
spirits, and repeats his offers of many good wishes to you. I
and my wife have determined, with the blessing of God, to
go up to Strasburgh about the 1st of October, and to visit you

[4 This has reference to a work on the celibacy of the clergy,
in reply to bishop Gardiner, to which reference is made in Letter
XXVII.]

[5 Some allusion is made to these troubles of Bucer, in Strype,
Cranmer, Book ii. c. 24. Vol. i. p. 362.]

our most affectionate friend. Your beloved parents are in tolerable health, and have only just written to you. From Bergzabern, September 13, 1544.

Yours,

M. COVERDALE.

LETTER XXII.

MYLES COVERDALE TO CONRAD HUBERT.

Dated from BERGZABERN, *Oct.* 3, 1544.

[Ex autogr. in MSS. Tom. I. p. 30. Scrin. Eccles. Argent.]

PEACE and joy in the Holy Ghost! How kindly you are disposed towards your country, most beloved Conrad, the letters which you sent to me last week for our young men afford abundant proof. I have served their cause with our prefect, in a small degree indeed, yet to this extent, that by his order ten florins have been advanced to our friend Erasmus, till the matter itself shall have been brought to a favourable result before the visitors; which the prefect says will not take place before Christmas. Moreover, he invited me and my wife, as he often does, to supper on the 27th of last month. During supper-time, in the course of conversation about many matters, we happened to mention that of the sacred ministry. To this conversation I would gladly have added something; but the wife of the prefect pleaded the cause of the Lord with such dexterity, that it was needless for me to say anything. But the prefect on the following day, which was the Lord's day, in speaking to the people, and using very strong language, told them that he was not much pleased with some secret proceedings of our rabble. Our young mother, I am thankful to the Lord, with her little daughter, has recovered. Farewell, and may happiness attend you! And if you have not received from the bookseller the copies of the books which I mentioned in a former letter, I beg that you will not get them; for I have already got a sufficient supply of them from Frankfort: but if you have already procured them, send them to me; and remember me

kindly to your wife Margaret.   Grace be with you!   From
Bergzabern, October 3.

Yours,

MICHAEL ANGLUS.

To Conrad Hubert, my brother
and greatly respected friend
in the Lord.

LETTER XXIII.

MYLES COVERDALE TO CONRAD HUBERT.

Dated from BERGZABERN, *Oct.* 11, 1544.

[Ex autogr. in MSS. Tom. II. p. 122. Scrin. Eccles. Argent.]

PEACE and joy in the Holy Ghost! If you have returned
well and happy to your home with your child and very dear
wife, it is a subject to me of great joy.   Your parents are
in good health, and, wishing you much health in the Lord,
desire that you should be informed that Margaret, your
brother's wife, is now restored to tolerable health; and also
that that person, namely, John's wife, who, when you were
here, had not been delivered, has, through the great mercy
of our heavenly Father, yesterday become the mother of
another and beautiful child.   I wish you to see that this
small bag of chesnuts be conveyed to the house of master
Richard.

Farewell, my dearest Conrad, and I pray you to commend me in your prayers to the Lord.   From Bergzabern,
October 11.

M. COVERDALE.

I do not doubt that you are yourself mindful, and also
diligently remind master Bucer, to write sometimes at his
convenience to our prefect, and also to have regard to our
friend Edmund; and I am desirous that you should forward
this business.

M. COVERDALE.

To the most excellent Conrad Hubert,
  minister of the gospel at St Tho-
  mas's church at Strasburgh.

33—2

LETTER XXIV.

MYLES COVERDALE TO CONRAD HUBERT.

Dated BERGZABERN, *Dec.* 9, 1544.

[Ex autogr. in MSS. Tom. I. p. 39. Scrin. Eccles. Argent.]

PEACE and joy in the Holy Ghost! I intended to have inquired, and so to have ascertained from you, when I was with you at Strasburgh, how and of what materials you make your ink; but owing to a press of business I omitted it. Wherefore I beg that you will either tell my wife, who is now with you, what materials I ought to procure for this purpose, or send me a list of them: also I earnestly beg that you will remind Bucer of the letter, which he promised he would give me to our prefect on the subject of our common religion, and of the situation of our friend Edmund. Your parents beg to be kindly remembered to you, as this letter will testify. I wish much health to your wife in the Lord, with her dearest child, and I earnestly commend my wife to you. From Bergzabern, December 9.

Yours,

MICHAEL ANGLUS.

To the very excellent Conrad Hubert,
preacher of the gospel at St Tho-
mas's.

LETTER XXV.

MYLES COVERDALE TO CONRAD HUBERT.

Dated from BERGZABERN, *Dec.* 26, 1544.

[Ex autogr. in MSS. Tom. I. p. 42. Scrin. Eccles. Argent.]

PEACE and joy in the Holy Ghost! Amidst the various causes of grief from other sources, with which the church is constantly afflicted, this most severe one is also to be added, that those persons are always, or at least in quick succession, labouring under the severest maladies, who possess both the power and the will to teach the people, and to comfort them with the counsels of the divine word. For Erasmus Bierus, the minister of the church at Bissweiler, (as also John, my beloved colleague here at Bergzabern,) is said to be reduced to such a state of debility from contraction of the limbs, that he can no longer discharge his sacred office before the people. Therefore Eschnavius, our most excellent prefect, being desirous of making provision for this distress, wishes that my pious brother and countryman, John Dodman, should be invited thither to the assistance of Erasmus, of your great kindness to whom I have heard with satisfaction; and who, I trust, has by this time made such proficiency in the German language, that I doubt not of his being able to discharge the duties of his office to the benefit of the church. I beg, therefore, that in your kindness to the church of Christ you would signify this to this same countryman of mine, Dodman, that, in case of his being summoned to Bissweiler, he may repair thither the more readily, under the certainty of receiving from the prefect an acceptable return. For a messenger has been sent for this very purpose to Strasburgh. Farewell, with many kind remembrances from my wife and your beloved brother, whose son John is now the bearer of this letter which is inclosed to you. I and my wife, together with your parents, desire to join in most affectionate remembrance to you in the Lord. From Bergzabern, December 26.

MICHAEL ANGLUS.

To the most pious and learned Conrad
Hubert, minister of the divine word
at St Thomas's at Strasburgh, his
dearly-beloved brother in the Lord.

LETTER XXVI.

MYLES COVERDALE TO CONRAD HUBERT.

Dated from BERGZABERN, *Feb.* 6, 1545.

[Ex autogr. in MSS. Tom. I. p. 40. Scrin. Eccles. Argent.]

PEACE and joy in the Holy Ghost! The letter, which
you had despatched to me on the twenty-first of December,
I received on the tenth of January, together with the parcel
of books of which you made mention in it. The principal
matter which I was desirous to have forwarded by your diligence with our prefect (for he was with you at that time at
Strasburgh) was this; namely, that in conformity with the
duty of his office he should put a stop to those most frivolous
public dances, and other hindrances of true piety of the same
description; and that he should take care, that at least during
the performance of the more solemn services of religion the
people should conduct themselves with less irreverence; and
during the time of the sermon, the prayers, and the singing,
they should not collect themselves together in so many corners
in every direction of the market and the burial-ground. But
now I cannot hope for anything better; for, alas! our magistrates here appear to be so lukewarm, and to divest themselves of all care for religion, although in other respects they
are most active in laying heavy burdens upon the people.

Our boys, although not all of them, have been confined
to their beds with a sort of unusual cough, attended with
headache and fever; but no one has had the disorder more
severely than my dearest pupil in the Lord, John Hubert,
your brother's little boy. But it has pleased the Lord in
his mercy graciously to restore him to us, after an illness of
eight days, safe and sound. We most of us indeed despaired
of the boy's life. Your parents received a letter eight days
ago from his father, in which he expresses no doubt of his
being able in a short time to satisfy every obligation. Both
your parents are very well, together with all your friends
here. Farewell, with the kindest remembrances from myself

and my wife in the Lord.   From Bergzabern, the sixth of February.

Yours,

MICHAEL ANGLUS.

*To the eminent patron of true piety
and literature, Conrad Hubert,
preacher at St Thomas's, Strasburgh.*

LETTER XXVII.

MYLES COVERDALE TO CONRAD HUBERT.

Dated from BERGZABERN, *Feb.* 16, 1545[1].

[Ex autogr. in MSS. Tom. II. p. 121. Scrin. Eccles. Argent.]

PEACE and joy in the Holy Ghost! I am happy, if you are well: we, together with your excellent parents, are in good health. But this, alas! has happened, in addition to the other misfortunes which afflict the church, that that Swiss, who was forced by Bader as minister upon the church at Lindau[2], and has been admitted by the senate as future minister of the parish, cannot be induced by their entreaties to administer the Lord's supper even once in the year. Wherefore that most unfortunate people is compelled, even against their will, to submit to the dictates of Schwenckfeld[3].

[1 There appears to be an error in the date of this letter, which speaks of Coverdale's wife as being at Strasburgh, whereas in the former letter he speaks of her as being with him at Bergzabern; and also in that immediately succeeding, which is dated only four days after this. It probably belongs to a later period, as the work, to which reference is made in it, was not published till 1547. See note 1, p. 520.]

[2 On the circumstances of this church, see Seckendorf, Vol. I. II. p. 128, &c.]

[3 Schwenckfeld held heretical opinions with regard to the person of Christ, as well as on the subject of the Lord's supper. See Seckendorf, Hist. Luth. Lib. II. pp. 52, 122, and Lib. III. pp. 268, 9. The person alluded to in the preceding sentence (who is probably the person alluded to also in Letter XXXII., and is named Frankwiler,) was a disciple of Schwenckfeld, and, as it appears, held his heretical opinions on the Lord's supper.]

My friend Edmund made me acquainted with this three days ago by letter. I wish you to acquaint my reverend master Bucer with the cause of this wound of the church, that he may be able to add it to his pious prayers in the Lord.

I have written to my wife an account of the seeds which our father wishes to be procured by you; and do you take care that, when my wife returns, she bring them to us. And if you can by any means procure even one copy of Bucer's answer to the bishop of Winchester[1] before the fair, I will take care that the Latin original shall be translated into English as soon as possible; which you need not doubt will be most acceptable to our brethren in the Lord throughout England. I wish, however, that it should be managed as secretly as possible, until it shall make its appearance both in Latin and English. Offer my prayers for the health of your wife and your little boy Samuel. My best wishes to your beloved father Conrad, the minister, and that distinguished ornament of the church, Paulus Fagius[2]. Farewell. From Bergzabern, February 16, 1545.

Yours with the greatest affection,

M. COVERDALE.

LETTER XXVIII.

MYLES COVERDALE TO CONRAD HUBERT.

Dated from BERGZABERN, *Feb.* 20, 1545.

[Ex autogr. in MSS. Tom. I. p. 43. Scrin. Eccles. Argent.]

MUCH health. During the interval which elapsed between the despatch of your letter of the 27th of December and my

[1 This refers to two letters addressed by Gardiner, bishop of Winchester, to Bucer, in answer to a book of Bucer against the celibacy of the clergy. To these letters Bucer prepared an answer, which was published in 1547; to which period possibly this letter ought to be referred. For an account of these works, see Strype, Memorials, Vol. II. part i. pp. 103—5. Ed. Oxf. 1822.]

[2 A learned divine of Strasburgh, who was invited over into England, and afterwards became professor of divinity at Cambridge. For some account of him see Strype's Cranmer, Book II. Chap. xiii.]

receipt of it, I myself had written to you in the business of
the church of Bissweiler, at the request of our prefect, in
behalf of my countryman John Dodman, on account of the
sickness at that time of our dear friend Erasmus.   Nor is a
long intermission of our mutual duty of correspondence in
any way agreeable to me.   For I venerate and am greatly
attached to this occupation of christian benevolence.   But I
confess that I am sometimes in need of a spur, inasmuch as
I am by nature dilatory, and continually overwhelmed with a
great press of business.   My messenger, when you see him,
will be able to inform you with regard to the state of affairs
here, and of my present condition.   The new schoolmaster
from Spires, who has been engaged by our senate at Bergzabern for four years, is daily expected.   My fellow-labourer
John is still suffering from contraction of the hands, and our
churches are constantly more and more troubled by the
ravings of the Anabaptists; which however as they are generally not thought much of, so also are they tolerated, not without the greatest misfortune to the people at large, as well as
to the princes themselves; while in the meantime the worship
of God is decaying and falling into contempt.   Farewell, with
many remembrances from my wife and your friends in the
Lord.   I and my wife salute your wife and your beloved
father.   From Bergzabern, February 20.

Yours in the Lord,

MICHAEL ANGLUS.

*To the learned and excellent Conrad
Hubert, my brother and most
beloved friend in the Lord at
Strasburgh.*

LETTER XXIX.

MYLES COVERDALE TO CONRAD HUBERT.

Dated from BERGZABERN, *June* 1545.

[Ex autogr. in MSS. Tom. I. p. 35. Scrin. Eccles. Argent.]

PEACE and joy in the Holy Ghost! Our illustrious prince
has so far considered the business of Matthew of Barbelrode[3],

[3 See Letter XVIII.]

that he was desirous that he should have devoted some more years to the studies and discipline of this place. But inasmuch as he is engaged to be married, and promises that he will lead a life in all respects worthy of a minister, the prince has consented that he should be put in charge of the church at Milhoffen; on this condition, however, that he pay exemplary attention both to his studies and his habits of life. This and other things to the same purport I gathered from the letter, which our prefect sent to me three days ago; who is of opinion that our friend Matthew can do nothing better than return to Strasburgh, and make his peace with all those persons, to whom he has given any trifling offence; for by these means he thinks that he will remove much cause of evil. The ministers at Deux-ponts have certified to the prince, that Matthew on his examination by them acquitted himself respectably; and he also promised himself, that he would make amends for his past life. I beseech you, therefore, with regard to this business, in order that the edifice of the church may be the more prosperously established for the future, that inasmuch as he has given proof of his repentance, you would solemnly warn him, encourage him after his fall, and give proof to him by a letter, written at least to our prefect, that he has recovered your favour. I make this earnest request to you, most kind Conrad, at the particular desire of our prefect, who has also written on this business to our common preceptor Bucer, to whom I desire my most respectful remembrances in the Lord. Farewell. Your parents, God be thanked, on their return hither safe and well, found all things satisfactory at home. Written from Bergzabern the third day after Pentecost.

MICHAEL ANGLUS.

*To the learned and pious Conrad
Hubert, my friend and beloved
brother in the Lord, at Strasburgh.*

LETTER XXX.

MYLES COVERDALE TO CONRAD HUBERT

Dated from BERGZABERN, *Dec.* 27, 1545.

[Ex autogr. in MSS. Tom. I. p. 37. Scrin. Eccles. Argent.]

PEACE and joy in the Holy Ghost! As soon as I knew that this messenger was going up to Strasburgh, I informed your dear parents of it, who, God be thanked, are in excellent health, and desire their kindest remembrances to yourself and your wife. Samuel's father also, with a prayer for every blessing on the return of the new year, has sent your grandson a piece of money together with a linen shirt, in proof of his paternal affection towards him. I am so overwhelmed at this time with my own affairs, that I do not write more at the present, hoping in the meantime that you will give me credit for my good intentions. My wife desires her remembrances to you and your wife in the Lord. Farewell. From Bergzabern, Dec. 27.

Yours,

MICHAEL ANGLUS.

To the very courteous Conrad Hubert, preacher at St Thomas's, Strasburgh.

LETTER XXXI[1].

MYLES COVERDALE TO CONRAD HUBERT.

Dated from BERGZABERN, *Feb.* 1546.

[From the Archives of the Church at Strasburgh.]

THE mercy and loving-kindness of God be with us all! Amen. The members of the church of Weissenheim have brought me, on account of the relict of the late pastor, some money, namely, 19 florins, 3s. 1d., reckoning the florin at 15 batzen; which money I was to convey to Strasburgh.

[1 The original of this letter is in German.]

Since therefore my pupil Lewis, the son of Eschnavius, is intending to journey thither, I have troubled him with it. My friendly request, therefore, is, that ye would receive the said money from him, and make it over to the above-mentioned widow, namely, Katharine; but in such form that she shall give me a quittance, to the effect that she has received such money from me through you: for I have been obliged to give a quittance to the members of the church at Weissenheim, as they brought the money to me. Likewise also the mayor of Barbelrode[1] has sent money to his son Matthew, with letters to you and to him; all which you will find separately in this linen bag, as also the other money apart, with its superscription. This do ye, for God's sake, at this time execute, and write me word again that all has been received. For this will I to you and yours in all good-will diligently render service. Herewith commending you to Almighty God. Dated Bergzabern, the Friday before Shrove Tuesday, anno 1546. We are all in good health and spirits (God be praised!) except that your dear mother is as usual sickly and infirm, but not more so than is her wont.

Your servant and brother in the Lord,

MICHAEL ANGLUS.

I will write further to you by Hannah Schirer, if possible.

LETTER XXXII.

MYLES COVERDALE TO CONRAD HUBERT.

Dated from WEISSEMBERG, *March* 9, 1546.

[Ex autogr. MSS. Tom. i. p. 32. Scrin. Eccles. Argent.]

PEACE and joy in the Holy Ghost! I entreat you again and again, my dearest Conrad, that you would attentively consider my writing against Frankwiler[2]; and if I have made any mistakes, either in my German, or in any other way, that

[1 See Letters XVIII. and XXIX.]

[2 This is probably the Swiss, the disciple of Schwenckfeld, concerning whom Coverdale writes in his letter to Hubert of the sixteenth of February, 1545. Simler.—See above, Letter XXVI.]

you would kindly correct them, and communicate your opinion to me. For you are scarcely aware in what jeopardy our church is, and what trouble Frankwiler is giving us; not to mention, how reluctant our friend Nicholas is, although equally solicited with myself, to oppose the progress of these evils. Do you proceed in your endeavours to assist the affairs of the Lord, if it be only by your advice. And if you have received the money, which three days ago I delivered to our prefect to be paid to you, namely, for Katharine the widow of Francis Osterhing, and for Matthew of Barbelrode, send me word, I pray, by our friend Edmund.

May the Lord Jesus preserve you all to his church! Amen.

In haste. Weissemberg, March 9, 1546.

LETTER XXXIII.

MYLES COVERDALE TO JOHN CALVIN.

Dated at FRANKFORT, *March* 26, 1548.

I CANNOT but avail myself, most illustrious sir, of the offered opportunity of saluting your worthiness. There was brought hither three days since, during the time of the fair, a certain little book in English, containing that Order of holy Communion, which the king's majesty has set forth, as suitable to the present time[3]. And as I perceived many persons were desirous of obtaining it, I forthwith translated it both into German and Latin. And therefore, when I

[3 The English work, the Order of the Communion, is printed in the volume containing the Liturgies of King Edward VI., published by the Parker Society. The translation into Latin by Coverdale, here mentioned, does not seem to have been printed; but there is a Latin translation extant, printed apparently in 1548, with the initials A. A. S. D. Th, probably indicating Alexander Alesse, who also translated into Latin the first Liturgy of King Edward VI. A.D. 1549. It is a very rare small volume, bearing the title of "Ordo distributionis sacramenti altaris sub utraque specie, et formula confessionis faciendæ in regno Angliæ. Hæc Londini evulgata sunt octavo die Martii Anni MDXLVIII." See "The ancient Liturgy of the Church of England," by Rev. W. Maskell, p. xlv.; also Burnet II. 247, and Strype, Mem. II. i. 96.]

understood the godly bearer of this letter to be a townsman of yours, I thought I should gratify your reverence by sending you this trifling present. One of the translations I intended for the Germans; the other, namely the Latin one, I am exceedingly anxious should be forwarded to your reverence. And should you feel inclined to make known to others this cause for congratulation, and first-fruits of godliness, (according as the Lord now wills his religion to revive in England,) you will be able to commit this token of my affection for you to the press more easily than I can. I am now on my return to England, having been invited thither after an exile of eight years. Farewell, most excellent master, and affectionately salute your wife, who deserved so well from me and mine, when we went up to Strasburgh. Frankfort, March 26, 1548.

MICHAEL (*alias* MILO) COVERDALE, *Anglus.*

LETTER XXXIV.

MYLES COVERDALE TO PAUL FAGIUS.

Dated at WINDSOR CASTLE, *Oct.* 21, 1548.

PEACE and joy in the Holy Ghost! Your letter, most excellent sir, dated on the 22nd of August, I received from my wife on the 8th of this present month, with exceeding compassion for those individuals, whom this dreadful tyranny[1] so greatly distresses. I also shewed your letter yesterday to the most reverend the archbishop of Canterbury; who, as he has undertaken to educate your dear son (whom he has just sent away to Canterbury, by reason of the plague that is raging at this place) both in religion and learning, at his own expense; in like manner, reflecting upon the lamentable condition of your churches, he truly sympathises in your misfortune: wherefore he desired you most especially to come over to us, rather than to go away either into Turkey or Hungary. Oh, my master, if you should seek a refuge any

[1 Namely, the persecutions in Germany by Charles V., to enforce compliance with the Interim.]

where else than with us, since the faithlessness of mankind is every where so great, how will that most excellent gift, which the good and gracious God has bestowed upon you, grow cool! If the most reverend archbishop, whose answer I inclosed in my letter to you, had foreseen so much danger to the church, truly what I wrote to you would have been no impediment. You must think, therefore, that we are both of us sorry for what we did, although there was nothing stated in those letters, but what the occasion then called for. For myself, indeed, my master, I am in no little apprehension both for yourself and for our churches and schools, deprived of your most happy ministrations. Wherefore, although our rulers may not invite you by name, eminent as you are among the best scholars of Germany, and this probably, as I have before hinted to you, from secret motives; yet we, who know you well, entreat you most solemnly to come over to us, where you need not doubt but that you will be most acceptable, and therefore treated with the greatest kindness. Farewell. From the king's castle, which we call Windsor. Oct. 21, 1548.

Yours from my heart,

M. COVERDALE.

LETTER XXXV.

BISHOP COVERDALE TO CONRAD HUBERT.

Dated from BERGZABERN, *Sept.* 20, 1543, [probably 1555[2].]

[Ex autogr. MSS. Tom. I. p. 41. Scrin. Eccles. Argent.]

PEACE and joy in the Holy Ghost! When I was on my journey from Wesel to Frankfort, my very dear friend John Abel attacked me in terms of sufficiently strong reproof, under the supposition that I had received from you a most

[2 It is evident that the date of this letter is wrong, and that it was written at a later period, after his second settlement at Bergzabern. On leaving England in February 1555 he went to Denmark, and from thence to Wesel, where he resided some time as preacher to the exiles there; from thence he removed to Bergzabern. It was immediately on his arrival at that place that this letter was written.]

affectionate letter, to which I had not condescended to return
any answer.   Upon which I forthwith sent my servant with
a letter to the magistrates of Bergzabern.   But in the mean
time, while my servant was away, this letter was delivered
to me, with the others which were inclosed in it.   Upon the
return therefore of the messenger to Frankfort, I at length
left that place on the 15th of September, and by the kindness
of God arrived here this day; whither also Eschnavius, our
prefect, had arrived on the same day.   But although I have had
an interview with him, the business itself is referred to the
prince for his determination, on his arrival, which is looked
for to-morrow.   The issue of the affair, whatever it may be
which God may grant to it, shall be announced to you by
letter, either from myself or from your dear brother John.
I constantly, as you deserve, dwell upon the sincerity of
your mind, and recognise in you in the strongest manner
the benevolent feelings which you entertain towards me.
Farewell, the friend of my friend and brethren, and my
most sincere brother in the Lord; and salute for me your
wife, together with your beloved Samuel.   Sent from Bergzabern, September 20.

MILO COVERDALUS, *Anglus,*

Nuper Exon.

To the most learned and excellent
Conrad Hubert, my very delightful
friend and brother, at Strasburgh.

With regard to the business, concerning which you
requested me to inquire relating to the most illustrious
duchess of Suffolk[1], her very distinguished husband, whom I
spoke to on this subject at Frankfort, assured me that her
grace, as far as money was concerned, owed nothing at all
either to our excellent father Bucer, or to any other persons.
But when I shall return to Wesel, from whence I must now
bring up my dear wife to this place, I will make a diligent
examination into the whole business.

[1 Catharine Willoughby, wife of Charles Brandon, duke of Suffolk,
who was a great friend to Bucer when he was at Cambridge, and
during the reign of Mary, resided at Wesel in exile with her husband.
See Strype, *passim,* and particularly Memorials, III. i. p. 233. Ed. 1822.]

LETTER XXXVI[2].

BISHOP COVERDALE TO ARCHBISHOP PARKER.

Dated from LONDON, *Jan.* 29, 1564.

[MS. Library C. C. College, Cambridge, Vol. Epist. Principum[3].]

MY duty considered in right humble and faithful wise. These are in like manner to beseech your grace, most reverend father and my singular good lord, that as my good lord of London, tendering as well my weak and feeble age, as also my poor travail in God's husbandry within his diocese, hath most gently conferred upon me the benefice of St Magnus, in London, being in value an hundred marks or thereabouts, so it may please your grace to join with his lordship in suit for me to the queen's most excellent majesty, that in favourable consideration, how destitute I have been of a competent living in this realm ever sith my bishoprick was violently taken away from me, I being compelled to resign; and how I never had pension, annuity, or stipend of it these ten years; how unable also I am either to pay the first-

[2 The following letter from bishop Grindal to Sir William Cecil, relating to Coverdale, belongs to this period:

(Lansdowne MSS. No. 6. Burghley Papers, Art. 85.)

I PRAY you, if it chance any suit to be made for one Evans to be bishop of Llandaff, help to stay it, till some examination be had of his worthiness. If any means might be found, that things wickedly alienated from that see might be restored, it were well. If any competency of living might be made of it, I would wish it to father Coverdale, now lately recovered of the plague. Surely it is not well that he, *qui ante nos omnes fuit in Christo*, should be now in his age without stay of living. I cannot herein excuse us bishops. Somewhat I have to say for myself; for I have offered him divers things, which he thought not meet for him. Your warrant in Hatfield Park, or Enfield Chace, would serve my turn very well. God keep you! From Fulham, Dec. 20, 1563.

Yours in Christ,

EDM. LONDON.

To the honourable Sir William Cecil, knight,
secretary to the queen's majesty.

[3 See also Strype's Parker, Vol. I. pp. 295, 6. Ed. Oxon.]

[COVERDALE, II.]

34

fruits, or long to enjoy the said benefice, going upon my
grave, as they say, and not like to live a year, her majesty,
at the contemplation of such most reverend, honourable, and
worthy suitors, will most graciously grant me her warrant
and discharge for the first-fruits of the said benefice. And
as I am bold most humbly to crave your grace's help herein,
so am I fully purposed, God willing, to shew myself again
as thankful, and in my vocation during this my short time
as faithful and quiet as I can. Thus having uttered my
boldness, I most humbly commit your grace and all yours
to the mighty protection of God. From London, Jan. 29,
[1564.]

MYL. COV. Quond. Exon.

[To this letter is appended also, in bishop Coverdale's hand-writing,
the following extract from a subsequent letter to the archbishop, mentioning that his petition had been complied with:]

And whereas I was bold of late to write unto your
grace for your honourable help for the procurement of the
first-fruits of St Magnus, I am now advertised by message
from the right honourable the lord Robert Dudley, that the
queen's majesty hath graciously granted me my suit already;
thus remaining in your grace's obedience, and most humbly
craving the continuance of your favourable love, I beseech
your honour of a gracious answer to the former part.

LETTER XXXVII.

BISHOP COVERDALE TO SIR WILLIAM CECIL.

Dated from LONDON, *Feb.* 6, 1564.

[Lansdowne MSS. No. 7. Burghley Papers, Art. 60.]

MY duty considered in right humble wise unto your honour.
These are in like manner to beseech the same, that whereas
my lord of London, tendering as well mine age as my simple
labours in the Lord's harvest, hath very gently offered me
the pastoral office and benefice of St Magnus in London;
even so it may please your honour to be means for me to
the queen's most excellent majesty, that in favourable consideration, not only how destitute I have been ever sith my

bishoprick was taken from me, and that I never had pension, annuity, or stipend of it these ten years and upward; but also how unable I am, either to pay the first-fruits, or long to enjoy the said living, I going upon my grave, not able to live over a year, her majesty at the contemplation hereof may most graciously grant me the first-fruits of the said benefice, which her highness must needs have again anew, when I am gone.   Heretofore (I praise God for it!) your honour hath ever been my special help and succour in all my rightful suits.   If now, that poor old Myles may be provided for, it please your honour to obtain this for me, I shall think this enough to be unto me as good as a feast.   Thus most humbly beseeching your honour to take my boldness in good part, I commit you and all yours to the gracious protection of the Almighty.   From London, February 6, [1564.]

MYLES COVERDALE, Quond. Exon.

To the right honourable sir William Cecil, knight, chief secretary to the queen's most excellent majesty, and of her highness's most honourable council.

LETTER XXXVIII.

BISHOP COVERDALE TO SIR WILLIAM CECIL.

Dated from LONDON, *March* 18, 1564.

[Lansdowne MSS. No. 7. Burghley Papers, Art. 67.]

As it hath pleased your honour of a very charitable motion to further mine humble suit unto the queen's most excellent majesty, for the obtaining of the first-fruits of St Magnus, and as the same first-fruits amount to the sum of lx^{li}. xvi^s. x^d. ob; so I humbly beseech your honour, that joining with my singular good lord, the lord Robert Dudley, ye will help to obtain the signing of the warrant which I here send unto your honour, as it is drawn by the orderly course of the court of first-fruits and tenths.   I am herein the bolder, because it hath pleased my said lord of his goodness to send me word by Mr Aldersley, that the queen's highness hath

34—2

granted my said petition already. I have, therefore, used the counsel of my dear friend, Mr Peter Osborne, in the draught of this writing engrossed: which as I most humbly send here unto your honour, to be ordered by your godly and charitable wisdom ; even so beseeching you to continue your accustomed favour towards me, I humbly and most heartily commit your honour and all yours to the mighty protection of God. From London, the 18th of March, [1564.]

Your own ever to use and to command in Christ Jesu,

MYLES COVERDALE, *Quond. Exon.*

To the right honourable sir William Cecil, knight, chief secretary to the queen's most excellent majesty, and of her highness's most honourable council.

LETTER XXXIX.

BISHOP COVERDALE TO THE REV. Mr ROBINSON, CHAPLAIN TO ARCHBISHOP PARKER.

[Lambeth MSS. No. 959. 58.]

MY duty considered in right humble and most hasty wise. Whereas I am summoned to appear, with others, to-morrow afore my lord's grace, at Lambeth, I beseech your worthiness to be means for me unto his grace, that at this present I may be dispensed with; not only for that I am un-wieldy, and could neither well travel by land, nor altogether safely by boat, but also for other considerations which this bearer, my dear friend, shall signify unto you by mouth. Thus being desirous of your gentle answer, I commend you and all yours to the gracious protection of God. March 25, 1566.

Your own in the Lord,

MYLES COVERDALE, *Quond. Exon.*

To the right worshipful and godly learned Mr Robinson, chaplain to my lord of Canterbury his grace.

GHOSTLY PSALMS

AND

SPIRITUAL SONGS.

Goostly Psalmes and Spirituall Songes

drawen out of the holy Scripture, for the coforte
and consolacyon of such as loue
to reioyse in God and
his worde.

Psal.

O prayse the Lorde, for is it a good thinge to
synge prayses unto oure God.

Collo. iii.

Teach and exhorte your awne selbes with Psalmes and Hymnes and Spirituall Songes.

Jaco.

Yf eny of you be mery, let him singe Psalmes.

To the boke.

Go lytle boke, get the acquaintaunce
Amonge the louers of Gods worde
Geue them occasyon the same to auaunce
And to make theyr songes of the Lorde
That they may thrust under the borde
All other ballettes of fylthynes
And that we all with one accorde
May geue ensample of godlynes
Go lytle boke amonge mens chyldren
And get the to theyr companye
Teach them to synge ye comaundementes ten
And other ballettes of Gods glorye
Be not ashamed I warande the
Though thou be rude in songe and ryme
Thou shalt to youth some occasion be
In godly sportes to passe theyr tyme.

[GHOSTLY PSALMS AND SPIRITUAL SONGS.

This edition of this very rare volume is here presented from a copy of the original in the library of Queen's College, Oxford, by the obliging permission of the Provost and Fellows of that Society; and the following account of it is extracted from a valuable work, entitled, "A list of the Bible and parts thereof in English from the year M.DV. to M.DCCCXX, by Henry Cotton, D.C.L. Oxford, 1821." "It is," observes this learned writer, "perhaps the only copy now remaining, and appears to have been unnoticed by all our bibliographers, except by Foxe, in the first edition of the book of Martyrs. In that edition, at the end of the Injunctions issued by king Henry VIII., anno 1539, is a catalogue of books forbidden; and among those attributed to Coverdale occurs, 'Psalmes and Spiritual Songes drawn out of the holy Scripture.' No mention however is there made, whether these Psalms were in prose or verse. This list of prohibited books seems to have been omitted in all subsequent editions of Foxe's history; at least it is not contained in those of the years 1576, 1583, 1641, and 1684; nor is it given by Wilkins in his Concilia, although the Injunctions themselves are there reprinted." Cotton, p. 157—8. note. It is evident, therefore, that this work must have been printed before 1539.

It would appear, therefore, that this must have been amongst the earliest, if not the very earliest attempt at a metrical Version of the Psalms in our language. Dr Cotton mentions also one in 1542; a version of Psalm xxv. by Queen Elizabeth; and "David's harpe newly stringed by Theodore Basille;" but this last is not a metrical version; it is Becon's piece, published under the name of Theodore Basille. (See Becon's Works, *Early Writings*, Park. Soc. Ed. p. 262.) In 1549, the year in which Sternhold died, thirty-seven Psalms were published by Day, under the title of "Psalmes of David, drawn into English metre by Thomas Sternholde." About this time metrical versions of the Psalms became common, as is shewn by Dr Cotton, p. 56, &c.

This edition is printed from the original with no other alteration, except the omission of the musical notes, and the substitution of the present for the old Gothic type. The ancient spelling has been preserved throughout, except in the Address to the reader.]

MYLES COVERDALE UNTO THE CHRISTIAN
READER.

Matt. iv.
Mark i.

Luke xvii.

It grieveth me, most dear reader, when I consider the unthankfulness of men, notwithstanding the great abundant mercy and kindness of Almighty God, which so plenteously is heaped upon us on every side. For though Christ our Saviour goeth now about from place to place as diligently as ever he did, teaching in every country, and preaching the gospel of the kingdom, healing all manner of sicknesses and diseases both of body and conscience among the people; yet is the unthankfulness of the world so great, that where ten are cleansed, and have remission of their sins, there is scarce one that cometh again unto Christ, and saith, "Lord, gramercy;" as the poor Samaritan did in the gospel of Luke, which when he saw that he was cleansed, turned back again, and with a loud voice praised God, and fell down upon his face at Christ's feet, and gave him thanks.

And by this we may perceive, what causeth us to be so unthankful as we are; namely, because we do not call to mind, neither consider, that we are cleansed, as this man did. For if we would open our eyes, and remember well, what kindness it is that the Father of mercy hath shewed us in Christ, and what great benefits he hath done, and daily doth, for us in him and for his sake; we would not only fall down upon our faces and give him thanks, but with loud voices would we praise him, and in the midst of the congregation would we extol his name, as David and Asaph do almost in every psalm. For doubtless whoso believeth that God loveth him, and feeleth by his faith, that he hath forgiven him all his sins, and careth for him, and delivereth him from all evil; whosoever he be, I say, that feeleth this in his heart, shall be compelled by the Spirit of God to break out into praise and thanksgiving therefore: yea, he shall not be content, nor fully satisfied in his mind, till other men know also what God hath done for him, but shall cry and call upon them, as David

doth, saying : " O praise the Lord with me, and let us mag- Psal. xxxiv.
nify his name together.   I sought the Lord, and he heard
me, yea, he delivered me out of all my fear." And in the
same psalm : " O taste and see how friendly the Lord is :
blessed is the man that trusteth in him." And in another
place : " O come hither and hearken, all ye that fear God ; Psal. lxvi.
I will tell you what he hath done for my soul."

O that men would praise the goodness of the Lord, and
the wonders that he doth for the children of men !   O that
we would remember what great things the Father of mercy
hath done, doth daily, and is ever ready to do for our souls !
O that men's lips were so opened, that their mouths might Psal. l.
shew the praise of God !   Yea, would God that our minstrels
had none other thing to play upon, neither our carters and
ploughmen other thing to whistle upon, save psalms, hymns,
and such godly songs as David is occupied withal !   And if
women, sitting at their rocks[1], or spinning at the wheels, had
none other songs to pass their time withal, than such as
Moses' sister, Glehana's wife, Debora, and Mary the mother Exod. xv.
1 Sam. ii.
of Christ, have sung before them, they should be better oc- Judg. v.
Luke i.
cupied than with *hey nony nony, hey troly loly,* and such
like phantasies.

If young men also that have the gift of singing, took
their pleasure in such wholesome ballads as the three children
sing in the fire, and as Jesus the Son of Sirac doth in his
last chapter, it were a token, both that they felt some spark
of God's love in their hearts, and that they also had some
love unto him ; for truly, as we love, so sing we ; and where
our affection is, thence cometh our mirth and joy.   When
our hearts are tangled with the vain lusts of this corrupt
world, then, if we be merry and are disposed to gladness,
our mirth is nothing but wantonness and inordinate pastime ;
and when we are sad, our heaviness is either desperation, or
else some carefulness of this vain world.

Contrariwise, if our minds be fixed upon God, and we
subdued to the holy desires of his Spirit ; then, like as our
hearts are occupied in the meditation of his goodness and
love which he beareth toward us, even so are our tongues
exercised in the praise of his holy name : so that when we

[1 rock : an instrument used in spinning.]

are merry, our pastime and pleasure, our joy, mirth, and
Eccles. iii. gladness is all of him. And as for our hemnes[1], when we
are sad, (as every thing must have a time,) it is either patience
in trouble, repentance for offences done in time past, compassion upon other men, or else mourning for our own infirmities, because our body of sin provoketh us so oft to do
the will of the flesh. And thus God causeth both the mirth
Rom. viii. and sorrow of them that love him to work for their profit,
as all other things turn to their best.

Psal. cxlvii. Seeing then that, as the prophet David saith, it is so
good and pleasant a thing to praise the Lord, and so expedient for us to be thankful; therefore, to give our youth
of England some occasion to change their foul and corrupt
ballads into sweet songs and spiritual hymns of God's honour,
and for their own consolation in him, I have here, good
reader, set out certain comfortable songs grounded on God's
word, and taken some out of the holy scripture, specially out
of the Psalms of David, all whom would God that our
musicians would learn to make their songs! and if they
which are disposed to be merry, would in their mirth follow
Coloss. iii. the counsel of St Paul and St James, and not to pass their
James v. time in naughty songs of fleshly love and wantonness, but
with singing of psalms, and such songs as edify, and corrupt
not men's conversation.

As for the common sort of ballads which now are used
in the world, I report me to every good man's conscience,
what wicked fruits they bring. Corrupt they not the manners of young persons? Do they not tangle them in the
snares of uncleanness? Yes, truly, and blind so the eyes of
their understanding, that they can neither think well in
their hearts, nor outwardly enter into the way of godly and
virtuous living. I need not rehearse, what evil ensamples of
idleness, corrupt talking, and all such vices as follow the
same, are given to young people through such unchristian
songs. Alas! the world is all so full of vicious and evil livers
Gen. vi. already, it is no need to cast oil in the fire. Our own
nature provoketh us to vices, God knoweth, all-to sore: no
man needeth enticing thereto.

1 John ii. Seeing then that we are commanded not to love this
world, neither the lusts thereof; seeing, I say, that all the

[1 hemnes: hymns.]

pleasures and joys that the world can imagine, are but vanity, _{Psal. lxii.} and vanish away as doth the smoke; what cause have we then to rejoice so much therein? Why do we not rather take these worldly lusts for our very enemies, that stop the way betwixt us and that everlasting joy, which is prepared for us in heaven? Why do we not rather seek the things that are above, where Christ is at the right hand of God, as St Paul saith? _{Coloss. iii.}

Wherefore let not the wise man rejoice in his wisdom, _{Jer. ix.} nor the strong man in his strength, neither the rich man in his riches; yea, (I dare be bold to warn them that will be counselled,) let not the courtier rejoice in his ballads, let not youth take their lust and pastime in wantonness and ignorance of God, or in misspending the fruits of their fathers' labour: but let us altogether, from the most unto the least, be glad, rejoice, and be merry even from our heart, that we have gotten the knowledge of the Lord among us, that we are sure of his love and favour, and that our names are written _{Luke x.} in heaven.

The children of Israel in the old time, when God had delivered them from their enemies, gave thanks unto him, and made their song of him, as thou seest by Moses, Barak, _{Exod. xv. Judg. v.} David, and other more. Why should not we then make our _{2 Sam. xxii} songs and mirth of God, as well as they? Hath he not done as much for us as for them? Hath he not delivered us from as great troubles as them? Yes, doubtless. Why should he not then be our pastime, as well as theirs?

As for such psalms as the scripture describeth, (beside the great consolation that they bring into the heart of the spiritual singer,) they do not only cause him to spend his time well by exercising himself in the sweet word of God; but through such ensamples they provoke other men also unto the praise of God and virtuous living. And this is the very right use wherefore psalms should be sung; namely, to comfort a man's heart in God, to make him thankful, and to exercise him in his word, to encourage him in the way of godliness, and to provoke other men unto the same. By this thou mayest perceive, what spiritual edifying cometh of godly psalms and songs of God's word; and what inconvenience followeth the corrupt ballads of this vain world.

Now, beloved reader, thou seest the occasion of this my

small labour.   Wherefore, if thou perceivest that the very word of God is the matter thereof, I pray thee accept it, use it, and provoke youth unto the same.   And if thou feelest in thine heart, that all the Lord's dealing is very mercy and kindness, cease not then to be thankful unto him therefore: but in thy mirth be alway singing of him, that his blessed name may be praised now and ever.   Amen.

———————

GOOSTLY PSALMES AND SPIRITUALL SONGES.

TO THE HOLY GOOST.

O HOLY Spirite our comfortoure,
For grace and help, Lorde, now we call;
Teach us to know Christ our Savioure,
And his Father's mercy over all.
From his swete worde let us not fall;
But lyft up our hertes alway to the,
That we may receave it thankfully.

Nowe seynge we are come together,
To heare the wordes of verite;
In understandynge be thou guyder,
That we may folowe the voyce of the.
From straunge lernynge, Lorde, kepe us fre,
That we thorowe them be not begyled:
Kepe our understandynge undefyled.

We praye the also, blessed Lorde,
Enflame our hertes so with thy grace,
That in our lives we folowe thy worde,
And one forgeve another's trespace.
To amende our lyves, Lorde, geve us space:
With thy godly frutes endewe us all,
That from thy worde we never fall.

Let us not have thy worde only
In our mouthe and in our talkynge;
But both in dede and verite
Let us shewe it in our lyvynge.
Make us frutefull in every thynge,
And in good workes so to encrease,
That whyle we lyve, we may the please.

O Lorde, lende us thy strength and power,
To mortifie all carnall luste:
In all our trouble sende us succour,
That we faynt not in the to truste.
And make us stronge to suffer with Christe,
Beynge pacient in adversite,
And in all thynges thankfull to the.

ANOTHER OF THE SAME.

COME, holy Spirite, most blessed Lorde,
Fulfyl our hartes nowe with thy grace;
And make our myndes of one accorde,
Kyndle them with love in every place.
O Lorde, thou forgevest our trespace,
And callest the folke of every countre
To the ryght fayth and truste of thy grace,
That they may geve thankes and synge to thee,
                    Alleluya, Alleluya.

O holy lyght, moste principall,
The worde of lyfe shewe unto us;
And cause us to knowe God over all
For our owne Father moste gracious.
Lorde, kepe us from lernyng venymous,
That we folowe no masters but Christe.
He is the verite, his worde sayth thus;
Cause us to set in hym our truste.
                    Alleluya, Alleluya.

O holy fyre, and conforth moste swete,
Fyll our hertes with fayth and boldnesse,
To abyde by the in colde and hete,
Content to suffre for ryghteousnesse:
O Lord, geve strength to our weaknesse,
And send us helpe every houre;
That we may overcome all wyckednesse,
And brynge this olde Adam under thy power.
                    Alleluya, Alleluya.

ANOTHER OF THE SAME.

Thou holy Spirite, we pray to the,
Strengthe oure fayth and increase it alwaye;
Comforth oure hertes in adversite
With trewe beleve bothe nyght and daye.

Kirieleyson.

Thou worthy lyght, that art so cleare,
Teache us Christe Jesu to knowe alone;
That we have never cause to feare
In hym to have redempcyon.

Kirieleyson.

Thou swete love, graunt us altogether
To be unfayned in charite;
That we may all love one another,
And of one mynde alwaye to be.

Kirieleyson.

Be thou our confortoure in all nede;
Make us to feare nether death nor shame;
But in the treuth to be stablyshed,
That Sathan put us not to blame.

Kirieleyson.

UNTO THE TRENITE.

God the Father, dwell us by,
And let us never do amysse;
Geve us grace with wyll to dye,
And make us redy to thy blysse.

From the devel's myght and powre,
Kepe us in fayth every houre;
And ever let us buylde on the,
With hole herte trustynge stedfastly.

Oure fleshe is weake, the devell is stronge,
He wolde overthrowe us ever amonge.
Without the can we never spede;
Now helpe us therfore in our nede.

Amen, amen, let it be so;
The shall we synge Alleluya.

Jesus Christe, now dwell us by
And let us never do amysse.
Holy Goost, now dwell us by,
And let us never do amysse.

THE TEN COMMANDEMENTES OF GOD.

THESE are the holy commaundements ten,
Which God oure Lorde gave so strately,
By Moses his servaunte, unto all men,
Upon the hygh hyll of Sinia.

Kirieleyson.

Exod. xx.

Thou shalt have none other God but me;
Set thou thy trust in me alone;
Love and dred me unfaynedly,
With harte and mynde at all season.

Kirieleyson.

Deut. v.

Thou shalt not take my name in vayne,
But call on it in all thy nede:
From othes and lyes thou shalt refrayne,
That my name be not dishonoured.

Kirieleyson.

Heb. iv.

The Saboth day halowe thou to me,
As I rested fro my workynge:
So cease thou from all vanite,
That I maye worke in the all thynge.

Kirieleyson.

Ephes. vi.

Honoure thy father and mother also,
With men that are in auctorite:
Obeye them all, where ever thou go;

Rom. xiii.

So shall thy lyfe be longe truely.

Kirieleyson.

Matt. v.
Rom. xii.

Thou shalt not kyll, nor hate any man,
Nor yet beare malyce in thy mynde.

Do thy enemyes the best thou can,   Matt. v.
And to all men se thou be kynde.
                  Kirieleyson.

Thy wedlocke shalt thou kepe truly,
And keepe other men to do the same;
That whordome and dishonestie
May be destroyed and put to blame.
                  Kirieleyson.

Thou shalt not steale thy neghbour's good,
Nor get it with false marchaundyse;
But worke with thyne hande to get thy food,   Ephes. iv.
And to sustayne the poore helplesse.
                  Kirieleyson.

Agaynst no man beare false witnesse,
And speake no evell to hurte his name:
But yf he fall thorowe his weaknesse,   Gal. vi.
Do thou thy best to cover his shame.
                  Kirieleyson.

Thou shalt not thy neghbour's house desyre,
His wyfe, servaunt, nor mayde also;
But shalt be glad his good to forbeare,
As thou thyselfe woldest be done to.   Matt. vii.
                  Kirieleyson.

ANOTHER OF THE SAME.

MAN, wylt thou lyve vertuously,   Matt. xix.
And with God reygne eternally,
Man, must thou kepe these commaundements ten
That God commaunded to all men.
                  Kirieleyson.

I am thy God and Lorde alone;
Without me shalt thou other have none.
Thy herte shall trust on me alwaye,
Love and feare me both nyght and daye.
                  Kirieleyson.

Thou shalt honoure my name with spede,
And call on it in all thy nede.

[COVERDALE, II.]
        35

Heb. iv.

Thou shalt halowe the Saboth daye,
That I maye worke in the alwaye.

Kirieleyson.

Matt. xv.

Honoure thy father and mother also;
Obey thou them where ever thou go.

Matt. v.

No man's persone desyre to kyll;

Heb. xiii.

And thy wedlocke shalt thou fulfyll.

Kirieleyson.

Ephes. iv.

From thy neghboure steale thou nothynge,

Exod. xx.

Nor false witnesse agaynst hym brynge.
Thy neghbour's house thou shalt not desyre,
His wife and good shalt thou forbeare.

Kirieleyson.

THE CREDE.

We beleve all upon one God;
Maker of heven and erth he is truly.
Oure father deare he hath hym made,
That we all his chyldren myght be.
He provydeth for us dayly,
Body and soule defendeth he strongly.
All mysfortune shall from us fle,
No harme shall happen to any of us.
He careth for us both daye and nyght;
He is oure keper most gracyous:
Al thynge stode in his powre and myght.

We beleve all on Christe Jesu,
His owne Sonne and oure Lorde most deare;

John xiv.

Which in Godhead, power, and vertue
Is alway lyke to his Father.

Luke ii.

Of the glorious Virgyn Mary
Was he borne a man undoutedly,

Matt. i.

Thorowe the Holy Gooste's workying fre:

Mark xv.

For he deed and buried truely,

Mark xvi.

He rose up the thyrde daye alone;

Luke

To heaven ascended he myghtely,

Matt. xxv.

And shall come to judge us echone[1].

[¹ echone: each one.]

We beleve all on the Holy Goost;
Lyke the Father and Sonne in Trenite;   1 John v.
In all our trouble oure comforte most,
And in all oure adversite.
One holy church beleve we all,   Ephes. iv.
Which is fylled with sayntes great and small;
And for synne can it never fall.
Of synnes there is clene remission: John xx.
Our flesh shall aryse without doutynge: 1 Cor. xv.
There is prepared for us everychone
A lyfe that is everlastynge.

ANOTHER OF THE SAME.

In God I trust, for so I must;
He hath made heaven and earth also;
My Father is he, his chylde am I;
My conforte he is, I have no mo:
In all my nede he maketh me spede;
His powre is with me alwaye,
To keepe me every daye.
There is no evell can have his wyll
Agaynst my health nor yet my wealth,
But it muste come to my furtheraunce.
He is my kynge, that ruleth all thynge;
The devell can make no hynderaunce.

So do I trust on Jesu Christ,
His Sonne conceaved of the Holy Goost;   Matt. i.
Borne of Marye a virgin fre,   Luke ii.
For all my synnes to paye the cost.
For deed was he and buried truely;   Mark xv.
The gates of hell hath he broken,
And heaven hath he made open.
He rose truely the thyrde daye fre;   1 Cor. xv.
He went up ryght to the Father of myght;
And shall apeare at domes-daye: Mark xvi.
For judge shall he all the worlde truely,   Acts i.
And dryve myne enemyes all awaye.

I also truste on the Holy Goost,
Lyke the Father and Sonne in Trenite;   1 John v.

35—2

My conforth best in all evell rest,
In all my nede my chefest remedie.
A Church holy I beleve truely,
Which is but one generall:
For synne can it never fall;
A company of sayntes they be.

John xx.

Of synfulnesse true forgyvenesse
Is from amonge them never.

1 Cor. xv.

Our fleshe verely shall ryse in glory;
So shall we lyve with God for ever.

OF THE PATER NOSTER.

O FATHER ours celestiall,
We praye to the;
Thou wylt have us on the to call
In spirite and verite.
Thy godly name be sanctified
In great honoure
Amonge us all; and halowed
Also every houre.
The kyndome of thy grace drawe nye,
That thou mayst dwell alwaye in us
With thy holy Spirite continually,
That we remayne not vicious:
But as thou hast geven us thy Spirite,
So let us ever do good thorowe it.

Acts xxi.
Matt. vi.

We praye the also, blessed Lorde,
Let thy will be done
Amongst us here with one accorde,
As in heaven all season.

Luke xi.

And let us never oure wyll fulfyll,
But thyne alwaye:

Gen. vi.

For ours is wycked and geven to evell,
Truely both nyght and day.

Matt. vi.

And geve us ever oure dayly bred,
Both for oure body and soule also;
And let us with thy worde be fed,
That we be never kepte therefro.

Luke xi.
Matt. vi.

Lorde, sende us true shepherdes therefore,
To fede us thy shepe evermore.

Forgeve our dettes and synfulnesse,
Lorde, we the praye;
Where we have greved the more or lesse,
Ether by nyght or daye.
For we forgeve them that greve us,   Matt. xviii.
Or do us evell;
Trustynge that thou wylt be gracyous,
Thy promyse to fulfyll.
In no tentacyon, Lorde, us brynge,   Matt. vi.
Nor suffre us for to fall from the;
But be oure keepe in every thynge,
And kepe us from all ioperdy
Both of our body and soule also,   Luke xi.
And delyver us whereever we go.

ANOTHER OF THE SAME.

O oure Father celestiall,
Now are we come to praye to the:
We are thy chyldren, therefore we call;
Hear us, Father, mercifully.
Now blessed be thy godly name,
And ever amonge us sanctified:
There is none other but this same,
Wherby mankynde must be saved.
                                    Kirieleyson.

Thy kyngdome come: reigne thou in us,   Matt. vi.
For to expell all synne awaye;
Let not Sathan dwell in thy house,
To put the forth by nyght nor day.
Fulfylled be thy godly wyll   Luke xi.
Among us all, for it is ryght;   Acts xxi.
As they in heaven do it fulfyll,
So let us do both daye and nyght.
                                    Kirieleyson.

Our dayly bred geve us this daye;   Luke xi.
And let us never perysh for nede.
The litle byrdes thou fedest alwaye;   Matt. vi.
Thyne own chyldren than must thou fede.

Matt. xviii.

Our dettes are great; forgeve us, Lorde,
As we oure detters all forgeve;
And let us alwaye be restored
To thy mercy, that we may lyve.

Kirieleyson.

Tentacyon is sore in use,
And strongly now are we proved;
Good Lorde, thou mayst us not refuse.
We pray the with us to abyde:
Not that alone, but helpe us out
From parels all and ioperdy:
Let no evell sprete put us in doute
Of thy favour and great mercy.

Kirieleyson.

BE GLAD NOW, ALL YE CHRISTEN MEN.

Be glad now, all ye christen men,
And let us rejoyce unfaynedly.
The kyndnesse cannot be written with penne,
That we have receaved of God's mercy;
Whose love towarde us hath never ende:
He hath done for us as a frende;
Now let us thanke him hartely.

Rom. v.

Psalm li.

Psalm xiv.

I was a prysoner of the devell;
With death was I also utterly lost;
My synnes drove me dayly to hell;
Therein was I borne; this may I bost.
I was also in them once ryfe;
There was no virtue in my lyfe,
To take my pleasure I spared no cost.

Rom. iii.

Rom. iii.
Gen. vi.

Unto my workes I trusted to sore:
But they coulde not helpe, nor yet fre wyll;
My herte was not the better therefore,
For I was alwaye geven to evell.
My conscience drove me to despayre;
It was so vexed all with feare;
There was no helpe, but synke to hell.

Than God eternall had pitie on me,
To ryd me fro my wyckednesse. *Luke i.*
He thought of his plenteous great mercy,
And wolde not leave me comfortlesse.
He turned to me his fatherly herte, *Ephes. i.*
And wolde I shoulde with hym have parte
Of all his costly ryches.

He spake to his deare beloved Sonne,
The tyme is nowe to have mercye;
Thou must be man's redempcyon,
And lowse hym from captivite.
Thou must hym helpe from trouble of synne;
From paynfull death thou must hym wynne,
That he may lyve eternally.

God's Sonne was redy so to do; *Phil. ii.*
Into this worlde he cam to me;
Borne of a virgen pure also, *1 Tim. i.*
Because he thought my brother to be.
For in my shape he dyd apeare, *Luke ii.*
Me to delyver whole from feare, *Heb. ii.*
And from all evell to make me fre. *Phil. ii.*

These lovynge wordes he spake to me:
I wyll delyver thy soule from payne;
I am desposed to do for the,
And to myne owne selfe the to retayne.
Thou shalt be with me, for thou art myne; *John xiv.*
And I with the, for I am thyne;
Soch is my love, I can not layne.

They wyll shed out my precyous bloude,
And take away my lyfe also;
Which I wyll suffre all for thy good:
Beleve this sure, where ever thou go.
For I wyll yet ryse up agayne; *Matt. xx.*
Thy synnes I beare, though it be payne,
To make the safe and fre from wo.

I wyll go from this worldly lyfe *John xvi.*
To my deare Father, with him to lyve:
Yet am I with the in batell and stryfe;
Pure Spirite of truth I wyll the geve,

Which shall the conforte in hevynes,
And lede the into godlynes :
Thus wyll I all thy synnes forgyve.

Matt. xxviii.   Soch thynges I have taught and done,
Shalt thou both teach and do also.
Geve thankes for thy redempcyon,
And knowlege my worde, where ever thou go;
And kepe the well from straunge lernynge,
Which maye the to destruction brynge;
So wyll I never departe the fro.

NOW IS OURE HELTH COME FROM ABOVE.

Now is oure health come from above,
For God hath shewed us his mercy :
We cannot deserve to have his love;
Yet Christ hath brought us liberte
Frō all oure synnes and wickedness,
Oure naughtie lyfe and wātōnes,
And wyll not cōdēne us truly.

Acts xv.   What God had commaunded in the lawe
Were we not sufficient for to do;
For oure stomakes it was to rawe;
Ephes. ii.   God's wrath reigned in us also.
Rom. viii.   Oure flesh was weake, it had no myght;
We coulde not geve the Sprete his ryght;
Oure flesh wolde not consent therto.

Yet had we a false meanyng therbye,
And thought the law was geven therfore;
As who saye we were all so fre
God's lawe to fulfyll evermore.
Gal. iii.   The law is but a scolemaster,
Which doth oure naturall evell declare,
That causeth us to synne so sore.

For all this must the lawe be donne;
Els had we ben all utterly lost.
Gal. iv.   Therefore hath God sent his deare Sonne,
Which was made man to paye the cost.

The hole law hath he well fulfylled; Matth. v.
His Father's anger hath he stylled,
To do it else no man coulde boost.

The lawe therefore sheweth us oure synne, Rom. vii.
And smytteth oure conscience to the grounde:
But when the gospell commeth therin,
It lyfteth us up, and maketh us sounde.
Our synne is great, but mercy is more; Rom. v.
Our conscience oft doth greve us sore,
But Christe hath stopped that bloudy wounde.

When I consyder this in my mynde,
What God in Christe hath done for me;
I can in no wyse be unkynde,
Nor use myself unchristenly.
I am compelled godly to lyve,
My neghbour's fautes to forgeve, Ephes. iv.
As Christ dyd for me mercyfully.

So are good workes the very frute
Of hym that beleveth stedfastly.
A good tre with good frutes breaketh out,
As the gospell doth testifie.
For lyke as fayth hangeth whole on God,
So shulde our workes do other men good: Matt. vii.
For fayth without them can not be.

O hevenly Father, grant thy grace
Thy name in us to be sanctified:
Thy kyngdome come; thy wyll alwayes Matt. vi.
Amonge us all be fulfylled.
Fede us, and forgeve all our evell; Luke xi.
Lede us not in tentacion styll;
From evell delyver us at oure nede.

CHRIST IS THE ONLY SONNE OF GOD.

CHRIST is the only Sonne of God,
The Father eternall:
We have in Jesso founde this rod,
God and man naturall;

He is the mornynge star;
His beames sendeth he out farre,
Beyonde other starres all.

Luke i.

He was for us a man borne
In the last parte of tyme;
Yet kepte the maydenheade unfolorne
His mother that bare hym:
He hath hell gates broken,
And heaven hath he made open,
Bryngynge us lyfe agayne.

Thou only maker of all thynge,
Thou everlastynge lyght,
From ende to ende all rulynge,
By thyne owne godly myght;
Turne thou oure hartes unto the;
And lyghten them with the veritie,
That they erre not from the ryght.

Let us increase in love of the,
And in knowlege also;
That we belevynge stedfastly
John iv.
May in spirite serve the so,
That we in our hartes may savoure
Thy mercy and thy favoure,
And to thyrst after no mo.

Awake us, Lorde, we praye the;
Thy holy Spirite us geve,
Which maye oure olde man mortifie,
That oure new man maye lyve.
So wyll we alwaye thanke the,
That shewest us so great mercye,
And oure synnes dost forgeve.

MEDIA VITA.

In the myddest of our lyvynge
Death compaseth us rounde about:
Who shulde us now sucour brynge,
By whose grace we maye come out?

Even thou, Lorde Jesu, alone:
It doth oure hartes sore greve truly,
That we have offended the.
O Lord God, most holy,
O Lord God, most myghtie,
O holy and mercyfull Savioure,
Thou most worthy God eternall,
Suffre us not at our last houre
For any death from the to fall.

Kirieleyson.

In the myddest of oure dyenge
We are vexed with helle's payne.
Who shulde helpe us out of this thynge,
With stronge fayth to resyste agayne?
Even thou, Lorde Jesu, alone.
For whan we crye and call on the,
Thou art moved than with mercye.
O Lorde God, most holy,
O Lorde God, most myghtye,
O holy and mercyfull Savioure,
Thou most worthy God eternall,
Suffre us not at oure last houre
For any hell from the to fall.

Kirieleyson.

In the myddest of oure helle's payne
Oure owne synnes vexe us greatly.
Who shulde save us from despayre agayne,
That we maye holde by thy mercye?
Even thou, Lorde Jesu, alone:
For thy deare bloude ryght plenteously
Was shed out for oure synnes frely.
O Lorde God, most holy,
O Lorde God, most myghtye,
O holy and mercyfull Savioure,
Thou most worthy God eternall,
Suffre us not at oure last houre
Thorow despare from the to fall.

Kirieleyson.

BY ADAM'S FALL.

By Adam's fall was so forlorne
The whole nature of mankynde,
That we were poysoned or we were borne;
And no helpe thereto could we fynde,
Tyll Christ Jesu
By his vertue
For oure dette his deare bloude hath spent,
That we were in
By Adam's synne,
When he brake God's commaundement.

Gen. iii.
Seynge Eve was sore begyled
By the serpente's tentacyon,
Because she God's worde despysed,
Brought mankynde to destruccyon;
Agaynst this dede
It was great nede,
That God shulde us to comforte geve
Rom. viii.   His owne deare Sonne,
Rom. iii.   And mercy troane[1],
By whose death we all myght lyve.

Rom. v.
Lyke as in Adam a straunge det
Had brought us to destruccyon;
So are we now delyvered from it
In Christe, our ryght salvacyon.
Lyke as we all
By Adam's fall
Were ordened with ryght to dye;
So in God's Sonne
Redempcyon
Have we found eternally.

Rom. v.
So dyd he then geve us his Sonne,
When we were yet his enemys;
Which for us on the crosse was done:
Matt. xxvii.
1 Cor. xv.
And so the thyrde daye dyd aryse,

[1 mercy troane; mercy-seat. Rom. iii. 25. "Whom God hath
set forth for a mercy-seat." Coverdale's Translation.]

To justifie
Eternally
All us that trust fast on his myght. Rom. iv.
Why shulde we than
Drede any payne?
He is now oure owne by ryght.

He is his Father's eternall Worde,
The way, the lyfe, and veritie; John xiv.
He is the Savioure and the Lorde,
Whom he hath geven us frely
To be oure health,
Oure helpe and wealth,
And not to trust in any man. Psal. lxii.
For there is none,
But he alone,
That us sucoure or comforth can.

Man is all wicked by nature;
There is no helpe with hym to fynde.
Who seketh helpe in a creature,
And not in God with harte and mynde,
He buyldeth on sonde,
And may not stonde,
When tyme cometh of tentacyon.
Therefore to trest Psal. cxviii.
On God is best,
And the most sure foundacyon.

He that hopeth in God stedfastly, Rom. x.
Shall never be confounded:
For doutles God's worde can not ley,
Though all men shulde resist it.
Great trouble and care
Is every where;
This worlde's sorowe is infinite:
Yet sawe I never
Him perish for ever,
That fast on God's worde trusted.

O Lorde, I praye the hartely
For thy great mercyfull kyndnesse;
Thy wholsome worde take not fro me, Psal. cxix.
Because of my unthankfulnesse.

Psal. xxxviii.

My synne is great,
I acknowlege it:

Psal. cxlv.
Eccles. ii.

But thy mercy excelleth all thynge.
Therefore will I
Hope styll in the,
To thy blysse that thou mayest me brynge.

WAKE UP, WAKE UP.

WAKE up, wake up, in God's name,
Thou worthy fayre christente;
And shewe thy brydgrome's great fame,
For that he hath done to the;
Which hath his word now sent
And opened it once agayne;
As thou mayest se in many a place,
Where now is preached his grace
So truly and so playne.

John viii.

Thy olde enemye that Sathan,
The father of all lesynge,
Seketh all the meanes that he can
The veritie downe to brynge.
If any man speake thereof,
It must cost hym his bloude:
For many soch men he dryveth alwaye,
And some he slayeth now every daye;
Yet all doth hym no good.

He can not leave his cruelnesse,
But threateneth daye and nyght;
His mynde is whole the to oppresse,
That thou mayest feare his myght.
But stonde thou fast in God,
O worthy fayre christente:
He is thy helpe and sucoure;
Whoso doth the displeasure,
He toucheth God's owne eye.

Exod. xiv.

Beholde, how God hath ever done
For Israell in theyr nede.
He drowned kynge Pharao ryght sone,
With all that them troubled:

The walls of Hierico fell,
So sone as God's folke came:
Thy Lorde God is so myghty,
That he can helpe the swyftly,
And put thy foes to blame.   *Josh. vi.*

The Madianites dyd all theyr best
To trouble God's people deare:
The Amaleckes wolde not let them rest,
But helde them styll in feare.
Israel cryed to God,
Which helped them louyngly
By Gedeon his servaunt:
There fell a hundreth thousande   *Judg. ix.*
And twenty thousande truly.

Remember, how God kepte David   *1 Sam. xxiii.*
From Saul, that wicked kynge;
How oft he hym delyvered,
Which caused David to synge.   *2 Sam. xxii.*
He had also great harme   *2 Sam. xv.*
Even of his naturall sonne,
That made great laboure hym to slaye;
But God delyvered hym alwaye,
And hanged fayre Absalon.   *2 Sam. xviii.*

Note also how God helped
The good kyng Abia;
And hym strongly delyvered
From Hieroboam alwaye.
Though he was sore vexed
Of hym a longe season,
As sone as he complayned,   *2 Chron. xiii.*
Five hundreth thousande were slayne deed,
And all destroyed ryght sone.

So hath God helped ryght well
Assa, that faythfull kynge;
That we his sucoure myght fele
In every troublous thynge.
His enemyes were many,
And stronge in all men's syght,
A thousand tymes a thousande: *2 Chron xiv.*
Yet were they not so stronge to stonde,
But fell all thorow God's myght.

Consyder how God delyvered
The kynge Ezechiam,
Which was very oft sore threatened
With Sennacherib by name.
2 Kings xix.
1sai. xxxvii.
2 Chron.
xxxii.
Of thousandes even an hundreth
Foure score and .v. he brought:
Yet were they sone destroyed than;
God's aungell slewe them every man,
And brought them all to nought.

2 Chron. xx.
Heare to how strongly God fought
For his kynge Josaphat,
When Ammon all his power brought,
And Moab's hoost was thereat.
Israel called to God;
He was theyr helpe onely;
The heythen were so plaged,
That one dyd slaye another deed,
God's folk gat the victory.

Thus all God's enemyes peryshed,
God slewe them all sodenly.
His hand is not yet shortened,
O worthy fayre christente:
He can the well defende;
Thy heeres are told truly:
Let Sathan do all that he maye,
Yf thou holde fast God's worde alwaye,
He shall not forsake the.

I CALL ON THE, LORDE JESU CHRISTE.

I CALL on the, Lorde Jesu Christ,
I have none other helpe but the:
My herte is never set at rest,
Tyll thy swete worde have conforted me.
And stedfast fayth graunt me therfore,
To holde by thy worde evermore
        Above all thynge,
        Never resistynge,
But to increase in fayth more and more.

Yet once agayne I call on the;
Heare my request, O mercyfull Lorde:
I wolde fayne hope on thy mercye,
And can not be thereto restored,
Excepte thou with thy grace oppresse
My blynde and naturall weaknesse.
          Cause me therefore
              To hope evermore
On thy mercy and swete promises.

Lorde, prynte into my harte and mynde
Thy holy Spirite with ferventnesse;
That I to the be not unkynde,
But love the without faynednesse.
Let nothynge drawe my mynde from the,
But ever to love the earnestly:
              Let not my harte
              Unthankfully departe
From the ryght love of thy mercye.

Geve me thy grace, Lorde, I the praye,
To love myne enemyes hartely;
Howbeit they trouble me alwaye,
And for thy cause do slaundre me.
Yet, Jesu Christe, for thy goodnesse,
Fyll my harte with forgevenesse;
              That whyle I lyve
              I maye them forgeve,
That do offende me more or lesse.

I am compased all round aboute
With sore and stronge tentacyon:
Therefore, good Lorde, delyver me out
From all this wycked nacyon.
The devell, the worlde, my flesh also,
Followe upon me where I go;
              Therefore wolde I
              Now fayne delyvered be:
Thy helpe I seke, Lorde, and no mo.

Now seist thou, Lorde, what nede I have;
I have none els to complayne to:
Therefore thy Holy Goost I crave,
To be my guyde wherever I go;

That in all my adversitie
I forget not the love of the;
     But as thou, Lorde,
     Hast geven me thy worde,
Let me therein both lyve and dye.

OF THE BIRTH OF CHRIST.

Now blessed be thou, Christ Jesu;
Thou art man borne, this is true:
The aungels made a mery noyse,
Yet have we more cause to rejoyse.
                   Kirieleyson.

Luke ii.

The blessed Sonne of God onely
In a crybbe full poore dyd lye:
With oure poore flesh and oure poore bloude
Was clothed that everlastynge good.
                   Kirieleyson.

He that made heaven and earth of nought,
In oure flesh hath oure health brought;

Phil. ii.

For oure sake made he hymselfe full small,
That reigneth Lorde and Kynge over all.
                   Kirieleyson.

1 John i.

Eternall lyght doth now appeare
To the worlde both farre and neare;
It shyneth full cleare even at mydnyght,
Makynge us chyldren of his lyght.
                   Kirieleyson.

The Lorde Christ Jesu, God's Sonne deare,
Was a gest and a straunger here;
Us for to brynge from mysery,
That we might lyve eternally.
                   Kirieleyson.

Into this worlde ryght poore came he,
To make us ryche in mercye:
Therefore wolde he oure synnes forgeve,
That we with hym in heaven myght lyve.
                   Kirieleyson.

All this dyd he for us frely,
For to declare his great mercy :
All Christendome be mery therfore,
And geve hym thankes evermore.

Kirieleyson.

OF THE RESURRECTION.

CHRISTE is now rysen agayne
From his death and all his payne :
Therfore wyll we mery be,
And rejoyse with hym gladly.

Kirieleyson.

1 Cor. xv.

Had he not rysen agayne,
We had ben lost, this is playne :
But sen he is rysen in dede,
Let us love hym all with spede.

Kirieleyson.

Now is tyme of gladnesse,
To synge of the Lorde's goodnesse :
Therefore glad now wyll we be,
And rejoyse in hym onely.

Kirieleyson.

ANOTHER OF THE SAME.

CHRIST dyed and suffred great payne,
For oure synnes and wickednesse ;
But he is now rysen agayne,
To make us full of gladnesse.
Let us all rejoyse therfore,
And geve him thankes for evermore,
Synginge to hym, Alleluya.

Alleluya.

There was no man that coulde overwynne
The power of death, nor his myght :
And all this came thorow oure synne,
Wherfore we were dampned by ryght.
By occasyon of which thynge
Death took us into his kepynge ;
We coulde not escape out of his syght.

Rom. v,

Alleluya.

36—2

But the Lorde Jesu, God's owne Sonne,
Takynge on hym oure weake nature,

John i.

Hath put awaye oure synnes alone,
And overcome death thorow his power.
As for death and his great myght,
Christ hath overcome it all by ryght;
It can do us no displeasure.

Alleluya.

It was a marvelous great thynge,
To se how death with death dyd fyght:
For the one death gat the wynnynge,

1 Cor. xv.

And the other death lost his myght.
Holy scripture speaketh of it,

Heb. ii.

How one death another wolde byte;
The death of Christ hath wonne by ryght.

Alleluya.

1 Cor. v.

This same is the ryght paschall lambe,
That was once offred for oure synne:
Into this worlde mekely he came,
From Sathan's power us to wynne.

Rom. iv

For oure wickednesse wolde he dye,
And rose us for to iustifie;
The mercy of God was great therein.

Alleluya.

GLORIA IN EXCELSIS DEO.

To God the hyghest be glory alwaye,
For his great kyndnesse and mercy;
That doth provyde both nyght and daye
Both for oure soule and oure body.
To mankynde hath God great pleasure,
Now is great peace every where;
God hath put out all emmyte.

Ad Patrem.

We love and prayse and honoure the,
For thy great glory; we thanke thy grace,
That thou, God, Father eternally,
Art oure defender in every place.

Thou art to us a mercyfull Father,   Rom. viii.
And we thy chyldren altogether;
Therfore we geve the thankes alwayes.

Ad Filium.

O Jesu Christ, thou onely Sonne
Of God Almyghty thy heavenly Father,   Rom. iii.
Our full and whole redempcyon,   1 John ii.
Thou that hast stilled God's displeasure;
O God's Lambe, that takest synne awaye,   John i
When we have nede, helpe us alwaye;
Graunt us thy mercy altogether.

Ad Spiritum Sanctum.

O Holy Goost, our confortoure
In all oure trouble and hevynesse;
Defende us all from Sathan's power,
Whome Christ hath bought from wofulnesse:
Kepe oure hertes in the verite,
In oure tentacyon stonde us by,
And strength alwaye oure weake bodies.

MAGNIFICAT, WHICH IS THE SONGE OF THE VIRGIN MARY. Luke i.

My soul doth magnyfie the Lorde,
My spret rejoyseth greatly
In God my Savioure and his worde;
For he hath sene the lowe degre
Of me his handmayden truly.
Beholde now, after this day,
All generacyons shal speake of me,
And call me blessed alwaye.

For he that is onely of myghte
Hath done great thynges for me;
And holy is his name by ryghte:
As for his endles mercy,
It endureth perpetually,
In every generacyon,
On them that feare hym unfaynedly
Without dissimulacyon.

He sheweth strength with his great arme,
Declarying hymselfe to be of power;
He scatereth the proude to theyr owne harme,
Even with the wicked behavoure
Of theyr owne hertes every houre.
He putteth downe the myghtye
From theyr hye seate and great honoure,
Exaltynge them of lowe degre.

The hongrye fylleth he with good,
And letteth the ryche go emptie,
Where his owne people want no foode:
He thynketh upon his mercye,
And helpeth his servaunt truely,
Even Israel, as he promysed
Unto oure fathers perpetually,
Abraham and to his sede.

NUNC DIMITTIS, WHICH IS THE SONGE OF SIMEON. Luke ii.

With peace and with joyfull gladnesse,
And with a mery harte,
Accordynge to thy swete promesse,
Lorde, let me now departe:
Now geve me leave, that I may dye;
For I wolde be present with the.

For myne eyes have seen the Savioure,
That is sent out from the;
Thou hast satisfied my harte therfore,
That thou hast shewed hym me,
Which is oure onely salvacyon,
Oure helth and oure redempcyon;

Whome thou hast prepared ryght well,
And shewed hym openly
Before the face of all people,
Preachynge thy worde planely;
Kepynge no man from thy kyngdome,
That thorow hym wyll therin come.

He is the true and onely lyght,
Which moved with mercy
Restoreth the Gentyls to theyr syght,
Lyghtenynge theyr hartes truly.
He is the glory of Israel,
Thy people whom thou lovest so well.

THE XI. (XII.)[1] PSALME OF DAVID.

Salvum me fac Domine.

AGAYNST FALSE DOCTRYNE AND YPOCRITES.

HELPE now, O Lorde, and loke on us,
How we are brought in lowe degre.
Thy sayntes are dryven from every house,
Where are fewe faythfull lefte truly :
Men wyll not suffre thy trueth to be known,
Thy fayth is almost overthrowen
Amonge men's chyldren piteously.

It is but lyes and vanite,
That one preacheth now to his brother;
They flatter with theyr lyppes falsely,
And one dyssembleth with another.
Thus shewe they with theyr mouth one thynge,   Jer. viii.
And yct have they another meanynge
Within theyr hertes altogether.

O that the Lorde wolde once rote out
All soch disceatful lyppes speakynge;
Which wyll not have that men shulde doute
In thynges that are of theyr makynge.
We ought to speake by auctorite,   Jude.
Oure tonge shulde prevayle, they say proudly;
Who shulde rule us or oure doynge?

[1 This Psalm, which is the twelfth according to the notation of the
Hebrew Text, is numbered the eleventh in the Septuagint version
and the Vulgate, the notation of which was generally followed by
Bishop Coverdale.]

Therfore, sayeth the Lorde, now wyll I ryse,
I se the poore are oppressed;
Theyr sore complaynte wyll I not despyse,
But wyll them helpe shortly in dede.
I wyll set them at lybertie,
My worde shal be preached planely;
They shall no more be disceaved.

Psalm xviii.

Sylver seven tymes tryed in the fyre
Is purified and made deare therby:
So is God's worde alwaye nearer,
Whan it is persecute cruelly.
The Lorde's wordes are pure and ryght,
And wyll not be kepte downe by myght,
But wyll apeare the more planely.

O Lorde, defende thou them therfore,
And preserve us gracyously
From this generacyon evermore,
That persecute us so cruelly:
For whan vanite and ydilnesse
Is set by amonge men, doutless
All are full of the ungodly.

THE SECONDE PSALME OF DAVID.

Quare fremuerunt gentes.

Acts iv.
Psalm lxxi.
& lxxxiii.

WERFORE do the heithen now rage thus,
Cōspyryng together so wyckedly?
Wherfore are the people so malicious,
Vayne thynges to ymagyn so folyshly?
The kynges of the earth stonde up together,
And worldly rulers do conspyre
Agaynst the Lorde and his Christ truly.

The enemies.

They saye, Let us breake up theyr bondes,
And let us cast theyr yocke awaye;
Theyr lawes wyll make us lose oure londes,
Therfore none soch wyll we obeye.

The prophet.

But he that in heaven hath residence,
Shall laugh them to scorne and theyr pretence;

Prov. i.

The Lorde shall mocke them nyght and daye.

The Lorde shall talke with them together
In his great anger and wrath truly;
And also he shall trouble them ever
Thrugh his displeasure at them daylye.
Yet have I ordened and set my kynge   God the Father.
On my hyll Syon to have rulynge,
Theyr heade and governoure for to be.

I wyll shewe forth the commaundement,   Christ the Son.
Wherof the Lorde hath sayd to me:
Thou art my Sonne, whome I have sent,   God the Father.
This day have I begotten the.
Axe me, and I shall geve the soone   Heb. i. & v.
All heithen in possession,
Throwout the worlde, wherever they be.   Acts xiii.

Forsoth thou shalt rule them together
With a rodde of yron made strongly;   Rev. ii. & xiv.
Lyke erthen vessell brent in the fyre,
Shalt thou them breake that resyst the.   Isai. xxx.
Therfore, ye kynges, now understonde,   The prophet.
Be wyse and resyst not the Lorde's honde;
Be content, ye judges, warned to be.

With feare se that ye serve the Lorde,
Reioyse before hym all with drede;
Kysse ye the Sonne and his swete worde;
The Lorde wyll els be sore greved.
Than shall ye peryshe from the verite;
His wrath shall be kyndled shortly: Jer. xvii.
They that truste in hym are all blessed.

THE XLVI. PSALME OF DAVID.

Deus noster refugium.

OURE God is a defence and towre,
A good armoure and good weapē;
He hath been ever oure helpe and sucoure,
In all the troubles that we have ben in.
  Thorfore wyl we never drede,
  For any wonderous dede

By water or by londe,
In hilles or the see sōde;
Oure God hath them al in his hōd.

2 Cor. i.

Though we be alwaye greatly vexed
With many a great tentacyon;
Yet, thanked be God, we are refreshed,

John xiv.

His swete worde conforteth oure mansion.
    It is God's holy place;
    He dwelleth here by grace;

Psalm ii.

    Amonge us is he
    Both nyght and daye truly;

Acts iv.

He helpeth us all, and that swyftly.

The wicked heithen besege us straytly,
And many great kyngdomes take theyr parte:
They are gathered agaynst us truly,

Psalm lxvi.

And are sore moved in theyr herte.
    But God's worde as cleare as daye
    Maketh them shrenke alwaye.
    The Lorde God of power
    Stondeth by us every houre;
The God of Jacob is oure stronge towre.

Psalm lxvi.

Come hether now, beholde, and se
The noble actes and dedes of the Lorde;
What great thynges he doth for us daylye,
And conforteth us with his swete worde.
    For whan oure enemyes wolde fyght,
    Than brake he theyr myght,
    Theyr bowe and theyr speare,
    So that we nede not feare,
And brent theyr charettes in the fyre.

Therfore, sayeth God, take hede to me,
Let me alone, and I shall helpe you.
Knowe me for youre God, I saye onely,
Amonge all heithen that reigne now.

Psalm xlvi.

    Wherfore than shulde we drede,
    Seyenge we have no nede?

Rom. viii.

    For the Lorde God of power
    Stondeth by us every houre;
The God of Jacob is our stronge towre.

THE CXXIII. (CXXIV.) PSALME OF DAVID.

Nisi quia Dominus.

EXCEPT the Lorde had bene with us,
Now maye Israel say boldly;
Excepte the Lorde had ben with us,
When men rose up agaynst us fearsly;
   They had devoured us quyck doutlesse,   Prov. i.
   And had overwonne us confortles,
They were so wroth at us truly.

The waves of waters had wrapped us in;
Oure soule had gone under the floode.
The depe waters of these proude men
Had ronne oure soules over where they stode.
   The Lorde be praysed every houre,
   That wolde not suffre them us to devoure,
Nor in theyr tethe to sucke oure bloude!

Oure soule is delyvered from theyr power,
They can not have that they have sought.
As the byrde from the snare of the fouler,
So are we from theyr daungers brought.
   The snare is broken, and we are fre;   Prov. xviii.
Psal. cxxi.
   Oure helpe is in the Lorde's name truly,
Which hath made heaven and earth of nought.

THE CXXXVI. (CXXXVII.) PSALME.

Super flumina Babilonis.

AT the ryvers of Babilon,
There sat we downe ryght hevely;
Even whan we thought upon Sion,
We wepte together sorofully.
For we were in soch hevynes,
That we forgat al our merynes,
And lefte of all oure sporte and playe:
   On tho willyc trees that were thereby
   We hanged up oure harpes truly,
And morned sore both nyght and daye.

They that toke us so cruelly,
And led us bounde into pryson,
Requyred of us some melody
With wordes full of derision.
When we had hanged oure harpes alwaye,
This cruell folke to us coulde saye:
Now let us heare some mery songe,
   Synge us a songe of some swete toyne,
   As ye were wont to synge at Sion,
Where ye have lerned to synge so longe.

To whome we answered soberly:
Beholde now are we in youre honde:
How shulde we under captivite
Synge to the Lorde in a straunge londe?
Hierusalem, I say to the,
Yf I remember the not truly,
My honde playe on the harpe no more:
   Yf I thynke not on the alwaye,
   Let my tonge cleve to my mouth for aye,
And let my loose my speache therfore.

Jer. xlix.

Ezek. xxv.

Obad. i.
Yee, above all myrth and pastaunce,
Hierusalem, I preferre the.
Lorde, call to thy remembraunce
The sonnes of Edom ryght strately;
In the daye of the destruction,
Which at Hierusalem was done
For they sayd in theyr cruelnes,
   Downe with it, downe with it, destroye it all;
   Downe with it soone, that it may fall,
Laye it to the grounde all that there is.

Isai. xiii.
O thou cite of Babilon,
Thou thy selfe shalt be destroyed.
Truly blessed shall be that man,
Which, even as thou hast deserved,
Shall rewarde the with soch kyndnesse,
As thou hast shewed to us gyltlesse,
Which never had offended the.
   Blessed shall he be that for the nones[1]
   Shall throwe thy chyldren agaynst the stones,
To brynge the out of memorie.

   [1 for the nones: for the nonce, for the purpose.]

THE CXXVII. (CXXVIII.) PSALME.

Beati omnes qui timent Dominum.

BLESSED are all that feare the Lorde,
Worshyppynge hym both nyght and daye,
Ordrynge theyr lyfe after his worde,
And walkyng ever in his waye.

For thou shalt get thyne owne lyvynge,   Gen. iii.
And eate thy bred without ydelnesse;
Even with thy handes laborynge,
So shalt thou have prosperous increase.

Thy wyfe as the vyne shall be frutefull
Within the walles of thy dwellynge;
Thy chyldren shall stonde about thy table,
Lyke olyve braunches floryshynge.

Lo, thus shall that man be blessed,
And happye shall he be alwaye,
That leadeth his lyfe in the Lorde's drede,
And feareth hym both nyght and daye.

From Sion shall the Lorde blesse the,
And pleasure shalt thou have amonge,
Beholdynge the great prosperite
Of Hierusalem all thy lyfe longe.

The Lorde shall so prolonge thy lyfe,   Job xlii.
That thy chyldre's chyldren thou shalt se;
In Israel shalt thou se no stryfe,   Tobit xiv.
But peace and great felicite.

THE SAME PSALME.

Beati omnes.

BLESSED are all that feare the Lorde,   Psalm
Worshippynge him both nyght and daye,   xxxiii.
Ordrynge theyr lyfe after his worde,
And walkynge ever in his waye.

For thou shalt get thin owne lyving,
And eat thy bred without ydelnes,
Evē with thin owne hādes workyng.
And thou shalt have prosperous increace,
And want nothynge to thy harte's ease.

Thy wyfe also shall be frutefull
Within the walles of thy dwellynge:
As the vyne-tre plenteous and full,
Shall she fayre chyldren to the brynge,
Which rounde aboute thy table shall stonde,
Lyke fayre plantes of the olyve-tre.
Lo, thus shall he blessed be founde,
That worshippeth and feareth the Lorde truly,
Havynge God's lawe before his eye.

The Lorde shall do the goode alwaye
From the holy hyll of Sion:
Thou shalt delyte both nyght and daye,
Beholdynge the prosperous fortune
Of Hierusalem all thy lyfe longe;
And thy chyldre's chyldren shalt thou se.
Thus shall the Lorde thy dayes prolonge,
To se the peace and felicite,
Wherin all Israel shall be.

Job xlii.
Tobit xiv.

THE L. (LI.) PSALME OF DAVID.

Miserere mei Deus.

O LORDE God, have mercy on me,
After thy marvelous great pite:
As thou art full of mercy,
Do away all my iniquite;
And washe me frō all fylthynesse
Of my great synnes and wantonesse;
For they are many within me,
And ever I fele them hevye:
My synne is alwaye before myne eye;
I have alone offended the;
Before the have I lyved synfully:
In thy worde stondest thou stedfastly,
Thoughe thou be judged wrongfully.

Psal. xxxii.
Job xiii.
Luke xviii.

Se how I am conceaved in synne,
My mother hath brought me forth therin;
A chylde of wrathe by nature borne,   Ephes. ii.
And without the Lorde am forlorne.
To the treuth thou hast a pleasure alwaye,
And helpest my blyndnesse every daye,
To knowe thy wysdome gracyously,
That thou hast hyd so secretly.
With ysope fayre sprenkle thou me,
Washe thou me clene; so shall I be
Whyter than snowe: mende thou my cheare,
My weery bones to helpe from feare,
Which thou thyselfe hast brused so neare.

Loke not upon my wreched lyfe,
Forgeve my synnes that are so ryfe: Ezek. xxxvi.
Lorde, make in me a ryght pure harte,   Acts ii.
A good conscience let be my parte;
A godly spirite renew in me,
And cast me not away from the;
Thy holy Spirite let me have styll,
To be my conforte in all evell;
And let me have ever the gladnesse
Of thy health in all hevynesse:
Thy myghty Spirite holde thou in me;
I wyll helpe synners turne to the,
Thy way wyll I teache them hartely.

God, rydde me from bloud-gyltynesse,
Thou God of all my healthfulnesse.
So shall my tonge geve prayse to the,
Thy ryghtuousnesse to honoure in me.
Lorde, open thou these lyppes of myne,
That my mouthe maye to thy prayse inclyne.
Thou hast no pleasure in offrynge;   Mic. vi.
For els I thought them the to brynge.
Burnt offrynges are not to thy paye[1],
They please not the, though they be gaye;
They are nothynge worth in thy syght:
God's offrynge is of moche more myght;
A Spirite all troubled is his ryght.

[1 pay: satisfaction, content.]

Isai. lxvi.

A contrite harte that is brought lowe
Shalt thou, Lorde God, awaye not throwe :
That dost thou alwaye so regarde,
That it shall ever of the be harde.
To Sion, Lorde, be gracyous,
After thy kyndnesse plenteous ;
That the walles of Hierusalem
Maye be buylded and brought from shame.

Rom. xii.

Then thou shalt be pleased doutlesse
With the offrynge of ryghtuousnesse,
With the brent offrynges of thy wyll :
Then shall good men theyr calves kyll,
Therwith thyne alter to fulfyll.

THE SAME PSALME.

Miserere mei Deus.

O God, be mercyfull to me,
Accordynge to thy great pitie ;

Psal. xxxii.

Washe of, make clene my iniquite :
I knowlege my synne, and it greveth me ;
Agaynst the, agaynst the only
Have I synned, which is before myne eye :
Though thou be judged in man's syght,

Rom. iii.

Yet are thy wordes founde true and ryght.

Beholde, I was all borne in synne,
My mother conceaved me therin :
But thou lovest treuth, and haste shewed me
Thy wysdome hyd so secretly.
With fayre ysope, Lorde, sprenkle thou me ;
Washe thou me clean ; so shall I be
Whyter than snowe : cause me reioyse,
Make my bones mery, whō thou madest lowse.

Lorde, turne thy face from my wickednesse ;
Clense me from all unryghtuousnesse :

Ezek. xxxvi.

A pure harte, Lorde, make thou in me,
Renewe a ryght spirite in my body :
Cast me not out away from the,
Nor take thy Holy Goost fro me ;

Make me reioyse in thy savynge health,
Thy myghty Spirite strength me for my wealth.

Thy waye shall I shewe to men full of vyce,
And enstructe them well in thy service :
That wicked men and ungodly
May be converted unto the.
O God, O God, my Savioure,
Delyver me from the synne of murther :
My tonge shall reioyse in thy mercye ;
Open my lippes, and my mouth shal prayse the.

Thou wylt have no bodely offrynge ;   Mic. vi.
I thought them els to the to brynge.
God's sacrifice is a troubled spirite ;
Thou wylt not dispise a harte contrite.   Isai. lxvi.
With Sion, O God, deale gently,
That Hierusalem walles may buylded be :
Than shalt thou delyte in the ryght offrynge,
Which men shall with theyr calves brynge.

THE CXXIX. (CXXX.) PSALME.

De profundis.

OUT of the depe crye I to the,
O Lorde, Lorde, heare my callynge ;
O let thyne eares enclyned be
To the voyce of my complaynynge.
Yf thou, Lorde, wylt deale with stratenesse,   Job ix.
To marke all that is done amysse,   Psal. cxliii.
Lorde, who may abyde that rekenynge ?

But there is mercy ever with the,   Exod. xxxiv
That thou therfore mayest be feared :
I wyll abyde the Lorde paciently ;
My soule loketh for hym unfaynted,   Psal. cii.
And in his worde is all my trust ;
So is my hope and conforte most,
His promyse shal be fulfylled.

As the watchemen in the mornynge
Stonde lokynge longe desyrously,

That they myght se the fayre day sprynge;
So wayteth my soule for the Lorde dayly.
Therfore let Israel wayte styll,
Untyll it be the Lorde's wyll
To lowse them from adversite.

Psal. lxxxvi.   For with the Lorde there is mercy,
And great plenteous redempcyon;
1 John ii.   Allthough we synne oft wickedly,
Yet hath he for us a sure pardon.
He shall redeme poore Israel,
Isai. xliii.   And hym shall he delyver full well
From all the synnes that he hath done.

THE XXIV. (XXV.) PSALM OF DAVID.

Ad te Domine levavi.

I LYFT my soule, Lorde, up to the,
My God, I trust on the alone;
Let me never confounded be,
Rom. ix.   My enemys els wyll mocke me soone.
Isai. xxviii.   They shall not be shamed that trust on the;
Psal. xxxi.   But they that scornefull despysers be,
Those shalt be put to confusyon.

Shewe me, O Lorde, thy godly wayes,
And lerne me the ryght pathes to the;
In thy verite leade me alwayes:
Thou art God my Savioure truly.
Lerne me, for in the is all my trust,
My hope, my beleve, and conforte most,
All the daye longe continually.

Remembre, Lorde, thy great mercy,
And thy great plenteous kyndnesse.
Call to thy mynde, Lorde, we praye the,
Thy gracious favoure and gentylnesse:
For in these thynges thou excellest greatly,
Even from the begynnynge eternally;
Thou art so ryche in mercyfulnesse.

My fautes and my ungodlynesse,
My synfull youth and cruell bearynge,
As thou art, Lorde, full of goodnesse,
Remembre not this my evell lyvynge;
But after thy mercy thynke on me,
And after thy great benignite
Forgyve thou all my mysdoynge.

The Lorde is iuste, full of goodnesse   Psal. xxxvii.
To synners that leave theyr cruell lyvynge:
For though they fall oft thorowe weaknesse,
Yet to his waye he wyll them brynge.
He shall lerne meke men his gracyous wyll;
And teach them his waye to come thertyll,
And set theyr fete fast for slippynge.

All wayes of the Lorde are full truly
Both of mercy and faythfulnesse.
For as he promyseth mercyfully,
So payeth he all without doubylnesse
To soch as regarde his worde and wyll,
And are ever redy to fulfyll
Theyr covenaunt with hym and theyr promesse.

For thy name's sake, Lorde, I praye the,
Forgeve me my great wickednesse.   Isai. xliii.
The Lorde shall lerne that man truly,
That feareth hym with all lowlynesse:
He shall be teachynge hym ever the waye,   Jer. xxxii.
That pleaseth hym both nyght and daye;
His conscience shal be in quyetnesse.

His chyldren shall possesse the londe;
It shall be theyr heretage and ryght:
They shall never want by see nor londe,
The Lorde wyll fede them thorow his myght.   Psal. xxxvii.
He is a defence both lovynge and deare,
For every man thath hym doth feare,
Shewynge them his covenaunte day and nyght.

Myne eyes shall on the Lorde be set,
Tyll he se his tyme and season
To drawe my fete out of this net,
That holdeth me so fast in pryson.

Beholde thou, and have mercy on me;
For I am forsaken in mysery,
And full of great affliction.

The cares of my harte and sorofulnesse
Increase ever dayly more and more.
Leade me out of my hevynesse,
And my poore state beholde therfore:
Forgeve thou all my synnes, and se,
How many they are that trouble me,
And persecute me with furiousnesse.

Preserve my soule, and delyver me,
Lest I be brought to confusion;
For I have put my trust in the.
Let godlynesse kepe me all season;
My hope is in the, and shall be styll.
Oh God, delyver poore Israel
From all theyr trouble and affliction.

THE LXVI. (LXVII.) PSALM.

Deus misereatur nostri.

God be mercyfull unto us,
And sende over us his blessynge;
Shewe us his presence glorious,
And be ever to us lovynge;
That men on earth may knowe thy waye,
Thy savynge health and ryghteousnesse;
That they be not led by nyght nor day,
Throwe the pretexte of trewe justice,
To seke salvacyon where none is.

Therfore the people mought magnifie the:
O God, let all folke honoure thy name;
Let all the people reioyse gladly,
Because thou dost ryght without blame.
The people dost thou judge truly,
And ordrest every nacyon:
Thou hast directe the earth iustly,
Ever sense the fyrst creacyon,
With thy godly provision.

O God, let the people prayse the;
All people, God, mought geve the honoure;
The earth also ryght plenteously
Mought increase ever more and more;
And God, which is oure God over all,
Mought do us good and pleasure.
God blesse us now both great and small,
And all the worlde hym honoure,
Fearynge alwaye his myght and power.

THE XIII. (XIV.) PSALME OF DAVID.

Dixit insipiens.

THE foolish wicked men can saye,
They holde of God ryght perfectly;
Yet are they farre out of the waye;
For in theyr hartes they hym deny:
Corrupte and abominable are they also
In al the thynges that they do;
There wyll not one do good truly.

The Lorde dyd loke here downe fro heaven,   Gen. xi. &
Men to consyder and theyr doynge;   xviii.
To se yf any men were geven,
To God's knowlege above all thynge;
Yf there were any, that perfectly
Regarded God so earnestly,
To folowe his worde in his lyvynge.

Then sayd God these wordes moreover:
Is every man gone so farre by,
Swarved so farre now all together
From the ryght waye so parlously;
So unprofitable and peryshed,
That no man wyll do good in dede,   Rom. xiii.
No not so moche as one truly?

Are they out of theyr myndes so farre,
All these workers of wickednesse?
Beholde now, for they nothynge care
My people to devoure for gredynesse,

As one shulde eat a pece of bread :
The Lorde's feare is out of theyr heade,
They do not regarde it moch doutlesse.

Wherfore they shal be feared truly
With feare incomparable and endlesse.
O ryghteous man, thou mayst be mery ;
For they that beseged the gyltles,
Theyr bones hath God shaken altogether.
How shalt thou despyse them for ever !
For God hath left them confortles.

God is in iust men's company,
And in the ryghteous nacyon.
But wicked men mocke them dayly,
For none other cause nor reason,
But for because they folowe the mynde
Of the poore afflicte, which was God's frende,
To trust in the Lorde's redempcyon.

Isai. lix.

Rom. xi.

O wolde God that the savynge health
Wolde come from the hyll of Sion ;
That Israel myght have his wealth,
And God to lowse hym from preson !
Then shulde Jacob be full of joye,
And Israel shulde make full mery,
Because of his redempcyon.

THE CXLVI. (CXLVII.) PSALME.

Lauda, Hierusalem, Dominum.

PRAYSE thou the Lorde, Hierusalē,
Prayse thou thy God, O Sion :
For all thy strength stondeth whole in hym ;
He barreth and kepeth thy gates alone,
Endewyng thy chyldrē in the
With goodly gyftes plēteously,
Blessyng thy cōgregacion.

He doth endewe thy borders all
Rounde about the with peace and rest :
His provision for the is not small ;
With wheate he feadeth the of the best.

He sendeth his worde into the earth;
Swyftly renneth his commaundement forth;
All thynges obey hym, most and least.

Psalm xxxiii.
& cxliv.

Lyke woll doth he cast downe the snowe,
Scatrynge the frost lyke as asshes;
Lyke morsels of bread his haile doth he throwe,
That no man maye byde the coldnesse;
With a worde meltynge them all agayne,
And leadeth his wynde backe to geve rayne;
So droppe the waters downe with moystnesse.

This same is he that tolde ryght well
His pleasures to Jacob, his deare frende;
His lawes and decrees to Israell,
That they myght kepe them in theyr mynde.
With no nacyon hath he dealte thus,
Nor bene to them so gracyous,
His godly worde them for to sende.

Exod. xx.

Deut. iv.

THE CXXXII. (CXXXIII.) PSALME.

Ecce quam bonum.

BEHOLDE and se, forget not this,
How joyfull and pleasaunt a thynge it is,
Brethren to dwell all together,
And to be of one mynde ever.
For they are lyke that precious unction,
Which, beynge powred on the head of Aaron,
Ran in his bearde, into Aaron's bearde,
And to his skirtes it descended.

This brotherly love is so noble vertue,
That it is lykened unto the dew,
Which fell on the hyll of Hermon,
And on the fayre hyll of Sion.
For there the Lorde gave his blessynge,
And shewed his lyfe everlastynge.
So where as love is unfayned,
There is the Lorde's blessynge in dede.

CHRISTE, QUI LUX.

O CHRIST, that art the lyght and daye,
Thou discoverst the darkness of nyght;
The lyght of lyghtes thou art alwaye,
Preachyng ever the blessed lyght.

Thou holy Lorde, to the we praye,
Defende us all in this darke nyght;
Let us have rest in the alwaye,
And graunt us all a quyet nyght.

Let not hevye slepe on us fall,
Nor let the feynde take us awaye;
Let nor oure fleshe consent withall,
To make us gyltie by nyght nor daye.

Let oure eyes take theyr slepe naturall,
But let oure hartes wake to the styll:
With thy ryght honde defende us all,
Thy servauntes true that love the well.

Loke on us, Lorde, our defender;
Put them downe, that wolde us no good:
Kepe thy servauntes in good ordre,
Whom thou hast bought with thy deare bloude.

Lorde, call us now unto thy mynde,
In this body that is so hevy;
Thou, that doest ever oure soule defende,
Be present now with thy mercy.

God the Father for evermore,
With Jesu Christ his Sonne only,
And the Holy Goost oure Confortoure,
Be thanked alwaye hartely.

O HEVENLY LORDE.

O HEVENLY Lorde, thy godly worde
Hath longe bene kepte alwaye from us:
But thorow thy grace now in oure dayes
Thou hast shewed the so plenteous,

That very well we can now tell,
What thy apostles have written al;
And now we se thy worde opēly
Hath geven anthyechrist a great fall.

It is so cleare, as we may heare,
No man by ryght can it deny,
That many a yeare thy people deare
Have bene begyled perlously
With men spirituall, as we them call,
But not of thy Spirite truly;
For more carnall are none at all,
Than many of these spirites be.

They have bene ever sworne altogether,
Theyr owne lawes for to kepe alwaye:
But, mercyfull Lorde, of thy swete worde
There durst no man begynne to saye.
They durst them call great heretikes all,
That dyd confesse it stedfastly;
For they charged, it shulde be hyd,
And not be spoken of openly.

O mercyfull God, where was thy rod,
In punyshynge soch great tyranny?
Why slepte thou then, knowynge these men
Resist openly the veritie?
But the prophetes saye, thou art alwaye
Full of mercy and gentylnesse;
For nyght and daye thou suffrest, that they
Myght turne from theyr olde wickednesse.

Neverthelesse they dyd oppresse
Thy worde and thy true preachers:
For theyr evell syght thou sent thy lyght,
Yet slewe they all soch teachers.
Then seynge they resisted alwaye
Thy grace offred so lovyngly;
Thou madest it mete for the poore in sprite,
That now receave it thankfully.

For there are none, but they alone,
That knowe the for theyr Savioure:
All other withstonde thy godly honde,
And slaundre thy worde every houre.

Well is hym therfore, that feleth his sore,
Sekynge no helpe but in thy bloude;
Receavynge grace of the alwayes,
Knowynge of hymselfe to have no good.

We thanke the, Lorde, for thy swete worde,
And for thy kyndnesse shewed therin;
For thy mercy, Lorde, we praye the,
Strength us therwith agaynst all synne.
And, Lorde, oppresse unthankfulnesse,
That we never do forget the:
Graunt us thy Spirite, to lyve throwe it
In vertue ever, whyle we dye.

LET GO THE WHORE OF BABILON.

LET go the whore of Babilon,
Her kyngdome falleth sore;
Her mechauntes begyne to make theyr mone,
The Lorde be praysed therfore.
Theyr ware is naught, it wyll not be bought,
Great falsheed is foūde therin:
Let go the whore of Babilon,
The mother of al synne.

No man wyll drynke her wyne any more,
The poyson is come to lyghte;
That maketh her marchauntes to wepe so sore,
The blynde have gotten theyr syghte.
For now we se God's grace frelye
In Christ offred us so fayre:
Let go the whore of Babilon,
And bye no more her ware.

Of christen bloude so much she shed,
That she was dronken withall;
But now God's worde hath broken her head,
And she hath gotten a fall.
God hath raysed some men in dede,
To utter her great wickednesse:
Let go the whore of Babilon,
And her ungodlynesse.

Ye ypocrites, what can ye saye?
Wo be unto you all!
Ye have begyled us many a daye;
Heretikes ye did us call,
For lovynge the worde of Christ the Lorde,
Whom ye do alwaye resiste.
Let go the whore of Babilon,
That rydeth upon the beast.

Ye proude and cruell Egipcians,
That dyd us so great wronge,
The Lorde hath sent us delyveraunce,
Thoughe ye have troubled us longe.
Youre Pharao with other mo
Is drowned in the Reed See.
Let go the whore of Babilon,
With her captivite.

Ye Canaanites, ye enemyes all,
Though ye were many in dede;
Yet hath the Lorde geven you a fall,
And us delyvered.
Even in youre londe do we now stonde,
Oure Lorde God hath brought us in:
Let go the whore of Babilon,
And fle from all her synne.

Dagon, Dagon, that false ydoll,
The Philistine's God,
Which hath deceaved many a soule,
In soch honoure he stode:
But now the Lorde with his swete word
Hath broken hym downe before the arke.
Let go the whore of Babilon,
And forsake the beeste's marke.

Balaam, Balaam, thou false prophet,
Thou hast cursed us ryght sore;
Yet into a blessynge hath God turned it,
No thanke to the therfore.
For thy helpe thou woldest lye,
Though God make the to saye the soth[1].
Let go the whore of Babilon,
And turne you to the trueth.

[1 soth: sooth, truth.]

Thy God be praysed, O Daniel,
For his goodnesse so great :
The gredy prestes of the idoll Bel
Were wonte to moche to eate,
And that prively, no man did se ;
But now the kynge hath spied theyr cast.
Let go the whore of Babilon,
For Bell is destroyed at the last.

O glorious God, full of mercye,
We thanke the evermore ;
Thou hast shewed us thy verite ;
Thy name be praysed therfore.
For thy swete worde, O gracious Lorde,
Let us be ever thankfull to the ;
And send the whore of Babilon
Into captivite.

Rejoyce with me, thou heaven above,
And ye apostles all ;
Be glad, ye people, for Christe's love,
That the whore hath gotten a fall.
Be thankfull now, I requyre you,
Amende youre lyves, whyle you have space.
Let go the whore of Babilon,
And thanke God of his grace.

THE SONGES CONTEYNED IN THIS BOKE.

Imprynted by me Johan Gough.

Cum privilegio Regali.

APPENDIX

CONTAINING

THE ORIGINALS OF THE LETTERS WRITTEN IN LATIN.

CONTENTS.

EPISTOLA XII.

MILO COVERDALUS AD HENRICUM BULLINGERUM.

S. P. D. Occupationibus est factum meis et quadam corporis impotentia, (ut interim taceam rei familiaris inopiam,) ne una cum clarissimis viris D. Butlero dominoque Richardo iter istic nunc facerem. Quam ægre autem vobis jam absum, paucis equidem non dicam. Valde enim cupio præsens vestram contemplari ecclesiam. Quando vero id mihi non datur, præstolabor benignam Dei Patris voluntatem; contentus interim bonum illius Spiritum per vestrum in verbo suo ministerium degustasse, atque ita vobis in Christo usum esse familiariter. Defuisset plane quod nunc ad te scriberem, præceptor integerrime, si non habuissem in memoria, quam tu benigne nostras literas, et quidem crassiores, sub calendis Octobris emissas acceperis, bonique consulueris. Unde vides, qualem pariat balbutiem infelix educatio, nimirum aliena ab omni prorsus vel linguarum vel compositionum ornamento. Ceterum habeo gratiam, quod gravissimis alioqui studiis occupatus, me tamen in literis D. Richardi dignatus sis resalutare. Denique insignes hos viros, veræque pietatis et studiosos et patronos, omni quo possum animi candore vobis commendo; certus, gaudium illud in S. S. vobis utrinque non defuturum, ubi una in Domino conveneritis. Quod ut feliciter fiat, ille faxit, qui pectora vestra sincero sui amore jampridem curavit esse conjunctissima. Bene vale. Argentorati, sexto calendas Augusti. Salutat vos plurimum uxor mea in Domino.

Tuus,

MILO COVERDALUS.

EPISTOLA XIII.

MILO COVERDALUS AD CONRADUM HUBERTUM.

Pax et gaudium in Spiritu Sancto! Quando per temporis angustiam prolixiori scripto uti non datur, frater in Domino carissime, dummodo nobis nunquam non adsit gratissima tui

38

memoria, facilius te scio bene volenti amiculo ignoscere.   Heri
enim a prandio, quum alioqui plures mihi scribendæ essent
literæ, hunc hodie primo ad vos diluculo profecturum intel-
ligebam.   Miraris tu quidem, et merito, quid esset, si qui
apud tuos[1] nunc ago, literas tibi dare prorsus intermitterem.
Verum in Septembri cum literis vestris communitus huc vocatus accederem, plane effeci, quanquam scripto satis brevi, ut
quæ tum hic gererentur, ipse admodum non ignores.   Joannes
item, frater tuus carissimus, quæ postea in mei et ecclesiæ
hujus causa subsequebantur, nobis interim absentibus, haud
dubie indicavit.   Siquidem, confecto jam negotio, descendi
statim ego in inferiorem Germaniam, uxorem inde carissimam
allaturus.   Rediens tandem, atque nunc plura expertus, quæ
antea præsens parum animadverteram, video (proh dolor!) præsentem ecclesiarum, quæ hic sunt, calamitosam esse nimis
conditionem, imo fere deploratam : usque adeo principes
connivere, factiones horrendissimæ pullulascere, atque adeo
ipsi Dominici gregis pastores lascivire videntur.   Proinde
utinam ipse, ita ut carrissimus etiam parens, Dei adhuc beneficio superstes, percupide optat, nobis vel biduum adesses!
Nam et plurima sunt, quæ ego quoque in sinum tuum habeo
committenda.

Quod si tua humanitas carissimo nostro Abelo adfuerit in
vasis nostri quærendi negotio, quod civis cujusdam Mogunti-
nensis errore et incuria Argentoratum, ut audio, quum Spiram
adferri debuisset, est advectum, rem certe feceris nobis nunc
peregrinis gratissimam.   Vale, et conjugi et Samueli carissimo,
præceptori item nostro integerrimo D. D. Petro Martyri, etc.
multam ex me et uxore salutem nuntiabis.   Vale iterum.
Tabern. d. 24 Decembris.   1543.

MICHAEL ANGLUS[2],

Minister ecclesiæ Tabern.

[1 Hubertus e Tabernis Montanis erat oriundus.—Simler].

[2 Vel potius et rectius *Milo Coverdalus,* (ut ipse notat Hubertus
ad epistolæ inscriptionem,) nuper Exon. episcopus, qui cur nomen
Michaelis Angli sibi sumpserit, plane ignoro, nisi forte Milo et Michael
unum idemque lingua Anglica sonant.   Erat autem ludo literario ecclesiæ Taberno-montanæ præfectus, ut Joannes Dodmannus Anglus ad
Bissweilerianam ecclesiam, Germanice quoque docendam, vocabatur,
Edmundus vero ad scholæ Landaviensis ministerium.—Simler.]

EPISTOLA XIV.

MILO COVERDALUS AD CONRADUM HUBERTUM.

Pax et gaudium in Spiritu Sancto! In prioribus meis literis scripsi parentem tuum carissimum vobis ante octo dies adfuturum. Quid autem illi obstitit, ipsemet vos coram faciet certiores, cui et vii florenos xiique batzones numeravi; eo nimirum, ut tu pro tua, qua es erga me, humanitate id pecuniarum meis creditoribus solutum efficias; qua in re me multum sane tibi demereberis. Novisti quid per te acceperim ex D. Vindelino, Rihelio, Cephalæo, et Jacobo Jucundo. Præter hos item creditores habui Christophorum, (bibliopolam illum, qui sub prætorio officinam habet D. Vindolino proximam,) et senem illum Joannem Grymmum, qui præ foribus templi majoris duas habet ab occidente officinas. In summa, quicquid est, Germanica tibi hæc schedula significantius ostendet. Tu quæso ægre ne feras, quod integritatis tuæ officiis porro uti non desinam; tete enim mihi videre obtulisse, ut te fruar in Domino.

Cura, te oro, ut Cephalæus chartam illam mittat, cujus memini in meis ad illum literis: itidem et Jacobus Jucundus eos ut tradat tibi libros, quorum nomina in hac scribuntur schedula. Et ex nostratibus si quid literarum extorquere poteris, id ut facias rogo: nec hoc solum, sed et mensam illam, quam missurus est Edmundus noster, ad nos quam primum adferendam cures velim. Bene vale. Salutamus plurimum ego et uxor mea te et tuam carissimam in Domino. Iterum vale. E Tabernis Montanis, prid. Calend. April.

MICHAEL COVERDALUS.

Cal. April. Hoc mane, cum obsignaturus eram has literas, accessit ad me carissimus pater tuus, qui per corporis impotentiam institutum iter aggredi nunc non potest. Brevi tamen ad te profecturum non desperat: nec se male habere videtur usque adeo, Deo sit gratia! Quare non est, quod vos hoc nomine magis sitis solliciti: nam accessisset etiam nunc, si auriga non negasset personæ suæ vecturam.

38—2

EPISTOLA XV.

MILO COVERDALUS AD CONRADUM HUBERTUM.

Pax et gaudium in Spiritu Sancto! Literas tuas 11 Martii datas, Conrade carissime, reddidit mihi Edmundus noster; cujus equidem negotium, ut in hujusmodi docendi ministerium admitteretur, pro mea virili ante tres menses laboravi. Dominus item Jesus, cujus agitur causa, huic nostro instituto non defuit: nec de prosperrimo successu possum dubitare, etiamsi pueros insulsissime educatos offenderit, valde- que arduus sit illi ingressus in scholam Landaviensem hoc potissimum nomine. Quod ad causam nostratium puerorum, qui istic sunt, attinet, ego ante quindecim dies, absente D. Nicolao, quum illustrissimus princeps adesset, Spiram descen- surus, hanc ipsam, quod potui, peregi; non quidem apud salutatum principem, sed, præsente et audiente principe, apud præfectum nostrum: qui mihi illustrissimi principis nomine hoc dedit responsum, nempe ab illius celsitudine decretum jam esse, ut in proxima visitatione, quam nos in Maio futuram putavimus, huic rei optime consulatur. Præterea, nos una cum parentibus tuis longe carissimis utcunque valemus, vestri et illius quæ istic est in Domino ecclesiæ parum immemores; quod et vos vicissim pro nobis indesinenter facere non dubi- tamus. Vale. E Tab. Mont. d. 10 Aprilis, 1544.

Tuus in Domino,

MICHAEL ANGLUS.

EPISTOLA XVI.

MILO COVERDALUS AD CONRADUM HUBERTUM.

S. Summam erga me ostendit amicitiam beatus ille, præclarus quidem, juvenis, qui non solum huc, imo ad Taber- nas Montanas, istinc ad me attulit literas, verum etiam in se accepit has pecunias per fidum internuntium ad vos perferen- das. Vix paucis dicam, quam invitus ipse eas hactenus tenuerim: parens enim tuus, ut scis, attulisset. Quæ cuique debeatur summa, intelligis ex illa schedula, quam in literis meis Cal. Aprilis ad te misi; ut nunc pluribus te verbis interturbare

non sit opus. Saluta mihi et uxori meæ tuam, quæso, carissimam. Libenter audimus filiolum tuum revaluisse. Bene vale.

Tuus ex animo,

MICHAEL ANGLUS.

Interim pro mutua inter nos in Domino amicitia oro, ut
ex Vindelino, Cephalæo, et Jacobo Jucundo eos quam primum
habeam libros, quorum memini in superioribus meis literis.
Iterum vale. Raptim. Wissenburgæ. Idibus Aprilis, 1544.

EPISTOLA XVII.

MILO COVERDALUS AD CONRADUM HUBERTUM.

GRATIAM et pacem a Domino! Cum internuntius hic
carissimus mihi per literas significasset, se tam paucos post
dies istuc profecturum, parentem tuum carissimum conveni,
de cujus ad vos profectione non aliter constat, quam quod
circiter Ascensionis festum vos tandem invisere decrevit.
Pedibus enim nunc melius valet. Mater item, etsi molesta
quadam scabie teneatur, animo tamen pulchre valere videtur.
Dominus autem, qui nunquam non sanctus est in omnibus
suis operibus, pro bona sua voluntate, ante octo dies Joanni
fratri tuo prolem illam suavissimam ademit, quam circiter
Natalem ediderat illi uxor. Cras, Domino volente, sacram
illius cœnam peracturi sumus. Negotium catechismi, quod
ante duas septimanas in templo aggrediebamur, feliciter (Deo
sit gratia!) et non sine frugi experimur nunc succedere. Faxit
ille Optimus Maximus, ut magis ac magis in sui gloriam in-
crementum accipiat, quod nos plantare et rigare orsi sumus.

Quod ad pecunias illas attinet, quas hic tibi traditurus
est D. Valent. Brentius, in literis meis prid. Cal. Aprilis misi
una ad te schedulam, qua significabam quid cuique debeatur.
Quare tu hoc meum, quæso, cura negotium, et ut chartam ac
libros, quibus nunc opus habemus, mittantur, diligenter
admone Vindelinum, Cephalæum, et Jucundum. Ad Vindelinum
et Cephalæum dedi nunc literas privatim, non autem ad
Jacobum Jucundum. Quare pro mutua inter nos amicitia
abs te effectum velim, ut Donati minoris exemplaria duodecim,
totidemque Collo : Formu : Seobaldi Heiden, et Buco. Virgilii

exemplaria vi aut viii, ab illius quoque officina habeam ; utque
una cum charta Cephalæi et libris Vindelini ad nos per-
ferantur.   Quod utinam quam primum fieret !   Non enim
credis, quanta librorum necessitate et chartarum penuria
laboramus.   Wissenburgum saltem hæc esse advecta optarem,
si fieri posset.   Nec te sane in tam sancto ministerio occu-
patum his rebus impedirem, si esset, cui istud negotii liceret
tuto committere.   Bene vale, salutatus plurimum ab uxore
mea, quæ tuam quoque carissimam pl. salvere jubet.   Iterum
vale.   E Tabernis Montanis, xi Calend. Maii.   1544.

MICHAEL tuus COVERDALUS.

EPISTOLA XVIII.

MILO COVERDALUS AD CONRADUM HUBERTUM.

Pax et gaudium in Spiritu Sancto !   Quanto nos beneficio
affecerit Dominus, quod huc carissimum nobis in illo præceptorem D. Bucerum nunc miserit, præ animi mei alacritate
vix satis vel prædicare vel scribere possum.   Ad triduum
enim usque exhibuit nobis, non sine summis laboribus, multa
et pietatis et caritatis officia : unde et ecclesias nostras non
parum stabilitas fore, certus scio, in Domino.   Hæc autem
Christophorus noster suo melius ore, quam ego scriptis, sig-
nificabit.   Ad carissimorum parentum ædes D. Bucerum bis
duxi ; quod quantum illis refocillamenti attulerit, utriusque
parentis, imo et fratris, affectus satis indicarunt.   Nostrum
vero oppidulum (proh dolor !) ex superiori, qui ante dies octo
contigit, grandine maximum suscepit damnum.   Sed si veram
hujus flagelli rationem habeamus, bonitas profecto Dei, qui
susceptum filium erudire solet, ad pœnitentiam nos invitat.
Quod ad Matthæum, prætoris in Roda filium, attinet, (quando-
quidem in literis ad nos datis, quam bene illi in Domino
volueris, satis ostendisti,) mihi etiam sane consultum neque
huic ipsi neque ecclesiæ Dei esse videtur, ut ante annum
saltem vigesimum secundum ad sacrum ministerium assumatur.
Rationes, quibus eo adducor, ut hoc asseram, plures sunt,
quam ut paucis commemorem.   Denique ante Pentecosten
decrevit carissimus parens vos invisere : quo forsan nuntio,
si Dominus faverit, plura de ecclesiæ nostræ conditione, cui

tu candide faves, libenter scribam.   Optima illa vidua, matris
tuæ soror carissima, duos istuc aureos, quos Christophoro tradidi, misit: alterum dono dedit Samueli, suavissimo filiolo, alterum
in eum misit usum, ut inde conopus illi ematur, atque ad nos,
cum opportunum fuerit, transmittatur.   Vale, salutatus plurimum a parentibus et uxore mea in Domino.   Tuam cx nobis
pl. salvere jubebis.   Iterum vale.   E Tab. Mont. 22 Maii.

Tuus,

MICHAEL ANGLUS.

EPISTOLA XIX.

MILO COVERDALUS AD CONRADUM HUBERTUM.

PAX et gaudium in Spiritu Sancto !   Etiam si plura mihi
ad te scribendi argumenta non essent, volui tamen vel salutem
adscribere tibi, vir in Domino carissime, ne ex longa, qua
jam usus sum, intermissione literarum me tui immemorem
putes.   Parentes tui carissimi satis commoda sunt valetudine,
teque una cum uxore pl. salvere jubent.   Religionis negotium
magis ac magis in dies hic valiturum non dubito : hujus enim
specimen aliquod expertus, hæc scribo, ut qui ecclesiæ Dei
optime cupis, et illi nobiscum gratias agas, et pro majori
successu preces indesinenter effundas.   Hoc autem ab te vehementer peto, ut quid valeat D. Bucerus in turbulentissimo hoc
seculo, certior factus, nos itidem ut sciamus efficias.   Pacis
spem satis malam prænunciant rumores, quos hic audimus.
Nam ut aiunt Cæsarem nullam velle pacem admittere, (imo
ne hortatu quidem principum,) ita et Juliacensis fertur in
Brabantiam finesque Hollandicos de integro jam summa vi
grassatum esse.   Horrendissima profecto initia !   Faxit Deus,
ut tantis malis incitati, nostramque ingratitudinem vere ag-
noscentes, citra omnem fucum resipiscamus.   Salutatos mihi
libenter optarem, quotquot isthic sunt nostratium, præsertim
vero D. Ricardum, &c.   Meis item verbis D. Vindelino, D.
Conrado parocho, Sturmioque, et Severo salutem si nuntia-
veris, gratissimum erit.   Vale.   Idibus Augusti.   E Tabernis
Montanis, 1544.

M. COVERDALUS.

EPISTOLA XX.

MILO COVERDALUS AD CONRADUM HUBERTUM.

Pax et gaudium in Spiritu Sancto! Si quid edidit communis noster præceptor D. Bucerus in hostes jam evangelii, præsertim in Wintoniensem Anglum, te unice oratum volo, ut mihi quoque aliquid sit editionis hujusmodi. Valemus, Dei beneficio, omnes. Parentes te cum tua in imminentem jam vindemiam exspectant, plurimumque salvere jubent. Vale. E Tab. Mont. prid. Cal. Sept. 1545.

MICHAEL ANGLUS.

EPISTOLA XXI.

MILO COVERDALUS AD CONRADUM HUBERTUM.

Pacem et gaudium in Spiritu Sancto! Magnum humanitatis tuæ specimen præbes, virorum eruditissime, qui literis tuis suavissimis, veluti calcaribus, Michaelem (vel si mavis Milonem) tuum, pigre alias incedentem, ad feliciores progressus incitare non desistis. Literæ tuæ III. Cal. Sept. datæ bona nobis fide ad III. Novembr. ejusdem redditæ sunt; ex quibus intellexi D. Bucerum, præter nostram vero omnium opinionem, nondum rediisse. Quo nomine et nos magno affectos esse dolore ne dubites. Ceterum pro tanto viro universam ecclesiam multis jugiter precibus agere scio; atque Dominum pro solita eum misericordia liberaturum, non est quod desperemus. D. Nicolaus sanus et lætus domum rediit, teque pl. resalutat. Circa Cal. Octobris constituimus ego et uxor, superis bene juvantibus, isthuc ascendere, vosque nostri amantissimos invisere. Parentes tui carissimi satis commoda sunt valetudine, atque adeo præsentes ad te literas dedere. E Tab. Mon. Idibus Septembr. a. inc.

Tuus,

M. COVERDALUS.

EPISTOLA XXII.

MILO COVERDALUS AD CONRADUM HUBERTUM.

Pax et gaudium in Spiritu Sancto! Quam non male velis patriæ tuæ, Conrade carissime, testimonio sunt literæ, quibus superiori septimana adolescentulis nostris ad nos dedisti. Illorum nos causam, etiamsi parum, eo tamen promovimus apud Præfectum, ut hujus jussu Erasmo nostro x floreni in subsidium ministrentur, donec res ipsa coram visitaturis meliorem habuerit exitum: id quod Præfectus ante Natalem non esse futurum prædixit. Præterea ad cœnam diei mensis hujus xxvii me et uxorem, ita ut sæpius solet facere, invitavit. Inter cœnandum de pluribus conferentes, in sacri ministerii mentionem incidimus. Cui equidem colloquio libenter ipse aliquid addidissem; sed uxor Præfecti tanta dexteritate causam Domini agebat, ut mihi verba facere opus non esset. Præfectus vero sequenti die, qui erat Dominicus, orationem habens ad populum, gravissimisque verbis usus, ostendebat sibi parum placere, quæ popellus noster clanculum illo factitare solet. Puerpera nostra (gratiam habemus Domino) cum sua filiola revaluit. Vale feliciter, atque librorum exemplaria, quorum in superioribus literis memini, si a bibliopola nondum acceperis, ne quæso sumas; horum enim mihi tandem satis allatum est e Francofordia: sed si jam habes, ad nos mitte; atque Margaretam tuam nostro nomine pl. jubeto salvere. Gratia tecum. Amen. Tab. Mont. iii Octobris. Anno [1544].

Tuus,

MICHAEL ANGLUS.

EPISTOLA XXIII.

MILO COVERDALUS AD CONRADUM HUBERTUM.

Pax et gaudium in Spiritu Sancto! Si cum prole et uxore carissima sanus atque lætus domum redieris, est id nobis vehementer gratum. Parentes tui prospera sunt valetudine, tibique multam in Domino salutem optantes, significatum volunt, Margaretam, fratris tui uxorem, mediocriter nunc revaluisse, atque adeo mulierem illam, nempe Joannis con-

jugem, quæ vobis præsentibus nondum pepererat, felicem novæ
et pulchræ prolis matrem heri esse factam, non sine summa
Patris summi clementia. Hunc castanearum sacculum ad ædes
D. Ricardi allatum cures velim.

Vale, mi D. Conrade suavissime, et me precibus tuis Domino, quæso, commenda. E Tab. Mont. xi Octobris [1544].

M. COVERDALUS.

Non dubito, quin memor sis, dominumque Bucerum diligenter admoneas, ut pro sua opportunitate ad Præfectum
nostrum aliquando literas mittat, atque adeo Edmundi nostri
rationem habeat, cujus rei te promotorem esse cupio.

EPISTOLA XXIV.

MILO COVERDALUS AD CONRADUM HUBERTUM.

PAX et gaudium in Spiritu Sancto! Rogassem, atque
adeo abs te didicissem, adhuc præsens Argentorati, quonam
pacto, quibusvis rebus atramentum conficere soleas: pluribus
tamen negotiis obrutus neglexi. Quare pl. oro, ut eorum,
quæ ad hanc rem comparanda sunt, uxorem meam adhuc
præsentem, vel schedula quadam, facias certiorem: præterea
D. Bucerum et literarum, quas ad Præfectum nostrum polli-
citus est se daturum, (nempe in communi pietatis negotio,) et
conditionis Edmundi nostri aliquando, ut admoneas, vehementer abs te peto. Hoc enim mihi gratius nihil facere potes.
Parentes tui te pl. salvere jubent, vel his testantibus literis.
Uxori tuæ cum prole carissima multam precor salutem in
Domino, meamque vobis ex animo commendo. Vale. E
Montanis Tabernis, 9 Dec. [1544].

M. tuus ANGLUS.

EPISTOLA XXV.

MILO COVERDALUS AD CONRADUM HUBERTUM.

PACEM et gaudium in Spiritu Sancto! Ad summos alioqui dolores, quibus nunquam non afficitur ecclesia, accedit et

hoc acerbissimum, quod morbis semper gravissimis, vel saltem
subinde, tenentur, qui populum docere sacrisque monitis
erigere et possint et velint. Erasmus Bierus, Bissweilerien.
ecclesiæ minister, (ita ut collega hic meus Taberno-Montanus,
Joannes carissimus,) contractis membris eo (proh dolor!) im-
potentiæ dicitur pervenisse, ut apud populum officio fungi
ecclesiastico non valeat. Proinde Æschnavius, Præfectus noster
integerrimus, huic malo consulere cupiens, optat eo in auxilium
Erasmi vocari pium illum confratrem nostrum, Dodmannum
Anglum, de quo et tuam integritatem optime meritam esse
haud illibenter audio : quem item in lingua Germanica tantopere jam promovisse speramus, ut cum frugi ecclesiæ etiam
posse inservire non dubitemus. Tu igitur pro tuo, quo es
in ecclesiam Christi candore, eidem nostrati Dodmanno hæc
significes oro, ut Bissweilerum accersitus eo libentius se con-
ferat, mercedem a Præfecto reportaturus non ingratam.
Nuntius enim hanc ipsam ob causam missus est Argentoratum.
Vale, salutatus pl. ab uxore mea, et a fratre tuo carissimo,
cujus filius Joannes et has tibi tradendas attulit nunc literas
inclusas. Uxorem tuam cariss. una cum parentibus nostris
verbis amantissime salutari cupimus ego et mea multum in
Domino. VII Cal. Januarii. E Tab. Mont. [1544].

MICHAEL ANGLUS.

EPISTOLA XXVI.

MILO COVERDALUS AD CONRADUM HUBERTUM.

S. P. PAX et gaudium in Spiritu Sancto! Literas quas
26 Dec. ad me dederas, ad 10 Januarii accepi, una cum
librorum fasciculo, cujus tu in eisdem feceras mentionem.
Quod et tibi per alios meo nomine significatum esse non
dubito. Causarum quidem præcipua, quam vestra diligentia
promotam apud Præfectum nostrum (adfuit enim tunc vobis
Argentorati) ex animo cupiebam, hæc erat; nempe ut va-
nissimas populi hujus saltationes, aliaque istiusmodi pietatis
impedimenta pro officio suo aboleret, faceretque, ut saltem
tempore sacrioris ministerii minori cum contemptu adessent,
nec suis privatis colloquiis tot undique fori et cœmeterii an-
gulos gregatim, dum concionatur, dum oratur, dum canitur,

occuparent. Nunc autem sperare non possum meliora. Adeo
enim (proh dolor!) hic frigere, omnemque pietatis curam
prorsus exuisse videntur præfecti nostri, in miseris hominibus
gravissime onerandis alioqui studiosissimi.

Pueri nostri, quanquam non omnes, tussi quadam inso-
lenti, ut et capitis dolore, nimium etiam calentes, misere
decumbunt: gravius autem nullum hactenus hic tenuit mor-
bus, quum carissimum meum in Domino tironem, Joannem
Hubertum, fratris tui filiolum. Quem Dominus tamen pro sua
clementia post octiduanum morbum benigne nobis restituit
nunc sanum et incolumem. Nos sane plerique de vita pueri
desperabamus. Ante octiduum acceperunt istinc parentes tui
literas, quibus se pater brevi satisfacturum non dubitat.
Valet uterque parens una cum omnibus, quos hic habes,
amicis feliciter. Plurimum vale, salutatus ab uxore mea in
Domino. E Tab. Mont. 6 Febr. [1545].

Tuus,
MICHAEL ANGLUS.

EPISTOLA XXVII.

MILO COVERDALUS AD CONRADUM HUBERTUM.

S. P. Pax et gaudium in Spiritu Sancto! Si vales, bene
est; nos una cum parentibus tuis longe carissimis omnes quidem
valemus. Hoc autem ecclesiæ (proh dolor!) ad cetera accessit
mala, quod Suevus ille a Badero ad ministerium ecclesiæ
Lindaviensis intrusus, etiam a senatu in futurum parochum
nuper admissus, rogantibus illis, eo adduci non possit, ut vel
semel in anno sacram Domini cœnam administret. Itaque
populus ille miserrimus cogitur, vel invitus, in verba Schwenkfeldii jurare. Cujus me rei ante triduum certiorem fecit
Edmundus meus per literas. Hoc tu vulnus ecclesiæ, quam
creverit, D. Bucero, præceptori meo observando, significes
velim, ut habeat, quod piis precibus in Domino addat.

Scripsi uxori meæ, quæ parens noster semina abs te
cupiat comparata. Tu vero cura, ut mea rediens ad nos
adferat. Et si qua ratione efficere possis, ut responsionis
Buceranæ ad Wintoniensem vel unum mihi exemplar sit ante
nundinas, dabo operam, ut Latinus Brittannice etiam quam

primum calleat, idque amicis et fratribus in Domino per
Angliam gratissimum fore ne dubites ; quod tamen clanculum
omnibus optarem effectum, donec ut Latine, ita et Anglice
prodeat. Uxori tuæ castissimæ atque Samueli filiolo multam
precare salutem. Carissimum patrem Conradum parochum
simul et insigne illud ecclesiæ ornamentum, D. Paulum Fagium,
meis verbis multum salutatos velim. Vale. È Tabernis Montanis, 14 Cal. Mart. a. 1545.

Tuus ita ut suus,

M. COVERDALUS.

EPISTOLA XXVIII.

MILO COVERDALUS AD CONRADUM HUBERTUM.

S. D. P. INTEREA dum ad me perlatæ essent H. T.
literæ 6 Cal. Januarii datæ, scripseram ipse ad te meas in
negotio ecclesiæ Bissweilerianæ pro Joanne Dodmanno nos-
trate, prout D. præfectus optaverat, ægrotante tunc D. Erasmo
nostro carissimo. Nec me certe oblectat diuturnum a mutuo
scribendi officio silentium. Veneror enim et exosculor hoc
christianæ benevolentiæ studium. Calcare tamen subinde me
opus habere fateor, ut qui et natura tardus, et pluribus per-
petuo negotiis obrutus sum. Quæ geruntur apud nos, et ego
hic nunc qua sum conditione, potest præsens internuntius
facile significare. Exspectatur in diem novus ille ludimode-
rator Spirensis, quem senatus Taberno-Montanus noster in
quadriennium conduxit. Conservus meus D. Joannes manuum
adhuc contractione laborat, nostrisque ecclesiis magis atque
magis facessunt negotium Anabaptistarum furiæ ; qui tamen
passim ut magni habentur, ita et non sine maximo totius tam
populi quam ipsorum etiam principum infortunio tolerantur,
ruentibus interim et omnino contemptis Dei Optimi Maximi
ministeriis. Vale, salutatus plurimum ab uxore mea et tuis in
Domino. Salutamus ego et mea conjugem tuam simul atque
parentem cariss. E Tab. Mont. 10 Calend. Martii [1545].

Tuus in Domino,

MICHAEL ANGLUS.

EPISTOLA XXIX.

MILO COVERDALUS AD CONRADUM HUBERTUM.

Pax et gaudium in Spiritu Sancto! Negotium Matthiæ
Rodensis ita pensitavit princeps noster illustrissimus, ut cupe-
ret illum plures istic annos studiis et disciplinæ addidisse.
Verum quando fide astrictus est conjugali, et se vitam in
omnibus ministro dignam ducturum pollicetur, annuit princeps,
ut ecclesiæ Milhoffen præficiatur, ea tamen lege, ut optimis
et studiorum et vitæ rationibus uteretur.   Hæc et consimilia
intellexi ex literis, quas mihi relegabat ante triduum Præfectus;
cui nihil videtur Matthæo nostro consultius, quam ut Argentoratum repetens, cum iis isthic omnibus redeat in gratiam
reconciliatus, quos nuper affecit offendiculo; hac enim ratione
magnas mali occasiones amputaturum illum arbitratur.   Bi-
pontini ministri testati sunt principi, Matthiam illis ad quæsita
examinatum non inepte respondisse.   Ipsemet etiam prioris
se vitæ pœnitentiam acturum et illis promittebat.   Qua in re
ut felicius firmetur in futurum ecclesiæ ædificium, vos quæso
prioris suæ petulantiæ argutum sancte illum admonete, lapsum
erigite, et vestrum se favorem recuperasse, literis, ad præfectum saltem datis, ostendite.   Hoc te unice rogo, Conrade
humanissime, quod ut facerem unice hortatus est D. præfectus,
qui hac de re literas etiam misit ad Bucerum, communem
nostrum præceptorem, quem ex me officiose in Domino salutatum cupio.   Bene vale.   Parentes salvi et incolumes, Deo
sit gratia, domum redeuntes omnia salva offenderunt.   Dat.
Zaberniæ, die tertia a Pentecoste. [1545].

MICHAEL ANGLUS.

EPISTOLA XXX.

MILO COVERDALUS AD CONRADUM HUBERTUM.

Pax et gaudium in Spiritu Sancto! Cum scirem hunc
internuntium istuc ascensurum, parentes tuos carissimos feci
certiores, qui nunc, Deo sit gratia, optima sunt valetudine,
teque et uxorem pl. salvere jubent.   Pater item Samueli tuo
omnia precatus felicissima, (id quod anno inchoante facere

solent amici,) in paterni favoris argumentum una cum lineo
indusio quamdam misit monetam. Ego vero meis fere obrutus negotiis, plura non scribo, sperans te pro tuo candore
animum meum interim boni consulturum. Salutat te et tuam
cariss. uxor mea in Domino. Vale. E Tab. Mont. 27 Dec.
[1545].

Tuus, MICHAEL ANGLUS.

EPISTOLA XXXI.

MILO COVERDALUS AD CONRADUM HUBERTUM.

PAX et gaudium in Spiritu Sancto ! Rogo te etiam atque
etiam, mi D. Conrade carissime, ut scriptura mea in Franc-
wilerum[1] diligenter perpensa, si quid vel in lingua Germanica
vel alia quacunque ratione a me in hoc negotio peccatum sit,
humaniter corrigas, meque tuæ sententiæ facias certiorem.
Vix enim credis, quam nostra periclitetur ecclesia, et quantum
nobis negotii exhibeat Francwilerus; ut interim taceam, quam
parum promptus sit noster Nicolaus (æque rogatus atque ego)
istis malis occurrere. Tu rebus Domini profuturus, perge vel
consulendo. Et si eas acceperis pecunias, quas ante triduum
Præfecto nostro tradidi tibi reddendas, (nimirum pro Catharina
Francisci Osterlingii vidua, et pro Matthæo Rodensi,) mihi
quæso per Edmundum nostrum renuntia.

Dominus Jesus vos omnes ecclesiæ suæ incolumes con-
servet. Amen.

Raptim. Wyssenburgæ, ix Martii a. 1546.

Tuus, MICHAEL ANGLUS.

EPISTOLA XXXIII.

JOANNI CALVINO M. COVERDALUS.

OBLATA occasione, virorum clarissime, non potui integritatem tuam non salutare. Ante triduum allatus est huc in
mediis nundinis libellus quidam Britannicus, illum Sacræ
Communionis Ordinem, quom regia majestas pro temporis

[1 Num hic Suevus ille Schwenkfeldii discipulus, de quo v. Milonis
Epist. ad Hubertum, xvi. Febr. 1545. Simler.]

adhuc ratione instituit, complecteus. Cujus equidem rei quum plures viderem percupidos, traduxi statim in linguam et Germanicam et Latinam. Atque adeo cum intelligerem pium hunc hominem vestratem esse, arbitrabar me tibi rem facturum haudquaquam ingratam, si humanitatem tuam hoc qualicunque manusculo donarem. Alteram enim traduction em Germanis, datam alteram, nempe Latinam, humanitati tuæ transmissam ex animo cupiebam. Tu si hanc felicitatis rationem et pietatis initium aliis significare volueris, (prout nunc Dominus religionem suam in Anglia vult renatam,) prælo hoc mei in te amoris pignus committere poteris facilius. Ego nunc post octo annorum exilium vocatus rediturus sum in Angliam. Vale, præceptor integerrime, et uxorem tuam de me et mea, cum Argentoratum ascendimus, optime meritam benigne saluta. E Frankofordia, 26 Martii 1548.

MICHAEL (*alias* MILO) COVERDALUS, *Anglus.*

EPISTOLA XXXIV.

MILO COVERDALUS AD PAULUM FAGIUM.

PACEM et gaudium in Spiritu Sancto! Literas tuas, virorum integerrime, 22 Augusti datas, ab uxore mea 8 hujus mensis accepi, vestri plurimum commisertus, quos dira ista tyrannis tantopere exagitat. Scripta item tua heri reverendissimo Cantuariensi ostendi, qui ut carissimum filium tuum (quem etiam modo Cantuariam misit ob sævientem hic pestem) suscepit suis porro sumptibus et pietate et literis educandum, ita calamitatem ecclesiarum vestrarum animadvertens, vicem revera vestram dolebat maxime : quare et te præsertim nobis adesse maluit, quam vel in Turciam abire vel in Ungariam. O mi præceptor! si tu alio quam ad nos aufugeris, cum tanta sit hominum ubique perfidia, quam frigebit donum illud præstantissimum, quod reposuit in te Deus Optimus Maximus! Si reverendissimus tot ecclesiæ pericula prævidisset, cujus ego responsum literis meis ad te inserebam, revera mea tibi scripta nunquam fuissent impedimento. Cogita igitur utrumque nostrum facti pœnitere, etiamsi nihil sit in illis literis scriptum, quod tum non ferebat occasio. Ego sane, mi præceptor, et tibi et ecclesiis nostris atque scholis felicissimo ministerio tuo destitutis non parum timeo. Proinde etsi principes nostri te nominatim, qui clares inter Germaniæ studiosiores, non vocent ob latentes forsan causas (ut antea scripsi); nos tamen, qui te satis novimus, per immortalem Deum te obsecramus, ut huc te conferas, ubi te gratissimum fore, atque adeo humanissime tractatum iri, ne dubites. Bene vale. Ex arce regia, quam vocamus Windsor, 21 Octobris, a. 1548.

Tuus ex animo,

M. COVERDALUS.

EPISTOLA XXXV.

MILO COVERDALUS AD CONRADUM HUBERTUM.

PACEM et gaudium in Spiritu Sancto! Quum ascenderem Vesalia Francofordiam, 7 Idus Sept. adortus est me jurgio satis quidem acri amicus meus carissimus Joannes Abelus, ut qui literas me a vobis suavissimas accepisse putaverat, nec tamen respondere voluisse. Proinde misso statim famulo scripsi ad magistratum Taberniensem. Interea vero dum famulus abesset, redditæ sunt mihi hæ literæ una cum reliquis illis inclusis. Nuntio igitur Francofordiam reverso, ad 17 Cal. Oct. tandem illinc solvens, hodie Dei Optimi Maximi beneficio huc adpuli, quo et Eschnavius præfectus Taberno-montanus die etiam hodierno accesserat. Quem etsi convenerim, ipsum tamen negotium ad principem, cujus adventum cras fore prædicant, refertur absolvendum. Quem postea exitum Deus O. M. dederit, vel meis vel Joannis, fratris tui carissimi, scriptis humanitati tuæ significabitur. Ego interdum animi tui erga me candorem merito amplexus, insignem etiam in vobis agnosco benevolentiam. Vale, amicorum et fratrum amice et frater in Domino sincerissime, conjuge tua pudicissima diligenter ex me salutata una cum Samuele carissimo. Dat. Zabernis Montanis, 12 Cal. Octobr.

MILO COVERDALUS, *Anglus,*
nuper Exon.

Quod ad rem illam attinet, de qua illustrissimam Suffol-
cianam per me cupis interrogatam, maritus certe illius, vir
adprime illustris, quem hujus negotii causa alloquutus sum
Francofordiæ, certo se scire dicit, illustrissimam nihil omnino
debere (quod æs alienum spectat) vel optimo patri Bucero vel
aliis. Ego vero quum rediero Vesaliam, unde et uxorem me
cariss. huc adferre nunc oportet, rem omnem diligentius ex-
piscabor Domino fortunante.

INDEX.

M